Praise for *The Handbook of Media Audiences*

"This book offers helpful background readings for media research courses. Summing up: recommended."

Choice

"This much-needed volume provides the most up-to-date, cutting-edge research and scholarship on one of the most researched but still little understood media concepts, that of 'the audience'. Virginia Nightingale has done an excellent job in bringing together a diverse body of contributors who write from various perspectives across media and theories of audience. Essayists point to the ways in which our relationships with media are entwined with how we think about ourselves as citizens and architects of our own here and now, no longer simply in thrall to other people's versions of the world but creating our own."

Karen Ross, University of Liverpool

"At a time when our relations to media are in flux and established notions of audiences under question, this volume offers an invaluable guide to the state of our present knowledge, the questions we now need to ask, and the concepts and methods we can use to tackle them. Admirably comprehensive and with original contributions from leading scholars in the field, this is a volume that everyone should have on their shelf."

Graham Murdock, Loughborough University

Global Handbooks in Media and Communication Research

Series Editor: Annabelle Sreberny (School of Oriental and African Studies, London)

The Global Handbooks in Media and Communication Research series is co-published by Wiley Blackwell and the International Association for Media and Communication Research (IAMCR). The series offers definitive, state-of-the-art handbooks that bring a global perspective to their subjects. These volumes are designed to define an intellectual terrain: its historic emergence; its key theoretical paradigms; its transnational evolution; key empirical research and case study exemplars; and possible future directions.

Already published

The Handbook of Political Economy of Communications edited by Janet Wasko, Graham Murdock, and Helena Sousa

The Handbook of Global Media and Communication Policy edited by Robin Mansell and Marc Raboy

The Handbook of Media Audiences edited by Virginia Nightingale

The Handbook of Development Communication and Social Change, edited by Karin Gwinn Wilkins, Thomas Tufte, and Rafael Obregon

About the IAMCR

The International Association for Media and Communication Research (IAMCR) (http://iamcr.org) was established in Paris in 1957. It is an accredited NGO attached to UNESCO. It is a truly international association, with a membership representing over 80 countries around the world and conferences held in different regions that address the most pressing issues in media and communication research. Its members promote global inclusiveness and excellence within the best traditions of critical research in the field.

The Handbook of Media Audiences

Edited by

Virginia Nightingale

WILEY Blackwell

Table of Contents

Contents

Notes on Contributors

Adam Arvidsson is associate professor of sociology at the University of Milano. He has published extensively on brands and the history of consumer culture (*Brands: Meaning and Value in Media Culture*, Routledge, 2006). His present work is concerned with the potential of new open economic forms and their likely impact on the global economy. His new book is *The Ethical Economy: Business and Society in the Twenty-First Century* (coauthored with Nicolai Peitersen; Columbia University Press, 2010).

Fatimah Awan is a research fellow in media users and creative methodologies at the University of Westminster, London. She taught media studies for a number of years at Southampton Solent University and undertook her PhD at Bournemouth University (see www.artlab.org.uk). Her research interests include the sociology of young people and contemporary media, and new qualitative methods which use visual and creative techniques.

S. Elizabeth Bird is professor, Department of Anthropology, University of South Florida. Her books include *For Enquiring Minds: A Cultural Study of Supermarket Tabloids* (1992); *Dressing in Feathers: The Construction of the Indian in American Popular Culture* (1996); *The Audience in Everyday Life* (2003); and *The Anthropology of News and Journalism: Global Perspectives* (2009), and she has published over 60 articles and chapters in media studies, popular culture, and folklore.

Kristina Busse has a PhD in English from Tulane University and teaches in the Department of Philosophy at the University of South Alabama. She has been an active media fan and has published a variety of essays on fan fiction and fan culture. Kristina is coeditor, with Karen Hellekson, of *Fan Fiction and Fan Communities in the Age of the Internet* (2006), and founding coeditor of *Transformative Works and Cultures*, an online-only international peer-reviewed journal about fan cultures and fan works.

Richard Butsch is author of *The Making of American Audiences from Stage to Television 1750–1990* and *The Citizen Audience: Crowds, Publics and Individuals*. He also is editor of *Media and Public Spheres* and *For Fun and Profit: The Transformation of Leisure into Consumption*. He is currently working on a history of screen culture and a study of changes in American representations of and respect for manual labor and laborers in the twentieth century.

Nico Carpentier is Senior Lecturer in the Social Sciences Department of Lough-borough University, and was previously an assistant professor in the Communication Studies Department of the Vrije Universiteit Brussel (VUB – Free University of Brussels). He is co-director of the VUB research center CeMeSo and vice president of the European Communication Research and Education Association (ECREA). His theoretical focus is on discourse theory, and his research interests are situated in the relationship between media, journalism, politics, and culture, especially toward social domains such as war and conflict, ideology, participation, and democracy.

Jackie Cook teaches communications at the University of South Australia, where she specializes in radio studies and new uses of digital media. She maintains a regular round of broadcasting commitments, and is currently designing media-training modules for doctoral-level research students.

Nick Couldry is professor of media and communications at Goldsmiths, University of London, and director of its Centre for the Study of Global Media and Democracy. He is the author or editor of nine books, including most recently *Why Voice Matters: Culture and Politics after Neoliberalism* (Sage 2010) and the revised paperback edition of *Media Consumption and Public Engagement: Beyond the Presumption of Attention* (with Sonia Livingstone and Tim Markham, Palgrave 2010).

David Deacon is professor of communication and media analysis in the Communication Research Centre, Department of Social Sciences, Loughborough University. He has published widely on political communication, media sociology, and communication theory and is coauthor of *Researching Communications: A Practical Guide to Media and Cultural Analysis*, which has just been published in its second edition (Arnold, 2007). His latest book is *The British News Media and the Spanish Civil War: Tomorrow May Be Too Late* (Edinburgh, 2008).

Jennifer Deger is an Australian Research Council Future Fellow in the Department of Archaeology and Anthropology at the Australian National University. An anthropologist and experimental filmmaker, Deger's work explores the intercultural lives of images. She has published widely on art and anthropology, indigenous aesthetics and collaborative media production including her book *Shimmering Screens: Making Media in an Aboriginal Community* (University of Minnesota Press: 2006).

Kirsten Drotner is a professor of media studies at the University of Southern Denmark and founding director of DREAM: Danish Research Centre on Education and Advanced Media Materials. Author or editor of 22 books, her research interests include media history, qualitative methodologies, and young people's media uses.

Recent books are *Researching Audiences* (coauthored with Kim Schrøder, Catherine Murray, and Steve Kline; Arnold, 2003); *The International Handbook of Children, Media and Culture* (coauthored with Sonia Livingstone; Sage, 2008); and *Informal Learning and Digital Media* (coedited with Hans S. Jensen and Kim Schrøder; Cambridge Scholars' Publishing, 2008).

David Gauntlett is professor of media and communications in the School of Media, Arts and Design, University of Westminster. He is the author of several books, including *Moving Experiences* (1995, 2005); *Media, Gender and Identity* (2002, 2008); *Creative Explorations: New Approaches to Identities and Audiences* (2007); and *Making is Connecting: The Social Meaning of Creativity, from DIY and Knitting to YouTube and Web 2.0* (2011). He produces the popular website about media and identities, Theory. org.uk, and the hub for creative and visual research methods, ArtLab.org.uk.

Anna Gibbs is associate professor at the University of Western Sydney. She has published numerous essays on affect theory and mediatized forms of contagion and mimesis (or mimetic communication). Her most recent work, with Maria Angel, is on the corporeality of writing in the new media arts.

Gerard Goggin is professor of media and communications in the Department of Media and Communications, the University of Sydney. His books include *New Technologies and the Media* (2011), *Global Mobile Media* (2011), *Internationalizing Internet Studies* (with Mark McLelland; 2009), *Cell Phone Culture* (2006), and *Digital Disability* (with Christopher Newell; 2003).

Jonathan Gray is associate professor of media and cultural studies at the University of Wisconsin–Madison. He is the author of *Show Sold Separately: Promos, Spoilers, and Other Media Paratexts*; *Television Entertainment*; and *Watching with the Simpsons: Television, Parody, and Intertextuality*. His coedited collections include *Satire TV: Politics and Comedy in the Post-network Era*; and *Fandom: Identities and Communities in a Mediated World*.

Joshua Green is a Senior Strategist at Undercurrent, a consultancy based in NYC. He is coauthor of *Spreadable Media: Creating Value and Meaning in Network Culture* (with Henry Jenkins and Sam Ford, NYU Press 2013) and *YouTube: Online Video and Participatory Culture* (with Jean Burgess, Polity Press 2009).

Wendy Griswold is the Bergen Evans Professor in the Humanities and professor of sociology at Northwestern University. She is the author of *Regionalism and the Reading Class* (University of Chicago Press, 2008); *Cultures and Societies in a Changing World*, 3rd edn (Pine Forge Press, 2008); and *Bearing Witness: Readers, Writers, and the Novel in Nigeria* (Princeton University Press, 2007).

Annette Hill is professor of communication and media at the department of Communication and Media, Lund University, Sweden. She is the author of *Reality TV: Audiences and Popular Factual Television* (Routledge, 2005); and *Restyling Factual*

TV: The Reception of News, Documentary and Reality Genres (Routledge, 2007). Her previous books include *Shocking Entertainment* (1997); and *TV Living: Television, Audiences and Everyday Life* (with David Gauntlett 1999), and she has written a variety of articles on audiences and popular culture. She is the coeditor of the *Television Studies Reader* (with Robert C. Allen; Routledge, 2003).

Henry Jenkins is the Provost's Professor of Communications, Journalism and Cinematic Arts at the University of Southern California and formerly the co-director of the Comparative Media Studies Program at MIT. He is the author or editor of 13 books on various aspects of media and popular culture, including *Convergence Culture: Where Old and New Media Collide*. He is currently writing a book on "spreadable media" with Joshua Green and Sam Ford. He blogs at henryjenkins.org.

Emily Keightley is lecturer in communication and media studies in the Department of Social Sciences, Loughborough University. She has published in relation to both conceptual and methodological issues in memory studies. Most recently this includes "Remembering Research: Memory and Methodology in the Social Sciences" (*International Journal of Social Research Methodology*, 2010). She is currently working on the book *Creative Memory* with Michael Pickering, which explores and reconceives the relationship between memory and imagination. She is also editing a collection on the mediation of time in modernity.

Elizabeth Lenaghan is a doctoral student in Northwestern University's School of Communications (Media, Technology, and Society) working on book collectors and material culture.

Sonia Livingstone is the author or editor of a dozen books and 100+ academic articles and chapters on media audiences, children and the internet, domestic contexts of media use, and media literacy. Recent books include *Children and Their Changing Media Environment* (coedited with Moira Bovill; Lawrence Erlbaum, 2001); *Young People and New Media* (Sage, 2002); *Audiences and Publics* (Intellect, 2005); *The Handbook of New Media* (coedited with Leah Lievrouw; Sage, 2006); *Public Connection?* (coedited with Nick Couldry and Tim Markham; Palgrave, 2007); and *The International Handbook of Children, Media and Culture* (coedited with Kirsten Drotner; Sage, 2008). She was president of the International Communication Association, 2007–2008.

Peter Lunt is a social psychologist and media scholar; he is professor of media and communications at Brunel University, London. His main research interests are in media audiences, public participation through popular culture, and media and social theory. He has also written widely on consumption, and his work is often at the interface between social identity as citizens and as consumers. His recent publications include a book on Stanley Milgram published by Palgrave, and he is currently working on a book on media regulation with Sonia Livingstone which will be published by Sage.

Mirca Madianou is a lecturer in the Department of Sociology, University of Cambridge, and a fellow of Lucy Cavendish College. She is the author of *Mediating the Nation* (UCL Press/Routledge, 2005) and several other articles on news audiences, nationalism, transnationalism, and media consumption. She is currently the principal investigator on the ESRC-funded project "Migration, ICTs and Transnational Families."

Patrick D. Murphy is Chair and Associate Professor of the Department of Broadcastng, Telecommunications and Mass Media, School of Communications and Theater, Temple University. He has published on the topics of media and globalization, media reception and ethnographic method, and Latin American cultural theory. He is coeditor of *Negotiating Democracy: Media Transformation in Emerging Democracies* (SUNY, 2007); and *Global Media Studies: Ethnographic Perspectives* (Routledge, 2003).

Michelle Naffziger is a doctoral student in Northwestern University's Sociology Department working on education and inequality and on reading groups. All correspondence should be addressed to Wendy Griswold, Department of Sociology, Northwestern University.

Philip M. Napoli is professor of communications and media management in the Graduate School of Business, and director of the Donald McGannon Communication Research Center, at Fordham University in New York. He also serves as a Knight Media Policy Fellow with the New America Foundation and as a docent in the Department of Communication at the University of Helsinki. His research interests focus on media institutions and media policy. His books include *Audience Economics: Media Institutions and the Audience Marketplace* (Columbia University Press, 2003); and *Audience Evolution: New Technologies and the Transformation of Media Audiences* (Columbia University Press, 2010). His research has been supported by organizations such as the Ford Foundation, the National Association of Broadcasters, the National Association of Television Programming Executives, the Social Science Research Council, and the Center for American Progress.

Virginia Nightingale held the position of associate professor with the School of Communication Arts at the University of Western Sydney until retiring in 2009. Now an independent scholar, her publications include *Studying Audiences: The Shock of the Real* (Routledge 1996); two books published in collaboration with Karen Ross, *Media and Audiences: New Perspectives* and *Critical Readings: Media and Audiences* (both Open University Press, McGraw-Hill, 2003); and, in collaboration with Tim

Dwyer, the anthology *New Media Worlds: Challenges for Convergence* (Oxford University Press Australia, 2007).

Brian O'Neill is head of research for the Faculty of Applied Arts, Dublin Institute of Technology, and former head of its School of Media. His research interests include media literacy and media policy in relation to digital broadcasting, new media technologies, and information society issues. He is a member of the DRACE research group (www.drace.org), originally part of COST A20, and is a contributing editor of its volume *Digital Radio in Europe: Technologies, Industries and Cultures* (Intellect, forthcoming).

David Rowe is professor of cultural studies at the Centre for Cultural Research at the University of Western Sydney. His principal research interests concern media and popular culture, including broadcast and online sport, tabloidization, cultural policy, and urban leisure. His books include *Popular Cultures: Rock Music, Sport and the Politics of Pleasure* (Sage, 1995); *Globalization and Sport: Playing the World* (Sage, 2001); and *Sport, Culture and the Media: The Unruly Trinity* (2nd edn; Open University Press, 2004).

Andy Ruddock lectures in communications and media studies at Monash University, Melbourne. He is the author of *Understanding Audiences* (2001) and *Investigating Audiences* (2007). Andy has published numerous articles on audience-related media subjects, including sport fandom, political celebrity, moral panics, and drinking, in journals such as *The European Journal of Cultural Studies*, *Convergence*, *Popular Communication*, *Social Semiotics*, *Sociology of Sport Journal*, *Journal of Sport and Social Issues*; and *Sociology Compass*.

Cornel Sandvoss is senior lecturer in the Department of Sociology at the University of Surrey. He is author of *Fans: The Mirror of Consumption* (Polity, 2005); and *A Game of Two Halves: Football, Television and Globalization* (Routledge, 2003); and is coeditor of *Fandom: Identities and Communities in a Mediated World* (New York University Press, 2007), and *Bodies of Discourse* (Peter Lang, 2010). He is also coeditor of *Popular Communication: The International Journal of Media and Culture*.

Shawn Shimpach is assistant professor in the Department of Communication at the University of Massachusetts, Amherst. He is the author of the book *Television in Transition: The Life and Afterlife of the Narrative Action Hero* (Wiley-Blackwell, 2010). His research has also appeared in such journals as *Social Semiotics* and *Cultural Studies* and in the collection *Media and Public Spheres*.

Series Editor's Preface

Welcome to the Global Handbooks in Media and Communication Research series. This grew out of the idea that the field needed a series of state-of the-art reference works that was truly international. The International Association for Media and Communication Research (IAMCR), with a membership from over 80 countries, is uniquely positioned to offer a series that covers the central concerns of media and communications theory in a global arena.

Each of these substantial books contains newly written essays commissioned from a range of international authors, showcasing the best critical scholarship in the field. Each is pedagogical in the best sense, accessible to students and clear in its approach and presentation. Theoretical chapters map the terrain of an area both historically and conceptually, providing incisive overviews of arguments in the field. The examples of empirical work are drawn from many different countries and regions, so that each volume offers rich material for comparative analysis.

These handbooks are international in the best sense: in scope, authorship, and mindset. They explore a range of approaches and issues across different political and cultural regions, reflecting the global reach of the IAMCR. The aim is to offer scholarship that moves away from simply reproducing Westcentric models and assumptions. The series formulates new models and asks questions that bring communication scholarship into a more comprehensive global conversation.

The IAMCR (http://iamcr.org) was established in Paris in 1957. It is an accredited NGO attached to UNESCO. It is a truly international association, with a membership around the world and conferences held in different regions that address the most pressing issues in media and communication research. Its members promote global inclusiveness and excellence within the best traditions of critical research in the field.

This series supports those goals.

Annabelle Sreberny
Past President of IAMCR and Series Editor
London, December 2010

Acknowledgments

In 2007, the International Association of Media and Communication Research and Wiley-Blackwell reached agreement to publish a Global Media and Communication Studies Handbook series. As chair of the IAMCR Audience Section, I was invited to put together a proposal for a *Handbook on Audience Studies*. This book is the result.

I would like to begin by acknowledging the authors who responded so positively and excellently to my request for papers that addressed quite specific aspects of the field of audience studies. Most, but not all, have attended and presented papers at IAMCR conferences. However when commissioning chapters, my priority was to ensure first that as many as possible of the most significant academics studying audiences in 2010 were approached; second, that the diverse concerns that motivate academics to study audiences were included; and, third, that the anthology be able to make a significant impact both by reviewing the past of audience studies and also by providing directions and insights for future research. By presenting a range of perspectives from which audiences have been and are currently being studied, it is hoped that future audience researchers will find inspiration for innovative research designs and strategies. I am sincerely grateful to all the contributing authors for agreeing to participate in the project, and for their patience with the pace of my editing.

I wish to recognize the vision and hard work that Professor Annabelle Sreberny, president of IAMCR 2008–2010, has devoted to securing the agreement with Wiley-Blackwell, and convey my personal thanks that, along with the Political Economy Section, the Audience Section was invited to develop one of the initial proposals. I would also like to acknowledge the support and encouragement of staff from Wiley-Blackwell, particularly Elizabeth Swayze and Margot Morse, who have been more than generous with their time and good advice.

Virginia Nightingale

Introduction

Virginia Nightingale

For most people, the study of audiences consists of little more than the information they read in the media, ironically "as audiences." The most consistently reported audience information is provided by ratings agencies that monitor shifting audience allegiances across the mediascape. Since audience ratings are primarily intended for industry consumption, they are often of limited interest to audiences themselves. So the main source of public information about audiences comes from journalists reporting on media activities that they represent as "dangerous," addictive, or shocking. Today these include cyber bullying, internet "addictions," online "stranger danger," and accessing prohibited content online, whether this is pornographic, political, or revolutionary. Such popular discourses on audiences are counterintuitive in terms of the day-by-day safe encounters with media that most people enjoy, and more importantly they distract us from what is really important about audiences, in particular the ways being an audience is essential to cultural participation, the ways it affects how we understand ourselves (our identity) and our power to control the world around us, and the ways familiarity with media use prepares us to take advantage of technological change as it sweeps through our everyday worlds. These are the types of issues addressed by the international scholars who have contributed to this book.

The contributors to this book hold a complex view of media audiences. They study people being audiences with diverse media technologies. They dissect the details of participation with media, the ways people engage with media content, and the implications they have for the experience of citizenship and public life. They explore how different methods of audience research might be used so that the realities of audience experiences can be better represented to the broader public. And they explore the challenges that particular audiences pose for research. The wealth of experience and knowledge they provide, and the futures they imagine for

The Handbook of Media Audiences, First Edition. Edited by Virginia Nightingale.
© 2014 John Wiley & Sons, Ltd. Published 2014 by John Wiley & Sons, Ltd.

audience research in general, stand in marked contrast to the views held by some new media commentators who argue that because people can now broadcast themselves online, the need for audience research is at an end. This view is based on a narrow understanding of broadcast media audiences as passive recipients of broadcast messages, and it overlooks the emphasis on the "active audience" that has been so influential in audience studies for the last quarter of a century and more.

Still, many media scholars today do feel impatient and more than a little bored with the term *audience*, and by implication with audience research. There is a sense that the term is inadequate to explain the sorts of things people do with media now that social media and web 2.0 have transformed the media landscape. For example, Jay Rosen[1] (2006) introduced "the people formerly known as the audience," describing them as

> those who *were* on the receiving end of a media system that ran one way, in a broadcasting pattern, with high entry fees and a few firms competing to speak very loudly while the rest of the population listened in isolation from one another – and who *today* are not in a situation like that *at all*.

The point of Rosen's intervention is not so much to challenge the study of audiences as to confront the complacency of those media professionals who have not quite cottoned to the fact that the broadcasting era is over and that people behave and "expect" differently in a media world where producing media for one's own consumption constitutes everyday media use. As he puts it,

> [T]here's nothing wrong with old style, one-way, top-down media consumption. Big media pleasures will not be denied us. You provide them, we'll consume them and you can have yourselves a nice little business.... But we're not on your clock any more! (Rosen 2006)

By contrast, Axel Bruns (2007) has substituted the term *produser* for Alvin Toffler's older term, the *prosumer*. For Bruns, terminology *is* an issue, and he argues,

> To overcome the terminological dilemma which faces us as we attempt to examine processes of user-led content creation, we must introduce new terms into the debate. The concept of *'produsage'* is such a term: it highlights that within the communities which engage in the collaborative creation and extension of information and knowledge that we examine on this site, the role of consumer and even that of end user have long disappeared, and the distinctions between producers and users of content have faded into comparative insignificance. In many of the spaces we encounter here, users are always already necessarily also producers of the shared knowledge base, regardless of whether they are aware of this role – they have become a new, hybrid, *produser*.

The produsage issue is a complex one, and Bruns has chosen to explain it as an extension of the 1970s self-sufficiency drives that informed Toffler's term *prosumer*.

Where Toffler emphasized the interplay of production and consumption, Bruns refers to the interplay of media production and usage. However, just as *prosumption* registered the activities of very particular groups of interests and people, so *produsage* references quite discrete groups of "communities" that engage in collaborative media production activities. What seems to be forgotten in the debates about new media audiences is that produsage is not a new media phenomenon, as the photographs in this introduction, taken in the 1940s, should remind us. The photographs were taken by an amateur radio enthusiast and photographer, Reg Bennett,[2] and capture the excitement of his infant daughter, Lynda, as she successfully tuned a radio and heard broadcast sound, possibly for the first time. According to Lynda Bennett, her father took his hobby further than most and actually made all the (broadcast) radio sets her family used. He also developed and printed his photographs. Clearly Reg Bennett provides an early example of produsage which, in hardly altered form, has returned today in our uploading and sharing of podcasts, photos, and home videos; our secret ambitions for professional recognition; and our connection to other produsers.

Photographs from the family collection of L. Bennett, with permission.

These photos take us back to a time in the history of radio when hobbyists still made their own radio sets and picked up two-way signals on headphones. Making simple "crystal" sets was a widely enjoyed but nevertheless minority hobby until at least the 1950s, and along with two-way radio, remains a viable hobby for amateurs today. Amateur photography has enjoyed an even more devoted following, if anything growing in strength in the internet environment, where, ironically, the capacity to publish or share photographs online has been used to advocate the replacement of the audience with the produser. Then again, film and television have also inspired dedicated amateur production, as was the case with "guerrilla television" and some off-network cable channel broadcasting (Downing 2001). Many diaspora communities (see e.g. Naficy's [1993] account of video production and distribution by the Iranian communities in Los Angeles) have proved extremely innovative in their capacity to express their media cultures whether in music and music cassette distribution (Wallis and Malm 1984), video, or print forms. And this is before the strong intervention of community media (Meadows et al. 2007) is even mentioned. The argument that produsage replaces the audience holds only if the long history of the audience amateur is ignored.

So, if audience research has always worked in a context where produsage is occurring, why is the current emphasis on it felt to be a challenge to the future of audience studies? What seems to confuse many audience researchers is the pervasiveness of produsage in the contemporary experience of new media, which far outstrips the intervention made by amateur production in the past. When the millions of people with Twitter or Facebook accounts "tweet" or post photographs, videos, comments, and the like to their Facebook wall, it is unclear whether they are acting as new media audiences, locked into frameworks of engagement defined by site managers, or as produsers contributing to the making of the patchwork of communications that "is" Facebook? Should Facebook users (for example) be treated as a mass audience or as a produser community … and would it make any difference to the research that could – and, more importantly, should – be carried out by media scholars?

These and many other issues are taken up and debated by the contributors to this book, as they address the ways their research projects and practices have responded to the challenges of the transition from broadcast to digital communications systems. The book is unusual in that it does not set out to provide a template for how audience research should be done. Instead, it works on the assumption that better research will evolve if future researchers have a solid understanding of the complexity of *audience* and *audiences*, and of the research traditions that have informed our practice over the last century. The position the book takes is that there is no "one-size-fits-all" way of doing audience research. Instead the field works best by identifying particular "audience problems" and applying the best theories and research methods at our disposal to solving them.

The book is divided into four loosely thematic parts. The first part looks at the ways the digital revolution has affected the pragmatics of engaging with media content, such as reading, listening, and viewing, and introduces some of the characteristic ways of engaging with new media, such as searching, sharing, and going mobile. It identifies the problems new media audiences pose for audience research design. The authors link their analyses of these modes of audience engagement to issues of theory and research practice specific to particular media contexts and reflect on the historical development of media-specific audience practices. The second part examines theories of audience formation and engagement. It introduces readers to the breadth of theoretical debate about the nature of audiences and modes of engagement. Issues addressed include the nature of audience "publics" and the citizen audience, the importance of theories of practice and cultural participation, a new analysis of reception theory, and an assessment of the relevance of affect theory for the study of audiences. The third part turns to audience research methodologies. It includes chapters on the ways audiences are researched by the advertising industry, and traces the ways new research technologies now challenge how ratings research is conducted. It explores the importance of quantitative methods, the history of effects studies, the contribution of cultivation analysis, and the call for increased use of "creative and visual" methods in audience research. Finally, it provides an overview and reassessment of media ethnography in audience studies. The final part looks at how leading audience researchers have approached "doing" research in conditions that raise particular issues concerning the capacity of audiences to participate in the research. The chapters explore how the interest of child audiences, globally dispersed audiences, ethnically diverse audiences, and indigenous communities might be incorporated into researcher attitudes and research design. The last three chapters return to the problems faced by those who research mass audiences, and provide examples of particular audience situations that transcend media platforms and interpolate live audiences as media "content." They explore ways of doing research about live audiences, news, and sport.

Part I: Being Audiences

Reading, listening, and viewing are easily recognizable as abilities that audiences draw on to engage with media content. This Part begins by evaluating their contemporary significance. In Chapter 1, Wendy Griswold, Elizabeth Lenaghan, and Michelle Naffziger analyze the cultural value and status of books and reading just as the material form of the book is subject to digitization, and as more reading takes place using computer screens than the printed word. They point out that the introduction of digital media has not (yet) made the book redundant, largely because reading books is accorded such importance as social practice. The fundamental importance of reading as an entry point to cultural participation consolidates its status as a key cultural value. Book clubs and reading groups that encourage not just reading but also discussion of what is read are proliferating. Griswold and her coauthors argue that claims that the computer screen, the internet page, and the reading tablet (e.g. Amazon's Kindle or Apple's iPad) threaten to displace the book-object and the value attached to reading in Western culture are exaggerated. Instead, reading is becoming ever more fundamental to participation in social and cultural life.

Learning to listen, by contrast, does not enjoy the same privileged status as reading in school curricula and estimations of cultural value – but this could be changing. In Chapter 2, Jackie Cook offers some reasons for this. As she puts it, "Listening, among the earliest of the human communicative senses to develop, is culturally among the last to be taken seriously," with the result that "[t]here are no definitive ways of critiquing, or discussing, or teaching, or even understanding, any aspect of the arts of all this mediated listening." For this reason, the little research that has been done has primarily used conversational analysis, a research method borrowed from linguistics, but this does not help us to understand listening any better because it confines us to questions of cognition, comprehension, and interpretation. Cook argues that the soundscapes that accompany human life are "sticky" in that they are not easily forgotten. As a result, memories of sound pattern our experiences of listening, and the temporality of sound, plus the quality of the way it connects people with time and with the world, suggest that new methods for researching sound and listening are urgently needed. The invention of new listening experiences invites us all to pay more attention to the listening experiences of audiences.

In spite of its long history, Shawn Shimpach argues that viewing has yet to be fully understood from an audience perspective. He argues that what is missing, particularly in the context of digital media viewing, is respect for the ways viewing has become "productive." In Chapter 3, Shimpach traces theories of viewing from the "unruly space" of nickelodeon spectatorship to the "gaze" of the classical Hollywood era, the "glance" for broadcast television, and the "new media user." He suggests that viewing cannot be divorced from the spaces where it occurs, and that it "is always constructed in relation to political and cultural discourses." Our understanding of viewing is undergoing transformation as digital and mobile media continue to promote diverse forms of distracted viewing, and as the economic and cultural "value" of viewing changes.

The first three chapters argue that the onset of the era of digital communications is transforming the economic and cultural value associated with "old" ways of being audiences such as by reading, listening, and viewing. However, studies of new media audiences demonstrate that digital communications have brought about the mediatization of additional domains of human activity, bringing them into the ambit of audience research. Virginia Nightingale (Chapter 4) argues that this is the case with "search" … a survival activity for the human race which, online, is mediated by search engines. She documents the activities of an email group, dedicated to online search, which formed to solve some shared family history research problems. The email group was linked not just to each other but also to several of the major family history research sites. These sites devote considerable time and effort to maintaining the appeal of their search activities, not least by offering a diversity of "positions" from which to engage with the site. This elaborated positioning of site users includes roles such as members, subscribers, and collaborators. While all remain positions of "recipience" in relation to site management (thus positioning them as audiences), they experience varying degrees of "power" in terms of their relationship to the historical records available at the sites. Nightingale explores the ways the group, working together, established a highly productive micro system of social networking and information sharing outside the parent sites.

In Chapter 5, Joshua Green and Henry Jenkins explain the concept of "spreadable" media with reference to the way Susan Boyle's first appearance on the TV show *Britain's Got Talent* became a YouTube phenomenon. As mentioned above, this is another example of a domain of human activity, in this case sharing good things and giving small gifts, being mediatized and taking on new significance as an audience activity (even if its significance is not yet fully understood). Green and Jenkins return to the dilemma with which this introduction began – the question of whether "spreading" online content is better understood as "consumption" or "production." They argue that it would be wise to pause before hastily classifying such activities as "progressive or reactionary, exploitative or resistant" in part because the shift in the value we attach to cultural content may in future be linked more to its capacity for "circulation and appraisal" than to "interpretation and appropriation."

The changing value of "circulation and appraisal" is reinforced when we start to look at the impact "going mobile" has had on how we understand "mobile" audiences and what's involved in being part of a "mobile audience," rather than simply being a user of mobile technology. In Chapter 6, Gerard Goggin argues that "'going mobile' has become central to the processes of contemporary audience engagement." He explains this position by situating the emergence of the mobile audience in the history of telephony and documenting examples of the use of the telephone for content delivery long before the mobile phone was ever imagined. The expansion of mobile telephony has encouraged a return to the use of telephony for the delivery of media content, and greatly expanded the scope and quality of downloadable content. As a result, mobile media are now understood as a companion platform for online media and broadcast media. So rather than the term *audience* disappearing, it seems to be attracting new modalities and expanding in relevance, and, even more importantly, revealing the specialization creeping into the generic term *new media user*. The challenge for media academics is to identify and document what is likely to prove enduring about new ways of being "media active" as an audience.

Part II: Theorizing Audiences

The six chapters in Part II allow us to identify some of the diverse theories and understandings commonly called on in the interpretation of audience practices. All begin by recognizing that interactive digital media are changing the contexts and situations in which audience is enacted. Interactive digital media (e.g. web 2.0 and social media) force researchers to reconsider the ways audience and audiences are understood. In Part I, this reconsideration involved re-evaluating established ways of being an audience, and, second, identifying some of the new media activities that can justifiably now be encompassed by the term *audience*. In Part II, the challenge of digital media takes a different path. In an article I published in 2004 (Nightingale 2004), I felt reasonably confident that the contexts of audience fell fairly neatly into the following typology: publics, markets, communities, and fandoms. While this typology remains vaguely useful today, it is painfully obvious that it fails to account for the globally dispersed audiences of cyberculture. Social networking and the types of collaborations Pierre Lévy (1997) has characterized as "immanence," where a "large, self-organizing community is a molecular group" that uses "every resource of microtechnology" to enhance "its human wealth, attribute by attribute" (p. 41), just don't fit this pattern. When compared to audiences of the broadcast era, these new audience groups are ephemeral, engage in fragments, and are more goal oriented. They make no distinction between entertainment and news, and between politics and pleasure, but they have motivated many academics to think long and hard about some of the cultural work that was previously achieved courtesy of the link between audiences and publics.

The first three chapters in this part discuss the implications of interactive digital media in terms of the influence they exert on the quality of public life and experiences of cultural and political citizenship. Richard Butsch (Chapter 7) provides an introduction to the "public" and the history of its link with audiences. His concern is that as digital media are more widely used, the capacity for a rich civic life may be compromised, at least in part because we have not yet fully appreciated the role that broadcast media have played as spaces for public discourse. With broadcast media in decline, and digital media promoting higher levels of political factionalism, it may become harder to establish the civic consensus needed to maintain social order, especially since many governments in the West have promoted a shift to forms of consumerism that promote individualist excess at the expense of commitment to common values and communal well-being.

The theme of government responsibility for creating the conditions for cultural citizenship is taken up by Sonia Livingstone and Peter Lunt in Chapter 8, and linked to the articulation of a responsibility for audience research to be more "proactive" in challenging the remorselessness with which the "citizen" of social policy is replaced by the "consumer-citizen" and often the "consumer." Drawing on their research, they demonstrate the repeated reluctance of policy makers to embrace ideals of cultural citizenship, especially in the context of media regulation. They argue that it is time for those of us engaged in audience research to become more proactive and outspoken, both in the research we undertake and in pursuing the interests of those on whose behalf the research was motivated, and that we need to identify the new powers that audiences need to enjoy the qualities of "access, equity, empowerment and opportunity" that make life meaningful.

Nico Carpentier (Chapter 9) takes issue with the extent to which the proliferation of "user-generated content" can be equated with political or cultural "participation." He argues that "the participatory potential of media technologies remains dependent on the way that they are used and the societal context of which they are part," and that if we closely examine the contemporary mediascape, it is obvious that it is composed as much of "old media" as of "new." So, while people are generating "user content," they are doing so in a context still heavily influenced by broadcast media and the institutions that govern it. For this reason, he sees parallels between the participatory media practices developed in the context of "old" media and the online practices associated with the production of user-generated content. Carpentier distinguishes between participation in media production (active engagement) and interaction with media content (passive engagement) and demonstrates how, depending on whether the goals of an organization are internal or external to the group, participation and interaction set up relations with participating members that facilitate the pursuit of organizational goals while still controlling member activities.

The study of audiences is not confined to issues of publics, citizenships, and participation. While theories of "the public" have historically been important to the study of audiences, it is not the only theoretical perspective that has informed current perspectives on audiences. The next three chapters open up the theoretical field of audience studies to some very different theories, issues, and ideas. Nick Couldry (Chapter 10) argues for a return to social science, and in particular to "practice theory" because it offers the opportunity to trace the ways different audience practices assist the maintenance of the "mediated center" so important for the smooth operation of social, political, and economic process. Couldry emphasizes the important point that many audience practices may not be "about" the actual content of the media but instead may be a way of gaining access to other resources – whether human, informational, or material. This insight is increasingly evident in much internet use, and Couldry argues that audience research needs to move away from its fixation on texts and instead adopt "an open-minded, practice-based approach to whatever it is that people are doing with, or around, media."

In Chapter 11, Cornel Sandvoss discusses "reception" and "reception theory," and its centrality for understanding audience engagement. He demonstrates that it remains one of the foundational elements of audience studies. Theories of reception are important because they explore the diversity of "positions" available to the "reader" of a text, but Sandvoss is keen to move beyond this limited understanding of its role. Through his analysis of the contribution of the Constance School to reception theory, Sandvoss argues that an outstanding achievement of reception theory "is to have developed methodological strategies for the study of the empirical reader or media consumer in his or her everyday context." For Sandvoss, the way ahead lies in "combining the ethnographic tradition of media reception studies with the evaluative aesthetic analysis of the act of reading."

Another theory growing in importance for media studies is *affect theory*. In Chapter 12, Anna Gibbs suggests that the significance of affect theory for audience research lies in a refocusing of audience research practice on "communication and flow" rather than on "the subjects and objects produced within it." One of the many important insights emerging from affect theory concerns the ways that affect contagion can sweep through global populations and nations. Gibbs explains that some affects, particularly anger, fear, and enjoyment, are highly contagious. When mediated by audiovisual media, they can very quickly "infect" whole communities, nations, and even global populations, sometimes with catastrophic effects. Affect doesn't need words to be communicated … the visual image is sufficient to spread immediate fear and panic – or joy and euphoria – amplified by the addition of sound. Affect theory therefore allows us to identify a range of events and media "effects" that have so far escaped sustained academic analysis within audience studies.

Part III: Researching Audiences

The seven chapters in Part III deal with the methods used to research audiences. Their variety reminds us of the public lives of audiences and the "scenes" in public life where their activity has social and cultural significance. In some cases, these "scenes" are gaining rather than diminishing in importance – such as in advertising and, given the power of emerging software technologies for audience measurement, in ratings research. In general, the chapters offer a rationale for the methods they advocate and an account of their past use. Just as in other parts, the writers here appreciate the scale of the transformation currently affecting the media and look to the improvement of audience research practice resulting from greater clarity of purpose. So here we turn to discussions of brands and advertising, of ratings, of the benefits of quantitative research and the reinvention of "effects" research, of cultivation analysis, of research using performance and media production activities, and of media ethnography.

The first of the scenes addressed in this part, the world of advertising, is introduced by Adam Arvidsson (Chapter 13), who explains the history of advertising research and the genesis of brand advertising. As he notes, the management of audiences through advertising research has generated criticism for its administrative bias. But Arvidsson argues that changes are occurring in the advertising industry as it comes to terms with the new possibilities offered by social media. In this context, the significance of the emergence of brands as the new focus of advertising (the brand as itself a medium offering access to an environment of consumption), and as the means by which collaborative relationships with audiences are established, is explained.

Another "industry scene" where audience research has been criticized for its administrative bias is ratings research. In Chapter 14, Phillip Napoli explains this criticism as arising from different ideological positions about consumption and consumer rights. Today, he argues, the old broadcast ratings' emphasis on tracking "exposure" to media content, divorced from consideration of the significance of media content for audiences, is on the wane. Importantly, new types of measures of audience engagement are emerging, and many of these may prove as useful for academic as for industry researchers. Overall his view is that the future promises exciting new possibilities, especially "to investigate new and different questions related to both media audiences and media institutions … and, ultimately, to expand the parameters of ratings analysis in the years to come."

Both advertising and ratings research have relied primarily on quantitative research methods and statistical analysis, and arguably this has added to the suspicion many academic researchers have felt about the capacity of quantitative methods to represent the views and interests of audiences. When research participants cannot speak for themselves but are confined to expressing their views through surveys and questionnaires, some researchers have felt that the voice of the audience is silenced. In Chapter 15, David Deacon and Emily Keightley take issue with this view and argue that the reluctance of media and audience researchers to use quantitative methods threatens to weaken the overall strength of the audience research interventions that academics make. They advocate combining the use of "extensive" and "intensive" methods in audience research because whereas intensive methods are needed to understand the social, cultural, and political significance of media issues for audiences, extensive methods provide more reliable options for extrapolating from the data and making a forceful case in policy debates.

One area where audience researchers have not shied away from using quantitative methods has been in the study of media "effects." In chapter 16, Brian O'Neill explains that effects research has been criticized for its functionalism, its individualism, and its inability or reluctance to engage with issues of wider concern to society, and for reflecting what the media industry wants to know about audiences rather than the media concerns and criticisms of audiences. Against this, O'Neill points out that it is effects research that generates most press coverage and defines popular criticism of the media. Like the three earlier chapters in this part, O'Neill argues that the current media research environment offers great scope for moving beyond the old ideological debates that have divided the field, and to search for new ways to do pertinent and useful studies of media effects. For O'Neill, "[T]he challenge for effects researchers will be to meet policy makers' expectations for straightforward answers with intellectually rigorous policy guidance" while retaining respect for the complexity of audiences.

In Chapter 17, Andy Ruddock turns to *cultivation analysis*, which was initially intended to explain the "cultural effects" of viewing violent media content on television. It attempted to do this by using a combination of both quantitative and qualitative methods, and, within the limits of its own research design, was able to explain the gender and race politics of media violence and the ideological stance of the media industries in the United States. By documenting the number of violent acts broadcast, and the gender and race of victims and perpetrators, early cultivation analysis laid the foundations for future research about violence and the media. Ruddock believes that this early emphasis remains relevant today. But, in addition, he notes that today it's much easier to gain access to audience commentary on broadcast TV shows from the shows' websites. This opens an opportunity for collaboration between cultivation analysis and fan studies.

In Chapter 18, Fatimah Awan and David Gauntlett contest the heavy focus in audience research on methods that require audiences to express their views in words, whether written (as in questionnaires, surveys, diaries, and writing letters) or spoken (as in interviews and focus groups). They argue instead for the inclusion of more visual and creative ways for research participants to express themselves, and document a range of studies where (for example) children have been involved in producing short videos, playing games, and constructing objects using Lego. Awan and Gauntlett argue that using creative and visual methods offers audience research new directions for the future and access to richer and more complex data about audiences.

The final research method included in this part is media ethnography, the method of choice for researching communities and subcultural groups as audiences. Patrick Murphy begins Chapter 19 by questioning the importance of distinguishing between doing "ethnographic research" and doing research that is somewhat ethnographic or that incorporates fragments of ethnographic method. His aim is less to judge whether or not research methods are ethnographic than to open discussion about the particular tensions within ethnography that have resulted in its methods being separated from its mode of presentation (as written narrative). Murphy argues that the way we understand "the field" in media ethnography holds the key to the current ferment in media ethnography. Two of the reasons why Murphy proposes this are the "deterritorialization of culture" that has accompanied global media culture, and the fact that yesterday's "natives" are no longer cut off from an understanding of the wider cultures in which they are situated. This means that research subjects have greater awareness of who they are and of what's at stake in talking to an ethnographer. As a result, Murphy sees the field as "dissolving" in terms of traditional understanding of "the field," as researchers experiment with ways of doing ethnography online, with geographically dispersed groups, and even with characters in game worlds. As it breaks the bonds with its past, media ethnography stretches out to occupy new territories.

Part IV: Doing Audience Research

In certain situations, "doing" audience research means coming to terms with the fact that either the people participating or the type of audience activity addressed places constraints on the way research is carried out. The chapters included in this part offer examples of such situations. Even though each chapter deals with a differently "situated" audience, they all reflect on a theme that is of enduring importance in audience studies – the interplay of audience-ing and identity. These chapters look beyond simplistic understandings of audience engagement as "usage" and reflect on the diverse ways that audiences and media are active in the constitution of identity.

In Chapter 20, Sonia Livingstone and Kirsten Drotner introduce us to two quite different audience "situations." First, they report on a series of studies about child audiences, alerting us to the relevance of differences in age and power, and the particular rights of children as research subjects. They argue that we cannot afford to ignore the size and economic value of children's culture and what's happening to it globally, because children are the future and a "creative, emotional, and ethical force shaping continuities and change for societies everywhere." To the situation of the child audience, they add the complications associated with comparative research, because the child audiences they discuss were researched as part of an international project. The nature and complexity of the global audience, in terms of the different communication futures that children are able to imagine, have not received sufficient academic attention, in their view, and they call for more comparative research.

The next audience "situation" included in this part is that of the fan and fan communities. The study of fans holds a unique position in audience research. In Chapter 21, Kristina Busse and Jonathan Gray trace its genesis and development from two main influences: first, from forms of audience research that, from the 1980s, advocated integrating audience research and reader response criticism; and, second, from cultural studies' embrace of "the popular" as an academically legitimate field of research. Fan research offered immediate access to people who had developed deep and lasting attachments to popular culture texts and characters, and who, importantly, were only too willing to talk about them. In addition, fans were not averse to expressing their own creative interests by reworking popular culture artifacts and did not hold back from repurposing copyrighted materials for their own ends. As a result, they were only too ready to take advantage of the opportunities offered by the internet to extend their media production and to share it online. Busse and Gray point out, however, that the internet has made it possible for many more people to express their fandom as individuals rather than through fan communities, and this has resulted in a differentiation of ways of being a fan. This differentiation has not yet extended in any systematic way outside the realms of popular culture texts, in spite of the fact that many other "audience situations" support audience communities that strongly resemble fandoms.

In Chapter 22, Mirca Madianou addresses the reception situations faced by "ethnically and culturally differentiated audiences." Madianou argues that it is essential that research about ethnically diverse audiences take an "audience-centered" perspective in order to recognize and respect the internal differences among people of shared ethnic and/or cultural backgrounds. She proposes that studies of transnational audiences and media, which in the past have been used to construct and essentialize ethnic cultures, should question our assumptions about the nature of "culture" and of "essentialism."

Jennifer Deger (Chapter 23), an anthropologist working with Indigenous Australian communities, demonstrates the intimacy and immediacy of ethnographic research practice in documenting her experiences of watching DVDs with her Yolngu family-by-adoption. This chapter confirms the benefits of long-term observation and thick description as the means by which the researcher can start to ask better, more relevant questions of his or her research subjects. In this case, Deger draws attention to the fact that her research subjects understand their identity in terms of "a being-in-relationship to others, never in terms of the individuated self." This alters the basic presuppositions on which most individualized Western viewing is based, because for this community the stories become ways of "constituting the social on local terms." The chapter demonstrates in situ research processes noted by Murphy (Chapter 19) and Madianou (Chapter 22).

Annette Hill (Chapter 24) introduces the situation of the (televised) live audience. Initially taking a historical perspective, Hill reviews the changing conventions about what has constituted acceptable behavior for live audiences in the past, before addressing the problem of the television studio audience and other situations where the audience itself becomes "the show." She is particularly interested in the work of magicians and hypnotists, whom she describes as "audience handlers" because for the show to succeed, the audience has to be complicit in the construction of the skills of the performer. The active participation of the audience is essential as the success of the media event as a cultural experience rests on co-performance and co-production by both performer and audience. Hill points to the potential in this type of research for the study of the production of belief in additional contexts such as televangelism and political debate.

In Chapter 25, S. Elizabeth Bird points to the importance of research about audiences and news. As she notes, there is a body of research about news and its presentation, but this has often ignored the actual interests and involvements with news of people as audiences. Instead, journalism and public opinion research focused on whether people can remember and regurgitate news stories, whether they like or dislike certain news stories, and, most importantly, what might be done to produce the sorts of responses to news stories others desire. While everyone is dependent on news reporting for information about the world we live in, the research on news audiences has demonstrated that there is little consensus about what is news and what is not on the part of the people of its audiences. The ways journalists define and classify news stories hold little interest for audiences, who not infrequently are looking for points of relevance and identification. Their interest in news seems rather to involve attempts at "constituting the social on local terms," as Jennifer Deger put it in her description of Yolngu viewing. While news presents a challenge for audience research, it offers an important avenue for understanding the ways people apprehend the significance of social, political, economic, and cultural events and their significance for the ways they live their lives.

Like news, sport is a ubiquitous audience experience, and as David Rowe (Chapter 26) points out, it draws our attention to the range and diversity of sport now crowding into television's diverse platforms. We watch sport on national, commercial, and cable TV channels. We go online to check scores and find information about players' histories. Mobile phone companies encourage us to download results and scores. Rowe suggests that the proliferation of sport in the media is no accident. Sport, he proposes, has been called upon to "enliven television in the face of pressures on audience time and competition from other media." For its aficionados, sport generates intense emotion and affect. It documents the interplay of aggression and creativity, submission and defiance. It legitimates bending the rules and seeing what you can get away with. Metaphorically, Rowe argues, televised sport enacts the qualities and characteristics needed to succeed in the world of global capitalism.

Notes

1   Rosen and Bruns are mentioned in several chapters, particularly in Green and Jenkins (Chapter 5) and Couldry (Chapter 10).
2   Email from Lynda Bennett, 24/4/10: "My dad's full name was Reginald Howard Bennett, but he was known by everyone as Reg Bennett so if you mention his name, then Reg Bennett it must be! It was probably taken in the summer of 1948 in our back garden in Wood Green, North London...I thought you might like to see the sequence that Dad took at the time - there were 5 pictures all told, but unfortunately I moved during the taking of the last one. Dad thought of himself as an above-average amateur photographer and he entered the photos into a newspaper competition but sadly for him he never won anything with them. The radio would have been hand-made by him. In the days of valves, it wasn't that difficult for people with the confidence, skill and, of course, a soldering iron, to make them themselves."

References

Bruns, A. 2007 Produsage. Retrieved from http://produsage.org

Downing, J.D.H. 2001 *Radical Media: Rebellious Communication and Social Movements*. Sage, Thousand Oaks, CA.

Lévy, P. 1997 *Collective Intelligence: Mankind's Emerging World in Cyberspace*. Trans. Robert Bonnono. Perseus, Cambridge, MA.

Meadows, M., Forde, S., Ewart, J. and Foxwell, K. 2007 Empowering audiences: transformative processes in Australian community broadcasting. *Australian Journalism Review*, 29, 1, pp. 27–40.

Naficy, H. 1993 *The Making of Exile Cultures: Iranian Television in Los Angeles*. University of Minnesota Press, Minneapolis.

Nightingale, V. 2004 Television audiences: publics, markets, communities and fans. In J.D.H. Downing, ed. *Sage Handbook of Media Studies*. Sage, Thousand Oaks, CA, pp. 227–249.

Rosen, J. 2006 The people formerly known as the audience. Retrieved from http://journalism.nyu.edu/pubzone/weblogs/pressthink/2006/06/27/pplfrmr.html

Wallis R. and Malm, K. 1984 *Big Sounds from Small People: Music Industry in Small Countries*. Pendragon, New York.

Part I
Being Audiences

1

Readers as Audiences

Wendy Griswold, Elizabeth Lenaghan, and Michelle Naffziger

"Reading," an instantly recognizable and socially valued activity, has boundaries that are difficult to discern. Changes in both the delivery of written words and the breadth of access to them have drawn attention to the instability of concepts like "the reader" and "the book/text." There is nothing new about this. When a letter from a student abroad in London arrived in a colonial Nigerian village, a literate community member would transmit its contents to the nonliterate parents. Who is the reader here? Is it the person who mechanically translates the letter from written to oral form, or the parents who memorize the contents and scrutinize the words for what is said and left unsaid? What is the text, the words on paper or the set of connotations and implications drawn by the parents? Online reading and electronic media present such questions in a different technological form and context, but they remain the same questions. The analyst may take an expansive or restrictive view of the process and practices, but the absence of bright lines between reading and some other activity (e.g. scanning blogs or downloading podcasts of news reports) is a constant.

That being the case, the following discussion is shaped by several choices. First, we are not focusing on literacy – as in who develops the capacity to decode writing – but on the practices of reading. Second, in keeping with most of the social scientific and indeed the popular uses of the term, we define *reading* to be leisure time reading; literacy is required for an increasing percentage of occupations worldwide, but to say someone is "a reader" or "likes to read" refers to their leisure pursuits rather than to their occupational requirements. Third, we draw primarily on the research involving traditional genres, especially "the book." While the ways in which texts can reach their potential audience are rapidly evolving and multiplying, books continue to be the model that new media emulate, as when electronic reading devices, like Apple's iPad and Amazon's Kindle, replicate the printed page.

The Handbook of Media Audiences, First Edition. Edited by Virginia Nightingale.
© 2014 John Wiley & Sons, Ltd. Published 2014 by John Wiley & Sons, Ltd.

A reader is an individual, and readers are aggregates of individuals, but an audience is a collectivity, a mass phenomenon whose attributes are not the sum of individual components. So what might conceiving of readers as "an audience" offer us? Conceptualizing readers-as-audience encourages an emphasis, first, upon the social, economic, and political context in which reading takes place; and, second, upon the agency of readers as constructors of meaning, images of passivity having been superseded by those that emphasize interpretive agency.[1]

Cultural studies, to take a prominent disciplinary example, has looked at readers in context since its mid-twentieth-century inception. Hoggart (1957) considered television, along with "degraded" media such as magazines, a threat to the traditional rhythms and values of British working-class life, while Wertham (1955) argued that comic books endangered the sensibilities and morality of young Americans. By the mid-1980s, the image of vulnerable readers gave way to an emphasis on resilience and resistance (Willis 1977; Morley 1980; Fiske 1989). This made way not only for readers to be understood as more active interpreters of texts, but also for less canonical interpretations of texts to gain legitimacy, as in Radway's (1984) seminal look at how women readers of romance novels rationalize their practice and understand its meaning in ways not suggested by the ontological boundaries of the text itself.

Both linguistic and cultural studies theories find contemporary analogs in reader response criticism and reception studies. Emerging directly from the structuralist and poststructuralist movements (including Barthes 1968/1977), reader response criticism emphasizes the individual reader's role in constructing the meaning of texts. Reception studies, while also emphasizing the individual's role in meaning making, go to greater lengths to situate individual responses within a larger cultural context. In its earliest incarnations, both reader response criticism and reception studies found inspiration in the work of Jauss (1982) and Iser (1974, 1978), whose phenomenological approaches to reading were seen as a departure from the Marxist emphasis on production (see also Fish 1980). Feminist and ethnic studies scholars, rejecting the concept of the "universal reader," have explored discrete, marginalized text communities (Radway 1997; Bobo 1992; Currie 1999; Sonnet 1999, 2000).

An audience perspective, then, suggests that the analyst might conceive of readers, or of a readership, as a collective body. The readers-as-audience may share socioeconomic and/or demographic characteristics, may be targeted as a group, and may respond to or resist literary messages. Furthermore, members of the collectivity may influence one another through interaction or because of a shared identification. The scale of the audience (from universal to micro) is an empirical question, as is the degree of agency the group exercises. Beyond what they share with all audiences, readers have specific and defining attributes as well. These include both the material conditions that reading entails and the social practices and institutions surrounding reading. An audience for a live concert, for example, is interacting with a transient cultural object compared with a book's stability and availability; a theater audience has the potential for collective effervescence while a reading audience is an abstraction from what are typically private engagements with texts. Following is a consideration of how these specific attributes impact the readers-as-audience model.

Books as Material Objects, Reading as Physical Practice

Taking into account the material properties of books means considering how the physical act of reading is directly tied to the physicality of books themselves. The burgeoning field of book history contains a number of steps in this direction. McKenzie (1985) and McGann (1983) helped to move textual studies beyond the impulse to create essentialist distinctions between different types of texts (i.e. print vs. digital) and back toward a rhetoric of material forms. McGann, in particular, has specified what he terms "the poetics of the book" to discuss the production and distribution of books in terms of their material properties (page format, paper, typeface etc.). As Chartier (2002) has since argued,

> Readers, in fact, never confront abstract, idealized texts detached from any material-
> ity. They hold in their hands, or perceive, objects and forms whose structures and
> modalities govern their reading or hearing and consequently the possible compre-
> hension of the text read or heard. (p. 48)

Chartier, like McGann, emphasizes the importance of the institutional structures governing the reception and production of books, concluding,

> We must insist that there is no text outside the material structure in which it is given to
> be read or heard. Thus there is no comprehension of writing, whatever it may be, which
> does not depend in some part upon the forms in which it comes to the reader. (p. 51)

The material culture approach, which focuses on these forms, offers a position from which to theorize the physical role of the book, even though it sometimes concentrates on the book-as-object to an extent that obscures the complexities of the surrounding social world. Other studies maintain a balance between attention to the physical properties of the book and the social world in which books circulate.[2] Some of the most successful efforts look at archival evidence from the beginnings of book printing and circulation to explore the role of books in the development of society and culture (Johns 1998; Swann 2001; Andersen and Sauer 2004; Brown 2007; Chartier 2007). In addition to detailing what books were printed and read in the burgeoning print cultures of early modern Europe and colonial America, these studies also detail how books were purchased, circulated, and displayed in both private and public places. This attention to the consumption and social rituals surrounding books, necessarily, pays close attention to their representation as material objects.

Another trend in recent research has responded to the perceived threat that digital content poses for the book as physical object by focusing on how the material forms of both historic and contemporary texts carry meanings that cannot be found in their digital reproductions. Journals such as *Modern Intellectual History* and *PMLA*, for example, have published special issues on book history that, according to editorial introductions, were inspired by just these concerns (Price 2006; Bell 2007). Lerer's (2006) epilogue to *PMLA*'s effort explicitly addresses this growing attention in both the scholarly and popular understanding of books. He counters decades-old predictions of the book's demise with centuries-old accounts of the joys of reading in bed, suggesting that he "can't imagine curling up with a computer" and elaborating, "I can imagine falling asleep in front of a screen but not 'over' one, the preposition *over* powerfully carries with it both the physical place of the reader and the imaginative space generated by that place" (p. 234, emphasis in original).

Lerer's attempt to distinguish the book from its digital form, based entirely on its physical properties, is echoed in the more popular accounts of journalists and bloggers, whose chronicles of the latest e-book ventures suggestively call into question the sorts of casual (though valued) facets of reading culture that might be lost to e-reading technology. These accounts include the serendipitous pleasures of digesting the titles consumed by fellow readers in coffee shops or on public transport, judging the tastes of potential lovers from the books in their collection, or taking in the smells and sights of public research libraries (Crain 2007; Grafton 2007; Dominus 2008; Donadio 2008). The significance of the loss of such encounters and the gains of digitalization is explored by professional organizations such as the (now) transatlantic Institute for the Future of the Book.[3]

Together, both print and digital as well as the academic and popular attempts to examine the significance of the physical form of the book point toward a contemporary desire to acknowledge and understand the importance of books as material objects. The consequences of such study not only help us to understand the role that books play in the larger social milieu in which reading takes place, but also indicate that the value of reading may not be solely determined by the content of books alone. Rather the materiality of books might determine both the propensity for, and the pleasure in, reading.

Books as Social Objects, Reading as Social Practice[4]

Historically a culture's "reading class" (Griswold, McDonnell, and Wright 2005) has been populated by a small minority, usually of men engaged in commerce or in religious or government administration. So a reading class is not the same as a broad-based reading culture, and indeed reading classes often flourish without reading cultures. Qing Dynasty China, for example, was administered by a reading class populated by the bureaucrats known as the *literati*, while most Chinese were illiterate. The manuscript culture of medieval European monasteries and the Koranic interpretation of conservative Islamic cultures of the past and present offer clear examples of elite reading classes separate from reading cultures. Readers, therefore, have been a privileged minority throughout most of human history. Although written records and communications became established in certain institutional niches, most people continued to occupy themselves with basic tasks – farming and hunting, tending children, and fighting – for which reading and writing were not much help. Reading was mainly useful for activities involving coordination and memory – administration, trade, and organized religion – and early readers were the people involved in these activities: rulers and their staffs, merchants, and priests. Even in so-called literate societies, the vast majority, including almost all women, almost all rural people, and most slaves, did not read.

Every society that has writing has a reading class, but not everyone who can read is a member. All societies with written language have a reading class, but few have a reading culture. A reading culture is a society where reading is expected, valued, and common. A reading class has a stable set of characteristics that include its human capital (education), its economic capital (wealth, income, occupational positions), its social capital (networks of personal connections), its demographic characteristics (gender, age, religion, ethnic composition), and – the defining and noneconomic characteristic – its cultural practices. Only during the past two centuries, and only in northwestern Europe, North America, Japan, and a few cities elsewhere, did reading become routine. It took the Industrial Revolution for reading to become a common leisure time activity, because when industrialism began to give way to the postindustrial society, reading became a vehicle to achieve secure employment in better jobs. In this handful of places, the reading culture also became a "reading audience" in which the majority of the adult population participated. So while the term *readers* could refer to each and any of these reading formations, it may be useful to reserve the term *reading audience* for readers whose reading experiences settle on a particular type of reading material.[5] For some material the reading audience may both be considerable and be largely independent of the reading class. An example is the immense reading audience for evangelical Christian fiction (E. Smith 2007). For other materials, such as academic research texts, the reading audience may be quite tiny.

In countries with essentially total adult literacy, something like half of all adults read books now and then, and something like 15% are heavy readers, the heart and soul of the reading class.

Surveys of reading conducted in various high-income countries over the past 50 years have repeatedly found that about 80 to 90 percent of the population reads *something*; 50 to 60 percent of the population reads books as a chosen leisure activity; and 10 to 15 percent of the population are avid readers, who borrow and buy the lion's share of books, magazines, newspapers, and other media consumed. (Ross, McKechnie, and Rothbauer 2006, pp. 17–18)

The NEA (2004) survey found that about 17% of Americans are *frequent readers* (reading 12–49 books/year), while only 4% are *avid readers* (reading 50+ books per year). Internationally, these figures vary somewhat – Scandinavians and Japanese are particularly heavy readers, while southern Europeans read less – but the basic pattern is roughly the same in developed countries: most people can read and do so as their work or daily lives require, about half read for leisure, and a few read a great deal.

The demographic patterns for developed countries are consistent as well. Readers in general (the 50% or so who read books) and the reading class (the 15% or so who read a lot) are highly educated; their amount of education is by far the strongest predictor of whether or not someone reads. They also tend to be urban, affluent, middle-aged, and female. The picture is often different in developing countries, where male literacy is invariably higher than female literacy and where older cohorts may have considerably less education than younger ones. Developed or not, individual countries often vary along religious and ethnic lines too; some minorities (e.g. African Americans) read less than average even when education is controlled, while others (Jews in North America and Europe) read more.

Readers have distinctive social characteristics as well. They tend to be very involved in cultural and civic life. Surveys show that readers have high rates of participation in the arts. Perhaps more surprising, given popular images of bookworms as introverts being lost in their reading, readers score higher than nonreaders on virtually all measures of civic and political participation: voting, membership in associations, and volunteerism. It is this tendency toward active participation, along with the characteristics of education and affluence, that give the reading class power and influence far beyond its relatively modest numbers.

So while elegies for the "death of the book/print/reading" hearken back to a time when the book/print/reading lived and flourished, taken in historical perspective, this period was a mid-nineteenth- to mid-twentieth-century anomaly. Today, as the use of electronic media increases, we are seeing a return to the norm: a thin slice of "readers" cut from a loaf of nonreaders. These nonreaders are literate, reading constantly for their work and for some of the business of everyday life, but they do not lose themselves in books, they rarely subscribe to newspapers or magazines, and they are seldom called *readers* by family and friends.

Institutions Bringing Social and Material Together

A vast institutional apparatus supports reading and readers, and these institutions perpetuate the social prestige of reading. Education is the most familiar example. Much of the early work of Bourdieu (1984) concentrated on how schools and schooling naturalize and justify social inequality. Similarly discussions of "the canon" emphasize the privileging of "good reading," while the response of multicultural education has aggressively broadened the definition of quality, and some proponents of popular culture want to do away with it altogether. Religion is another institutional field that legitimates, even makes sacred, certain texts and certain ways of reading. Christianity, Judaism, and Islam are all "religions of the book," organized around scriptures believed to be divinely inspired or written. The third of the major institutional fields is commerce. Books were one of the first products of a consumer society. Urbanization and modernization bring newspapers, bookstores, and a reading public. Today books and other texts circulate globally and, especially in electronic format, almost freely, although authoritarian regimes still try to control them. The fourth institutional field that supports reading is the state itself, and virtually all levels of government. No form of cultural practice has anything approaching the extent of relentless government support and promotion as reading. At all levels from the local to the transnational, governments promote reading and literature through, for example, support of public libraries and promotion of literary festivals (Augst and Carpenter 2007). The authority of the regime is built on and supported by the sacred status of books.

Books and reading shape consumption practices well beyond the actual sale of reading materials. A wealth of consumer products beyond media spinoffs accompanies a reading phenomenon like the *Harry Potter* or the *Twilight* series. Many bookstores incorporate coffee shops and "third places" for community gathering.[6] More rarified spaces exist: the Library Hotel in New York City offers its guests over 6000 volumes of books organized throughout the hotel by the Dewey Decimal System. Interior decorators follow Anthony Powell's (1971) advice on elite domestic spaces: "Books do furnish a room."[7] Institutional supports, from the stable (education, public libraries), to the episodic (literary festivals), to the trendy (the Library Hotel), support, create, and reward readers, thereby shaping both the reading audience and those who do not read themselves but observe this audience. Consider how this works in two different fields: the macro-institutional level of schools, and the micro-interactional level of book groups.

Reading and schools

When scholars consider the practice of reading in the context of schools, their work builds from the fundamental assumption that reading is intimately tied to the development, transformation, or maintenance of the social order. Research in this area asks what students read; how this varies by ability, race, or class; what values are associated with the content of reading; and how particular values or reading practices are translated into costs or benefits for students and, more broadly, various groups within society.

Reading can be understood as a mechanism for developing human capital in the form of cognitive skills and linguistic tools (Bernstein 1964, 1973; Coleman 1988). Sociologists take gaps in reading ability as evidence of broader race- and class-based inequalities (Farkas 2000; Jencks and Phillips 1998). Exacerbating differences in ability, in some tracked school systems teachers teach standard literature to high school students in higher tracks but young adult fiction to students in lower tracks (Oakes 1986; Gamoran 1993).

Looking beyond the question of ability, some scholars understand the practice of reading, and reading certain texts, in terms of status culture and as a form of capital that can be mobilized for social advantages (Weber 1946; Collins 1971; Bourdieu and Passeron 1977; Bourdieu 1984). Regarding cultural capital as an indicator and/or basis for class position, Bourdieu argued that class-based attitudes, preferences, and behaviors are conceptualized as "tastes" which can be mobilized for social selection. Dominant groups use such cultural capital to define their boundaries and justify exclusion even in the eyes of the excluded. Schools are a key venue for the translation of cultural capital into social advantages. Collins (1971) goes so far as to suggest that their primary function is to teach status cultures in the form of "vocabulary and inflection, styles of dress, aesthetic tastes, values and manners" (p. 1010); such education will be advantageous when "the fit is greatest between the culture of the status groups emerging from schools, and the status group doing the hiring" (p. 1012).

Many studies consider reading as one component of cultural capital. As such, these analyses test for effects of participation in high-status culture activities on school achievement (see DiMaggio 1982; Farkas et al. 1990; Lareau and Weininger 2003, among many others). Parent-to-child reading is considered essential for student school success. Educators and public officials regard the practice of parents reading to children as virtually sacred. What is read matters less than how they read with their families. Parent-to-child reading is understood both as developing human capital and as preparing children for successful interactions in schools. When children read with their parents, they learn to take and use meanings according to shared community rules (Heath 1983, 1996). When children get to schools, these meanings influence their chances of success.[8]

Scholars also assess how actors value reading by focusing on battles over *what* students should read. Primary, secondary, and postsecondary reading content all serve as battlegrounds for contestation. Actors can and do engage in these battles on both through challenges to entire curricula or specific disciplinary canons, and through opposition to particular books. In a review of research on higher education, Stevens, Armstrong, and Arum (2008) find that because universities grant status and legitimate knowledge, university actors and content become the target of political contestation. Small-scale battles, often targeting school libraries, tend to focus on battles over particular books in the form of censorship. Censorship may result from a moral reform movement or from class-based efforts at social reproduction (Beisel 1990), or it may be based on shifting evaluations (e.g. the depiction of African Americans and the removal from school curricula of books that use the word *nigger* such as *Huckleberry Finn*). Control over reading can be used as a tool for social reproduction, but at the same time actors imbue freedom to read with a democratic ethos. Librarians shifted from being "moral censors" in the late 1800s to being "guardian[s] of the freedom to read" in the early twentieth century (Geller 1984, p. xv).

Book groups

Book groups "constitute one of the largest bodies of community participation in the arts" (Poole 2003, cited in Burwell 2007, p. 285). A Google.com search on the phrase "book club" produces 23,700,000 hits. Book clubs are growing rapidly, with estimates of 500,000 in the United States as of 2002, 50,000 in the United Kingdom (Hartley 2002), and 40,750 in Canada (Sedo 2002). Further, Sedo has estimated the individual membership of book clubs in the United States at 17,230,933 and in Canada at between 244,500 and 489,000. As this growth continues, more and more people will experience and interpret specific books in groups rather than solely as individuals.

Reading in groups for both black and white women dates back to nineteenth-century literary societies and is intimately connected to social reform (McHenry 2002; Murray 2002; Long 2003; Kelly 2008). In her study of the Boston Gleaning Circle, the first postrevolutionary reading group not connected to a particular institution, Kelly (2008) finds that women used the space of the reading circle to puzzle through the rights and responsibilities of women citizens. They developed their reading and social practices based on transatlantic traditions and cultural institutions and engaged in and informed this discourse. Women in this group were dedicated to "the improvement of the mind" (p. 8). The group would write as they read and share those communications with one another. They used one another to understand their world: "meeting in this social way to search for truth" (p. 9).

Long's (2003) survey of 73 contemporary reading groups in Houston showed that members of book clubs generally match the demographic criteria of readers outlined by Griswold, McDonnell, and Wright (2005). Long found that book club members are generally highly educated, affluent, stable, and traditional with regard to marriage and religion. Indeed, ethnographic work on book clubs generally focuses on groups of women readers (see also Eberle 1997, 2007).

Considering the homogeneity of reading group membership, texts serve as sites for "encounters with difference" that are "more likely to occur through textual engagement than through encounters with other members" (Burwell 2007, p. 285). Readers work collectively to make sense of books in relation to their own subjectivities and experiences:

> [P]articipants in book groups create a conversation that begins with the book each woman has read but moves beyond the book to include personal connections and meanings each has found in the book, and the new connections with the book, with

inner experience, and with the perspectives of the other participants that emerge
within the discussion. (Long 2003, p. 144)

One way that groups of readers use texts is to look for guidance on how to identify and handle problems, both public and private. Readers look to books for
"equipment for living" (Burke 1973), but sometimes readers produce surprising
interpretations of seemingly straightforward texts. Some readers challenge conventional interpretations of genres, such as those who read romances to defy traditional gender roles (Radway 1983, 1984). Long (2003) argues that the groups she
studied did more than passively look to books for advice on how to live. Instead,
she found that groups constructed collective reflections on life that resonated with
their experiences and with an ideal sense of how the world should be; reading
group discussions are "creative cultural work" enabling members "to articulate or
even discover who they are: their values, their aspirations, and their stance toward
the dilemmas of their worlds" (p. 145).

While the typical reading group takes place in a private home, libraries are
increasingly starting book clubs. Library science journals abound with articles
providing advice on what makes a book club effective, why libraries should offer
them, and how effective book clubs operate. For example, in *Teacher Librarian*, Hall
(2007) shares lessons learned from running a "really popular book club," which
include incorporating movies, field trips, even a sleepover and other activities to
keep students excited about and engaged in the club's book choices (see also Solan
2006; Priddis 2007). Some educators also argue for the establishment of book clubs
in school to encourage participation and better engage young readers. Heller
(2006) found that when first graders discuss nonfiction books in a book club–like
setting, children retell the facts they've learned as well as employ narratives to
make sense of the information they encountered in this genre of book. And
Twomey (2007), building on past research on how book club members reshape
their understandings of the social world, advocates incorporating books clubs in
education to encourage critical thinking.

A growing body of scholarship considers the impact of television talk show host
Oprah Winfrey's popular book club on how and what America reads and the effects
of that reading (Sedo 2002; Hall 2003; Striphas 2003; Farr 2004; B. Smith 2007).
Oprah's book club, which is broadcast as part of *The Oprah Winfrey Show*, appeared
in two incarnations, first from 1996 to 2002 and then again from 2003 until the
present. In its second incarnation, Oprah rebranded the book club as Traveling
with the Classics, focusing on literary classics and incorporating travel to sites in
the chosen books.

In her book on this subject, Farr argues that through her book club, Oprah advocates a "cultural democracy" because she encourages her readers to "challenge
given standards of taste in social contexts" (2004, p. 107). Farr understands this
cultural democracy as founded on "aesthetic freedom" (p. 101). Oprah expands the
base of who can read, what they should read, and how they should read as she uses

novels to "invite social interaction as well as intellectual engagement and personal transformation [which] affirms a wider and more generous standard for evaluating fiction" (p. 102). Oprah's book club reaffirms that "reading, valuing, and assessing literature is, and has long been, a democratic activity" (p. 103). Similarly, Fuller (2007) finds that a popular Canadian radio broadcast, *Canada Reads*, promotes a combination of reading practices that are both academic and widely engaged in by face-to-face book groups. He encourages researchers to develop "nuanced analyses of non-academic reading practices and theories capable of explaining the pleasures, politics, and social relations that reading practices both shape and resist."

The internet provides an infrastructure to support both online and face to face reading groups. The website www.ReadersCircle.org lists author events and 764 book groups open to new members in the United States, United Kingdom, Canada, Australia, and New Zealand. Readers are now organizing and sharing titles they have read through more than two dozen social-networking sites by names such as aNobii, Booktribes, LibraryThing, Shelfari, Squirl, and All Consuming (Schubert 2007). Such groups represent another way for readers to connect to one another as they engage with texts. In her study of an online mystery book group, Fister (2005) finds that though virtual, the group she studied actively works to build and maintain community. Club members share book recommendations and reviews with one another, building an international network of friendships in the process. Relationships sometimes extend beyond books as well, through the "sunshine club," a subcommittee of members who offer extra support and encouragement to members going through hard times. For Fister, who estimates that thousands of online reading groups have formed, these groups provide "a sense of community with books at the center" (p. 309). And in an online survey of 252 members of face-to-face and online reading groups, Sedo (2002) finds that virtual groups and face-to-face groups share many similarities. Members in both kinds of groups enjoy the intellectual stimulation provided by participation in these groups. She argues that virtual group members most appreciate the exposure to new books, while face-to-face members value sharing ideas and learning from one another. Face-to-face groups tend to meet once a month for between two to four hours at a time, while virtual groups sometimes discuss books daily. "The virtual meetings allow the reader to transcend physical, geographical and time boundaries, enriching her interpretations of the book" (Sedo 2002, p. 16).

Death and Resurrection

If predictions about the death of print, the death of the book, and even the death of reading are correct, exactly what is imagined to have died? In popular and academic discourse, the death of the book is linked to four things: literacy, reading, print, and "the book." No one supposes that the actual ratios of illiterates to literates is increasing, but what the Jeremiad predictions of the "death of literacy" focus on is a decrease in the literacy competence required by the labor market, which they assume is and will have a destructive impact on international competitiveness.

In the case of reading, the argument is that people are literate but they simply don't read. By read, all studies mean read in leisure time, not reading for work or school, and many studies refer to "serious" or "literary" reading, distinguishing between this and more popular or ephemeral reading materials. The National Endowment for the Arts issued a grim report in 2004: "The report can be ... summarized in a single sentence: literary reading in America is not only declining rapidly among all groups, but the rate of decline has accelerated, especially among the young." As for print, Gomez (2008), a writer turned publisher who has worked in e-books and online marketing, says this shift is already happening as new technologies cause declines in old media, not just books but also magazines, newspapers, network television, and movie attendance. Print material will go the way of music, "ending up as a digital file, instead of as a physical thing" (p. 16). Gomez argues that authors "won't ultimately care" any more than musicians do because "it's the writer's words that touch us, not the paper those words were printed on." In these critiques, a cultural object has emerged, not "books" but "the book," that incorporates all of these: literacy, leisure reading practices, and print. The "dead" metaphor "incorporates" quite literally "the book" as body, its materiality.[9]

While the death of "the book" is related to the death of print, the emphasis here is not simply on materiality – print versus digital media – but also upon the form itself. "Books" are linear, while digital "content" is splayed out and may be accessed at any point. Commenting on an article in *The Economist*, Gomez concedes that good points are raised, but is disgusted that

> [a]fter extolling all of the virtues of electronic books, the writer trots out the standard 'the book is perfect' argument.... *The Economist* classifies all readers as similar, noting that the most important thing to them was not to be interrupted while they're reading. This is a silly if not insane notion. Readers are changing ... some people will continue to hug novels in bay windows on autumn days, basking in the warm glow of a fireplace with a cup of chamomile at their side. But many more will embrace the convenience and advanced usability that digital technology and electronic reading provides. (pp. 26–27)

He argues – without evidence – that the novel itself will change into "short, pithy bursts." So far this prediction is not borne out by the types of new writing available. Most novels remain linear narratives just as in the past. So debates over the death or nondeath of reading are unabashedly premised on technological change and ignore the social dimensions of reading. There are two aspects to this debate that warrant further attention. One is the variation in global reading audiences. The second is the social position of reading.

Research about global reading audiences concentrates on the literacy of adult populations; the degree of tertiary education; the inequality of education by gender; book and newspaper production per capita; reading surveys; and any other indicators of unequal distribution of reading practices, such as different religious or cultural traditions. Such research suggests that there are four types of reading cultures, each with specific configurations of reading audiences: advanced, restricted, emerging, and potential reading cultures:

- *Advanced reading cultures* occur in countries with substantial tertiary education (above 50%) and established reading practices (as indicated by newspaper circulation, book production, library use, and survey data).
- *Restricted reading cultures* occur where lower percentages of the population access tertiary education and reading practices in general are weaker. They are characterized by well-established reading classes but considerably less middle-class or mass reading. This is the case in Italy and some Muslim countries.
- *Emerging reading cultures* are similar but demonstrate rapidly increasing participation in tertiary education and attempts to redress historical inequalities of region and gender. Some countries, like Portugal, have introduced explicit programs to increase reading.
- *Potential reading cultures* tend to be found in nations that are changing slowly or where improvements are disrupted by war. These are countries, like Nigeria and Sierra Leone, with very low rates of participation in tertiary education, that are unable to provide a secure social basis for a reading class beyond the narrow elite.

The global situation demonstrates considerable diversity, but would seem to herald an increase in elite reading classes at the expense of reading cultures. However, we should bring technology back into the picture at this point because it seems likely that the new media, user-generated content (UGC), and web 2.0 are not bringing about the death of reading, or a postprint age, or the disappearance of the book in ink-on-dead-trees form, but are changing the nature and type of reading experiences available.

First, consider the demographic likenesses and differences between the new media class and the established reading class. To a large extent, they include the same people. In terms of internet use, the digerati *are* the literati. Heavy users of new media and heavy readers are (above all) highly educated, and they tend to be affluent and urban as well. They represent advantaged groups in most societies, yet the two classes are not entirely congruent. This leads us back to the issue of "reading audiences" and, more specifically, to the question of who reads e-books. Historians do (Grafton 2007), and so do students and academics, though, as McKiel (2007) notes, even these prefer print books.

Students are judging e-books as inferior to finding and using regular books – a process that they understand well and find easy to do. They also judge e-books to be

inferior to books because of the portability and ease of use for reading print books. …
The e-book collection is not primarily purchased as a collection of books that would
be read cover-to-cover.… Until e-book reading devices are preferred to printed books
and are commonly available, the e-book collection will not be seen as preferable
when the intent is to read an entire work. (p. 3)

As argued earlier, reading for pleasure distinguishes both the reading class, and
the reading audience of the present and future. Yet McKeil finds that it is academic,
not public, libraries that use e-books. Public libraries "serve a much higher proportion
of their patrons with content that is read cover to cover, much of it fiction. The
primary mission of an academic library is the provision of content for research and
teaching" (p. 2). And while it has been the mission of Apple iPad, Sony Reader, and
Amazon.com's Kindle to change this, it is not clear what success they have had.
Neither Sony nor Amazon reports sales (Amazon's reluctance on this is especially
surprising given their heavy promotion of the Kindle).[10]

According to the PEW Report (2007) 8% of American adults are technology
"Omnivores…Web 2.0 devotees, highly engaged with video online and digital content. Between blogging, maintaining their Web pages, remixing digital content, or
posting their creations to the websites, they are creative participants in cyberspace."
They are predominantly men (70%) and in their twenties (53%). Students and academics, sometimes reluctantly, use new media forms for ready access to information, but there is little evidence that any group of leisure readers is relying primarily
on e-books, reading online, or other forms of new media for their reading.

The core of the reading class is very different in composition. It is mostly middle-
aged people, especially women (55–60%). In terms of the PEW (2007) study, they
are closest to the "connected but hassled" group; they are online to manage their
work and domestic affairs, but not to read in what little leisure time they have.
Given these differences, and despite the fact that they draw from the same pool of
educated and advantaged readers, the new media class seems unlikely to replace
the reading class (young men will not become middle-aged women), and the reading
class seems unlikely to convert wholesale to digital books.

A second reason why the reading class is not dying is social, specifically the
social life of books – which is not quite the same as the social life of information.
A wealth of research suggests that technology per se rarely produces social or cultural change (print using movable type may have been the exception to the rule).
More typically, technological innovations facilitate people doing what they were
already doing, only more efficiently. So if what people "were already doing" is getting information, then media other than books-on-paper may be preferable. But
people do other things with books. Most notably, they entertain themselves, and
nothing has beaten the book in terms of portability and use in all personal spaces –
the bath, the bed, and public transportation. They use books in interactions –
bringing the marked-up copy to the book club – and as objects of loan, trade, and
gift. They collect and display books, and in these activities the material nature of

the book is paramount. They signal interests, passions, and other identity markers through the books they carry, the books they are observed reading on planes and in coffee houses (this doesn't work for Kindles, although an e-book reader might signal something else, like technology geek). None of these aspects of the social life of books is conveyed in the books-as-vehicles-for-information model, and to confuse these is to misunderstand the reading audience and its desires.

The third reason is cultural. Reading is a sign of status and has explicit connections to the realm of the sacred.[11] For this reason, it is accorded immense social honor, even by those who are not themselves part of the reading class. This is why there are so many institutional supports for reading, seen most dramatically in literary festivals and One Book programs.[12]

Readers and Social Honor: A Lesson from Africa

A West African case vividly illustrates the social prestige accorded to readers everywhere (Griswold, McDonnell, and Metz 2006). Ghanaian and Nigerian internet users of all ages were surprised when asked if their online time affected their reading. They uniformly insisted that the internet had no impact on reading, unless it was to support it by providing access to information about authors and books. They did think that their internet use competed for time with a number of things – they mentioned phone calls, hanging out with friends, watching television after school, and writing letters – but not with reading. This is consistent with what seems to be the case in the West: internet use has a negative relationship with television watching, but either no impact or a slightly positive one on reading. Although the internet–reading relationship may be similarly noncompetitive, the reasons for this are somewhat different. In the West, the positive relationship between internet use and reading is an example of the more general point that educated people do more of just about everything. Surveys have shown that middle-class people don't just participate more in highbrow culture; they also participate in just about every form of cultural activity (Erickson 1996; Peterson and Kern 1996). We suspect the same is true for West Africans. In West Africa, to a far greater extent than in the West, reading and going online occupy different physical, temporal, social, and especially cultural spaces from each other.

In Nigeria and Ghana, people read for pleasure in their homes, in private vehicles (for those lucky enough to ride in them), or – for students – in the school library. They go online in cybercafés. They read after their evening meal, or in the early morning. They also read at work, more or less surreptitiously, and on their way to work if the vehicle is not too crowded. Adults, especially job seekers, use the internet in the daytime, and students – the most frequent users – go online in the mid-afternoon and early evening. Electrical failures drive Nigerians and Ghanaians from their televisions to their local cybercafés. Loss of power has less impact on reading, which does not require electric light during the day. West Africans view reading as a private activity (even if surrounded by other people), while they regard going online as a social activity. Internet use is in public and often in groups. Moreover, going online is inherently social, maintaining ties to distant friends, relatives, and strangers (even scams are social). Middle-class women are a significant portion of the West African reading class but a negligible portion of the internet class.

Going online is new, trendy, and associated with youth and globalization, yet tainted for Nigerians by its association with scams. West Africans hold no comparable reservations about reading. On the contrary, the occasional persecution of journalists and writers has established them as cultural heroes. Reading is established, institutionally encouraged, and associated with elite practices and with wisdom and has the attractions of honor. Thus the two activities occupy different cultural positions; they do not compete in West African culture. Nigerians and Ghanaians read for information, for study, for self-improvement, for entertainment, and to enact and demonstrate their social status. They go online to maintain or initiate social connections, for fun, for practical reasons (school and job searches), and to enact and demonstrate their cosmopolitanism. The functions of the two activities overlap but are by no means congruent. West Africans regard reading as more serious, the mark of a refined person, someone of substance and gravity, while using the internet is fun, practical, and the mark of the young and the trendy.

There is every reason to believe that this separation between the sacred status of reading and the more profane (though possibly glamorous) states of other media use persists everywhere. Technological change does not unsettle longstanding cultural hierarchies but augments them. More generally, readers – whether we are talking about committed members of the reading class, reading audiences for specific kinds of materials, or the general literature population – exist in a network of social relations, material contingencies, status cultures, demographic relationships, micro-interaction contexts, global exchanges, and individual bodies that seek emotional and physical pleasure. Their reading cannot be reduced to information gathering, sheer escapism, or any other single dimension. Scholarship that acknowledges complexity will be on sounder footing than predictions based on a single angle of vision.

Notes

1   Both early twentieth-century pragmatism (Park 1922; Dewey 1927) and later studies of mass communications (Lasswell 1927) and "uses and gratifications" (Blumler and Katz 1975; Katz 1990) influenced the reading-in-context approach. Schmidt, for example, advocated a "systems-oriented" approach to literature that locates readers as actors who inscribe meanings based on their cultural and structural context (1998, pp. 646–650). Other empirical studies of literature have taken more cognitive approaches to understanding how readers derive meaning from texts, for example by using experimental

designs to isolate how readers use textual features (such as word order or line breaks) and personal experiences to identify the important elements of a narrative (Miall 2006; see also Wolf 2007). More squarely in the mass communications tradition is work on marketing and consumer culture that looks at new systems for measuring audience behavior as shaping producer and consumer choice. Chris Anderson's (2006) "long-tail" theory, for example, looks at how seemingly infinite choices for consumer content (represented by online retailers such as Amazon, eBay, and Netflix) suggest new models for marketing and publicity that allow for greater consumer agency in determining a product's popularity or distribution. In the literary field, such methods have been used to study the adoption of the Bookscan Audience Measurement System in the American publishing industry (Andrews and Napoli 2006). Looking at how retailers' preferences for more accurate Bookscan technology forced publishers to change their longstanding practice of using bestseller lists to measure the success of newly published literature, these types of studies locate readers as an economic audience whose aggregate choices inform the behaviors of publishers and retailers.

2   Levenston (1992) and Danet (1997) are examples of studies that focus explicitly on the material aspects of their object of study at the expense of considering the larger social world from which these objects are derived.

3   See www.futureofthebook.org, sponsored by the University of Southern California and the MacArthur Foundation. In addition to regularly blogging on matters related to the evolution of print and media on their if:book site, the Institute's projects include maintenance and development of Sophie (a project of reading and writing rich media texts in a networked environment), CommentPress (a digital reading tool allowing users to comment on already-published texts in a conversational, networked manner), and MediaCommons (a site for scholars to post commentary and research on media-related themes). Their collective attempts to both probe and problematize the manner in which digital technologies engage material forms suggest the significance of physicality in even the most virtual realms.

4   Parts of this section are drawn from Griswold (2008).

5   As one study of reading audiences put it, "Audiences are not simply aggregates of readers. They are complicated social and textual formations; they have interpretive tendencies and ideological contours" (Klancher 1987, p. 6).

6   It is revealing that in the third (1999) edition of his 1989 book, Ray Oldenburg added "bookstores" to the list of public gathering spaces in the subtitle.

7   Anthony Powell's 1971 novel, *Books Do Furnish a Room*, which takes its title from a commonplace, was the tenth novel of his 12-volume cycle, *A Dance to the Music of Time*.

8   Cook-Gumperz (2006) identifies an early-modern link between literacy and virtue which still persists today. According to this approach, reading can be considered one aspect of a distinct interpretation of cultural capital in education as the ability for families to comply with institutional expectations (Lareau and Weininger 2003). Lareau finds that student success in elementary and secondary schools varies by class and depends on parents' ability to meet school expectations for parental involvement (see Lareau and Horvat 1999; Lareau 2000).

9   OED Incorporate: I. trans. 1. To combine or unite into one body or uniform substance; to mix or blend thoroughly together (a number of different things or one thing with another). [f. late L. incorpor{amac}t-, ppl. stem of incorpor{amac}re to embody, include, f. in- (IN-2) + corpor{amac}re to form into a body, CORPORATE v.]

10 On September 11, 2008, Jeffrey A. Trachtenberg reported in *The Wall Street Journal*'s Technology page that "The online retailer [Amazon.com] has steadily refused to provide any information regarding the number of Kindles in use.... Sony hasn't released sales figures for its device."

11 For a historical analysis of the overlap between reading and the sacred, especially as manifested in library architecture, see Augst (2007).

12 One of the most dramatic examples of collective reading is the multiplicity of "One Book, One City [or state, or community, or university, etc.]" programs. The idea started in 1998 when Nancy Pearl, a librarian and the head of the Washington State Center for the Book, launched a program called "What if All Seattle Read the Same Book?" Although Pearl and her colleagues thought the venture might fall flat, "One Book" programs were irresistible, tapping into readers' desires for intelligent discussions, libraries' desires to increase visibility in the community, and mayors' desires to associate their cities with the prestige of literature. "One Book" programs have proliferated in the United States and have spread to Canada, the United Kingdom, and Australia. In the United States, the Library of Congress attempts to maintain a list of the more prominent programs, although of course the plethora of university and institutional programs slip below the radar. See http://www.read.gov/resources/ for a current listing.

References

Andersen, J. and Sauer, E., eds. 2004 *Books and Readers in Early Modern England*. University of Pennsylvania Press, Philadelphia.

Anderson, C. 2006 *The Long Tail: Why the Future of Business Is Selling Less of More*. Hyperion, New York.

Andrews, K. and Napoli, P. 2006 Changing market information regimes: a case study of the transition to the bookscan audience measurement system in the U.S. book publishing industry. *Journal of Media Economics*, 19, 1, pp. 33–54.

Augst, T. 2007 Faith in reading: public libraries, liberalism, and the civil religion. In T. Augst and Carpenter, K., eds. *Institutions of Reading: The Social Life of Libraries in the United States*. University of Massachusetts Press, Amherst, pp. 148–183.

Augst, T. and Carpenter, K., eds. 2007 *Institutions of Reading: The Social Life of Libraries in the United States*. University of Massachusetts Press, Amherst.

Barthes, R. 1968/1977 The death of the author. In R. Barthes, *Image-Music-Text*. Trans. S. Heath. Fontana, London.

Beisel, N. 1990 Class, culture, and campaigns against vice in three American cities: 1872–1892. *American Sociological Review*, 55, pp. 44–62.

Bell, B. 2007 Symposium: what was the history of the book? Introduction. *Modern Intellectual History*, 4, 3, pp. 491–494.

Bernstein, B. 1964 Elaborated and restricted codes: their social origins and some consequences. *American Anthropologist*, 66, 6, pp. 55–69.

Bernstein, B. 1973 *Class, Codes, and Control*. Vol. 2, Routledge & Kegan Paul, London.

Blumler, J. and Katz, E., eds. 1975 The Uses and Gratifications approach to mass communications research. *Annual Review of Communication Research 3*. Sage, Beverly Hills, CA.

Bobo, J. 1992 The Color Purple: black women as cultural readers. In D. Pribham, ed. *Female Spectators*. Verso, London.

Bourdieu, P. 1984 *Distinction: A Social Critique of the Judgment of Taste*. Trans R. Nice. Harvard University Press, Cambridge, MA.

Bourdieu, P. and Passeron, J-C. 1977 *Reproduction in Education, Society and Culture*, vol. 5. Trans R. Nice. Sage Studies in Social and Educational Change. Sage, Beverly Hills, CA.

Brown, M. 2007 *The Pilgrim and the Bee: Reading Rituals and Book Culture in Early New England*. University of Pennsylvania Press, Philadelphia.

Burke, K. 1973 Literature as equipment for living. In *The Philosophy of Literary Form: Studies in Symbolic Action*. University of California Press, Berkeley.

Burwell, C. 2007 Reading Lolita in times of war: Women's book clubs and the politics of reception. *Intercultural Education* 18, 4, p. 281.

Chartier, R. 2002 Labourers and voyagers: From text to reader. In D. Finkelstein and A. McCleery, eds. *The Book History Reader*. Routledge, London, pp. 47–58.

Chartier, R. 2007 *Inscription and Erasure: Literature and Written Culture from the Eleventh to the Eighteenth Century*. Trans. A. Goldhammer, University of Pennsylvania Press, Philadelphia PA.

Coleman, J. 1988 Social capital: Its origins and applications in modern sociology. *Annual Review of Sociology* 24, pp. 1–24.

Collins, R. 1971 Functional and conflict theories of stratification. *American Sociological Review* 36, pp. 1002–1019.

Cook-Gumperz, J. 2006 *The Social Construction of Literacy*. Cambridge University Press, New York.

Crain, C. 2007 Twilight of the books: What will life be like if people stop reading? *The New Yorker*, December 24, pp. 134–141.

Currie, D.H. 1999 *Girl Talk: Adolescent Magazines and Their Readers*. University of Toronto Press, Toronto.

Danet, B. 1997 Books, letters, documents: The changing aesthetics of texts in late print culture. *The Journal of Material Culture*, 2, 1, pp. 1–38.

Dewey, J. 1927 *The Public and its Problems*. Holt, New York.

DiMaggio, P. 1982 Cultural capital and school success: The impact of status culture participation on the grades of U.S. high school students. *American Sociological Review* 47, pp. 189–201.

Dominus, S. 2008 Snoopers on the subway, beware digital books. *The New York Times*, March 31.

Donadio, R. 2008 It's not you, it's your books. *The New York Times*, March 30.

Eberle, T. 1997 Cultural contrasts in a democratic nonprofit organization. The case of a Swiss reading society. In S. Sackmann, ed. *Cultural Complexity in Organizations: Inherent Contrasts and Contradictions*. Sage, Beverly Hills, CA, pp. 133–155.

Eberle, T. 2007 Facets of power in a swiss reading society. Paper presented at the Oslo Culture and Power Conference, December 13–15, Oslo, Norway.

Farkas, G. 2000 Teaching low-income children to read at grade level. *Contemporary Sociology*, 29, pp. 53–61.

Farkas, G., Grobe, R. P., Sheehan, D. and Shuan, Y. 1990 Cultural resources and school success. *American Sociological Review*, 55, pp. 127–142.

Farr, C. K. 2004 *Reading Oprah: How Oprah's Book Club Changed the Way America Reads*. State University of New York Press, Albany.

Fish, S. 1980 *Is There a Text in This Class? The Authority of Interpretive Communities*, Harvard University Press, Cambridge, MA.

Fiske, J. 1989 *Understanding Popular Culture: Reading the Popular*. Routledge, London.

Fister, B. 2005 "Reading as a contact sport": Online book groups and the social dimensions of reading. *Reference and User Services Quarterly*, 44, 4, pp. 303–309.

Fuller, D. 2007 Listening to the readers of "Canada Reads". *Canadian Literature*. Retrieved from http://vnweb.hwwilsonweb.com/hww/jumpstart.jhtml?recid=0bc05f7a67b17 90e88760b1524ddb2e097f3da6269d7e79301faf99f3ae3ec58f8669f2d1b0e8f94&fmt=C $3Citation$yArticle Citation in WilsonWeb.

Gamoran, A. 1993 Alternative uses of ability grouping in secondary schools. *American Journal of Education*, 102, pp. 1–21.

Geller, E. 1984 *Forbidden Books in American Public Libraries, 1876–1939: A Study in Cultural Change, Contributions in Librarianship and Information Science No. 46*. Greenwood Press, Westport, CT.

Gomez, J. 2008 *Print Is Dead: Books in Our Digital Age*. Macmillan, London.

Grafton, A. 2007 Future reading: digitization and its discontents. *The New Yorker*, November 5, pp. 50–56.

Griswold, W. 2008 *Cultures and Societies in a Changing World*, 3rd edn. Pine Forge Press, Thousand Oaks, CA.

Griswold, W., McDonnell T. and Wright, N. 2005 Reading and the reading class in the twenty-first century. *Annual Review of Sociology*, 31, pp. 127–141.

Griswold, W., McDonnell, T. and Metz, E. 2006 Glamour and honor: the relationship between reading and the internet in West African culture. *Information Technologies and International Development*, 3, 4, pp. 37–52.

Hall, R.M. 2003 *The "Oprahfication" of Literacy: Reading "Oprah's Book Club."* National Council of Teachers of English, Washington, DC.

Hall, S. 2007 How I learned to run a really popular book club (and what I learned about its effect on students' reading skills and attitude). *Teacher Librarian*, 35, 1, p. 32.

Hartley, J. 2002 *The Reading Groups Book*. Oxford University Press, Oxford.

Heath, S.B. 1983 *Ways with Words*. Cambridge University Press, New York.

Heath, S.B. 1996 What no bedtime story means. In D. Lawrence, R. Brenneis and K.S. Macaulay, eds. *The Matrix of Language: Contemporary Linguistic Anthropology*. Westview Press, Boulder, CO.

Heller, M.F. 2006 Telling stories and talking facts: first graders' engagements in a nonfiction book club. *Reading Teacher*, 60, 4, pp. 358–369.

Hoggart, R. 1957 *The Uses of Literacy*. Penguin, Harmondsworth.

Iser, W. 1974 *The Implied Reader*. Johns Hopkins University Press, Baltimore.

Iser, W. 1978 *The Act of Reading*. Johns Hopkins University Press, Baltimore.

Jauss, H.R. 1982 *Toward an Aesthetic of Reception*. Trans. T. Bahti, University of Minnesota Press, Minneapolis.

Jencks, C. and Phillips, M. 1998 America's next achievement test: closing the black-white test score gap. *The American Prospect*, September–October, pp. 143–152.

Johns, A. 1998 *The Nature of the Book: Print and Knowledge in the Making*. University of Chicago Press, Chicago.

Katz, E. 1990 A propos des medias et de leurs effets. In I. Sfez and G. Coutlee, eds. *Technologies et Symboliques de la Communication*. Presses Universitaires de Grenoble, Grenoble.

Kelly, M. 2008 "The need of their genius": women's reading and writing practices in early America. *Journal of the Early Republic*, 28, 1, p. 1.

Klancher, J. 1987 *The Making of English Reading Audiences*. University of Wisconsin Press, Madison.

Lareau, A. 2000 *Home Advantage: Social Class and Parental Intervention in Elementary Education*, 2nd edn. Rowman & Littlefield, New York.

Lareau, A. and Horvat, E. 1999 Moments of social inclusion and exclusion. *Sociology of Education*, 72, 1, pp. 37–53.

Lareau, A. and Weininger, E.B. 2003 Cultural capital in educational research: a critical assessment. *Theory and Society*, 32, pp. 567–606.

Lasswell, H. 1927 *Propaganda Technique in the World War*. Knopf, New York.

Lerer, S. 2006 Epilogue: falling asleep over the history of the book. *PMLA*, 121, 1, pp. 229–234.

Levenston, E.A. 1992 *The Stuff of Literature: Physical Aspects of Texts and Their Relation to Meaning*. State University of New York Press, Albany.

Long, E. 2003 *Book Clubs: Women and the Uses of Reading in Everyday Life*. University of Chicago Press, Chicago.

McGann, J. 1983 *A Critique of the Modern Textual Criticism*. University of Chicago Press, Chicago.

McHenry, E. 2002 *Forgotten Readers: Recovering the Lost History of African-American Literary Societies*. Duke University Press, Durham, NC.

McKenzie, D.F. 1985 *Oral Culture, Literacy and Print in Early New Zealand: The Treaty of Waitangi*. Wellington, NZ: Victoria University Press.

McKiel, A.W. 2007 *ebrary's Global eBook Survey*. Ebrary report.

Miall, D. S. 2006 *Literary Reading: Empirical and Theoretical Studies*. Peter Lang, New York.

Morley, D. 1980 *The Nationwide Audience*. British Film Institute, London.

Murray, H. 2002 *Come Bright Improvement! The Literary Societies of Nineteenth-Century Ontario*. University of Toronto Press, Toronto.

National Endowment for the Arts. 2004 *Reading at Risk: A Survey of Literary Reading in America*, Research Division Report no. 46. Ed. T. Bradshaw and B. Nichols, Research Division. National Endowment for the Arts, Washington, DC.

Oakes, Jeannie. 1986 Keeping track. *Phi Delta Kappa*.

Oldenburg, R. 1989/1999 *The Great, Good Place: Cafés, Coffee Shops, Bookstores, Bars, Hair Salons, and Other Hangouts at the Heart of a Community*. Marlowe, New York.

Park, R.E. 1922 *The Immigrant Press and Its Control*. Harper, New York.

Pew Internet and American Life Project. 2007 *A Typology of Information and Communication Technology Users*. Pew Internet and American Life Project, Washington, DC.

Poole, M. 2003 The women's chapter: women's reading groups in Victoria. *Feminist Media Studies* 3, 3, pp. 263–281.

Powell, A. 1971 *Books Do Furnish a Room*. Heinemann, London.

Price, L. 2006 Introduction: reading matter. *PMLA*, 121, 1, pp. 9–16.

Priddis, M. 2007 The well read librarian: book discussion resources. *Indiana Libraries*, 26, 3, pp. 76–77.

Radway, J. 1983 Women read the romance: the interaction of text and context. *Feminist Studies*, 9, 1, pp. 53–78.

Radway, J. 1984. *Reading the Romance: Women, Patriarchy, and Popular Literature* University of North Carolina Press, Chapel Hill.

Radway, J. 1997 *A Feeling for Books: The Book-of-the-Month Club, Literary Taste, and Middle-Class Desire*. The University of North Carolina Press, Chapel Hill.

Ross, C.S., McKechnie, E.F.L. and Rothbauer, P.M. 2006 *Reading Matters: What the Research Reveals about Reading, Libraries, and Community*. Libraries Unlimited, Westport, CT.

Schauber, E. and Spolsky, E. 1986 *The Bounds of Interpretation: Linguistic Theory and Literary Text*. Stanford University Press, Stanford, CA.

Schmidt, S.J. 1998 A systems-oriented approach to literary studies. In G. Altman and W. Koch, eds. *Systems: New Paradigms for the Social Sciences*. Walter de Gruyter, Berlin, pp. 646–670.

Schubert, S. 2007 Building a better book club. *Business*, 2, 8, p. 50.

Sedo, D.R. 2002 Predictions of life after Oprah: a glimpse at the power of book club readers. *Publishing Research Quarterly* 18, 3, pp. 11–22.

Smith, B.K. 2007 Branded literacy: the entrepreneurship of Oprah's Book Club. In B. Daniell and P. Mortensen, eds. *Women and Literacy: Local and Global Inquiries for a New Century*. Lawrence Erlbaum, New York.

Smith, E.A. 2007 "Jesus, my pal": reading and religion in middlebrow America. *Canadian Review of American Studies*, 37, pp. 147–181.

Solan, R. 2006 *Reading Raps: A Book Club Guide for Librarians, Kids, and Families*. Libraries Unlimited, Westport, CT.

Sonnet, E. 1999 Erotic fiction by women for women: the pleasures of post-feminist heterosexuality. *Sexualities*, 2, 2, pp. 167–187.

Sonnet, E. 2000 What the woman reads: categorising contemporary popular erotica for women. In J. Hallam and N. Moody, eds. *Consuming for Pleasure: Selected Essays on Popular Fiction*. John Moores University Press, Liverpool, pp. 246–267.

Stevens, M.L., Armstrong, E.A. and Arum, R. 2008. Sieve, incubator, temple, hub: empirical and theoretical advances in the sociology of higher education. *Annual Review of Sociology*, 34, pp. 127–151.

Striphas, T. 2003. A Dialectic with the everyday: communication and cultural politics on Oprah Winfrey's book club. *Critical Studies in Media Communication*, 20, 3, pp. 295–316.

Swann, M. 2001 *Curiosities and Texts: The Culture of Collecting in Early Modern England*. University of Pennsylvania Press, Philadelphia.

Trachtenberg, J.A. 2008 [Article]. September 11, *Wall Street Journal*, Technology page.

Twomey, S. 2007 Reading "woman": book club pedagogies and the literary imagination. *Journal of Adolescent and Adult Literacy*, 50, 5, pp. 398–407.

Weber, M. 1946 The rationalization of education and training. In H.H. Gerth and C. Wright Mills, eds. *From Max Weber: Essays in Sociology*. Oxford University Press, New York.

Wertham, F. 1955 *Seduction of the Innocent*. Museum Press, London.

Willis, P. 1977 *Learning to Labour*. Saxon House, Farnborough.

Wolf, M. 2007 *Proust and the Squid: The Story and Science of the Reading Brain* Harper, New York.

2

Listening for Listeners
The Work of Arranging How Listening Will Occur in Cultures of Recorded Sound

Jackie Cook

Listening

The act of listening to recorded sound – whether music, talk, or performance – is one of those aspects of human communication eclipsed by so many else-where-derived models and sources of explanation, as to have almost entirely escaped any means of definition founded upon its own practices. No one knows for certain what makes good, bad, or even ordinary listening, despite the vast production mass of sound materials within radio, recorded music, and, more recently, DIY sound-recording and presentation formats. Internet podcasting, telephone voice messaging, or even karaoke – each has its own enthusiastic consumer base, and there are many more innovations yet to come. So why is there so little work on understanding what it is all about? Even radio broadcast managers can't easily explain what makes a good radio presenter, or a program worth listening to, placing their trust in someone said, quite simply, to have a "good ear" or a "great sound." There are no definitive ways of critiquing, or discussing, or teaching, or even understanding any aspect of the arts of all of this mediated listening.

There are, of course, ways of examining how a specific audio product should be made to "sound." Radio presenters and singers, for instance, learn to create impact upon audiences by using voice techniques which suit their particular format. Yet all of these evolved elsewhere, for entirely other purposes: "elocution" or voice

The Handbook of Media Audiences, First Edition. Edited by Virginia Nightingale.
© 2014 John Wiley & Sons, Ltd. Published 2014 by John Wiley & Sons, Ltd.

production exercises used by actors or public speakers to improve their confidence and audibility in front of live audiences; breath control and phrasing taught by singing coaches; and the persuasive tone, pace, and rhythms learned in retail marketing. When it comes to analyzing how the "sound" of an audio product "works" on its audiences, once again the techniques come from somewhere else. For assessing radio or telephone talk, the academic methodology of conversational analysis (CA) can be useful (see e.g. Hutchby 1996). It focuses on the power relations negotiated among speakers in talk settings, and can help reveal who is controlling a spoken dialogue, and how they are doing it. CA, however, is as yet mostly unadapted to the particular circumstances of professionally "presented" and sound-managed talk, which differs in a number of ways from the "natural" talk of everyday conversations. The same is true of discourse analysis, which evolved out of the linguistic and rhetorical repertoires used first to describe how language systems work, and then how they reflect power relations between "producers" and "receivers" (see especially Fairclough 1989, 1992, 1994, 1995; Gee 2005). While this can be applied to language-based "sound texts," more is needed when the focus shifts to how speech is listened to, or how the various forms of music appreciation work to predispose listeners. Formal induction to classical composition techniques can alter the ways a symphonic concert is heard. The fan subcultures behind so many strands of popular performance are widely understood to add to a listener's pleasure. The act of listening to broadcast sport, broadcast sports chat, or broadcast sports talkback is so compelling that it has become part of the "sports spectatorship" experience. Behind these activities, however, lie complex production techniques used to maximize audience enthusiasm and pleasure. Most of us know little about them – and understand even less.

In any act of mediated sound transmission, be it for speech, music, or even ambient sound, the arrangements made to optimize the act of listening, to pull in the largest and most interested and enthusiastic audience, are in themselves a communicative element. Listening, among the earliest of the human communicative senses to develop, is culturally among the last to be taken seriously. While any pregnant mother-to-be becomes aware of her capacity to command a listening response from her child in utero, the act of listening is largely regarded as one seamlessly and "naturally" in place, and requiring no further serious address. Yet broadcasters, musicians, and public performers of every possible type know just how carefully they themselves "listen back" in order to perfect the structuring of the sound they want. When you see a singer place a hand over their own ear, they are attempting exactly this process of "hearing themselves as heard." The politician rehearsing a key speech, the religious leader perfecting the enactment of a public ritual, the auctioneer out to command top price, and even the new pet owner learning to control a nervous animal, are each consciously redisciplining their "sound" to suit their listeners. The focus and expertise required of the trained sound producer, from recording engineer to radio presenter, tell us that listening is an active, discriminating, critical, evaluative act.

To refocus attention onto this disregarded communicative act, this chapter takes up a very small aside made by UK radio analyst Paddy Scannell (1996). He was trying to capture for study the sound phenomena which characterize the many established formats of broadcast radio. He noticed that, while radio formats move in and out of favor, those that are out of fashion somehow remain curiously extant. They continue to exist, as a kind of potential sound entity. Rather like a neglected musical score, they can always be recuperated and reactivated. The comment alerts us to the ways in which our many acts of listening never quite pass out of the cultural repertoire. Individuals might, for a range of reasons, choose once again to aggregate as listening audiences, in the name of this or that audio enactment. It is not only possible, as US radio historians know to their profit, to re-record and market old radio shows or music recordings, but also there are successful re-enactments of shows past: modern performances working from original scripts, using presentational techniques and technologies decades out of date. Sound is among the most evocative and directly emotional of our sense stimuli. Its capacity to command nostalgic pleasure is widely known, tapping deep veins of audience memory and enthusiasm.

This discussion examines what it means in today's heavily mediated world to have such an open field of listening potential. On the one hand, we confront an exciting array of new sound products, as well as onward, adaptive, and perhaps recombinant use of the old – all at a personalized level. On the other hand, there is the more worrying consideration of what might be happening to our culture of sound production, given this curious gap in our capacity to understand and talk about what it is we are doing as we arrange to activate this, or that, form of listening, and ignore, or suppress, others.

To test this "open field" across some of its best-established yet least regarded sound products, this study examines and theorizes four types of recorded sound use.

Sound Archives: What We Know and Understand of "Sounds Past"

Unearthing how we listen to mediated sound, through accessing archived material, reveals a great deal about our listening behaviors. Few of us today listen attentively to "old sounds" – those no longer common on daily airwaves, or easily download-able as MP3 files. Aficionados of the great performers of the past, such as jazz or early rock fans, are more likely than most to seek out and replay old recordings – but even they rarely consider the sorts of sounds these artists were seeking at the point of production. Books, films, and even TV programming have established niches for "classic" or nostalgia product, but listening to the century of recorded sound available to us is still a more difficult enterprise.

There is a commonly held view that the "sounds of today" are producing an ever-accelerating evolution of fast-paced, dynamically voiced, full-spectrum sound. This is a taste developed in commercial radio's music programming formatted around multitracked, pulsing sound, with presenter vocalization and ad-break editing to match. Listeners feel invited to "speed up" their listening. There is in effect an evolutionary audio dynamic in play, in which pace is a sign of the energy of modernity – and analysts of today's listening have made much of this (see e.g. Potts 1989, 1995). Yet try challenging radio listeners to access something like a 1948 drama: perhaps an edition of the crime thriller *Dragnet*, produced for the US Armed Forces network. Today's listener struggles with the pace of delivery used over 60 years ago. They cannot keep up with the plot. They confuse one character with another. They are no longer receiving a daily education in how to process audio narrative through voice alone. Add to this some intriguing early work from discourse analyst Theo van Leeuwen (1984, 1985) which tested the speed of delivery of radio advertisements against that of news bulletins. He found, to his own surprise, that the news was spoken faster than the commercial copy – so that critical processing of information was invited more for the advertisement than for the news. It is findings such as those which signal the need to work analytically into audio texts – in a range of ways.

Sound archive work challenges media experts to listen critically to commercially available compilations of past sound materials, and to voice their responses. What has changed – and what do such changes mean, for the ways we now present recorded sound? As we "record," we are arranging for certain forms of listening to occur – forms which will endure into the future, when very different listening(s), and reuses, may occur. The "listening" we have already lost has had consequences: it has changed our orientation toward aural and audio texts, and our preferred ways of interpreting them. Such changes have rarely resulted, however, from conscious "listening production" decisions, or from audience demand. Incidental changes, such as technological innovation, force redirection of audio content production – which is then attributed to changes in "public taste." Even sound media professionals and analysts responsible for selecting what gets produced may not be in control – or even fully aware – of the impact of audio presentation at the most basic level: that of its sound composition.

Audio/Spectating: Sportscasting and the Formation of Mass Audiences

I am driving south from Alice Springs (South Australia) on the afternoon of a football Grand Final, hoping against hope that somewhere on that long, flat highway, some slight elevation will put my car's radio aerial in touch with a broadcast signal....

Thirty minutes out of the mining town of Coober-Pedy a voice suddenly crackles in. The excitement of that far-off scene fills the car. Suddenly, I am in two places. Despite the wide empty country through which I am driving, I am with that crowd, and focused on that team, on that field....

How is radio able to make this happen? Broadcast sport is a compelling listening experience. Sportscasters carry the game and its emotional swings vividly to those not present, so that radio's particular form of listening has contributed to the extraordinary success of mass sporting events in the modern era, constructing the now largely delocalized fan culture of sport followers. Comparing contemporary radio sportcasts to other forms of sports programming reveals a rapidly expanding sports broadcast repertoire – not all of it actually about listening to sport.

Soundscapes: The rise and rise of personal audio media

Personal music compilations have been possible since the arrival of the cassette recorder in the 1970s, and are now easily transferable through a wide range of digital devices and networks. They raise interesting questions about the social uses of a mobile sensorium of the affect that music carries. The ways we listen to popular music have produced certain uses of mobile, personalized, listening devices, uses which evolved somewhere between the resources of broadcast radio, the music recording industry, technologies for home dubbing, and the cultural positioning of popular song as soundtrack to our adolescent emotional and social-relational development. Outcomes of an ongoing ethnographic sampling of contemporary music compilation habits help question how people select and use favorite music tracks as they listen in still-evolving personal auditory spaces, such as on public transport, or use sound to represent "the life" of a deceased friend or family member at funeral or memorial services.

Podcasting: Changing the social centrality of selves by "voicing your/self"

The personalized, expressive space opened up through podcasting is a way for every voice to establish its own expertise, and to command an audience through the sheer power of its voicing. What remains to be established is which podcasts are succeeding, and what it is that distinguishes them from others. This is a new mix of personalized opinion, hyperexpressivity, and a vastly reopened "address," with a keen embrace of new forms and new levels of self-assertion. We are still learning to listen critically for these effects as they evolve – and may yet need to intervene upon the social, cultural, and perhaps psychological consequences which flow from them.

In each case, the focus is once again upon Scannell's hypothesis: that producing sound texts is about arranging for a certain kind of listening to occur. This work, in all of its variant locations and media types, is about listening out, for listening in. It is designed to capture the reception, in the production – and finding ways to talk about it.

The Sound of Sounds Past: Uses of the "Listening Room"

By entering the many sound archives within any given culture, we can examine those formats which have endured and been central to audio output. With today's digital audio-editing processes, sound files which have been able to exert audience "pull" consistently across time are now able to flow across space, letting audiences not only relive performances of the past, but also work them into new forms of listening pleasure.

Scannell's work reminded us of our ability to re-activate from the sound notation of the day the social and cultural phenomena behind each original audio composition. Listeners who regard sound texts as significant and memorable know there is a kind of semiotics in sound: a set of significations layered into the recording, carried not just in the content but also in its performance, expressivity, editing, and production values. Sound as lain down for us in a given recording technology cues our listening in certain ways: it makes us acutely aware of some things, and less certain of others. It invites our focus, distributes our attention or sympathies, and evokes our emotional responses. Yet consciousness of this "audio poetics" has largely disappeared even among expert media readers, so that knowledge of sound practices remains informal, without a descriptive or evaluative vocabulary, despite the attempts in various resource locations to design and disseminate a universal system.

It is, of course, possible to argue that this lack of any standardized descriptive repertoire is an advantage to the field. In a study of the radio voicing of sentiment, the presenter styling of music request programming as practiced by 1990s "Love-God" presenter Richard Mercer (Cook 2002), I have argued that what preserves the immediacy and emotionality of popular romantic music and its applicability to the sentimental lives of listeners is that it rests on an untutored listening. When audio texts have no critical registers, music is "felt" rather than understood. So too the relations which come to exist – carefully positioned to exist in just such ways – between radio presenters and their committed audiences. The quasi-intimacy built between broadcaster and listener, or music performer and fan, is mediated through conscious construction of a presentational persona and styled vocalization, as well as through the various technological affordances of the medium of contact. Listeners, however, "hear" them and use them as true and real forms of intimacy and interpersonal contact (Thompson 1995).

It appears, then, that relational qualities of the social and interpersonal can be "heard," and so responded to, in the various forms of audiorecorded material. Producing and deciphering "sound signs" comprise a cultural act, a learned behavior. Fiumara (1990) has outlined the act of listening as a kind of directed attentiveness: the deployment of an educated ear, likely to be listening for, so preemptively "hearing" and consensually co-producing the messages it ultimately "receives." Test yourself on your car radio, which scans the spectrum until it locates a radio source. Most listeners select, or reject, a "lock on" in less than two seconds. Our listening tastes are acute, and fiercely critical.

To hypothesize an active or co-productive listening raises two issues. There is a kind of arranged or laboratory-simulated listening, where teachers or media industry trainers arrange a "listening room" experience, its aims pre-established. Listening conditions are carefully controlled. Sound files are selected and arranged, and listeners cued to hearing some special feature. Such teacherly or producerly acts of compilation and airing are intrinsic to both the audio classroom and industry production: they are powerfully persuasive because of their apparent capacity to deliver a predicted response. Audio responsiveness, the emotional and cognitive processing stimulated in listeners, is already socially and culturally inculcated, and the reason the producer(s) selected the texts. They know the ways audiences will react when confronted by this, or that, set of sound sequences, audio allusions, or intertextual or generic sound references, just as we do in textual or visual codes.

What this means is that even with no exposure at all to a "listening room" audio education, each person's set of auditory "pre-dispositions," in Bourdieu's terms (1977, 1984), rests on an entire habitus – even an acquired listening hexis or set of physical orientations toward this or that set of sounds, established socially and culturally. Audio literacies and skills in listening are informally acquired, with little consciousness of any regulatory apparatus or set of instructional or interpretive directions, despite the years of cultural effort most of us expend in producing them. Listening room experiences can help begin the process of raising that cultural and discriminatory apparatus into consciousness, enabling a comparative analysis of what otherwise appear to be personal or individual tastes and preferences. A critical listening foregrounds how these have been culturally embedded in the first place – and how limited and limiting they might prove to be. Above all, critical listening reminds us that within a contemporary Western perspective, such sounds and listening processes were selected and produced to establish precisely the "personalized" reception we each locate in ourselves. Only once the context of one's own "active listening" is established can there be an appreciation of which listening contexts dictate the particulars of an audio framing. Different eras, and different cultures, build very different forms of aural address: calculated ways of "signing" a given sound text with the values needed for its reception. In a fluid and multicultural modern context, these are audio values which any given listener may, or may not, share.

Within that context, sound archive materials produced within other spaces, or eras, challenge the modern listener. It is in testing for these differences that the power of the personalized hearing of today can be detected – the good news being that any set of stimulus sound texts can raise audio consciousness. The "something other" which shocks us into awareness is infinitely variable.

Calculating how context influences audio texts is not, however, easy. Talk texts, for instance, have often been formatted and scripted as forms of "secondary orality" (Ong 1982) to further control the act of listening. Sound files which capture, or claim to capture, the spontaneous speech of nonprofessionals are especially valuable – and, at least in the early days of sound recording, rare. The idea of an unmediated modern self is more contentious, despite the seeming accessibility and even interactivity of today's media – since everyone is influenced by the all-too-familiar forms of "sound scripting" via media exposure. There are certainly audio sectors which seek immediacy and authenticity in their audio presentation, but how far this is an unscripted, uncued capture remains contentious. One rich field involves community members for whom instruction in the act of listening is still a major part of everyday life: children.

Broadcaster Keith Smith's immensely popular *Pied Piper* series of radio interviews with Australian children of the 1950s and 1960s invariably positioned the children as neophytes in an adult world. They were to be heard as naïve and spontaneous revealers of family secrets, uncomprehending and often quirky interpreters of adult realities – and always sources of humor.

There was, however, a rigorous formula at play within this prescription for the program. Veteran Australian actress Jacki Weaver (2007) relates in her biography how she was selected as one of "Mr. Smith's" child subjects – and how far the spontaneity of the child's comments, the quintessential motif of the programming, was actually a "command performance."

> Keith Smith, the radio star, came talent-scouting to our school to choose children to be on his very popular national show called 'The Pied Piper' and I was recommended to him by my teacher. After auditioning me, Keith Smith then nabbed me to do several episodes. It was supposed to be ad-lib and spontaneous but he did run us through the questions beforehand and, if the cute riposte didn't quite measure up, he'd be rather stern and say, 'That's a boring answer. Think of something better than that!' (p. 20)

This programming was structured around the tastes and expectations of an adult audience, built over the many earlier *Children's Hour* programs. Avuncular presenters and biddable children licensed participation by child listeners in strictly delimited ways. The formula is clearest in comparison to those now rare occasions when children appear on mainstream radio. Compare a set of street interviews produced by ABC broadcaster Richard Margetson (2009), covering the Pokemon gaming phenomenon in the late 1990s. These "vox pop" sound bites from children (presented as computer-gaming "experts") capture the frenzied global release of a new Pokemon game character, and show adults as bemused bystanders. Margetson's interviewer–interviewee relation with these children positions them as the sole source of any analysis of the Pokemon fad. Only the child can explain the attraction of this product. Those adults who have enabled them to attend this massive "visibilization" (audibility) of product demand for the Nintendo enterprise are now the naïve observers – a role which Margetson himself models, as he struggles to capture the Pokemon experience for his listeners.

RICHARD MARGETSON: This is total madness here – I can't believe it! You say you've had 1800 downloads here today.... I'll wade through the hundreds of children. ...

POKEMON TECHNICIAN: They pressure their parents to get more Pokemon in the future ... it's child demand marketing. It's a question of what interests the children. ...

RICHARD MARGETSON: Are you the parent of a Pokemon child?

WOMAN ONE: Yes I am. ...

RICHARD MARGETSON: When did the 6 year old start playing?

WOMAN ONE: A couple of months ago – the older one is 12 and he started playing. ...

WOMAN TWO: This is really the phenomenon of the school holidays – we had to come down from the Barossa, we had to plan our trip. ...

CHILDREN: Hellooooo Pikechu....

RICHARD MARGETSON: (aside) Pikechu looks remarkably like a broad bean. ...

(MUSIC TRACK PLAYS):   I will travel across the land, Searching for advice. ...

SMALL BOY: It's cool. ... you tell all your friends about Pokemon, then you might get them interested. ... then – they might get a card, and then you can play with them. ...

RICHARD MARGETSON: Are you a Pokemon Grandmother? Do you understand it?

OLDER WOMAN: No – I just go along with it – he's very good at explaining it....

SECOND SMALL BOY: You got all these different little animals, and you can gain experience points? You fire, and gain experience points, and like, the evolution of one Pokemon is like, better than another Pokemon. ...

OLDER WOMAN: He's very good – he's only 9. ...

WOMAN THREE: We have this totally new language in the house which I don't understand a bit of: it's a – a new cult! (she laughs) (Margetson 2009)

Carefully edited to achieve a coherence that street interviewing rarely achieves uncut, this short social documentary, constructed in the round of production for a daily talk-and-music radio show, displays a great deal of expertise in both verbal scene setting and astute short sound grab interviewing. Margetson is able to make what he persistently describes as "madness" into a coherent whole, building a clearly articulated message. It is one suited to his audience of older, socially conscious ABC listeners, perennially concerned with issues of parenting and anxious to keep up with trends. The questioning and the editing together, however, position the children as occupying some strange parallel universe. Adults are present only to arrange transport and make the odd claim of parental pride. The ambient sound belongs totally to the children present: the entire clip is filled with crowd noises, and Pokemon character performers and music tracks, all producing a sense of dynamic excitement. Margetson remains the representative of the uncomprehending adult, but is able to crack open just a little the attractions of this interesting new media form. At core, however, it remains yet another separation between the worlds of child and adult. Listeners to this audio document "hear" a new form of audio as they are told about a new form of visual pleasure – and learn that it is not for them. That fleeting occupancy of the unfamiliar position of the alienated listener makes this a powerful text.

Sound texts of the past, or *sounds-past*, can help reveal how far listenership is attuned to the auditory practices of its time, practices always largely inaudible – until shocked or "estranged" into consciousness. Sounds-past make clear to us the constraints acting upon earlier listening, and also those acting to produce today's audio tastes. If the Babel of daily audio encounters has imposed a cultural sameness upon a diverse and multivalent sound mediascape, listening room experiences, no matter their provenance, can provide ways of revealing our listener selves to ourselves.

Audio/Spectating: Sounding Out Sports Events

As just one example of audio uniformity, today's radio broadcasting of major sports events is so familiar as to appear transparent. This is a mediation which translocates us into "the experience" of a sports event, and yet endlessly adds to the act of its own dis-appearance (inaudibility) new layers of interpretive and informational enrichment. A format which began with a man and a microphone, positioned in the stands high above the field of play, using binoculars, a player list, and a lot of creative guesswork to keep track of the passage of the ball, has today become a complex team effort. Co-commentators, ex-player celebrities, sideline coaches, stringers, and statistical analysts work together on a near seamless sports talk construct. The mix engages many other sports-programming types which have now evolved: sports news, sports chat, sports talkback, sport–comedy–panel shows, sports game shows, and match analysis. The experience of "listening" to sport has become a crucial element of the modern staging of games.

Sports commentary

The dominant feature of the presentation style used in sports commentary has never been, as might be expected, its descriptiveness, but the pace of its delivery. The origins of game calls on radio tell us much of what listeners found pleasurable. The BBC, convinced that no one could visualize a broadcast game and make sense of it, experimented with publishing gridded diagrams of the football field to give listeners visual cues to help map the progress of the ball across the field. They understood very little of the process of audio representation of complex actions. Then, as now, listening to a game was not a matter of somehow imagining the action in every detail, but of sharing in the spectator response. Listeners wanted to experience the high points and releases of tension and anticipation, as the game advantage flowed back and forth between the contesting sides. The excitement, not the precise action of each player, is registered in the commentator's delivery. His vocalization, pace of description, and accelerating volume signal the flow of the game. These are the qualities which build and control listener response – along with the various idiosyncrasies and tag lines which characterize the performance of the most famous commentators, and make them memorable. These can become so much a part of sports presentation as to stand in for the qualities of the game itself. Broadcast cricket was considered by many radio listeners to be so perfectly suited to the commentary of Alan McGilvray that his retirement produced a popular song which stated outright that "The game is not the same – without McGilvray!" In the New Zealand Rugby Union, the entire nation in the 1950s would hold its breath as broadcaster Winston McCarthy timed the agonizingly slow delivery of a penalty or conversion kick with the phrase "Wait for it. … Wait for it…. It's a goal!"

To capture this enactment of a game's emotional affect in print transcription demands all of the codings available in CA linguistic notation. The challenge of representing tone, pace, and various forms of vocal accentuation in print mode helps foreground the complex mix of performative elements used in producing the commentary voicing. As a caller describes just one sequence of play, the speech will shift from the medium-paced, near-conversational tones used to report indecisive midfield play, to the heightened and rapidly accelerating "breakout" of a successfully executed run down the field – and, finally, the ecstatic and optimal-volume excitement of a goal. So extreme are the vocal techniques used in game commentary, especially in the faster paced and directly competitive sports, that the performance literally has "nowhere to go" to intensify – and sometimes even to sustain – its peaks of excitement. Listeners hear the human voice at its limits, or beyond those limits, in terms of the everyday acceptability of vocal range. Volume and pace regularly exceed norms – think of horse-racing calls – but so too does the range of vocal pitch considered acceptable in the male voice. Sports commentary is one of the few circumstances in modern English where the falsetto range can be used by men without losing authority.

To supplement the capacity of one voice, many ancillary techniques are now used to evoke listener response. New elements in sports commentary are introduced only in part to allow the game caller to avoid hyperventilation and vocal exhaustion. Handover rituals to second commentators "spread out" the task of calling the game, generalizing its translation into audio format, and so successfully modeling it as a dialogue to be taken up by the listening audience. This is sport to be talked about – during, after, and even before an actual game. Subsidiary flows of information and "feeds" are added. Sideline stringers conduct on-the-run reports after injuries, or investigate tactical huddles with coaches. The "stats man" intervenes on the commentary to fill injury time or other stoppages with the kind of authority discourses which guarantee the authenticity of the commentator's call.

Beneath this on-the-run, high-energy audio representation of a sporting event lies something more complex than simple description. Sports commentary shares features with other forms of structured listening from both media and social conversational exchange, where talk enacts the competitive ethos of masculinity. What Hutchby (1996) described as "confrontation" talk is used in a number of locations within sports radio, each in its way displaying and confirming masculine authority. Call-in chat on sports radio extends the life of the weekend game-round into and through the midweek hiatus – even into the out-of-season layoff. Conducting endless postmortem discussions on earlier games, and promoting those yet to be played, these shows confirm the centrality of sport within men's social and emotional lives, and extend the availability of the pleasures it offers. Authoritative expertise is made available to the nonplaying but still "expert" and committed (audio) spectator, through the ways mediated sports talk is enacted.

Commercial radio in particular has produced sports talk and talkback programming with a mix of qualities which confirms authority claims, yet invites listener–caller participation. Built in interesting ways over the "patter" routines of comedy-cross-talk vaudeville entertainers – think of Abbott and Costello in their radio days, or the "Mr Gallagher–Mr Sheen" recordings of the 1930s – these two-hander joint broadcasts split the enactment of sporting authority. They set up a relatively cool and abstract "straight guy," whose expertise is almost always founded in a heroic sporting past, against the more pugnacious, more contentious, and more everyday opinions of the enthusiast, standing in for the sports-mad listener. Those who call in take up the same tactical variants on the enactment of authority, replicating this or that performance of the "in-the-know" sporting self.

What is under construction is an imagined community – one then appropriated by both the program sponsors through their advertising copy, which mimics the program's talk types and vocalizations, and the broadcasting station itself, which tailors station identity sound bites and top-of-the-hour newsreader handover banter so that it matches, and confirms, the performance. For listeners, a clear sound-self emerges: one able to phone in and contribute directly to the on-air enactment of sporting selfhood, but also likely to "spread" this self into the wider community. The chat produced here, and the selves formed and confirmed within it, enact this sporting identity well beyond the confines of this single listening experience. The technique builds continuity for the sporting self, whose features and behavioral codes and values correspond across both the mediated and the physical experiences of sport spectatorship. It is not, however, the only space in which such modeling is occurring, even at the level of sound alone.

Compiling a Sound Self

As the digitization of audio-recording technologies delivers more and more ways of re-recording and playing back programmed sound, the auditory spaces of modern culture expand in interesting ways. How people select and "use" favorite music tracks, broadcast talk presentations, or personal sound files designed to express their opinions and responses to social issues and experiences has become a part of identity work which is still not well defined. This has grown as much through user demand and individual or subcultural creative impulse as through any planned or designed catering of enabling technologies. In part because of the sheer range of activities involved, it has been difficult to capture the totality of this burgeoning cultural work performed by the listening self.

The smaller, commonly disregarded media of audio digitization have achieved their impact by quite literally "privatizing" the processing of the listening self. This development has been quite diverse in form: the use of unobtrusive ear buds with personal mobile audio players, the specialist industry which evolved online to provide "personal" ring tones for mobile phones, the "sound-canceling" earphone technology which preserves a pristine personal sound scape – each arising at the very moment of accelerating auditory intrusion, from commercial "muzak" to the idea that the "personal" mobile phone licenses fully public "private" conversations.

Sound spaces which once merely offered information now resonate with new forms of audio creativity. The lifts in one Australian city carpark use an audio-mnemonic coding to enable car parkers to remember which floor they are on. Each level of the building is characterized as a planet in the Solar System, and warns returning drivers in suitably robotic tones, "You-are-now-leav-ing-Mars-and-approach-ing-Ven-us...."

"Voiced" space is already altering our ways of understanding our own mobility. The GPS navigation systems installed in cars not only offer the choice of differently voiced and accented advisory commentary, but also are shifting user perceptions of the spaces through which they move. They define landmarks not in the conventional modes of an individual, personal past ("It's near the church where your sister got married...") but through a commercial index of possible consumer sites ("On the next corner, there will be a McDonald's restaurant...").

If this is a relatively new example of the commercialization of our social environment, the recorded music industry's intervention into our emotional state has a long history. The various soundtracks which now play in our lives keep us attuned to an emotional pitch which no longer affords precisely with the reality of our location or actual condition. It suggests selves which are more saturated in emotionality and expressivity than is feasible within everyday living. Rather than the social alienation predicted for a hyperconnected but physically disengaged world, what seem to be emerging are practices which accentuate both social connectedness and personal expression.

Grounding the Flow-Through Experience:
Personal Sound Systems on Public Transport

Personal mobile music players, as noted since the rise of the transistor radio and Sony Walkman (Hosokawa 1984; Chambers 1990; Bull 1999), offer a complex and two-way process promoting both social exclusion and inclusion. They are clearly used to preserve personal space, and yet go beyond this, focusing their users onto a sense of their own "valuable" interiority. Pressures from the anonymous sociality of modern urban life have forced the construction of selectively styled identity, even style-tribe affiliation of the type identified by Maffesoli (1984), inside anonymous transient spaces. Here identity is made safe by the audio amour-guarding of personal mobile sound systems. Who can tell whether the demure, uniformed schoolgirl on the train is listening to acid rock? Who among his workmates will know if the construction worker on the road gang has a taste for Schubert *lieder*? Personal sound systems become a form of cultural resistance work. They enable us to contest the auditory assaults on personal tastes and preferences represented by modern urban public spaces and the sheer volume of their incidental operating sound. At the same time they sustain a personalized expressivity in the autonomy of the particular "sonorous envelope" they allow us to carry through those otherwise alien sound scapes.

For some, especially in the more extreme locations of population density and urgency of movement, these are important matters. In Hong Kong, cashed-up citizens with near-immediate access to the latest in digital devices have been quick to develop ways of taking up these new audio systems. They use them not only to pace their journeys on crowded public transport, even measuring progress against the sequencing of their personal music compilation, but also deliberately select upbeat or quieter tracks to suit the varying audio ambience of their surroundings. Stress reduction, and more complex forms of emotional recharging or release, can be created by these "cut-off" or barrier uses of sound. The same devices, however, can also work in reverse, re-establishing social contact when the surrounding pressures suddenly alter or intensify to levels which require re-engagement in the social.

One notorious sound–media incident on Hong Kong's public transport system, still debated in public media, involves the use of sound-and-vision recording via a handheld mobile phone. A man was recorded by a fellow traveler rebuking a younger bus passenger who had asked him to speak more quietly into his mobile phone. This – rare – public enactment of wrath subsequently arrived on YouTube, from where it was fully launched into public media debate. The footage, remarkable more for its soundtrack of sustained abuse than for any visual excitement, was played and replayed on radio and television, and enthusiastically accessed online, as Hong Kong citizens examined how far they found such "personal" expressions of intergenerational anger and rebuke acceptable or not in a public venue. The "Bus Uncle" case became a defining moment in how the personal intersects with the public in Hong Kong's crowded spaces. So widespread was the ensuing debate that the "Bus Uncle" himself, later identified as one Roger Chan Yuet-tung, subsequently entered politics ("Political Animal" 2010; "Hong Kong Uncle" n.d.). Without the recording capacities of personal mobile telephones, the moment would have remained ephemeral and unremarkable.

This one event highlighted how one person's oral performance can now compel a form of auditory voyeurism – partly in spite of the attempts not to listen (everyone focused on their personal sound devices), but partly because of them (anyone able to record and transmit the event). It is in the audio field that the transformation is at its clearest. What was originally an involuntary "overhearing" became recast as a wider, cultural, "listening in." Those present – and, through the affordances of the network of digital recording and onward-transmitting devices, that meant everyone – were suddenly confronted by their unwitting role as public audience. A public space usually so characterless that it demanded the expressive coloration of personal sound systems had suddenly and irruptively become hyperpersonalized. Someone else's expressivity had exploded onto the scene. It was as if the volume of all those MP3 players and mobile phones and handheld game devices had suddenly hit maximum – and revealed what everyone was listening to. The seemingly safe extension of the personal into the core of the public, offered by the unobtrusive design of handheld pocket and palm devices, unexpectedly re-entered the broadcast format – and nobody liked what they heard.

The Auditory Epitaph: Music at Modern Funeral Services

The contribution of audio texts, and memories of those texts, to the sense of a "completed" self is at its most intense when they are used to represent "the life" of a deceased friend or family member at funeral or memorial services. Here they are used to carry the emotional load of the narrative of a lost life: to speak an understanding of that life to those who remain. With today's retreat from formal or institutionalized religious ritual, and even from emotional expressivity carried in the spoken word, the affective loading of music and music lyric have very rapidly – within a single generation – come to occupy the space once held by officiating clergy, carefully composed eulogies, and strict conventions on "suitable," inevitably somber, choral tributes.

Music selections at modern funerals are more likely to be drawn from the favorite tracks of a given social cohort or generation, than from the hymn lists, as a recent new media report makes clear:

> The West Australian reports that football theme songs and rock anthems by *AC/DC* and *Metallica* are now the most requested at WA funerals. West Australian funeral directors say they had noticed a rise in more contemporary funerals where heavy metal

had replaced traditional hymns for final send-offs.... *Def Leppard, Motley Crue* and *Led Zeppelin* are also popular. Mark Rae, of Chippers in Subiaco, said, "Families ask us to make sure we play the music really loud, while we are bringing the coffin through to really make that statement".... "I have been here 15 years and when I first started about 80 per cent of funerals were very traditional and religious." (West Australian n.d.)

Music selections for funerals have been changing everywhere, according to a Reuters report in the *Sydney Morning Herald* (March 11, 2005). Robbie Williams has topped the UK funeral music chart, leaving Mozart trailing in his wake, according to a survey. Williams's song "Angels" was the record most Britons would like played at their funeral, with Mozart's *Requiem* coming in at five in digital broadcaster Music Choice's poll of top 10 British funeral songs. Frank Sinatra's "My Way" was second, just ahead of Monty Python's "Always Look on the Bright Side of Life." This move to music selected to express the character and tastes of the deceased is now so common that the funeral industry includes vast music resource collections in their online advertising – including a clear sense of the range of genres likely to be in demand:

Recognising the importance of music, Tobin Brothers has developed an extensive Recorded Music Library of around 1,300 titles, to help families choose that special song, hymn or piece of music for the service. Click on the links below to view the entire music catalogue or select a catergory [*sic*] of interest. (Tobin Funerals n.d.)

The bereaved are offered a selection from Tobin Brothers' entire catalogue of 1300 songs, or genre selections from popular songs, classical music, orchestral/instrumental music, or sacred music/gospel songs and hymns. Music is being used to signal key moments of the life trajectory traveled by the deceased, pinpointing remembered moments of triumph or tragedy. Mourners are expected to understand and connect with the emotional cues carried by the familiar performers, lyrics, or genres of their generation or social cohort. This is "mood music" at its most powerful, carrying all the communal intensity of focus and affect once signed by religious ritual, but understood today as expressive of a "unique" human identity. To this degree, funerary music – and, alongside it, the elevated emotional loading of purpose-written or selected verse – is part of the act of "voicing the self," to which this discussion finally turns.

"Voicing Your/Self": The DIY Audio World of Podcasting

The world of the audio podcast is beginning to mature, as the initial enthusiasm for this new form of sound entertainment shifts from the endless vanishing stream of broadcast radio to the self-select "audio library" of web-based sound file downloads. Not only is the audio pod now supplemented, as bandwidth expands, by video and the accelerated "viraling" of the web 2.0 networks, but also format listings have begun to emerge. These replace early-adopter "anything goes" offerings with more structured and genre-conscious productions. Podcast audiences are emerging, with specialized tastes. There are hit pods and dominant formats, and producer-presenters who are amassing significant listenerships.

Already it is clear that professional media outlets are winning this sector. Big-name performers from earlier media, unashamedly out to prolong their celebrity and turn a further profit from their accumulated productions, have taken over from the free-for-all of the initial podcast community. Not that podcasters are unwilling to admit them. Mark Hunter (2007) for *Podcast User Magazine* acknowledges the arrival online of British comedian, actor, and latterly training-video presenter John Cleese:

> What happens when old school meets new media? How does a Cambridge-educated, Academy Award-nominated, Emmy-winning comedian and actor reach out to a global fan base from the comfort of his California ranch? Would you be surprised to know that the answer to both questions is 'podcasting'?…
>
> Cleese recently bumped into a young fan in the States who very enthusiastically explained how important his podcast was to her. She told him how she can watch and listen to him whenever she pleases, enabling her to fit a slice of Cleese into her daily schedule … with just a couple of clicks she was able to subscribe to his podcast, and with that the penny dropped … he's now considering ways to provide regular content that fits into people's modern media consumption patterns.

Despite the work done by this report to assimilate Cleese into the podcaster world, his arrival there shows the reverse: that the professionalizing of that field is well underway. A quick Google search of any of the popular podcast listings online shows sports channels, news shows, and comedy team formats now well in the lead – rivaled, thanks to the arrival of video, only by the highly predictable presence of sex and pornography. The pod-osphere has moved on from the profiling that Candace Lombardi provided in 2006, when she characterized the pod consumer in the following terms:

> To whom should you be targeting your podcasts? Apple Computer users, Trekkies and maybe Nike lovers….. Macworld is the No. 1 most-visited content site by people who download audio podcasts, according to media research group Nielsen/ NetRatings, while StarTrek.com is the most visited content site among video pod-cast downloaders.

The sustained writing-into-presence here of the podcast enthusiast – edgy, design-savvy Mac users; hardcore sci-fi fan-cult followers, and the lower-end demographic of sneaker wearers – maintains the original image of slightly IT-nerdy creative innovation which early podcasters liked to wear as their badge of authenticity.

Typically the podcast still presents, despite its growing professionalism, as a specialist online space, positioning itself as quirky and socially radical, and committed to doing things differently. The casual personalization of the pod, with everyone always on first-name terms, their enthusiasms just like yours, and their lifestyle just a little enhanced, typifies the genre. The Singapore POD called Mr Brown captures the style precisely. Highly personal in tone and content, often courageous, and acutely observing of the nuances of everyday life, it is offered in the slightly-self-mocking tones of the popular newspaper or magazine columnist – but carefully credentialed with all of the right sorts of attributes. Even the not-so-accidental erasures cue listeners to the sorts of in-joke which characterize the long-term podcaster:

> I, mrbrown, am the accidental author of a popular Singapore website, mrbrown. com, that has been documenting the dysfunctional side of Singapore life since 1997. When not writing, I play Xbox Live, PC games, World of Warcraft, DoTA, Team Fortress 2, Soul Caliber 3 on PS2, watch too many movies and anime, buy too many gadgets, rear fish and ride my bikes. (Lee Kin Mum 2010)

Mr Brown varies his pod topics between world-political comment, beautifully realized social history on life in Singapore (as in his pod on his younger brother's wedding), and heartbreaking accounts of life with his children – especially his autistic daughter. None of this capacity for warm and human emotional expressivity prevents him, however, from specializing in slightly wry, amused, and always amusing comment on the current political scene.

> The Greater Grace Temple in Detroit put three SUVs on stage for a service focused on getting God to convince Congress to approve a bailout for the US auto industry. I didn't know God had a soft spot for SUVs. (Lee Kin Mum 2010)

One way to approach the "listening" evoked by podcasts is to watch the interactants' replies, posted back to the websites. Are they hearing just the content, ideas, and information, or the expressivity as well – the ways in which things are said, and the personality behind the voicing? Many of these sites are dependent upon voicing technologies rather than recording their actual author(s), so that "scripted" attributes such as wordplay and wit, rhetorical forcefulness, audacity, and over- and understatement mimic the techniques of the columnist, or the radio presenter or TV host with a crew of writers. Even small levels of secondary orality impact upon what is "heard" and so persistently "listened for." Online talk texts and pod format effects are having to work hard to pull away from established broadcast techniques – and, as listener-users or wannabe producer-creators, we have to learn to listen critically for new elements as they evolve.

Pod audiences have developed according to two principles: the affordances of the technologies of delivery and listening, and the social spaces into which each pod product was directed. A quick sampling of two children's story pod sites points the way. The massively successful Storynory.com (n.d.), produced by experienced media professionals and reliably carrying conventional children's narratives, old and new, onto the internet, contrasts in interesting ways with BabyMonsters.com, which promotes itself as the storying space of a child elaborated by her parents into an altogether edgier source of collaborative contributions. The first re-mediates traditional children's narrative. The second voices the imaginative powers of children's own storying. To understand podcasting, we need to learn to listen actively for those sorts of progressions across the full range of new audio spaces. This, then, is the new listening room: part of the digital sounding chamber in which the next audio habitus is under production. New cultural practices are already regulating the social responses of listeners, and will inexorably, across time and the many new spaces of audio production and reception, be augmented by the creative, the unexpected, or the unfamiliar – and incorporated into the known. What was previously unvoiced or unsounded is more likely than ever before to find a social use. Uplifted and reapplied in new assemblages, older audio resources will reconnect. This new open-endedness maximizes both hybridity and creative transformation. With all of these auditory spaces very much still under construction, we will be listening as never before.

Conclusion

None of what has been covered here is in any way exhaustive of the topic. Listening is, when conceived as the "open field" which I postulated at the beginning, an endless, and endlessly developing, source of social and cultural activity. In its mediated production alone, without any of the myriad forms of "natural" sound work in which we all engage, it has vast repertoires of historical, contemporary, and specialized applications. As these spin into all of the new sound production and listening spaces of the digital era, expect to be confronted by entirely unexpected listening challenges – and to witness our range of listening techniques adapt to each of them.

Quite where this all may be headed remains to be heard – but I am interested in a recent comment by van Leeuwen (2008), who, in beginning an analysis of contemporary discourses of time, notes that we are moving into what he calls a saturational polyvalence when it comes to postmodernity's many avenues of "mechanizing" the forms of time which measure our lived day. Time has become, van Leeuwen suggests, "polyrhythmic." Each of us exists within a number of simultaneous time frames, and faces the challenge of somehow coordinating the demands of each of these strands of time in which we swim with those of other spaces, other selves, and other demands.

There is, I suggest, an equivalent polyrhythmic quality in the contemporary soundscape: one which already defines our listening behaviors, and is more likely to intensify as our access to and control over digitized sound sources and audiofile management techniques further develop. Only by coming to an understanding of what our personal listening has been, why it is as it is, and what it might have been, can we begin to perform the complex listening practices of our globally sound-charged future. So keep listening. There is a great deal more to be heard.

References

Bourdieu, P. 1977 *Outline of a Theory of Practice*. Cambridge University Press, Cambridge.

Bourdieu, P. 1984 *Distinction: A Social Critique of the Judgement of Taste*. Harvard University Press, Cambridge, MA.

Bull, M. 1999 The dialectics of walking: Walkman use and the reconstruction of the site of experience, in consuming culture. In J. Hearn and S. Roseneil, eds. *Power and Resistance*. Macmillan, Basingstoke, UK, pp. 199–220.

Chambers, I. 1990 A miniature history of the Walkman. *New Formations*, 11, pp. 1–4.

Cook, J. 2002 Lovesong dedications. *M/C: A Journal of Media and Culture*, 5, 6. Retrieved from http://www.media-culture.org.au/0211/lovesongdedications.html

Fairclough, N. 1989 *Language and Power*. Longman, London.

Fairclough, N. 1992 *Discourse and Social Change*. Polity Press, Cambridge.

Fairclough, N. 1994 Conversationalisation of public discourse and the authority of the consumer. In R. Keat, N. Whitely and N. Abercrombie, eds. *The Authority of the Consumer*. Routledge, London, pp. 253–268.

Fairclough, N. 1995 *Media Discourse*. Edward Arnold, London.

Fiumara, G.C. 1990 *The Other Side of Language: A Philosophy of Listening*. Routledge, London.

Hong Kong Uncle. N.d. Retrieved from http://www.youtube.com/watch?v=EsYRQkmVifg

Hosokawa, S. 1984 The Walkman effect. *Popular Music*, 4, pp. 165–180.

Hunter, M. 2007 Podcast user magazine. *Podzine*, May 16.

Hutchby, I. 1996 *Confrontation Talk: Arguments, Asymmetries and Power on Talk Radio*. Lawrence Erlbaum, Hillsdale, NJ.

Lee Kin Mum. 2010 Mr Brown podcast. Retrieved from http://www.mrbrown.com/blog/podcast/

Maffesoli, M. 1984 *Essais sur la violence banale et fondatrice*. Méridiens Klincksieck, Paris.

Maffesoli, M. 1996 *The Time of the Tribes*. Sage, London.

Margetson, R. 2009 Pokemon street interviews. Transcribed with the broadcaster's permission, October, ABC Radio 5AN, Adelaide South Australia.

Ong, W. 1982 *Orality and Literacy: The Technologising of the Word*. Methuen, London.

Political animal: Bus Uncle eyes more than votes. 2010 *South China Morning Post*, March 21.

Potts, J. 1989 *Radio in Australia*. University of New South Wales Press, Kensington.

Potts, J. 1995 Schizochronia: time in digital sound. In S. Davies et al., eds. *Essays in Sound 2: Technophonia*. Contemporary Sound Arts, Sydney, pp. 17–22.

Scannell, P. 1996 *Radio, Television and Modern Life: A Phenomenological Approach*. Blackwell, Oxford.

Storynory.com. N.d. Free audio stories for kids. Retrieved from www.Storynory.com

Thompson, J.B. 1995 *The Media and Modernity: A Social Theory of the Media*. Polity Press, Oxford.

Tobin Funerals. N.d. Music selection. Retrieved from http://www.tobinbrothers.com.au/index.asp?menuid=140.130

Van Leeuwen, T. 1984 Impartial speech: observations on the intonation of radio newsreaders. *Australian Journal of Cultural Studies*, 2, 1, pp. 84–98.

Van Leeuwen, T. 1985 Persuasive speech: the intonation of the live radio commercial. *Australian Journal of Communication*, 7, pp. 25–34.

Van Leeuwen, T. 2008 *Discourse and Practice: New Tools for Critical Discourse Analysis*. Oxford University Press, Oxford.

Weaver, J. 2007 *Much Love, Jac*. Allen & Unwin, Sydney.

West Australian. N.d. Retrieved from http://au.news.yahoo.com/thewest/

3

Viewing

Shawn Shimpach

In the half-light the faces of the audience detach themselves into little pallid ovals.
Mary Heaton Vorse, *Outlook* 98 (1911/2002)

[I]f only you could see what I've seen with your eyes.
Roy Batty (Rutger Hauer), *Blade Runner* (Ridley Scott, 1982)

Viewing

The verb *viewing* hardly seems adequate. The range of activities claimed for the practice of coming into contact with today's media beg for something more. Indeed, the recent modifiers *mobile* and *interactive* suggest the need to expand the types of activity associated with mere viewing. But if some notion of an even more "active audience" constitutes received wisdom about the act of viewing media today, it does so as it always has, in relation to the media form being viewed, and assumptions about the location and conditions of that viewing. Viewing is located at the intersection of "media," "text," "audience," "reception," and "subject." It is implicitly (and functionally) defined at the recipient end of a transmission model of communication in which it is occasioned only by the prior and distinct production and distribution of a media text.

In the context of this volume, *viewing* needs to be distinguished from other terms used to describe the encounter with media. Viewing implies, first of all, a (sighted) subject's encounter with a visual medium: an encounter that in turn implicates the subject, the medium, and the conditions of that encounter. This is where the practice of viewing draws its power, for it is the privileged moment

The Handbook of Media Audiences, First Edition. Edited by Virginia Nightingale.
© 2014 John Wiley & Sons, Ltd. Published 2014 by John Wiley & Sons, Ltd.

and location where all the parts of a media practice ultimately come together. Viewing implies exhibition, reception, and depending on the subject being theorized, cognition, interpretation, behavioral effects, or needs gratified. In addition, it often includes hearing and certain phenomenological sensations and can imply embodiment, ideological positioning, subject (re)formation, or simply stimuli response.

Second, viewing implies a singular, idealized, individual process. It is an activity, a verb. This is as opposed to an *audience*, an entity only in the aggregate. An audience is a thing, a noun. When an audience is said to be active, the first activity implied is viewing. While audience, perhaps more inclusively, represents a categorical and structural position within a larger, institutionalized process (see Ang 1991), viewing suggests a localized process, which is largely constituted by the viewing subject's activity. Viewing is more specific, suggesting a position to occupy alongside a process to activate. Viewing delimits the media it implies to those that can be seen (thus excluding radio, mp3, etc., as well as Braille) and also arguably excludes the printed word such that *reading* implies a different practice with different associations.

Third, viewing implies an extended, on some level deliberate, even contemplative, practice in a specific space often presumed to be intended for the purpose of viewing or at least to include it, in a sustained, more or less intentional encounter. This viewing process has been variously laboratory tested, ethnographically observed, and retroactively theorized. The viewing process is understood differently depending on the weight assigned the viewing environment, assumptions about the medium viewed, and the role allowed the viewing agent. Many studies of viewing have typically combined assumptions about the space of viewing with the specificities of a given medium, rendering the viewing subject in terms of a medium's supposed essence; thus the "spectator" focusing his "gaze" on the classical Hollywood cinema, the domestic "couch potato" allowing her distracted "glance" to bounce off network television, and the mobile "user" who "interacts" with video games and cellular phones. The viewing subject and the practice of viewing are observed and/or imagined from there. In this way the study of viewing is much more often the study of what is being viewed in combination with the specificities of where. While this intersection of space, medium, text, and subject is powerful and compelling, this construction of viewing nevertheless positions viewing and the viewing subject at the end of the process of communication and does not typically consider viewing to be itself a constitutive and productive practice. The viewing subject is constituted as such only in relation to a series of prior and distinct practices. Viewing has much less often been conceived of as itself a distinct and generative set of practices constituting its own terrain and distinct outcomes.

To clarify the contributions and limits of such assumptions, it is worth considering several moments in the history of viewing media, using the United States as our example, for how they bring viewing space into considerations of the texts being viewed and the viewing subject, whose presumed activities have constituted the basis for retroactive theories of media and viewing.

Nickelodeon: Unruly Social Space

> Behind us sat a woman with her escort. So rapt and entranced was she with what was happening on the stage that her voice accompanied all that happened – a little unconscious and lilting obbligato. It was the voice of a person unconscious that she spoke – speaking from the depths of emotion; ... Outside the iron city roared: before the door of the show the push-cart venders bargained and trafficked with customers. Who in that audience remembered it? They had found the door of escape.... And for the moment they were permitted to drink deep of oblivion of all the trouble in the world. (Vorse 1911/2002)

Such rapt attention describes a physiologically distinct conceptualization of viewing film that was understood to be implicit in the very technology, wherein the mechanized replacement of one still photo by another – with brief interludes of darkness between – is perceived as smoothly moving images because of its physical apprehension by an embodied viewer (through an effect known for years as *persistence of vision*). Beyond this marvelous coincidence of the mechanical and the physiological, observers of early filmgoing paid particular attention, first to the assortment of languages, mixing of ethnicities, genders, ages, and class makeup of the attending viewers gathered, publicly, in a darkened theater space. Such information was usually considered alongside interpretations of the films being screened and the conditions of the viewing space as they were observed and reported. Viewing for these observers not only involved an encounter with a visual medium but also was constitutive of cultural and moral experiences tied directly to questions of citizenship then very much in flux (Uricchio and Pearson 1993; Abel 2006).

Such concerns about the viewing experience, however, substantially predate the cinema, recalling debates about public "stimulation of the passions" resulting from theater, exhibitions, traveling shows and tours, and later museums and tourism. Concerns were mixed with admiration for the potentially "uplifting" educational and cultural benefits of viewing such displays. Theater in the United States, for example, was conceived already by the later eighteenth century as a "politicized public space" where Americans could be engaged in "intense and widespread political participation" (Butsch 2008, p. 25). So intense, indeed, that the possibility of unruly, potentially violent, crowd activity became associated with theatergoing throughout the nineteenth century. By the end of that century, the theater was composed of separate spheres, where one could experience cultural refinement, stimulating entertainment, or, for a lesser entrance fee, burlesque titillation. In each case, the specificities of viewing were closely associated with the class and political proclivities of the viewing subject in conjunction with the conditions of the viewing space. Meanwhile, traveling exhibitions, world's fairs, and museums offered opportunities to broaden one's cultural awareness (and enjoy the sense of privilege that accompanied the gaze onto what was often presented as radical otherness) even while it potentially threatened to offend delicate sensibilities and undermine social taboos with displays of nudity, death, and grotesquerie (Schwartz 1995; Thomson 1996). Here viewing implied a participation in practices of cultural citizenship connoting world and worldly knowledge, personal enlightenment and uplift, and bodily affect and titillation.

By the last decade of the nineteenth century, individual viewers could pay to view short reels of film through a viewfinder on contraptions such as Edison's coin-activated Kinetoscope. Found in penny arcades and the like, they featured brief visual encounters – often lasting less than 20 seconds – showing actors kissing, cock fights, shirtless boxers, exotic dancers, and so on. Movies of this era have since been described as a "cinema of attractions" for their textual emphasis on sensation, movement, spectacle, and implied direct address with comparatively little attendant effort made toward narrative immersion or realist characterization (Gunning 1990). This early cinema required a form of viewing that embraced modernity, sought sensation, and was not married to story as the sole evocation of realist entertainment (Musser 1990). Beyond the practically applied demonstration of persistence of vision, viewing the cinema of attractions offered immediate sensation, both emotional and reportedly phenomenological (Musser 1990; Sobchack 1992), while locating the viewer on the leading edge of scientifically produced, commercialized amusements.

Motion pictures in the first decade of the twentieth century could vary dramatically depending upon where and when they were viewed. Projectionists sought to vary their programs or edit footage in creative new ways, while in-house music and live narration varied by venue. No one film was guaranteed to be the same at each viewing (Bowser 1990; Musser 1990). By the time motion picture exhibition took hold as a regular, projected visual display, offered initially in improvised storefront theaters at prices low enough to allow the Nickelodeon label to catch on, viewing was a multifaceted undertaking, with protocols derived from other cultural practices. The location and the text featured as only parts of the overall activity. In addition to attracting a strikingly diverse audience to an airless, darkened space after – for many – a grueling day of hard work, the theater management typically allowed or encouraged practices that complicated a straightforward viewing experience. As Butsch (2008) has summarized,

> The shortness of each film, for example, created momentary intermissions for conversation and movement.... Live and participative entertainment, such as piano players and creative projectionists or sing-a-longs, combined with people eating and talking, and entering and exiting at will, would have disrupted any spellbinding effect. (p. 47)

Whether to facilitate reel changes or sociability, viewing in the boisterous nickelodeon involved participation in a distinct set of practices involving not only the cinematic text, but also the sociability and community associated with the space of exhibition, in which the interaction between film and subject was but one part. In the storefront nickelodeons, the audience could redefine the viewing experience, casting it in a distinctly ethnic, national, political, or social light. Early viewing was therefore an intensely social, interactive experience where the thrill of the moving image was but a part of what it meant to be viewing (Gomery 1992; Butsch 2008).

Retroactively, this audience experience has been regarded as an alternative public sphere accessible to ages, genders, ethnicities, and languages normally excluded from the public sphere (as well as from accepted, middle-class cultural experiences of refinement). Film viewing during this moment was not solitary, internal, or psychological, but social, external, public, and sociological (Hansen 1991). Viewing was an experience not simply of making sense of a projected, visual text, but a social and cultural activity involving the potential for social mobility, Americanization, and danger (moral, political, and physical). Viewing in the context of the nickelodeon era therefore involved audiences as "sociable publics" rather than focused spectators, while individual films could be very different experiences depending not only on the venue in which the viewer encountered the film but also on the viewer's cultural capital and knowledge of narratives drawn from other sources (Uricchio and Pearson 1993). Despite darkened space and on-screen activities, viewing always included interactions with fellow filmgoers in the space of the theater (Hansen 1991). Moreover, as descriptions of movie going began to populate the era's journalism, viewing became part of a practice of entering into a distinctly new, modern form of public (Shimpach 2007).

By the 1910s, while this era's cinema worked out what Singer (2001) has described as "a film-narrative language that was still having trouble making itself fully understood" (p. 270), nationally distributed periodicals offered their predominantly middle-class readership assistance in the form of motion picture tie-ins, feature articles, advertisements, and even fiction. For example, the nationally popular *McClure's* magazine published a short story in 1914 that featured a fictional young woman who over the course of the story receives instruction on viewing film from a provocatively single man. Watching a typical (if fictitious) melodramatic Western together, the man recognizes the "smartly dressed" young woman's evident antipathy to the apparently simplistic story and unrealistic acting. He suggests she draw on her evident cultural capital through recourse to allegory and symbolism via such established culturally worthy intertexts as Henry James, Maeterlink, and even the Bible. Watching her struggle, he says, "Oh, you haven't got the idea," and offers, apparently quite convincingly, "The story's sound enough. Dress it up for yourself" (Webster 1914).

Singer (2001) wonders, in such instances, "Did spectators use [magazines] to make sense of film narratives they found baffling? Did filmgoers – and filmmakers – rely on tie-ins as a means to ease proto-classical cinema's semiotic growing pains?" (p. 270). What, in other words, constituted the full act of viewing at this time? Did it include also the reading of magazines and newspapers? Did it include a background in the liberal arts and humanities? How important were, the "instructive portraits of refined film-going, either for those unaccustomed to the experience, or for those seeking an upscale, heterosocial mode of attending the cinema" that filled the pages of magazines at this time (Stamp 2000, p. 106)? While I have argued elsewhere that such instances provide evidence for the assumption of audience labor from the earliest days of the cinema, they also suggest that viewing has always been presumed to involve more than a completely innocent encounter with an instance of media (Shimpach 2005). Here viewing presumed a variety of activities and practices far in excess of the medium, text, and even site on offer. Viewing at this time was a practice that required diligence, effort, and a level of autodidacticism.

As theater size began to increase and movie-going became a more widely socially acceptable undertaking, viewing motion pictures in the space of the movie theater took on characteristics understood to be increasingly medium specific. A large group of people gathered at the same place, watching the same thing, signified in specific ways to observers at the time. As Gustav Le Bon noted about the theater, so too was it true of the cinema that "the entire audience experiences at the same time the same emotion" (Le Bon quoted in Butsch 2008, p. 42), suggesting a powerful and potentially dangerous relationship wherein the viewer was positioned between the screen and the era's alarmist notions of crowd psychology.

In 1916 Münsterberg drew on the then current notion of the powers of suggestion, through which the specific perceptual process associated with the motion pictures, he argued, left the viewer "certainly in a state of heightened suggestibility." He wrote that "the intensity with which the [photo]plays take hold of the audience cannot remain without social effects ... the mind is so completely given up to the moving pictures" (quoted in Langdale 2002, p. 154). Such an approach began a tradition of "effects" research based on the operative mechanism of suggestibility that "located control of effects in the media rather than in the audience" (Butsch 2008, p. 45) and constituted the viewing subject as the sum of behaviors that could be effected. The Progressive era thus produced a longstanding approach to viewing in the era of so-called mass communication in which statistically measurable audiences were individually subject to the effects of media produced prior to and separate from the moment of viewing. At the same time, the experience of simultaneously being part of a gathered crowd and also "given up" to the movies, defined the viewing experience.[1] Viewing had no meaning in itself and was not itself productive except in variously contextualized relationships to a media apparatus.

Classical Hollywood: The Gaze

The mass of mainstream film, and the conventions within which it has consciously evolved, portray a hermetically sealed world which unwinds magically, indifferent to the presence of the audience, producing for them a sense of separation and playing on their voyeuristic fantasy. Moreover, the extreme contrast between the darkness in the auditorium (which also isolates the spectators from one another) and the brilliance of the shifting patterns of light and shade on the screen helps to promote the illusion of voyeuristic separation. Although the film is really being shown, is there to be seen, conditions of screening and narrative conventions give the specta- tor an illusion of looking in on a private world. Among other things, the position of the spectators in the cinema is blatantly one of repression of their exhibitionism and projection of the repressed desire onto the performer. (Mulvey 1986, p. 201)

Restructuring of the motion picture industry in the United States soon involved ver- tical integration linking production, distribution, and exhibition within the same companies. Exhibition sites were soon characterized by the rapid construction of large movie palaces, dedicated buildings featuring seating for hundreds, offering elab- orate concessions and services, even themed decor (e.g. Greek or Egyptian), with full, live orchestras to accompany silent films, and all organized around the feature film as the center of the evening's entertainment (Koszarski 1990). By the start of the 1930s, theaters were moving to electronic speaker systems allowing the film sound to be not only synchronized with the image, but also standardized at the point of production so that the viewing experience (at least of the film and its soundtrack) would be the same no matter at which theater it was viewed (Gomery 1992).

Such a transformation in the site of exhibition was accompanied by new proto- cols for the practice of viewing. Ticket prices increased, theater locations moved, and practices of middle-class decorum were increasingly expected and enforced. The movie-viewing experience was much more singularly encompassed by the feature film display, and consequently, much less social. Middle-class decorum – itself derived in bourgeois counterdistinction to European aristocratic viewing practices characterized by displays of disinterest and nonchalance (Johnson 1995) – borrowed from the "respectable" theater, increasingly replaced the raucous socia- bility of the working-class nickelodeon. Although more people could be seated within a given movie theater, the enforcement of middle-class decorum; the dark- ened hall; the enormous, brightly illuminated screen lit from a projector apparatus shooting over the viewers' heads from behind; and the narrative structure and formal style of the film itself all conspired to produce an individual, internal experience of the film. Viewing was now a supposedly solitary (if still public) and fully absorbing activity in which viewers were isolated by darkness, their attention directed singularly toward the screen.

These changes were the result of the latest stage in a process of product stand- ardization that was accompanied by the refinement of narrative and formal practices, culminating in what has been identified as the classical Hollywood style and narrative (Bordwell, Staiger, and Thompson 1985). Hollywood films finally made their narrative language understood by focusing attention on a single, inter- nally coherent storyline, featuring a consistently characterized, psychologically motivated, action- and goal-oriented protagonist whose exploits the film would follow (Bordwell 1987). At the same time, production techniques and filmmaking style were relatively standardized and designed to be self-effacing with so-called invisible editing, cause-and-effect narrative sequencing, and story and characterization borrowed from realist conventions of the nineteenth-century novel. All these practices were designed specifically to focus viewer attention on the story. The text was put together to enable the viewer to get "lost" in the world of the narrative and forget she or he was viewing a film (Bordwell, Staiger, and Thompson 1985).

Spectatorship

This transformation in the viewing experience has been retroactively (and elaborately) theorized as *spectatorship*. The *spectator* is an idealized, universalized subject produced as an actual effect of the text (at least when experienced in these conditions). The spectator shifted the emphasis of film theory onto a highly psychologized (or psychoanalyzed) viewing subject whose process of viewing involves regression, absorption, the indulgence of voyeurism, and other subconscious desires which, as Kuhn (1984) has suggested, characterize the viewing of cinema as "a set of psychic relations." While this represents a significant departure from the Progressive era characterization of the motion picture audience as, again in Kuhn's (1984) words, "a group of people who buy tickets at the box office ... who can be surveyed, counted and categorized according to age, sex, and socio-economic status" (p. 23), it nevertheless ultimately draws on some strikingly similar assumptions. On reading Kuhn's distinction in viewing between spectator and audience, Staiger (1992) has noted "the notion of context – psychological versus social – changes the event [of viewing] into two different situations" (p. 49), and indeed assumptions about the significance of one or the other context have led attendant scholarship in dramatically different directions with seemingly different sets of priorities and emphases. Yet both the spectator and the film audience share important characteristics.

They both imply, if in different ways, the significance of the viewing space to practices of viewing. As Morley (1995) proposes, "[F]ilms have had to be seen in certain places, and the understanding of such places has to be central to any analysis of what film-viewing has meant" (p. 170). Therefore the transformations of the nickelodeon into the picture palace should correspondingly change the very experience and practice of viewing film. Motion picture viewing in the context of the picture palace heightened the perceptual experience of viewing originally described by Münsterberg, where

> the massive outer world has lost its weight, it has been freed from space, time, and causality, and it has been clothed in the forms of our own consciousness. The mind has triumphed over matter, and the pictures roll on with the ease of musical tones. It is a superb enjoyment which no other art can furnish. (Langdale 2002, pp. 153–154)

With a decidedly more Freudian conclusion, Baudry (1986) could largely agree, writing later that taking into account "the effects which result from the projection of images ... the cinematographic apparatus brings about a state of artificial regression" (p. 313).

Apparatus Theory

In what became known as *apparatus theory*, the combination of the classical Hollywood form and the dominant viewing situation of the cinema produced the conditions for theorizing the filmic spectator as isolated from the outside world and artificially induced to experience regression. Such an approach to viewing cinema drew on what were perceived as unique characteristics of the cinematic experience to define the ways the cinema functions as an institutional apparatus, a structure of interlocking parts and functions that position the viewer – now spectator, or subject – in specific and consistent relation to (and through) the apparatus. Hence Mulvey begins her now canonical description of "visual pleasure and narrative cinema" by linking cinema viewing, the Hollywood text, and a Freudian notion of *scopophilia*. Such an understanding of viewing depends on the specificities of the movie palace. The interrelated assumptions about viewing context and medium viewed, the institutional apparatus, and the medium-specific choice of narrative style (both more historically and culturally specific than credited) collude to produce a viewing subject as the product of these arrangements. Drawing from analogies to Lacanian psychoanalytic theory, the spectator, under these kinds of conditions, was positioned as an "all-perceiving subject" whose viewing entailed an all-encompassing "gaze" upon the projected filmic narrative that characterized the subject effect of the apparatus. Initially for Mulvey, this gaze was gendered, a specifically male gaze imposed by the cinematic viewing experience causing all spectators to identify voyeuristically with a masculinist gaze at woman (Mulvey 1986).

Apparatus theory supposes a consistent and rather monolithic cinematic experience for the viewer that allowed film theory to focus on variations in the textual aspects of film while presuming the spectator-in-the-text subject of the address. Ultimately as film theorists applied and practiced this approach to spectatorship, the cinematic apparatus became, on the one hand, self-evident, and, on the other, too automatic, producing a spectator theorized as constructed solely through the ideological positioning performed by the narrative cinematic text, although, as Stam (2000) notes, "at once constituting and constituted by the text" (p. 230). The viewer and the text were here mutually constitutive rather than distinct from each other. This led, finally, to the conclusion that this approach deprived the spectator of any perspective for social or political action except during privileged moments when vision was fleetingly disturbed by a pressure the text could not contain (MacCabe 1985, p. 11). Nevertheless, at their best, such notions of spectatorship figured a complex (if always evasively abstract) practice, experience, and subject of viewing. As Stam (2000) has summarized,

> If spectatorship is on one level structured and determined, on another it is open and polymorphous. The cinematic experience has a ludic and adventurous side as well as an imperious one; it fashions a plural, 'mutant' self, occupying a range of subject positions. One is 'doubled' by the cinematic apparatus, at once in the movie theater

and with the camera/projector and the action on screen. And one is further dispersed through the multiplicity of perspectives provided by even the most conventional montage. Cinema's 'polymorphous projection-identifications' on a certain level transcend the determinations of local morality, social milieu, and ethnic affiliation. Spectatorship can become a liminal space of dreams and self-fashioning. Through the psychic chameleonism of spectatorship, ordinary social positions, as in carnival, are temporarily bracketed. (p. 233)

Lost in even this account is the original notion that the "subject" of the cinema was not really meant to be the same as the "viewer," even if it has been theorized from some imagined conditions of viewing involving the cinematic space. The spectator-subject is actually a reading strategy for addressing the ideological implications of the filmic text. Like much of reception studies, while interested in the effect of the text upon viewer, the theory is actually devised to apprehend the text in its complexity and merely presume the "actual" viewer at the end point of the process described. Here it is the text, or qualities of the text, historically and culturally situated, that is investigated, while the viewer acts as one of the possible contexts at a given historical moment. Thus, Mayne (1993) has suggested,

By bracketing the 'real viewers' altogether, such theories undertake what is ultimately an impossible task. However much one can insist upon the theoretical need for separating the ideal spectator from the real viewers of motion pictures, the two categories are not so easily separated. Instead of theorizing the difficulty, the slippage between the two supposed incommensurate terms, much film theory has ignored the problem altogether by dismissing one or the other as irrelevant or secondary. (p. 56)

The cinematic spectator figured ultimately as a strategy for textual analysis rather than the study of viewing.

Growing dissatisfaction with this approach in some realms led to different ways of examining the act of viewing the classical Hollywood cinema, often couched in terms that implied that the actual activity of real viewers would be queried. Thus Bordwell, introducing an approach to understanding cinematic narrative informed by cognitive psychology posited that "a film, I shall suggest, does not 'position' anybody. A film cues the spectator to execute a definable variety of *operations*" (Bordwell, quoted in Mayne, p. 55; emphasis in original). Initially this appears to offer a very different assumption about the viewing subject, suggesting that viewing is a "motivated activity." However, as Bordwell describes the process, it is the film text that "cues" the spectator to follow various "protocols" relating to "schemata" associated with narration or other types of filmic organization. Ultimately this cognitive approach, in addition to raising the not insignificant question of whether "viewing or perceiving can be separated, except in a most theoretical way, from interpreting or reading" (Staiger 1992, p. 64), relies upon an unexamined cultural context in which such "cues" can signify in the first place and in any event focuses on the text being viewed, while the viewing is read off from that text and the "cues" it offers. As Barker (2006) concludes,

> Bordwell in the end is really interested in the formation of films, not the formation of audiences – therefore, he only explores the *conditions of comprehension*. He therefore curtails his account to just the cognitive, and excludes consideration of sensuous (the impact of films on our *bodies* through sound, light, etc.), aesthetic (all the forms in which we experience films as *beautiful* or *horrible*), emotional (the dimensions of caring, etc.), and imaginative (the ways in which audiences build larger worlds beyond the cues provided) aspects of film viewing. (p. 134; emphasis in original)

Nevertheless, the ostensible stability of the formal, narrative, and stylistic elements of Hollywood's productions continue to inform understandings of those films' viewers in a number of studies. It is often, for example, against Hollywood films that the difference of other textual and viewing practices can be registered and characterized (e.g. Gopalan 2002; Larkin 2008). Other efforts have focused on the viewing experience in relation to what has been described as the incompleteness of the Hollywood text as a precondition for successful international circulation and reception implicitly suggesting that viewing involves completing the story by filling the gaps with local knowledge and beliefs, in ways that are crucial to the contemporary functions of the globally successful culture industries. Olson (1999), for example, argues that Hollywood productions are imbued with a "narrative transparency" that he defines as "any textual apparatus that allows audiences to project indigenous values, beliefs, rites, and rituals into imported media or the use of those devices" (p. 5). While his phrasing would seem to offer the text more agency than the viewer, he implies a viewing practice where once again the story is sound enough – just dress it up for yourself. The films remain the center of his analysis, while their economic value is contingent upon the work done by viewers to "localize" them.

Exhibition studies

At the same time, drawing on approaches developed from the take-up of British cultural studies while cognizant that films result from strategies derived from an institutionally endorsed understanding of motion pictures audiences (like Olson's), critical attention has also turned to the observable practices of audiences attending movies. This has led both audience studies and exhibition studies to increasingly focus on the specific contexts of viewing, the associated practices, and the cultural assumptions that accompany motion picture viewing. What has emerged endorses an understanding that viewing is never a singular or a straightforward activity. Indeed as Acland's (2003) account of viewing at a typical multiplex illustrates, isolating a singularly distinct act of "viewing" can be challenging:

Public movie performances are occasions for eating ... for sneaking snacks and drinks, for both planned and impromptu socializing, for working, for flirting, for sexual play, for gossiping, for staking out territory in theater seats, for threatening noisy specta- tors, for being threatened, for arguments, for reading, for talking about future movie- going, for relaxing, for sharing in the experience of the screening with other audience members, for fleeting glimpses at possible alliances and allegiances of taste, politics, and identity, for being too close to strangers, for being crowded in your winter clothes, for being frozen by overactive air-conditioning, for being bored, for sleeping, for dis- appointment, for joy, for arousal, for disgust, for slouching, for hand holding, for drug taking, for standing in lines, for making phone calls, ... and for both remembering and forgetting oneself ... cinemagoing is banal, it is erotic, it is civil, it is unruly; it is an everyday site of regulated and unregulated possibility. (pp. 57–58)

Exhibition studies that focus on the space of viewing have led scholars such as Hark (2002) to deduce "discourses of movie-going pleasure" that "metonymically link movie-going [and thus viewing] with other cultural experiences and encom- pass connotations generated both by the place of exhibition and the filmed narra- tive on the screen" (p. 7). Such accounts begin to suggest the complexity and diversity of everyday practices subsumed under the label *viewing*. Moreover, they imply a range of practices not readily determined merely by some combination of media text and spatial location.

The limits of a definition of viewing that rests on the empirically observable become clear when even observable behaviors are cloaked behind a veil of the private and domestic, as has been presumed in the case of television viewing.

Broadcast Television: The Glance

The benefits of television can be derived only when you are looking at it directly and not doing anything else. The housewife will not very long remain a housewife who attempts to watch television programs all afternoon and evening instead of cooking or darning socks. (Samuel Cuff, General Manager WABD [DuMont affiliate], 1946, quoted in Boddy 2004, p. 51)

Recall the first stand-alone episode of *The Honeymooners* ("TV or Not TV," 1955).[2] Here was a commercial network program – at the dawn of network television – humorously depicting the prevalent cultural anxieties about introducing television into the home. This single, half-hour episode included allusions to such concerns as the debt associated with this expensive new consumer electronic device, the potentially addictive nature of the programming, the infantilizing and feminizing effects this commercialized domestic medium was claimed by some to exert, the rearranging of schedules in order to watch favored programs, the conflicts between friends and family members all wishing to watch (or not watch) at the same time, the potential for disruption to gendered domestic relations ("I don't want to look at these same four walls," Alice insists to Ralph; "I want to look at Liberace!"), and so on.[3] Amidst this checklist of (then) new media anxieties, a scene in the second act depicts Ralph Kramden elaborately conditioning his environment in anticipation of watching television at home for the first time. Before ever watching, he apparently intuits that environment is crucial to the viewing experience, carefully arranging snack foods and beverages for an entire evening's viewing in easy reach, opening each one, measuring them to no more than an arm's length away. Similarly, he adjusts his seating, in relation to not only the screen but also the snacks. He does all this before even seeking out the listings for that night's programming. His friend, Ed Norton, goes further, unable to enjoy the children's science fiction programming he wants to view (*Captain Video*)[4] without an array of props and costumes (space helmets, ray guns) as part of his viewing experience. While this leads to conflict between the two friends (and signifies broader anxieties over television's alleged lethargy-inducing or infantilizing powers), it also clearly acknowledges and demonstrates that what is on screen (something the entire episode never shows) constitutes at most merely a part of the experience of viewing. The space of viewing and the activities within that space are the sites of the episode's humor.

The viewing of perhaps no other medium has been so interwoven with discourses about the space of its viewing as has television. The overriding determinant of the distinct activity of viewing television as opposed to earlier visual media forms consists of television's presumed viewing context of the private, domestic home. This single factor, the space of viewing, has determined interpretations of the televisual text and characterized most predominant assumptions about the television viewer. And yet this domestic space, so closely associated with television viewing, leaves investigations of actual viewing practices open only to speculation, secondhand reporting, or various small-scale observations. The television viewer, we understand from anecdote, familiar experience, and voluminous research, is characterized primarily by the fact that she or he is viewing while simultaneously at home (although exceptions abound; e.g. McCarthy 2001; Govil 2004). This marks a significantly different practice than the viewing of cinema. Petro (1986) once characterized perceptions of the difference by noting,

> When viewing a film, the spectator centers attention on the screen, becoming absorbed in the narrative and with the characters. When watching television, however, viewing seems to be marked by discontinuous attention, by the spectator's participation in several activities at once in which televiewing may not even rank as third in importance. (p. 5)

And, as Allen (1992) notes, "The expression *watching television* subsumes a wide variety of modes of engagement with the television set, from rapt attention to occasional glances in the direction of the screen while you are doing something else" (p. 102). The idea is that the home, the domestic space, already constitutes a site of labor, of consumption, and, perhaps overridingly, of distraction. Watching television is presumed to be interrupted by the call of domestic duties, from ironing, vacuuming, preparing meals, and cleaning windows to answering phones, doorbells, and emails, and from helping children (to eat, play, clean, do homework, get ready for bed, or sleep) to dozing off in the comfort of one's own sofa. At the same time, the televisual text, characterized on one hand by Williams's (1974) enduring concept of "flow," can just as readily be seen as complicit in these constant interruptions by itself consisting of constant interruptions.[5] On commercial channels, these consist of the program segments interrupted by "bumpers," promotions, advertisements, and identifications returning to another program segment which may not narratively conclude today, next week, or for 30 years. Rather than absorption, the state of television viewing in the home has been characterized by distraction.

At the same time, locating the primary site of television viewing within an already complex and ideologically overdetermined domestic sphere places new emphasis on gendered differences in viewing. In the scenario implied by Petro's example, the cinema's focused, absorbing mode of spectatorship offers a masculine cultural practice of comparatively high cultural value compared to television viewing, which becomes less culturally valuable, associated with commercialized vulgar popular culture, and offering a feminine cultural practice in its domestic, distracted, superficial glance. These assumptions coincide with a history of practices in which "mass culture is somehow associated with women while real, authentic culture remains the prerogative of men" (Huyssen 1986). Such gendered value judgments have placed television viewing in the middle of broader discourses characterizing the value and the politics of the domestic everyday. While Modleski (1983) could once link daytime programming aimed primarily at women to patterns of domestic labor in what she termed the "rhythms of reception," Allen (1992) has more recently extended the observation (in perhaps inadvertently gendered language) to note that

> television's penetration into the private spaces of our lives, its unnoticed connection with the rituals and routines of daily life, inevitably make television viewing a part of our relations with the other people with whom we share those private spaces. (p. 134)

The focus on the domestic space as the site for television viewing has not only concerned scholars interested in knowing the processes involved in viewing. Indeed, cultural historians of television have amply demonstrated that this very notion of domestic viewing featured centrally and widely in early public discourse on television (Haralovich 1989; Spigel 1992). From popular magazines of the era to television critics, to industry correspondence and trade paper columns, television viewing's place in the home was a central issue from the start (Spigel 1992; Boddy 1993). The industrial rollout of television as an electronic appliance for the home, particularly in the United States, coincided with rapid suburbanization, the development of freeway systems, and changing domestic architectures. At the same time, television's perceived immediacy or "liveness," its ability to show viewers something happening right *now* but far away, in the privacy of their own homes, signaled a new mode of viewing that Williams famously labeled "mobile privatization" (Williams 1974).

Nevertheless, television industry executives worried about the effect of a mini-cinema in the domestic sphere and its possible impact on gendered domestic tranquility (Boddy 1993; Morley 1995). As an NBC employee argued in 1948, the domestic viewing necessitated by television's rollout after World War II as a postwar domestic consumer electronic appliance posed special problems because

> [t]he audience must watch a television play in order to receive full enjoyment. And if the housewife does that for too many hours each day and for too many days each week, the divorce rate may skyrocket, as irate husbands and neglected children begin to register protest. (Quoted in Boddy 1993, p. 21)

One solution was to borrow from radio broadcasting, placing an emphasis in early television on sound so that "although visual aids are used, clarifying lines of dialogue would accompany them in order to keep that portion of the audience which is unable to watch the program aware of what is transpiring" (quoted in Boddy 1993, p. 21). As radio was already adapted to fit perceptions of gendered domestic activity, this led to a conscious effort to instead focus on "radio with pictures" as a television broadcast model more likely to produce socially acceptable home viewers.

The extent to which such practices were implemented has led some to focus on sound as a neglected but crucial component of television viewing, allowing for very different practices than those associated with the cinema (Ellis 1982; Altman 1986). If the cinematic apparatus encouraged a deep, potentially regressive "gaze," then television viewing, characterized by interruption but cued through sound, could be argued to encourage a distracted "glance" (Ellis 1982). Caldwell (1995) has more recently called some of the assumptions (e.g. on a small, degraded picture compared with cinema; on an emphasis on sound; and on monotonous flow) into question, suggesting that "glance theory" ignores production and programming practices specifically designed to visually attract viewer attention amidst growing programming clutter.

Nonetheless, viewing is again derived from the combination of assumptions and observations about the intersection of the viewing space and the text being viewed. Viewing is abstracted from characterizations of reception conditions and textual generalizations in an attempt to define (the essence of) the medium. While "actual" viewing by "regular" viewers was, by definition here, hidden behind the privacy of individual, private homes, their practices and conditions were constituted from what could be assumed.

Anxiety over this led to a period of ethnographically inspired efforts to observe television viewing in the spaces where it actually takes place with special attention given to the class, gender, and geography of these viewers (Hobson 1982; Gray 1992). Viewing became a generalized practice of empirically observable behaviors in a specific space in relation to television programming, either to be measured and documented, or as in the era's approach to cultural studies, socially and historically situated. Ang (1991), after applying poststructural analysis to demonstrate the infinite regress of the actual viewer as constituted through empirical data gathering about television audiences, finally concluded that viewing could ultimately best be understood only in the context of "micro situations" that radically delimited context variables but also took into account a diverse array of practices and perhaps distractions in order to better summon something approaching an accurate description of television viewing (pp. 162–163). Few such studies, however, followed. Others were encouraged by a growing interest in the (more visible and thus observable) activities of fans of television programs, who engaged productively and intersubjectively (and certainly not passively) with their object of affection.

While fandom has taken on heightened visibility in the era of digital media and the internet, other forms of viewing have been characterized as practices of self-fashioning and exercises in the *conduct of conduct*, drawing on Foucault's late writing on governmentality so that television (and particularly the recent trend of "reality" programming) is located within a nexus of surveillance technologies that function to prescribe and proscribe conduct for viewers and imply forms of self-governing control. While such processes suggest complex interactions for self-fashioning in the context of always potential surveillance, often the television viewer is again simply located at the end of a transmission model where the only choice, the only existence of the viewer, is in relation to the already produced text or technology of television's now governing discourse (Ouellette and Hay 2008).

"New Media": The User

In the context of such influential and varied scholarship that constructs viewing from a combination of presumed viewing conditions and textual and/or technological essence of the medium viewed, what is to be made of the wholesale retreat from *viewing* as an applicable verb in the current environment of digital and "new" media? The latest media technologies suggest activities on the part of the viewer that would seem to undermine certain passive assumptions about the role of viewing. The implication is that the new media viewer is no longer absorbed or positioned, at least not in exactly comparable ways to earlier forms of viewing. Viewing in relation to new media technologies characterized by digital forms of content, mobility of use, and increased direct interaction is now reconceived as *using,*[6] *interacting,* and *searching.* Video games, personal computers, internet surfing, social networking, emailing, mobile telephony, and so on all increasingly abandon *viewing* as the appropriate verb to describe an individual's encounter with such media technology. Perhaps the rapid proliferation of new consumer devices that seem to qualify as sites of media has surpassed the immediate scholarly agreement upon the "essence" of such media so that we appear not yet to have settled upon a consistent set of attributes to characterize the text and/or tech from which we can read off a viewing experience. Like the early nickelodeon days, the civil rules of decorum have not yet linked with the regularized production of standardized new media texts in order to produce something consistently recognizable as a viewer.

The tendency to seek out alternatives to *viewing* as a symptom of a radically new form of activity occasioned by the invention of new media technologies seems to be belied by the existing scholarship that does seek to determine what it is these "users" *are* actually doing. Such efforts have typically conceived of these activities, again, as the effect of the texts now possible through new consumer technologies. For example, the interactive piecing together of a textual experience made possible by clicking through a hypertext is understood by examining what it is a hypertext is and what it seems to require of a user-viewer (Landow 2006). The activity of using-viewing is implied from the description of the textual properties. The interactivity of the internet or multi-user role playing game or first-person video game is understood by examining the ways in which these media imply the need for certain types of active usage (e.g. Ndalianis 2002; Carr et al. 2006). Studies of users of "transmedia" texts focus on the way the text itself is dispersed over multiple media, apparently requiring the user to seek it out in different virtual locations and construct individual experiences of the media to the extent the pieces are sought (Jenkins 2006). In all such cases, while the constructed viewer is understood to act very differently than the viewer of the cinema or television – at a minimum, moving his or her thumbs a great deal more – (a difference that is already diminishing as TV itself becomes only one stop on the transmedia superhighway), using-viewing is still produced as the effect of the (new media) text. Even empirical studies of actual users exist primarily to endorse readings of these new hyper-interactive texts and show us the users-viewers they imply.

The Place of Viewing

Could there be more to this retreat from viewing than a barrage of new tech devices? Already scholars approaching the question of viewing from very different standpoints have begun asking new kinds of questions, even when considering "old" media. Bobo (1989), for example, has shown the way some viewers encountered a film which "acquired certain meanings because of discourses originating outside of the film text itself" (p. 333), negotiated these discourses, and "were able to extract meanings of their own" (p. 341). Meanwhile, Staiger (2000) advocates "an approach [that] considers cognitive and affective activities of spectators in relation to the event of interpretation." Even more, she suggests, "A historical materialist approach [that] acknowledges modes of address and exhibition, but … also establishes the identities and interpretative strategies and tactics *brought by spectators to the cinema*" (emphasis in original). Such "reception" studies belie their own label, implying (though hesitating to articulate) something different from an activity occasioned only by the transmission of a previously produced text. They begin to suggest that the convention of defining viewing as an effect of the text they have encountered need not prevail. Thus Staiger concludes that "context factors, more than textual ones, account for the experiences that spectators have watching films and television and for the uses to which those experiences are put in navigating our everyday lives" (p. 1).

Mayne (1993) has observed that the desire to name "real viewers"

> is neither transparent nor innocent, for [such real viewers] are mediated by [the investigator's] questions, her analyses, and her narrative. It is inevitable that such projections exist in this kind of analysis, and unless those projections are analyzed, then we are left with an ideal reader who seems more real because she is quoted and referred to, but who is every bit as problematic as the ideal reader constructed by abstract theories of an apparatus positioning passive vessels. (p. 84)

Yet important work has been produced that not only takes viewing seriously, but also begins to suggest what "viewing" would look like if it were considered a constitutive and productive activity on its own, rather than merely the end of a chain. Hay (1996) has suggested that the space of the audience might be expanded to include a "geography of viewing." This geography, as Bratich (2008) has noted, would suggest that the place of viewing "refers both to the physical surroundings of reception (from social theater, to home, to mobile technologies) and to the metaphoric space of framing the audience (e.g., the end of a chain)" (p. 50 n. 12). This concurs with Ang (1996), who argued that

> the term 'reception' itself bears some limitations because, stemming from the linear transmission model of communication, it tempts us to foreground the spatial/ temporal moment of direct contact between media and audience members [i.e. viewing], and thus to isolate and reify that moment as the instance that merits empirical examination. A more thoroughly *cultural* approach to reception, however, would not stop at this pseudo-intimate moment of the text/audience encounter, but address the differentiated meanings and significance of specific reception patterns in articulating more general cultural negotiations and contestations. (p. 137; emphasis in original)

If, on the one hand, taking viewing seriously "has intensified our interest in the ways in which people actively and creatively make their own meanings and create their own culture, rather than passively absorb pre-given meanings imposed upon them" (p. 136), then, on the other hand, this is not yet enough, for "[t]exts, abstracted from subjective practices, [remain] the *condition* for activity (which [is] then reduced to decoding). The openness that allowed activity came from the semiotic structures of meaning-making rather than from subjective forces" (Bratich 2008, pp. 37–38). The viewing process – involving positioning, interpreting, or decoding, and whether absorbed, distracted, or interactive – therefore depends on an already existing notion of "viewing" at the recipient end, responding to a set of productions that precede it. Bratich argues that "to transform passive into active was a necessary first step, but now that activity needs another transmutation: from reactive to active" (p. 48). Such a necessity is perhaps all the more apparent as new consumer electronics and technologies of delivery simultaneously expand the number of textual offerings while collapsing practical differences between media. Viewing might be thought of as the site of intersection and inflection of multiple discourses and questions of technology, media, space, and subject.

This takes us rather a great way from the physical act of discerning a media text. The basis for "viewing" after all might still be presumed to be a process of biological stimulus in which the play of light and shadow encountered by a human eye and processed by a human brain figure as foundational events. Indeed, as Sobchack (2004) has insisted, the very meaning and sense we attribute to viewing are "carnal," owing to the "embodied and radically material nature of human existence and thus the lived body's essential implication" in this process (p. 1). For Sobchack (2004), this means that "the experience [of viewing] is as familiar as it is intense, and it is marked by the way in which significance and the act of signifying are *directly* felt, *sensuously* available to the viewer" (p. 8; emphasis in original). But such sensuous, carnal aspects of viewing[7] can only be understood as such if viewing takes place, as it were, largely within the subject, severing "perceptual experience from a necessary and determinate relation to an exterior world" (Crary 1994, p. 21). The physiology of viewing is therefore also neither empirical nor neutral, but historical. The embodied response to visual stimuli has no meaning outside a cultural and historical context. As Crary (1990) has argued, "[V]ision and its effects are always inseparable from the possibilities of an observing subject who is both the historical production *and* the site of certain practices, techniques, institutions, and procedures of subjectification" (p. 5). Perception and vision, therefore "have no autonomous history" but rather are subject to cultural and historical forces that define the terms of viewing (p. 6). This notion of subjective vision, then, registers again the complicating notion that "the quality of our sensations depends less on the nature of the stimulus and more on the makeup and functioning of our sensory apparatus" defined in both cultural and historic specificity (Crary 1994, p. 21).

Viewing, then, is always constructed in relation to political and cultural discourses. Embracing this fact might lead to new ways of understanding viewing and producing the viewing subject. Viewing, for example, might be usefully and effectively conceived as a form of labor performed in relation to the culture industries (Smythe 2001; Shimpach 2005; Jhally 2006), even entitling viewers to forms of recompense for their work. Andrejevic (2007), for example, notes that participatory elements of reality competition programming such as the world-popular *Idol* series amount to the construction of the viewing audience as a nationwide focus group, where the trick is to "offload the work onto the populace by portraying it as fun and empowering" (p. 242). If viewing has always involved "dressing it up for yourself" and "projecting indigenous values" in addition to attaining the necessary literacies and mastering the appropriate decorum in order to exchange leisure time for viewing pleasures, then the age of digital DIY media has only exaggerated the already contestable nature of the contract between producers and viewers of media. If the commodity value of visual media is dependent on the ability to hold a viewer's attention, then the practice of viewing itself has economic value (Crary 2000). The time spent, but also the extent to which the viewer contributes in various active ways to a media text's attention-worthiness, implicates the viewer in the production of a media text's value. Perhaps this labor of viewing could be recognized in exchange for new considerations of ownership and use, access and attribution.

Looked at another way, viewing might also look like a practice of cultural citizenship. Indeed, too much consideration of the media audience, according to Morley (2006), "quite ignores the crucial role of the media in the construction of what we might call 'cultural citizenship'" (p. 103). Currently,

> the media are present, seemingly, to generate or retard political participation as defined through knowledge of parliamentary democracy, policy processes, and the judiciary, but not in ways that acknowledge the media's place at the heart of neoliberalism, nationalism, and social movements. (Miller 2007, p. 73)

But, as Miller argues, "the freedom to participate in culture is contingent on both freedom from prohibition *and* freedom to act via political, economic, and media capacities" (p. 73; emphasis in original). If the viewer has always already been constructed out of the intersection of media texts with sites specific to the media experience, then within Miller's formulation the viewer is already coterminous with the cultural citizen in ways that need to be further explored. If viewing were to truly be understood as a constructive and constitutive practice rather than a predefined destination, labor and cultural citizenship are only two examples of the possibilities that viewing could hold as a productive and effective cultural practice.

If the verb *viewing* hardly seems adequate, it is not because new technologies have surpassed the limited range of activities it implies. Rather, it is because *viewing* has not yet been mobilized to its full potential.

Notes

1   Such an understanding of viewing the cinema continues to inform a diverse array of contemporary scholarship. For example, Larkin's (2004) investigation of cinematic practices in twenty-first-century Nigeria includes this straightforward explanation: "The cinema is based around a disparate group of people who come together for a few hours and then disperse. This relative anonymity is heightened by the fact that audience members sit in the dark, their identities merged with that of the larger crowd" (p. 360).

2   *The Honeymooners* was a U.S. television program on CBS. The four main characters, Alice and Ralph Kramden and Ed and Trixie Norton, were recurring characters in sketches on *The Jackie Gleason Show*. For one U.S. season, 1955–1956, 39 episodes were filmed as a stand-alone sitcom (rather than as sketches within the variety show). These episodes have been in near continuous rerun ever since.

3   For elaboration see Spigel (1992, pp. 88–89 and 125–126).

4   *Captain Video* was an actual half-hour space serial, it aired in the United States from 1949 to 1955 (on the DuMont network).

5   For "flow," see Williams 1974. For the "segmentation" of flow, see Ellis (1982, esp. p. 112).

6   *Using* in this sense is a term drawn from studies of the telecom industries and can imply not only the interactive use of such a media technology, but also the active participation in ultimately building the system and the creation of networks and associated technologies to extend and further facilitate uses perhaps not even originally conceived of for the communication technology (see Fischer 1994). In this sense, it differs substantially in implication from the term *viewing* or indeed even from the implications of most of the various definitions of *audience*. I am indebted to Martha Fuentes-Bautista for this insight.

7   Which can be accompanied by additional, related bodily reactions such as when vision induces arousal, sleepiness, a quickening of the heart, or the hairs of the neck to stand, goosebumps to form, tears to grow, or a scream to emit.

References

Abel, R. 2006 *Americanizing the Movies and 'Movie-Mad' Audiences, 1910–1914*. University of California Press, Berkeley

Acland, C.R. 2003 *Screen Traffic: Movies, Multiplexes, and Global Culture*. Duke University Press, Durham, NC.

Allen, R.C. 1992 Audience-oriented criticism and television. In R.C. Allen, ed. *Channels of Discourse, Reassembled: Television and Contemporary Criticism*, 2nd edn. University of North Carolina Press, Chapel Hill, pp. 101–137.

Altman, R. 1986 Television/sound. In T. Modleski, ed. *Studies in Entertainment: Critical Approaches to Mass Culture*. Indiana University Press, Bloomington, pp. 39–54.

Andrejevic, M. 2007 *iSpy: Surveillance and Power in the Interactive Era*. University Press of Kansas, Lawrence.

Ang, I. 1991 *Desperately Seeking the Audience* Routledge, London.

Ang, I. 1996 *Living Room Wars: Rethinking Media Audiences for a Postmodern World*. Routledge, London.

Barker, M. 2006 I have seen the future and it is not here yet...; or, on being ambitious for audience research. *The Communication Review*, 9, pp. 123–141.

Baudry, J-L. 1986 The apparatus: metapsychological approaches to the impression of reality in cinema. In P. Rosen, ed. *Narrative, Apparatus, Ideology*. Columbia University Press, New York, pp. 299–318.

Bobo, J. 1989 Sifting through the controversy: reading *The Color Purple*. *Callaloo*, 39, pp. 332–342.

Boddy, W. 1993 *Fifties Television: The Industry and Its Critics*. University of Illinois Press, Urbana.

Boddy, W. 2004 *New Media and Popular Imagination: Launching Radio, Television, and Digital Media in the United States*. Oxford University Press, Oxford.

Bordwell, D. 1987 *Narration in the Fiction Film*. Routledge, New York.

Bordwell, D., Staiger, J. and Thompson, K. 1985 *The Classical Hollywood Cinema: Film Style and Mode of Production to 1960*. Columbia University Press, New York.

Bowser, E. 1990 *The Transformation of Cinema, 1907–1915: Vol. 2. History of the American Cinema*. University of California Press, Berkeley.

Bratich, J. 2008 Activating the multitude: audience powers and cultural studies. In P. Goldstein and J.L. Machor, eds. *New Directions in American Reception Study*. Oxford University Press, Oxford, pp. 33–56.

Butsch, R. 2008 *The Citizen Audience: Crowds, Publics, and Individuals*. Routledge, New York.

Caldwell, J.T. 1995 *Televisuality: Style, Crisis and Authority in American Television*. Rutgers University Press, New Brunswick, NJ.

Carr, D., Buckingham, D., Burn, A. and Schott, G., eds. 2006 *Computer Games: Text, Narrative, and Play*. Polity, Cambridge.

Crary, J. 1990 *Techniques of the Observer: On Vision and Modernity in the Nineteenth Century*. MIT Press, Cambridge, MA.

Crary, J. 1994 Unbinding vision. *October*, 68, pp. 21–44.

Crary, J. 2000 *Suspensions of Perception: Attention, Spectacle and Modern Culture*. MIT Press, Cambridge, MA.

Ellis, J. 1982 *Visible Fictions: Cinema, Television, Video*. Methuen, London.

Fischer, C.S. 1994 *America Calling: A Social History of the Telephone to 1940*. University of California Press, Berkeley.

Gomery, D. 1992 *Shared Pleasures: A History of Movie Presentation in the United States*. University of Wisconsin Press, Madison.

Gopalan, L. 2002 *Cinema of Interruptions: Action Genres in Contemporary Indian Cinema*. British Film Institute, London.

Govil, N. 2004 Something spatial in the air: in-flight entertainment and the topographies of modern air travel. In N. Couldry and A. McCarthy, eds. *Mediaspace: Place, Scale and Culture in a Media Age*. Routledge, London, pp. 33–52.

Gray, A. 1992 *Video Playtime: The Gendering of a Leisure Technology*. Routledge, London.

Gunning, T. 1990 The cinema of attractions: early film, its spectator and the avant-garde. In T. Elsaesser, ed. *Early Cinema: Space, Frame, Narrative*. British Film Institute, London, pp. 56–62.

Hansen, M. 1991 *Babel and Babylon: Spectatorship in American Silent Film*. Harvard University Press, Cambridge, MA.

Haralovich, M.B. 1989 Sit-coms and suburbs: positioning the 1950s homemaker. *Quarterly Review of Film and Video*, 11, pp. 61–84.

Hark, I.H. 2002 General introduction. In I.R. Hark, ed. *Exhibition: The Film Reader*. Routledge, London, pp. 1–16.

Hay, J. 1996 Afterword: the place of the audience; beyond audience studies. In L. Grossberg, J. Hay, and E. Wartella, eds. *The Audience and Its Landscape*. Westview Press, Boulder, CO, pp. 359–378.

Hobson, D. 1982 *Crossroads: The Drama of a Soap Opera*. Methuen, London.

Huyssen, A. 1986 Mass culture as woman: modernism's other. In T. Modleski, ed. *Studies in Entertainment: Critical Approaches to Mass Culture*. Indiana University Press, Bloomington, pp. 188–208.

Jenkins, H. 2006 *Convergence Culture: Where Old and New Media Collide*. New York University Press, New York.

Jhally, S. 2006 *The Spectacle of Accumulation: Essays in Culture, Media, and Politics*. Peter Lang, New York.

Johnson, J.H. 1995 *Listening in Paris: A Cultural History*. University of California Press, Berkeley.

Koszarski, R. 1990 *An Evening's Entertainment: The Age of the Silent Feature Picture, 1915–1928: Vol. 3. History of the American Cinema*. University of California Press, Berkeley.

Kuhn, A. 1984 Women's genres. *Screen*, 25, 1, pp. 18–28.

Landow, G.P. 2006 *Hypertext 3.0: Critical Theory and New Media in an Era of Globalization*. Johns Hopkins University Press, Baltimore.

Langdale, A., ed. 2002 *Hugo Münsterberg on Film: The Photoplay: A Psychological Study and Other Writings*. Routledge, New York.

Larkin, B. 2004 Hausa dramas and the rise of video culture in Nigeria. In R.C. Allen and A. Hill, eds. *The Television Studies Reader*. Routledge, London, pp. 354–366.

Larkin, B. 2008 *Signal and Noise: Media, Infrastructure, and Urban Culture in Nigeria*. Duke University Press, Durham, NC.

MacCabe, C. 1985 Class of '68: elements of an intellectual autobiography 1967–81. In C. MacCabe, ed. *Tracking the Signifier: Theoretical Essays: Film, Linguistics, Literature*. University of Minnesota Press, Minneapolis.

McCarthy, A. 2001 *Ambient Television: Visual Culture and Public Space*. Duke University Press, Durham, NC.

Mayne, J. 1993 *Cinema and Spectatorship*. Routledge, New York.

Miller, T. 2007 *Cultural Citizenship: Cosmopolitanism, Consumerism, and Television in a Neoliberal Age*. Temple University Press, Philadelphia.

Modleski, T. 1983 The rhythms of reception: daytime television and women's work. In E.A. Kaplan, ed. *Regarding Television*. American Film Institute, Los Angeles, pp. 67–75.

Morley, D. 1995 Television: not so much a visual medium, more a visible object. In C. Jenks, ed. *Visual Culture*. Routledge, New York, pp. 170–189.

Morley, D. 2006 Unanswered questions in audience research. *Communication Review*, 9, pp. 101–121.

Mulvey, L. 1986 Visual pleasure and narrative cinema. In P. Rosen, ed. *Narrative, Apparatus, Ideology*. Columbia University Press, New York, pp. 198–209.

Musser, C. 1990 *The Emergence of Cinema: The American Screen to 1907: Vol. 1. History of the American Cinema*. University of California Press, Berkeley.

Ndalianis, A. 2002 The rules of the game: Evil Dead II … meet thy Doom. In H. Jenkins, T. McPherson and J. Shattuc, eds. *Hop on Pop*. Duke University Press, Durham, NC, pp. 503–516.

Olson, S.R. 1999 *Hollywood Planet: Global Media and the Competitive Advantage of Narrative Transparency*. Lawrence Erlbaum, Mahwah, NJ.

Ouellette, L. and Hay, J. 2008 *Better Living Through Reality TV*. Blackwell, Malden, MA.

Petro, P. 1986 Mass culture and the feminine: the 'place' of television in film studies. *Cinema Journal*, 25, 3 pp. 5–21.

Schwartz, V.R. 1995 Cinematic spectatorship before the apparatus: the public taste for reality in fin-de-Siècle Paris. In L. Charney and V.R. Schwartz, eds. *Cinema and the Invention of Modern Life*. University of California Press, Berkeley, pp. 297–319.

Shimpach, S. 2005 Working watching: the creative and cultural labor of the media audience. *Social Semiotics*, 15, 3, pp. 343–360.

Shimpach, S. 2007 Representing the public of the cinema's public sphere. In R. Butsch, ed. *Media and Public Spheres*. Palgrave Macmillan, New York, pp. 136–148.

Singer, B. 2001 *Melodrama and Modernity: Early Sensational Cinema and its Contexts*. Columbia University Press, New York.

Smythe, D. 2001 On the audience commodity and its work. In G. Meenakshi and D.M. Kellner, eds. *Media and Cultural Studies Keywords*. Blackwell, Oxford, pp. 253–279.

Sobchack, V. 1992 *The Address of the Eye: A Phenomenology of Film Experience*. Princeton University Press, Princeton, NJ.

Sobchack, V. 2004 *Carnal Thoughts: Embodiment and Moving Image Culture*. University of California Press, Berkeley.

Spigel, L. 1992 *Make Room for TV: Television and the Family Ideal in Postwar America*. University of Chicago Press, Chicago.

Staiger, J. 1992 *Interpreting Films: Studies in the Historical Reception of American Cinema*. Princeton University Press, Princeton, NJ.

Staiger, J. 2000 *Perverse Spectators: The Practices of Film Reception*. New York University Press, New York.

Stam, R. 2000 *Film Theory an Introduction*. Blackwell, Malden, MA.

Stamp, S. 2000 *Movie-Struck Girls: Women and Motion Picture Culture after the Nickelodeon*. Princeton University Press, Princeton, NJ.

Thomson, R.G. 1996 Introduction: from wonder to error – a genealogy of freak discourse in modernity. In R.G. Thomson, ed. *Freakery: Cultural Spectacles of the Extraordinary Body*. New York University Press, New York, pp. 1–22.

Uricchio, W. and Pearson, R.E. 1993 *Reframing Culture: The Case of the Vitagraph Quality Films*. Princeton University Press, Princeton, NJ.

Vorse, M.H. 1911 Some picture show audiences. *Outlook*, 98, June 24, pp. 441–447. (Reprinted in G.A. Waller, ed. 2002 *Moviegoing in America*. Blackwell, Malden, MA, pp. 50–53.)

Webster, H.K. 1914 The shower. *McClure's*, September 1914, pp. 59–65, 187–192.

Williams, R. 1974 *Television: Technology and Cultural Form*. Wesleyan University Press, London.

4

Search and Social Media

Virginia Nightingale

Introduction

In the days of mass broadcasting and publishing, audiences located texts by switching on electronic equipment, buying print media, or visiting the cinema. They could expect these activities to deliver texts worthy of consumption. Libraries, museums, galleries, and encyclopedias managed specialized collections, and provided access to less widely available information through cataloguing and curatorial initiatives. The work of locating texts and filtering good from bad was undertaken, in the first instance, by media gatekeepers such as editors, publishers, and broadcasters, and secondarily by the scions of taste: curators, librarians, and critics. Today many of these institutions have licensed the digitization and management of online access to their collections to independent internet businesses. The result has been the exponential growth of companies that specialize in the sale of public data. Certain niche categories such as family history records, photographic collections, and personal records (particularly involving legal information) have proved to be extremely good "honeypots" in terms of attracting subscriptions from masses of users. Subscription and pay-per-view payments for easy and usable access to records and images have generated the financial capital needed for massive investment in search software which public instrumentalities (e.g. national and state records offices) would struggle to match. The result has been a revolution in the sorts of search activities available to the general public, and in the types of the research tasks people are able to undertake, particularly when working collaboratively. But just how do audiences fare in the business of finding records and other information relevant to their highly personalized search quests? And what aspects of the old order of public records depositories, libraries,

The Handbook of Media Audiences, First Edition. Edited by Virginia Nightingale.
© 2014 John Wiley & Sons, Ltd. Published 2014 by John Wiley & Sons, Ltd.

museums, and galleries remain important adjuncts to the scope of online search? These are the questions addressed in this chapter.

Transforming Search

Halavais (2009) has suggested that an estimation of how society is changing as digital technologies are absorbed into its fabric can be obtained by examining the operation of search engines. He has argued, "The ways in which attention is concentrated and distributed are changing rapidly, and the search engine is today's equivalent of the post office or telephone exchange" (p. 57). Except that search engines play a much more interventionist role than this metaphor implies, and in some of their forms they filter online content in ways that resemble the gatekeeping role of critics and curators whose education has been limited to reading popularity charts. Search engines privilege certain sorts of information through the algorithms they use to identify and select search results (Battelle 2005, among others). As a result, responsibility for locating, evaluating, and publicizing texts considered worthy of consumption is devolving, irrevocably, to audiences, thus accelerating the "disintermediation" (Evans and Wurster 2000; Nightingale 2007) of media industries and professions that characterized the mass era (Lévy 1997). So audiences now are expected to find their own texts in the labyrinth posed by the world of webs: the surface-level "World Wide Web," the "dark" or "deep" web of unindexed sites that evade the mainstream web crawlers, and increasingly the mobile net (see Goggin, Chapter 6, this volume). This change has led Halavais (2009) to describe contemporary society as a "search engine society." He argues that economically, politically, and culturally, our social organization is increasingly dependent on search engines for quick and efficient location of texts, products, services, and entertainment in general.

Search is fundamental to engagement with world wide webs. Opening a web browser (e.g. Internet Explorer, Firefox, or Mozilla) positions us to engage in search activities. While browsers provide access to sites we know or have previously visited, and provide means to store addresses for sites we want to return to by bookmarking them as favorites, they don't help us find sites we hope or believe might exist but that we have never before visited – at least not unless we use them in conjunction with a search engine. Shaw (2007) defines a search engine as "a coordinated group of programs" that "uses a *webcrawler* (a robotic program) to visit millions of web pages to retrieve data that is then compiled into an indexed database that can be searched for matches to the queries you send to it" (p. 11). This makes web search very efficient and fast, but it does not necessarily ensure that the search results are communicatively rich in terms of meaningfulness for the user. Battelle (2005) has described the limitations of search engine software that relies only on page-ranking algorithms and outlined a range of different approaches to searching that, at least in 2005, it was thought might prove useful in the future.[1] Many of these possibilities, particularly for diverse types of domain search, have now been realized, and more specialized search engines than the mainstream (e.g. Google and Yahoo) are available, such as those designed to search business information, books, email addresses, medical trends, and more (see http://thesearchenginelist.com). Semantic search (e.g. AskMeNow), domain search (e.g. Google Books), and "clusty cloud" searches (e.g. Vivisimo) and hundreds of others have made search more complex but also more interesting as an audience activity. Increasingly, new search technologies are deployed "within" sites to help users find information archived there. This wider deployment of search technologies has been assisted by companies such as Amazon, which allows "innovative developers to leverage Alexa's Web index to create new search tools on a pay-per-use model" (Tapscott and Williams 2006, p. 208).

The excitement around the expansion of new search technologies has limited much contemporary analysis of the internet experience to search engine usage. Search service providers, like Google, have attracted critical analysis for the power they hold to make and break small businesses seeking to operate effectively online (e.g. Battelle 2005). Instruction manuals (e.g. Hock 2007; Shaw 2007) have proliferated, catering to the needs of web content producers wanting to ensure that their sites attract maximum attention (known as *search engine optimization*, or SEO). More recently, Halavais (2009) has expanded the horizon for studies of "search" by labeling contemporary society a "search engine society." In particular, he discusses the ways our dependence on search engines is changing patterns of attention, our views about censorship and privacy, and the ways the search for knowledge affects our understanding of democracy and its operation. Correctly, in my view, he sees that the introduction of social networking and "sociable search" as accelerating public attention to the internet, its content, and online advertising. And, interestingly, this wider horizon allows us to recognize the relevance of shifting our investigations to include the deployment of search technologies within sites that rely on the search activities of their members and/or subscribers. In this context, search engine optimization is redundant since the site itself manages access to the archives of data that attract mass audiences.

Many of the most successful web 2.0 sites (e.g. Amazon, eBay, and other shopping sites; Wikipedia; and Ancestry.com) combine search technologies such as "collaborative filtering" and "crowd sourcing" with social networking. Halavais (2009) describes the resulting search activity as "sociable search" – "an idea that is making its way into every sort of site on the web" – and for this reason, he is of the opinion that, in order to effectively research the ramifications of changing search technologies, "the 'site' for observing sociable search is not the individual website but the information ecology at large" (p. 179). For Halavais, therefore, web 2.0 and sociable search represent a change in the climate of the web's ecosystem. However, as will be demonstrated, far from being a single ecosystem, the World Wide Web, like the natural world, is made up of interlocking informational micro ecologies that shift and change with the web climate. As mentioned earlier, the web is not one web but a series of webs, including the increasingly important "mobile web," and investigating the relationships between certain similar websites may facilitate identification of significant "prosumer communities" (Tapscott and Williams 2006) that operate across suites of websites.

Search and discovery

Social media sites linked to the mobile Net, for example Facebook and Twitter, offer new directions for internet search through the creation of software applications (apps) that deliver search "results" while minimizing the need for users to even understand with certainty what is it they're looking for. This type of search is currently referred to as "discovery," to distinguish it from page rank and other semantic search options. Recently this has led to speculation that the integration of advertising with social media (as on Facebook) has the potential to render search giants, like Google, obsolete. In an opinion piece for the online magazine *Techcrunch.com*, Reddy (2010) distinguished between Google-style search that is basically a form of information retrieval, and a "discovery" search model that "will not be constrained by the fact that you have to actually look for something ... you simply have to log into Facebook" for things you are presumed to want to be always already available.

The distinction between *search* and *discovery* is reminiscent of older metaphors for web usage. Early search metaphors included terms such as *surfing* and *hunting and gathering*. The surfing analogy encouraged novices to engage with the internet, even if they had no idea what they were looking for or likely to find. It justified the time spent exploring the affordances of a new medium offering new modes of communication, established familiarity with internet culture, and was assumed to help people understand what web search had to offer. People "surfed" the cyber-world's uncharted seas, and likely as not, chanced upon information of "interest" that others had uploaded. This was, in a sense, "discovery" search – time spent just getting to know the parameters of search and its possibilities; time spent becoming familiar with the types of information available online and how to use it. A second metaphor entered the lexicon a little later. The term *hunting and gathering* is borrowed from anthropology, where it is used to describe pre-agricultural economic organization. As a metaphor for web search, the terminology registers the complementarity of two opposing approaches to search. "Hunting" is strategic and involves "tracking down" something you know you want. "Gathering" involves reaping the rewards that nature (or the work of others) has provided. So "surfing" was the precursor for the more strategic search actions implied by "hunting and gathering" and is still re-enacted in the "combat," "warcraft," and "communal" activities that characterize many online gaming communities, multi-user environments, and virtual world communities (Castronova 2007; Boellstorff 2008, ch. 2).

Now, the search for resources has always depended on chance and serendipity, but as Zielinski (2006) has noted, this does not mean that it "defies all systematic order" because "trails are not simple phenomena. They are impregnations of events and movements, and even prehistoric hunter-gatherers needed to learn much in order to decode, read and classify the signs" (pp. 26–27). The activities associated with search are reflected in the value attached to the search outcomes achieved, and successful "hunting" delivers an emotional satisfaction far removed from the acceptance of received "gifts" of information, as demonstrated by Zielinski's quotation from the nineteenth-century Italian scientist Cesare Lombroso:

> When we embarked on our collection of facts, we often felt as though we were groping in the dark, so that when a bright and clear goal appeared our joy was that of a hunter whose enjoyment of success is doubled when he catches his prey after much toil and trouble. (Lombroso 1909, quoted in Zielinski 2006, p. 219)

From an audience perspective, however, the differences between search and discovery, the ways they are entwined, and their respective value for people in their engagements with each other (whether web-mediated or real-world ones) invite closer scrutiny. A recent broadcast television advertisement in Australia for the website Ancestry.com.au explicitly plays on the theme that "You don't have to know what you're looking for – you just have to start looking,"[2] disavowing the necessity for prior training and experience. However, this leads us to question whether the "enjoyment of success" might be lessened by discoveries that are too easy and quests that fail to challenge the searcher.

Search, Social Media, and Family History Research

Successful software applications designed for Facebook users can quickly attract millions of subscribers. This has been the case with the application FamilyLink, launched in 2007. The discovery-based advertising model ensures that FamilyLink's subscription services are "pushed" to Facebook members, who may, indeed, have no idea what they're looking for! The routine acknowledgment of kinship relations between Facebook members provides FamilyLink.com with a receptive virtual market for its products. By responding to a relative's invitation to confirm that they are a member of your family, you are prompted to download the FamilyLink "app." Downloading FamilyLink means that you start receiving emails inviting you to access its family history research services, and to explore your particular family history by subscribing to their advanced family search options. You don't need to initiate this search since FamilyLink presents you with a list of "results" based on your surname. However, trying to access details of the listed records requires payment of a subscription before you can examine their relevance in any detail.

The marrying of online family history research (FHR) with Facebook and Twitter's social networking via FamilyLink represents a competitive move in the FHR environment. The partnership with Facebook and Twitter has positioned FamilyLink to solicit memberships and subscriptions from mobile web users. Through recent partnership arrangements with the US site (WorldVitalRecords. com), the British site (FindMyPast), and the Australian site (Gould Genealogy and History of Australia) FamilyLink has secured access for its subscribers to a formidable set of records. Even though the established FHR sites have increased the scope and ease of use of social networking since about 2007, they have been slow to exploit the advantages that FamilyLink has identified in Facebook and Twitter.

The established FHR sites

The priority for the longer established sites seems to have been to compete on the basis of records held, their "searchability," and the quality of their online genealogy software. In the last year, for example, FindMyPast, based in the United Kingdom, has acquired the Reunited network of sites that importantly included GenesReunited, along with other domain-specific relationship-tracking services. Like FamilyLink.com and Ancestry.com, GenesReunited is only as attractive to subscribers as the information uploaded by subscribers to their family trees. That information is "pushed" to other subscribers through its "hot tips" and contact activity notification services. By acquiring GenesReunited, FindMyPast upgraded its own impressive collection of records and licensing agreements with additional subscribers, subscriber data, and improved social networking. Through its partnership with FamilyLink, mentioned above, FindMyPast is the first of the mainstream sites to announce links with the mobile net as it extends its operation into several new markets (Yvette, blog post for FamilyLink,[3] April 29, 2010).

By contrast, Ancestry.com (n.d.), the current market leader in FHR, only recently registered the importance of social networking for its future competitive position, announcing, "We are beginning to deploy tools and technologies to facilitate social networking and crowd sourcing, a means of leveraging collaborative efforts." Ancestry.com specialized initially in North American records, but now offers services through a network of national sites covering the United States, United Kingdom, Canada, Australia, Germany, Italy, France, Sweden, and China. Notwithstanding its announcement in May 2010, Ancestry.com has in fact been slowly adding refinements to its social-networking options for many years, but pay-per-view and subscription based search have remained its primary focus. These refinements include "discovery" options offered as "Ancestry Hints." The subscriber is offered two options: access to family trees submitted by other subscribers' complete with lists of saved records, photos, videos, and stories that appear to reference the same person; or access to additional records Ancestry has identified as of possible relevance. In addition, subscribers have access to bulletin boards, family name sites, and other Ancestry members through its secure notification emails. The attraction of other people's sites lies in the ease of transferring data rather than laboriously uploading details of each person individually. Basing your research on other people's searches has some disadvantages, not the least being the inheritance of their mistakes and false assumptions.

FHR as work: from individual to collaborative action

Globally, FHR site members are busy, day and night, piecing together the fragments of family histories disrupted by the migrations, wars, misfortunes, and chance encounters of previous centuries that they hope will explain the trajectories that led to their current life circumstances and potentially explain their racial origins, likes and preferences, and sometimes even career choices. The genealogy sites, in general, draw on simple forms of social networking to link site members and to accelerate the discovery of search outcomes. They merchandise related services such as magazines, DNA testing, genealogy software, and printing options (book production based on genealogical research, etc.), and they sponsor a range of television programs and *Who Do You Think You Are?* road shows and conventions to promote their services and those of local genealogists. So, unlike FamilyLink's recursive return to its parent sites, Facebook and Twitter, the mainstream FHR sites look beyond the web and situate themselves in real-world activities more reminiscent of fan behavior. It is, in fact, tempting to see the mainstream sites as constructing a fandom for FHR.

The primary work undertaken for the sites by subscribers is family tree research and construction. Each tiny addition a researcher uploads to a family history research (FHR) site, regardless of how sporadically a person searches, is fed into a system of record sharing that allows others to make some further tiny advance, with each addition enriching a global project that few individual members fully comprehend. Most of the sites have integrated collaborative filtering into their search design so that site members are able to readily take advantage of research findings, stories, photographs, and other family documents uploaded by other site members. In addition, Ancestry and FamilySearch, alongside other smaller scale and localized family history research sites (e.g. the confederation of Online Parish Clerks in the UK), enlist site members as volunteers in the transcription of digital images of original records. Ancestry.com, for example, operates a World Archives Project that enlists the assistance of enthusiastic site members (a form of *crowd sourcing*)[4] in the partial transcription of records from digital images of original documents obtained under license from public records offices. These partially transcribed records are offered free to site members but access to the digital image is reserved for subscribers. Ancestry claims that over 50,000 members have joined its volunteer World Archives Project workforce (Crista Cowan, email, May 12, 2010).

From an audience perspective it is therefore clear that the FHR sites create distinctions between their users on the basis of the user's financial "investment" (subscription) in the site. The concept of "user" is not sufficient to grasp the differences in "situation" this represents. Though all users occupy a "recipient" position vis-à-vis a site's suite of services, there are marked differences between users, members, and subscribers (including subtleties linked to levels of subscription) in terms of the search opportunities they are securing with their "investment." In addition, some site members take on the role of "voluntary worker" when they respond to the site's "crowd sourcing." This elaboration of user "positions" indicates that there is a level of self-interest for site subscribers in submitting their "work" to the site, before we even begin to take higher level commitments, such as securing information and documents for future generations, into account.

Getting Involved: A Personal Account

I began my own family history research as a leisure pursuit in Sydney, Australia, in 1998.[5] For the first nine years, I worked comparatively independently, sharing my research either by snail mail or email with a handful of others to whom I had discovered I was distantly related, who shared my enthusiasm for recovering our family's history, and with whom I exchanged information and documents. While some recourse was made to bulletin boards and newsgroups (such as Rootsweb and Cindy's List) and the FamilySearch site operated by the Church of Latter Day Saints (www.familysearch.org), my research breakthroughs occurred primarily as a result of the online availability of the indexes to the NSW State Registry of Births, Deaths and Marriages records. These indexes allowed me to locate records that could subsequently be accessed by visiting libraries, my local genealogical society, or the NSW State Records Office (for microfiche and immigration records) or by paying for the services of transcription agents. Searching was slow and time consuming. It frequently involved travel – locally to state archives and libraries, and interstate or overseas to towns and cities where particular records might be held. Success was never guaranteed as the discrepancies between what is promised by a resource and what is actually available are unpredictable.

Making connections

In about 2007, this situation changed. That year Ancestry.com released access to the 1841 British Census, a significant development for Australian researchers because by the 1840s convict transportation to Australia was being wound back and the resulting labor shortage was redressed by large-scale assisted migration from the United Kingdom. Suddenly it was possible to trace not only the families of origin of those few Australian convicts who had taken care to preserve knowledge of their family origins in official documents, but also those of the free and assisted migrant families who had begun to arrive in large numbers. Also at about this time the social networking offered by Ancestry and GenesReunited expanded in scope and became easier to navigate. Faster internet access speeds allowed people from all over the world to more easily contact each other and share records, documents, and the results of their past family history research. In addition, uploading information, stories, and photographs to the family research sites was simplified, so the records and data sets held by the genealogy sites were suddenly augmented by the research that site members had been conducting for years. To put it another way, the site membership and its records became an additional data set – one now capable of answering back and of working independently of the parent sites. The threshold for social networking and sociable search in FHR had been crossed, and sites began to exploit the user-generated content their subscribers had uploaded.

Researching the Marsh family

In my case, the 1841 Census delivered information about the parents and siblings of one of my convict ancestors, William Marsh (1811–1879), and offered the possibility of tracking what had happened to his parents, brothers, and sisters remaining in England. Using email addresses, at first obtained through the Ancestry permissions system that served as its precursor to social networking, I had been in contact with several English and US researchers descended from sisters of my ancestor. As Ancestry's social networking established itself with site members, we started sharing our new and existing information and posting it online. We were quickly joined by others who, thanks to the FHR sites we were using, noticed this activity. By late 2007, the size of the group of excited researchers investigating the Marsh family had increased to between 12 and 15. At this point it became difficult to keep track of what information had been shared with whom, and from which member of the original family each researcher was descended. At my suggestion, we solved this problem by creating our own email group, which each newly discovered distant "cousin" was invited to join, and by sharing contact details. At its most productive, our email group included researchers from Great Britain, the United States, Canada, Australia, and New Zealand. Group members differed greatly in education and life experience, but by combining our different skills, we achieved some remarkable research outcomes for amateur family historians. My experiences with this group and its activities evolved into a participant observation[6] when I started archiving the group's emails at the end of 2007.

Family photograph: William Marsh (1811–1879).

The Email Group

> Hi All, it's J. again. Just to say I've been looking into why it took so long between William's conviction and transportation. Haven't found definite proof yet but have discovered there was a 'Hulk' moored on the south side of the Thames especially for holding child prisoners. Sometimes for years. (JB, February 2, 2008)

By collaborating, the group eventually recovered the life stories for all the siblings of my convict ancestor. In addition, our activity led to the discovery of old photographs and letters written as long ago as the 1850s. We solved the problem of why the transportation of my convict ancestor was delayed for five of his seven years' sentence when we uncovered books and other research documents about the establishment of Child Hulks in 1824, to separate boy prisoners from the older men. And we confirmed our suspicions by visiting (virtually and really) the National Archives at Kew to check microfiche records held there. An inscription in a family Bible recovered in the United States enabled us to locate the British military service record for one of my ancestor's brothers, who served in India in the 1850s. Together we traced the circumstances of his death by suicide in 1871 through newspaper and hospital records and assistance from the Cambridge Records Office. We visited information about the Poor Laws and the workhouses where some of our British ancestors had finally given up their struggles with life. In 2008, we welcomed a contingent of researchers from New Zealand to the group. They revealed what had become of a daughter we could not trace for one of my ancestor's sisters. She had migrated to New Zealand, where she and her husband had run a successful bakery chain servicing New Zealand's gold rush. Their pioneering work in the South Island has recently been featured in local history publications there (MH, email, September 14, 2009). The establishment of the email group accelerated the process of ancestor tracking, enabled us to search local records simultaneously on different continents, and led to the recovery of documents and privately held information that would otherwise have remained out of global circulation.

The email group experience[7]

> Just to let you know that I'm still here & enjoying the emails.... I think I must know now how a peeping Tom feels!!! Because I have nothing to contribute I feel as though I'm looking into other people's lives ... not just the ancestors ... and find myself getting quite excited about the whole thing!!!! (KT, December 12, 2007)

> Just lately it seems I only have time to myself late in the evening. Then my mind gets overactive, and then I can't sleep thinking of all the different topics we are discussing, does anyone else have this problem or is it only me. (J.B-W, February 2, 2008)

In terms of levels of experience of the internet itself, development of research skills, what individual members wanted to achieve, and the degree of past research completed and available to share, the group was far from a level playing field. Participating in an email group was a novel experience for some members, and it took some time for everyone to feel comfortable with this mode of communication. Members who had barely started their research on the Marsh line were initially a little daunted by the amount of information offered, sometimes feeling that they lacked the means to reciprocate. Once established, however, our email group was the source of almost daily contact between members for approximately three years, even though, as one might expect, discovery of new information was not evenly distributed over time, and the amount of information that any one group member had to share also varied.

The diversity within the group actually encouraged members to expand our initial project to include topics and issues of more general interest, such as family news and events, how to use computer software, differences in time and weather, house and garden tips, good TV programs, interesting internet media (podcasts, You Tube videos, and professional photography), and anything else that happened to crop up in the course of everyday life. As time went by, the group process became one of anchoring the everyday activities of the group within the context of the world of the worldwide web, and for the worldwide web to be more securely integrated with group members' experiential worlds.[8] It also meant that our search activities diversified beyond the context of family history research, to include whatever group members had an interest in discussing at any given point in time.

The constant "chatter" of the daily emails formed the bulk of the email traffic generated by the group. It played an important role in our search activities by providing the everyday ebb and flow of interaction that facilitated our independent work on preferred research tasks, and it delivered a confidence and security that our search efforts would be appreciated by other group members. It "wallpapered" over the periods of inactivity that occasionally descended on the group. Comments like "Boy, it sure is quiet these days!" (MT, email, February 18, 2008) helped to prompt others to respond, even if only to comment on the comment until, as mentioned below, viral content replaced them.

Sharing and caring

Whew! I think I spurred as many emails regarding this wedding as we did regarding the family tree!! Haha! I haven't definitely set the date but it will be around the last of April/first of May before it gets too hot.... Everyone is invited, of course! (MT, January 31, 2008, Arkansas, US)

I can only say that [a cancer victim] must not lose hope. Also he must keep up his nutrition. If he doesn't provide the body with proteins and nutrients then it cannot repair itself after the radiation. I'm sure that you have already researched and know this and more without me telling you, but these are the 2 most important lessons learned after 3 yrs on the Oncology ward. (MT, January 17, 2008)

The sharing of information about family events and experiences, in particular, contributed to a climate of acceptance, caring, and familial commitment within the group. It could draw on personal experience to offer comfort when family members were seriously ill, yet generate lots of chatting and joking about happier topics. Such sharing could be quietly reflective, on the one hand, or relate to the planning and enjoyment of a significant life event. The wedding (mentioned above) became a means to discuss what we share in common and to reflect on the ways our preferences and tastes have been shaped by the different regions and climates where we live, and, of course, to joke about how the wedding might be celebrated if held in the country where the emailer lives. It also became one vehicle (among many) for confronting the realities of the group's distributed nature, alongside what group members love and enjoy about the geographical areas where they reside. And, far from the least significant, it was occasionally used as a vehicle to express patriotism and to explain the niceties of national identity.

Patriotism and national identity

M., Can't find anything on "Barley the Bushwacker"... In Australia a bushwacker is
one who lacks the social graces, not sophisticated. City people used it more as a term
of derision for country people, and I think the early British Colonists used it in a
similar derogatory manner when referring to the Australian Born. Then it is also
possible you might also be the victim of an Australian "leg pull." (JZ, May 17, 2009)

A secondary "research" aim emerged for the group out of the email chatter – that of
exploring the everyday implications for our personal circumstances of decisions
made by our ancestors a century and a half ago. So, as the seasons change, the cli-
matic differences and references to their effects on gardens and gardening plans are
regular topics for discussion. If adverse weather conditions (e.g. tornados in Arkansas,
snow in England, floods in northern NSW, and bushfires in Victoria) threaten a
region close to the home of a group member, emails expressing concern are immediately sent off and information regarding geographic details and local impressions
are forwarded. The celebration of National Days and religious and cultural festivals
usually prompt at least one group member to explain the origins and history of the
event commemorated. The celebration of New Year seems to highlight the realities
of the time zone differences because when one member is preparing for New Year's
Eve celebrations, others prepare for bed on the night of January 1. If one "cousin"
should happen to telephone another, there is email comment about accent or collo-
quial differences. As Miller (2000) noticed when analyzing the websites created by
Trinidadian students studying overseas, intercultural communication online encourages an exaggeration of national differences and recourse to a sometimes jingoistic
nationalism that in many respects is out of character for its protagonists.

Differences over more contentious issues, relating to religion and politics, have
at times ruffled feathers within the group, causing some members to withdraw
from the group discussion. Some group members typically keep a watching brief
on the email chatter, and step in only when something of interest emerges. For
some group members, it is only the "eureka" moments related to the Marsh project
that attracts comments. Some group members have quietly withdrawn from the
group completely, while others cease to participate once they have completed
the research task that led them to the group. The core membership of the group,
however, uses the group chatter to perpetuate the sense of familial belonging
established when the group began.

"Computering"

Sorry to bother you as I know you are receiving a lot of email lately [what have we
started]. but could you run through the group email send please as I cannot work out
how to do it. That is why I have been quiet. I am receiving everything but cannot

send to group. And how come messages come through twice. [just reply when you get time] (RM, December 14, 2007)

Thanks for all the information on computering, I am printing your advice off, so that I can refer back anytime, I am getting my own Marsh Computer Manual. Keep the lessons going please! (J.B-W, February 12, 2008)

A certain amount of sharing that occurred during the early days of the group was highly task specific. It addressed the unequal experience of group members when it came to computing and internet skills, and emerged only as we became more adventurous in our research ambitions. The "lessons" mentioned above included tasks such as deleting earlier messages from emails, cutting and pasting, creating and updating an email group, and downloading and accessing attachments. The differences of experience reflected both the age of group members (all but a few in their late 50s or early 60s) and the diversity of our education and work experiences. For example, since writing is fundamental to my academic practice, the production of stories based on our research seemed like a good idea, yet when approached about this, other members were much less comfortable with writing as a means of summarizing their research outcomes. They were, however, much more meticulous than me in uploading information to the FHR sites and sharing photographs.

Photographs

That was S. my youngest, She is going to like gardening like her mother when she grows up, the violets were in a friends yard, the verbena was found while traveling back roads on a Sunday outing, and the Daisy's and cock's comb are what survived the kittens playing in my flower beds. HaHa! I plan to get a better digital camera this year to be able to send prettier pics, the Dogwood and Redbud will be blooming just around the corner! (MT, January 22, 2008)

Just having a little chuckle as I was looking through photo's, look at the difference in J.'s (my 3yr. old grandson) birthday cakes. On his first b'day I planned and ordered a beautiful cake, by his 3rd he had a little cupcake, we were in Tasmania and had been at the Cadbury chocolate factory and a cruise and were too tired to eat, but he had to have a cake. (VW, February 18, 2008)

Whether we shared contemporary photographs documenting the here and now, or very old photographs retrieved from family collections, photos provided access to worlds both past and present. While photographs of historical value to the group are often (though not always) uploaded to the FHR sites, contemporary photographs (especially photographs of ourselves and our family members) seldom are, due to privacy concerns. Sharing photographs has been the source of great pleasure within the group, but it is also time consuming for both giver and receiver. Initially photos served to introduce members to each other, and to open discussion about inherited traits, physical similarities, and aspects of lifestyle (such as house renovation and gardening successes). Over time travel snapshots became more important, especially for group members who had fewer opportunities to travel. Taking photographs of places where our ancestors once lived became the explicit rationale for some travel experiences. Holiday snapshots inevitably result in comments about which similarities might point to our shared family origins.

Photographs and the Internet

I am having trouble printing out the scanned photo's people are sending me. I will have to keep trying as I am quite new to all this. (VW, January 17, 2008)

My computer is running again – what a disaster – my hard drive died – apparently its been ailing for some time, as the last lot of back ups I did have been corrupted, so at the moment I don't know what I have saved and what I will have to get again. Anyway I have now upgraded my hard drive to 120G, and come the school holidays my daughter is buying a 500G external hard drive and I am getting her old 160 G, so I will back up to the external hard drive. But the lesson is backup ! backup ! backup! And now I can't get my Office 97 to work with XP, I know there is something I have to reset on the computer, but do you think I can remember what it is. (JZ, March 24, 2008)

Sharing photographs represented a second level in the group's "computering" discussion, as everyone sorted out how to take better photos, scan old photos, and upload and best share photos. Some were moved to buy new computing, scanning, and printing equipment to store hard copies of selected images; others just ignored the photos; and still others filed them on hard disks and computers. Some, as in the email above, saw the solution in upgrading and external storage rather than in being more selective. Even though all the major family history research sites provide opportunities for uploading and sharing photographs, the scope and volume of photographic sharing undertaken by the group speak to the domestic nature of the activity. It also meant that some treasured personal photos, not directly relevant to our family research, were shared. An obvious solution to the problems we experienced sharing photos would have been to upload albums of photos to an online social-networking site like Facebook or Flicker. However, this suggestion prompted surprisingly reluctant responses from group members, reflecting considerable distrustful of social media sites – a distrust that does not extend to uploading information to FHR sites. The unwillingness of group members to join Facebook meant that only a handful of us used it to share photographs, and eventually everyone resumed using email. In spite of the frustrations, sharing photographs of families and holidays, homes, and gardens remains an important activity for the group and a way of staying in touch.

Viral content

I have to confess that some of the e-mails I receive do get deleted rather quickly – I mean the "funny" ones and the "please forward to 20 friends and return to me as well" type. Life is too short to be spending time on such as those…! (Email, April 21, 2010)

Within a short space of time, the sharing of photographs was supplemented by an apparently inexhaustible supply of viral jokes,[9] chain letters, political propaganda, recipes, and house-cleaning tips. The group had discovered the mixed blessings of "spreadable media" (Chapter 6, Green and Jenkins, this volume). The significance for the group of the web's viral content stream is perhaps best understood as an evolution from consensual sharing to an informal "gift economy" (Mauss 1925 / 1966; Murdock 2007). Members used the viral content to confirm their commitment, especially when they had little to contribute to the group's primary research. Even though never explicitly articulated, the group seemed implicitly to decide it was better to send a message about friendship, or something interesting that someone else had passed on to them, than to make direct comments about the quietness of the group. The group tapped into the internet's "gift economy" of recycled content and repurposed it for group maintenance. Metaphorically, the viral content stream resembles a new flow permeating everyday life and constituting a continuum for the life of the group. It linked the group to a wider information ecology, as each viral message shared connected our group to other groups of friends who had thought to send on these gifts. (See Green and Jenkins, Chapter 5, this volume, for their discussion of "spreadable media.")

Search and Discovery in the Email Group

Untangling the maze of emails generated over the last three years indicates the group's activity to have been variable and in many respects unpredictable as members increasingly worked on research tasks more marginal to the primary FHR focus of the group.[10] In the first six days of December 2008, for example, over 140 emails were exchanged between group members, covering three FHR investigations then current in the group plus several of interest only to specific members, at least 50 messages containing viral content or responses to viral content, and at least 20 sent between individual members arranging local meetings or excursions. By contrast, in the first six days of 2009, barely one email a day was exchanged, and all involved the spreading of viral content. Group activity died off dramatically during 2009 from approximately 200 emails per month from January to March down to between 50 to 100 midyear, and to closer to 30 emails per month for the last three months of the year. By mid-2009, the group had resolved most of its questions about the Marsh family, and, interestingly, spreading viral content failed to sustain group activity once the primary search project had been resolved.

"Eureka" moments

> Following on from J.'s amazing 'Eureka' moment yesterday, for those of you that are interested, it looks as if Emily Mary Lowin had more kids. (JB, April 21, 2010)

Reflecting on the activity of this email group over the three years, it seems obvious that the group's Marsh research project was pivotal in generating and maintaining interest and excitement in the group. Now that there are no pressing research problems to resolve, the group's activity has slowed to a standstill. The peripheral activities (sharing photographs and spreading viral content) that had been so important for sustained enthusiastic group solidarity and for successful collaborative action proved inadequate on their own to sustain the group. The "eureka moments" that characterized the group during the height of its activity have become muted in intensity and much less frequent. The emotional payoff for time spent researching this family's history began to fade. By comparison, when the group had begun to self-manage its research project outside the FHR sites and to engage with the wider FHR ecosystem of information sources, family history had been experienced as a "bug" it's hard to shake, leading to comments like "It feels empty running to my mailbox nowadays and finding it void. It is just so addictive; this *Ancestry* stuff!!" (MT, January 17, 2008), and "Glad you found all the information on the workhouse interesting. I am obsessed with that subject" (J.B-W, March 8, 2008). Such statements direct our attention to the emotional significance of search and discovery, including the doubling of joy felt when a problem is resolved "after much toil and trouble" (Zielinski, 2006, p. 219).

Affect[11] and search: a brief reflection

The search process becomes "obsessive" or "addictive" because it works mostly in the realm of positive affects: interest-excitement; enjoyment-joy; and surprise-startle. Each of these affects is referenced in the Ancestry.com.au advertisement cited earlier.[12] It begins by referencing interest ("I wanted to find out about my great-great-grandfather"), followed by surprise ("I found ... a record that showed he was a convict ... it's funny! No one ever told me about that"). Enjoyment-joy is referenced primarily nonverbally: through the excitement in the woman's voice, its contrast with the gravitas of the male voiceover, and the enthusiasm of the recommendation the woman gives Ancestry. During the early stages of FHR, when the subscriber doesn't already have a lot of information at hand, this affect script,[13] from interest to surprise to joy, is repeated with search after search until it becomes naturalized. This script is also reproduced in FHR television programs like the now international format *Who Do You Think You Are?*[14] In this case, emotional contagion works overtime as viewers identify with a celebrity's search for lost ancestors and recovery of lost family knowledge. So group members described FHR as a "bug" that gets into your system, in which having a "eureka moment" is felt as intense joy and contrasts markedly with feeling sad or "empty" on days when there were no messages or updates. In my own case "search obsession," the desire to replicate the "eureka moment" has led me to repeat past successful searches when I can't find what I'm looking for, just to remind myself that, when I do find it, I'll be glad I kept looking! This seems to suggest that, in certain circumstances, the search process may come to represent an ability to generate positive affects and to evade feelings of emptiness and loss. Certainly redemption from loss (of family history, knowledge of the past, and actual loved ones) is an outcome returned to repeatedly in the FHR literature, online newsletters, television shows, and conventions.

Attention and Time

Now, clearly, a person can't continue reproducing "eureka moments" indefinitely, especially if it means resorting to reproducing past searches to maintain the excitement level. And equally clearly the size and scope of the FHR sites are such that to remain successful, their business plans need to keep subscribers interested, searching, finding and uploading more and more information. As mentioned earlier, Halavais (2009) has described this as "attention seeking," noting,

> In an attention economy, those hoping to capture the desires and interest of consumers have struggled with this new structure, and continue to try to understand how to profit from the ways search reconfigures our information and the greater communication landscape. (p. 57)

It is clear that the FHR sites act strategically to maintain interest and excitement through the services they offer. They have proved exemplary in their capacity to leverage the labor of their subscribers and the content they generate. In fact, they effectively make "investment" in the site a precondition for engagement with it. In this informational ecosystem, subscribers pay twice: first, for access to the records and services offered; and, second, through the unpaid time and labor devoted to researching and uploading their results to the websites. Yet there is a strong component of self-interest in this audience labor. As subscribers, their own search experiences are enhanced by the scope and scale of records available at the site, and also by the capacity that social networking offers to share research findings with interested others. And in the case of voluntary work, there is a potential payoff in the possibility that information that is currently hidden will be revealed.

The sites also manage attention by direct address to the general public using established media, particularly television, to familiarize the mass television public with the conventions of family research and the sorts of questions a family history researcher might want to answer. As Arvidsson (2004) has pointed out, "Immaterial content, like brands, can travel between different environments and across media platforms (and … this capacity for technological convergence is precisely what is now being exploited by the culture industries)" (p. 96). Both Genes Reunited and Ancestry have exploited linkages with television companies. The TV series *Who Do You Think You Are?*[15] has played a pivotal role in driving new members to its spinoff products. The quest-like undertaking that online family history research becomes once the searcher sets out is previewed in the individual emotional journeys experienced by the program's celebrity searchers. Several of the large genealogy sites sponsor[16] this and similar programs and advertise during them. *Who Do You think You Are?* is now not just a television show, but also a magazine and annual "road show" convention event. And new television shows are in the pipeline. Recently, S&N Genealogy (n.d.) invited family researchers who had reached a brick wall in their research to submit their dilemma for consideration for a new TV show (*Trackers*) designed to showcase experts with skills "in genealogy and people finding."

For most family history researchers, the free labor carried out for the FHR sites is counted as a "labor of love" that is more than repaid by the richness of the shared information available and the contact with other distantly related researchers. However this free labor is extremely time consuming, and the time taken over family history research is an important factor in understanding search. Commenting on the nature of media time, Zielinski (2006) has asked,

> Who owns time? Between the beginning of the twentieth century and the beginning of the twenty-first century, there was a marked shift in the quality of political and economic power relations that both involved the media and drove their development: away from rights of disposal over territory and towards rights over disposal of time; less with regard to quantity, and more in connection with refining its structure, rhythm and the design of its intensity. (p. 29)

The FHR environment represents a complex informational micro system within the broader context of search engine society, where refinement of the "structure, rhythm, and design" of the search experience has proved extremely successful. Structurally FHR has identified the importance of fast and efficient access to data, and leveraged social networking and crowd sourcing in ways that complement the services offered to subscribers. It constitutes a "context of consumption" (Ardivsson 2004, p. 78; Lury 2004); it is a veritable genealogical shopping mall designed to consume the time of its visitors. It manages rhythm through the sending of email messages to subscribers notifying them of site activity by people they have nominated as "family members"; and through monthly newsletters and advertisements, mainstream television series, and the variety of associated products available. And intensity is managed through affect scripting of the experience of genealogical search, and through the "emotional contagion" (Gibbs, Chapter 12, this volume) generated by imaginative identification with the celebrities who take part in the television shows.

Conclusion

In his final chapter, Halavais (2009) contemplates the future of search after Google. He notes,

> Developments in the industry are rapid, but incremental. Each of the major players will continue to try to improve basic search, but the potential for expansion is really not at the broadest level, but in projects that can effectively exploit particular vertical search markets. (p. 189)

I have suggested here that the family history research environment constitutes just such a market. FHR sites manage membership and subscriber numbers that are unimaginably large and growing daily. They are on the cusp of leaping from the internet to the mobile web, leveraging relationships with Facebook and Twitter to launch mobile media apps for the iPhone (and presumably the iPad). They rely on user-generated content (UGC) to maintain the attractiveness of their social networking, to recruit new members, and to maintain their subscriber numbers. As internet production companies, they offer product ranges that differ dramatically from the types of operation required in the broadcast era, and they work with very different types of professionals. But, importantly, they still rely on advertising revenue, they use ever more sophisticated audience measurement to monitor site-relevant activity levels, and they license site-related merchandising to horizontally integrated spinoff companies. The relation they establish with their members and subscribers exceeds concepts like *prosumer* and *produser*. But the experiences shared by the members of the Marsh research email group, documented above, demonstrate that the joy of discovery and success is amplified when the task undertaken escapes the artificial borders put in place to protect the proprietary site interests. The information delivered by the sites is welcome but not as highly valued as the information that is harder to reach. That difficulty of access often involves the user leaving the safety of the World Wide Web and tracking records still held by individual researchers or locked in archives where one still has to prove you *do* "know what you're looking for."

Notes

1 I have discussed the work of Battelle (2005) in Nightingale (2007).
2 Slogan from an Ancestry.com advertisement broadcast repeatedly on Australian TV in 2010.
3 "Leading US, UK, and AU Genealogy Companies Announce New Venture," FamilyLink, by Yvette on April 29, 2010, at 7:08 P.M. The National Genealogical Society Conference in Salt Lake City, Utah, provided the backdrop for a joint announcement by three leading players in the world genealogy market. FamilyLink.com, Inc.'s WorldVitalRecords Australasian operation is to be taken over by leading UK family history website findmypast.

co.uk and run in partnership with Gould Genealogy and History of Australia. The website currently known as WorldVitalRecords.com.au will be relaunched next month under the new name of findmypast.com.au. It will initially provide subscription access to mainly Australian and New Zealand content. The plan is then to fully integrate both content and features from the findmypast.co.uk website as soon as possible   (http://blog.familylink.com/353/leading-us-uk-and-au-genealogy-companies-announce-new-venture-at-national-genealogical-society-conferencee).

4   "Crowdsourcing" is defined by Halavais (2009) as referring to "online structures that promote mass collaboration" (p. 162).

5   To research this chapter, I subscribed to four of the family history sites and have undertaken volunteer work for Online Parish Clerks and for Ancestry to explore their crowd sourcing firsthand. In addition, I have visited many additional sites, investigated management structures and personnel shifts from site to site, and tried to keep abreast of the many takeovers and collaborative initiatives the sites are involved in.

6   Reading Tom Boellstorff's (2008) account of using participant observation in an ethnographic exploration of Second Life, I was struck by the similarities to this project. In my participant observation, the emphasis was on "participation" first, as I registered some time into the life of this email group so that it offered an opportunity to "observe" the activity of a group of amateur researchers, all committed to family history research, grappling to come to terms with the challenges of online internet search and research.

7   From late 2007 to the present, I have collected and saved almost all of the emails posted by the group. The emails and the collections of photographs and certificates shared by the group have also been saved. I have also saved a small selection of the web's viral content circulated among group members.

8   This process is reminiscent of the ways mobile telephony has been described as involving "the virtual colonizing of more and more settings of everyday life" (Ito 2005, p. 8).

9   Text of a viral joke passed on at least five times before reaching our group (on August 18, 2009) with animations and formatting removed:

Two brooms were hanging in the closet and after a while they got to know each other so well, they decided to get married. One broom was, of course, the bride broom, the other the groom broom. The bride broom looked very beautiful in her white dress. The groom broom was handsome and suave in his tuxedo. The wedding was lovely. After the wedding, at the wedding dinner, the bride-broom leaned over and said to the groom-broom, "I think I am going to have a little dust broom!!!"

    "Impossible !!" said the groom broom. (Are you ready for this? Brace yourself; this is going to hurt), "we haven't even <u>swept together</u>!"
(Oh for goodness sake… laugh, or at least groan. Life's too short not to enjoy… even these silly little cute…and clean jokes.)
Sounds to me like she's been "sweeping" around!!!!!!!!!!!!!!!!

10   Due to the length of time over which the group emails were collected, the exact number of emails exchanged remains uncertain. The exact content of each email is also not necessarily reflected in the subject line of the message, especially since (to save time) some group members might use a current subject line to send a message that addressed a range of threads introduced since their last posting to the group.

11 See Gibbs, Chapter 14, this volume, for in-depth discussion of the human affects and affect scripting.

12 The full transcription of the script of this TV spot advertisement is as follows:

Middle-aged woman speaking to camera, family tree printout scrolling behind her: "I wanted to find out about my great great grandfather, so a friend told me to give Ancestry.com.au a go. I found all kinds of historical documents including a record that showed he was a convict. It's funny. No one ever told me about that!"

Older male voiceover, stronger Australian accent, photographic collage of family history photos: "Visit Ancestry.com.au and discover the world's largest online family history resource."

Middle-aged woman again: "You don't have to know what you're looking for, you just have to start looking."

Older male voice again: "Your discovery starts right now, at Ancestry.com.au."

13 See Gibbs, Chapter 21, this volume, for further discussion of affect scripting.

14 *Who Do You Think You Are?* was first produced in the United Kingdom but is now also franchised to SBS in Australia and NBN in the United States. It is sponsored by Ancestry.

15 *Who Do You Think You Are?* is currently produced by Wall to Wall, a member of the Shed Media group, "an independent television production company that produces event specials and drama, factual entertainment, science and history programmes for broadcast by networks in both the UK and US" (http://en.wikipedia.org/wiki/Wall_to_Wall, accessed 4/02/2010). The program was first broadcast in the United Kingdom in 2005, where five series of the program have been made. Local versions of the program have also been produced in Canada (2007), Australia (2008 and 2009), Ireland (2009), and South Africa and Sweden. NBC broadcast the first US series in March 2010, featuring among others Sarah Jessica Parker, Susan Sarandon, and Spike Lee. The number of episodes in a series varies, depending on the interest of the stories. Wikipedia claims, for example, that Michael Parkinson's story was abandoned because it was judged to be too boring (http://en.wikipedia.org/wiki/Who_Do_You_Think_You_Are%3F).

16 RootsMagic.com (United States) sponsors the Generations program (www.Rootsmagic.com); and Ancestry.com and FindMyPast sponsor *Who Do You Think You Are?* and a new initiative, featuring noncelebrity searchers and currently in production, called *Trackers*. The number of reality television spinoffs serving the family history research community continues to grow.

References

Arvidsson, A. 2004 *Brands: Meaning and Value in Media Culture.* Routledge, Oxford.

Battelle, J. 2005 *The Search: How Google and Its Rivals Rewrote the Rules of Business and Transformed Our Culture.* Penguin, New York.

Boellstorff, T. 2008 *Coming of Age in Second Life: An Anthropologist Explores the Virtually Human.* Princeton University Press, Princeton, NJ.

Cowan, C. 2010 Re: Ancestry World Archives project. Email message, May 12.

Evans, P. and Wurster, T.S. 2000 *Blown to Bits: How the New Economics of Information Transforms Strategy*. Harvard Business School Press, Boston.

Halavais, A. 2009 *Search Engine Society*. Polity, Cambridge.

Ito, M. 2005 Introduction: personal, portable, pedestrian. In M. Ito, D. Okabe, and M. Matsuda, eds. *Personal, Portable, Pedestrian: Mobile Phones in Japanese Life*. MIT Press, Cambridge, MA.

Lévy, P. 1997 Collective Intelligence: mankind's emerging world in cyberspace. Trans. Robert Bonnono. Perseus, Cambridge, MA, pp. 13–19.

Lury, C. 2004 *Brands: The Logos of the Global Economy*. Routledge, London.

Mauss, M. 1966 *The Gift: The Form and Reason for Exchange in Archaic Societies*. Cohen & West, London. (Original work published in 1925)

Miller, D. 2000 The fame of Trinis: websites as traps. *Journal of Material Culture*, 2000, 5, pp. 5–24.

Murdock, G. 2007 Digital technologies and moral economies. In V. Nightingale and T. Dwyer, eds. *New Media Worlds: Challenges for Convergence*. Oxford University Press, Melbourne.

Nightingale, V. 2007 New media worlds? Challenges for convergence. In V. Nightingale and T. Dwyer, eds. *New Media Worlds: Challenges for Convergence*. Oxford University Press, Melbourne.

Reddy, B. 2010 How Facebook will crush Google. Retrieved from http://techcrunch.com/2010/05/15/facebook-google/

S&N Genealogy. N.d. Email news. Retrieved from http://www.genealogysupplies.com/email_news.htm

Shaw, M.D. 2007 *Mastering Online Research: A Comprehensive Guide to Effective and efficient search strategies*. Readers Digest Books, Cincinnati, OH.

Tapscott, D. and Williams A.D. 2006 *Wikinomics: How Mass Collaboration Changes Everything*. Portfolio/Penguin, New York.

Yvette. 2010 Blog post for FamilyLink. Retrieved from http://blog.familylink.com/353/leading-us-uk-and-au-genealogy-companies-announce-new-venture-at-national-genealogical-society-conferencee

Zielinski, S. 2006 *Deep Time of the Media: Towards an Archaeology of Hearing and Seeing by Technical Means*. Trans. G. Custance. MIT Press, Cambridge, MA.

Websites

Ancestry: www.ancestry.com

Ancestry corporate: http://corporate.ancestry.com/about-ancestry

Cindy's List: www.cindislist.com

Family Link: www.FamilyLink.com

Family Search: www.familysearch.org

Find My Past: www.findmypast.com

Genes Reunited: www.genesreunited.com

Gould Genealogy and History of Australia

Roots Web: www.rootsweb.ancestry.com

S & N Genealogy (Publishing Company): www.sandn.net

Search Engine List: http://thesearchenginelist.com

World Vital Records: www.worldvitalrecords.com

5

Spreadable Media
How Audiences Create Value and Meaning in a Networked Economy

Joshua Green and Henry Jenkins

Every time a new consumer joins this media landscape, a new producer joins as well because the same equipment – phones, computers – lets you consume and produce. It is as if when you bought a book they threw in the printing press for free. It's like you have a phone that can turn into a radio if you pushed the right buttons.

Clay Shirky, TED conference (2005)

The people formerly known as the audience wish to inform media people of our existence, and of a shift in power that goes with the platform shift you've all heard about. Think of passengers on your ship who got a boat of their own. The writing readers. The viewers who picked up a camera. The formerly atomized listeners who with modest effort can connect with each other and gain the means to speak – to the world, as it were. Now we understand that met with ringing statements like these many media people want to cry out in the name of reason herself: If all would speak who shall be left to listen? Can you at least tell us that?

Jay Rosen (2006)

By now, we've all heard the news – trumpeted to us via blogs and tweets – that web 2.0 has set us free! Powerful new production tools and distribution channels are enabling the mute to speak and the invisible to be seen, are realizing long-deferred hopes for a more participatory culture, embodying the "technologies of freedom" predicted so many years ago by Hans Magnus Enzensberger (1970/2000) and Ithiel de Sola Pool (1984), fulfilling John Fiske's (1994) claims about ongoing

The Handbook of Media Audiences, First Edition. Edited by Virginia Nightingale.
© 2014 John Wiley & Sons, Ltd. Published 2014 by John Wiley & Sons, Ltd.

"technostruggles" between "the people" and "the power bloc." In short, all of our dreams are coming true.

Not so fast, warn Jose Van Dijck and David Nieborg in their essay, "Wikinomics and Its Discontents" (2009). They dissect and critique recent web 2.0 manifestos (including Jenkins 2006) that describe fundamental shifts in the economic and cultural logics shaping the media landscape. Citing a Forrester survey of American adult online consumers which found that 52 percent were "inactives" and only 13 were "actual creators" of so-called user-generated content, Van Dijck and Nieborg conclude, "The active participation and creation of digital content seems to be much less relevant than the crowds they attract.... Mass creativity, by and large, is consumptive behavior by a different name" (p. 855). What, they ask, has changed – if anything – in a world where "the majority of users are in fact those who watch or download content contributed by others" and where this segment of "spectators and inactives" represents the most "appealing demographic to site owners and advertisers" (Van Dijck and Nieborg 2009, p. 861). They find the shift away from a language of *audiences* or *consumers* and toward *users* profoundly misleading, since the latter term merges passive ("merely clicking") and active ("blogging and uploading videos") modes of engagement.

In this chapter, we will do what academics do best – complicate things. In particular, we are going to complicate the recurring fantasy of a world without "gatekeepers" or "audiences." We also want to complicate arguments that the "digital revolution" has amounted to little more than a rebranding and repackaging of consumer culture. Rather than seeing the changes the internet has wrought as transforming audiences into producers and "setting them free" from the tyranny of one-way chains of communication, we argue these changes are shifting how we value audiences, how we understand what audiences do, and how they fit into the networks of capital, both economic and cultural, that constitute the current media landscape.

Even though we are excited about the prospect of lowering the barriers of entry to cultural production, we think audiences do important work as audiences and not simply as producers. We believe that forms of participation closer to "merely clicking" than to "blogging and uploading videos" still reflect a changed relationship between media makers and their audiences. Unlike Rosen, we believe that there are still people who are "listening" and "watching" the media produced by others, but, like Yochai Benkler (2006), we argue that they listen and watch differently in a world where they know they have the potential to contribute than in a world where they are locked out of active meaningful participation.

In focusing on adult populations, Van Dijck and Nieborg may underestimate some changes in cultural production. A 2007 survey by the Pew Center for the Internet and American Life found that 64 percent of American teens online had produced media, with 39 percent circulating that content beyond friends and family (Lenhart et al. 2007). Over the past five years, Pew has seen dramatic increases in youth media production (more than 10 percent), suggesting that the trend is toward more and more active participation, not toward a return to more traditional patterns of consumption. Yet, Van Dijck and Nieborg are right that we do not yet – and may never – live in a world where every reader is already a writer, every consumer already a producer, and every audience already Rosen's "people formerly known as." Indeed, we respect Matt Hills's (2002) warning that, at times in our efforts to redeem fans from the old mass culture critiques, the concept of "cultural producer" has been "pushed to do too much work" in the hopes of "removing the taint of consumption and consumerism" (p. 30).

On the other hand, there is a risk of making DIY media making the be-all and end-all of participatory culture, reducing other kinds of participation – those involving evaluating, appraising, critiquing, and recirculating content – to "consumptive behavior by a different name." This is a particular risk of the "ladder of participation" models prepared by groups such as Forrester, which put more dramatic and visible modes of production higher up the scale. In doing so, such hierarchies ascribe greater "participation" to those who create cultural artifacts, seeing their fellow participants as less engaged and suggesting that those who engage in no productivity are "inactives" and "lurkers."

Yet, as Van Dijck and Nieborg rightly point out, every mouse click or video view is logged and even these inactive lurkers are ultimately (unwillingly?) generating data to refine content delivery systems or recommendation engines, and ultimately drive up the popularity of online media businesses. The emergence of social networks transforms each of these everyday acts of consumption, giving them greater public visibility, increasing their social dimensions, and ultimately expanding their economic and cultural impact.

At its core, this chapter is about how value and worth get appraised and ascribed through circulation. We don't mean the kinds of circulation basically concerned with consumers as receptacles for content both mass produced and mass distributed. The consumer is an eyeball in front of the screen (in television terms), a butt in the seats (in film or sports terms), or whatever other body part media companies hope to grab next. Instead, we are concerned with a far more participatory and much messier understanding of circulation; what happens when a large number of people make active decisions to pass along an image, song, or bit of video that has taken their fancy to various friends, family members, or larger social networks? Increasingly, all of us – media "producers" and consumers alike – are also media appraisers and distributors.

We are proposing the concept of "spreadable" media[1] as a way to understand how contemporary audience practices produce value. *Spreadability* represents an alternative to now widely deployed metaphors which describe how audiences engage with content. Some, like viral media or memes, also seek to explain how media circulates. Others, such as "stickiness," hold onto the perceived value in aggregating eyeballs to a particular location. All three of these concepts, however, underestimate audience members' active agency in shaping what messages spread, the routes they take, and the communities they reach. Spreadability stresses the technical affordances that make it easier to circulate some kinds of media content than others, the social networks that link people together through the exchange of meaningful bytes, and the diverse motives that drive people to share media.

How Susan Spread

The strange case of Susan Boyle, the Scottish village matron who rose to sudden fame and became a top-level recording star primarily on the basis of pass-along content, aptly illustrates spreadability at work. If nothing else, Boyle now supercedes hipster rock groups like Arctic Monkeys and OK Go as the poster child for so-called viral media. But the Boyle case also illustrates how the collective choices of audiences make content culturally meaningful, socially fungible, and economically valuable.

Thirty-two million viewers tuned in to watch the 2009 season finale of *American Idol*, making it one of the most highly viewed two-hour blocks on broadcast television that year. By contrast, the original Susan Boyle video, depicting her initial performance on *Britain's Got Talent*, was streamed more than 86 million times on YouTube (at the time of this writing). But these are figures reflecting the viewership of the original upload only; YouTube is a place where success often encourages duplication. Indeed, a cursory glance showed more than 75 different uploaded copies of Boyle's audition performance of the song "I Dreamed a Dream," available on the service and uploaded by users from Brazil, Japan, the United States, the Netherlands, and various parts of the United Kingdom. There are edited copies, high-definition copies, and copies with closed captioning and subtitles in various languages. Many of these versions have themselves been viewed millions of times. And this scan considers only YouTube alone, ignoring the other large online video sharing platforms such as Chinese site Tudou (where a quick glance shows at least 43 copies), or Dailymotion (where there are 20 easily found copies of her first audition video). No matter how you look at it, the viewership of the Susan Boyle video dwarfs that of the highest-rated show on American broadcast television.

American Idol embodies how television was being reconceptualized during an earlier moment of media convergence (Jenkins 2006). This television show has driven viewers across multiple media platforms, with content designed to sustain the interests of casual and dedicated viewers alike, and its voting mechanism constitutes an explicit invitation for viewer participation. *American Idol* has remained one of the highest-rated series on American television for the better part of a decade and has become a global franchise with its format duplicated everywhere from Australia to India, from Scandinavia to the Arab world.

Britain's Got Talent is, in many regards, *Idol's* sister program: it is created by the same production company (FremantleMedia), also featuring prickly judge Simon Cowell and following a somewhat similar mechanic in winnowing down amateur contestants.[2] Further, the episodes break down into bite-sized chunks, melodramatic mini-dramas that can be appreciated outside of the program's larger framework. *Britain's Got Talent*, however, has a particular penchant for the Cinderella story, featuring unlikely – in this case, eccentric and middle-aged – contestants with remarkable abilities who finally gain recognition. This scenario worked the previous season around Paul Potts, a gap-toothed opera singer from a working-class background. The Susan Boyle video introduced a character, set up ridiculing expectations, swept the rug out from under those expectations with a spectacular performance of a popular West End song, and then showed viewers the reactions of both judges and audience. It was content ready-made to spread.

While Boyle's performance was broadcast in Great Britain, it was not offered commercially to viewers in the United States and the many other parts of the world. Despite this, once it surfaced online the video's circulation and discussion occurred at a feverish pace: we were seeing broadcast content with grassroots circulation. Boyle's entry into the American market was shaped by the conscious decisions of millions of everyday people who choose to pass her video along to friends, families, workmates, and fellow fans.

We can't reduce Boyle to a by-product of the old broadcast model. The Susan Boyle phenomenon would not have played out the same way if there wasn't YouTube, if there weren't online social networks, if there wasn't Twitter. YouTube makes it easy to embed content on blogs or Facebook, services such as Bit.ly allow supporters to reduce the length of a URL to something that will fit in a tweet, and Twitter allows them to alert their social networks. Rather than focus on individual technologies and their effects, however, our focus is on the integrated system of participatory channels. Susan also spread because the participating public has collectively and individually become literate about social networking, because we are linked to more people and have more regular contact with them, and because we now often interact with each other through sharing meaningful bits of media content.

The most popular YouTube version reached 2.5 million views in the first 72 hours and reached 103 million views on 20 different websites within the first nine days of its release. Meanwhile, Boyle's Wikipedia page attracted nearly half a million views within the first week. What allowed the Susan Boyle video to travel so far so fast was that it could travel so far so fast. Most of the people who saw and decided to pass the video along enjoyed a sense of discovery. They could anticipate sharing Boyle's performance with people who probably hadn't seen it already, precisely because the content was not yet on commercial television. The fans found Susan Boyle before the networks did, and there was an infrastructure in place – across multiple communication systems – that allowed anyone to share this content with minimal effort.

Choosing to spread media involves a series of socially embedded decisions: that the content is worth watching; that it is worth sharing with others; that the content might interest specific people we know; that the best way to spread that content is through a specific channel of communication; and, often, that the content should be circulated with a particular message attached. However, even if no message is attached at all, just receiving a piece of media content from someone we know gives the text a range of new potential meanings. As we listen, read, or view that material, we think about not only what the producers might have meant but also what the person who sent it our way was trying to communicate.

Going Viral

The top-down hierarchies of the broadcast era now coexist with a diverse network of platforms offering grassroots participation. As marketers and media companies struggle to make sense of their role in this transformed media landscape, the idea that media content might "go viral" – spreading through audiences, not via purposeful sharing but by infecting person after person who comes into contact with it – has emerged as a popular cultural logic. Viral media captures the speed with which new ideas circulate, while at the same time seeming to account for the perceived randomness and unpredictability of the things which pique the public imagination – be they videos of cats playing keyboards or Photoshopped pictures of world leaders. The promise is simple, if deceptive – create a media virus and watch it infect the public.

In the marketing world, the viral media analogy can be traced in part back to the success of Hotmail, which, by automatically appending to every message a short invitation for recipients to sign up for the service, grew with exponential success.[3] Steve Jurvetson and Tim Draper (1997), whose venture capital firm had invested in the company, wrote that Hotmail had spread like a virus. Eric Ransdell, in a 1999 piece for *Fast Company*, wrote, "The email service has spread around the world with the ferocity of an epidemic. By passing along emails with a clear (but inoffensive) marketing message, current users were infecting potential users. And the rate of infection increased rather than decreased as time went on."

Significantly, Jurvetson and company suggest the spread of Hotmail *resembled* a biological epidemic, not that the medium actually *was* a virus. Rushkoff's book *Media Virus* (1994) does, however, advance such a proposition. Rushkoff describes media texts as Trojan horses, packages that surreptitiously bring messages into our minds: "These media events are not *like* viruses. They *are* viruses," the only intention of which is "to spread its own code as far and wide as possible – from cell to cell and from organism to organism" (p. 9; emphasis in original). There is an implicit and often explicit proposition that this spread of ideas and messages can occur without the user's consent and perhaps against their conscious resistance: people are duped into passing a hidden agenda while circulating compelling content. Rushkoff describes contemporary culture as a "datasphere" or "mediaspace" – "a new territory for human interaction, economic expansion, and especially social and political machination" (p. 4) – that has arisen because of the rapid expansion of communication and media technologies. And it is through this interconnected system that viral media spread:

> Media viruses spread through the datasphere the same way biological ones spread through the body or a community. But, instead of traveling along an organic circulatory system, a media virus travels through the networks of the mediaspace. The 'protein shell' of a media virus might be an event, invention, technology, system of thought, musical riff, visual image, scientific theory, sex scandal, clothing style or even a pop hero – as long as it can catch our attention. Any one of these media virus shells will search out the receptive nooks and crannies in popular culture and stick on anywhere it is noticed. Once attached, the virus injects its more hidden agendas into the datastream in the form of *ideological code* – not genes, but a conceptual equivalent we now call "memes." (pp. 9–10; emphasis in original)

Rushkoff links this still emerging concept of viral media to the famed British evolutionary biologist Richard Dawkins's notion of the "meme," which Dawkins introduces in his book *The Selfish Gene* (1976). Dawkins proposes the meme as the cultural equivalent to the gene – the smallest evolutionary unit. He proposes, "Cultural transmission is analogous to genetic transmission," (p. 189) and,

> Just as genes propagate themselves in the gene pool by leaping from body to body via sperms or eggs, so memes propagate themselves in the meme pool by leaping from brain to brain via a process which, in the broad sense, can be called imitation. (p. 192)

For advertisers and those in the creative industries, this is an especially attractive idea: create a designer germ, and turn the hapless public into the unknowing carriers of your message. In a moment when the meme pool – the cultural soup which Dawkins describes as the site where memes grow – is overflowing with ideas, being able to create or harness a meme allows an advertiser to ride participatory culture. At its heart, this idea absents human beings (and their agency) from our understanding of how content spreads. While Dawkins stresses that memes (like genes) aren't wholly independent agents, such notions often describe such content as "self-replicating."

As we saw in the Boyle example, people make conscious choices about what media they are passing along as well as the forms and forums within which they circulate them. Audiences have shown a remarkable ability to turn advertising slogans and jingles against their originating companies. They do so by writing fan fiction or editing fanvids, but they also do so by forwarding a clip along to their mates with an ironic comment or even simply a smiley face. Talk of "memes" and "media viruses" gave a false sense of security at a time when the old attention economy is in flux and in the face of widespread uncertainty about what might motivate audience engagement in this new context. Such terms promise a pseudo-scientific model of audience behavior, one which keeps power firmly in the hands of media producers. In practice, they mystify the process, obscuring the complex factors now shaping the creation of value through the circulation of content within these new social networks.

The concept of "spreadability" preserves what was useful about the earlier models – the idea that the movement of messages from person to person, and from community to community, over time increases their effectiveness and expands their impact. This new "spreadable" model allows us to avoid the language of "infection" and "self-replication" which overestimates the power of media companies and underestimates the agency of audiences. In this emerging model, audiences play an active role in "spreading" content: their choices, their investments, and their actions determine what gets valued.

Spreadability assumes a world where mass content gets repositioned as it enters different niche communities. When material is produced according to a one-size-fits-all model, it necessarily imperfectly fits the needs of any given audience. As content spreads, then, it gets remade, either literally through various forms of sampling and remixing, or figuratively via its insertion into ongoing conversations and interactions. Such repurposing doesn't necessarily blunt or distort the original communicator's goals. Rather, it may allow the message to reach new constituencies where it would otherwise have gone unheard. Yet by the same token, it is also not necessarily reproduced uncritically, since people have their own varied agendas for spreading the content. No longer "hosts" or "carriers," consumers become grassroots curators and advocates for personally and socially meaningful materials. Under these conditions, media content which remains fixed in location and static in form doesn't generate public interest and thus drops out of these ongoing conversations. In short, if it doesn't spread, it's dead!

Spreadability Made Simple

Let's identify some basic characteristics of the spreadable media model.

First, spreadability seeks to *motivate and facilitate* the efforts of fans and enthusiasts to "spread" the word. Contrary to speculation that the Boyle phenomenon would be short-lived, the release of her initial album, *I Dream a Dream* (Columbia Records), months later generated record advance sales, surpassing the Beatles and Whitney Houston on Amazon's charts (Lapowsky 2009). In fact, Boyle sold more than 700,000 copies in her first week of release, swamping 2009 *American Idol* winner Adam Lambert with the largest opening week sales of any album released that year, and she remained in the top ranks for several months. As Columbia Records chair Steve Barnett explained, "The reason that this record really did what it did, was that people wanted to get it and own it, to feel like they're a part of it" (Sisario 2009). Barnett's comments suggest the deeper investment audiences often feel toward performers they helped to discover and promote.

Second, spreadability seeks to expand audience awareness by *dispersing the content* across many potential points of contact. Susan Boyle would have reached nowhere close to as many viewers if ITV or FremantleMedia had locked down the content, rather than allowing Boyle's video to come at us through every available participatory channel. Most of us would have had no clue that *Britain's Got Talent* was on the air, let alone that there was a fascinating personal drama to be experienced, if Boyle's video had not spread throughout our social networks.

Third, spreadability depends on creating *a diversified experience* as brands enter into the spaces where people already live and interact. As the Susan Boyle video was circulated, its footage was inserted into all kinds of ongoing conversations. Because of Boyle's explicit acknowledgment of Christianity, she became the focus of online prayer circles. Science blogs discussed how someone with that body could produce such a sound. Karaoke singers debated her technique and reported on an incident when she was thrown out of a karaoke bar because she was now seen as a professional performer. Reality television blogs debated whether her success would have been possible on US television given the rules of *American Idol* which exclude people her age from competing. Fashion blogs critiqued and dissected her makeover for subsequent television appearances. Boyle's video circulated because she was meaningful on many different levels, and, after a while, all of this started to "go meta," so that people were spreading Susan's videos to talk about how fast they were spreading.

Fourth, spreadability maps the flow of ideas through *social networks*. Boyle's circulation represents the expanded communication power which now rests in the hands of communities of participants defined around a wide array of different interests and affiliations. Mizuko Ito et al. (2009) draw an important distinction between friendship-based and interest-based networks. Participants are motivated by different goals depending on which kind of online community we are describing. In the case of Boyle, some people were passing her along as a gesture of friendship (something like a Facebook gift), while others attached her to their pet interest (religion, motherhood, Karaoke, science, reality television, British culture, and so forth).

Under spreadability, grassroots intermediaries become advocates for brands and evangelists for content. By *grassroots intermediaries*, we mean unauthorized and self-appointed parties who actively shape the flow of messages within their community, often becoming strong advocates for brands, performers, and franchises.

Fifth, spreadability restores some aspects of the *push model* through relying on audiences to circulate the content within their own communities. A spreadable message comes to us: we don't have to seek it out. Most of us probably encountered the Boyle video because someone sent a link or embedded it in their Facebook feed or their blog. The Boyle video came to us in the middle of other social exchanges, much as an advertisement comes at us as part of the flow of television content. Yet, there's a difference – when an advertisement is pushed at us, it feels like an intrusion or an interruption. When we receive spreadable media content from a discerning friend, we often welcome it because it has been framed in regard to the interests that drew us to that network in the first place.

Sixth, spreadability depends on *increased collaboration* across and even a blurring of the distinction between economic and noneconomic exchanges. While the circulation of the Boyle video no doubt created the market for her album, it was not authorized by the production company or network. Boyle stars in a British program which had no commercial distribution in the United States. Americans couldn't turn on a television network – cable or broadcast – and watch the next installment of *Britain's Got Talent*. They couldn't go on Hulu and stream that content. And they couldn't go on iTunes and buy episodes. Market demand was dramatically outpacing supply. A potential US audience could, however, consume illegal downloads of the series via various torrents, video-sharing sites, or fan distribution sites, which could circulate the content without negotiating international deals. In some cases, socially networked advertisers and content providers may actively solicit our participation, but the public is participating now, whether producers, networks, or brands want us to or not. The result is an ongoing negotiation around what forms of participation are acceptable and how much the public is willing to tolerate constraints on their participation.

And, finally, spreadability takes for granted an almost infinite number of often *localized and many times temporary networks*, through which media content circulates. The broadcast mind-set assumes one-to-many communication; the spreadability paradigm assumes that compelling content will circulate through any and all available channels, moving us from peripheral awareness to active engagement. What some marketers are calling transmedia planning seeks to coordinate the dispersal of this information by systematically tapping a broad range of media channels, but the same process is at play at the grassroots level, with or without active coordination.

Looking at the way Susan Boyle spread around the Internet (and the globe), we can see the complex modes of audience-ship that emerge within participatory culture. It isn't simply that Susan Boyle is an amateur who has become a producer – indeed, her performance on *Britain's Got Talent* falls well within a traditional framework for the production of a particular type of television (the talent quest), and in the end, she becomes a recording star because a record company offered her a contract based on her media exposure. But the value of Boyle as a performer emerged through many different types of audience behaviors as people forged connections through and spoke to the world about what they were "consuming."

Understanding Appraisal

So, all of this begs the question: is spreadability "consumptive behavior by a different name," to return to Van Dijck and Nieborg's critique of participatory culture? From one point of view, what we have described here is still very much consumption and not production. These audience members might have created a great number of things – blog posts, Tweets, YouTube comments, emails, and fan groups on Facebook – but mostly they were appraising and evaluating content produced by others.

While we often use the concept of *appraisal* in an economic sense to talk about the relative exchange value of different objects, the same term gets used to discuss processes of curation. For instance, appraisals performed in archives or museums may be just as concerned with the historical, cultural, or symbolic value of an artifact, and often with whether the artifact is worth preserving for future generations, as it is with the item's monetary value. Here, museums and archives may be reluctant to take gifts donated by the general public if the costs of preserving an artifact exceed its symbolic worth or cultural significance. As we talk about the various forms of grassroots appraisal, we need to recognize the ways that these two notions – assessing economic value and determining cultural or sentimental worth – are increasingly connected, as the artifact (whether a physical object or a media clip) travels through different kinds of exchanges involving groups who are applying different systems of evaluation and who may be pursuing fundamentally divergent goals and interests.

Our distinction between value and worth comes from Lewis Hyde's book *The Gift* (1983). Hyde sees commodity culture and the gift economy as alternative systems for measuring the merits of a transaction. He writes, "A commodity has value…. A gift has worth" (p. 78). By *value*, Hyde primarily means "exchange value," a rate at which goods and services can be exchanged for money. Such exchanges are measurable and quantifiable because they represent agreed upon standards and measurements. By *worth*, he means those qualities we associate with things on which "you can't put a price." Sometimes, we refer to what he is calling "worth" as sentimental or symbolic value. It is not an estimate of what the thing costs but rather what it means to us. Worth is thus variable, even among those who participate within the same community – even among those in the same family – hence the complex negotiations which occur around possessions when a beloved member of a family passes away.

In that sense, *worth* is closely aligned with *meaning* as it has been discussed in cultural studies – the meaning of a cultural transaction cannot be reduced to the exchange of value between producer and consumer, but also has to do with what the cultural good allows them to say about themselves and what it allows them to say to the world. We capture something of "worth" when we talk about consumers making "emotional investments" in the television programs they watch or claiming a sense of "ownership" over a media property.

So, as consumers appraise media content, they are involved in a complex set of negotiations between commodities and gifts, value and worth. The decision to share the content with our friends transforms it into a form of gift, which enters us into a system of reciprocal social relations. We are not simply creating meaning based on what the content says; we are also creating meaning through the exchange of that content, which constitutes and reaffirms our interconnections with others in our network. This is true even if we are sharing content we have purchased as a commodity, just as we have all had the experience of buying a consumer good at a store in a commercial transaction and giving it to a family member as a gift. As Hyde notes,

> The boundary can be permeable.... Put generally, within certain limits what has been given us as a gift may be sold in the marketplace and what has been earned in the marketplace may be given as gift. Within certain limits, gift wealth can be rationalized and market wealth can be eroticized. (1983, pp. 357–358)

Hyde's use of the word *eroticized* here is especially evocative, meant to refer to the ways that the exchange of goods gains emotional intensity as it mediates between participants. In the current media landscape, the same content often circulates both illegally and legally, and may be both available for purchase and free for the taking; we weigh a range of economic and social factors each time we decide whether to pay or not for the media we consume and share with others.

Historically, of course, these decisions were private and individualized – the work of "choosy shoppers." Robert Kozinets notes, however, the emergence of "communities of consumption" as these once private decisions are taking place with social networks, noting "groups of consumers with similar interests actively seek and exchange information about prices, quality, manufacturers, retailers, company ethics, company history, product history, and other consumer-related characteristics" (1999, p. 10). Kozinets argues that commercial transactions are increasingly being policed by what such consumption communities are willing to tolerate, and shaped by their norms and values:

> Loyal customers are creating their tastes together as a community. This is a revolutionary change. Online, consumers evaluate quality together. They negotiate consumption standards. Moderating product meanings, they brand and rebrand together. Individuals place great weight on the judgment of their fellow community of consumption members.... Collective responses temper individual reception of marketing communications.... Organizations of consumers can make successful demands on marketers that individual consumers cannot. (1999, p. 12)

Just as the decision about what kind of computer or car to buy may now be shaped by the evolving consensus of a consumption community, the decision about what television content to watch is shaped by the emerging norms of our social networks, whether those organized around fan communities or those around other kinds of social identities: religious groups, racial and ethnic groups, political groups, and other interest-driven networks assert their own sense of what kinds of media content are meaningful and valuable.

The kinds of appraisals conducted on YouTube are much closer to those performed by curators at museums, archives, and libraries than those performed by dealers in antiques or secondhand books. Whether uploading to YouTube is an act of gift giving is a separate question given the range of hopes and expectations which surround these contributions, including many involving economic gain and some involving social advancement. At the local level, consumers appraise this content often trying to figure out who is circulating it and with what goals as they decide which content to watch and to spread through their social networks. The dispersal of the content allows us to track shifts in attention and interest with greater sociocultural depth than would have been possible in an era of traditional broadcasting where we might count the number of eyeballs watching a program but not map its integration into social interactions. Some content circulates within a clearly defined and relatively confined niche where it aligns with localized interests, while other content (the Boyle video, for example) may spread across a range of different interest groups and niches, suggesting material which has a much more generalized interest within the culture.

Are these transactions valuable within consumer capitalism? Yes and no. Increasingly, companies are seeking to monitor (though some would describe it as surveillance) these networked transactions as they seek to better anticipate what kinds of content consumers value, how much value they put on it, and in what contexts they are willing to pay for content. The issue of audience "engagement" has become a vital question as some branches of the entertainment industry experience what they perceive as a crisis point in their relations to consumers. In his book *Democratizing Innovation*, Eric Von Hippel (2005) talks about "lead users," early adapters and adopters whose decisions help manufacturers anticipate future uses or identify potential bugs or flaws in a newly issued product. At the same time, Brown, Kozinets, and Sherry (2003) have described a process of "retro-branding," as nostalgia-seeking consumers sift back through what much of the culture has left behind, identifying materials which still have worth and, perhaps, value. More and more, these networked acts of reappraisal are also fueling decisions about what kinds of content to produce and distribute and identifying potential markets for goods that their corporate owners may have otherwise abandoned as worthless.

Here, we are describing how value and meaning gets generated around what Raymond Williams (1977) might describe as the "residual," that is, materials "formed in the past, but ... still [potentially] active in the cultural process" (p. 40). Just as *appraisal* has cultural as well as economic meanings, the term *residual* also works on both levels. In accounting, residual value is another term for *salvage value*, the value which remains with an asset after it has been fully depreciated. In the entertainment industry, a residual is a form of profit sharing through which talent continues to receive compensation when their work gets recirculated or reperformed in supplemental markets. In both uses, then, *residual* refers to economic value which is generated through the afterlife of material objects and media performances. These multiple meanings of residual suggest that the ongoing sentimental attachment and cultural interest in these goods may still generate profit on the initial investments long after their initial exchange and uses have started to vanish from our memories.

On the other hand, corporations are threatened by their loss of control over cultural circulation, often describing unauthorized sharing in morally charged terms as "theft" or "piracy," and as "disruptive" of existing economic logics (such as those which might roll out content at different paces in different markets or specify different prices for different consumption niches). In the case of the Boyle video, the initial phase of distribution, as we've suggested, failed to generate revenue the production company or network could capture. It increased Boyle's visibility and, in the long run, inspired the audience that has purchased her albums at extraordinary rates, but there must have been some gnashing of teeth in closed-door meetings as executives had to decide whether to allow the video to circulate or to try to shut it down. If contemporary media audiences are reappraising content, industry practices, economic terms, and legal standards which shape their consumption, media industries are reappraising their historic relations with consumers and the economic and legal practices which allowed them to measure and monetize attention.

The Ecology of Media Consumption

Major commercial producers are having trouble adjusting their economic models to take advantage of alternatives to broadcast distribution, because they don't know how to value the work audiences perform when they are not simply "consuming" content. No wonder, talk of the media viruses has been embraced by professional media producers – it preserves the illusion that they can master some arcane process and design a self-propagating consumable. But the term's popularity indicates corporate struggles to understand the new roles audiences perform within the dynamic networks of distribution and circulation. To understand the rapid success of Susan Boyle as a product of audiences enmeshed in social and cultural practices of meaning making from and via media content, rather than as the acts of bodies "infected" with a media virus, requires a re-evaluation of the way value flows through the media landscape, a re-evaluation which requires more than collapsing the lines between producers and consumers.

Models which emerge from researching social networks and online culture, such as Axel Bruns's (2007) "produsage," offer a useful alternative. Bruns's model is borne out of studies of the collaborative construction of online sites such online news services such as Slashdot and the Wikipedia, as well as social-networking platforms such as MySpace and Facebook. *Produser* merges *producer* and *user*. He argues that increasingly users are generating the content they enjoy and constructing the networks through which it circulates. Online content sharing sites like Flickr or YouTube are co-created and mutually sustained through participants' use of these platforms – through contributing content, making certain content popular, and creating links between different parts of these networks (Bruns 2007). "Produsage" provides, he argues, for "the possibility of having producer/consumer relationships reversed and duplicated to the point where multiple such relationships describe the interconnection between any two nodes in the network," seeing audiences as active agents appraising, distributing, advertising, contextualizing, packaging, and critiquing content for others within their networks.

Built on a user subjectivity that suggests a more active participant than the audience subjectivity of the broadcast media (Marshall 2009), Bruns's model is perhaps not completely translatable as a model for understanding broadcast audience behavior. But it does provide us with a starting point for mapping the various roles participants play in the value chain of media production. As the Boyle example suggests, audience members are using the media content at their disposal to forge connections with each other, to mediate social relations, and to make meaning of the world around them. Audience members, both individually and collectively, exert agency in the spreadability model. They are not infected with media messages; they select material that matters to them from the much broader array of media content on offer (which now includes user-generated as well as industrially produced materials). They do not simply pass along static content; they transform or recontextualize the content so that it better serves their own social and expressive needs. Content does not remain in fixed borders but rather circulates in unpredicted and often unpredictable directions, not the product of top-down design but rather the result of a multitude of local decisions within diverse cultural spaces. "Consumers" do not simply consume; they recommend content they like to their friends, who recommend it to their friends, who recommend it on down the line. Nothing spreads widely in the new digital economy unless it engages and serves the interests of both audiences and producers. Otherwise, the circulation gets blocked by one side or the other, either through corporations constructing roadblocks (legal or technical) upon its spread or through audiences refusing to circulate content which fails to interest them.

As we noted in the introduction, Van Dijck and Neuborg relied on a Forrester Report which sought to classify and evaluate different forms of participation, suggesting that the most active contributors represent a very small percentage of the user base for any web 2.0 platform. Most often within the industry, this insight is represented as a pyramid of participation, which shows how the population of users narrows as you reach activities which demand more time, money, resources, skills, and passion. Bradley Horowitz (2006) has described how his company modeled consumer participation in Yahoo Groups:

> 1% of the user population might start a group (or a thread within a group). 10% of the user population might participate actively, and actually author content whether starting a thread or responding to a thread-in-progress. 100% of the user population benefits from the activities of the above groups (lurkers).... We don't need to convert 100% of the audience into "active" participants to have a thriving product that benefits tens of millions of users. In fact, there are many reasons why you wouldn't want to do this. The hurdles that users cross as they transition from lurkers to synthesizers to creators are also filters that can eliminate noise from signal.

Such a model is consistent with Van Dijck and Neuborg's account, seeing production as the highest form of consumer participation, and seeing consumers as having more or less fixed positions. As we have seen, what gets read as less demanding forms of participation may still generate of new values, meanings, relationships, and circuits of circulation and distribution.

The game designer and theorist Richard Bartle (2003) has proposed a much more "dynamic" and "ecological" model to talk about how participants with very different motives and modes of play interact within massively multiplayer game worlds. Bartle broke players down into Achievers (who "like doing things that achieve defined goals"), Socializers (who are interested in interacting with other players), Explorers (who seek to expand their knowledge of how the virtual world works), and Killers ("who want to dominate others"). What gave his account its nuance, though, was the ways he understands the interplay between these different modes of participation – often the activities of one group provided the preconditions for the pleasures sought by others. Sometimes these groups competed, sometimes they collaborated, but it would be difficult to label one group as passive and the other active or to describe one form of activity as more, or less, valuable than another. Moreover, any individual player might shift their status, might adopt new goals and roles, or might embrace new forms of participation in the course of their engagement with the game world. Sometimes a player is performing; sometimes she is the audience. Similarly, we might imagine an *ecology of spreadable media*, where consumers are curators, critics, commentators, distributors, fans, and producers, facilitating each other's engagement and participation.

Consumption Politics

Spreadability may look threatening to corporate rights holders who seek to monetize the eyeballs who access their content, yet it may be more attractive to groups of all kinds – churches, educators, nonprofit groups, political organizations, campaigns, and advertisers – which seek to lower the friction of circulation and thus allow their messages to reach larger publics. Consider, for example, the case of Brave New Films, the group established by progressive documentary producer Robert Greenwald (*OutFoxed: Rupert Murdoch's War on Journalism*; *Iraq for Sale*; and *Walmart: The High Cost of Low Price*). Greenwall created his films as tools for activist mobilization, early on embracing Netflix as an alternative distributor of his content and encouraging his supporters to host what he calls "house parties" where the videos are publicly displayed and discussed "in churches, schools, bowling allies, pizza parties, wherever there was a screen" (Greenwald, director's commentary, Brave New Films boxed set).

Greenwall encouraged his supporters not simply to show his films but also to discuss them – inserting the videos into ongoing conversations within the community, and tapping social networks to rally the audience. He was more invested in getting the word out than in capturing revenue, though he uses the web to attract donations to help support the production of subsequent titles. Increasingly,

Greenwall's team are sharing their videos through social-networking sites such as Facebook and encouraging young followers to remix and recirculate their content.

Greenwall's approach is consistent with what Jessica Clark and Pat Aufderheide (2009) have written about as "public media 2.0." The term *public media*, Clarke and Aufderheide argue, refers to media which mobilize and facilitate publics. Clark and Aufderheide describe how giving publics greater control over the circulation of media may enable their deeper investment:

> Rather than passively waiting for content to be delivered as in the broadcast days users are actively seeking out and comparing media on important issues, through search engines, recommendations, video on demand, interactive program guides, news feed and niche sites. This is placing pressure on many makers to convert their content so that it's not only accessible across an array of platforms and devices, but properly formatted and tagged so that it is more likely to be discovered. (2009, p. 6)

Sounding like our spreadability model, their report discusses the ways such content offers resources to sustain public conversations, how consumers deepen their involvement through acts of curation and circulation, and how spreading the word may help prepare them to take action around the issues being discussed.

Our goal here is not to reopen longstanding debates about the similarities between publics and audiences. Our point is simply that we have no trouble describing a range of actions that help increase the visibility of such political messages as civic participation. We place a value on the person who accesses a Brave New Film video and organizes a house party, but we also recognize the value of people who attend, participate in the discussion, make a contribution, or help spread the word about what they heard. Their value does not come simply from producing films and videos – though Greenwall's group certainly welcomes video responses that help sustain the conversations they have started. Acts of curation, conversation, and circulation also help spread his progressive messages and thus are understood as part of the political process, so why should we see consumption as valuable only when it becomes production rather than when it alters the discursive contexts or shifts the circulation of media messages?

We are describing shifts in the media landscape which are still taking shape, and it would be surprising if we fully understood their long-term implications. Neither of these models which see consumption as exploitation or as resistance fully account for this new media ecology. We see consumption as participation, with the understanding that participation carries multiple and perhaps even contradicting political valances.

Participants are certainly implicated in the cultural and economic systems through which they operate, just as they are implicated in the social networks through which they help to circulate content. In some cases, their actions further the interests of media companies, directly or indirectly creating value around one or another piece of media content they are helping to spread. The goal of many media companies is not just to capture their eyeballs but also to harness their collective intelligence and tap their capacity to circulate messages.

Yet, we would be mistaken if we saw this as "consumptive behavior under a different name," since even those actions which look and feel like classic consumption – localized acts of appraisal – may nevertheless operate differently when conducted through public and collaborative processes. Even the simple act of clicking a mouse may gain new significance when it is part of the meaning making and value negotiation that occur within a social network. Not all of the value is produced for the companies; these consumption communities increasingly work together to identify common interests and exert direct and indirect influence on the kinds of media being produced and distributed. There is a reason that media companies feel threatened by these kinds of practices which they cannot fully control and which may undercut their business models.

These same processes may make Susan Boyle into an international recording star and help Robert Greenwall organize his "house parties" in support of progressive causes. We should be less concerned with labeling these processes as progressive or reactionary, or exploitative or resistant, than in trying to understand how they operate and mapping their influence across a range of different contexts. This focus on the processes of circulation and appraisal may be as much a part of what audience research means in the twenty-first century as more traditional focuses on interpretation and appropriation have been for cultural studies over the past two decades.

Notes

1   This article builds on the spreadable media framework the authors have developed in collaboration with Sam Ford, Xiaochang Li, and Ana Domb. We are currently writing a book exploring these themes.
2   Of course, *American Idol* was itself based on the British talent show *Pop Idol*.
3   The service collected 1 million users in its first six months but swelled to 12 million subscribers by the time it was sold to Microsoft only 18 months later (Ransdell 1999).

References

Bartle, R. 2003 *Designing Virtual Worlds*. New Riders, San Francisco.
Benkler, Y. 2006 *The Wealth of Networks*. Yale University Press, New Haven, CT.
Brown, S., Kozinets, R.V. and Sherry, J.F. Jr. 2003 Teaching old brands new tricks: retro branding and the revival of brand meaning. *Journal of Marketing*, 67, July, pp. 19–33.
Bruns, A. 2007 Produsage, generation C, and their effects on the democratic process. Paper delivered at the Media in Transitions 5 Conference, MIT, Cambridge, MA, April 27–29.
Clark, J. and Aufderheide P. 2009 *Public Media 2.0: Dynamic, Engaged Publics*. Center for Social Media, American University, Washington, DC. Retrieved from http://www.centerforsocialmedia.org/resources/publications/public_media_2_0_dynamic_engaged_publics/

Dawkins, R. 1976 *The Selfish Gene*. Oxford University Press, Oxford.

De Sola Pool, I. 1984 *Technologies of Freedom: On Free Speech in an Electronic Age*. Harvard University Press, Cambridge, MA.

Enzensberger, H.M. 2000 Constituents of a theory of the media. In P. Marris and S. Thornham, eds. *The Media Studies Reader*. New York University Press, New York. (Original work published in 1970)

Fiske, J. 1994 *Media Matters: Everyday Culture and Political Change*. University of Minnesota Press, Minneapolis.

Hills, M. 2002 *Fan Culture*. Routledge, London

Horowitz, B. 2006 Creators, synthesizers, and consumers. *Elatable*, February 15. Retrieved from http://blog.elatable.com/2006/02/creators-synthesizers-and-consumers.html

Hyde, L. 1983 *The Gift: Imagination and the Erotic Life of Property*. Vintage, New York.

Ito, M., Baumer, S., Bittani, M., et al. 2009 *Hanging Out, Messing Around, and Geeking Out: Kids Living and Learning With New Media*. MIT Press, Cambridge, MA.

Jenkins, H. 2006 *Convergence Culture: Where Old and New Media Collide*. New York University Press, New York.

Jurvetson, S. and Draper, T. 1997 Viral marketing: viral marketing phenomenon explained. Draper Fisher Jurvetson's *Netscape Newsletter*, January 1.

Kozinets, R.V. 1999 E-tribalized marketing? The strategic implications of virtual communities of consumption. *European Management Journal*, 17, 3, pp. 252–264.

Lapowsky, I. 2009 Susan Boyle's upcoming debut album bigger than the Beatles and Whitney, hits no. 1 on Amazon list. *New York Daily News*, September 4. Retrieved from http://www.nydailynews.com/entertainment/music/2009/09/04/2009-09-04_susan_boyles_upcoming_debut_album_bigger_than_the_beatles_and_whitney_hits_no_1_.html

Lenhart, A., Madden, M., Smith, A. and MacGill, A. 2007 Teens and social media. Pew Internet and American Life Project, December. Retrieved from http://www.pewinternet.org/Reports/2007/Teens-and-Social-Media.aspx

Marshall, P.D. 2009 New media as transformed media industry. In J. Holt and A. Perren, eds. *The Media Industries: History, Theory, and Method*. Wiley-Blackwell, West Sussex, UK, pp. 81–89.

Ransdell, E. 1999 Network effects. *Fast Company*, 27, August.

Rosen, J. 2006 The people formerly known as the audience. *PressThink*, June 27. Retrieved from http://journalism.nyu.edu/pubzone/weblogs/pressthink/2006/06/27/ppl_frmr.html

Rushkoff, D. 1994 *Media Virus: Hidden Agendas in Popular Culture*. Ballantine, New York.

Shirky, C. 2005 Speech presented at TED conference. Retrieved from http://www.ted.com/talks/clay_shirky_how_cellphones_twitter_facebook_can_make_history.html

Sisario, B. 2009 Susan Boyle, top seller, shakes up CD trends. *New York Times*, December 1. Retrieved from http://www.nytimes.com/2009/12/03/arts/music/03sales.html

Van Dijck, J. and Nieborg, D. 2009 Wikinomics and its discontents: a critical analysis of web 2.0 business manifestos. *New Media Society*, 11, p. 855.

Von Hippel, E. 2005 *Democratizing Innovation*. MIT Press, Cambridge, MA.

Williams, R. 1977 *Marxism and Literature*. Oxford University Press, New York.

6

Going Mobile

Gerard Goggin

A central thread in the understanding of audiences over the past two decades has been the realization that, while audiences may be generated by various media and their producers, framers, curators, vendors, investors, and regulators, their actual construction revolves around modes of engagement. Accordingly, preceding chapters of this *Handbook* examine reading, viewing, and listening. These old styles of engagement have been revitalized and expanded by internet-specific forms of engagement such as search associated with the rise and rise of the internet. In this chapter, I discuss "going mobile." Like search, mobile engagement has its antecedents in many older forms of communication, culture, and media. However, going mobile takes on distinctive forms and increasing centrality when it comes to the contemporary audience. With the rise of various portable mobile and wireless technologies over the past two decades, new kinds of audience have been shaped around distinct and important new processes of engagement centering on the use of mobile devices. Going mobile, like this, is not only significant for the enormous audiences of mobile phone and mobile media users – but also increasingly involved in the reshaping of media and its audiences across the board.

Mobile Phone Culture

The most obvious kind of "going mobile" is associated with cellular mobile phones. In 2010, the number of mobile phone subscriptions worldwide topped the 5 billion mark. So the mobile phone is a global technology, used by many subscribers (even poor ones) across the world, and even in relatively poor countries or those places with historically scant communications infrastructure. Since its

The Handbook of Media Audiences, First Edition. Edited by Virginia Nightingale.
© 2014 John Wiley & Sons, Ltd. Published 2014 by John Wiley & Sons, Ltd.

commercial deployment in the late 1970s and early 1980s, the mobile or cell phone has moved through a number of distinct, though overlapping phases (Goggin 2006), with each stage adding layers of complexity to the audience processes of "going mobile."

The mobile phone clearly builds upon a media form that has not often previously been associated with the formation of audiences: the telephone. Since their inception in the late nineteenth century and through much of the twentieth century (up until the 1980s), the people who used the telephone instrument were regarded as "subscribers." When thought about as a collective, telephone subscribers were probably most often considered to amount to a community when it came to media policy, and when telephone communication and its social correlates were studied – for instance, by sociologists or communication scholars (de Sola Pool 1977; Fischer 1992; Rakow 1993). Once the role of the telephone was established and stabilized as a technology, subscribers were hardly ever imagined as an audience – at least not in the way that audiences were conjured up, measured, and argued about with television, radio, performance, or even print media – with some interesting exceptions.

Between its invention and adoption as a person-to-person technology, various uses of telephony were trialed that included, for instance, broadcast, concerts, performances, and news – things that *did* involve the idea of an audience. A famous instance is the Telefon Hirmondó service established in Budapest in 1893, which transmitted daily programming of various sorts of news and announcement as well as concerts. For the next two decades, Telefon Hirmondó attracted sizable audiences of telephone subscribers with a "hybrid of newspaper practices, conventional modes of oral address, and telephone capabilities that anticipated twentieth-century radio" (Marvin 1988, p. 231). Telefon inspired the establishment of a similar venture in Rome, a "speaking journal" called *Araldo Telefonico* (the *Telephone Herald*). *Araldo Telefonico*

> copied the Hirmondò schedule: news, various shows and emissions above all from theatres in Rome, popular programs such as the weather forecast, foreign language lessons, and, especially, the time signal that represented a genre in early Italian radio broadcasting too. (Balbi and Prario 2009, p. 163)

As Balbi and Prario note, "Telephone networks are built to allow one person to communicate with another one; on the other hand, in *Araldo*'s networks there is only one subject that has to communicate, or better, to spread information, to all the others (broadcasting)" (p. 163). We will return to these considerations and distinctions from the early decades of the telephone – and from these experiments with what we might call *telephone media* – later in this chapter when we encounter mobile media, but for the present let us consider the appearance of the mobile phone.

Initially, the mobile phone distinguished itself as a form of radio telecommunications that allowed people to make telephone calls to each other, first with equipment in motor vehicles, and by the mid- to late 1980s via handheld phones (Katz and Aakhus 2002). There were two obvious attributes of going mobile that are evident even in this early stage of first-generation analogue mobile phones: portability and personalization (Katz 2003; Ito, Okabe, and Matsuda 2005; Goggin 2006).

The installation of mobiles in cars, trucks, and other vehicles meant that voice telephony was now portable. This portability increased qualitatively and took on new dimensions when mobiles could be carried with a bulky kit, and then, of course, things changed even more radically once mobiles could be carried on one's person, placed in a pocket or handbag, or worn against, or even under, one's skin (Fortunati, Katz, and Riccini 2003; Schroeder 2008). If we take questions of embodiment and affect seriously at all, in terms of how audiences work, then mobiles suggest many new possibilities indeed for engagement – not to mention a slew of challenges (Vincent and Fortunati 2009). Portability has led to ongoing discussions about mobile media use that turn on place and space. Mobiles are used in more places than existing media have been. Often it is difficult to know where someone using a mobile actually is. From early on in the development of mobile phone culture, place has been a preoccupation among users, those with a commercial interest in mobiles, and scholars. Now mobiles themselves come equipped with spatial, location, and place-sensitive technologies – so interaction with place becomes an important part of the processes of engagement of mobile audiences (Nyíri 2005; Goggin and Wilken 2011).

Along with portability came a new relationship of telephones to their users (Green et al. 2001). Especially once mobiles became lighter, able to be carried by one person alone, increasingly affordable, and necessary for a greater proportion of the population, they took on the guise of a personal technology. *Personal* in the sense that one telephone number was associated with a particular individual, rather than a workplace or household. *Personal* in the sense that individuals saw their mobiles as a site of personal investment, representation, identity, and even obligation (Katz and Aakhus 2002; Katz 2003; Hjorth and Chan 2009). *Personal* by signifying that both users and nonusers were involved in new ways of creating the social. That is, accompanying the mobile come new ways of connecting people to their culture and society; in a profound sense, the mobile is intimately involved in how society, and the social, is put together (Latour 2005; Ling 2008). The personal nature of mobiles has accrued much significance as the technology has increased in importance as a means of audience formation. With mobile media has come a new mode of addressing people as audiences. The technology, and the concomitant development of the mobile culture associated with it, theoretically allows each of its members to be individually communicated with, often at any time of the day (the "always on" audience) – and also to respond in various ways.

The addressability of the individual audience member has a significance that we still have not fully grasped. For a long time a range of parties – scholars, advertisers, media companies, producers, and artists – interested in audiences have sought to understand the great question "What does the audience want?" by parsing this as an inquiry into the desires of individual audience members. And then they respond to their own question by approximating an answer, and then comes a cataloguing and analysis of the habits, preferences, income, tastes, and characteristics of each potential viewer, listener, or user. In the field of interactive television, for instance, a great time of technical, media industry, and scholarly energy was spent during the 1990s with discussion of technologies such as the interactive television service VEIL, which allow viewers to "interact" with television via a remote control–like device. Such limited kinds of interactivity often revolve around allowing, or encouraging, viewers to make purchasing decisions, while actually watching television advertisements:

> Creating a whole new experience in watching television. VEIL allows devices to interact with televisions and computer monitors. It's typically used in marketing promotions and children's toys. (http://www.veilinteractive.com)

Such interactive technology is now well established in controlled, networked environments of subscription television – where the television company bills each customer-individual, can identify their household, and so has some access to their billing records. VEIL, for instance, claims to foster

> the marriage of all types of media. Allowing the capture of data from all forms of video and print, VEIL provides the consumer the chance to bridge what they see on-screen or in print, to the world-wide-web and beyond. Never before has a technology been able to make this giant, and historic leap into complete media convergence. (http://www.veilinteractive.com/CoInfo/SweetSpot.htm#)

Mobiles as well as handheld game devices, and remote controls, feature prominently among VEIL's "data capture" devices. Digital broadcasting, for different technical and commercial reasons, also affords customers new kinds of interactivity. So too do various technologies associated with the internet, which allow identification of individuals, and build up audiences from new kinds of internet cultures and technologies – the audiences of blogging (Bruns and Jacobs 2006), for instance, or Twitter (Crawford 2009). Mobile personalization partakes of these convergent media developments, but it is quite distinctive for a number of reasons.

It is not only a question of the association of the individual with their mobile device, but the possession of one – or, in some cases, several – subscriber identity module (SIM) cards, and the billing relationship of the subscriber to a phone carrier or service provider. The mobile phone was bound up with a set of new policies, markets, and technologies to do with telecommunications, the liberalization and creation of markets, and deep shifts in regulation and the state (Hills 1986; Curwen 2002). An early consequence of this was the derogation of the term *subscriber* in favor of the preferred term, *customer*. As the term suggests, the rise of telecommunications from the 1970s onward had to do with new technologies that went well beyond voice telephony – and especially involved data transmission and the role of telecommunications networks evolving into data rather than voice networks (Mansell 1993). It is data transmission and networks that really deepen the importance of mobiles, and mobile-izing, for audience.

The importance of portability, personalization, place conjuring, and other mobile phones qualities were crystallized for processes of audience engagement with the advent of text messaging. Short message service (SMS) was a low-bandwidth data application that worked as a send-and-forward messaging technology over mobile phones. It proved not only phenomenally popular, but also a very flexible technology. SMS became a source of fascination because of the argot associated with it, and the particular communicative and cultural bearings, that saw it associated first with youth cultures, then generally as an emblem of mobile culture (Kasesniemi 2003). In youth cultures, its asynchronous qualities allowed users to function as small audiences for each other, communicating via text message. In larger contexts, famously in protests, in meeting people via anonymous texting, or in emergency situations, text messaging allowed a viral, mass circulation or even mass broadcast of short messages (Pertierra et al. 2002; Yu 2004; Goggin 2006; Castells 2009).

The encounter between the nascent audiences of mobile culture, and those older audiences, for instance of television, could literally be observed in the use of SMS in participation television formats. Audience members were enabled to vote in reality television and quiz format programs such as *Who Wants to Be a Millionaire?* (the subject of the British-Indian hit movie *Slumdog Millionaire*), or comment and send images (via multimedia messaging service, or MMS) for incorporation in the programs as they were being broadcast. These processes of mobile engagement were new, insofar as the programs, to be successful, now required viewers to interact via their mobile phones. However, such interactivity retraced early forms of media, such as talk radio, or phone-in television – formats that relied on listeners and viewers to telephone the host, and in turn being reinscribed as spectacles staged, and communicative architectures deployed, as very much part of the show (Nightingale and Dwyer 2006; Spurgeon and Goggin 2007).

SMS has been a resilient, flexible, and surprisingly versatile part of mobile phone culture, that has been crucially important, not only for its profitability but also for being an early, and indeed enduring kind of mobile media (Donner 2009a). In the massive growth of mobile phones in developing countries especially, we find SMS playing a critical role in crystallizing audiences for mobile media in ways that create new relationships between work or business and leisure or entertainment. In many developing countries, more profoundly even than elsewhere (given the affordability and availability issues with computer-based internet access), the mobile supports workers and their families, or micro entrepreneurs, as much as it allows the circulation of jokes, or images, or news (Donner 2009b).

Mobile Media Audiences

If early uses of SMS in television harked back to the decades-long history of telephones in processes of audience engagement, the diverse and nascent forms of other mobile media called up other histories and made alliances with other contemporary technologies. This is nicely illustrated in the case of mobile television.

On the face of it, mobile television could simply be conceived as the broadcast of television programs to a mobile phone – or other wireless or handheld device – rather than broadcasting such programs to a television set in the lounge room, or bedroom. Certainly this is what mobile phone carriers and television broadcasters had in mind when mobile television officially became available in the 2004–2006 period.

Yet this deceptive simple proposition of broadcasting television signals and programs to mobile phones has proven rather difficult to make a reality. As well as technical, regulatory, and business difficulties (Curwen and Whalley 2008), a central problem has been constituting an audience. Here, as often in the case of media and technology, a story of failure, at least at one point in time, tells us much about industry assumptions.

In South Korea, where it was adopted quite early mobile television has attracted considerable numbers of viewers. However, in most countries where it has been introduced, while it certainly has adherents who enjoy watching particular types of programs on their mobile devices, it has struggled to build in popularity. This is perhaps because much of the content that is actually broadcast to mobile handhelds, or offered by mobile phone carriers as television, is so closely related to the major entertainment and news media brands that dominate subscription and free-to-air television around the world. There is only limited made-for-mobile content that really seeks to take advantage of the particular characteristics of mobile phone culture and the handsets and networks typically supporting it.

Mobiles are a crucial part of the imagined if still emerging audience for television of the future: the idea of watching programs when, where, and how one wishes to do so. Of course, as the foregoing suggests, this kind of easy, elective, or voluntaristic mobility has proven much more difficult to realize. With "official" mobile television stalled in many ways, it is "unofficial," do-it-yourself forms of television that are being constructed by mobile audiences that seem to hold the key to the future. To start with, many mobile users are involved in the collective creation of new forms of televisual experience. Since 2001, mobile phones have shipped with cameras, and the use of mobile handsets as video cameras has been wildly successful with users (Koskinen, Kurvinen, and Lehtonen 2002). Thus, users commonly take video using their phone, and, rather than distributing these materials via still relatively slow and expensive cellular mobile networks, upload videos via wireless or landline internet to video-sharing sites such as YouTube (Burgess and Green 2009). There are important mobile dimensions, then, to the processes of audience engagement that characterize postbroadcast television. Another logic of audience engagement highly influential in the reconfiguration of television is time shifting, especially through file downloading and sharing. While IP (Internet Protocol) television networks are being constructed in many countries around the world, a key revenue stream of next-generation broadband networks, the user-generated forces unleashed via the contemporary internet demonstrate that viewers do indeed wish for greater choice in programming. Television and video programs are downloaded onto mobiles (what is termed *off-deck*), but laptops, with greater size screen, better resolution, and more memory, are more widely used than handhelds.

Mobiles, then, are playing a powerful role in the formation of a very new and interesting television audience formation, already dubbed "social television" (Ducheneaut et al. 2008). A term used only since 2007, *social television* refers to the way in which recommendations, commentary, links, feedback, file sharing, friendship groups, micro blogging, status updates, and the various apparatuses of social media actually provide the connective tissue and the content for television (Schatz et al. 2007). The idea of social television is that the audience is not only active. Rather, the audience is much more multifarious and porous than it ever has been. There is a teeming life of digital, social media interaction around social television that exceeds the scope of the fan cultures previously supported by television magazines or, more recently, websites or even the kind of user appropriation of choice in television viewing that downloading using peer-to-peer programs such as bittorent represents. Social television is that irruption of the great plenitude of television possibilities across many platforms where users really do become produsers, as Axel Bruns puts it (Bruns 2008).

Social television is not simply a wonderful, new era of audience freedom and potentialities. There is a sense in which it is a requirement of the contemporary system of media convergence and cross-platform televisions. That is, there is actually a need for such intricately networked, elaborately interwoven audiences to be in the foreground of co-producing television. This is because the future of television exists across so many platforms now: web 2.0, digital video broadcast, digital television, set-top boxes, online web video sites, IP television, and mobile television.

In the advent of mobile media, then, there is at least a twofold role of "going mobile" underway in the new modes of audience engagement. Mobiles are a "fourth screen," after the silver screen, the television screen, and the computer screen. The mobile screen can support new kinds of media – as the example of mobile television illustrates. Here is a familiar media form, television, in the process of being rethought and reconfigured for the mobile device. Mobile phone screens are, of course, quite small – although companies, such as Nokia, have deliberately designed phones with larger screens to improve viewing for potential audiences. There are also major issues of resolution, sound, acoustics, and audio quality (Oksman 2009). Then there are the issues that come from the fact that mobiles are associated with different kinds of spaces, experiences, rituals, social and cultural contexts, and even power relations than television sets (Oksman et al. 2007). For instance, we use mobile phones on buses and trains, in queues, in classrooms or libraries, in nightclubs or family events, at home or away from home, away from work or at work, first thing in the morning or in the middle of the night. Broadcasters and phone companies target offerings – television events such as sport, events of national or international significance (Barack Obama's inauguration, for instance), great moments in television (the eviction on a *Big Brother* program), or series – so that potential mobile viewers can enjoy short-form made-for-mobile videos (*mobisodes*), or live television, or "snack television," in ways that fit the habitus of the mobile phone user.

These quite recent forms of mobile media – really only appearing from 2001 onward – are developing their own distinct audiences. Yet, especially because of trends in convergent media, "going mobile" is very much about the new ways that mobile media figures in the complex ensemble of internet, broadcasting, and mobile telecommunications networks and devices. Here processes of audience engagement characterizing mobility are beginning to go far beyond anything imagined by those reworking television for broadcast to mobile devices – or, indeed, commencing the adaptation of other media forms (e.g. novels, books, and news) to cellular mobiles. Just as text messaging inaugurated a new kind of engagement, so too now mobile social media are intimately involved in the grand visions for change in television cultures. Mobile-izing became central to what occurred next for online media audiences, as we shall see with the Apple iPhone phenomenon.

Audiences with Mobile Computers: iPhones, Smartphones, and Apps

Mobile phones have been difficult devices for many to manipulate, and to reprogram in the way that users of computers, and especially users of the internet, expect to be able to do. This awkwardness obtains even with smartphones, which have for some years offered keyboard-like devices, or other innovations in user interfaces and input, to make mobile internet and mobile computing a more enjoyable experience (Funk 2001)— and something that bears a closer resemblance to the user experiences of computers. Of course, there is an irony in this. As mentioned earlier, mobiles have actually been an eminently customizable device (Hjorth and Chan 2009). Users have personalized them, adorned them with their favorite keepsakes, and changed their faces and colors. Mobile lovers regularly change ringtones, screensavers, or desktop layouts. And, of course, they care intensely about the mobile as a signifier of fashion and identity.

Regarding the mobile phone as an object or machine that is programmable and networked in accordance with individual user preference has proved difficult for developers, designers, and carriers. What has compounded the problem is the lack of an open market in mobile phone applications at the consumer level. The typical scenario of mobile software is that applications – notably games – can be downloaded via mobile internet (wireless access protocol, or WAP) sites, or via premium mobile content, and then can run on the device (memory permitting). There are also many internet websites that offer applications for mobiles. Certainly there are some mobile users who do regularly download such applications (evidence a burgeoning mobile content industry) – but the process is not especially user friendly.

Enter the iPhone Apps Store. Using the iTune interface and user experience, the Apps Store has made it much easier to be aware of, choose, pay for, and download applications for the iPhone, making it so much easier for consumers to find and buy computer applications that were easy to work on mobiles. Hence Apple's pitch: "Applications unlike anything you've seen on a phone before." Both via the internet and using the iPhone itself, the experience of finding applications is much enhanced. Not only is the iPhone a signal adaptation of the internet and mobiles, but also it itself is highly adaptable by its users. The applications and programming options of the iPhone themselves feature very visibly in iPhone culture, as the Apple promotion suggests – as users try, swap, and discuss applications. It has also meant that the iPhone is an important new platform for developers, a community who have often found developing applications for mobiles a frustrating experience. Indeed, the iPhone has faced serious criticisms from developers. In the first place, Apple launched the iPhone without allowing access to third-party developers. This allowed it to announce the release of a software development kit with some fanfare. The basic terms upon which Apple engages with iPhone application developers are still quite controversial, and seen by many as too restrictive, and slanted in Apple's favor.

With Apple's easing of the restrictions on developers, a number of applications for the iPhone's three-element accelerometer have been developed. The iPhone's accelerometer is a sensing device that is able to gauge the orientation of the phone, and make appropriate changes in the screen. For instance, someone viewing photos of their iPhone can rotate the device 90 degrees, from portrait to landscape layout and the display will detect the movement and change accordingly. The iPhone is equipped with two additional sensors: a proximity sensor and an ambient light sensor. There are now a myriad of uses for the iPhone's adaptation of sensing technology, including applications that allow you to play games swinging the phone, such as iBowl ("Simply swing your iPhone like a bowling ball and see how many strikes you can get"). Here the iPhone is clearly adopting gaming practices and moves familiar from Nintendo's Wii remote, the wireless controller for the popular video game console (Johnson 2008).

The burgeoning culture surrounding the iPhone centers upon its great potential for adaptability through downloading of apps, flexible configuration, and new logics of sensing, motion, and touch. However, while the iPhone facilitated a novel combination of mobile, computing, and internet cultures, it is just one example in a crowded field of smartphones, many of which existed or were in development before Apple's "Jesus phone" was launched in mid-2007. The present competitor to iPhone is Google's Android, built on an open source software platform. Then there is the Canadian firm Research in Motion's Blackberry. Not to mention various other smartphones and apps stores offered by established and new mobile phone vendors from Nokia (and its Ovi apps stores) through HTC Touch devices (challenged by Apple in 2010 for alleged patent violation) to Samsung.

Thus the *iPhone moment*, as it can be usefully termed, represented an important new phase, if not paradigm shift, in mobile-izing. With the iPhone, and other such devices, the mobile supports radically new kinds of media engagement, in which, for instance, the audiences can do the following:

1. Bring together a range of their media, cultural and everyday activities, from the kinds of things that mobile phones brought together (address books, phone calls, text messages, games, radio, music, and photos) to new things that were not previously so much the province of mobile devices (especially computing, the internet, and social media).
2. Change the very nature of the device itself – as with apps, a phone becomes a spirit level, or a breathalyzer, or a music instrument one can play; many of these apps make for a great metamorphosis of the mobile phone – which assumes any shape or form (of course, within limits!) that the software can turn it into.
3. Use the mobile phone as a platform for cultural production and exchange, in ways reminiscent of the internet but also in ways that extend online culture.

Many of these things have been evolving for quite some time with mobiles, but with the resurgence of the smartphone, catalyzed by the iPhone, we find compelling new affordances (Gibson 1977) seized by, and reshaping, mobile audiences.

Locating the Audience

A great theme of mobile phones has been the place of the user. Scarcely a day can pass in the vicinity of people using their mobile phones, when one escapes overhearing the question – "Where are you?" – or the other side of the conversation, namely, the utterance "I'm here." Placing oneself is the starting point for appreciating how "going mobile" brings new questions of the locations of audiences and their members into consideration.

The personal nature of mobile phones, discussed above, saw many ideas and practices concerning place come into play in the formation of mobile audiences. Fundamentally, there is an unpredictability and uncertainty about where the other person – the "B" calling party – to a mobile phone conversation is actually

located – unless they are in line of sight, in range of hearing, or otherwise percep-
tible through the senses. Thus much of the discourse about mobile phones when
they appeared and went through a period of domestication in the 1980s and 1990s
(and even in the 2010s) revolves around the fact that we often do not know with
any deal of conviction where a mobile user is situated. We don't know where those
forming part of our conversation, whether communicative ecologies or media cultures (if we are speaking to someone), a group or audience to which we might be
seen to belong (a group of friends texting each other), a group of people who we
hardly know at all, or those circulating information via Twitter, friends of friends
or strangers we might encounter through social-networking software on mobiles,
might actually be located. This is doubtless true of many other kinds of audiences
also – where we do not know where others watching the same television show, or
playing the same computer game actually are – but it takes upon particular significance and forms for "going mobile" (e.g. see Ling 2004; Ling and Pedersen 2005).

It is important to recognize this everyday sociotechnical shaping of location as
an early and enduring element of "going mobile," before we proceed to discuss the
technologies of location that have emerged recently – and their implications for
audiences. We can start to understand such technologies by recalling the nature of
mobile phone networks. Such networks are "cellular" in nature – hence the English
word *cell phone* used to describe mobiles in North America and elsewhere. The
technical nature of cellular mobile networks has meant that the network is divided
up into "cells," and the base station transmits signals to all the handsets within the
cell. When a handset passes across the boundary of a cell, then there is a handover
of transmission that goes unnoticed to the user. What this means is that a mobile
network can identify a handset within a cell – this is necessary to be able to transmit to and receive signals from the device. This is the basis for what have been
called "location-based services."

In addition to the capability of mobile networks to identify and locate devices,
and through this users, mobile handsets now include other kinds of location and
positioning technologies – notably: global positioning technologies that rely upon
satellite networks, and underlie satellite navigation (satnav) applications that are
popular not only in cars but also on mobile phones too; contingent local network
connections that rely upon the Bluetooth protocol; various new networks that are
crossing over with cellular mobile networks such as a range of sensing and con-
text-aware technologies, Radio Frequency Identification, and other networks.
Mobile phones and wireless and mobile media are now the site of an explosion of
location-based applications, services, and the creation of new affordances that
work at the interface of multiple networks, systems, and devices.

Consider two examples of "going mobile." First, the popularity of satellite navigation devices in cars (manufactured by companies such as Garmin and TomTom)
has rekindled enthusiasm for the ideas that mobiles can assist in navigation
and way finding. The combination of cellular mobile location capabilities, GPS,
directory databases, and maps allows users with most advanced mobile phones to

find where they are and where they want to go. Then, from this, users can also reuse this data, or create their own, to participate in user-generated content – another important aspect of contemporary participatory culture where mobiles add new dimensions (Haddon et al. 2005; Carpentier, this volume; Green and Jenkins, this volume). For instance, users can annotate the locations they have visited, and upload this information to a shared software platform or site. Such user-generated mapping is common in what is called the "geospatial web" (Scharl and Tochtermann 2007), and it amounts to a new kind of intersection between mobiles and internet that might be termed the "geomobile web" (Crawford and Goggin 2009). Second, there is the case of mobile social software (or *mososo*), by which users of mobile devices interact with each other because the devices can detect other users in their vicinity (Crawford 2008). Like location-based applications, mobile social software has been some time in the making – as early feted examples in the late 1990s and 2000s like the Lovegety (in Japan; see Crawford 2008) and Dodgeball (in the United States; see Humphreys 2007) indicate. Mobile social software predated, or at least was synonymous with, early versions of internet-based social-networking systems (Friendsters, Orkut) and, while now being intertwined with Facebook, MySpace, Twitter, Flickr, and the many other social media technologies standard on mobiles, still have their own dynamics (Goggin 2010). In the United States from 2009 onward, a number of mobile social software applications, including Whrrl, Brightkite, and Centrl, attracted significant numbers of users. Sporting the motto "Discover the World around You," Loopt, for example, promises to "turn your phone into a social compass":

> Loopt shows users where friends are located and what they are doing via detailed, interactive maps on their mobile phones. Loopt helps friends connect on the fly and navigate their social lives by orienting them to people, places and events. Users can also share location updates, geo-tagged photos and comments with friends in their mobile address book or on online social networks, communities and blogs. (http://www.loopt.com)

Going mobile, then, is not only a matter of locating the audience. It is about the audience locating each other, and in doing so, constituting itself.

Mobile Gaming and Locative Media

As we have seen, new logics of going mobile may be observed in relation to the user invention of mobile television, profound changes catalyzed by iPhones and smartphones, and in the practices and affordances of location. Perhaps more radical still are the subtle and far-reaching changes to the dynamics of audience occurring with mobile gaming. Mobile games have a set of histories, the most obvious and perhaps best known of which are games embedded into mobile phone handsets, such as the famous Snake game that shipped on Nokia handsets in the 1990s (Parikka and Suominen 2006). Games became established as a key, if apparently trivial, episodic, or inconsequential, part of mobile phone use. Game developers, entertainment companies, mobile carriers, and handset manufacturers all quickly sensed the lucrative potential of deploying games on the mobile's platform.

As mobile phones developed, so too did the possibilities for games and gaming. Mobiles started to attract a great deal of interest, as a potentially distinctive and sophisticated platform for games, at a time when the games industry internationally began consolidating its position as a vastly profitable area of consumer electronics and entertainment, and a key site of contemporary culture. Perhaps the most publicized mobile game at this time was Botfighter, developed by the Swedish company It's Alive (which later became Daydream). Botfighter was a classic first-person shooter game with a twist. Botfighter used the location capability of mobile phones – namely, their ability to locate a device within a cell of the GSM system – for players to interact with and shoot each other. Botfighter also used a web interface, but it heralded the use of the mobile to allow players to roam a city, finding and fighting other players, that really captured the imagination of its users and also the general public. Launched in Stockholm, Botfighter was sold to mobile operators in countries as diverse as Turkey and Ireland, and was apparently very successful in Russia, its debut coinciding with the 2002 Moscow Theatre hostage crisis. Once a player locates an adversary, they can shoot them through a text message. Botfighter was widely discussed by scholars, as it brought together various features that we see recurring and remediated in later mobile games: the role of location in mobile media; the use of SMS to provide billing and a business model; the production of new spatial relations in an urban setting; and the expansion of gaming outside the charmed circle that had come to characterize it in various ways, including pervasive gaming (De Souza e Silva 2009; De Souza e Silva and Hjorth 2009). A difficulty in developing games for mobile platforms has been the small screens, constraints on quality of graphics, battery life, fragmented nature of mobile media, and, associated with this, lack of standardization. Problematically, mobile gamers have been often regarded as casual, rather than hardcore, gamers (reminiscent of the characterization of mobile television as "snack TV"). Because of the typically short duration of use of mobile applications, design focused on brief games, rather than deep game experiences.

An increasingly important feature of gaming centers on possibilities for moving beyond individual or group console-based play to networked gaming. This has been tackled in different ways in mobile gaming. While downloading games has proved popular, it nevertheless put limits on collective gaming. Of course, the distinction between individual player downloadable mobile games and multiplayer networked games does not hold fast. Not only is downloaded game play often an experience shared with others, but also an individual player often experiences it as such; that is, they "enjoy perceived copresence, even though the game may not be connected to other players" (Kim et al. 2009, p. 14). Nonetheless, in the move to take mobile gaming beyond basic downloading, the role of the internet has been critical, whether this included games devised for, or adapted for, multiplayer play on the internet; connecting game devices, such as consoles to the internet (through embedding wifi transmitters, or plugs); or the ability of gamers to communicate via the internet, find key resources, and exchange parts of games via the internet. With 3G networks, and associated moves to bring together mobiles and the internet, greater attention was paid to networked gaming on mobiles. An early, mobile-centric mode of networked gaming is possible through Bluetooth connectivity and networks. B'ngo was a console-type games player for mobile phone that allowed up to eight players to compete with each other via Bluetooth and GRPS. Bluetooth networked games were a feature of Nokia's N-Gage platform, noted above in relation to the Snake game. However, Nokia too sought to create a relationship between N-Gage's mobile cellular platform and the internet's space of community and cultural formation for gaming.

The development of the multimedia mobile (Koskinen 2007) is only one trajectory that influenced the development of mobile gaming. The development of the mobile phone–based games market has come with considerable constraints compared to the video game market in general – not least the dominance of distribution of mobile games by carriers and large service providers (underscored by the centrality of the menu on devices as a locus of control, rather like the electronic program guide in subscription and digital television). Returning to the distinctive aspect of location when it comes to mobiles, there are now many examples of location-based games, that draw upon a combination of the available technologies I have earlier discussed – but which give these new and unexpected attributes.

Location-based gaming features in a range of different movements within gaming generally, whether as mixed-reality, alternative reality, or pervasive gaming. Context and location is central to pervasive games:

> One of the most exciting aspects in these games is that the context information is utilized to modify a game world or it is converted to game elements. In addition, gaming can be blended into the daily life and normal social situations of the players. (Korhonen, Saarenpää, and Paavilainen 2008, p. 21)

Nonplayers, for instance, can find themselves in the game space:

> [T]he pervasive games are often played in environments inhabited by people who are not playing the game. The game design must ensure that the game does not disturb too much players' social interaction outside the gameworld or disrupt nonplayers' ongoing activities. (Korhonen, Saarenpää, and Paavilainen 2008, p. 22)

Alternative reality gaming (ARG) involves interactive, participative narrative that uses the resources of places, players, media, and location technologies. A much-discussed ARG is Perplex City, a sprawling affair, first played in London, then in different cities around the world:

Welcome to Perplex City. A city obsessed with puzzles and ciphers. A game that blurs the boundaries between fiction and reality. Begin an incredible, immersive adventure that spills out into the real world. Interrogate suspects over the phone, search police files for evidence, decipher coded emails and check newspapers for clues – working with tens of thousands of players around the world. (http://www.perplexcity.com)

Devised by social multiplayer game outfit Mind Candy, the first season of Perplex City relied heavily upon players using mobile phones to send answers and photos back to base via SMS and MMS, while organizers sent back questions, unexpected tasks, and updates.

Perplex City is but one of a dizzying array of alternative reality games. What is evident is that mobile media often plays an important role in these – as a personal, portable technology and network infrastructure that allows multimedia communication, recording, and quotidian media production, that underlies and shapes the participatory structures of these nascent cultural forms. Mobiles also have a set of relations to place, space, and location, now proliferating with the intersection of technologies that traverse handsets and networks (Hjorth and Chan 2009; Licoppe and Inada 2008). Social, multiplayer gaming has become part of the mobile experience, if not as widespread as solely internet-based alternatives. Perhaps mobile gaming's greatest contribution has been to challenge dominant, gendered preconceptions of console and online gaming, about the duration, genre, and type of practice that characterize "real gaming," or genuine gamers and their communities and cultures. Mobile gaming tends to be episodic, or fragmentary; to reconfigure the large-screen, embodied experiences of many gaming locales; and, instead, to encourage awareness of context – indeed, through location technologies allowing incorporation of place into gameplay.

Conclusion: Theorizing Mobile Audiences

As I have outlined, "going mobile" involves a radical shift for thinking about audiences in overlapping and complex ways. The emergence of the mobile phone from the 1970s onward – now a global technology with billions of users, and a career into its fourth decade – has meant that scholars and students have been obliged to expand and reconsider fundamental ideas of what audiences are. While telephones were imagined as "media" from the late nineteenth century through to the 1920s, as historians have pointed out, the classic identity of the telephone and the people who were its subjects during the twentieth century was something else – rather more to do with communications, communities and citizens, or, with telecommunications reforms, markets, customers, and consumers (cf. Livingstone and Lunt, this volume). So the coming of the mobile phone, its insinuation into the nooks and crannies of everyday life, and by turns, piecemeal, programmatic, and incidental, attachment to other forms of media, has meant that "going mobile" has become central to the processes of contemporary audience engagement.

Once acknowledged as a component of contemporary audience "scene," mobile-izing looks reasonably intelligible. That is, if we have in mind the mobile phone cultures and practices from the classic period of the 1990s, where mobiles became widely diffused through the world, and their new ensemble of practices, contexts of use, and media investments achieved something of a promising if not stable form. However, as mobile phones are made over as mobile media, the customizable handset has become programmable, extensible, and connectable in ways that are still not clear. What will be significant and enduring about mobile media and decisive for how audiences actually congregate and function is still to unfold (cf. Feijóo et al. 2009), making it difficult to distinguish between the latest press release or breathless technophilic reporting, and what it is that makes "going mobile" special for audiences.

Interestingly enough, there is as yet little systematic work by researchers that draws together the various overlapping strands of going mobile and how it structures audiences. There is a vibrant, interdisciplinary body of work on mobiles, and steadily increasing critical attention and exploration of mobile media. We could really do with research dedicated to studying and theorizing mobile audiences, and the operations and actions of going mobile. One obstacle to such accounts is that mobile media, in their various forms and convergent hybridity, are still unfolding so little reliable information, for instance, about those who watch, discuss, or share mobile television, play mobile games, or enjoy – or detest or are indifferent to – mobile social software, or who rely upon mobile apps for work, education, and pleasure. Another obstacle is the wide range of disciplines and expertise of mobile researchers themselves, and the relative belated entry of cultural and media studies scholars into the field. Of course, in such challenges lie great possibilities —for grasping what going mobile encompasses, and also for understanding the precise ways in which it is implicated in the dynamics of contemporary audiences and their cultural politics.

References

Balbi, G. and Prario, B. 2009 Back to the future: the past and present of mobile TV. In G. Goggin and L. Hjorth, eds. *Mobile Technologies: From Telecommunications to Media*. Routledge, New York, pp. 161–173.

Bruns, A. 2008 *Blogs, Wikipedia, Second life, and Beyond: From Production to Produsage*. Peter Lang, New York.

Bruns, A. and Jacobs, J. 2006 *Uses of Blogs*. Peter Lang, New York.

Burgess, J. and Green, J. 2009 *The Uses of YouTube: Online Video and the Politics of Participatory Culture*. Polity, Cambridge.

Castells, M. 2009 *Communication Power*. Oxford University Press, Oxford.

Crawford, A. 2008 Taking social software to the streets: mobile cocooning and the (an-) erotic city. *Journal of Urban Technology*, 15, 79–97.

Crawford, K. 2009 These foolish things: on intimacy and insignificance in mobile media. In G. Goggin and L. Hjorth, eds. *Mobile Technologies: From Telecommunications to Media*. Routledge, New York, pp. 252–265.

Crawford, A. and Goggin, G. 2009 Geomobile web: locative technologies and mobile media. *Australian Journal of Communication*, 36, 1, pp. 97–109.

Curwen, P. 2002 *The Future of Mobile Communications: Awaiting the Third Generation*. Palgrave Macmillan, Basingstoke, UK.

Curwen, P. and Whalley, J. 2008 Mobile television: technological and regulatory issues. *Info*, 10, 1, pp. 40–64.

Donner, J. 2009a Blurring livelihoods and lives: the social uses of mobile phones and socioeconomic development. *Innovations: Technology, Governance, Globalization*, 4, pp. 91–101.

Donner, J. 2009b Mobile media on low-cost handsets: the resiliency of text messaging among small enterprises in India (and beyond). In G. Goggin and L. Hjorth, eds. *Mobile Technologies: From Telecommunications to Media*. Routledge, New York, pp. 93–104.

Ducheneaut, N.M., Oehlberg, L., Moore, R.J., Thornton, J.D. and Nickell, E. 2008 Social TV: designing for distributed, sociable television viewing. *International Journal of Human-Computer Interaction*, 24, pp. 136–154.

Feijóo, C., Maghiros, I., Abadie, F. and Gómez-Barroso, J-L. 2009 Exploring a heterogeneous and fragmented digital ecosystem: mobile content. *Telematics and Informatics*, 26, pp. 282–292.

Fischer, C. 1992 *America Calling: A Social History of the Telephone to 1940*. University of California Press, Berkeley.

Fortunati, L., Katz, J.E. and Riccini, R. eds. 2003 *Mediating the Human Body: Technology, Communication, and Fashion*. Lawrence Erlbaum, Mahwah, NJ.

Funk, J.L. 2001 *The Mobile Internet: How Japan Dialed up and the West Disconnected*. ISI Publications, Pembroke, Bermuda.

Gibson, J. J. 1977 The theory of affordances. In R.E Shaw and J. Bransford, eds. *Perceiving, Acting, and Knowing: Toward an Ecological Psychology*. Lawrence Erlbaum, Hillsdale, NJ, pp. 67–82.

Goggin, G. 2006 *Cell Phone Culture: Mobile Technology in Everyday Life*. Routledge, London.

Goggin, G. 2011 *Global Mobile Media*. Routledge, London.

Goggin, G. and Wilken, R. 2011 *Mobile Technology and Place*. Routledge, New York.

Green, N., Harper, R., Murtagh, G. and Cooper, G. 2001 Configuring the mobile user: sociological and industry views. *Personal and Ubiquitous Computing*, 5, pp. 146–156.

Haddon, L., Mante, E., Sapio, B., Kommonen, K-H., Fortunati, L. and Kant, A., eds. 2005 *Everyday Innovators: Researching the Role of Users in Shaping ICTs*. Springer, London.

Hills, J. 1986 *Deregulating Telecoms: Competition and Control in the United States, Japan, and Britain*. Pinter, London.

Hjorth, L. and Chan, D., eds. 2009 *Gaming Cultures and Place in Asia-Pacific*. Routledge, New York.

Humphreys, L. 2007 Mobile social networks and social practice: a case study of Dodgeball. *Journal of Computer-Mediated Communication*, 13, 1, article 17. Retrieved from http://jcmc.indiana.edu/vol13/issue1/humphreys.html

Johnson, J. 2008 Is the iPhone the next Wii? BoingBoing.net, March 7. Retrieved from http://gadgets.boingboing.net/2008/03/07/is-the-iphone-the-ne.html

Kasesniemi, E-L. 2003 *Mobile Messages: Young People and a New Communication Culture.* Tampere University Press, Tampere, Finland.

Katz, J.E., ed. 2003 *Machines That Become Us: The Social Context of Personal Communication Technology.* Transaction, New Brunswick, NJ.

Katz, J.E. and Aakhus, Mark E., eds. 2002 *Perpetual Contact: Mobile Communication, Private Talk, Public Performance.* Cambridge University Press, Cambridge.

Korhonen, H., Saarenpää, H. and Paavilainen, J. 2008 Pervasive mobile games: a new mindset for players and developers. In P. Markopoulos et al., eds. *Fun and Games.* Springer Verlag, Berlin, pp. 21–32.

Koskinen, I.K. 2007 *Mobile Multimedia in Action.* Transaction, New Brunswick, NJ.

Koskinen, I., Kurvinen, E. and Lehtonen, T-K. 2002 *Mobile Image.* IT Press, Helsinki.

Latour, B. 2005 *Assembling the Social: An Introduction to Actor-Network Theory.* Clarendon, Oxford.

Licoppe, C. and Inada, Y. 2008 Geolocalized technologies, location-aware communities, and personal territories: the Mogi case. *Journal of Urban Technology*, 15, pp. 5–24.

Ling, R. 2004 *The Mobile Connection: The Cell Phone's Impact on Society.* San Francisco: Morgan Kaufmann.

Ling, R. 2008 *New Tech, New Ties: How Mobile Communication Is Reshaping Social Cohesion.* MIT Press, Cambridge, MA.

Ling, R. and Pedersen, P.E., eds. 2005 *Mobile Communications: Re-negotiation of the Social Sphere.* Springer, Surrey, UK.

Mansell, R. 1993 *The New Telecommunications: A Political Economy of Network Evolution.* London: Sage.

Marvin, C. 1988 *When Old Technologies Were New: Thinking about Electric Communication in the Late Nineteenth Century.* Oxford University Press, New York.

Nightingale, V. and Dwyer, T. 2006 The audience politics of 'enhanced' TV formats. *International Journal of Media and Cultural Politics*, 2, pp. 25–42.

Nyíri, K., ed. 2005 *A Sense of Place: The Global and the Local in Mobile Communication.* Passagen, Wien.

Oksman, V. 2009 Media contents in mobiles: comparing video, audio and text. In G. Goggin and L. Hjorth, eds. *Mobile Technologies: From Telecommunications to Media.* Routledge, New York, pp. 118–130.

Oksman, V., Noppari, E., Tammela, A., Mäkinen, M. and Ollikainen, V. 2007 Mobile TV in everyday life contexts – individual entertainment or shared experiences? In P. Cesar et al., eds. *EuroITV.* Springer-Verlag, Berlin, pp. 215–225.

Parikka, J. and Suominen, J. 2006 Victorian snakes? Towards a cultural history of mobile games and the experience of movement. *Game Studies*, 6, 1. Retrieved from http://gamestudies.org/0601/articles/parikka_suominen

Pertierra, R., Ugarte, E.F., Pingol, A., Hernandez, J. and Dacanay, N.L. 2002 *Txt-ing Selves: Cellphones and Philippine Modernity.* De La Salle University Press, Manila. Retrieved from http://www.finlandembassy.ph/texting1.htm

Rakow, L.F. 1993 *Gender on the Line: Women, the Telephone, and Community Life.* University of Illinois Press, Chicago.

Scharl, A. and Tochtermann, K., eds. 2007 *The Geospatial Web: How Geobrowsers, Social Software and the Web 2.0 Are Shaping the Network Society.* Springer, London.

Schatz, R., Wagner, S., Egger, S. and Jordan, N. 2007 Mobile TV becomes social – integrating content with communications. In *Proceedings of the ITI 2007 Conference*, June 25–28, Croatia.

Schroeder, F. 2008 Caressing the skin: mobile devices and bodily engagement. In *Proceedings of 5th Mobile Music Workshop* 2008, May 13–15, Vienna, pp. 26–30.

De Sola Pool, I., ed. 1977 *The Social Impact of the Telephone*. MIT Press, Cambridge, MA.

De Souza e Silva, A. 2009 Hybrid reality and location-based gaming: redefining mobility and game spaces in urban environments. *Simulation and Gaming*, 40, 3, pp. 404–424.

De Souza e Silva, A. and Hjorth, L. 2009 Playful urban spaces. *Simulation and Gaming*, 40, pp. 602–625.

Spurgeon, C. and Goggin, G. 2007 Mobiles into media: premium rate SMS and the adaptation of television to interactive communication cultures. *Continuum*, 21, pp. 317–329.

Vincent, J. and Fortunati, L., eds. 2009 *Electronic Emotion: The Mediation of Emotion via Information and Communication Technologies*. Peter Lang, Oxford.

Yu, H. 2004 The power of thumbs: the politics of SMS in urban China. *Graduate Journal of Asia-Pacific Studies*, 2, pp. 30–43.

Part II
Theorizing Audiences

7

Audiences and Publics, Media and Public Spheres

Richard Butsch

From the 1930s through the 1950s, with the rise of fascism in Europe and the spread of broadcasting, intellectuals worried about the power of mass media to manipulate the public and their participation as citizens in democracy. Since the 1980s, the world has experienced again a rapid intensification of media and of politics and their relationships to each other. Media ownership has concentrated in a handful of global multimedia corporations; markets for media texts, technologies, and services have become global; and the new media of internet and mobile phones have spread and converged with television and computers. Politics has become more polarized in Europe, North America, and South America; across much of the world fundamentalist religious revivals have become political movements, shifted politics, and toppled governments: and the global balance of power was destabilized with the end of Soviet era. All this has revived concerns about media audiences and their relation to the public sphere, raising the question: are audiences publics, and in what ways and with what consequences?

To address these questions, this chapter explores the relationships between three social formations: publics, media, and audiences. The scholarly literature on the relationships between the three attempts primarily to conceptually or empirically categorize audiences as publics or not, as if this were a characteristic of these formations. This chapter, however, will take a different approach, exploring how contemporaries defined the audiences of their times as publics in a wide range of discourses, from research to law and policy to business to popular culture, reading these contemporary statements as primary historical documents. I presume that what matters historically and politically is whether people think of and act toward audiences as if they are publics or not. It is that which shapes how people, including audiences, act, and what consequences this has for democracies. To do this, I will concentrate primarily on the American context with which I am most familiar.

The Handbook of Media Audiences, First Edition. Edited by Virginia Nightingale.
© 2014 John Wiley & Sons, Ltd. Published 2014 by John Wiley & Sons, Ltd.

Publics: Some History of the Idea

Put simply, a public is an aggregate of people who engage in public discussion on issues of concern to the state. It is distinguished from government and from people engaged in private affairs, whether at home or in the marketplace. The social institutions that "house" such discussion constitute the public sphere (Weintraub and Kumar 1997; Emirbayer and Sheller 1999). Ancient Greek and Roman citizens assembled in fora to consider issues facing their city-state. These ideas and institutions faded from European culture in the Middle Ages, to gradually reappear in the early modern period. The Enlightenment re-established publics as a valued idea and emphasized reason as the necessary mode of deliberation among citizens (Habermas 1989). But the size of eighteenth-century nation-states made assemblies of even a select class impracticable. Thus, the press became integral to the concept of publics dispersed across a nation. In the twentieth century other media, in particular broadcasting, were added to this. But the growth of media raised concerns about its controlling publics rather than being a tool for publics.

The idea of publics has been largely prescriptive about what publics should be, "an objective standard for political critique" (Hansen 1993, p. xxvii). This normative quality grows from the idea that democracy depends upon citizens actively engaging in the discussion of issues and problems, and this in turn requires a structure that enables collective response, a public sphere. The concept of "ideal" publics was woven into the political discourse that was part of the formation of modern European nations, nationalism, and nationality since the seventeenth century, when governments were reconceived as deriving their authority from "the people," the idea of popular sovereignty (Calhoun 1975; Morgan 1989; Eley and Suny 1996). Social contract theory of the eighteenth century presumed popular sovereignty by challenging traditional justifications of kingly sovereignty based on divine right or the natural order as reflected in the patriarchal family, and claimed instead that society and government is based on a contract among men (Pateman 1989). English libertarians of the seventeenth and eighteenth centuries, such as Milton and Locke, argued that popular sovereignty necessitated free public speech for its exercise. By the late eighteenth century in both England and the United States, freedom of speech and of the press began to be accepted as necessary for political stability (Levy 1985; Nerone 1994). Continental political philosophy followed a similar path, evolving a more specific "public" from the vague concept of "the people." Bourgeois political thought since Descartes claimed that a collective rational deliberation, that is, a public sphere of rational individuals, is necessary to realize the principle that "reason alone has authority" (Negt and Kluge 1993, pp. 9–10).

By the nineteenth century, while the role of the public in governance had become widely accepted in Western Europe and North American, elites were increasingly concerned about broadening the voter franchise because they doubted the capacity of "the masses" of new industrial and urban workers to fulfill their role in a public. They feared that the masses would resort to what they perceived as disruptive traditional modes of collective action (i.e. as unruly and violent crowds rather than reasoning publics). This made it important to clearly define what might constitute a proper public. By the end of the nineteenth century, the new fields of crowd psychology and of sociology had identified publics as a safe social formation that did not threaten social order, and as distinct from other forms of collective behavior such as crowds and social movements (Tilly 2004), and from social forms such as mass society. This concept led to examining the role of media in relation to publics.

Among the first to refine the distinction between publics and crowds was the French jurist and social theorist Gabriel Tarde (1969), who wrote at the turn of the twentieth century. Theories of crowd psychology that circulated among intellectual elites of the time characterized crowds as irrational, easily suggestible, and prone to impulsive, violent collective actions. Tarde defined publics as dispersed and not susceptible to such crowd traits. He argued further that one can simultaneously participate in several publics, each acting as counterweights to each other so that, participating in each, we are likely to be more tolerant of all. The implication was that publics would therefore be less bound by emotional attachment to the group, and its members more independent and individual. When publics assembled, they were more rational and deliberative, and more civilized and tolerant, than crowds.

Tarde's ideas probably were known to American sociologist Robert Park (1972), who completed his dissertation in Germany in 1904 on the subject of crowds and publics. Returning to the United States, he introduced this crowd versus public distinction into American sociology. As a faculty member and then chairman of the preeminent University of Chicago Department of Sociology, he founded and shaped the field of collective behavior based on these concepts. Like Tarde, Park contrasted homogeneity of mind in the crowd to the individual differences retained in publics. He asserted that differences of viewpoint are critical to publics. Differences produce "prudence and rational reflection" before action. Without difference, he said publics dissolve into crowds whose drives are not contained by critical thought (Park 1955, p. 80).

John Dewey, a founder of pragmatic philosophy and a very influential public intellectual in the 1920s, was a contemporary of Parks who shared an interest in publics and in the American Progressive reform movement. Unlike Park, however, Dewey gave greater emphasis in his concept of publics to community rather than communication, and to action rather than discussion. He defined a public as a spontaneous group of people that arises as a result of a community being confronted by an issue and engaging in discussion about it. Most theorizing about publics concluded with some vague concept of public opinion that, in some unspecified manner, influenced governments. Dewey went beyond the formation of public opinion to say that through such discussion, people arrive at a collective decision and act to influence government (Dewey 1927).

Dewey's adversary in 1920s public debate was Walter Lippmann, a journalist and public intellectual. Lippmann's focus (1920) was on the limitations of the masses, whom he described as "absolutely illiterate, feeble-minded, grossly neurotic, undernourished and frustrated individuals," and unable to engage in reasoned discussion. Lippmann (1920) considered the "phantom public" a figment of Progressive intellectual imagination and instead argued for a "realistic" recognition of the need for elites to guide the masses, and use mass media to do so. Dewey and Lippmann were part of an interwar debate about government propaganda and corporate advertising, media, and the role of the masses in a democracy. Not only Lippmann but also many intellectuals, including some Progressives, and policy and corporate elites talked about the inadequacies of the working-class masses as citizens (Gary 1999, pp. 30–31).

From the interwar years to the postwar era, intellectual concerns shifted from the masses' limitations as publics to changes in the structure of society that transformed the population from communal entities into a mass (Giner 1976; Leach 1989). The word *mass* became commonplace in the 1950s, entering the conversation and vocabulary of the general reading population. Rather than referring to the working class, as *the masses* did, the term *mass* drew attention especially to middle-class, white-collar corporate workers and their suburban families. Books advancing these ideas were read well beyond academic circles: *White Collar, The Lonely Crowd, The Organization Man, The Man in the Grey Flannel Suit*, and so on. They shared claims, sometimes called the *problem of center and periphery*, that large modern societies require a set of intermediary institutions between the local and the national, and that mass media in particular had undercut these institutions and turned the population into a mass composed of isolated, anonymous, and identical individuals (Butsch 2008). In other words, the centralized power of mass society operates by mass media manipulating the mass of the population. As with earlier crowd psychology, theories of mass society continued to presume some version of the older psychological concept of suggestibility to explain why and which audiences were vulnerable to mass media manipulation.

In Europe, similar critiques were rooted in a concern that impersonal modern urban society was displacing traditional small communities. Such ideas were the founding problem of late nineteenth-century sociology, and central to the work of Marx, Durkheim, Weber, and others. Out of this grew mass culture critiques from a range of political viewpoints from conservatives such as Ortega y Gasset and T. S. Eliot to the Frankfurt school (Swingewood 1977). Habermas was immersed in this critique of mass culture when he was writing *The Structural Transformation of the Public Sphere* in the 1950s (see Habermas 1989). Not surprisingly, he contrasted modern capitalist mass media that were the subject of this critique, to an idealized version of eighteenth-century European publics.

Much of public sphere scholarship since the 1980s has been a critique of Habermas's thesis, contrasting his idealized version of Enlightenment publics with the historical reality. The principal thrust of these critiques has been that eighteenth-century publics were exclusionary and even its participants were not equal, most notably that the historical bourgeois public sphere was "essentially, not just contingently, masculinist" (Landes 1988, p. 7). Others added that private inequality of any sort produces unequal access to the public realm and dominance by superordinate groups. Critics, drawing on historical research of crowds and social movements since Habermas had written, preferred multiple public spheres of people with similar status or social identity who could use these spheres to mobilize their political strength and then engage in larger public debate or struggle (Emirbayer and Sheller 1999). Cultural studies scholars challenge the presumption that audiences are easily manipulated by mass media, while political economy approaches to media industries continue to emphasize Habermas's assumption about the power of media.

Media and Audiences as Public Sphere

Through the twentieth century, media of communication spread broader and deeper into everyday life and increasingly raised questions about the consequences for individuals, society, and political process. Criticisms of media, implicitly or explicitly, judged media in terms of their contribution to the vitality of a public sphere and their enabling people to fulfill their role as citizens, or in preparing people (children, immigrants, and the uneducated) to become citizens. Discourses on media audiences polarized into images of an ideal public of educated, informed, cultivated and civic-minded citizens who are capable and committed to their duty as citizens versus uneducated, ill-informed, pleasure-seeking, suggestible crowds or mass. The latter were invariably described as women, children, "inferior" races, and subordinate classes, while higher-class, northern and western European men were considered of strong enough character to be good citizens.

Correlatively, public discourses typically characterized each succeeding new communication medium as fit or unfit for a public sphere. These discourses have focused on technological determinants, private ownership versus public trust, or displacement and persuasion as media factors influencing the viability of publics. The visual media of movies and television were claimed to have a hypnotic effect on viewers that undercut their civic value. Language-based print and radio were considered ideal for the public sphere. The interactive conversational aspect of the internet has been cited as the latest ideal. An extension of the technological argument claims that the attraction power of a medium is so strong that it displaces more civic and beneficial activities. Media from the tabloid press at the turn of the twentieth century, to commercial television at midcentury, to the internet at the end of that century, have been charged with this failure. The extreme of displacement claims is the charge that certain media are addictive (Butsch 2008).

Private commercial ownership of the media has been criticized for a very long time as detrimental to a civilization and a nation. As early as the eighteenth century, authors talked about their reading publics as markets rather than as citizens, and began to write accordingly (Williams 1960). Public ownership positions the audience as citizens, while commercial ownership positions them as consumers. With the spread of broadcasting, most of the world's governments opted for public control. Public media have been cast as guardians of civic health and charged with delivering culture and knowledge to foster good citizenship. This in turn has been criticized as merely a veil for a subtle control of the masses that Foucault called governmentality (Burchell, Gordon, and Miller 1991) or as blatant dictatorial propagandizing. Alternately, private ownership, typified by the US example, has been widely criticized for the poor quality of media messages, changing media from cultural and civic resources into mere entertainments that debase the citizenry and reduce audiences to consumers. Habermas (1989) argued that when commodity exchange came to pervade public activity, rational-critical debate was replaced by consumption, and the "web of public communication unravelled into acts of individuated reception, however uniform in mode" (p. 161).

To define audiences as publics is to conceive them enacting their role of "good citizens." In public broadcasting, this is explicit in its premises and justifications, even when, in an authoritarian state, citizens are deemed passive servants of the state rather than active participants in the state. In the former, media produce a representative public sphere; in the latter, a democratic public sphere. Commercial media, on the other hand, by definition treat audiences as individual consumers. Treatment of them as publics has to be imposed through regulation or other constraints, producing ongoing tensions about what is the role of audience and what is the role of media. As commercial media have advanced and public media receded across the globe in the past two decades, the tension between defining audiences as citizen or consumer has generated continual debate about media audiences and the public sphere (Downing 2004).

Through the twentieth century, negative descriptions of media audiences replaced *crowd* with other terms, including *consumer* and *mass man*, but each new term continued to emphasize the emotionality and suggestibility of the audience. Whether audiences were considered publics also depended upon the medium and how people were believed to use it. Virtuous citizen audiences were expected to seek news and cultivation and act after calm deliberation. Mere consumers sought entertainment and self-indulgence, acted on emotion and impulse, and were invariably identified as lower class, women, children, and "lesser races."

Print as Public Sphere

From the origins of modern democracy, print media were considered important to publics (Habermas 1989; Darnton 2000). Emphasizing the necessity of information to public discussion, the Levellers of the English Revolution in a 1646

"Remonstrance" to Parliament declared, "[L]et the imprisoned Presses at liberty, so that all men's understandings may be more conveniently informed" (Levy 1985, p. 91). Milton claimed that public discussion was necessary to sound public decisions (Zaret 2000, p. 219). In eighteenth-century England and France, libertarians argued that a free press was necessary to people's participation in a democracy (Levy 1985, pp. 135–136). Thomas Jefferson wrote in 1787 that, if newspapers sufficiently informed the people, there would be fewer rebellions and other extralegal political actions (Nerone 1994, p. 55). In the mid-nineteenth century, John Stuart Mill (1958) wrote that to "surmount [the problem of population size] required the press, and even the newspaper press, the real equivalent ... of the forum" (p. 5).

Through the nineteenth century, newspapers underwent dramatic changes – in organization, technology, and marketing. But throughout, newspapers were acknowledged as central to the public sphere (Curran 2000, pp. 121–129). Early in that century, the American press was openly partisan, a voice for political parties and watchdog against its opponents in office. Transformation into capitalist enterprises through midcentury freed newspapers from dependence upon political parties, and they began to tout themselves as neutral arbiters in the political ring (Barnhurst and Nerone 2001). Late in the nineteenth century, competition between Pulitzer and Hearst gave rise to the derogatory designation of *yellow journalism*. This "degraded" press was contrasted to the "true legatees" of the public tradition, such as Adolph Ochs, who, when purchasing the *New York Times* in 1896, declared he would make the *Times* "a forum for the consideration of all questions of public importance and, to that end, to invite intelligent discussion from all shades of opinion" ("Business Announcement" 1896, p. 4).

This role of the press was incorporated into the sociological tradition of publics, which arose when metropolitan newspapers were at their height. Tarde argued that dispersed people formed publics through the common experience of reading the news and discussing it in public places such as cafés. He concluded that reading engendered discussion rather than disorder (Tarde 1969, pp. 307–8). Robert Park (1955), a former journalist, reacting to the yellow journalism of his day, emphasized that newspapers should provide the facts that must be the basis of discussion among members of a public. He wrote,

> The first typical reaction of an individual to the news is likely to be a desire to repeat it to someone. This makes conversation, arouses further comment, and perhaps starts a discussion ... [the] discussion turns from the news to the issues it raises. The clash of opinions and sentiments which discussion inevitably evokes usually terminates in some sort of consensus or collective opinion—what we call public opinion. (pp. 79, 116)

Walter Lippmann (1920) similarly emphasized newspapers' role in delivering information to publics, and caustically criticized the tendencies of tabloid journalism. He wrote,

The most destructive form of untruth is sophistry and propaganda by those whose profession is to report the news. The news columns are common carriers ... when a people can no longer confidently repair "to the best fountains for their information," then anyone's guess and anyone's rumor, each man's hopes and each man's whim become the basis of government. (pp. 10–11)

Movie Audiences as Crowds

Movie exhibition as an independent entertainment in the United States began about 1905 with the rapid proliferation of nickelodeons, small storefronts set up with a hundred or so chairs, a projector, and a screen, many of these in poor neighborhoods of the largest cities that were swelling with the turn-of-the-twentieth-century wave of immigration. Quickly a stereotype of nickelodeon audiences arose as lower-class immigrants, the working-class "masses," women, and children, the same populations that crowd psychology had already identified as emotional and suggestible. Concerns arose about the effects of movies upon new and vulnerable immigrants. Many advocated censorship of movies and succeeded in instituting censorship boards in several cities and states, as a means of social control (Grieveson 2004). These concerns were incorporated into early theory and research on movie going.

French crowd psychologist Gustave LeBon (1898/1960) had anticipated claims of movies' power of suggestion, stating, "Nothing has a greater effect on the imaginations of crowds of every category than theatrical representations. The entire audience experiences at the same time the same emotion" (pp. 67–68). His observation soon was applied to audiences for nickelodeon movies. In an address in 1911 in New York at the People's Institute, an organization devoted to helping lower-class immigrants, Reverend H. A. Jump claimed that movies operated through "psychologic suggestion." Jane Addams similarly claimed that her young working-class charges were powerfully influenced by nickelodeons. In the first psychological treatise about movies, *The Photoplay*, influential Harvard psychologist Hugo Münsterberg (1970) (Park was one of his students) gave scholarly legitimacy to the idea that movies "implant" thoughts in viewers' minds. A suggestion he said, "is forced on us ... something to which we have to submit." In *The Photoplay*, he wrote,

The intensity with which the plays take hold of the audience cannot remain without social effects ... the mind is so completely given up to the moving pictures ... the moral balance, which would have been kept under the habitual stimuli of the narrow routine of life, may be lost under the pressure of the realistic suggestion. (Münsterberg 1970, pp. 46–47, 95–96)

Through the 1910s and 1920s, reformers and academics alike wrote about movie influence upon the masses and particularly upon children. In the late 1920s one of these reformers, William Short, convinced the Payne Fund, a philanthropy devoted to promoting children's reading, to fund an ambitious research project on the power of movies over children (Jowett, Jarvie, and Fuller 1996). The project enlisted leading social scientists and produced one of the largest and most significant research studies of movie audiences, 13 research reports published in eight volumes. A popular summary published by a commercial publisher and reviewed in newspapers and magazines across the nation was intended to reach the educated public. Herbert Blumer (1933), soon to be one of the most important American sociologists, authored two of these volumes in which he describes the grip movies held on viewers as so strong that "even his efforts to rid himself of it by reasoning with himself may prove of little avail" (p. 74). He concluded that the effects of movies were determined by "the social milieu [of the moviegoer]" and were stronger in "socially disorganized areas," a phrase used by his University of Chicago colleagues to indicate working-class and immigrant neighborhoods (Blumer and Hauser 1933, pp. 201–202; Blumer 1935).

By the time the Payne studies were published in 1933, the movie industry was controlled by a handful of vertically integrated studios who preempted further criticism through industry self-censorship that cleansed controversial topics from the screens of most American theaters and many foreign ones. Also to avoid controversy, the industry publicized the idea that movies were purely entertainment, excluding them from the public sphere and treating their audiences as consumers rather than as citizens (Maltby 1993).

Broadcasting as Public Sphere

In striking contrast to public discourse about movies, broadcasting was framed from the beginning as an institution of the public sphere. From its inception in the 1920s, radio broadcasting was conceived on the model of the press and hailed as a boon to civic participation. Reflecting recognition of its importance in public affairs, most governments established publicly funded and controlled broadcasting systems. Even before broadcasting, when it was considered a two-direction communication wireless telephone, radio was framed as a public good. It was especially valuable for communication at sea. Two international conferences of nations in 1903 and 1906, gave priority to naval and military use over commercial use (Douglas 1987, pp. 137–141); in the United States, licensing of radio transmitters also predated broadcasting. Both developments privileged public use over private.

This alone did not define radio as a public sphere, since it held radio as a tool for government, not for citizens. With the arrival of broadcasting, however, radio was required to serve citizens. In Britain and its empire, the BBC took on the role of educating its listeners as citizens. It was founded "as a trustee for the national interest," and its first director defined its purpose "to build up knowledge, experience and character," of listeners to better fulfill their role as citizens. Again in 1932 a BBC report exhorted that "if democracy is to be a real democracy, it must be an educated democracy. ... Broadcasting ... can do more to ensure an educational democracy than any other single agent" (Bailey 2007, pp. 99, 100, 106; Pinkerton 2008).

In the United States shortly after the birth of broadcasting, Secretary of Commerce Herbert Hoover, who was in charge of regulating radio, defined it as a medium of free speech: "We seek to preserve the ownership of the road through the ether as public property ... to keep alive free speech; to avoid censorship; to prevent interference in the traffic" (*Wireless Age*, October 1924, p. 24). Not long after, the US Radio Act of 1927 required that broadcasters, to obtain and retain a license, must serve the "public convenience, interest and necessity" (Barnouw 1966). In the 1930s the US Congress, the Federal Communication Commission (FCC), and the courts began to construe the phrase as a requirement to provide citizens news and public information and a place for public debate, like the press (Barnouw 1968). A 1946 FCC report described radio as "an unequalled medium for the dissemination of news, information, and opinion, and for the discussion of public issues" (FCC 1946, pp. 39, 55). In 1954 the US Congress again reiterated that "the spectrum is a natural resource belonging to the entire national public ... the right of the public to service is superior to the right of any licensee to make use of any frequency or channel for his own private purposes" (p. 54). This conception of broadcasting serving the public interest continued until the deregulation era of the 1980s abandoned it for a market model (Polic and Gandy 1991).

Many radio programs during the 1930s positioned radio listeners as a public. In addition to news and commentary programs, American radio networks created and sustained many public forum programs that fulfilled the FCC requirement. These programs featured a panel of experts who presented their views on a current issue, often followed by questions and responses from a live studio audience. Many of these programs also encouraged people to listen in groups and engage in discussion among themselves. *American Forum of the Air* and *University of Chicago Round Table*, among others, distributed weekly summaries of their programs to aid such groups. The most ambitious *America's Town Meeting of the Air* provided handbooks for group listening, weekly mailings of transcripts of the previous broadcast and information to prepare for the next, and an advisor service to answer questions by mail (Butsch 2008).

These programs typically cooperated with the listening group movement. The movement was international, active in Britain and several European nations (Hill and Williams 1941). In Britain, the BBC developed administrative offices for this purpose, scheduled regular programs, and distributed free information to aid listening groups (Bailey 2007). *America's Town Meeting* mailed information on group listening to members of the YMCA, Chautauqua Literary and Scientific Circles, American Library Association, and WPA Adult Education. It succeeded more than any other program in establishing group listening to its shows. Groups were organized by PTAs, universities, high schools, boards of education, churches, libraries, and New Deal programs as well as the YMCA, and other such civic organizations (Hill and Williams 1941).

Participants in these groups fully adopted their role as citizen-listeners. A survey in 1940 found almost 2000 organized listening groups in the United States formed in the 1930s. Groups ranged from as few as five to ten meeting in homes to hundreds in public halls. About two-fifths of group members were not high school graduates. Members were earnest in their participation: they "believe in the social importance of discussion. They feel they are assisting to make democracy work" (Hill and Williams 1941, p. 69). A minister described his group:

> [W]e had a group of men who gathered in the local barbershop each week to listen to the *Town Meeting*, which always ended with a question for listeners to discuss. We stayed late some nights talking about the topic of the week. (Barfield 1996, p. 93)

A woman in an informal group wrote to *Town Meeting* that

> our discussions often became so heated that it was two or three o'clock before we could calm down enough to think of sleep. This year we decided to ask ten of our friends to meet with us. The group became so interested we decided to make a supper club of it, in order to give more time for discussion. (Hill and Williams 1941, p. 27)

Social psychologist Hadley Cantril found that half of *Town Meeting* listeners reported usually discussing issues after the program.

Pursuing this idea of audience discussions, Paul Lazarsfeld studied radio listening during the 1944 presidential election to learn how people were influenced by broadcasts. His famous two-step flow thesis conceptualized the evidence of people listening to broadcasts, but forming opinions about the issues through conversations. The influence of media messages was not direct from medium to listeners, but rather through "opinion leaders" who were influential peers and existed at all social levels (Lazarsfeld, Berelson, and Gaudet 1944; Katz and Lazarsfeld 1955; Simonson 2007). Public service programs allied with the group listening movement defined broadcasting as a public sphere – and many listeners enthusiastically embraced their role as publics.

Radio networks and program sponsors developed programs that also incorporated the language of radio as a public sphere (McCarthy 2005). Radio networks in 1932–1933 sustained broadcasts of the New York, Boston, Cleveland, and Philadelphia Symphonies and 10 other concert music series and continued this through the 1930s (Summers 1971). Through these programs the networks presented themselves as civic-minded philanthropists to the nation, cultivating and educating the public, much as the BBC presented itself. In a similar vein, the largest American corporations sponsored cultural and civic programming. Under the guidance of emerging modern advertising agencies, they crafted images of themselves as good corporate citizens contributing culture, prosperity and strength to the nation and its people. Firestone Tires, Ford Motors, General Motors, Armco Steel, Cities Services, Packard Motors, RCA, Sherwin Williams Paints, Carborundum Abrasives, Chesterfield Tobacco, and American Banks each sponsored concert series. Philco Radio, Scott Paper, Sun Oil, Pall Mall, Bromo Quinine, Jergens Lotion, and Campbell Soups sponsored news and commentary (Summers 1971). *Westinghouse Salutes* and GM's *Parade of the States* offered weekly eulogies for cities and states. DuPont's *Cavalcade of America* promoted the link between consumption and citizenship with its new advertising motto, "Better living through chemistry"; and GM delivered intermission messages about New Deal policies under the title "The American Way of Doing Things" during the General Motors *Symphony Concerts* from 1934 to 1937 (Bird 1999).

The imagined audience for these shows, despite their highbrow fare, was the masses. In a 1935 internal memo criticizing the musical selections for *Symphony Concerts*, GM president Alfred Sloan remarked that too many compositions "are very low in melody and appeal to the masses" and called for more popular music, to reach a less sophisticated audience (Bird 1999, pp. 43–44). With these sponsored programs and intermission talks, corporate executives used radio to construct a representative rather than deliberative public sphere, an example of Habermas's (1989) "refeudalization." They sought to create audiences of attentive and obedient listeners rather than citizens actively participating in debate and politics. Fear of such manipulation of the publics underlay another discourse, about propaganda, mass media, and mass society.

Television and Mass Society

While the predominant discourse into the 1940s hailed radio as a boon to citizens and democracy, other commentators were concerned that radio could manipulate people's minds as well as or better than the movies. The apparent effectiveness of propaganda during World War I generated a debate during the 1920s about governments and corporations using media to manipulate the masses (Ewen 1996; Gary 1999). In the 1930s some began to worry about the power of radio, as the Nazi government of Germany and the Fascist government of Italy used radio to broadcast government messages directly into every home (Isola 1995; Lacey 1996). In the United States, audience research pioneer Hadley Cantril conducted a series of experiments on the power of radio and concluded that "radio, more than any other medium of communication, is capable of forming a crowd mind among individuals who are physically separate from one another" (Cantril and Allport 1935, p. 21), making it an ideal tool for propagandizing the masses. He also argued that those with less education were more vulnerable, as had been claimed about movies. He used the "panic" response to the *War of the Worlds* broadcast in 1938 as a real-world event to demonstrate his thesis (Cantril 1941).

In the same decades, sociologists worried about the power of national radio to erode local communities and social networks that were fundamental to an active public. Robert Lynd and Helen Merrill Lynd observed that radio owners traded more active pursuits outside the home for passive listening at home. Listeners became more informed about national events, but less involved in local community and civic affairs (Lynd and Merrill Lynd 1929, pp. 269–271). Listener letters and cards indicate a strong connection to network celebrities that confirm this change (Butsch 2000). Listeners often expressed the feeling that the speaker on national radio was like a friend in their home. David Ryfe (2001) found similar responses in letters to FDR's "Fireside Chats" in the 1930s, imagining themselves as part of a national public when listening to him.

Katz and Lazarsfeld (1955) described the two opposed views at the time:

> When people first began to speculate about the effects of the mass media they showed two opposite inclinations. Some social commentators thought the mass media would do nothing less than recreate the kind of informed public opinion which characterized the 'town meeting' in the sense that citizens would once again have equal access to an intimate almost first-hand account of those matters which required their decision. People had lost contact with the ever-growing world, went the argument, and the mass media would put it back within reach. Others saw something quite different. In their view the mass media loomed as agents of evil aiming at the total destruction of democratic society. (pp. 15–16)

Both, however, had similar assumptions: their image first of all was of an atomistic mass of millions … prepared to receive the Message; and, second, they pictured every Message as a direct and powerful stimulus to action which would elicit immediate response. In short, the media of communication were looked upon as a new kind of unifying force.

By the time television arrived, the concerns about weakening local ties had blossomed into theories of mass society. Television was not welcomed, like radio, as a boon to the public sphere. Quite the contrary, from its beginnings in the United States shortly after World War II, it was scathingly attacked first for its cultural degradation and its displacement of more constructive activities, and then for its alleged power to persuade and manipulate viewers. Soon Cold War discourse spread fear of brainwashing and subliminal advertising, linking these to the vulnerability of audiences, especially of television. These criticisms became widely accepted even among heavy viewers. From the 1950s into the 1970s, many argued about and tried to measure how much television affected people's attitudes and behavior. But the very question accepted the premise that the medium was the independent variable and people were dependent upon it, entirely dismissing any idea of an autonomous citizen audience.

A positive discourse about television and the public sphere was proffered by broadcast networks and corporations as they continued their campaign to equate consumerism and citizenship (Glickman 2007, p. 206), even though consumers are conceived as individuals while publics are collective. Market research and public opinion research grew as one field with one method, asking questions, on the one hand, about products, and, on the other, about politics. Even Lazarsfeld published in 1945 *Printers Ink* an article entitled "Who Influences Whom: It's the Same for Politics and Advertising." He applied his two-step flow explanation both to the selling of toothpaste and political campaigns (Simonson 2007, p. 13).

Since the 1970s, Lazarsfeld's emphasis on agency in audiences has regained ascendance among media researchers. The new paradigms reconceived audiences as agents, focused on teens and young adults, and raised questions of power, all characteristics central to publics. Audiences again were seen conversing about what they saw on television, reconfiguring the meaning to fit their own experiences and values. This new approach was soon criticized for exaggerating the political significance of this dialogue. But it successfully redefined television audiences as engaging in practices of publics.

New Media Public Spheres

Over the last two decades, new media have dramatically changed the social environment of our everyday life. They also have generated another wave of great expectations and concerns about the place of media in a public sphere. Mass media were conceived as one-way communication, delivering information which publics could then use in conversation to develop public opinion. New media are interactive, conflating the information supply and conversation of this old conception and relocating both in a simultaneous virtual space. They disaggregate audiences, integrate media use into everyday life, and reconceive users' relation to media such that the term *audiences* barely describes the position (Simonson 2007, p. 243). Sonia Livingstone (2005) noted that new media so change the role of audiences that we need to rethink our conceptions.

New media is a catchall term whose very lack of specificity allows its application to a rapidly growing list of twenty-first-century media. They share a digital foundation that has enabled rapid convergence of video and audio technologies, such as movies, radio, and television, with phone and computer technologies. In the United States, this began in the 1980s with the spread of cable television, VCRs, and movie rental re-scaping traditional TV and movie viewing (Butsch 2000). Soon videogames transformed TV use by youth; as home computers became more common in the 1990s, gaming spread to computer and then to the internet. In the 1990s, mobile devices also proliferated: portable video game consoles joined music as mobile entertainments, laptop and notebook computers became increasingly successful, and mobile phones began to transform communication (Drotner 2005, pp. 189–190). MP3 technologies began connecting the internet to mobile digital technologies. Text messaging paralleled the change from computer email to instant messaging among youth. In this youth-driven development, the adult PDA technology trailed in market saturation. The historical sequences varied from nation to nation and from class to class, as latecomers leapfrogged over earlier technologies to lead in the spread of newer ones. But the general pattern of digitalization, integration, and mobilization applies around the world.

Media industries have accelerated their convergence as well. One consequence has been that media companies have become increasingly multinational, so that commercial media increasingly transcend and overshadow nation-bound public systems. The growth of satellite communication aided this transnational trend, as it made it more difficult for nations to regulate media within their borders. The internet presents governments with the same problem again. These developments also occurred in a changed political climate in many nations that favored privatization and deregulation over the trustee model of public media that had been widely accepted through most of the twentieth century.

New media have dissolved the dichotomy between public and private space, a social distinction underlying traditional concepts of public spheres. Formerly, publics have been conceived as people engaged in face-to-face interaction, requiring assembly in a public *space*. New media and especially mobile devices – wireless internet, mobile phones, MP3 players, and Blackberry – have uncoupled public conversation from face-to-face contact (Drotner 2005, pp. 189–190). More easily than ever before, individuals can have public conversations in private spaces and private ones in public spaces. Mobile users redefine the meanings of both public and private, both penetrating and blending with the other, with simultaneous participation in both at the same time: one by physical presence, and the other by media connectedness.

The internet and mobile media also have accelerated the trend to an environment in which we are immersed in media all the time and everywhere. In the 1990s, we talked about media embedded in everyday life. Immersion has turned embeddedness on its head. Today everyday life is immersed in media. Whatever we are doing, some form of media is present. However, spanning all our activities are these same media. The proliferation of embedded media has produced media immersion. Immersion has become a corporate strategy, the three-screen strategy, a leap beyond the old strategy of spinoffs, intended to keep people tuned to a program no matter where they are or what they're doing (Nightingale and Dwyer 2006).

Yet, despite this drastically modified media environment, current debates about new media echo past debates. Some see wonderful opportunities and possibilities of new media for broadening and deepening citizen participation. Others see dark clouds, as huge media corporations loom over us all like Big Brother, always watching us as we watch. On the positive side, the interactive capacities of new media have been hailed as the basis for a new form of public sphere. For most new media, both use and discourse about them are still very much in flux, but cheerleaders for the internet tend to be technological determinists. In the 1990s, many, mostly in the popular press, hailed the internet's public sphere promise. The British Labor Party, for example, claimed in 1995 that the internet could significantly alter UK democracy by giving "ordinary people" access to information and opportunity to voice their views. Some recent research has documented how the internet, as currently configured, has strengthened people's role as a public. Internet use was associated with people self-identifying as publics, being more politically informed, and engaging in more political discussion and civic participation (Dayan 2005; Mossberger, Tolbert, and McNeal 2008, pp. 81–89).

Critical literature is typically antideterminist, and sees these hopeful scenarios as utopian, temporary, and mutable. The dramatic expansion, concentration, and globalization of commercial media since the 1980s at the expense of public media have heightened alarm in this respect. This has revived fears from the 1950s. Changes in regulation can quickly limit access to websites ownership and availability, cutting the link between all users and all websites, and returning the internet from a many-to-many medium toward the old media one-to-many model (Jenkins and Thorburn 2003, p. 12). Other critics fear corporate use of the internet intruding into private life, as with consumer profiling and data mining (Gertz 2002). Some perceive a steady trend to commercialization that undermines the internet's value for users acting as publics. Barber (2003, p. 35) bemoans that the internet is quickly changing from text based to image based, repeating the old intellectual prejudice against image (spectacle) in favor of text (reading). Each of these criticisms is based in the presumption of corporate power and control over the nature of the internet wielded in such ways that its promising characteristics are stunted or eliminated. Another criticism is that the internet is not communication but cacophony, with many speaking but few listening. Access to operate a website is not access to an audience. The vast majority of websites are politically ineffective since they have no one listening, or have their "15 minutes of fame," and then the audience is gone (Jenkins and Thorburn 2003, p. 12) Clearly, the social, economic, and political context of new media are still too much in flux to draw conclusions that are more than temporary. Another concern is the digital divide between those with access and those without. Those with more education and income and those fluent in English and computer use and other skills may benefit, but others are excluded. Those with education and skills can digest and make use of internet access to information; those who lack such intellectual and research skills cannot (Bentivegna 2002, pp. 55–57).

Conclusion

Regardless of the capabilities or limitations of media technologies and organization, ultimately it is what people do with it that determines whether audiences are publics. What people do is influenced by their culture and their community. Public discourses on media have focused on the nature of the medium and the psychology of audience members. These discourses have no sociological imagination to understand the social context and sustenance of publics in a mediated world. Some scholars, most notably Peter Dahlgren (1991, 1995, 2003), have worked to develop this broader understanding, widening the lens to see the social context and civic culture. Dahlgren, in particular, has emphasized the civic culture on which a public sphere must rest. This shifts the focus to defining social practices appropriate to a public sphere, for example whether such practices need be restricted to the classic rational deliberative model of a bourgeois public sphere. Any collectivity, if it is to sustain itself, must have a culture. Oppositional readings of media messages require an oppositional culture to frame the reading, and a community that sustains that culture. Negotiated readings are based upon incongruities between preferred reading and personal experience, and people's interpretations of their experience also are a shared practice dependent on an alternative culture not written into the preferred message. In sum, no matter what the media, if people do not have customs of a public sphere they will not act as publics.

A strong civic culture encourages people to seek ways to act as publics even with minimal resources. Such are the cases in transitional moments in societies, such as seventeenth- and eighteenth-century England (Zaret 2000), late eighteenth-century United States (Warner 1990) and France (Ravel 1999; Darnton 2000), early and late twentieth-century Russia, twenty-first-century China (Wu 2007), and the Muslim world (Lynch 2005). In these conditions nascent publics, using limited and often prohibited resources, engaged in intensive public discourse on political issues of vital concern to them, typically in the face of repression by governments who did not recognize their rights as publics.

A weak civic culture may emphasize people's individual self-interests over the community or polity, one's role of consumer over citizen, or, to put it baldly, bread and circuses. These emphases have gained considerably in the wave of conservative governments in Europe and the United States of recent decades which have displaced government regulation and delivery of basic services with marketplace models that claimed citizens worked best *as* consumers, that voting was like buying, and that deregulated markets and businesses and privatized government services.

The question, then, is how to sustain a strong civic culture through good times as well as bad – but that is another topic and another body of literature.

References

Bailey, M. 2007 Rethinking public service broadcasting: the historical limits to publicness. In R. Butsch, ed. *Media and Public Spheres*. Palgrave, London, pp. 96–108.

Barber, B. 2003 Which technology and which democracy? In H. Jenkins and D. Thornburn, eds. *Democracy and New Media*. MIT Press, Cambridge, MA, pp. 33–48.

Barfield, R. 1996 *Listening to Radio: 1920–1950*. Praeger, Westport, CT.

Barnhurst, K. and Nerone, J. 2001 *The Form of News: A History*. Guilford Press, New York.

Barnouw, E. 1966 *A Tower in Babel: A History of Broadcasting in the United States: Vol. 1. To 1933*. Oxford University Press, New York.

Barnouw, E. 1968 *The Golden Web: A History of Broadcasting in the United States: Vol. 2. 1933–1953*. Oxford University Press, New York.

Bentivegna, S. 2002 Politics and new media. In L. Lievrouw and S. Livingstone, eds. *Handbook of New Media: Social Shaping and Consequences of ICTs*. Sage, London, pp. 50–61.

Bird, W. 1999 *'Better Living': Advertising, Media, and the New Vocabulary of Business Leadership, 1935–1955*. Northwestern University Press, Evanston, IL.

Blumer, H. 1933 *Movies and Conduct*. Macmillan, New York.

Blumer, H. 1935 Moulding of mass behavior through the motion pictures. *American Sociological Society*, 29, pp. 115–127.

Blumer, H. and Hauser, P.M. 1933 *Movies, Delinquency and Crime*. Macmillan, New York.

Burchell, G., Gordon, C. and Miller, P., eds. 1991 *The Foucault Effect: Studies in Governmentality*. University of Chicago Press, Chicago.

Business announcement. 1896 *New York Times*, August 19, p. 2.

Butsch, R. 2000 *The Making of American Audiences*. Cambridge University Press, Cambridge.

Butsch, R. 2008 *The Citizen Audience: Crowds, Publics and Individuals*. Routledge, New York.

Calhoun, C. 1975 Nationalism and the public sphere. In J. Weintraub and K. Kumar, eds. *Public and Private in Thought and Practice*. University of Chicago Press, Chicago, pp. 75–102.

Calhoun, C., ed. 1992 *Habermas and the Public Sphere*. MIT Press, Cambridge, MA.

Cantril, H. 1941 *The Invasion from Mars: A Study in the Psychology of Panic*. Princeton University Press, Princeton, NJ.

Cantril, H. and Allport, G. 1935 *The Psychology of Radio*. Harper & Brothers, New York.

Curran, J. 2000 Rethinking media and democracy. In J. Curran and M. Gurevitch, eds. *Mass Media and Society*, 3rd ed. Arnold, London.

Dahlgren, P. 1995 *Television and the Public Sphere: Citizenship, Democracy and the Media*. Sage, London.

Dahlgren, P. 2003 Reconfiguring civic culture in the new media milieu. In J. Corner and D. Pels, eds., *Media and the Restyling of Politics*. Sage, London, pp. 151–170.

Dahlgren, P. and Sparks, C., eds. 1991 *Communication and Citizenship: Journalism and the Public Sphere*. Routledge, London.

Darnton R. 2000 An early information society: news and media in eighteenth-century Paris. *American Historical Review*, 105, 1, pp. 1–35.

Dayan, D. 2005 Paying attention to attention: audiences, publics, thresholds and genealogies. *Journal of Media Practices*, 6, 1, pp. 9–18.

Dewey, J. 1927 *The Public and Its Problems*. Henry Holt, New York.

Douglas, S. 1987 *Inventing American Broadcasting, 1899–1922*. Johns Hopkins University Press, Baltimore.

Downing, J. 2004 Audience publics and audience markets. In J. Downing, D. McQuail, P. Schlesinger, and E. Wartella, eds. *The Sage Handbook of Media Studies*. Sage, Thousand Oaks, CA, pp. 230–234.

Drotner, K., 2005 Media on the move: personalised media and the transformation of publicness. In S. Livingstone, ed. *Audiences and Publics: When Cultural Engagement Matters for the Public Sphere*. Intellect Press, Bristol, UK, pp. 187–212.

Eley, G. and Suny, R., eds. 1996 *Becoming National: A Reader*. Oxford University Press, Oxford.

Emirbayer, M. and Sheller, M. 1999 Publics in history. *Theory and Society*, 28, 1, pp. 145–197.

Ewen, S. 1996 *PR! A Social History of Spin*. Basic Books, New York.

Federal Communication Commission. 1946 *Public Service Responsibility of Broadcast Licensees*, March 7.

Gary, B. 1999 *The Nervous Liberals: Propaganda Anxieties from World War I to the Cold War*. Columbia University Press, New York.

Gertz, J.D. 2002 The purloined personality: consumer profiling in financial services. *San Diego Law Review*, 39, pp. 943–999.

Giner, S. 1976 *Mass Society*. Academic Press, New York.

Glickman, L. 2007 The consumer and the citizen in *Personal Influence*. In P. Simonson, ed. *Politics, Social Networks and the History of Mass Communication Research: Rereading Personal Influence*. Sage, Thousand Oaks, CA, pp. 205–212.

Grieveson, L. 2004 *Policing Cinema: Movies and Censorship in Early Twentieth-Century America*. University of California Press, Berkeley.

Habermas, J. 1989 *The Structural Transformation of the Public Sphere: An Inquiry into a Category of Bourgeois Society*. Trans. T. Burger. MIT Press, Cambridge, MA.

Hansen, M. 1993 Foreword. In O. Negt and A. Kluge, eds. *Public Sphere and Experience: Toward an Analysis of the Bourgeois and Proletarian Public Sphere*. Trans. P. Labanyi, J. Daniel and A. Oksiloff. Minnesota University Press, Minneapolis.

Hill, F. and Williams, W.E. 1941 *Radio's Listening Groups: The United States and Great Britain*. Columbia University Press, New York.

Isola, G. 1995 Italian radio: history and historiography. *Historical Journal of Film Radio and Television*, 15, 3.

Jenkins, H. and Thorburn, D., eds. 2003 *Democracy and New Media*. MIT Press, Cambridge, MA.

Jowett, G., Jarvie I. and Fuller, K. 1996 *Children and the Movies: Media Influence and the Payne Fund Controversy*. Cambridge University Press, Cambridge.

Katz, E. and Lazarsfeld. P. 1955 *Personal Influence: The Part Played by People in the Flow of Mass Communication*. Free Press, New York.

Lacey, K. 1996 *Feminine Frequencies: Gender, German Radio and the Public Sphere, 1923–1945*. University of Michigan Press, Ann Arbor.

Landes, J. 1988 *Women and the Public Sphere in the Age of the French Revolution*. Cornell University Press, Ithaca, NY.

Lazarsfeld, P. 1945 Who influences whom: it's the same for politics and advertising. *Printers Ink*, 211, 10, pp. 32–36.

Lazarsfeld, P., Berelson, B. and Gaudet, H. 1944 *The People's Choice: How the Voter Makes up His Mind in a Presidential Campaign*. Columbia University Press, New York.

Leach, E. 1989 Just atoms massed together: the evolution of mass society theory from Ortega y Gasset to Riesman and Mills. *Mid-America*, 71, pp. 31–49.

LeBon, G. 1898/1960 *The Crowd: A Study of the Popular Mind*. Viking Press, New York.

Levy, L. 1985 *Emergence of a Free Press*. Ivan Dee, Chicago.

Lippmann, W. 1920 *Liberty and the News*. Harcourt, Brace, New York.

Livingstone, S, ed. 2005 *Audiences and Publics: When Cultural Engagement Matters for the Public Sphere*. Intellect, Bristol, UK.

Lynch, M. 2005 *Voices of the New Arab Public*. Columbia University Press, New York.

Lynd, R. and Merrill Lynd, H. 1929 *Middletown: A Study in American Culture*. Harcourt Brace, New York.

Maltby, R. 1993 The production code and the Hays Office. In T. Balio, ed. *Grand Design: Hollywood as a Modern Business Enterprise, 1930–1939*. University of California Press, Berkeley, pp. 37–72.

McCarthy, A. 2005 Governing by television? Public service films and the early TV archive. *Montage/AV*, 14, 1. Retrieved from http://www.montage-av.de/a_2005_1_14.html

Mill, J.S. 1958 *Considerations on Representative Government*. Bobbs-Merrill, Indianapolis, IN.

Mossberger, K., Tolbert, C. and McNeal, R. 2008 *Digital Citizenship: The Internet, Society and Participation*. MIT Press, Cambridge MA.

Münsterberg, H. 1970 *The Film: A Psychological Study*. Dover, New York.

Morgan, E. 1989 *Inventing the People: The Rise of Popular Sovereignty in England and America*. Norton, New York.

Negt, O. and Kluge, A., eds. 1993 *Public Sphere and Experience: Toward an Analysis of the Bourgeois and Proletarian Public Sphere*. Trans. P. Labanyi, J. Daniel and A. Oksiloff. University of Minnesota Press, Minneapolis.

Nerone, J. 1994 *Violence against the Press: Policing the Public Sphere in US History*. Oxford University Press, New York.

Nightingale, V. and Dwyer, T. 2006 The audience politics of 'enhanced' television formats. *International Journal of Media and Cultural Politics*, 2, 1, pp. 25–42.

Park, R. 1955 News as a form of knowledge, and news and the power of the press. In R. E. Park. *Collected Papers of Robert Ezra Park: Vol. 3. Society*. Free Press, Glencoe, IL.

Park, R. 1972 *The Crowd and the Public*. University of Chicago Press, Chicago.

Pateman, C. 1989 *The Disorder of Women*. Stanford University Press, Stanford, CA.

Pinkerton, A. 2008 Radio and the Raj: broadcasting in British India, 1920–1940. *Journal of the Royal Asiatic Society*, 18, 2, pp. 167–191.

Polic, J. and Gandy, O. 1991 The emergence of the marketplace standard. *Journal of Media Law and Practice*, 12, pp. 55–64.

Ryfe, D. 2001 From media audience to media public: a study of letters written in reaction to FDR's fireside chats. *Media, Culture & Society*, 23, 6, pp. 767–781.

Simonson, P. 2007 *Politics, Social Networks and the History of Mass Communication Research: Rereading Personal Influence*. Sage, Thousand Oaks, CA.

Summers, H. 1971 *A Thirty Year History of Radio Programs, 1926–1956*. Arno, New York.

Swingewood, A. 1977 *The Myth of Mass Culture*. Humanities Press, Atlantic Highlands, NJ.

Tarde, G. 1969 The public and the crowd, and opinion and conversation. In T. Clark, ed. *On Communication and Social Influence*. University of Chicago Press, Chicago.

Tilly, C. 2004 *Social Movements 1768–2004*. Paradigm, Boulder CO.

US Congress. 1954 *Network Broadcasting: Report of the Committee on Interstate and Foreign Commerce*, Eighty Fifth Congress, Second Session. Government Printing Office, Washington, DC.

Warner, M. 1990 *The Letters of the Republic: Publication and the Public Sphere in Eighteenth Century America*. Harvard University Press, Cambridge, MA.

Weintraub, J. and Kumar, K., eds. 1997 *Public and Private in Thought and Practice*. University of Chicago Press, Chicago.

Williams, R. 1960 *Culture and Society 1780–1950*. Columbia University Press, New York.

Wu, Y. 2007 Blurring boundaries in a 'cyber-greater China': are internet bulletin boards constructing the public sphere in China? In R. Butsch, ed. *Media and Public Spheres*. Palgrave, London.

Zaret, D. 2000 *Origins of Democratic Culture: Printing, Petitions, and the Public Sphere in Early-Modern England*. Princeton University Press, Princeton, NJ.

8

The Implied Audience of Communications Policy Making
Regulating Media in the Interests of Citizens and Consumers

Sonia Livingstone and Peter Lunt

Changing Regulatory Regimes and the Implied Audience

Most books with "audiences" as their subject matter do not, it must be said, address media policy and regulation, so the reader of this chapter may already be puzzled by our title. To take one prominent example, Abercrombie and Longhurst (1998) insightfully delineated the changing nature of audiences and audience research over the twentieth century, noting the near demise of the effects tradition (at least in Britain), the (short-lived) celebration of audience resistance, the rise of viewing as spectacle, the guerrilla actions of fans, and the diffused nature of today's diversified, socially embedded audiences. But they show little interest in contemporaneous changes in public service provision, media ownership, the global media economy, relations among media and state, the digital revolution, or, our focus here, regimes of regulation. On the other hand, in their contemporaneous volume on media policy, McQuail and Siune (1998) made little reference to research on audiences, although implicitly the audience is everywhere – in their inquiry into the role of citizens in a mediated democracy, the future of the masses in an individualized society, the prospects for national cultures under globalization, the role

The Handbook of Media Audiences, First Edition. Edited by Virginia Nightingale.
© 2014 John Wiley & Sons, Ltd. Published 2014 by John Wiley & Sons, Ltd.

of users in an interactive media landscape, and the protection of public service principles in liberalized media markets.

The policy landscape seems to have been bracketed off by audience researchers as practical rather than intellectual, parochial rather than grand in vision, and, most problematic, positivist (or administrative) rather than critical in purpose. Policy research has returned the favor. But in a context where almost everything is mediated, with little escaping the ubiquitous embrace of the digital age, we invite audience researchers to rethink their (dis)engagement with policy debates and to and engage theoretically, empirically, and critically with the national and international management of powerful media and communications institutions and processes. Some audience researchers do recognize the relation between policy and power. Ruddock's *Investigating Audiences* (2007) reads audience reception studies through the lens of such policy-relevant issues as harmful media content and the democratic potential of new technology, though he does not engage directly with the specific policies which research may either support or critique. Having reviewed the reception tradition, Nightingale (1996) follows Foucault in concluding that "for policy research, examination of the audience-industry relation as a technology of production, by means of which audience-text links are produced as marketable commodities, would seem a necessary beginning" (p. 149).

At least two recent trends link the study of audiences with media policy. Developments in public sphere theory and the revival of interest in civil society invite a rethinking of the connections among media, audiences (or publics), and public policy in order to find a positive response to the growing democratic deficit in Western countries. This has drawn a number of critical audience researchers into focused consideration of how policy may enshrine, or undermine, the communicative requirements of democratic engagement (e.g. Dahlgren 2004). Second, the confrontation of globalization theory with localized audience research (e.g. Liebes and Katz 1990) triggered recognition of "glocalization" on a far wider cultural scale than usually reached by audience theory (Tomlinson 1999). Indeed, belated recognition that global audiences are "big business" has stimulated attempts to move beyond Dallas Smythe's scathing, post–Frankfurt school critique of the commodified audience and to transcend the sterile opposition between cultural and political economy approaches to audiences (consider Buckingham 2000; Butsch 2000; Hagen and Wasko 2000; Seiter 2005).

These trends, in turn, invite some rethinking of the perception of policy-relevant research as practical, parochial, and positivist, especially since policy research often addresses audience-relevant themes – tastes and pleasures, harm and offense, the public interest, communication rights, consumption practices and contexts, and so forth. In seeking "to restore a sense of agency and politics to a process often described in rather technical and administrative terms," and so to advocate the critical and participatory principles of inclusiveness, legitimacy, public engagement, and the dispersal of power, Freedman (2008, p. 217) quotes Hesmondhalgh's conceptualization of media policy as the "common concern with collective subjectivity" (2005, p. 95). Whether or not all policy researchers concur with this definition, it suggests an agenda that critical audience studies could endorse, one that should not be left solely to the macro theory of economy or political science nor to administrative and market researchers.

To pursue this, we propose a twin strategy: first, to identify and critique the implied audience of communications policy making; and, second, to draw on the insights of critical audience studies to reshape that implied audience so it reflects the concepts and findings of academic audience research and, importantly, so that it enables mediated citizen interests and communication rights. In so doing, we hope to identify an alternative to the approach of Foucault-inspired "governmentality" theorists who regard "the audience" as a construct developed by industry and the state for their own purposes (Ang 1996; Ouellette and Hay 2008), and, further, who regard academic audience research as complicit in a vocabulary that seeks to contain and govern audiences. In other words, while recognizing that the concept of the audience is indeed problematically mobilized in the conduct of commercial and regulatory practices, we wish to explore the possibility that critical scholars need not turn their back on audiences per se but, rather, can avoid enrollment in these governmental processes by first critiquing institutional discourses and interests and, second, developing an alternative and critical account of audiences and their interests.

Thus this chapter explores whether the insights and findings of academic audience research can be used to analyze, critique, and engage with communications policy making. We take as our point of entry the *implied audience*, a term by which we mean to make explicit the commonplace but often unnoticed and, arguably, ungrounded assumptions that get mobilized in policy discourses about how people ordinarily relate to media and communications (Livingstone 1998). Unlike some of the explicitly contested elements in policy debates – the role of the state or the market, public service broadcasting, or the regulation of the press, to name but a few – the role of the audiences is little focused upon. As Webster and Phalen (1994) observe, "[A] review of the policymaking process does not reveal clearly articulated, systematically applied audience paradigms" (p. 19). But this does not, however, render implicit assumptions about audiences innocuous, for they influence both provision and the regulation of provision (Born 2004; Syvertsen 2004).

We write in the wake of the formation in the United Kingdom of a converged regulator, the Office of Communications (Ofcom), by the 2003 Communications Act. Ofcom's design as a principled, (almost) sector-wide regulator, established by act of Parliament and funded by industry to replace multiple regulators of diverse provenance and practices, was widely welcomed as a constructive response to the emerging challenges of a converged, global media market. Its primary duty – to further the interests of citizens and consumers, along with responsibilities in relation to public service broadcasting, universal service provision for broadband, the management of spectrum, and much more, with an intriguing addition of the promotion of media literacy – gave rise to new hopes and a perhaps unprecedented level of policy engagement and activism among critics, civil society groups, media reformers, and academics (Lunt and Livingstone, 2012).

Writing 20 years ago, Seymour-Ure (1987) scathingly described the confusion that was British media policy as "Now you see it, now you don't," listing a litany of regulatory inconsistencies across the media landscape, itself ill defined. The implication was that a sector-wide consistency is desirable, as was also echoed 10 years later by Collins and Murroni's (1996) update on the continuing multiplication of regulators and regulatory ineffectiveness. It may therefore seem surprising, the next decade having brought Britain a converged approach, that some now doubt the value of a single all-powerful regulator (Harvey 2006) and more have become critical of Ofcom's processes and achievements (Freedman 2008; Hardy 2008).

In a recent project, the "Public Understanding of Regimes of Risk Regulation," we examined how complex risks faced by the public are being addressed by changing regimes of regulation (Livingstone and Lunt 2007). These are changing not just because of technological and market developments in the media and communications sector, but also in response to wider political moves away from the social contract of welfare liberalism, moves that seek to disperse the power of the state upward (from nation to international organizations) and downward (to the third sector, or civil society, to a self-regulated private sector and to individual households; Black 2002; Jessop 2002; Clarke, Newman, and Smith 2007; Lunt and Livingstone 2007). Specifically, we asked, on the one hand, how the public is represented within the new culture of regulation, and, on the other hand, how the public understands its changing role and responsibility within communications and financial service regulatory regimes, with the latter potentially influencing personal responses to communications and financial risks. Thus we traced how Ofcom represents the interests of the public (audiences, and also those excluded from particular audiences), undertakes consumer education, and engages with stakeholders (including audiences). These are all regulatory roles for which critics have long called (e.g. Blumler and Hoffman-Riem 1992), but they require the regulator to achieve a complex, arguably even impossible, balance between economic regulation, consumer protection, and furthering citizen interests.

In practice, we observed Ofcom's predominant focus on market regulation, thus prioritizing a conception of the public as media-savvy consumers who demand quality, choice, diversity, and value anytime, anywhere. This audience-as-consumer can usefully highlight certain problems arising from technical and market innovations – for example, in the case of broadband, problems of digital illiteracy and digital exclusion. But, unlike alternative conceptions of audience-as-citizen, which we explore below, the consumer model does not pose any fundamental challenge to the "normal business" of what is, after all, primarily conceived as an economic regulator. It particularly struggles to assert any collective legitimacy for the public interest, public service, or public rights. And nor, despite considerable policy anxiety over the emerging array of risks facing ordinary people – newly worried about as the digitally excluded, the offended or misrepresented, the vulnerable or victimized, or the targets of new scams or privacy invasions – can the consumer model satisfactorily redress what Beck (1986/2005) has termed "the individualisation of risk," namely, that the navigational (or decision-making) task for the public gets ever harder, if potentially also more rewarding, while the risk of getting things wrong or of being left out falls as unequally as ever.

One might ask who should speak for audiences and publics here. To be sure, audiences occasionally represent their own interests in what are, at times, public-facing, transparent, and consultative regulatory deliberations. More often, their concerns are revealed through the controlled routes of customer care and complaint procedures, with some use of democratic channels such as protests to their Member of Parliament or participation in activist groups. Ironically, it seems that it is those media organizations and regulators whose interests may precisely conflict with "the public interest," who, nonetheless, have the resources to speak on behalf of the audience through the commission and conduct of substantial amounts of market or social research. As a result, it appears that, in the plethora of contemporary multistakeholder deliberations that Benhabib (1996, p.76) describes as "mutually interlocking and overlapping networks and associations of deliberation, contestation and argumentation," audiences are less often participant than co-opted, less heard than spoken for.

Although our immediate focus is British policy, discussions with colleagues internationally suggest that the various ways in which we have observed audience-related issues to come to the fore in policy debates have wider resonance, not least because, in a globalizing media landscape, neoliberal regulatory regimes are increasingly influential. In what follows, we outline two recent case studies in order to develop the argument for a critical academic engagement with policy making: one concerns the fraught and largely unsuccessful attempts of academics and civil society groups to get citizens' communication rights onto the policy agenda; and the other concerns the more successful efforts to promote media literacy, this ironically resulting in a policy that is both more modest and more easily co-opted in its claim to audience "empowerment."

Audiences as Citizens or Consumers? The Communication Rights Debate

In our first case study, we examine how the duty given to Ofcom to regulate in the interests of citizens and consumers came about during the passing of the Communications Act and has, subsequently, been debated. From our perspective as audience researchers, this debate has taken the form of a contest between two different conceptions of the public as audience – as citizen and as consumer – with both state and regulator variously cast as playing the role of mediator. Since the role of the regulator in furthering the interests of consumers is, in fact little contested, this debate more fundamentally forces onto the policy agenda the role of media and communications in enabling or impeding the interests of citizens in a democracy. While for media and communications scholars this raises complex and long-discussed questions about participation, civil society, and the public sphere, the regulator debates tend to distill key arguments in a highly focused manner but with a still-uncertain outcome that reflects the fragility of emancipatory democratic agendas in this field.

This case study is best introduced through a necessarily abbreviated narrative of events leading to the passing of the act, focused on a sequence of discursive struggles in which any reference to the interests of citizens was very nearly dropped (Puttnam 2006; Livingstone, Lunt, and Miller 2007a). We begin, perhaps arbitrarily, in December 2000, when the Communications White Paper was published which first proposed a converged regulator for, it stated, the benefit of consumers (by ensuring choice and value for money) and citizens (by ensuring standards, fairness, and privacy). After a period of consultation, debate, and, no doubt, lobbying, the Draft Communications Bill of May 2002 proposed that Ofcom should further the interests of customers of broadcasting and telecommunications services – no mention of either citizens or consumers. The public debate was, in consequence, greatly intensified, and in July 2002, Lord Puttnam's Joint Select Committee concluded a wide-ranging public consultation by rejecting the customer of the Draft Bill and recommending that Ofcom should have two principal duties – to further the interests of citizens and of consumers.

Doubtless in recognition of this struggle over the very terms by which ordinary people could be legally referred to, a "note on terminology" was jointly issued by the then Departments of Trade and Industry, and Culture, Media and Sport. This explained that the consumer interest referred to an economic focus on networks and services for the benefit of individuals; by contrast, the citizen interest referred to a cultural focus on content for the benefit of the community. In Ofcom's proposed (and eventual) institutional structure, these "twin peaks" of the public interest in communications were built into the institutional design of the regulator through the establishment of the quasi-independent Consumer Panel and the internal Content Board respectively. But, surprising to many, the Communications Bill of November 2002, Clause 3 (General duties of Ofcom) specified only that Ofcom was "to further the interests of consumers in relevant markets, where appropriate by promoting competition" – any mention of the citizen had again disappeared. A heated debate in the House of Lords followed in June 2003, with Lord Puttnam leading the case for the citizen interest against the government. In a triumph for civil society advocates – who had coordinated their activities under the banner of a body called "Public Voice" – Blair's Labour government lost the vote, despite its arguments that the citizen interest is already covered by the consumer interest, that the citizen is not a term that can appear in any UK law for it refers only to immigration status, and that this is all an unnecessary semantic distraction for everyone should trust Ofcom to do the right thing.

Thus in July 2003, the Communications Act was passed, requiring Ofcom "to further the interests of citizens in relation to communications matters; and to further the interests of consumers in relevant markets, where appropriate by promoting competition." Yet any victory was short-lived. As Black (2002) argues, the letter of the law is meaningful only through its interpretation, and a frustrated Ofcom immediately reinterpreted the Act by framing its mission statement thus: "Ofcom exists to further the interests of citizen-consumers through a regulatory regime which, where appropriate, encourages competition." This positioned Ofcom primarily as an economic regulator by, first, conjoining citizen and consumer as the citizen-consumer, and, second, foregrounding competition as the primary instrument to further the interests of both. Although widely contested (Redding 2005), this hyphenated formulation has only recently rather quietly disappeared from Ofcom's walls, reports, and website – itself extraordinary, as no publicly available minutes of the Board record a decision to change its mission.

More important than the mission statement, however, are Ofcom's actions. Ofcom rapidly established institutional structures and roles relating to consumer policy: it publicly reported its progress in meeting consumer concerns, it adopted a "consumer toolkit" developed by the Consumer Panel to ensure that consumer interests are taken into account at all stages in policy development, and it established a range of public-facing initiatives to offer advice to consumers directly. Strikingly, little equivalent activity or accountability was forthcoming regarding actions to further citizen interests. Repeated requests from academics and civil society groups to define and report on Ofcom's efforts to further the citizen interests received little response. Moreover, Ofcom's policy documents persistently confuse its duties, scattered with haphazard references to "consumers" (mainly), "citizen-consumers" (until recently), "citizens and consumers" (though generally in relation to consumer issues), and, just occasionally and not always appropriately, "citizens."

An example is its 2007 document, *Taking Account of Consumer and Citizen Interest: Progress and Evaluation – 12 Months On*. This elides the twin duties into one by stating, "Ofcom has a principal duty to further the interests of both citizens and consumers," and then provides a wealth of information regarding consumer-related activities. As for citizens, to paraphrase Seymour-Ure, it seems a case of "Now you see it, now you don't." The report outlines a planning process aiming "to develop a framework which Ofcom can use to prioritize and plan its consumer policy programme of work and response appropriately to consumer interest related demands." This is implemented through projects aiming "to develop a consistent and coherent framework to ensure citizen and consumer interests are taken into account appropriately throughout Ofcom's policy and decision making processes." The outcomes are then communicated in order "to ensure we articulate and communicate our decisions in a way that allows consumers to understand our decisions and explains what the outcomes are for citizens and consumers." Such inconsistencies are explained away in Ofcom's Consumer Policy Statement of December

2006, where it is stated that "consumer and citizen interests are closely related and that for many people, the distinction is not very important" (p. 8). It also stated, "Citizen-related policy is concerned with changing market outcomes in order to meet broader social, cultural or economic objectives" (p. 8). But this frames the citizen interest reductively as an intervention in the market or a response to market failure, and it omits from the list of (undefined) broader objectives that which to most observers is key, namely, the civic or political.

Belatedly in July 2008, Ofcom put out for consultation a discussion paper entitled *Citizens, Communications and Convergence*. As it said, "The purpose of this paper is to discuss and clarify Ofcom's role in furthering the interests of citizens. It sets out our thinking on this issue and we hope that it stimulates debate." Noting that "the fact that we have not published an equivalent statement on citizens has led some stakeholders to suggest that Ofcom lacks commitment in discharging its responsibilities in this area" (p. 4), the paper documents how Ofcom has, in practice, furthered the citizen interest in some key ways: public service broadcasting has been at the top of the agenda for the past five years; the question of universal service for broadband is rising up the agenda; community radio has been strengthened by Ofcom's efforts; and its digital dividend review, digital inclusion, and media literacy strategies, among others, have all furthered the citizen interest. But as Chair of the Content Board Philip Graf said to the civil society group Voice of the Listener and Viewer, these and other activities result in "a bit of a laundry list." What is still lacking is a coherent and principled framework for scoping, underpinning and extending the citizen interest in communications matters.

It is unclear that Ofcom possesses the necessary vision for such a framework, for it stated in the consultation that "we tend to think of a market as a vibrant, enticing place where consumers interact, but there is not an equivalent metaphor for the way that citizens interact in civil society" (p. 8). The "we" of this claim may be unfamiliar to those who have suffered from the credit crunch, fuel poverty, or even mobile phone scams. The excitement of the market is surely also foreign to those who fear the might of Rupert Murdoch, the end of regional television news, or the future for indigenous children's drama. Furthermore, those excited by prospects for democracy can indeed think of some engaging metaphors – consider the vibrancy of the Athenian public sphere or, in today's version, of the blogosphere. Here, surely, was an opportunity for scholars of the public sphere, of citizen activism and participatory democracy to advise the media regulator. But there were only 25 responses (few compared with many Ofcom consultations), of which eight were from individuals (one or two of whom self-described as campaigners), four from industry, four from groups advocating local or community television, two (or three – classifying such organizations is not always straightforward) from civil society groups specializing in media matters, two from academics (including the first author of this chapter, though some of the civil society responses were written by academics), and one each from Ofcom's Consumer Panel, the British Humanist Association, the Communication Workers' Union, a Councillor, and Friends of the

Lake District (concerned with the environmental impact of ill-regulated cables and overhead wires).

There is no space here to detail the nature of these responses, though we draw on some of them below in concluding this section. Beyond the obvious paucity of academic input, it is also noteworthy that several of the responses – particularly those from industry and from individuals – offered little or no comment on the "citizen interest" at all, instead treating the consultation as an occasion to advance their own agendas (silent calls, complaints about telephone number systems, broadcast transmission, etc.). Intriguingly, the Broadband Stakeholders Group advocated citizen over consumer interests since the latter generate bureaucratic regulations on industry (designed to protect individuals), whereas the public interest in the long term, they implied, is best served by encouraging (i.e. deregulating for) investment and innovation. British Telecommunications plc focused on the citizen interest in establishing a universal service obligation for broadband – one would not disagree, but again self-interest dictates the plea, in bold and italics, that in future "BT and its customers are not constrained in improving its services by more regulation." Several months after the consultation closed, little had resulted, although Ofcom's website promises for all consultations that "[t]he team in charge of the consultation will review all the responses we have received. They will then prepare a summary for our board or another group responsible for making the relevant decision. We usually aim to produce this summary within 2 weeks of the consultation closing." In the present case, therefore, it appears that Ofcom has little interest in this consultation, consistent with its tendency to prioritize consumer issues over citizenship issues.

More importantly, the challenge remains of defining citizenship interests and articulating an appropriate regulatory policy for furthering these interests as well as addressing the relative lack of public engagement in debates over regulatory policy. Our second case study, by contrast, examines a rather more successful area of policy, one where definitions abound and research is expanding exponentially. Nonetheless, viewed critically, this apparent success may offer little more to the fundamental cause of advancing audiences' interests.

Audiences as Empowered or Vulnerable? The Media Literacy Debate

In the United Kingdom, the media and communication regulator, Ofcom, broke new ground when it gained, unwillingly, the legal duty to "promote media literacy" in the Communications Act 2003. Since media literacy was not defined in the Act, an early task was that of definitions. Doubtless many advised at this point; and one of the present authors made an early decision, political as well as intellectual, to advocate a simple but broad definition to Ofcom (Livingstone

2003), following this up by attending meetings, events, and responding to public consultations instigated by the regulator (and, subsequently, by the European Commission). The definition offered was that framed by the National Leadership Conference on Media Literacy a decade earlier and widely adopted since – the ability "to access, analyse, evaluate and communicate messages in a variety of forms" (Aufderheide 1993). This appeared effective, for in first consultation on the subject, Ofcom's document, "Strategy and Priorities for the Promotion of Media Literacy," stated,

> So media literacy is a range of skills including the ability to access, analyse, evaluate and produce communications in a variety of forms. Or put simply, the ability to operate the technology to find what you are looking for, to understand that material, to have an opinion about it and where necessary to respond to it. With these skills people will be able to exercise greater choice and be able better to protect themselves and their families from harmful or offensive materials. (p. 4)

There are several interesting points about this statement. First, a simple definition (the first sentence) is framed as too complex and, thus, further simplified in the second sentence, hailing the common sense of the reader ("you") to dispel possible criticism. Second, this restatement significantly waters down the breadth of the first (and of the original): "ability" has become "a range of skills" (a translation that enables quantitative evaluation of policy effectiveness), "communicate messages" has become "produce communications" (arguably a shift from the interactive process of communication to the one-way process of sending messages "out there"), and "access" (which many now conceive in terms of navigational and interpretative competences) has become "operate the technology," communicating back to others is qualified as "where necessary." And, third, the overall purposes of media literacy are radically scaled back (in the third sentence) to center on consumer choice and protection from harm.

Ofcom's work on media literacy has been shaped by its operating principles as a regulator which include the need to consult, the statutory requirement to appoint consumer representatives to the consumer panel, to promote and conduct research into public attitudes and to promote public debate on communications issues. Consequently, over the past five years, Ofcom has provided a forum for researchers across the academy, industry, and third sector to debate media literacy issues, and has conducted a substantial body of new and valuable empirical research. However, it pays more attention to the access and use elements of its definition than to either evaluation or creation, and tends to frame media literacy as a matter of overcoming individual barriers to access or choice in the media environment rather than enhancing individual and collective opportunities to use diverse media platforms for creation, participation, or critical evaluation. This is, no doubt, consistent with expectations to be held of a largely economic regulator. So too is its evident preference for easily quantifiable measures of media literacy (e.g. can people activate the interactive button on the remote control; can they check the recency of a website; do they know who to complain to if content offends them?) over more ambitious conceptions of media literacy (e.g. does the use of digital media mean that more people are scrutinizing government, that global misunderstandings are being renegotiated, or that marginalized identities can now be expressed and valorized?).

Since governments and regulators in other countries are observing Ofcom's forays into this field rather carefully, apparently no longer content to leave media literacy to their ministries of education, a critical gaze at Ofcom's practice – especially its potential subordination of emancipatory to protectionist and, apparently, deregulatory objectives – is merited. It appears that the British debate has influenced the European one closely following on its heels. In the key legal framework in this sector, the European Commission's Audiovisual Media Services Directive (AVMS, approved by the EC in November 2007 as a revision of the Television without Frontiers Directive), media literacy is defined in strikingly similar terms to those of Ofcom above:

> Media literacy refers to skills, knowledge and understanding that allow consumers to use media effectively and safely. Media-literate people will be able to exercise informed choices, understand the nature of content and services and take advantage of the full range of opportunities offered by new communications technologies. They will be better able to protect themselves and their families from harmful or offensive material.

In this definition, critics will note, media literacy is wholly individualized, prioritizing consumers and consumer choice over citizens and citizens' rights, and prioritizing protection over participation. Similarly, the European Commission's definition of media literacy repeats that of Ofcom (and of the National Leadership Conference) except that it omits the crucial element of "creating" messages and it downplays communication to a personal rather than, say, a civic matter. Thus it defines media literacy as

> the ability to access, analyse and evaluate the power of images, sounds and messages which we are now being confronted with on a daily basis and are an important part of our contemporary culture, as well as to communicate competently in media available on a personal basis. Media literacy relates to all media, including television and film, radio and recorded music, print media, the Internet and other new digital communication technologies.

Yet content creation and interactive communication are not optional extras – in a digital world, these are central to informed opinion, freedom of expression, and the democratic right to participate and be heard. Just as writing was more contested and regulated than was reading in the nineteenth century, it seems that creating will be more contested compared with receiving content in the twenty-first century. Shouldn't more of the audience researchers currently fascinated by technological affordances that enable people not only to be active but also interactive, writing and rewriting texts via fanzines, blogs, editing software, digital storytelling, and so forth, now be defending these activities as rights that require some complex societal support beyond the capacity of individuals to provide – from copyright freedoms to editing expertise?

Against this background, alternative definitions of literacy are struggling to be heard. Notably, the European Charter for Media Literacy has been significantly informed by academics and media reform advocates. It identifies seven competences for media literate people, including all four elements of "access," "analyse," "evaluate," and "create," and it emphasizes social as well as individual benefits and civic as well as expressive dimensions of "creation," while also encompassing the exercise of informed cultural choice and the avoidance of harm (Bachmair and Bazalgette 2007). A similar balance between emancipation and protection is evident in statements on media literacy from the Council of Europe and UNESCO. The latter states,

> Empowerment of people through information and media literacy is an important prerequisite for fostering equitable access to information and knowledge, and building inclusive knowledge societies. Information and media literacy enables people to interpret and make informed judgments as users of information and media, as well as to become skillful creators and producers of information and media messages in their own right.

Since these bodies concur in their ambitious definitions – stressing equity, inclusiveness, participation, and critique at a societal as well as individual level, and the requirements on institutional providers and state actors as well as skilled individuals – it is all the more striking that the European Commission apparently does not. It is hard to escape the conclusion that while emancipation is a popular rhetoric, the hidden agenda of media literacy policy is, more simply, minimizing individual risks and maximizing consumer skills so as to legitimate industry deregulation. Consider this statement by the United Kingdom's then Minister of State for Culture, Media and Sport, Tessa Jowell, "If people can take greater personal responsibility for what they watch and listen to, that will in itself lessen the need for regulatory intervention" (2004, p. 23). Robin Foster, Ofcom's Partner for Strategy and Market Developments in 2005, put it similarly when he said, "We will have to learn to rely more on markets than ever before. And we need to rely more on individual consumers and on companies exercising responsibility in those markets, with increasing emphasis on self-regulation and co-regulation" (quoted in Livingstone, Lunt, and Miller 2007b). Or, last, note Ofcom's statement to the European Commission consultation on media literacy in 2006, that "media literacy is increasingly becoming a fundamental component of European and national regulatory policy agendas in the communications sector, especially as developments in the creation and distribution of content challenge current approaches to regulation in this area". Media literacy, one may conclude, is being co-opted by a neoliberal politics for reasons quite distinct from those for which academics and educators have long advocated it.

In short, it can be argued that media literacy is prominent on the policy agenda because increasing consumer knowledge and awareness is held to advance the goal of economic competition by legitimating the reduction of top-down regulatory intervention in a converging and globalizing media market while simultaneously sustaining a promise (rarely evaluated in terms of outcomes) of "empowerment" to the public. In Isaiah Berlin's terms, regulating for negative freedoms (most notably, reducing restrictions on industry and increasing choice for consumers) seems more favored by governments than regulating for positive freedoms, such as ensuring a democratically engaged polity. If this argument is accepted, it becomes less surprising that media literacy is prominent on the policy agenda of Western governments. As the EC's Information Society and Media Commissioner Viviane Reding said in a 2007 speech, "Everyone (old and young) needs to get to grips with the new digital world in which we live. For this, continuous information and education is more important than regulation."

A newly responsible, self-regulating audience is, it appears, being called for in these proclamations (Ouellette and Hay 2008), a key new player (albeit more spoken for than heard) in the emerging multistakeholder regime regulating twenty-first-century European media and communication policy. This implied audience provides a vital component in efforts to reduce state regulation and increase industry self-regulation (e.g. through the promotion of codes of conduct, editorial principles, technical solutions for the user, access controls, notice and takedown procedures, and so on). As we noted in the first case study, again the costs for the individual in this regime shift are little articulated, although Ofcom's 2006 EC consultation response (p. 4) does acknowledge that, "these schemes rely for their effectiveness on consumers actively taking measures to protect themselves and their families." But if they do not – if people do not become dutiful and sensible consumers (and audience researchers surely know that people are diverse, sometimes resistant, and, most important, motivated by life course goals and everyday contingencies more than government agendas) – it is unclear who bears the responsibility for any adverse consequences. It seems likely, from previous research on knowledge gaps, the digital divide, and cycles of disadvantage, that the burden of risk will fall most heavily on those least able to bear it.

Public policy struggles face two tasks: one is to effect change for the better, the other – King Canute like – is to hold back change for the worse. If, for the moment, one defines "better" and "worse" as perceived by actors themselves, one might conclude that, thus far, the emancipatory approach to media literacy has achieved moderate success in defining and extending policy definitions of media literacy and in critiquing, if not holding back, some of the most reductionist approaches. But it has had little practical impact so far in mobilizing new initiatives or effective programs of implementation that go beyond the commerce-led aims of media literacy as either protection (which thereby also, often inadvertently, clears the way for further market deregulation) or empowerment defined minimally as acquiring the skill set expected of modern consumers. The protectionist approach has done better – parents and teachers are now largely aware of online risks, many consumers use technical tools to control their access to potentially harmful or offensive contents, signposting commercial and offensive content is at least on the industry's agenda, self-regulatory content codes are being agreed, and efforts are underway to extend digital literacy to the young, the poor, and the elderly.

But it must be said that little headway has been made in advancing a conception of media literacy, long advocated by critical audience scholars, that, on the one hand, draws on existing knowledge of audiences as – if and when conditions are right – creative, critical, social, civic, ludic, and imaginative, and, on the other hand, characterizes media literacy in terms of some ambitious purposes for our highly mediated society. These purposes may be stated in summary as, first, enabling equality of opportunity in the knowledge society, which requires overcoming digital inequality and exclusion; second, active and informed participation in a revitalized democracy which requires critical engagement with the mediated public sphere; and, third, self-actualization for individuals and communities, achieved through enabling the lifelong learning, cultural expression, and personal fulfillment that is everyone's right in a civilized society. What such ambitions would require for their realization, in relation to media literacy specifically and the digital media landscape more generally is, we suggest, a question that should be of concern to audience researchers (among others) everywhere.

Re-imagining the Audience – in Whose Interest?

In this chapter, we have written as audience researchers more than as policy experts, but as audience researchers whose sensibilities have recently been exercised by "the audience" as imagined, usually implicitly but still influentially, by policy makers and policy advisors spanning academia, regulators, commerce, civil society, and the state. We have found it problematic that, when policy debates draw on audience research, it tends to be that produced by market or social organizations (think tanks, regulators, and the like) rather than critical academic research. It is also problematic that, despite the mantra of evidence-based policy, much policy deliberation – including within the academy – does not see beyond, or question, the implied audience, often because its focus is on the regulation of *provision* (a top-down perspective) rather than on regulating the *mediation* of social relations – both hierarchical and heterarchical, including individual/state, market/state, community, and local/global. We agree with Raboy et al. (2001, p. 97) that "at the intersection of policy studies and audience studies lie different approaches to a common problem" – the former taking a normative and the latter a descriptive approach to the relation between media and audiences or publics. Yet the normative rests, implicitly if not explicitly, on descriptive accounts of this relation, just as normative ideals may underpin the critical framing of empirical audience research.

Making the implied audience in policy deliberations visible is, therefore, a critical task for audience researchers. What does, and should, policy expect of audiences? Are they reductively conceived as mere receivers of provision, benevolent or otherwise? Have they responsibilities? Or skills? Is regulation influenced by or even undermined by critical audiences? If they exit without voice, where does that leave provision claimed to be "in the public interest"? Does policy permit them the opportunity to adjudicate on whether their rights (cultural recognition, freedom of expression, freedom from harm, plurality of views, privacy, and freedom from commercial exploitation) are being met? If they can participate, is this as members of civil society or, more minimally, as complaining consumers? Are they addressed as an aggregate or a collective, as a national or global, local or fragmented body, as mere receivers or as also creators of content? As we see it, much media policy scholarship has not yet grasped the import of critical audience studies, in which each of these activities on the part of audiences – and their implications for power, agency and subjectivity – has been thoughtfully explored.

Furthermore, audience researchers themselves may engage in policy debates through diverse routes – working as consultants or in collaboration with policy makers, as members of civil society organizations who may contest regulators' claims to represent audiences' interests, as producers of independent studies of audiences which may challenge the knowledge claims of regulators, as contributors to public consultations and other deliberative processes, and as critical commentators working within the academy itself. However, this diversity of forms of engagement is perhaps not matched by academics' actual level of engagement.

One must also consider critically when and why opportunities to engage arise. The evident crisis in citizenship participation, trust and authority is one reason. Another appears to be because the neoliberal agenda demands new individualized approaches to governance and risk management that, more than ever, have direct implications for, and rely on empirical work with, audiences themselves. For example, in rethinking how to fund public service broadcasting in an age of digital convergence, policy makers prefer to rest their judgments on what audiences appear to want (and what industry is prepared to pay for) rather than on what society may have a right to expect. To take another example, in determining policy for content regulation on the internet, policy makers seek to gauge parents' competence in guiding their children or to evaluate the effectiveness of technical tools for child protection rather than to build consensus regarding "community standards" or work to negotiate legal, moral, or cultural norms. Last, one must be skeptical about the chances of being listened to as an academic researcher. In multi-stakeholder deliberations, academics are merely one voice amongst many: they are not necessarily much valued or understood, may come too late, and tend to disagree among each other. Most problematically, opportunities for engagement and consultation create the danger of capture, whether inadvertent or complicit. While acknowledging these very real hazards, we conclude by asking what could and should be the contribution of academics, especially of critical audience researchers, to policy deliberations?

First, in working with audiences, researchers should listen carefully to their concerns, hopes, and criticisms so as effectively to ground recommendations to policy makers and broadcasters. Of course, we already listen to them carefully, and unlike market researchers, academic researchers seek to draw them out sensitively: we interpret their silences, we do not take their utterances necessarily at face value, and we contextualize what they say. But do we make this research count? To be sure, engaging in policy deliberation is time-consuming and usually frustrating. But to research audiences' concerns, hopes, and criticisms without acting on the knowledge we produce is hard to defend; and, as many of us know, our interviewees often expect that those in power will learn of our findings and that improvements will follow. For example, critical social science would critique the technological determinism implicit in much policy (to illustrate, Ofcom's consultations treat technology as a given, merely asking, for example, how the mobile phone or video-on-demand or the internet can further benefit consumers). But it takes work to develop a non-determinist alternative, to show how people's life contexts, social trajectories, civic aspirations, or material disadvantages lead them to use, or need, or hope for media and technologies that may or may not or should be on offer; and it takes work to identify how one might measure progress or failure in meeting what Ofcom, as we saw earlier, terms "broader social, cultural, [political and] economic objectives."

Second, audience researchers should draw on democratic theory to contest the consumer focus of media and communication regulation by articulating the public or citizen interest, analyzing this in terms of social, cultural, political, and economic spheres, and conducting an independent assessment of the extent to which current policies meet these interests. To take the case of the political sphere (the sphere Ofcom seems least keen to include), it would surely be uncontentious to propose that furthering the citizen interest should include

- increasing the diversity of voices in the news (not simply more news organizations repeating the same headlines; Mansell 2007);
- "facilitating civic understanding and fair and well-informed debate on news and current affairs" (as mandated in sn 264(6)(c) and (l) of the Communications Act but not as measured in simple charts of news viewing or reported satisfaction with output); and
- delivering the community media that provide "an important means of empowering citizens and encouraging them to become actively involved in civic society, … [for] they enrich social debate, representing a means of internal pluralism (of ideas), … [and provide] an effective means to strengthen cultural and linguistic diversity, social inclusion and local identity" (European Parliament 2008).

Academics might develop and strengthen such a list, noting also that in societies characterized by individualization, distrust, and disillusion, the media surely remain a significant shared resource for citizens.

Third, academics could more often advocate alternative conceptions of the means of achieving the public interest in communications; for example, by supporting those who argue for communication rights. Hamelink (2003, p.1) collects under the heading of "communication rights" or "communication entitlements" those rights recognized by the UN's Universal Declaration of Human Rights that relate to information and communication, arguing,

> Communication is a fundamental social process and the foundation of all social organization.... Communication rights are based on a vision of the free flow of information and ideas which is interactive, egalitarian, and nondiscriminatory and driven by human needs, rather than commercial or political interests. These rights represent people's claim to freedom, inclusiveness, diversity and participation in the communication process.

Is this an agenda that critical audience researchers could sign up to as, in one form or another, have communication activists (Padovani and Pavan in press), political economists (Garnham 2000), and some cultural scholars (e.g. Couldry 2007)? If so, some policy engagement is again required, for the latest World Summit on the Information Society (WSIS) discussions failed to support the right to communicate (Hintz 2007; Hamelink and Hoffmann 2008).

At the outset, we advocated the twin strategy of, first, identifying in order to critique the implied audience of communications policy making; and, second, drawing on the insights of critical audience studies so as to engage with that policy making better to meet the interests of audiences, especially the interests – even the rights – of audiences as citizens. Identifying the implied audience has involved considerable attention to semantics – definitions of citizens and consumers, definitions of media literacy. The same would apply for other cases (for example, the "public" of public service broadcasting or the "community" of community radio) (Lunt and Livingstone, in press). We hope to have convinced that while the implied audience is constructed discursively, it is simultaneously (and consequentially) materially embodied in legal/regulatory principles and in institutional practice. Claims about "the audience" shift as political economy and cultural climates shift, enabling different constituencies to argue their case and so advance their interests. Alternative terms used to refer to the audience seem to pinpoint these discursive shifts – Syvertsen (2004) debates citizens, audiences, customers, and players; Webster and Phalen (1994) debate audiences as victims, consumers, and commodities; Dayan, Mehl, Madianou, and others have contrasted audiences, publics, and users (in Livingstone, 2005); and, increasingly to the fore, many are debating audiences as citizens, consumers, or citizen-consumers (Clarke, Newman, and Smith, 2007). Such terminological choices inflect audiences differently, invoking characteristics of active or passive, attentive or inattentive, mass or fragmented, discerning or mindless, demanding or accepting, and sophisticated or vulnerable. This is not, we have argued, merely a matter of semantics, for the implied audience plays a significant role in public deliberations over policy, co-opting evidence or, more often, common sense in subtly legitimating one position or another (Lunt and Livingstone, 2012).

As for the second element of our strategy, it must be acknowledged that this is more contentious than the first, for it requires researchers to enter the policy fray directly, putting their independence, itself their legitimation to speak as "experts" in multistakeholder deliberations, in jeopardy. However, we are writing in the wider context of what we see to be a normative turn across the social sciences – a renewed concern to make research count and to bring critical voices into the sites of decision making. Leaving behind the clarity of Lazarsfeld's (1941) founding distinction between administrative and critical schools of communication is undoubtedly a hazardous undertaking. Carey (1978/2003, p. 440) fears the "silent embrace" between academic and policy makers, as illustrated in Rowland's (1983) classic critique of media effects research. But the prospects for staking a claim for inclusiveness, diversity, quality, participation, and recognition of the other increasingly seem too important to turn one's back on. As Cunningham (2003) says, in advocating a shift in cultural critique from the often idealistic rhetorics of resistance, anticommercialism and populism and toward the more pragmatic demands of access, equity, empowerment, and opportunity:

> Replacing shop-worn revolutionary rhetoric with the new command metaphor of citizenship commits cultural studies to a reformist strategy within the terms of a social democratic politics, and thus can connect it more organically to the well-springs of engagement with policy. (p. 19)

McGuigan concurs, aiming to leave behind the problematic "gulf between the political pretensions of cultural studies and its practical effects" (2003, p. 28) and instead exploring the potential for a post-Marshall notion of cultural citizenship and cultural entitlement as the principal goal of (critical) cultural policy – an ambition central to the discussion of the citizen interest in communication.

We need not express a particular view on these or other issues in order to make three final arguments: first, that audience studies has the expertise to contribute in the audiences' interest in these deliberations (including expertise in ways of enabling audiences to speak for themselves); second, that critical scholarship must always ask in whose interest the various decisions are (including asking how the burden of risk may fall if things go wrong, as they will); and, third, that the very independence of the academy means that we have insights, findings and critical perspectives that surely should contribute to shaping the key policy decisions to be made regarding the future of media and communications.

Acknowledgments

This chapter draws on the research project, Public Understanding of Regimes of Risk Regulation, funded by the Economic and Social Research Council (ESRC) as part of the "Social Contexts and Responses to Risk Network" (RES-336-25-0001), see http://www.kent.ac.uk/scarr/. For project website and publications, see www.lse.ac.uk/collections/PURRR/. We thank Tanika Kelay, Laura Miller, and Sarita Malik for their work on the project, and Richard Collins and Ranjana Das for their comments on an earlier version of this chapter.

References

Abercrombie, N. and Longhurst, B. 1998 *Audiences: A Sociological Theory of Performance and Imagination*. Sage, London.

Ang, I. 1996 *Living Room Wars: Rethinking Media Audiences for a Postmodern World*. Routledge, London.

Aufderheide, P. 1993 *Media Literacy: A Report of the National Leadership Conference on Media Literacy*. Aspen Institute, Aspen, CO.

Bachmair, B. and Bazalgette, C. 2007 The European charter for media literacy: meaning and potential. *Research in Comparative and International Education*, 2, 1, pp. 80–87.

Beck, U. 1986/2005 *Risk Society: Towards a New Modernity*. Sage, London.

Benhabib, S. 1996 Toward a deliberative model of democratic legitimacy. In S. Benhabib, ed. *Democracy and Difference: Contesting Boundaries of the Political*, Princeton University Press, Princeton, NJ, pp. 67–94.

Black, J. 2002 Critical reflections on regulation. Discussion paper, London School of Economics and Political Science, Centre for the Analysis of Risk and Regulation, London.

Blumler, J.G. and Hoffman-Riem, W. 1992 Toward renewed public accountability in broadcasting. In J.G. Blumler, ed. *Television and the Public Interest: Vulnerable Values in West European Broadcasting*. Sage, London, pp. 218–228.

Born, G. 2004 *Uncertain Vision: Birt, Dyke and the Reinvention of the BBC*. Secker and Warburg, London.

Buckingham, D. 2000 *After the Death of Childhood: Growing Up in the Age of Electronic Media*. Polity Press, Cambridge.

Butsch, R. 2000 *The Making of American Audiences: From Stage to Television 1750–1990*. Cambridge University Press, Cambridge.

Carey, J.W. 1978/2003 The ambiguity of policy research. In S. Braman, ed. *Communication Researchers and Policy-Making*. MIT Press, London, pp. 437–444.

Clarke, J., Newman, J. and Smith, N. 2007 *Creating Citizen-Consumers: Changing Publics and Changing Public Services*. Sage, London.

Collins, R. and Murroni, C. 1996 *New Media, New Policies: Media and Communications Strategies for the Future*. Polity, Cambridge.

Couldry, N. 2007 Communicative entitlements and democracy: The future of the digital divide debate. In R. Mansell, C. Avgerou, D. Quah and R. Silverstone, eds. *Oxford Handbook on ICTs*. Oxford University Press, pp. 494–513.

Cunningham, S. 2003 Cultural studies from the viewpoint of cultural policy. In J. Lewis and T. Miller, eds. *Critical Cultural Policy Studies: A Reader*. Blackwell, Oxford, pp. 13–22.

Dahlgren, P. 2004 Citizenship and the Media: cultivating agency via civic culture. In N. Carpentier, C. Pauwels and O. Van-Oost, eds. *Het On(be)grijpbare Publiek: The Ungraspable Audience: Een communicatiewetenschappelijke verkenning van het publiek*. VUB Press, Brussels, pp. 259–268.

European Parliament. 2008 Report on community media in Europe, A6-0263/2008, 24/06. European Parliament, Brussels.

Freedman, D. 2008 *The Politics of Media Policy*. Polity, Cambridge.

Garnham, N. 2000 Amartya Sen's 'capabilities' approach to the evaluation of welfare: its application to communications. In A. Calabrese and J-C. Burgelman, eds. *Communication, Citizenship and Social Policy*. Rowman & Littlefield, Boulder, CO, pp. 113–124.

Hagen, I. and Wasko, J., eds. 2000 Consuming audiences? *Production and Reception in Media Research*. Hampton Press, Cresskill, NJ.

Hamelink, C. 2003 Statement on communication rights. Paper presented at the World Forum on Communication Rights.

Hamelink, C. J., and Hoffmann, J. 2008 The state of the right to communicate. *Global Media Journal*, 7, 13.

Hardy, J. 2008 Ofcom, regulation and reform. *Soundings*, 39, 1, pp. 87–97.

Harvey, S. 2006 Ofcom's first year and neo-liberalism's blind spot: attacking the culture of production. *Screen*, 47, 1, pp. 91–105.

Hesmondhalgh, D. 2005 Media and cultural policy as public policy: the case of the British Labour government. *International Journal of Cultural Policy*, 11, 1, pp. 95–115.

Hintz, A. 2007 Civil society media at the WSIS: a new actor in global communication governance. In B. Cammaerts and N. Carpentier, eds. *Reclaiming the Media: Communication Rights and Democratic Media Roles*. Intellect, Bristol, UK, pp. 243–264.

Jessop, B. 2002 *The Future of the Capitalist State*. Polity, Cambridge.

Jowell, T. 2004 [Statement]. *Daily Mail*, January 21, p. 23.

Lazarsfeld, P. F. 1941 Remarks on administrative and critical communications research studies. *Philosophy and Science*, 9, pp. 3–16.

Liebes, T. and Katz, E. 1990 *The Export of Meaning: Cross-Cultural Readings of Dallas*. Oxford University Press, New York.

Livingstone, S. 1998 Audience research at the crossroads: the 'implied audience' in media theory. *European Journal of Cultural Studies*, 1, 2, pp. 193–217.

Livingstone, S. 2003 *The Changing Nature and Uses of Media Literacy*. London School of Economics and Political Science, London.

Livingstone, S., ed. 2005 *Audiences and Publics: When Cultural Engagement Matters for the Public Sphere*. Intellect Press, Bristol, UK.

Livingstone, S. and Lunt, P. 2007 Representing citizens and consumers in media and communications regulation: the politics of consumption/the consumption of politics. *Annals of the American Academy of Political and Social Science*, 611, pp. 51–65.

Livingstone, S., Lunt, P. and Miller, L. 2007a Citizens and consumers: discursive debates during and after the Communications Act 2003. *Media, Culture and Society*, 29, 4, pp. 613–638.

Livingstone, S., Lunt, P. and Miller, L. 2007b Citizens, consumers and the citizen-consumer: articulating the interests at stake in media and communications regulation. *Discourse and Communication*, 1, 1, pp. 85–111.

Lunt, P. and Livingstone, S. 2007 Regulating markets in the interest of consumers? On the changing regime of governance in the financial service and communications sectors. In M. Bevir and F. Trentmann, eds. *Governance, Citizens, and Consumers: Agency and Resistance in Contemporary Politics*. Palgrave Macmillan, Basingstoke, UK, pp. 139–161.

Lunt, P. and Livingstone, S. 2012 *Media Regulation: Governance and the interests of citizens and consumers*. Sage, London.

Lunt, P. and Livingstone, S. In press. *Media Regulation: Changing Relations Between Government, Media Industries, Citizens and Consumers*. Sage, London.

Mansell, R. 2007 Crossing boundaries with new media: introductory remarks for the panel on the responsibility of the media. Presentation to the United Nations General Assembly Third Informal Thematic Debate on Civilizations and the Challenge for Peace: Obstacles and Opportunities, New York, May 10–11.

McGuigan, J. 2003 Cultural policy studies. In J. Lewis and T. Miller, eds. *Critical Cultural Policy Studies: A Reader*. Blackwell, Oxford, pp. 23–42.

McQuail, D. and Siune, K., eds. 1998 *Media Policy: Convergence, Concentration and Commerce*. Sage, London.

Nightingale, V. 1996 *Studying Audiences: The Shock of the Real*. Routledge, London.

Ouellette, L. and Hay, J. 2008 *Better Living through Reality TV: Television and Post-Welfare Citizenship*. Blackwell, Oxford.

Padovani, C. and Pavan, E. In press. The emerging global movement on communication rights: a new stakeholder in global communication governance? Converging at WSIS but looking beyond. In D. Kidd, C. Rodriguez and L. Stein, eds. *Making Our Media: Mapping Global Initiatives toward a Democratic Public Sphere*, Hampton Press, Cresskill, NJ.

Puttnam, D. 2006 The continuing need to advance the public interest. In E. Richards, R. Foster and T. Kiedrowski, eds. *Communications in the Next Decade*. Ofcom, London, pp. 125–131.

Raboy, M., Abramson, R. D., Proulx, S. and Welters, R. 2001 Media policy, audiences, and social demand: research at the interface of policy studies and audience studies. *Television and New Media*, 2, 2, pp. 95–115.

Redding, D. 2005 On the cusp: finding new visions for social gain from broadcasting. *Political Quarterly*, 76, s1, pp. 146–158.

Rowland, W. R. 1983 *The Politics of TV Violence: Policy Uses of Communication Research*. Sage, Beverly Hills, CA.

Ruddock, A. 2007 *Investigating Audiences*. Sage, London.

Seiter, E. 2005 *The Internet Playground: Children's Access, Entertainment, and Mis-education*. Peter Lang, New York.

Seymour-Ure, C. 1987 Media policy in Britain: now you see it, now you don't. *European Journal of Communication*, 2, pp. 269–288.

Syvertsen, T. 2004 Citizens, audiences, customers and players. *European Journal of Cultural Studies*, 7, 3, pp. 363–380.

Tomlinson, J. 1999 *Globalization and Culture*. University of Chicago Press, Chicago.

Webster, J. G. and Phalen, P. F. 1994 Victim, consumer, or commodity? Audience models in communication policy. In J.S. Ettema and D.C. Whitney, eds. *Audiencemaking: How the Media Create the Audience*. Sage, London, pp. 19–37.

9

New Configurations of the Audience?

The Challenges of User-Generated Content for Audience Theory and Media Participation

Nico Carpentier

Introduction

User-generated content (UGC) is seen as one of the main innovations in contemporary media worlds. As part of a digital culture that emphasizes new participatory opportunities, it claims to pose a number of challenges for our reflections about media and, more specifically, for (the more traditional forms of) audience theory. As enthusiastic and sometimes messianic discourses of novelty often still engulf "new" media technologies and practices, in combination with calls to rearticulate (or renew) our present-day ideological and theoretical frameworks, there is an equally strong need to evaluate the novelty of these practices, to contextualize them by confronting them with media practices "from the past" (which are, as always, still very present), and to consider the applicability of the "old" (so-called outdated) theoretical frameworks to make sense of the diversity of participatory practices that characterize the media configuration of today.

In order to confront the thinking about UGC with "traditional" (and fairly "old") audience theory, the first part of this chapter will give a brief overview of the core structural components of audience theory, focusing on its active-passive, participation-interaction, micro-macro, community-society, and meso dimensions. In the second part, the specificity claims of UGC will be analyzed, in combination

The Handbook of Media Audiences, First Edition. Edited by Virginia Nightingale.
© 2014 John Wiley & Sons, Ltd. Published 2014 by John Wiley & Sons, Ltd.

with the problems that arise through these acclaimed specific characteristics. Finally, the specificity claims of UGC will be scrutinized by embedding UGC and its acclaimed specific characteristics into the core structural components of audience theory. This strategy not only will show the relevance of audience theory for the study of UGC, but also allows pinpointing the strengths and weaknesses of UGC by positioning it within the core dimensions of audience theory.

Core Structural Components of Audience Theory

There are, of course, many approaches for structuring the ways the concept of the audience has been theorized, and a "totalizing account [is] a logical impossibility" (Jenkins 1999). The starting point of this multimedia analysis is the identification of two major dimensions that are labeled the active-passive and the micro-macro dimension by Littlejohn (1996), who writes that

> disputes on the nature of the audience seem to involve two related dialectics. The first is a tension between the idea that the audience is a mass public versus the idea that it is a small community. The second is the tension between the idea that the audience is passive versus the belief that it is active. (p. 310)

These two dialectics (or dimensions) are the starting point of this theoretical reflection, while at the same time the argument will be made that each of the two dimensions need to be transcended. In the first part, the reduction of the active-passive dimension to processes of signification is transcended by combining this dimension with elements from the participation-interaction dimension. Secondly, the micro-macro dimension is expanded by introducing the community-society dimension. Moreover, within the micro-macro dimension, a meso level is (re) introduced.

The Active-Passive Dimension in the Articulation of Audience

The first dimension that structures the audience concept – the active-passive dimension – is very much linked to the debates on structure and agency, as Allor formulates it: "The field continues to oscillate ... between the voluntarism of a conception of the full human subject as agent of meaning making and the determinism of a conception of the individual as the object of socialization processes" (1988, p. 217). This connection also influences audience theory, as there is often a clear preference for one of the sides of the binary opposition (to refer to one of the core principles of Derrida's deconstruction). In other words, we should avoid "the trap that being active is always best for the audience" (Höijer 1999, p. 191).

The passive model of the actor has a long history, and is present in one of the most stubborn communication models in the history of communication studies: the sender–message–receiver model of Shannon and Weaver (1949) (see Nightingale 1996, p. 6). Later versions and variants – such as DeFleur's (1966) model – add a feedback loop, but these additions do not fundamentally alter the position of the receiver as "ending point" of communication processes. The research tradition that connects most closely with this approach is media effects research, which is mainly inspired by the concern and/or fear for the disadvantageous effects that the media might have on the receiver(s) – usually articulated as potential victims (Webster and Phalen 1997, p. 128) – in a number of specific fields.[1] In contrast, the approach of the human subject as an active carrier of meaning is echoed in the development of Eco's (1968) aberrant decoding theory, on the one hand, from 1973 Hall's encoding-decoding model (published in 1980), and the concept of the active audience (Fiske 1987) that emanated out of this model, on the other hand. Fiske emphasizes the social and negotiated aspects of meaning, in which meaning is interpreted as unstable (and always susceptible to reinterpretation) and contested; witness the definition of *text* that Fiske uses: "a text is the site of struggles for meaning that reproduce the conflicts of interest between the producers and consumers of the cultural commodity" (1987, p. 14). Also, the uses and gratifications theory by (among others) Katz, Blumler, and Gurevitch (1974) and the deduced models, as for example the expectancy value theory of Palmgreen and Rayburn (1985) and the social action model of Renckstorf et al. (1996), rely to a large degree on the concept of the active audience (Livingstone 1998, p. 238). The importance of the uses and gratifications theory is, however, not only this emphasis on the active audience member, who acts with utilitarian considerations. At least of equal importance is – from an analytical point of view – the complete reversal of the sender–message–receiver model (Nightingale 1996, p. 8). Audience preferences (based on the social usefulness) function as a gauge for "value judgments about the cultural significance of mass communications" (Katz, Blumler, and Gurevitch 1974, p 22).

The Participation-Interaction Dimension in the Audience Articulation

The "traditional" active-passive dimension discussed above often takes an idealist position by emphasizing the active role of the individual viewer in processes of signification. This position risks reducing social activity to these processes of signification, excluding other – more materialist – forms of human practices. In other words, the active dimension itself hides another dimension, which will be termed here the participation-interaction dimension.

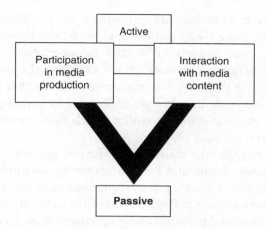

Figure 9.1   The two dimensions of audience activity.

The interaction component of audience activity refers to the processes of signification and interpretation that are triggered by media consumption. Obviously, the polysemic readings of media texts are an integrative part of this component. But also the identity work, where audiences engage with the media texts that are offered to them, is included in the interaction component of audience activity. This is, for instance, captured by the ritual, expressive, or mediating quasi-interactive aspects of the media (see, respectively, Carey 1975; McQuail 1994; Thompson 1995), where the symbolic-significatory linkage between media and audience is emphasized (Figure 9.1).

The participatory component of audience activity refers to two interrelated forms of participation, which can be termed participation "in" the media and "through" the media, in a similar way that Wasko and Mosco (1992, p. 7) distinguished between democratization "in" and "through" the media. Participation "in" the media deals with the participation of nonprofessionals in the production of media output (content-related participation) and in media decision making (structural participation). These forms of media participation allow citizens to be active in one of the many (micro-)spheres relevant to daily life and to put their right to communicate into practice. Second, these forms of micro participation are considered to be important because they allow people to learn and adopt a democratic and/or civic attitude, thus strengthening (the possible forms) of macro participation. Verba and Nie briefly summarize this as follows: "a participatory polity may rest on a participatory society" (1987, p. 3). Although mainstream media have attempted to organize forms of audience participation (Livingstone and Lunt 1996; Carpentier 2003; McNair, Hibberd, and Schlesinger 2003), alternative media have proven to be especially successful in organizing deeper forms of participation in the media (Girard 1992; Downing 2000; Rodriguez 2001; Bailey, Cammaerts, and Carpentier

2008). This approach, of course, also pressurizes the privileged position of the "traditional" white, male media professional, who finds himself located at one of the ends of the "professional elite" versus "member of the audience" dimension. One of the defining elements of, for example, the community media movement is precisely the anti-elitist discourse claiming that journalistic tasks must not (and should not) be taken on exclusively by media professionals but that members of the community – within which such media are active – can also take on this role (Girard 1992).

Participation "through" the media deals with the opportunities for extensive participation in public debate and for self-representation in the public spheres, thus entering the realm of enabling and facilitating macro participation (Couldry 2003). Starting from a broadly defined notion of the political, consensus-oriented models of democracy (and participation) emphasize the importance of dialogue and deliberation and focus on collective decision making based on rational arguments à la Habermas. Other authors (Fraser 1990; Mouffe 1994) stress more conflict-oriented approaches. They point to the unavoidability of political differences and struggles and see the media as crucial sites for struggles for hegemony (Kellner 1992, p. 57). Both consensus and conflict-oriented models enable one to stress the need for citizens to participate in these processes of dialogue, debate, and deliberation.

The Micro-Macro Dimension in the Audience Articulation

The second core dimension that was selected as an analytical starting point is the micro-macro dimension. This dimension is widely spread: in most definitions of the audience, the audience is referred to as an aggregate of individuals (the micro dimension) or as collective (the macro dimension). Littlejohn summarizes the two positions as follows: "In contrast to mass society thinking is the position that the audience cannot be characterized as an amorphous mass, that it consists of numerous highly differentiated communities, each with its own values, ideas and interests" (1996, p. 311). Other examples of such referrals to the micro-macro dimension can be found in a number of publications. Radway refers to the concept audience as "a collective label for the consumers of electronically mediated messages" (1988 p. 359), and Ang defines the audience – following Harré (1981) – as a "taxonomic collective": "an entity of serialized, in principle unrelated individuals who form a group solely because each member has a characteristic – in our case, spectatorship – that is like that of each other member" (1991, p. 33). Moores speaks of "several groups divided by their reception of different media and genres, or by social and cultural positioning" (1996, p. 2), and Dayan refers to "[a]udiences of this sort [namely, spectators] [that] are observational aggregates" (2005, p. 46).

As the definitions above indicate, the audience can also be charted using a variety of approaches to the "many" as its basis. In the micro approach, individuals are the building blocks of the audience, while in the macro approach the collective aspects are stressed:

> on the one hand [relating] to complete groups or social categories (a class, a community, a political public, etc.) and on the other to overlapping subsets of individuals within the total media audience which express this or that requirement from mass communication. (McQuail 1994, pp. 288–289)

Examples of audience articulations that are situated in the micro dimension can be found in the uses and gratifications theory and in the related models. As Dayan remarks, spectatorship has a similar aggregative dimension: "They are spectators added to other spectators – spectators in the plural" (2005, p. 46). Also Livingstone and Lunt's typology – which sees the television audience as aggregate of alienated viewers, consumer-viewers, or citizens-viewers – can be located within this micro approach of the audience (1996, pp. 18–19; see also Livingstone 2005, p. 31). At the other (macro) side of this scale, a series of articulations are significantly present: the audience as mass, the audience as market (segment), and the audience as public. The emphasis on the collective leads in all three cases to articulation of the audience as a living entity, "a huge, living subject" (Ang 1991, p. 61).

Communities and organizations

Both the micro and macro approach conceal a multitude of audience articulations that all relate to the collective, but in very different ways. To further expand this diversity of articulations, this text uses Tönnies's old *Gemeinschaft-Gesellschaft* dimension,[2] in which "society" is characterized according to Martin-Barbero by "an absence of identifying group relations" (1993, p. 29). Next to a number of audience articulations that construct the collective by the mere use of the media (which implies the absence of identifying group relations), a number of audience articulations are included which do imply (some type of) group identity. These articulations are discussed in the following part of this article, where a further distinction is made between the articulations of the audience as community and the organized audience.

The audience as community

A number of audience articulations previously discussed already contain (sometimes weak) references to the audience as community. At the political and economic domains, audiences are constructed as political communities (or publics) and markets at the macro level or as citizens and consumers at the micro level. For instance, in the typology of Livingstone and Lunt (1996), (part of the) audience is defined as an aggregate of citizens, which results in the creation of a linkage between what they call the citizen-viewer and the political community. In this part of the article, the focus is placed on audience articulations that put stronger emphasis on the community aspect. At the micro level, this relates to the audience articulation as social, virtual, and interpretative communities. Especially the so-called ethnographic turn (Livingstone 1998, p. 239) has led to increased attention for the interaction in small-scale communities such as, for example, the family, the peer group, the class room, the work environment, and the neighborhood. Examples of this are offered in the work of Morley (1986) and Walkerdine (1986) in connection to the social processes within the family related to, respectively, television and video. A similar emphasis on the family (as a moral economy) can be found in the domestication approach (Silverstone 1991; Silverstone and Hirsch 1992). The analysis of the impact of information and communication technologies (ICTs) on everyday life has shown that communities are formed not only in geographically defined spaces, but also in cyberspace, as virtual communities (Rheingold 1993). Third, more culturist approaches emphasize the existence of communities of meaning (Cohen 1989), meaning-making audiences (Dayan 2005), or interpretative communities (Lindlof 1988; Radway 1988). Within these audience articulations, the common frame of interpretation – sometimes combined with sociodemographic characteristics – is emphasized.

At the macro level, the articulations as community are more complex, and can be categorized in three different groups: class, gender, or ethnicity; ordinary people; and taste cultures or subcultures. Talking about television, Ang (1991) here suggests the term "cultural positioning and identifications" to describe the situation-transcending factors that people carry with them and that actualize in concrete situations such as "those along the lines of gender, class, ethnicity, generation, and so on, as well as cultural ideologies as to the meaning of television as a social and aesthetic phenomenon" (p. 184). Also, the articulation of the audience as ordinary people (negatively articulated with the elite or the power bloc) partly links up with this, when the audience articulation as ordinary people refers to a common popular culture (Hall 1980), or to "alliances of social interests formed strategically or tactically to advance the interests of those who form them" (Fiske, 1993, p. 10). Finally, the concept of taste culture can also be used for the articulation of the audience as community. With the incorporation of taste culture in his typology, McQuail refers not only to the definition of Gans (1967, p. 553) – in which a "taste culture" is seen as a collective of individuals grouped on the basis of their preference for a certain content, which also comprises media content – but also to the work of Lewis (1992) on music and subcultural identity. Such analyses lead to the articulation of the audience on the basis of subcultural identities, in relation to a dominant culture.

The meso level within the micro-macro dimension

The micro-macro dimension can not only be expanded by the community-society dimension. In defining this micro-macro dimension as a scale, space is also created for a meso level. This rather rare (but for that reason important) articulation leads to a definition of the audience as an organized audience. Here, too, a first version of this articulation of the audience is offered by McQuail (1994, p. 307) when he refers in his typology of the audience to the audience articulations as the already existing social group and to the fan club or group, and categorizes both as an "active social group." A more elaborate analysis of fan culture can be found in Jenkins's (1992, 2006) work, which makes it possible to connect fandom with the concept of the organized audience, as it is represented by the existence of fan clubs, fanzines, and congresses. More important in this context is the work of Reyes Matta, which has led to the development of an alternative model of communication based on active social participation (Reyes Matta 1981, 1986). A point of departure here is the right to communicate, which is explicitly appointed to (1) the entire society, (2) individuals, and (3) groups. These actors construct the social organization of the communication processes (on the international, national, as well as local levels) within which the media function. The messages that originate from these media will eventually reach the organized audience, which is defined as follows by Reyes Matta (1981):

> The entirety of the receivers should neither be perceived as individuals, nor as an amorphous, quantitative mass, but rather as social groups or institutions that are linked in an organizational or structural way with the society at large, such as labor unions, cultural groups, political parties, or new social movements. (Quoted by Servaes 1989, p. 59)

UGC and Participatory Media Practices

When studying the participatory potential of mediated communication and its context of structural organization, we can go back a long time in history (see e.g. Ostertag 2006). For instance, the start-up phase of radio was characterized by many examples of nonprofessional broadcasting. Not surprisingly, it was Bertolt Brecht's radio theory (see Brecht 2001) that provided the foundations for the dream of the transformation of radio as a tool of distribution into a tool of communication. But especially from the 1990s onward – and in some cases earlier, as for instance with Hakim Bey's TAZ (1985) – the focus of theoreticians of participation shifted toward the so-called new media. The development of the internet, and especially the web, would not only render most information available to all but also create a whole new world of communication, within its slipstream the promise of a structural increase of the level of (media) participation. Meanwhile, this dream seems to have come true, at least at first sight: while at first people still had to make the effort to construct their own web pages, the web 2.0 technologies now provide popular[3] and accessible ways to publish texts, images, and audiovisual material. Although a number of concepts have been launched, UGC seems to be one label commonly used to capture the changes in relation to these increased levels of audience activity.

Despite the popularity of the concept, clear definitions of UGC that move beyond the obvious statement that UGC deals with online or "website content produced by users" (Schweiger and Quiring 2006, p. 1) or with "services providing user-uploaded and user-generated audio and video content" (Principles for User Generated Content Services 2007) are rare. In its 2007 report "Participative Web: User-Created Content," the Organisation for Economic Co-operation and Development (OECD) makes a similar remark: "Despite frequent references to this topic by media and experts, no commonly agreed definition of user-created content exists" (p. 8). Even the concept itself has a number of variations.[4] And as an umbrella term, it covers many different practices and platforms, which the OECD report (2007) attempts to categorize as follows: Blogs; Wikis and Other Text-Based Collaboration Formats; Sites Allowing Feedback on Written Works; Group-Based Aggregation; Podcasting; Social Network Sites; Virtual Worlds; and Content or Filesharing Sites (p. 17). In order to deal with this diversity, the OECD report prefers to describe three distinguishing features of UGC. The report first emphasizes the "Publication Requirement," which implies that the UGC requires some type of (semi-)public distribution. A second distinguishing feature is the "Creative Effort," which refers to the "certain amount of creative effort [that] was put into creating the work or adapting existing works to construct a new one" (OECD, 2007, p. 8). Third, according to this report, the "Creation" takes place "outside of professional routines and practises," which "in the extreme" can imply that UGC is "produced by non-professionals without the expectation of profit or remuneration" (OECD 2007, p. 8). Especially the third characteristic situates UGC as a form of participation in the media production process.

This definition does raise questions about the specificity of UGC in relation to participatory practices in a diversity of other media contexts. Moreover, it also raises questions about the implications for audience theory, and whether the rise of UGC requires theoretical modifications, a question which will be addressed in the next part of this chapter. Especially when we keep in mind that "new" technologies often lead to the formulation of strong claims of novelty and uniqueness, in combination with processes of forgetfulness in relation to the importance of other social spheres and the societal roles of old technologies, care needs to be taken. One way to approach these issues is to study the (theoretical) discourses on UGC and their claims on specificity.

One of the main specificity arguments is based on the structural nature of the shift from one-to-many to many-to-many communication.[5] An example of this argument can be found in Jay Rosen's (2008) essay "The People Formerly Known as the Audience." Rosen argues that the (commercial) media system has lost control over its audiences, as it has been (re)transformed into "the public made realer, less fictional, more able, less predictable" (p. 165). He describes this change as follows:

> The people formerly known as the audience are those who were on the receiving end of a media system that ran one way, in a broadcasting pattern, with high entry fees and a few firms competing to speak very loudly while the rest of the population listened in isolation from one another – and who today are not in a situation like that at all. (Rosen, 2008, p. 163)

A similar position is taken by John Hartley (2008), who focuses on creative self-expression, suggesting, "Until recently, creative self-expression has been *provided* rather than *produced*; offered for a price on a take-it-or-leave-it basis by experts and corporations with little input by the consumers themselves" (p. 5; emphasis in original).

As already suggested above, UGC cannot be detached from the long history of participatory practices within the media. Mainstream media but especially alternative and community media have a long history of organizing participatory processes at the level of content and organization. And already during the UNESCO debates on the New World Information and Communication Order (NWICO), the debate on media and participation featured prominently, resulting in the following definition of participation as "a higher level of public involvement [than access] … in the production process and also in the management and planning of communication systems" (Servaes 1999, p. 85; see MacBride Commission 1980). At the same time, there is now clearly an increased diversity of participatory practices supported by an increased availability of technologies. Blogging, vlogging, webzines, internet radio (and television), podcasting, digital storytelling, and wiking are clear examples of these evolutions. Arguably, this is more a matter of modality than of novelty, where one can only wonder whether the increase in popularity and the widening of the net have not (negatively) impacted the intensities of the participatory processes (Carpentier 2007).

A second claim on specificity is based on the privileging of the "user," and his or her transformation into the "produser" (e.g., Bruns 2007; cf. the "prosumer" in Toffler 1980). This can be seen as part of a longer evolution of increased audience autonomy. At the theoretical level, more and more attention has been spent on the audience activity part of the active-passive audience dimension, first at the level of interaction with media content. Barthes's (1984) *Image Music Text* contains the seminal essay "The Death of the Author," which was a metaphor – not to be taken literally – implying that there was no privileged vantage point that fixed the interpretation of a text. Later, the participatory component of audience activity gained more strength, on the basis of which it is claimed that the Author has died for a second time, as we witness a convergence between the producers and receivers of discourses at the level of the production process. The old Author (here the media professional) is no longer solely in control of the production process, as the produser (of UGC) has overcome the rigid separations between both categories. It is this shift in the balance from audience activity as interaction with media content, to audience activity as participation in the production process, that supports this claim of specificity.

There are, nevertheless, a number of problems. The conflation of producer and audience complicates the notion of audience in two ways. Arguably, the notion of the user was introduced to emphasize online audience activity, where people were seen to "use" media technologies and content more actively. Paradoxically, it also protected the passive connotations of the signifier *audience* by creating a distinction between the signifiers *audience* and *user*, but at the same time the notions of the user and the produser problematically privilege online media worlds as sites of audience activity. Second, through the conflation of producer and audience, we are often led to believe that all audiences of participatory media are active participants, and that passive consumption is either absent or regrettable. Again, we can refer to alternative media studies, where a similar problem has been established: "It is a paradox, however, that so little attention has been dedicated to the user dimension, given that alternative-media activists represent in a sense the most active segment of the so-called 'active audience'" (Downing 2003, p. 625). In the case of new media participation, this has partially been compensated by the attention for the "lurker" in online communities, but the pejorative sound of this concept might be more of an indication of the problem than a solution. Moreover, the destructive consequences of this "free-riding behavior" was emphasized (Smith and Kollock 1999), although other (slightly more recent) publications have nuanced this negative framing (Nonnecke 2000; Nonnecke and Preece 2001; Walther and Boyd 2002).

A third claim is based on the convergence argument. In *Convergence Culture*, Jenkins (2006) locates the specificity of present-day media cultures in the combination of top-down business processes with bottom-up consumption and production processes. For Jenkins, convergence

> [r]epresents a paradigm shift – a move from medium-specific content toward content that flows across multiple media channels, toward the increased interdependence of communications systems, toward multiple ways of accessing media content, and toward ever more complex relations between top-down corporate media and bottom-up participatory culture. (2006, p. 243)

Analyzing fan cultures (including spoiling communities and fan fiction), Jenkins's argument is based on a multiple-media approach that overcomes the old-new media divide, in combination with attention for the intertwining of these fan cultures and corporate media. Very much in line with Fiske's (1989) position, Jenkins sees popular culture as a meeting place of active audiences and mainstream media, of participation and commodification. Again, the arguments in favor of the digital culture's specificity focus on the increased intensity and entanglement of these convergences, and not necessarily on the newness of digital culture.

Also at this level, a price is to be paid. Jenkins does point explicitly to the difficulties of avoiding incorporation: "To be desired by the networks is to have your tastes commodified" (2006, p. 62). The meeting of corporate culture and audience activity also has economic consequences, as the audience's leisure time is transformed into (free) labor (Terranova 2000) and consumers are disciplined into work (Zwick, Bonsu, and Darmody 2008). Third, the political-economic processes behind the convergence process also affect the participatory process itself, as the locus of control of many of the interfaces that facilitate and structure these participatory processes remains firmly in the hands of companies that are outside the participatory process. One illustration is the above-mentioned OECD report, which refers to the incorporation of UGC into the corporate world by what they call the "monetising" of UGC. The report distinguishes five models:

> Different UCC types (e.g., blogs, video content) have different although similar approaches to monetising UCC. There are five basic models: i) voluntary contributions, ii) charging viewers for services – pay-per-item or subscription models, including bundling with existing subscriptions, iii) advertising-based models, iv) licensing of content and technology to third parties, and v) selling goods and services to the community (monetising the audience via online sales). (OECD, 2007, p. 5)

Finally, the lack of formal organizational structures and the fluidity of these online participatory practices are invoked to claim specificity. Shirky's (2008) *Here Comes Everybody: The Power of Organizing without Organizations* is a good illustration of this line of argument, as it emphasizes the processes of collective action and community building that support the digital participatory culture, bypassing traditional organizational structures. Mass amateurization – "a world where participating in the conversation is its own reward" (Shirky 2002) – and mass collaboration are seen as main societal driving forces that have, for instance, displaced media professionalism. From this perspective, UGC sites become seen as temporary autonomous zones (Bey 1985), instable in space and time, and embedded within structural uncertainties where large groups of people join in collaborative projects, produce output, and then disperse again.

At the same time, this absence of formal organizational structures has a number of consequences for the participatory process itself, as it tends to limit the intensity of the participatory process, bracketing the issues related to power and decision making (see Carpentier 2007) and often assuming balanced power relations between all collaborators in informal organizations. This further complicates the notion of participation in media production, as there is a difference between

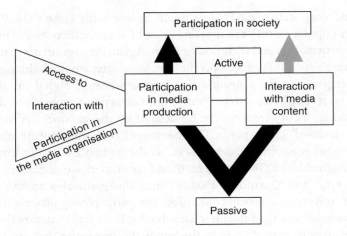

Figure 9.2   Participatory dimensions of audience activity.

participating in the content production process, participating in society, and participating in the decision-making processes of the content-producing organization. In other words, behind the participation in the media production lie two other dimensions, namely, participation in society and participation in the media organization. As Figure 9.2 shows, access to and interaction with the media organization do not necessarily imply participation in the media organization's decision-making structures. The risk described above relates to the reduction of participation at the organizational level to "mere" interaction, which in a way relates to the old feedback option discussed in the first part of this chapter (Figure 9.2).

In order to illustrate these differences, we can structure the organizations of participatory media practices into four ideal-typical models (Figure 9.3). These four models are constructed on the basis of two dimensions: the (formal or informal) membership of the participants of the organization (versus the absence of a membership structure), and the facilitation of access, interaction, and participation (versus the emphasis on access and interaction only). Arguably, only the first two models deal with organizations that facilitate participation at the micro level; in the other two cases, the label *semiparticipation* is preferred, which semantically excludes them from the sphere of (micro) participation in the strict sense. The first model deals with organizations that facilitate the participation of their members. These participatory processes concern people that organize their own participation. Classic examples are alternative radio stations (often linked to Amarc)[6] and the so-called Independent Media Centres (IMCs), where Indymedia[7] is the most famous example. Although in both cases different types of membership (with varying degrees of involvement) exist, this model presupposes an explicit link between the participants and the organization. In the second model, the members of the organizations take on a more facilitating role, which implies that

	Membership organization	Non–membership organization
Organization aimed at facilitating access, interaction, and participation at the micro level (that produce participatory outcomes at the macro level)	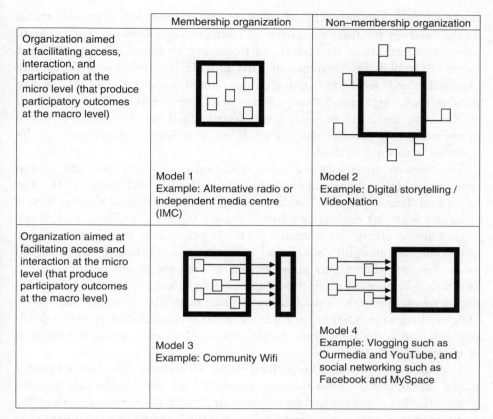Model 1 Example: Alternative radio or independent media centre (IMC)	Model 2 Example: Digital storytelling / VideoNation
Organization aimed at facilitating access and interaction at the micro level (that produce participatory outcomes at the macro level)	Model 3 Example: Community Wifi	Model 4 Example: Vlogging such as Ourmedia and YouTube, and social networking such as Facebook and MySpace

Figure 9.3   Models of (semi-)participatory organizations.

the objective of these organizations is to have others (meaning nonmembers) participate. Examples can (at least partially) be found in the sector of community media, as these media organizations are often oriented toward the facilitation of the participation of members of a specific community, where these members remain relatively detached from the actual organization. A mainstream media example is the British Video Nation project (see Carpentier [2003] and http://www.bbc.co.uk/videonation/), where the BBC – already in the early 1990s – organized a participatory television (and later web) project that resembles the contemporary YouTube format. Third, also the sector of digital storytelling produces a number of examples, when organizations like the Center for Digital Storytelling[8] support "their" participants in the creation of digital narrations (see Lambert 2002).

In the second group of models, the aim of the organization is not to allow for or support participatory processes; these organizations focus on access and/or interaction. In a relatively rare number of cases, this concerns organizations that have a membership structure (model 3). Examples can be found in the sector of community wifi, where these organizations aim to provide access to the internet for their members. In contrast, organizations that facilitate access and interaction (model 4) can frequently be found in many different forms. Examples are organizations that provide blog or vlog facilities, like Ourmedia and YouTube,[9] and websites aimed at social networking like Facebook and MySpace.[10] Many of the UGC sites are related to this fourth model. Also, instances of what is now often called *citizen journalism*, where nonprofessionals provide raw materials to professional newsrooms, can be included in this fourth model.

The claims of specificity and newness also raise questions about the need to revise or rethink audience theory. In his essay "The Work of Theory in the Age of Digital Transformation," Jenkins (1999) reflects on digital theory; how it struggles with "its multiplicity, hybridity and fluidity"; and how it is at the same time "evolving at a dramatic pace." Digital theory becomes "a way of envisioning meaningful change and keeping alive the fluidity which digital media has introduced into many aspects of our social and personal lives." Jenkins's reflection on the role of digital media (theory) does also affect non-digital media (theory), as the following quote from his conclusion illustrates: "Digital theory identifies historical antecedents for contemporary media developments and at the same time, defamilarizes older media and opens them to re-examination."

The question for audience theory then becomes if and how these "contemporary media developments" affect its core categories, and whether the new (digital) media practices require structural adjustments of audience theory. Jenkins (1999) points to changes that might affect what he calls the "theories of spectatorship," as they "assume a relationship between optical point of view and narrative identification" and "must be revised in light of the intense identification and participation experienced by players of Sega or Nintendo video games." He illustrates this argument as follows:

> When I feel the exhilaration of speed, spinning real fast and clearing the screen as the Tasmanian Devil, my pleasure has less to do with my moral alignment with those characters than with my ability to control them. Even given my ample facial hair and my sometimes anarchic sense of humor, I am not, in the end, terribly much like Taz.

Without ignoring the relevance of these arguments, the question that is posed here relates to the structural dimensions of audience theory, as discussed in the first part of this chapter. Following Jenkins's point that a totalizing account on digital media is slightly overambitious, I want to focus on UGC's impact on the structural dimensions of audience theory (which still is more than ambitious enough, given the diversity of UGC formats). If we look at the active-passive dimension of audience theory, it is hardly a surprising conclusion that UGC remains very well embedded within this debate (and dimension). UGC is clearly a celebration of audience activity. There is some attention for more passive use (see the lurkers debate mentioned above) and (even) for nonuse (e.g. Wyatt, Thomas, and Terranova 2002), although it seems difficult to escape the dominant approach of UGC audiences as produsers. This at the same time shows that the debates about UGC are also firmly embedded within the participation-interaction dimension, as UGC mainly emphasizes the participation of digital media users in the production process of content. Again, interaction with the content is (at the theoretical level) much less dominantly present, and reception analyses of UGC are (still) rather rare.[11]

The second main dimension of audience theory also seems to be able to accommodate the theoretical reflections on UGC. The micro-macro dimension is, for instance, very present in the analysis of blogging, where the concept of the blogger (e.g. Singer's analysis of the political j-blogger in Singer 2005) is combined with the concept of the blogosphere (e.g. Wallsten's 2007 analysis of agenda setting). Especially the notion of community plays a crucial role in theorizing UGC. First, the blogosphere (as a whole) is seen as a community, and references to the blogger community can sometimes be found. Lampa (2004), for instance, refers to the "imagined community of blogging" and "to the widespread notion of the transnational blogging community or ... the persistence of the blogger identity," claiming that this community "resides in the mind of the individual blogger as an online imagined community resulting from the shared experience of instant publishing." Other authors (e.g. Schaap 2004) link this blogger community to specific national communities. Third, similar arguments can be made for other kinds of platforms, applications, and activities like computer-supported collaborative work and web-based community applications (Bakardjieva and Feenberg 2002). One example can be found in Benkler (2006), when he refers to the "peer production community" (2006, p. 102) and to the "free and open source software development community" (2006, p. 123). This also immediately brings us to the importance of the organized audience, which in the discussions on UGC often refers to the informal organization of what the OECD calls the "creative effort." Quite often we can find examples of nonmembership organizations, where audience members can effectively produce media content, without allowing them opportunities for (equal) decision making. As Zwick, Bonsu, and Darmody (2008) argue, this will lead in some cases to corporate power working with the freedom of consumers to achieve its proper aims; the "challenge of new marketing 'govern-mentality' then becomes 'to ensure that consumer freedom evolves in the 'right' way'" (p. 184). Other cases, like Wikipedia, are not commercially motivated and remain successful examples of mass collaboration. As Fallis puts it, "By allowing anyone with Internet access to create and edit content... Wikipedia now includes millions of entries in many different languages" (2008, p. 1663). At the same time, as discussed above, more formal types of participatory online organizations do exist, also providing support for the presence of the meso level within the micro-macro dimension of audience theory.

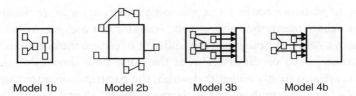

Model 1b   Model 2b   Model 3b   Model 4b

Figure 9.4   Models of (semi-)participatory organizations with networked participants.

This audience theory discussion also allows us to revisit the issue of the specificity and newness of UGC in relation to other forms of audience activity. Clearly, in many cases this specificity of UGC is related to issues of modality, where we find an intensification and massafication of already existing participatory practices. This intensification also has a number of consequences in relation to the participatory process itself, as the intensity of the participatory process, especially within the (decision-making processes of the) media organization itself, tends to be limited. However fascinating mass collaboration and informal organizations might be, they do not always offer the best guarantees for balanced power relations within the production process itself. This analysis is further strengthened by the convergence argument, which does imply that the power base of corporations has decreased through the need to negotiate with their consumers, but at the same time this negotiation also affects the intensity of the participatory process through the corporate use of governmentality strategies. The risk of incorporation and of what Penny calls "interpassivity," meaning the "Pavlovian interactivity of stimulus and response," is never far away (1995, p. 54).

Conclusion

The success of the new generation of media technologies – in combination with their presupposed interactive and even participatory nature – feeds the assumption that we are living another new communication revolution. But the discourse of novelty that accompanies these evolutions brings along a number of substantial problems. The attention has too often become focused on the participatory potential of new media, which brings us to ignore the capacities of "old" media. The newspaper, radio, and television appear to be media from the past century, not relevant enough to be incorporated in the debates on participation. This causes three crucial mistakes to be made. First, the cultural importance of the old media is underestimated, although they still play an important role in the everyday lives of many people. Blinded by the futurist megalomania, and by the hope for a better future, the taken-for-granted presence of the old media is often forgotten. Second, the institutional nature of the present-day media worlds is equally often ignored. A vast number of media products are still produced by media corporations, which are old top-down systems based on capitalist logics and not always in favor of the maximalist approaches toward participation and democracy. In this dazzling techno-optimism, it is often forgotten that the routines, identities, practices, conventions, and representations that circulate in the old media system have not been lost, but still co-structure the "new" media system. Third, the discourse of novelty feeds into the techno-logical-determinist model, assuming that media technologies are the driving forces of societal participation and that specific media technologies are per definition more participatory than others. Without wanting to underestimate the specificity of any kind of technology, or without positioning them as *"determined technologies"* (Williams 1974, p. 7), the participatory potential of media technologies remains dependent on the way that they are used and the societal context of which they are part.

From this perspective, Jenkins's (2006) argument to cross the old-new media divide is highly instrumental, not just to understand the role of media and UGC in everyday life. Also at the theoretical level, we need to be careful not to let the discourse of novelty smother the long theoretical tradition of studying the audience. Audience theory turns out to be quite stable in its capacity to facilitate the understanding of the diversity of relations between humans and media technology. The core theoretical dimensions that structure audience theory have not been downgraded by rise of the digital culture; on the contrary, they allow us to reflect on the changes that characterize the present-day media configuration, with its strong emphasis on informally organized audience activity (translated as participation in the production process, and not necessarily as participation with the organization and its decision-making routines or structures). However important these changes might be, many of them remain situated at the level of the intensification and massification of already existing participatory practices and models. For that reason, it would be regrettable to lose this long-lasting participatory tradition (at the levels of both theory and praxis).

One additional reason for keeping the history of participation in mind is that it has produced a number of radical examples that attempted to maximize media participation, at the levels of both content production and decision making (in formal or informal settings). These radical participatory projects have provided structural support for the democratic imaginary of full participation (see Pateman 1970), the phantasmagoric realization of which serves as the breeding grounds for civil society's attempts oriented toward democratization of the media. These radical participatory practices are the real temporary autonomous zones that Bey (1985) wrote about: the radical-democratic media archipelagos that are often carefully hidden away, and that dissolve before they can be incorporated by mainstream media corporations. As horizons, these radical media organizations (disregarding the technologies they use) remain a necessity to continue and to deepen the participatory processes that have been set in motion, and are now involving more people than ever.

Notes

1 Abercrombie and Longhurst (1998, p. 4) sum up the fields within which the research of effects is and has been active in six clusters: sexual activity, violence, children, elections/politics, gender, and race.
2 In this text, the term community-society dimension is preferred.
3 The Technorati website (http://technorati.com/about/) was tracking 112.8 million websites on March 24, 2008.
4 Such as user-created content (UCC) and consumer-generated media (CGM); see e.g. the Japanese *2006* White Paper of the Ministry of Internal Affairs and Communications (2006, p. 18).
5 To the regret of some; see Keen (2007).
6 See http://www.amarc.org.
7 http://www.indymedia.org.
8 See http:vwww.storycenter.org.
9 See http://www.ourmedia.org and http://www.youtube.com.
10 See http://www.facebook.com and http://www.myspace.com.
11 For one of my own examples of a reception study of UGC, see Carpentier (2010).

References

Abercrombie, N. and Longhurst, B. 1998 *Audiences: A Sociological Theory of Performance and Imagination*. Sage, London.

Allor, M. 1988 Relocating the site of the audience. *Critical Studies in Mass Communication*, 5, 3, pp. 217–233.

Ang, I. 1991 *Desperately Seeking the Audience*. Routledge, London.

Bailey, O., Cammaerts, B. and Carpentier, N. 2007 *Understanding Alternative Media*. Open University Press, Milton Keynes, UK.

Bakardjieva, M. and Feenberg, A. 2002 Community technology and democratic rationalization, *Information Society*, 18, 3, 181–192.

Barthes, R. 1984 The death of the author. In R. Barthes. *Image Music Text*. Fontana, London, pp. 142–148.

Benkler, Y. 2006 *The Wealth of Networks: How Social Production Transforms Markets and Freedom*. Yale University Press, New Haven, CT.

Bey, H. 1985 *The Temporary Autonomous Zone: Ontological Anarchy, Poetic Terrorism*. Autonomedia, Brooklyn.

Brecht, B. 2001 *Brecht on Film and Radio*. Ed. M. Silberman. Methuen Drama, London.

Bruns, A. 2007 "Anyone can edit": understanding the produser. Guest Lecture at State University of New York at Buffalo. Retrieved from http://snurb.info/index.php?q=node/286

Carey, J. W. 1975 A cultural approach to communication. *Journal of Communication*, 2, pp. 1–22.

Carpentier, N. 2003 BBC's Video Nation as a participatory media practice. Signifying everyday life, cultural diversity and participation in an on-line community. *International Journal of Cultural Studies*, 6, 4, pp. 425–447.

Carpentier, N. 2007 Participation and interactivity: changing perspectives. The construction of an integrated model on access, interaction and participation. In V. Nightingale and T. Dwyer, eds. *New Media Worlds: Challenges for Convergence.* Oxford University Press, Melbourne, pp. 214–230.

Carpentier, N. 2010 Produsers' on participatory websites. Ordinary young people and the politics of banality. In P. Dahlgren and T. Olsson, eds. *Young Citizens, ICT's and Democracy.* Nordicom, Stockholm, pp. 51–68.

Cohen, A. P. 1989 *The Symbolic Construction of Community.* Routledge, London.

Couldry, N. 2003 *Media Rituals: A Critical Approach.* Routledge, London.

Dayan, D. 2005 Mothers, midwives and abortionists: genealogy, obstetrics, audiences and publics. In S. Livingstone, ed. *Audiences and Publics: When Cultural Engagement Matters for the Public Sphere.* Intellect, Bristol, pp. 43–76.

DeFleur, M. 1966 *Theories of Mass Communication.* David McKay, New York.

Downing, J. 2003 Audiences and readers of alternative media: the absent lure of the virtually unknown. *Media, Culture and Society,* 25, pp. 625–645.

Downing, J., ed., with Ford, T. V. and Gil, G. 2000 *Radical Media: Rebellious Communication and Social Movements.* Sage, London.

Eco, U. 1968 *La Struttura Assente. La Ricerca Semiotica e il Metodo Strutturale.* Bompiani, Milano.

Fallis, D. 2008 Toward an epistemology of Wikipedia. *Journal of the American Society for Information Science and Technology,* 59, 10, pp. 1662–1674.

Fiske, J. 1987 *Television Culture.* Routledge, London.

Fiske, J. 1989 *Understanding Popular Culture.* Routledge, London.

Fiske, J. 1993 *Power Plays/Power Works.* Verso, London.

Fraser, N. 1990 Rethinking the public sphere. *Social Text,* 25/26, pp. 56–80.

Gans, H. J. 1967 Popular culture in America. In H. Becker, ed. *Social Problems: A Modern Approach.* Wiley and Sons, New York, pp. 582–598.

Girard, B., ed. 1992 *A Passion for Radio.* Black Rose, Montreal.

Hall, S. 1980 Encoding/decoding. In S. Hall, ed. *Culture, Media, Language: Working Papers in Cultural Studies, 1972–79.* Hutchinson, London, pp. 128–138.

Harré, R. 1981 Philosophical aspects of the macro-micro problem. In K.D. Knorr-Cetina and A.V. Cicourel, eds. *Advances in Social Theory and Methodology.* Routledge & Kegan Paul, Boston, pp. 139–160.

Hartley, J. 2008 YouTube, digital literacy and the growth of knowledge. Paper presented at the Media, Communication and Humanity Conference, 21–23 September, Media@ LSE, London.

Höijer, B. 1999 To be an audience. In P. Alasuutari, ed. *Rethinking the Media Audience.* Sage, Beverly Hills, CA, pp. 179–194.

Jenkins, H. 1992 *Textual Poachers: Television Fans and Participatory Culture.* Routledge, New York.

Jenkins, H. 1999 The work of theory in the age of digital transformation. Retrieved from http://web.mit.edu/cms/People/henry3/pub/digitaltheory.htm

Jenkins, H. 2006 *Convergence Culture: Where Old and New Media Collide.* New York University Press, New York.

Katz, E., Blumler, J. and Gurevitch, M. 1974 Utilisation of mass communication by the individual. In J. Blumler and E. Katz, eds. *The Uses of Mass Communications: Current Perspectives on Gratifications Research.* Sage, Beverly Hills, CA, pp. 19–32.

Keen, A. 2007 *The Cult of the Amateur: How Today's Internet Is Killing Our Culture.* Currency, New York.

Kellner, D. 1992 *The Persian Gulf TV War*. Westview Press, Boulder, CO.

Lambert, J. 2002 *Digital Storytelling: Capturing Lives, Creating Communities*. Digital Diner Press, Berkeley, CA.

Lampa, G. 2004 Imagining the blogosphere: an introduction to the imagined community of instant publishing. In L. Gurak, S. Antonijevic, L. Johnson, C. Ratliff and J. Reyman, eds. *Into the Blogosphere: Rhetoric, Community, and Culture of Weblogs*. Retrieved from http://blog.lib.umn.edu/blogosphere/imagining_the_blogosphere.html

Lewis, G.H. 1992 Who do you love? The dimensions of musical taste. In J. Lull, ed. *Popular Music and Communication*. Sage, Newbury Park, CA, pp. 134–151.

Lindlof, T.R. 1988 Media audiences as interpretative communities. *Communication Yearbook*, 11, pp. 81–107.

Littlejohn, S.W. 1996 *Theories of Human Communication*. Wadsworth, Belmont, CA.

Livingstone, S. 1998 Relationships between media and audiences. In T. Liebes and J. Curran, eds. *Media, Ritual and Identity*. Routledge, London, pp. 237–255.

Livingstone, S. 2005 On the relation between audiences and publics. In S. Livingstone, ed. *Audiences and Publics: When Cultural Engagement Matters for the Public Sphere*. Intellect, Bristol, pp. 17–41.

Livingstone, S. and Lunt, P. 1996 *Talk on Television, Audience Participation and Public Debate*. Routledge, London.

MacBride Commission. 1980 *Many Voices, One World: Report by the International Commission for the Study of Communication Problems*. UNESCO and Kogan Page, Paris.

Martin-Barbero, J. 1993 *Communication, Culture and Hegemony: From the Media to Mediations*. Sage, London.

McNair, B., Hibberd, M. and Schlesinger, P. 2003 *Mediated Access Broadcasting and Democratic Participation in the Age of Mediated Communication*. University of Luton Press, Luton.

McQuail, D. 1994 *Mass Communication Theory: An Introduction*. Sage, London.

Ministry of Internal Affairs and Communications. 2006 *Information and Communications in Japan: White Paper 2006*. Ministry of Internal Affairs and Communications, Tokyo. Retrieved from http://www.johotsusintokei.soumu.go.jp/whitepaper/eng/WP2006/2006-index.html

Moores, S. 1996 *Interpreting Audiences: The Ethnography of Media Consumption*. Sage, London.

Morley, D. 1986 *Family Television: Cultural Power and Domestic Leisure*. Comedia, London.

Mouffe, C. 1994 For a politics of nomadic identity. In G. Robertson, M. Mash, L. Tickner, J. Bird, B. Curtis and T. Putnam, eds. *Travellers' Tales: Narratives of Home and Displacement*. Routledge, London, pp. 105–113.

Nightingale, V. 1996 *Studying Audiences: The Shock of the Real*. Routledge, London.

Nonnecke, B. 2000 Lurking in email-based discussion lists. Unpublished PhD dissertation, South Bank University, London.

Nonnecke, B. and Preece, J. 2001 Why lurkers lurk. Paper presented at the Americas Conference on Information Systems, Boston.

Organisation for Economic Co-operation and Development (OECD). 2007 *Participative Web: User-Created Content*. OECD, Paris. Retrieved from http://www.oecd.org/dataoecd/57/14/38393115.pdf

Ostertag, B. 2006 *People's Movements, People's Press: The Journalism of Social Justice Movements*. Beacon Press, Boston.

Palmgreen, P. and Rayburn, J. D. 1985 An expectancy-value approach to media gratifications. In J. E. Rosengren, P. Palmgreen and L. Wenner, eds. *Media Gratification Research.* Sage, Beverly Hills, CA, pp. 61–73.

Pateman, C. 1970 *Participation and Democratic Theory.* Cambridge University Press, Cambridge.

Penny, S. 1995 Consumer culture and the technological imperative. In S. Penny, ed. *Critical Issues in Electronic Media.* State University of New York Press, New York, pp. 47–73.

Principles for User Generated Content Services. 2007 [Home page]. Retrieved from http:// www.ugcprinciples.com

Radway, J. 1988 *Reading the Romance: Women, Patriarchy and Popular Literature.* University of North Carolina Press, Chapel Hill.

Renckstorf, K., McQuail, D. and Jankowski, N. 1996 *Media Use as Social Action: A European Approach to Audience Studies.* Libbey, London.

Reyes Matta, F. 1981 A model for democratic communication. *Development Dialogue,* 2, pp. 79–97.

Reyes Matta, F. 1986 Alternative communication, solidarity and development in the face of transnational expansion. In R. Atwood and E.G. McAnany, eds. *Communication and Latin American Society: Trends in Critical Research, 1960–1985.* University of Wisconsin Press, Madison, pp. 190–214.

Rheingold, H. 1993 *The Virtual Community: Homesteading on the Electronic Frontier.* Addison-Wesley, Reading.

Rodriguez, C. 2001 *Fissures in the Mediascape: An International Study of Citizens' Media.* Hampton Press, Cresskill, NJ.

Rosen, J. 2008 Afterword: the people formerly known as the audience. In N. Carpentier and B. De Cleen, eds. *Participation and Media Production: Critical Reflections on Content Creation.* Cambridge Scholars Publishing, Newcastle upon Tyne, UK, pp. 163–165.

Schaap, F. 2004 Links, lives, logs: presentation in the Dutch blogosphere. In L. Gurak, S. Antonijevic, L. Johnson, C. Ratliff and J. Reyman, eds. *Into the Blogosphere: Rhetoric, Community, and Culture of Weblogs.* Downloaded from http://blog.lib.umn.edu/ blogosphere/links_lives_logs.html

Schweiger, W. and Quiring, O. 2006 User generated content on mass media web sites: just a kind of interactivity or something completely different? Paper presented at the annual meeting of the International Communication Association, Dresden, Germany, June 19–23. Retrieved from http://www.allacademic.com/meta/p12745_index.html

Servaes, J. 1989 *One World, Multiple Cultures: A New Paradigm on Communication for Development.* Acco & Leuven, Amersfoort.

Servaes, J. 1999 *Communication for Development: One World, Multiple Cultures.* Hampton Press, Cresskill, NJ.

Shannon, C. and Weaver, W. 1949 *The Mathematical Theory of Communication.* University of Illinois Press, Urbana.

Shirky, C. 2002 Weblogs and the mass amateurization of publishing. Retrieved from http:// www.shirky.com/writings/weblogs_publishing.html

Shirky, C. 2008 *Here Comes Everybody: The Power of Organizing without Organizations.* Penguin, New York.

Silverstone, R. 1991 From audiences to consumers: the household and the consumption of communication and information technologies. *European Journal of Communication,* 6, pp. 135–154.

Silverstone, R. and Hirsch, E., eds. 1992 *Consuming Technologies: Media and Information in Domestic Spaces*. Routledge, London.

Singer, J. B. 2005 The political j-blogger: "normalizing" a new media form to fit old norms and practices. *Journalism*, 6, 2, pp. 173–198.

Smith, M. A. and Kollock, P. 1999 *Communities in Cyberspace*. Routledge, London.

Terranova, T. 2000 Free labor: producing culture for the digital economy. *Social Text*, 18, pp. 33–58.

Thompson, J. B. 1995 *The Media and Modernity: A Social Theory of the Media*. Polity Press, Cambridge.

Toffler, A. 1980 *The Third Wave*. Bantam, New York.

Verba, S. and Nie, N. 1987 *Participation in America: Political Democracy and Social Equality*. University of Chicago Press, Chicago.

Walkerdine, V. 1986 Video replay: families, films and fantasy. In J. D. Burgin and C. Kaplan, eds. *Formations of fantasy*. Methuen, London, pp. 167–199.

Wallsten, K. 2007 Agenda setting and the blogosphere: an analysis of the relationship between mainstream media and political blogs. *Review of Policy Research*, 24, 6, pp. 567–587.

Walther, J. and Boyd, S. 2002 Attraction to computer-mediated social support. In C. Lin and D. Atkin, eds. *Communication Technology and Society: Audience Adoption and Use*. Hampton Press, Cresskill, NJ, pp. 153–188.

Wasko, J. and Mosco, V., eds. 1992 *Democratic Communications in the Information Age*. Garamond Press and Ablex, Toronto and Norwood, NJ.

Webster, J. G. and Phalen, P. F. 1997 *The Mass Audience: Rediscovering the Dominant Model*. Erlbaum, Mahwah, NJ.

Williams, R. 1974 *Television: Technology and Cultural Form*. Wesleyan Press, Oxford.

Wyatt, S., Thomas, G. and Terranova, T. 2002 They came, they surfed, they went back to the beach: conceptualising use and non-use of the Internet. In S. Woolgar, ed. *Virtual Society? Technology, Cyberbole, Reality*. Oxford University Press, Oxford, pp. 23–40.

Zwick, D., Bonsu, S. K. and Darmody, A. 2008 Putting Consumers to Work: "Co-creation" and new marketing govern-mentality. *Journal of Consumer Culture*, 8, 2, pp. 163–196.

10

The Necessary Future of the Audience ... and How to Research It

Nick Couldry

"The people formerly known as the audience are simply the public made realer, less fictional, more able, less predictable," writes Jay Rosen (2006). From this, it sounds as if abandoning the term *the audience* is a necessary first step to looking with clear eyes on everyday democracy in the media sphere. A rather less sanguine rule of thumb suggests that only one in a hundred people are active online content producers, with 10 "interacting" by commentary and the remaining 89 just viewing ... in other words, acting like an "audience" (van Dijck 2009). The need for a more accurate register of what people (outside of specialist institutions for producing and circulating media) are doing with media is clear.

Audience research is still a good term for this line of research. Even if it were true that everyone now can be a media producer (and this claim needs heavy qualification), this would consider only one factor unsettling the traditional "audience" in the digital age. Once we look at today's broader media environment, it becomes much less clear that "the audience" will disappear. On the contrary, the position of "the audience" in wider discourses about media is likely to persist, and because discourse informs practice, something rather like "audience" practices are likely to go on being reproduced within the larger landscape of media-related practice – even if that landscape is now much more diverse than we could have imagined 20, let alone 40, years ago. That is why the future of the audience is "necessary," which does not imply that it will remain simple. On the contrary, audience practice will be increasingly hard to track. This chapter considers the difficulties of that task, and some solutions, drawing on the potential contribution of "practice theory" to media research (Couldry 2004).

The Handbook of Media Audiences, First Edition. Edited by Virginia Nightingale.
© 2014 John Wiley & Sons, Ltd. Published 2014 by John Wiley & Sons, Ltd.

The "Necessity" of the Audience

Let me start with the "necessity" of the audience. For many, the demise of "the audience" is linked to the demise of what we have called *the media*, that is, the bundle of central media institutions that seemed for decades to be necessary reference points in everyday life but that, for multiple reasons, are now under challenge. Predictions of the death of "the media" are, however, greatly exaggerated because they ignore the accumulated historical forces (technological, economic, social, and political) that have underpinned the construction of "the media" from the huge range of outputs we call "media" (Couldry 2009). The fate of "the media" is indeed closely tied to that of "the audience." The audience (and the media) only emerged out of a quite particular settlement of symbolic and discursive resources that stabilized in the early twentieth century. As early histories of radio show, radio was originally understood by many as supporting a diffused many-to-many structure (Barnouw 1990, pp. 30–40; Chapman 2005, pp. 122–123), not a centralized one-to-many broadcasting structure. But fairly quickly, the centralized model came to dominate in radio as in previous media (e.g. the press), and with television the many-to-many moment never occurred. The notion of mass media became entrenched, but mass media are not "just there": their extraordinary symbolic privilege and power need to be legitimated. The beliefs, attitudes, and actions that help us "live with" media institutions are integral to the wider organization of economic, social, and political production, indeed to the sustaining of the modern nation-state. I have previously considered this question through the idea of "the myth of the mediated centre" (Couldry 2003), that is, the claim that the media are our privileged access point to society's center or core, to what's going on in the wider world. This myth about media enfolds another myth about social "order," "the myth of the center": the idea that societies, or nations, have not just a physical or organizational center – a place that allocates resources – but also a generative center that explains the social world's functioning and is the source of its values.

The myth of the mediated center is not simply an explicit ideology imposed from above; it is a form of understanding we enact in our talk, action, and thoughts. In the process of its own reproduction, the myth of "the media" is also reproduced. The idea of the media as a central access point to the social seems like a condensed answer to Durkheim's 100-year-old question about what bonds sustain a society as a society. This mythical work requires the attention of a national audience, "the audience."

But what if the very ideas of "the media" and "the mediated center" are imploding, as the interfaces we call media are transformed? Three dynamics – technological, social, and political – are potentially undermining our sense of the media as a privileged site for accessing a common world. *Technologically*, there is the multiplication of outputs, interfaces, and intertextual linkages, in other words, convergence: where in this complexity can we find anything as simple as "the audience" or "the media"? But it is easy to exaggerate the irrelevance of traditional media (Couldry 2009, pp. 442–443); it is easy also to forget the dependence of media's economic models (Turow 2007) not only on tracking individual "produsers" but also on *centripetal* forces that continue to drive attention to common media as the site of "what's going on." From this perspective, celebrity culture, while full of noninstitutional production (by fans, gossip websites, and the like), works, at another level, as a connective tissue, tying together countless media products into a "media world" (Couldry 2000, pp. 42–48). *Socially*, the rise of social-networking sites (SNS) suggests a new type of mediated "center" (indeed, a new type of "live" connection) in which the focus is not central media institutions, and through them the state and a social center, but ourselves, our friends and family, and our horizontal social world. There is no doubt that social-networking sites are a development of fundamental importance for our understanding of media and audiences, but we must not forget media industries' intense interest in colonizing social-networking space. Rather than expecting SNS to undermine "the media" and horizontally deconstruct "the audience," it is more plausible to suggest that SNS, as sites for performance and mutual engagement, will develop in close linkage with central media in a sort of double helix. *Politically*, there is no doubt that the state and those competing for state power will have to take SNS seriously, and it is not yet clear how SNS will work as an effective site of political communication. But it is equally clear that political pressures for some such adaptation and for some continuation of centrally produced news and entertainment infrastructures are intense: how would political communications work if governments and political parties could not assume they had centralized means of getting national audiences' attention?

In these various ways, it is clear that the fate of "the audience," however patched together from old and new practice, will be closely tied to the wider forces of economic social and political governance that still depend on the construction of the "mediated center." To argue that "the audience" is not a natural but profoundly historical phenomenon (Butsch 2009) does not imply that its reproduction is any less necessary under contemporary conditions. For the rest of this chapter, I will assume that *the audience* – defined broadly as the domain of media-related practice outside production within specialist institutions – remains of key importance for media research, and particularly for understanding contemporary media's social consequences. This is not to deny that *how* we understand the audience will undergo important shifts!

The rest of this chapter is in three main sections: first, a brief review of the perspective on audience research which underlies its argument; second, a discussion of the basic principles of practice theory, which suggests a new approach to the complexities of the contemporary audience; and, third, some examples that not so much map the emerging field of the audience – it is not yet in a position to be mapped – as indicate some key dimensions of audience practice, and their methodological implications.

Signposts from Early Audience Research

Critical research on media audiences (Hall, Morley, Ang)[1] in the 1980s quickly developed into an independent empirical tradition that came to interface with anthropological research (Ginsburg 1994; Ginsburg, Abu-Lughod, and Larkin 2002) and social psychology (Livingstone 1990). But the radical implications of audience research for the overall field of media research only became clear in the 1990s. A key turning point was Ien Ang's questioning of "what it means, or what it is like, to live in a media-saturated world" (1996 p. 72). This more widely focused research question had been anticipated also by writers on "mediation" (Silverstone 1999, 2006; Madianou 2005) interested in the dialectic of social processes focused around media.[2] In the 1980s and early 1990s, work on the domestication of media technologies in the home was also important in extending early audience research (Silverstone and Hirsch 1992), while my own early research pursued "mediation" from the perspective of power, asking "what it means to live in a society dominated by large-scale media institutions" (Couldry 2000, p. 6).

Two attempts over the past decade to shift the paradigm of audience research are worth noting here. First, Abercrombie and Longhurst (1998) challenged what they saw as an existing paradigm of media research dominated by ideological questions (the "incorporation/resistance" paradigm) and replaced it by a "spectacle/performance" paradigm that foregrounded the various levels of engagement people have in different aspects of media culture. Abercrombie and Longhurst's work overlapped in some respects with Alasuutaari's (1999) account of a "third generation" of audience research whose priority was to "get a grasp on our contemporary 'media culture'" (p. 6). But this "generational" formulation risked disguising the radical nature of the shift underway by holding onto a relatively traditional notion of "audiences" as its initial reference point.

Meanwhile, media anthropologist Liz Bird's book *The Audience in Everyday Life* (2003) argued that "we cannot really isolate the role of media in culture, because the media are firmly anchored into the web of culture, although articulated by individuals in different ways. The 'audience' is 'everywhere and nowhere'" (pp. 2–3). Bird usefully distinguishes between saying that our culture is media saturated, and saying that, as individuals within that culture, our own practice is media saturated, which is quite a separate question (2003, p. 3). This should put us on guard against assuming that "media cultures" involve a universal cultural system; better to look instead at the whole range of practices in which media consumption and media-related talk are embedded, including practices of *selecting out* media inputs (Hoover, Schofield Clark, and Alters 2003). While the latter may not be what normally we refer to by *media culture*, they are nonetheless significant practices *oriented to*, or *related to*, media. Maybe an approach to audiences that is less media-centric and more open to the complexity of audience practice's embedding in social life (Ruddock 2007) is more useful at a time when people's interactions with media are undergoing radical change (Jenkins 2006).

Analyzing Media as Practice

We can take these new insights about audiences further by drawing on the development of "practice theory" in wider social research. I have advocated this approach in detail elsewhere (Couldry 2004), and it draws on a broad philosophical and theoretical background that there is no space to review here (Schatzki 1999; Reckwitz 2002). A key point about this approach which fits practice theory well for grasping "what's going on" in a fast-changing media environment is that it aims to be *as open as possible* in analyzing what practices are out there. Instead of starting out from the simple division of media research into studying "the text" or the production or reception of "the text," it explores in a more open way the mass of things people do and say (and indeed believe) that are oriented to, or related to, media. To do this, it listens very closely to how people understand what they are doing, and what "practices" their actions comprise. Actions *are* linked into a "practice" not just by explicit understandings (e.g. the understanding that "breaststroke" and "butterfly" both belong to the practice of swimming) but also by common rules, aims, and beliefs, not all of which may be explicit (Schatzki 1999, p. 89). Take the media case: undoubtedly there are a whole mass of media-related practices in contemporary societies, but how are they divided up into specific practices, and how are those practices coordinated with each other? These questions can only be settled by investigating the details of everyday language and action.

Taking as our starting point what people are doing with, or in relation to, media has quite radical consequences. It distances us from industry or marketing hype; it distances us also from the normal media studies assumption that what audiences do ("audiencing"; see Fiske 1992) is already a distinctive set of media-focused practices rather than an artificially chosen "slice" through daily life that *cuts across* how people actually understand the practices in which they are engaged. And it insists we look very closely at the categorizations of practice that people themselves make, "in practice" as it were.

But doesn't this undercut the argument of my first section that media-related practice is shaped on a larger scale by certain myths about media institutions' relations to a social "center"? Certainly within a practice-based approach we have to consider the forces that order practice more widely, but this has already been considered in practice theory by the sociologist Ann Swidler (2001), who asks, "[H]ow [do] some practices anchor, control, or organise others" (p. 79)? Swidler approaches ordering first from the point of view of definitions: some practices are defined as part of a larger practice which provides their key reference points, so for example political marketing, lobbying, and campaigning are part of the wider practice of politics. Swidler also looks at ordering as a question of dynamic change: some practices "anchor" others, because changes in the former automatically cause the latter's aims to alter. So a ceremony or ritual may anchor a whole series of practices that participate in it. Anchoring practices, in other words, *produce* new forms of categorization and distinction relied upon in other practices, and so they reproduce our sense that the space of practices is ordered, not chaotic. From this perspective, we can see the "myth of the mediated center" as one of the most fundamental anchoring devices in the media field since it helps make sense of the act of being part of an audience itself, as a form of "necessary" attention. How this myth works in detail cannot be assumed in advance: it has to be tracked down in the details of practice. Against this background, let me turn more explicitly to how in the digital media age we can continue to research what audiences do.

The Varieties of Audience Practice

The value of practice theory, as we have seen, is to ask open questions about what people are doing and how they categorize what they are doing, avoiding preconceptions which would – automatically and from outside – read their actions as, say, "consumption" or "being-an-audience." One possibility already suggested is that, in many cases, "media consumption" and "audiencing" form part of practices which are not themselves "about" media. Let me consider this initial point in relation to "traditional" media, ignoring the transformations of digital convergence. I will come to convergence shortly.

Traditional Media

Watching a football game on television (an apparently simple media "object") might for one person be best analyzed as part of their practice as a football fan; for another, it may be not their own passion to watch football, but an obligation or pleasure shared with others that explains their watching, for example in a public space as an expression of group solidarity or at home as an expression of family solidarity; another person may simply be filling in time, a practice that like some magazines is instantly "putdownable" (Hermes 1995) as soon as an interesting interruption occurs. Making this general point is hardly new (Bausinger 1984; Morley 1992), and two decades ago Virginia Nightingale (1992) showed the different practices of men and women within apparently the same act of "watching Rugby League football." But it illustrates how variable are the meanings of a simple act of media consumption.

The practice into which the act of watching televised football is inserted radically affects what aspects of that act interest us as researchers. It will probably only be in the case of the football fan that the "way" she or he reads the game's text is of much interest, since it is only here that the watching of the game forms a central, nonsubstitutable part of a wider practice (football fandom). Political economy approaches are background in all the above cases, but probably only important background in the case of the football fan, where media economics structure the games available to him or her and even aspects of the format of the game itself. At another level, the fact that people perform a huge range of practices (from fandom to family interaction to group solidarity in a pub to just waiting for something else to do) via the act of watching televised football is itself an example of the time–space coordination of practices through media schedules, just as with the act of "watching the news." A media-related descriptive core remains common in each case, although in other cases this descriptive core may be less certain: reading a celebrity magazine is more ambiguous and heterogeneous (is it just passing time, a deliberate search for humor, information seeking, or what?). Answers depend on who is reading the magazine and where, and on whether and how they put the contents of that celebrity magazine to later use.

The Consequences of Media Convergence

Media convergence creates completely new challenges for the analysis of audience practice. As Sonia Livingstone (2004) argued, the internet challenges traditional notions of audience because mass communication and peer communication now occur in the same media (see also Schroder et al. 2003). However, this has not ended but has *renewed* the challenge of working out what people are doing in relation to media texts or images. Indeed, the challenge grows with online material, because of its almost infinite intertextual proliferation and because of people's varied trajectories across the online textual universe. One advantage of online media is that audiences often leave traces of their consumption practice, as they comment on and interact around a text (Livingstone 2004, p. 85). And we will go on, as Livingstone points out, needing to understand how audiences watch, listen to, and read media.

The problem that media convergence poses for any common domain we might call *audience research* is rather that the practical contexts and technological supports for these basic acts of consumption are increasingly variable. Or, as Henry Jenkins (2006) puts it, underlying media (recorded sound, printed text, etc.) may stay basically the same, but the delivery platforms through which we access them are subject to huge and unpredictable change (pp. 13–14). This matters even for those more interested in textual processes than other dimensions of what audiences do, since it affects the intertextual space in which a particular text is consumed; within a practice paradigm, however, these uncertainties become fundamental.

No one can predict how exactly the trajectory of media convergence will develop. But, if we compare media provision in rich nations toward the end of the first decade of the twenty-first century with media provision in those same nations in the decades when all or most of this book's authors were growing up, media have undergone at least three fundamental transformations. Until the 1990s in principle and until the 2000s for all but a few consumers, the space of media was segregated along three dimensions:

- Mode of address
- Function
- Context dependence

The telephone used to be fixed in one part of the living space, and the television in another (each a distinct spatial context), and each medium was sharply differentiated in function and mode of address. You might discuss by phone what you saw earlier that evening on television, but it was not conceivable that you could use the same device to speak to friends and watch TV. Now it is, and the device, in principle, could be either a television or a phone, part of the living room furniture or something you carry on your person wherever you go. In terms of mode of address, we can now readily imagine the same delivery platform enabling conversation (one-to-one), reception of centrally transmitted content (one institution to many), self-publicity (one individual to many), and simultaneous group exchange (many-to-many), perhaps some of these even simultaneously and interchangeably. In terms of function, the same device (some version of a phone or TV) may serve for real-time interaction, reception of common broadcasts, recording transmitted material, recording original material (new images, text, video, and sound), and archiving any of that recorded material, however sourced. In terms of context dependence, we can reserve most such devices for a fixed place or context (a living room, bedroom, kitchen, and so on) or take them with us into any number of different contexts, as we move.

So we now have, built on top of a still limited range of basic media (Jenkins 2006, p. 13), a *media manifold* comprising a complex web of delivery platforms. The media manifold is something we can all imagine, even if its actuality is uneven. We can imagine it for two reasons distinctive to our era: first, because all media are already, or are on the way to becoming, digital, and so convertible into information bits of the same type; and, second, because the internet comprises a space – an infinite space of archiving and a large, but not infinite, bandwidth of transmission – where producers and audiences of all sorts can be in touch with each other.

Accessing the Media Manifold

The question is how we access and use that media manifold. People may vary hugely in what they access overall and how they access particular media materials. The question of "how" itself involves dimensionality, since some people will generally be one-dimensional users (consuming one medium at a time), while others will be multidimensional users (accessing multiple media at the same time and perhaps interchangeably through the same device or devices). It should be clear that we need to tread carefully when describing such complexity. We can no longer assume that "watching TV" is the same thing for one audience as for another, even at the basic level of the protocols (Jenkins 2006; Gitelman 2007) through which the act is performed, without even considering the wider issues of context discussed for traditional media in the last section.

Practice theory, because it is open in its approach to classification and typification, can help us deal with this complexity, not least by looking out for the emergent classifications of this complexity in everyday practice itself. At a time of potentially rapid change, practice theory can operate on two levels, first, in helping us grasp better the varying practice contexts in which a basic practice – say, watching a football game – is embedded (see above); and, second, it can help us to grasp how a less determinate practice such as "going on Facebook" (Livingstone 2008; Brake 2009) is categorized variously by social actors themselves. In the second case, practice theory alerts us to emergent rules of classification which will themselves help shape the field of media practice as it restabilizes. The concerns of practice theory are therefore not incidental, but *internal*, to current transformations in audiencing.

Think of the various factors which constrain our access to the media manifold. All can be traced to practices of various sorts, but only some derive from our practices as media users. Some factors are institutional. There is the packaging of certain media functions in particular devices with particular availability conditions, so that what is available *together* via the same device and within a time sequence of reasonable length is, in effect, limited (so internet use on my standard mobile phone is possible but heavily constrained by both cost and speed). There is the economic push and pull whereby certain functions are subsidized by producers and others are made prohibitively expensive, at least in certain circumstances. There are also regulatory factors, for example those linked to government and civil society concerns about what media contents should be accessible to children.

But *other* important factors that constrain our access to the media manifold may derive from what audiences do. Habit, just as much as access and relative cost, is crucial here (Couldry, Livingstone, and Markham 2007). Habits involve not only simple acts of repetition but also the regular linking together of whole bundles of actions as part of wider lifestyles and ways of coordinating work, family responsibilities, and leisure. Practices are the key to grasping how the infinite manifold of possibilities that media now offer are "actualized" in particular places and markets by particular socioeconomic groups. The very meaning of the term "convergence culture" (Jenkins 2006) – indeed, its usefulness – depends on the fine-grained sociological detail of how these potentials of audience activity work out in practice (Ouellette and Wilson forthcoming)

Wider Contexts and Practices of Engagement

Within a practice paradigm, we can widen our lens when looking at "the audience." There are large domains of everyday life whose relation to audiencing is little researched: media use in education; individuals' uses of media references in telling stories about themselves, their family, or historical events; and the uses of media in the legal system and in work practices generally. All of these differ from simple media "production" or "reception," yet they are part of the wider space of "audiencing" in a media-saturated age. Because practice theory opens up our research on "audiencing" to the study of many diverse practices (law, education, and so on) for their uses of media, the understanding of "anchoring" (Swidler 2001) becomes particularly important: how media practices are anchored within other wider practices, and vice versa. One factor that helps shape the contexts which anchor a particular media-related practice is engagement.

Engagement by audiences in media contents is important to only some media-related practices, as we noted with the example of watching football on TV. But where film audiences *are* engaged in texts, the process, conditions, and expressions of engagement are highly variable: engagement is part of the "practical logics" in which any act of viewing or reading is embedded (Barker and Brooks 1998, p. 137). In other cases, where engagement seems to be a given (e.g. heavy TV viewers), close examination reveals that the *screening out* of textual information may matter more than engagement with specific contents that pass in front of viewers (Lembo 2000).[3] So engagement is complex and dependent on the varieties of practice – and this is without even considering the many varieties of engagement itself (see Takahashi 2007 for an important study).

Convergence has potentially altered the dynamics of engagement, too. It has changed the spaces in which engagement can be transmitted to other audience members, and, through the easy linkability of online material, it has also enabled much more elaborate "objects" of engagement to be registered: with a few links, I can show others that I like a long list of websites, blogs, films, places, news items, music tracks, and so on. Convergence has therefore altered the performance of engagement, and not just for fans who have been served for some time by specialist discussion lists and websites, but for general audience members who have easy access to the playful enthusiasms of others through online clearinghouses such as YouTube.

These are changes potentially in the overall landscape of audience experience, although their significance, once again, needs to be tracked into how audience practices are organized. It is easy to exaggerate the degree of change here and forget that, while YouTube is a fascinating connective space for researchers' speculation, we still know too little about who (and how many) people post on it, and under what conditions.[4]

Dimensions of Audience Practice

Granted that research into audiences has become more complex in an age of convergence, what are likely to be the important dimensions along which we distinguish audience practice in the future? Drawing on the previous discussion, there are three dimensions of audience practice which we must try to keep distinct:

- The texture of people's audience practices
- The media contents accessed through those practices
- The wider uses and practice contexts served by, or associated with, those practices

By *texture*, I mean the rhythms, density, and patterning of what people do to access or use media. A pioneering study on the texture of people's "audiencing" was David Morley's *Family Television* (Morley 1986). In recent years, there has been a revival of interest in questions of texture, even if that exact term is not always used. So Hoover, Schofield Clark, and Alters (2003) have introduced the distinction between households that are "suffused" by media and households that are more "differentiated" in their patterns of media consumption. In relation to television, Ron Lembo has distinguished between "continuous" and "discrete" viewers (2000, pp. 142–143). Clearly, it makes a great difference whether any particular act of media consumption is part of a continuous flow or a discrete act, anticipated in time or marked off from the day's activities in some other way: the patterning of media use in time may also be overlaid on the patterning of space (Bakardjeva 2005; Bengtsson 2006). As possibilities of convergence become embedded in every-day routines, questions of texture, even with traditional media, become more complex: does a continuous television viewer watch with a simultaneous online stream of communication (through the television), and if so, what is it used for? How does someone's discrete television viewing relate, if at all, to that person's separate computer use? Similar questions of breadth and frequency of use arise in measuring degrees of internet take-up (see Selwyn, Gorard, and Furlong 2005 for an important study of internet nonusers and minimal users).

Internet use poses its own distinctive questions of texture, too: we need to know more about how people consume online texts, to what degree and with what time expenditure they follow up hypertext links, and so on (Livingstone 2004, p. 80). Out of more detailed knowledge on these matters may emerge a new sense of the "genres" of new media usage which at present eludes us (Livingstone 2004, p. 81). Indeed, the capacity of convergent media to remediate other media (Bolter and Grusin 2000) raises the important question of whether audience members will cease, or in some cases are already ceasing, to care about the medium through which they access a particular content – say a TV series, available to be watched on a conventional TV, downloaded on a laptop, or watched in clips on your mobile phone (Jenkins 2006). Bolter and Grusin in their pioneering study of remediation commented on the paradoxical tendency of media to be erased (from our awareness) through the very process of remediation (2000, p. 5); it remains to be seen whether this will be reflected in the categorizations made, or not made, in everyday audience practice.

The same applies when we look at the second dimension of audience practice – the media contents accessed through audience practices. There is not much we can say in the abstract about this dimension: we need instead to study in much more detail the range of trajectories across the media manifold that people take. There is little work in audience studies of this sort from the pre-convergence era on which we can build. In remedying this gap, we will need to look more closely at the relative thickness and thinness of the intertextual activity around particular texts, for example a US comedy show versus a nature documentary. Degrees of intertextual activity will in turn need to be related to different types of viewers, with some less prone than others to pursuing such links. Now that intertextual interests are both easily pursuable and displayable (for example, through social-networking sites or YouTube), such practice becomes a more central topic of audience research, and a clue perhaps to developing better typologies of audience practice. There are obvious connections here with separate debates on changing media literacies.

Turning to the third dimension of audience practice – wider uses and purposes – we have already discussed this when considering the various practices in which the apparently simple act of watching televised football can be inserted. Presumably this too becomes more complex to chart when the textures and contents of audience practice are more variable. Wider purposes, as we saw earlier, can be analyzed in terms of the practices articulated with a particular act of watching; it is also important to note what apparently relevant practices are not articulated with the act of watching, since this is how boundaries in the overall field of practice are constructed. Rapid changes are underway: the practice of "going on Facebook" was virtually unknown six or seven years ago but already is associated with "practical logics" (Barker and Brooks 1998) and purposes of its own.

To close this section, let me consider briefly three underlying types of audience practice which condense these dimensions into recognizable everyday acts. One (blogging) emerged in the internet age, the other two emerged with convergence: Facebook and watching television other than on a television set, although the latter of course is related to a much older practice.

Blogging on the face of it is a surprising inclusion in a chapter on audience research since it is an act of production. Jokes abound on the average readership of blogs being between one and two (one being the producer). But there are areas where blogging has developed as a recognizable practice, and here what is striking is the *social* dimension of the activity, that is, its basis in *mutual* consumption of each other's blogs, for instance blogging among music fans (Hodkinson 2007; compare Schmidt 2007 on blogs generally). Indeed, a recent study has drawn on practice theory, particular the concept of "rules," to map blogging practice with some precision (Schmidt

2007, pp. 1411–1414). By contrast, websites which are explicitly interactive and audience targeted may prove, on close analysis, to be almost entirely one-way communication (Livingstone 2007 on UK government websites aimed at young citizens). The case of blogging – prima facie, an individually focused form of online production – illustrates the value of a practice-based approach in clarifying what is going on, and how it contributes to the audience landscape: the fact that a practice prima facie is an act of production does not mean it is not embedded in a wider practice where production and consumption are inseparably linked. So audiencing does not disappear, but its regular context may change, sometimes quite radically.

Social-networking sites (e.g. Facebook, MySpace, Bebo, and Orkut) are socially oriented production sites, that is, individual productions aimed at specific audiences. They illustrate well the hybrid complexity of media practices in an age of convergence. The Facebook process combines archiving (of photos, music clips, etc.), personal display, mutual audiencing, and commentary. In addition, depending on the users involved, Facebook sites may be inert and hardly developed, or the center of active social discussion and live chat. For young people at school, SNS may generate a sense of mediated social "liveness" focused around shared objects of discussion and exchange. How this complex multimedia practice develops into wider practical logics is at present uncertain, but already it is clear that the range of practices involved (and the constraints which practitioners see cutting across their productions) are complex (Livingstone 2008; Brake 2009). Since unwelcome audiences (potential employers, for example) are also viewing these sites, there is clearly some instability to the phenomenon. But as an amplification of audience practice – a space for the display of taste and cultural knowledge – SNS are clearly an important part of the emerging audience landscape.

Amidst all these new developments, we need also to know more about how the once discrete act of watching TV is being transformed, if at all, by our increasing ability to perform it through multiple platforms and in multiple spatial settings. Is TV viewing online a different practice – because, for example, of its greater potential intertextuality – from watching on a traditional TV set? And how is the internet capability of new television sets actually being incorporated into habits of viewing? Clearly, there are no answers as yet on this, but we are looking here toward the horizon of basic audience research of the future. The value of practice theory in guiding our questions should by now, I hope, be clear.

Conclusion

Let me recap. I started from the myth of the mediated center that helped stabilize an earlier domain of audience practice, and the new uncertainties that beset it, but argued that there are good reasons to suppose that something like "the audience" will survive in the context of renewed versions of that wider myth. Nonetheless, the complexity of interfaces and intertextuality in the digital media age makes tracking audience practice increasingly difficult and subtle. I then explored some approaches to that task that drew heavily on a practice-based approach to media research. To conclude, let me ask how, more widely, we should understand the broader challenges for future audience researchers. Two points are worth making.

First, what we lack and urgently need to develop are more international comparative studies of media culture and audience practices.[5] There is every reason to expect that a comparative frame both within and between nations will disrupt our assumptions about the dominant forms of audience practice (Algan 2005; McMillin 2007). To assume a "Western" dynamic of change as our reference point for analysis is patently inadequate. The examples and speculations offered earlier in this chapter were offered merely as illustrations of possibilities and must, of course, be reworked in the light of detailed empirical work in a variety of countries. It is much too early to say whether we are in the middle of a major transformation in the practices of information *consumption* – a "viewing" or "downloading" "revolution" to match the "reading revolution" which some have seen in the late eighteenth century in Europe (Wittmann 1999) – or something very different and less drastic. The complexity of the institutional and other factors involved in such a long-term change emerges from studies of earlier periods: see for example Wuthnow (1987) on the role of the book in emergent democratic culture in the West. We need instead a more open attention to the range of ways in which convergence may be working both within societies (but between classes, genders, ethnic groups, and so on) and between societies.

Indeed – and this is the second point – the connective dimension of "convergence" suggests a disturbing possibility, at least for those who want to tell a simple story of what convergence means: that, as communication across space and life contexts becomes easier, the contextualization of communication practices becomes increasingly uncertain and variable (Lievrouw 2001, p. 18). Far from generating a convergence "culture" with its suggestion of an integrated whole, contemporary media's connective properties may facilitate the pluralization and fragmentation of lifeworlds (Lievrouw 2001, p. 18), reinforcing earlier arguments for skepticism about "cultures" as unified spaces of shared meaning making (Hannerz 1992). At the very least, it will become more, and not less, important to understand the role of anchoring or metapractices in so far as they actually, or prospectively, order the space of audience activity.

To move ahead in audience research, we will need what Divya McMillin has called "renewed scrutiny of the ground" (2007, p. 157) and a close attention to the agency and reflexivity of the people we call *audience members*, as they cope with the complexities of the media manifold. A media-centric approach will serve us poorly; so too will an approach which ignores the large-scale struggles over the myth of the mediated center. An open-minded, practice-based approach to whatever it is that people are doing with, or around, media is likely to serve us best in these uncertain times for audience research.

Notes

1 For key references, see Hall (1980), Morley (1980, 1992), and Ang (1996).
2 I will put to one side here the recent debate between proponents of the term *mediation* and proponents of the now more popular term *mediatization*; see Lundby (2009).
3 For a useful review of this issue, see Longhurst (2007, pp. 42–48).
4 For an early snapshot, see Burgess and Green (2009).
5 Scholars have been calling for such work for some time: see Krotz and Tyler Eastman (1999, pp. 7–8) on public viewing of TV and Schmidt (2007, p. 1421) on blogging cultures.

References

Abercrombie, N. and Longhurst, B. 1998 *Audiences: A Sociological Theory of Performance and Imagination*. Sage, London.

Alasuutaari, P., ed. 1999 *Rethinking the Media Audience*. Sage, London.

Algan, E. 2005 The role of Turkish local radio in the construction of a youth community. *The Radio Journal – International Studies in Broadcast and Audio Media*, 3, 2, pp. 75–92.

Ang, I. 1996 *Living Room Wars*. Routledge, London.

Bakardjeva, M. 2005 *Internet Society: The Internet in Everyday Life*. Sage, London.

Barker, M. and Brooks, K. (1998) *Knowing Audiences: Judge Dredd, Its Friends, Fans and Foes*. University of Luton Press, Luton.

Barnouw, E. 1990 *Tube of Plenty*. Oxford University Press, New York.

Bausinger, H. 1984 Media, technology and daily life. *Media, Culture and Society*, 694, pp. 343–352.

Bengtsson, S. 2006 Framing space: media and the intersections of work and leisure. In J. Falkheimer and A. Jansson, eds. *Geographies of Communication*. Nordicom, Goteborg, pp. 189–204.

Bird, S.E. 2003 *The Audience in Everyday Life: Living in a Media World*. Routledge, London.

Bolter, J. and Grusin, R. 2000 *Remediation: Understanding New Media*. MIT Press, Cambridge, MA.

Brake, D. 2009 Shaping the "me" in MySpace: the framing of profiles on a social network site. In K. Lundby, ed. *Digital Storytelling, Mediatised Stories*. Peter Lang, New York, pp. 285–300.

Burgess, J. and Green, J. 2009 *YouTube*. Polity, Cambridge.

Butsch, R. 2009 *The Citizen Audience*. Routledge, London.

Chapman, J. 2005 *Comparative Media History*. Polity, Cambridge.

Couldry, N. 2000 *The Place of Media Power: Pilgrims and Witnesses of the Media Age*. Routledge, London.

Couldry, N. 2003 *Media Rituals: A Critical Approach*. Routledge, London.

Couldry, N. 2004 Theorising media as practice. *Social Semiotics* 14, 2, 115–132.

Couldry, N. 2009 Does "the media" have a future? *European Journal of Communication*, 24, 4, pp. 437–450.

Couldry, N. Livingstone, S. and Markham, T. 2007 *Media Consumption and Public Engagement: Beyond the Presumption of Attention*. Palgrave / Macmillan, Basingstoke, UK.

Fiske, J. 1992 Audiencing: a cultural studies approach to watching television. *Poetics,* 21, pp. 345–359.

Ginsburg, F. 1994 Culture/media: a mild polemic. *Anthropology Today,* 10, 2, pp. 5–15.

Ginsburg, F., Abu-Lughod, L. and Larkin, B. 2002 *Media Worlds: Anthropology on New Terrain.* University of California Press, Berkeley.

Gitelman, L. 2007 *Always Already New: Media, History and the Data of Culture.* MIT Press, Cambridge, MA.

Hall, S. 1980 Encoding/decoding. In S. Hall, D. Hobson, A. Lowe and P. Willis, eds. *Culture, Media, Language.* Unwin Hyman, London, pp. 128–138.

Hannerz, U. 1992 *Cultural Complexity.* Columbia University Press, New York.

Hermes, J. 1995 *Reading Women's Magazines.* Sage, London.

Hodkinson, P. 2007 Interactive online journals and individualization. *New Media and Society,* 9, 4, pp. 625–650.

Hoover, S., Schofield Clark, L. and Alters, D. 2003 *Media, Home and World.* Routledge, London.

Jenkins, H. 2006 *Convergence Culture.* New York University Press, New York.

Krotz, F. and Tyler Eastman, S. 1999 Orientations towards television outside the home. *Journal of Communication,* 49, 1, pp. 5–27.

Lembo, R. 2000 *Thinking through Television.* Cambridge University Press, Cambridge.

Lievrouw, L. 2001 New media and the "pluralization of lifeworlds": a role for information in social differentiation. *New Media and Society,* 3, 1, pp. 7–28.

Livingstone, S. 1990 *Making Sense of Television.* Pergamon Press, Oxford.

Livingstone, S. 2004 The challenge of changing audiences: or, what is the audience researcher to do in the age of the internet? *European Journal of Communication,* 19, 1, pp. 75–86.

Livingstone, S. 2007 The challenge of engaging youth online: contrasting producers and teenagers' interpretations of websites. *European Journal of Communication,* 22, 2, pp. 165–184.

Livingstone, S. 2008 Engaging with the media – a matter of literacy? *Communication, Culture and Critique,* 1, 1, pp. 51–62.

Lundby, K., ed. 2009 *Digital Storytelling, Mediatized Stories.* Peter Lang, New York. Madianou, M. 2005 *Mediating the Nation.* UCL Press, London.

McMillin, D. 2007 *International Media Studies.* Blackwell, Malden, MA.

Morley, D. 1980 Texts, readers, subjects. In S. Hall, D. Hobson, A. Lowe and P. Willis, eds. *Culture, Media, Language.* Unwin Hyman, London, pp. 163–173.

Morley, D. 1986 *Family Television.* BFI, London.

Morley, D. 1992 *Television, Audiences and Cultural Studies.* Routledge, London.

Nightingale, V. 1992 Contesting domestic territory: watching Rugby League on television. In A. Moran, ed. *Stay Tuned: An Australian Broadcasting Reader.* Allen & Unwin, Sydney, pp. 156–165.

Ouellette, L. and Wilson, J. Forthcoming. Women's work: affective labor and convergence culture. *Cultural Studies.*

Reckwitz, A. 2002 Toward a theory of social practices. *European Journal Social Theory,* 5, 2, pp. 243–263.

Rosen, J. 2006 The people formerly known as the audience. Retrieved from http://journalism.nyu.edu/pubzone/weblogs/pressthink/2006/06/27/ppl_frmr.html

Ruddock, A. 2007 *Investigating Audiences*. Sage, London.

Schatzki, T. 1999 *Social Practices: A Wittgensteinian Approach to Human Activity and the Social*. Cambridge University Press, Cambridge.

Schmidt, J. 2007 Blogging practices: an analytical framework. *Journal of Computer-Mediated Communication*, 12, pp. 1409–1427.

Schroder, K., Drotner, K., Kline, S. and Murray, C. 2003 *Researching Audiences*. Arnold, London.

Selwyn, N., Gorard, S. and Furlong, J. 2005 Whose internet is it anyway? Exploring adults (non-)use of the internet in everyday life. *European Journal of Communication*, 20, 1, pp. 5–26.

Silverstone, R. 1999 *Why Study the Media?* Sage, London.

Silverstone, R. 2006 Media and communication. In C. Calhoun, C. Rojek and B. Turne, eds. *The International Handbook of Sociology*. Sage, London, pp. 185–204.

Silverstone, R. and Hirsch, E., eds. 1992 *Consuming Technologies*. Routledge, London.

Swidler, A. 2001 What anchors cultural practices. In T. Schatzki, K. Knorr Cetina and E. von Savigny, eds. *The Practice Turn in Contemporary Theory*. Routledge, London, pp. 74–92.

Takahashi, T. 2007 Japanese young people, media and everyday life: towards the dewesternizing of Media Studies. In S. Livingstone and K. Drotner, eds. *International Handbook of Children, Media and Culture*. Sage, London.

Turow, J. 2007 *Niche Envy*. MIT Press, Cambridge, MA.

Van Dijck, J. 2009 Users like you? Theorizing agency in user-generated content. *Media Culture and Society*, 31, 1, pp. 41–58.

Wittmann, R. 1999 Was there a reading revolution at the end of the 18th century? In G. Cavallo and R. Chartier, eds. A *History of Reading in the West*. Polity, Cambridge, pp. 284–312.

Wuthnow, R. 1987 *Communities of Discourse*. Harvard University Press, Cambridge, MA.

11

Reception

Cornel Sandvoss

At the heart of contemporary media studies and the study of audiences lies a curious paradox: our discipline is premised on the assumption that media, and mediated texts, matter and that they impact how we make our lives, individually and collectively, and make sense of the world around us. Technical questions of media production and distribution aside, the inherent aim of critical media and communication studies is to explore how recipients of mediated texts create meaning. Yet, at the very time that audienceship has become ever more prevalent as the amount of mediated communication in our lives has steadily increased throughout modernity, the concept of the "audience" seems to have lost its analytical utility. As audiences are everywhere, they become increasingly indistinguishable and ultimately invisible – being an audience member has become synonymous with being an individual or social subject.

Indeed, some recent contributions, such as David Gauntlett (2007) in proposing the label of *media studies 2.0*, have praised efforts to avoid the label *audiences* altogether. Gauntlett's claim that media studies is too often about the media and that we hence ought to look at media consumers beyond narrow textual engagements is a curious one that implies no less than the redundancy of media and communication studies, and that forgets that disciplines that study the self individually and collectively beyond processes of reception have long existed in the form of history, philosophy, psychology, and sociology.

Media and communication studies have, of course, always been an interdisciplinary project drawing on all these disciplines as well as subjects dedicated to the study of texts, signs, and textual formations such as linguistics, various philologies, and most notably literary theory. Yet it is precisely the synthesis between these two fields – the science of the subject (history, philosophy, psychology, and sociology) and the science of the sign (linguistics and literary studies) – upon which the intellectual case of the discipline rests. What distinguishes our field from these disciplines is the study of the *interplay* between (social) subject and (textual) object or, put simply, *the process of reading*. In this sense, the study of reception lies at the heart of its conceptual and methodological project. This chapter aims to outline and critically assess the conceptual contributions of reception theory to our understanding of this interplay between text and reader.

What Is Reception Theory?

The task of assessing the contribution of reception studies and reception theory to the (contemporary) study of media audiences is further complicated by the fact that these terms have come to describe a range of diverse and only partially related theoretical traditions, with the parameters of definition ranging from shared aesthetic or conceptual concerns to research unified by methodological traditions or even the common geographical focus of leading proponents. While acknowledging that it would be "inappropriate to identify any unitary origin of reception studies," Livingstone (1998, pp. 237–238) – in a definition encompassing most of the research on audiences associated with media and cultural studies – describes reception studies as the body of work that focuses "on the interpretive relation between audience and medium, where this relation is understood within a broadly ethnographic context." Behind the definition of a shared methodology, however, lie deep running conceptual distinctions in which ethnographic traditions concerned with everyday life routines and practices are distinguished from approaches to mass communication informed by behaviorism and the search for (quantifiable) "effects" drawing on experimental and quasi-experimental research.

Staiger (2005), in contrast, offers a more universal definition of reception studies that incorporates such diverging methodological and conceptual traditions. To Staiger, reception studies are defined by not being "a hermeneutics or truth-finding of the meaning of the text. The enterprise it engages is historical and theoretical. How does a text mean? For whom? In what circumstances? With what changing values over time?" (p. 2). Following this broad definition, Staiger identifies a number of approaches as fundamentally concerned with the question of reception, including psychological approaches such as behaviorism, which in a positivist tradition explores processes of communication such as conditioning, stimulus, and response; cognitive psychology, focusing on the schemata of human experience derived from social experience that mediate between stimuli and response; psychoanalysis, which in contrast conceptualizes the development of unconsciousness and consciousness, drawing on Freud's tri-part model of self; and sociological models of reception that include studies of communication drawing on functionalism and conflict theory, both informing some of the conceptual traditions of the more narrow field outlined by Livingstone (1998).

Despite little, and frequently no, interchange between these strands of reception research, this broad definition illustrates *how* the analytical and normative agenda of one line of research has shaped and informed those in others. As little as the behaviorist experimental psychological research focusing on media effects conducted by the likes of Albert Bandura has in common with the conceptual and methodological traditions of the reception studies outlined by Livingstone (1998), the notion of "media effects" has become a major focal point which many such studies have sought to refute, thereby unwittingly subscribing to the frame of analysis that follows the notion of effect. Effects or their absence have thus become the primary prism through which such studies have sought to study and conceptualize reception. The notions of *audience activity* and *negotiation/appropriation* have thus continued to reflect the binaries of the effects model in emphasizing the absence of the singular, immediate effects proposed by behaviorism. While most in our field will find it difficult to deny the accuracy of these reception studies, the more interesting question is which questions fail to be asked when processes of receptions are defined by the effects discourse.

In her narrower definition of reception studies, Livingstone (1998) identifies six trajectories that point to questions that have been marginalized in the canon of audience research. Of these six trajectories, only one – the turn toward a poststructural concept of the interplay between texts and audiences – sees the text and the processes of meaning construction in its reading as a central focus. In other approaches, often in response to the converging concern over the structural power of the text in both behaviorism and Marxist ideology critique, the text and actual processes of reading move to the background in a shift toward attributing to audiences forms of agency seemingly isolated from the text. In these approaches, the act of reading is conceptualized not primarily as a realm of meaning constructing but as the space in which conflicting fields of power (audience agency versus textual stimuli or the structures of cultural production) collide.

Even in the focus on media consumption as everyday life agency, inspired by Michel de Certeau (1984) and informed by the anthropology of Clifford Geertz and Victor Turner, the shift toward the cultural symbolic in everyday life has analyzed meaning constructing only as indicator of symbolic importance, or functional utility. While Geertz himself still focused on the narrow form of rituals as de facto cultural texts, this focus has continuously gravitated from the symbolic form (text) to ritual and practice (audience activity) in reception studies within media and communication research as exemplified in Henry Jenkins's (1992, p. 284) summary of studies of fan culture as "exceptional readings" – a notion of meaning construction *in spite of* rather than *through* the text. Forms of communication seen as most palatable are those most ineffective and thus literally lacking in effect, such as forms of polysemic popular culture that are open to easy negotiation and appropriation.

Here an interesting distinction to literary theory emerges: in contrasts to media texts in the above approaches, the texts investigated in literary theory are examined as a form of art that, like all forms of art, is evaluated, interpreted, and curated by a diametrically opposing measure: not through an absence of effects but in relation to its impact on those encountering it – a concern that literary reception studies shares with most theories of art including those that disregard reception, such as critical theory (cf. Hohendahl and Silberman 1977). In the following, I therefore draw on Holub's (1984) narrower definition of reception studies as reception theory, referring in particular to the concepts and theories of reception studies developed (primarily by West German) literary theory.

Reception Aesthetics and Literary Theory

While Umberto Eco (1962/1989) is widely credited with the poststructuralist shift in literary theory that centered attention on questions of context, intertextuality and the process of interpretation, theories of reading, and the role of the reader date back as far as narrative and aesthetic theory itself. As Holub reminds us, Aristotle's *Poetics* "by its inclusion of catharsis as essential category of aesthetic experience" already implied a theory of the reader (1984, p.13). More narrowly, the precursors to late twentieth-century reception studies include Russian formalism, phenomenology, structuralism, hermeneutics, and early twentieth-century sociology of literature (cf. Barner 1975; Grimm 1975; Hohendahl and Silberman 1977; Holub 1984). A few lines of continuity between this last group of sociological studies and contemporary media audience research are worth noting. Levin L. Schücking (1966) examined the canonization of literature through various material as well as ideological forces in reference to modern institutions such as schools, universities, book clubs, or libraries (cf. Grimm 1975), thus not only moving toward a pre-Bourdieuian sociology of taste but also introducing an analytical focus that resonates with the contemporary notion of interpretive communities that has enjoyed popularity in the study of audience subgroups such as fan cultures (cf. Jenkins 1992). In his emphasis on the fulfilment and pacification of fantasy in the engagement with the object of art, fellow twentieth-century sociologist Leo Löwenthal (1971) addressed affective processes in the engagement between self and text, a further central theme of contemporary fan studies. Löwenthal sought to bring together the micro and macro much as many contemporary reception studies have tried to do, if in a distinctly comparative and theoretical-historical mode that explores changing patterns of reception over time. Recognizing that the interplay between literature, other forms of textuality, and historiography is an important contribution links Löwenthal's work to that of Julian Hirsch. In his study of the genesis of fame, Hirsch (1914) interrogated how the formation of literary taste and processes of canonization shape the reception of literary works, identifying processes of reception as fundamental to the formation of literary fame. To rephrase Hirsch, and drawing on Genette's (1997) terminology, the paratexts we encounter from the youngest age reiterate the genius of Shakespeare before we have encountered any of his works, thus affirming judgments in scholarly literature and leaving us little room but to endorse the aesthetic and artistic merit of Shakespeare's writings in our own reading. Much as contemporary studies of fans of scholarly rather than literary texts, such as Matt Hills's (2002) analysis of fan-academics, or Alan McKee's (2007) study of fans of cultural theory, have done, Hirsch by implication invites the critical examination of how all forms of knowledge and aesthetic judgment are themselves inherently tied up in, and constituted through, processes of reception, in readers', viewers', and listeners' encounters of literary and nonliterary texts alike.

The seemingly linear trajectory that emerges here between the early sociology of literature and contemporary audience research, however, takes an important new direction through the work of reception theorists Hans-Robert Jauss and Wolfgang Iser. Like contemporary audience research, Hirsch and Schücking lacked a theory of reading in bypassing the actual process of meaning construction. As Hohendahl and Silberman (1977) note,

> [T]aking obvious aim at then current fashion of intellectual history, Schücking demanded the abandonment of all abstract and idealistic models in favour of an analysis of communicative processes, despite the fact he had no theoretical model of communication at his disposal. (p. 36)

To develop such a model is the particular merit of the Constance School, despite its work being only occasionally recognized in media audience research and rarely featuring in media and culture studies textbooks. Much like the similarly broad label *Frankfurt School*, the *Constance School* serves as an umbrella term for a multidisciplinary and multiconceptual body of work that originated under the roof of the University of Constance in the final three decades of the West German state.[1] Here I will focus only on those aspects of Hans Robert Jauss's and Wolfgang Iser's work that have been central to a theory of reading that bears relevance to contemporary literary and nonliterary reception studies alike, thereby neglecting other figures associated with the school such as Karlheinz Stierle and Manfred Fuhrmann, or those outside it who have sought to move reception aesthetics from the hermeneutical to the empirical such as Norbert Groeben or Siegfried Schmidt.

Reception and the Horizon of Experience

Hans-Robert Jauss may be a surprising starting point toward the development of a theory of reading in that his primary interest was one of a historical, and hence macro, rather than a psychological or micro nature. As a literary historian, Jauss's (1982) declared target, which he attacked with some zeal, was both the descriptive and simultaneously canonizing literary chronology that, in its focus on the production of literary works, saw its aim in the compilation of information as "literary history arranges its material unilinearly, according to the chronology of great authors, and evaluates them still in accordance with the schema of 'life and works'" (p. 4), positioning them within the frame of a national literature. Yet in his critique of this literary chronology, Jauss formulates the need to develop a conceptual and methodological understanding of aesthetics and by extension processes of reception:

> It is not only rare but almost forbidden that a literary historian should hold judgements of quality concerning the works of past ages. Rather, he prefers to appeal to the ideal of objectivity of historiography, which only has to describe "how it really was." His aesthetic abstinence has good grounds. For the quality and rank of the literary work result neither from the biographical or historic conditions of its origin [*Entstehung*], nor its place in the sequence of the development of the genre alone, but rather from the criteria of influence, reception and posthumous fame, criteria that are more difficult to grasp. (p. 5)

In his attack on historiography, Jauss finds two natural allies in Marxist-teleological and formalist approaches to literary history. Yet, both fail at the hurdle of offering sufficient epistemological ground for the analysis of reception processes. Given the interplay between structure and agency in such processes, Jauss inevitably pleads for a nonreductive methodology that is incompatible with Marxist literary theory as literature cannot fully be referred back "to concrete conditions of the economic process" (1982, p. 12). His critique is primarily aimed at scholars such as Georg Lukács and Lucien Goldmann, because their commitment to the concept of *Widerspiegelung* – the reflection of reality in socialist realism – meant that "literary production remains confined to a secondary function, only always reproducing in harmonious parallel with the economic process ... only allowing already previously known (or ostensibly known) reality to be *once again recognized*" (p. 14; emphasis in original). Hence, Jauss concludes that Marxist aesthetic theory, ironically, forgoes the ability to understand the revolutionary and subversive character of art – much as the study of past literature only allows revisiting material and social conditions that have since been overcome.

Jauss finds an alternative in the work of Russian formalism and in Viktor Shklovskii's notion of *defamiliarization* in particular:

> Art now becomes the means of disrupting the automatization of everyday perception through estrangement or defamiliarization.... [T]his theory made art criticism into a rational method of conscious renunciation of historical knowledge and thereby brought forth critical achievements of lasting value. (1982, pp. 16–17)

However, the emphasis on, and awareness of, *form*, as Holub (1984) notes, directs the "attention to the process of interpretation itself" (p. 16) and enables us to see the work of art in *its* history, yet not necessarily "the work of art in *history*" (Jauss 1982, p. 18; emphasis in original).

236   *Cornel Sandvoss*

Both Marxist and formalist literary theory thus marginalize the reader:

> Orthodox Marxist aesthetics treat the reader – if at all – no differently from the author.... The Formalist school needs the reader really only as a perceiving subject that follows the directions of the text in order to distinguish the (literary) form or discover the (literary) procedure. (pp. 18–19)

The common failure of both Marxism and formalism to develop a meaningful theory of the relationship between art and history is therefore overcome by conceptualizing the audience as an active agent in the reception of art and hence in the formation of history. As Jauss notes, "In the triangle of author, work and public, the last is no passive part, no chain of mere reactions, but rather itself an energy formative of history" (p. 19).

Jauss conceptualizes this interplay between the aesthetic and historical through his key conceptual formulation: the *horizon of expectation*. The *horizon of expectation* describes the vantage point of the reader or audience that is constituted by the sum of their lifeworld experiences, including their experience of other literature and the respective conventions and genre categories emerging from such past encounters. Jauss in fact uses *horizon of experience* and *horizon of expectation* seemingly synonymously, and the former seems to constitute the basis of latter. Unlike the earlier use of the term by Karl Mannheim (1935), to distinguish between quotidian experiences in stable societies and the disruption of such experiences in unstable ones, as well as in the positivism of Karl Popper, to Jauss the term therefore delineates different types of aesthetic experience.

In Jauss's formulation, the aesthetic value of a given text derives from the gap, or "aesthetic distance," between the text and the audiences' horizon of experience. Aesthetic value is, therefore, no longer seen as text immanent, but always dynamic and relational, and manifested as well as measured in the horizontal change that is required by the audience in the reception of the text. Jauss is thus able to maintain the types of classifications that derive from the attribution of aesthetic value, such as the distinction between (high) art and entertainment that, post Bourdieu (1984), cultural studies have rejected outright. This rejection of aesthetic value in cultural studies are grounded in the (correct) assertion that Bourdieu's analysis, in the wider context of poststructuralism, revealed any essentialist aesthetic value in the (art) object of consumption as the fictitious vehicle of social distinction and stratification (cf. Sandvoss 2007). However, Jauss's "relational aesthetics," manifested in the triangle of author, work, and public, avoids the pitfalls and inherent conservatism of essentialism, hence rescuing aesthetics as an evaluative category in the analysis of texts by locating aesthetic value firmly in the relational and changing process of reception:

> The distance between the horizon of expectation and the work, between the familiarity of previous aesthetic experience and the "horizontal change" demanded by the

reception of the new work, determines the artistic character of a literary work, according to an aesthetics of reception: to the degree that this distance decreases, and no turn toward the horizon of yet-unknown experience is demanded of the receiving consciousness, the closer the work comes to the sphere of culinary or entertainment art [*Unterhaltungskunst*]. This latter work can be characterised by an aesthetics of reception as not demanding any horizontal change, but rather is precisely fulfilling the expectations described by the ruling standard of taste, in that it satisfies the desire for the reproduction of the familiarly beautiful ... if, conversely, the artistic character of the work is to be measured by the aesthetic distance with which it opposes the expectations of its first audience, then it follows that this distance, at first experienced as a pleasing or alienating new perspective, can disappear for later readers, to the extent that the original negativity of the work has become self-evident and has itself entered into the horizon of future aesthetic experience, as a henceforth familiar expectation. (Jauss 1982, p. 25)

Given that Jauss offers one of the very tools to maintain textual evaluation that is not at the mercy of the textual canon of disciplines which have traditionally perceived new forms of communication media as a threat to artistic value and, no less importantly, to the maintenance of their own discipline, it is surprising that the *horizon of expectation* remains a rarely visited concept in media and cultural studies. Tony Bennett's (1982) study of the reception of the James Bond franchise remains a notable exception here, as does Will Brooker's (2000) analysis of different readings of *Batman*, drawing on reception aesthetics (if primarily though Iser and Ingarden). In my own work, I have sought to illustrate how Jauss's distinction also sheds a critical light on processes of popular media consumption and fandom (Sandvoss 2005a).

Yet, Jauss's model of reception aesthetics has far from escaped critique within its own discipline (cf. Wehrli 1970; Harth 1971; Mandelkov 1974; Hohendahl and Silberman 1977). Holub (1984) takes Jauss to task over this key notion in his work being "so vaguely defined that it could include or exclude any previous sense of the word" (p. 59). Jauss's lack of reference to Mannheim or Popper does not, however, constitute an epistemological problem per se, nor is the *horizon of expectation* a summative category formulated on the basis of lifeworld and aesthetic experience as vague as Holub suggests. In that it ultimately seeks to destabilize the fundamental assumption on which Jauss's model rests, I also do not share Paul de Man's (1986) far-reaching claim that "the hermeneutics of experience and the hermeneutics of reading are not necessarily compatible" (p. xvii) – a charge that is amplified by de Man pointing to Jauss's lack of interest in the play of the signifier so central to the work of Roland Barthes. Epistemologically, de Man's critique rests upon the insistence of traces of essential textual qualities that distinguish the experience and reception of art and the world – a point to which we will return in Fish's critique of Iser's work below. A similar mistake is made by Jauss himself in seeking to maintain the "horizon of experience" not only as an individual but also as a universal intersubjective category that positions the work of art historically.

The *horizon of expectation* here is not one derived from the empirical reader, but one that sits uncomfortably between hermeneutics and objectivism. As Holub (1984) summarizes the epistemological problem, Jauss avoids

> psychology only by reintroducing an objectivist moment ... as long as he insists on the possibility of a reconstruction of the horizon of expectations and sets out to accomplish this reconstruction with evidence or signals from the works themselves, he is going to be measuring the effect or impact of works against the horizon that is abstracted from those works. (p. 61)

This, however, is an issue and limitation on the particular application of the concept of the *horizon of expectation*, in the writing of the particular reception-oriented literary history Jauss proposes, and hence a substantive issue within the realm of literary theory, yet not one that undermines the analytical value of the dynamic, relational definition of aesthetic value rooted in the interplay between text and *horizon of expectation*.

Holub's second concern is of a more pragmatic and methodological nature as he questions whether one could find a meaningful measure of the "disappointment" or elusion of existing horizons of expectation. It questions how defamiliarization and estrangement manifest themselves in the process of reading; here, Jauss's focus on literary history and an intersubjective *horizon of expectation* indeed remains vague. In moving our focus to the *horizon of expectation* of individual readers and micro processes of reading, it is less the work of Jauss than of his colleague Wolfgang Iser that charts the way toward the required analytical tools for an investigation of horizontal change through communication.

Wolfgang Iser's Analysis of Processes of Reading

If Jauss's main influences lie in formalism and a broadly hermeneutical model, Iser (1971, 1975) draws in contrast on phenomenology and in particular Roman Ingarden's (1973) work on concretization and reconstruction. Despite differences of concept and focus, Iser's work further pursues the aesthetic position developed by Jauss. Like Jauss, Iser (1975) directs his argument against an exclusively text-and/or author-focused tradition that fails to account for the very process through which literature and any other text comes to life: the act of reading. As he notes,

> If, as the art of interpretation would like us to make believe, the meaning was hidden within the text, one wonders why texts engage in such a hide-and-seek game concerning their interpretation; moreover why a once-reached interpretation is subject to transformation over time, despite the letters, words and sentences of the text remaining the same. (p. 229)

Consequently, he concludes that "the meanings of literary texts are only generated in the act of reading" (p. 229). Furthermore, in investigating this act of reading and interpretation, Iser explores the distinction between different types of texts, with the literary text, as he notes, being naturally fictitious; yet, this does not mean it bears no relation to reality, but rather that literary texts "constitute the seemingly familiar world in a form that differs from our experiences" (p. 232). "The reality" of a literary work is thus not constituted in representing an existing reality, but in offering insights into this reality. As in Jauss's work, literature is thus assessed by its ability to broaden or alter existing perceptions of the world through a form of negative, defamiliarizing aesthetics.

Much like the media reception studies emphasizing the active audiences that were to follow, Jauss engaged with the outcome of the reading process rather than with the act of reading that enables horizontal change itself. In contrast, Iser engages with a fundamental question for studies of textuality, exploring how these challenges are manifested in the reader's engagement with the text. The implicit premises of his argument are as follows: if one accepts that a given text is read by different readers in possibly diverging ways, however little or much they diverge, it follows that in the act of reading and meaning construction, the reader engages with elements that require textual interpretation. Only a radically essentialist model of textual value in fundamental conflict with any empirical research conducted on audiences could dispute such a position. If, as Eco (1994), we also maintain that texts, while not possessing a single meaning, nevertheless limit meaning construction – however minimally – what follows is that all texts contain both determinate and indeterminate elements. This interplay between determinate and indeterminate elements and their role in the process of reading are the key focus of Iser's theoretical contribution (1970, 1976).

Iser describes these indeterminate elements as textual gaps (*Leerstellen*), drawing on Ingarden's notion of "spots of indeterminacy." However, where Ingarden (1973) attributes the literary work with a metaphysical, essential quality through which the accuracy of the reader's attempts at filling these gaps – described by both Ingarden and Iser as the process of "concretization" – can be judged, for Iser (1975, 1978) the process of concretization fulfills a very different purpose. It is not meaning as such resulting out of readers' perceptions and ideation that he sees as a marker of the aesthetic quality of a text, but how the *process* of meaning construction through normalization takes places.

Two types of gaps occur in the act of reading. The first is the *Leerstelle* itself, which translates literally as a "blank space." Since the fictitious text does not represent actual but ideational objects, it evades verification. It is at this point that aspects of indeterminacy become part of all literary texts because these aspects cannot be related back to any lifeworld situation to the degree that they would become fully congruent with it (Iser 1975). Literary texts are therefore always anchored in the act of reading not the world per se, and thereby situated in the interaction between self and text:

> When the reader works through the different perspectives offered by the text, he can only resort to his own experience when drawing conclusions over what is being communicated in the text. In projecting the world of the text onto the reader's experiences a highly differentiated scale of reactions emerges which is witness to the tension that result out of the confrontation between the reader's actual and potential experience. (Iser 1975, p. 232)

The literary text therefore always points to a second type of gap: that between the schematized aspects of texts (in which *Leerstellen* open up) and the lifeworld experience of the reader. By the very nature of fictional texts, this second type of gap thus always creates a need for the reader to relate the experience of the text – and thus fill its gaps – to what, returning to Jauss's term, we might call *horizon of experience*. Iser describes this process as *normalization*. This process oscillates between two extreme possibilities:

> Either the literary world seems fantastic, because it contradicts our experience, or it seems trivial, because it merely echoes our own. This illustrates not only how heavily our experiences are at play in the realization of the text's meaning, but also that the process also always impacts upon our experiences. (Iser 1971, p. 8)

To Iser, aesthetic value is thus constituted through aesthetic distance: the more immediate the process of normalization, the less the text's aesthetic value. If a text serves as mere reflection of a known reality, its literary quality vanishes; the more the text evades our expectations and experiences in contrast, and the more it requires a reflexive engagement by the reader with his or her experiences, the greater its aesthetic value. The act of reading literary works is thus one of reflexive self-discovery as "the construction of meaning…enables us to formulate ourselves and thus discover an inner world of which we had hitherto not been conscious" (Iser, 1978, p. 158). This process is facilitated by the literary text that

> [t]akes its selected objects out of the paradigmatic context and so shatters their original frame of reference; the result is to reveal aspects (e.g. of social norms) which had remained hidden as long as the frame of reference remained intact. (Iser, 1978, p. 109)

Iser, like Jauss, thus subscribes to a form of aesthetic judgment that avoids positivist and absolute claims; aesthetic judgment instead is relative to a given reader or group of readers – their aesthetics are one of negativity in which art is ultimately judged by its potential to facilitate emancipation. This Brechtian vision of estrangement and defamiliarization creates a noteworthy and meaningful link between reception studies and the concerns of the Frankfurt School, which media and cultural studies have too readily made out to be incompatible. While Holub (1984) speculates that it was the evidently shared ground between his notion of the *horizon of expectation* and Adorno's (1970/2003) negative aesthetics that led Jauss to neglect his key conceptual contribution in his later works, Iser once more revives the concept of negativity, turning it into a valuable tool of contemporary textual criticism rather than a mere nihilist statement.

In his analysis of the act of reading, Iser thus not only challenges the dismissal of the negative aesthetics and negativity, but also, in returning to fundamental concerns of the Enlightenment and modernity, shares two key areas of concern with the tradition of empirical, qualitative audience studies: the reflexive project of the self (Giddens 1991) and emancipation. For Iser and qualitative audience studies alike, the potential for audience emancipation is rooted in what Iser calls "textual gaps" and audience studies calls *polysemy*. Yet, behind such different labels, Iser offers a radically different account of textual openness that addresses a fundamental theoretical conundrum for media audience research. The model of emancipation employed in media and cultural studies deemphasize the significance of the text in favor of audience activity largely autonomous from the text through which emancipatory practices are manifest. This means that qualitative audience studies ultimately assume the potential of social, cultural, or political emancipation to lie outside the text – a move not without irony in a discipline dedicated to the study of media and communication.

The difference between Iser's notion of polysemy and the common usage of the term in audience studies is, I have suggested (Sandvoss 2005a, 2005b), one we can summarize as the difference between quantitative and qualitative polysemy. Empirically and methodologically qualitative audience studies since David Morley's (1980) seminal study of the current affairs program *Nationwide* have explored quantitative notions of polysemy in asking how different readers construct meanings from the same text. The most polysemic text is hence one incorporating the greatest number of possible and actual readings. While this concept of the multiplicity of meaning coincides with Iser's concept of multiplicity of meaning through textual gaps in classical literary texts – such as James Joyce's *Ulysses* and *Finnegan's Wake* – the difference between the two becomes clearer as we turn to the reading of popular mass media texts. To Iser (1975), *Leerstellen* are not a question of lack of schematized aspects within the text – rather, both *Ulysses* and *Finnegan's Wake* are pertinent examples of how indeterminacy is only heightened through density of description. What marks the aesthetic quality of the text – its *qualitative* polysemy – is how such gaps are concretized in the process of reception. Quantitative and qualitative polysemy do not necessarily coincide. In fact, quantitative polysemy often invites a process of reading based on instant normalization because polysemic texts derive their appropriatability from a lack of aesthetic distance. As aesthetic quality is located in the act of reading, rather than in the text, the very structures of sustained regular consumption of a wide range of (mass-)mediated texts, reflective of their technologies of production and consumption, facilitate the immediate, nonreflexive normalization in which the gap between the schematized aspects of the text and our horizon of experience disappears.

This particular reading position is exemplified in the case of (media) fandom: when audiences, through a series of readings, rereadings, and appropriations of the text, develop a familiarity with the particular textual object of their affection, the resulting lack of aesthetic distance between text and reading renders such texts instantly normalized and hence trivial – no reflexive, horizon-changing engagement in the process of reading is required; rather, because the text matches the reader's horizon of experience, it functions as a fan object (Sandvoss 2005a, 2005b). In reflecting all that is known to the reader, and in failing to challenge expectations, such texts are easily appropriated to the reader's specific reading positions and horizons of experience. While polysemic in the range of readings they offer, they nevertheless represent banal acts of noncommunication. Notably, such lack of aesthetic distance is not a feature of the text in and for itself, but constituted in the act of reading. The scholar and fan of Shakespeare alike, to return to Hirsch's example – having detailed textual and contextual knowledge of and familiarity with their favorite Shakespearean texts – will over time near or even reach the point where the gap between *horizon of expectation* and schematized aspects of the text are closed, so that the process of normalization becomes automatic to the degree that the text is rendered as banal. In other words, the aesthetic value of a given text is never universal and fluctuates not only between different readers, but also between different instances of reading by the same reader. Iser's work thus serves as an important reminder that the shift from the question of what media do to the people to what people do with media has too quickly bypassed the crucial middle ground of reading: how media texts and audiences interact in the process of meaning production.

Critique and Application of Reception Aesthetics

The combined contribution to reception theory by the Constance School thus offers a meaningful evaluative framework of reception in two respects crucial to the analysis of processes of communication. First, it presents a theory of reading that promises to overcome the obvious empirical, methodological, and conceptual limitations of different forms of textual analysis while nevertheless maintaining the text as an important category of critical scholarly investigation. Second, it offers an evaluative framework by rescuing the notion of aesthetic value from an essentialist stranglehold while at the same time, in proposing a model in which aesthetic values are relative to the particular pairing of text and reader, avoiding the pitfall of intersubjective aesthetic judgment that has been unmasked as a means of social and cultural distinction.

Yet the conceptual and theoretical tools that Iser and Jauss offer are not applicable to the study of contemporary media without a qualification – and, like Jauss's work, Iser's theory of reading has attracted substantive critique. In Jauss's case, such critique has primarily been of interest to literary theorists as it has focused on the validity of the intellectual project of literary history, as much as on the protection of hermeneutics as the indispensable methodological and conceptual basis of the discipline. The critique of Iser's work, in contrast, is of immediate relevance to applying its lessons to the study of contemporary mediated texts.

Before turning to this critique, we should note that different aspects of both Jauss's and Iser's work respectively are more suitable for application in the study of contemporary media audiences than others. Iser's analysis of the act or reading, in its focus on the micro, seems more compatible with the methodological traditions of ethnographic or even experimental media reception studies than Jauss's notion of the "horizon of experience," which at least in his own work is rarely applied to the level of the individual, let alone the empirical reader. Yet, conceptually the "horizon of experience" applies rather more easily to the different forms of textuality across the range of contemporary print, broadcast, digital, and interactive media than Iser's notion of textual gaps which are identified as specific to literary, fictional texts.

His brief discussion of the differences between Henry Fielding's novel *The History of Tom Jones: A Foundling* and its screen adaptation, which Holub rightly calls a "terribly unsophisticated way of looking at films," leaves little doubt that Iser does not envision his notion of gaps extending to visual or audiovisual texts. Yet Iser's self-imposed limitation on the scope of his own conceptual contribution is based on an underestimation of the degrees of ideational activity required in viewing and interpreting texts "which are more textual than Iser cares to acknowledge" (Holub 1984, p. 105), as the discipline of film studies will witness.

In a similar manner, while Iser's analysis of ideational activity in the reading of fictional texts may be accurate, the basis on which he draws the distinction between fictional and factual texts is problematic. It assumes a mode of immediacy in the representation of facts that bypasses the very act of reading that Iser explores. To achieve this, Iser has to assume an objective external reality that is merely suspended in the writing and reading of fictional texts. This highly problematic premise is reflective of the initial phenomenological basis of Iser's work and is further and fatally undermined by our empirical knowledge that expository texts are not beyond interpretation either, nor do they offer – with literary and other forms of social or cultural theory as a case in point – a singular, verifiably correct reading.

Both these qualifications echo a central point in Stanley Fish's (1981) acrimonious critique of Iser's work. Fish identifies the Achilles' heel in Iser's analysis of the reading process: to maintain the distinction between determinant and indeterminate elements, Iser presupposes the existence of an external reality which can be encountered and experienced in a nonmediated fashion. The essence of the debate is quickly summarized:[2] Fish's metacritical objection is one to which Iser cannot possibly find an answer, since while the readings of a text may be limited, it is impossible to see how any form of interpretive activity can be reduced to the recognition of objective, determinate elements that somehow evade mediation. Iser's distinction between perception and mediation thus collapses – and with it, seemingly, the conceptual tenets of Iser's model. Yet, Fish's critique has more profound consequences for Iser's application of his own model in the figure of the implied reader than it has for its adaptation to empirical audience research. In the former case, Iser's reliance on notions of schematized aspects is a mistake which, as Samuel Weber (1986) notes, ultimately leads him to reassert the principle of authorial intent as the yardstick in evaluation of the act of reading.

However, while Fish's (1981) critique problematizes Iser's distinction between definite and indefinite elements in the text, he is nevertheless confronted with the empirical and epistemological reality that no text can accommodate indefinite readings. I have discussed the possibility of such a text, which would no longer be polysemic but neutrosemic, in detail elsewhere (Sandvoss 2005a, 2005b). While some mediated texts – or, rather, what below I will call *textual formations* – come close to the state of neutrosemy, it remains a theoretical impossibility as even if every single reading of a given text by the same and different readers varied, the text would retain a however minimal signification value. Fish is correct in as far as this may not amount to any universally shared interpretation that would reveal determinate elements within the text, but, subjectively on the level of the individual reader certain elements remain that are perceived as (if not being objectively so) part of an external reality rather than the ideational process of reading.

Despite Fish's critique (1981) of the epistemological premises of Iser's work, Iser's aesthetic postulations thus remain unscathed: in light of Fish's correct objections, we should not distinguish between determinate and indeterminate elements of texts – the terminology implying the objectivity of such positions – but rather between "known" and "unknown elements" in the process of reading, between elements that are *perceived* by the individual reader to be determinate because they match his or her *horizon of expectation*, and those elements that differ from past experiences and perceptions and hence require the reflexive engagement of interpretations of text and readers' experiences aimed at concretizing and hence normalizing the text. This indeed renders the figure of the implied, rather than the empirical, reader as a methodological tool unsustainable, yet it only further underscores the evaluative core of Iser's reception aesthetics that derives from his correct assumption of varying yet not indefinite readings of a given (literary) text.

Fish's contribution to this debate is hence instructive for our purposes on two counts: first, it questions the strict distinction between literary and other texts that Iser draws, and invites us to reflect on the extent to which the aesthetic principles formulated by both Iser and Jauss are applicable to all mediated texts. Second, by questioning the phenomenological foundations of Iser's project, Fish's critique points toward the important question of method.

In the first instance, it frees us from the uncomfortable need to differentiate diverse forms of mediated textuality into texts that we perceive as art and others that may be expository or fictional, but not artistic, in character. The grounds on which such distinctions could be undertaken remain highly problematic: either we would need to resort to an essentialist definition of art which fundamentally contradicts the aesthetics of reception that both Iser and Jauss propose and that shifts the notion of aesthetic value back toward the author and the text in and for itself; or we would follow a definition of art as socially constructed, and therefore part of the forms of social stratification that Bourdieu (1984) outlines. The latter, of course, is largely shaped by the form and medium. Texts circulated via broadcast media such as radio, and in particular television or online media, have traditionally been viewed as commanding lesser, if any, artistic merit compared to those taking the form of physical media such as the book, and in particular the novel, or those requiring an in situ presence in a public venue such as theater, opera, or even the cinema, with films more readily awarded the label of art than, say, a television series. To draw such a priori distinctions between art and other forms of communication undermines the notion of aesthetics value constituted in the process of reception. A television series such as *The Wire*, but also a less critically acclaimed show, may do more to challenge individual viewers' horizons of expectations than the repeated reading of a given novel or attendance of an opera. Similarly, many expository texts pose a greater challenge to existing horizons of expectations than fictional texts. The representation of the Holocaust is one of many examples of how such reception aesthetics can and should inform media reception studies. It seems fair to speculate that the aesthetic value of documentaries about the Holocaust such those by Claude Lanzman (*Shoah*) or Marcel Ophüls (*Hôtel Terminus*, and *The Sorrow and the Pity*) lies in the fact that they challenged many viewers' knowledge, expectations, and sometimes experiences of the Holocaust, the role of the Vichy regime, the industrial organization of death camps, and postwar collaboration with Nazi war criminals as part of Cold War efforts, offering a dramatic contrast to the quickly emerging stereotypical representation of Nazi figures across a range of Hollywood war films, or the 1979 NBC television series *Holocaust* (cf. Kaes 1990). The latter, though, for all its trivializing representation of literally unimaginable evil, in turn offers an example of how a text collided with existing perceptions, requiring a reflexive engagement by viewers in an attempt to normalize the text. Taken to its logical conclusion, then, the work of the Constance School, despite itself being still bound by the disciplinary tradition of literary studies, thus developed a framework that facilitates a form of analysis of mediated texts that is sorely missing in media reception studies: a concept of dynamic, relative aesthetics that allows us to develop an evaluative frame for the study of all textuality regardless of their medium or form. The principle of aesthetic value thus applies to all forms of communication, regardless of whether they are perceived as artistic or not. Indeed, despite the distinction he drew earlier, Iser broadens the universal applicability of reception aesthetic in such a manner when he notes that "communication would be unnecessary if that which is to be communicated were not to some extent unfamiliar" (1978, p. 229).

In expanding our definition to encompass more than literary texts, we also need to consider the nature of mediated textuality and the implications of reception aesthetics in its study. Jauss's *horizon of expectation* in particular provides us with a timely tool to study textuality in the age of media convergence: as narratives have increasing expanded across different media (see e.g. Brooker 2001), convergence culture is marked by transmedia storytelling in which reception practices of a text within one medium need to be analyzed in relation to the intertextual and inter-medial contexts of such a text (cf. Jenkins 2006). Hence, the *horizon of expectation*, in its sensitivity to the interplay between different texts and experiences and how this interplay shapes readers' expectations and normalization of mediated texts, is an important analytical category for studying audiences in an age of intertextuality heighted by technological change and serves as a powerful reminder of the need to study the interplay between different texts to take into account the various forms of paratextuality that inform (popular) media consumption (Gray 2010). Indeed, one of the crucial differences between the analysis undertaken by literary theorists and contemporary media reception scholars is that the latter are con-fronted with radically blurred textual forms. The novel, for instance, possesses clear textual boundaries: its beginning and end are marked by the physical form of the book, which commonly encourages reading from cover to cover. Many con-temporary mediated forms of textuality lack such clear textual boundaries: televi-sion programs are part of the medium's flow (Williams 1974; see also Corner 1999), particular shows usually consist of numerous episodes spanning several sea-sons, and the internet's hypertextuality abandons the principle of linear narrative progression altogether. Consequently, the construction of textual boundaries has shifted from producers to media consumers (Sandvoss 2005a, 2005b), with not only the process of meaning production but also the selection and definition of what narrative elements are perceived to be part of the text firmly in the hands of the reader. When talking about textual configurations whose impact upon the audience we are interested in, these configurations – such as a given television show, someone's favorite sports team, a given political party, or a discourse about a particular topic – tend to constitute textual fields within which audiences select given textual episodes for inclusion and exclusion. The moment that the single text as a recognizable and identifiable category seems increasingly to disappear in a converging media environment is hence precisely the moment when reception aesthetics becomes an essential methodological and conceptual tool in the study of media audiences.

Its aesthetics of negativity takes on even greater relevance in the times of con-vergence, for such aesthetics are not only constituted with a given text but also, as Jauss's notions of the *horizon of expectation* reminds us, within and across genres, and are positioned within the modes of reading itself. As I have argued in relation to fan audiences, the *horizon of expectation* takes on the role of a textual habitus vis-à-vis the exponential multiplication of media content as fans (and other media consumers) select texts on the basis of their affinity to their experiences and expectations, deriving pleasures and a sense of belonging from familiarity, recognition, and (self-)reflection (Sandvoss 2003, 2004, 2005a, 2005b); fans do so by selecting between the different texts surrounding their fan objects, thereby gravitating to the state of noncommunication Iser laments, as they privilege given texts for precisely their familiarity and their lack of challenge to existing experiences.

In the context of converging mediated communication where single individual texts are ever harder to define or only constituted on an individual level, the temptation to study audiences in separation from texts is only heighted by the methodological difficulties faced for the contemporary researcher by acts of reading. Much, as Alphons Silbermann (1973) noted, classical literature studies seemingly felt overburdened trying to understand the author's work in its interaction with his audiences – and hence rather ignored this interplay altogether – contemporary audience studies may understandably shun studying reading processes that have become ever more complex and individualized. However, such methodological choices have profound conceptual and empirical consequences: In presenting a model of how emancipation and empowerment are rooted not only in audiences' *autonomy from* the text – as the common model of "active audiences" suggests – but also potentially in audiences' *engagement with* the text, reception aesthetics underlines the importance to establish which texts are read as much as how meaning is created in the process of reading. Media reception studies must thus not lose sight of the text as an analytical category, if it does not want to limit its analytical scope to merely attesting the absence of quantifiable negative media effects. Reception aesthetics here charts the way to reconcile the critical traditions of the fields of media and cultural studies – and not least the culture critique of the Frankfurt School – with the study of media consumption as a complex, but nevertheless potentially emancipatory, process.

Yet, it is in the methodological realm that media reception studies have in turn much to contribute to reception aesthetics by providing the missing empirical pieces to the large puzzle of media reception. The implied reader of Iser's work hinges entirely on forms of clearly defined textual boundaries that are lacking in convergent media. Moreover, it relies on the problematic distinction between intersubjectively recognized schematized aspects and textual gaps. Similarly, Jauss's continued commitment to hermeneutics diminished the applicability of his conceptual innovation of the *horizon of expectation* in his later work (Jauss 1972, 1977). The conceptual innovations in literary theory that Iser and Jauss proposed ultimately pointed beyond the singularly text-based methodology of their own discipline (cf. Warning 1975). One of the most significant achievements of media reception studies, in turn, is to have developed methodological strategies for the study of the empirical reader or media consumer in his or her everyday context. However, to move to an ethnography of reading and media consumption, rather than an ethnography of readers and media consumers, we need to refine our conceptual-methodological toolkit by combining the ethnographic tradition of media reception studies with the evaluative aesthetic analysis of the act of reading. This requires the further innovation of methods facilitating the study of *which* texts are read (beyond often crude media diaries) as much as *how* they challenge existing horizons of expectations. In a world in which mediated communication is becoming an ever more central and present aspect of our lifeworlds, meeting these methodological challenges will be crucial in studying media texts and their reception, not least so that we can, like literature studies always have, become concerned with their quality once more.

Notes

1   A comprehensive summary of its body of work lies beyond the scope of this chapter, but can be found in the work of Holub (1984, 1992), Warning (1975), and Grimm (1975).
2   See Holub (1992) for a detailed discussion of Fish's critique and Iser's response.

References

Adorno, T.W. 1970/2003 *Ästhetische Theorie*. Suhrkamp, Frankfurt am Main.

Barner, W. 1975 Wikungsgeschichte und tradition: ein beitrag zur methodologie der rezepionsforschung. In G. Grimm, ed. *Literatur und Leser: Theorien und Modelle zur Rezeption Literarischer Werke*. Philipp Reclam, Stuttgart.

Bennett, T. 1982 Texts and social process: the case of James Bond. *Screen Education*, 41, pp. 2–14.

Bourdieu, P. 1984 *Distinction: A Social Critique of the Judgement of Taste*. Routledge and Kegan Paul, London.

Brooker, W. 2000 *Batman Unmasked: Analysing a Cultural Icon*. Continuum, London.

Brooker, W. 2001 Living on Dawson's Creek: teen viewers, cultural convergence, and television overflow. *International Journal of Cultural Studies*, 4, 4, pp. 456–472.

Corner, J. 1999 *Critical Ideas in Television Studies*. Oxford University Press, Oxford.

de Certeau, M. 1984 *The Practice of Everyday Life*. University of California Press, Berkeley.

de Man, P. 1986 *Resistance to Theory*. University of Minnesota Press, Minneapolis.

Eco, U. 1962/1989 *The Open Work*. Hutchinson Radius, London.

Eco, U. 1994 *The Limits of Interpretation*. Indiana University Press, Bloomington.

Fish, S. 1981 Why no one's afraid of Wolfgang Iser. *Diacritics*, 11, 1, pp. 2–13.

Gauntlett, D. 2007 Media studies 2.0. Retrieved from http://www.theory.org.uk/mediastudies2.htm

Genette, G. 1997 *Paratexts: The Thresholds of Interpretation*. Cambridge University Press, Cambridge.

Giddens, A. 1991 *Modernity and Self-Identity: Self and Society in the Late Modern Age*. Polity Press, Cambridge.

Gray, J.A. 2010 *Show Sold Separately: Promos Spoilers and Other Media Paratexts*, New York University Press, New York.

Grimm, G. 1975 Einführung in die rezepionsforschung. In G. Grimm, ed. *Literatur und Leser: Theorien und Modelle zur Rezeption Literarischer Werke.* Philipp Reclam, Stuttgart.

Harth, D. 1971 Begriffsbildung in der literaturwissenschaft. *Deutsche Vierteljahresschrift für Literaturwissenschaft und Geistesgeschichte* 45, pp. 397–433.

Hills, M. 2002 *Fan Cultures.* Routledge, London.

Hirsch, J. 1914 *Die Genesis des Ruhmes: Ein Beitrag zur Methodenlehre der Geschichte.* Johann Ambrosius Barth, Leipzig.

Hohendahl, P.U. and Silberman, M. 1977 Introduction to reception aesthetics. *New German Critique,* 10, pp. 29–63.

Holub. R.C. 1984 *Reception Theory: A Critical Introduction.* Routledge, London.

Holub, R.C. 1992 *Crossing Borders: Reception Theory, Poststructuralism, Deconstruction.* University of Wisconsin Press, London.

Ingarden, R. 1973 *The Cognition of the Literary Work of Art.* Northwestern University Press, Evanston.

Iser, W. 1971 Indeterminacy and the reader's response in prose fiction. In J.H. Miller, ed. *Aspects of Narrative.* Columbia University Press, New York.

Iser, W. 1975 Die appellstruktur der texte: Unbestimmtheit als wirkungsbedingung literarisher prosa. In R. Warning, ed. *Rezeptionästhetik. Theorie und Traxis.* Wilhelm Fink Verlag, München.

Iser, W. 1978 *The Act of Reading: A Theory of Aesthetic Response.* John Hopkins University Press, Baltimore.

Jauss, H.R. 1972 *Kleine Apologie der ästhetischen Erfahrung.* Universitätsverlag, Konstanz.

Jauss, H.R. 1977 *Ästhetische Erfahrung und literarische Hermeneutik.* Fink, München.

Jauss, H.R. 1982 *Toward an Aesthetic of Reception.* University of Minnesota Press, Minneapolis.

Jenkins, H. 1992 *Textual Poachers: Television Fans and Participatory Culture.* Routledge, New York.

Jenkins, H. 2006 *Convergence Culture: Where New and Old Media Collide.* New York University, New York.

Kaes, A. 1990 History and film: public memory in the age of electronic dissemination. *History and Memory,* 2, 1, pp. 111–129.

Livingstone, S. 1998 Relationships between media and audiences: prospects for audience reception studies. In T. Liebes and J. Curran, eds. *Media, Ritual and Identity: Essays in Honor of Elihu Katz.* Routledge, London.

Löwenthal, L. 1971 *Erzählkunst und Gesellschaft: Die Gesellschaftsproblematik in der deutschen Literaratur des 19. Jahrhunderts.* Luchterhand, Neuwied.

Mandelkov, K.R. 1974 Probleme der wirkungsgeschichte. In P.U. Hohendahl, ed *Sozialgeschichte und Wirkungsästhetik: Dokumente zur empirischen Sozialforschung.* Athenaum Verlag, Frankfurt a.M.

Mannheim, K. 1935 *Mensch und Gesellschaft im Zeitalter des Umbaus.* Sijthoffs Uitgeversmaatschappij, Leiden.

McKee, A., et al. 2007 The fans of cultural theory. In J.A. Gray et al., eds. *Fandom: Identities and Communities in a Mediated World.* New York University Press, New York.

Morley, D. 1980 *The 'Nationwide' Audience.* British Film Institute, London.

Sandvoss, C. 2003 *A Game of Two Halves: Football, Television and Globalization,* Comedia/ Routledge, London.

Sandvoss, C. 2004 Technological evolution or revolution? Sport online live internet commentary as postmodern cultural form. *Convergence: The Journal of Research into New Media Technologies,* 10, 3, pp. 39–54.

Sandvoss, C. 2005a *Fans: The Mirror of Consumption.* Polity Press, Cambridge.

Sandvoss, C. 2005b One dimensional fan: toward an aesthetic of fan texts. *American Behavioural Scientist,* 49, 3, pp. 822–839.

Sandvoss, C. 2007 The death of the reader? Literary theory and the study of texts in popular culture. In J.A. Gray et al., eds. *Fandom: Identities and Communities in a Mediated World.* New York University Press, New York.

Silbermann, A. 1973 Von den wirkungen der literature als massenkommunikationsmittel. In W. Kuttenkeuler, ed. *Poesie und Politik. Zur Situation der Literatur in Deutschland.* Kohlhammer, Stuttgart.

Staiger, J. 2005 *Media Receptions Studies.* New York: New York University Press.

Warning, R. 1975 Rezeptionästhetik als literaturwissenschaftliche pragmatik. In R. Warning, ed. *Rezeptionästhetik. Theorie und Traxis.* UTB/Wilhelm Fink Verlag, München.

Weber, S. 1986 Caught in the act of reading. In S. Weber, ed. *Demarcating the Disciplines: Philosophy, Literature, Art.* University of Minnesota Press, Minneapolis.

Wehrli, M. 1970 Deutsche literaturwissenschaft. In F.P. Ingold, ed. *Literaturwissenschaft und Literaturkritik im 20. Jahrhundert.* Kandelaber, Bern.

Williams, R. 1974 *Television: Technology and Cultural Form.* Fontana, London.

12

Affect Theory and Audience

Anna Gibbs

Media as Biomedia

The "affective turn" (Clough 2007) which has taken place in cultural studies over the last 15 years is progressively emerging in related fields of study, and seems likely to add a new dimension to audience research, even as it struggles with the rapid redefinition of its object as publics or, in some new media discourse, as users. To date, affect has been a category that has made more impact in media theory than in audience studies – in fact, affect theory has not yet been seriously adopted at all by audience research.

What, then, is *affect*? Two main theories of affect have been taken up in the humanities since the 1990s. The Spinozan-Deleuzian line of thought, developed by Brian Massumi (1993) and others, has affect emerging as an asubjective force in a perspective from which the human appears as an envelope of possibilities rather than the finite totality or essence represented by the idea of the individual organism. This is the view from which Massumi can describe *affect* as an energetic dimension or "capacity," and *emotion* as a selective activation or expression of affect from a "virtual co-presence" of potentials on the basis of memory, experience, thought, and habit (2003). Massumi's work is completely consonant with what has been called the *new vitalism*, a philosophical and sociological mode of thought which draws in part on the work of nineteenth-century French sociologist Gabriel Tarde, whose work was formative in the thought of Deleuze and Guattari. New vitalism focuses not on the molar domain of traditional, Durkheimian sociology, which deals with representations, but on the molecular domain of flows or fluxes, operating "beneath" them. In this domain, form is but a trace in the wake of flux, and it is rather *change* that is the object of study. This is the

The Handbook of Media Audiences, First Edition. Edited by Virginia Nightingale.

[i]nfinitesimal level of beliefs and of desires, of the power of affection of these asso-
ciative, attractive, collectively inventive forces that do not subjugate individuals without subjectivising them, without forming the possibility of new assemblages,
without reopening totally new processes of individuation. (Alliez n.d., p. 5)

In this optic, the individual appears as "the whole cosmos conquered and absorbed
by a single being" (Alliez 1999, my translation), and therefore always a collectivity,
while the social is what is abstracted from the individual, or what is virtual in it.
This formulation aims to avoid the traditional sociological (Durkheimian) distinction between the individual and the social: it sees both as constituted by relations
of force, which is itself constituted by differential relations. In other words, as in
Leibniz's monadology, it sees that it is relations that explain terms, and not terms
that explain relations. It is, as Alliez (n.d.) suggests, a "microsociology" (p. 4).

What this means for audience research is the prioritization of the analysis of
communication and flow over the subjects and objects produced within it. While
imitation (to which I will return) appears to be of one person by another, it is in
reality imitation of something abstracted from the other and which forms part of
a self-propagating flux or flow (cf. Deleuze and Guattari 1987). But it also implies
that not only what is abstracted from human beings, but also what is abstracted
from animals, plants, and things, constitute the social world and might be said to
have forms of agency which, although not the same as human agency, are still
available to them. But the distinction between things of a technological kind and
human beings has become extremely problematic, as the technology we incorporate into our lives begins to modify us – our capacity for attention, our desires, and
the way we remember. Indeed, something of this sort seems to be implied in the
titles of several recent books on image cultures, for example W. J. T. Mitchell's
What Pictures Want (2005) and Ron Burnett's *How Images Think* (2005).

The power of the image lies in part in its speed of reach. A small number of
experimental studies that measured data such as Galvanic Skin Response have found
that humans react physiologically to images faster than we can cognitively process
and make sense of them. Primarily affective rather than representational in their
modus operandi, media both aim directly at the human nervous system and are
entirely dependent on it for their existence (as Nightingale [1997] puts it, the media–
audience loop forms "non-anthropomorphic cyborgs"). Television "cathects" (in
Nightingale's suggestive psychoanalytically inflected usage) aspects of the human in
order to function, and I have argued elsewhere that what it primarily cathects is
human affect (Gibbs 2002). We could think of this investment of media in the human
body in a number of different ways: in the terms suggested by Mark Seltzer (1992)
when he writes of the "miscegenation" of bodies and machines, and of nature and
culture; or we could adapt Eugene Hacker's term "biomediation"; or, again, Bolter
and Grusin's concept of "remediation" (1999), all of which have the advantage of
moving beyond earlier models of the cyborg (such as Donna Haraway's) in the way
they describe how media repurpose the human (Angel and Gibbs 2005).

Using sensory appeal and the creation of novelty to attract interest, media amplify affect in their audiences by their ubiquitous use of faces, voices, and music, and, in the case of television especially, by the rhythms of editing which also sustain attention by continually activating the orientation reflexes. This broadcasting of human emotion then produces complex feedback loops between image, individual, and audience in which causes and effects become interchangeable (Gibbs 2007). Communication can then be conceived as "the articulation between the nervous, technical, and social systems which constitute the total human fact" (Stiegler 2006). What this generates is a complex system in which, because we act "in concert" (Burnett 2005) with technology, media, and things, "technology and the practical use to which we put it always exceeds the intentional structures that we build into it" (Burnett 2002; cf. Gibbs 2008).

What the Spinozan-Deleuzian view leaves out, however, is the highly differentiated work performed by the "categorical" or "discrete" affects which actually makes possible the focus on change in the "minoritarian" dimension of Tarde's microsociology, introduced below. Affect, after all, never occurs in the body simply as affect in general, or as affect opposed to or different from cognition, but always as a particular affect. This prospect is opened by the work of American psychologist Silvan Tomkins (1962, 1991, 1992) and taken up by Eve Kosofsky Sedgwick and Adam Frank (1995), who introduced it into cultural studies in their introduction to *Shame and Its Sisters: A Silvan Tomkins Reader*. According to American psychologist Silvan Tomkins, author of the comprehensive, four-volume work on affect theory, *Affect, Imagery, Consciousness* (1962, 1992), affects are correlated sets of facial, physiological, and neurological responses to internal events (perceptions, other affects, memories, and so on) and external events. Drawing on Darwin's evolutionary theory of the affects developed in *On the Expression of the Emotions in Man and Animals* (1998), Tomkins identified nine discrete affects, whose hyphenated names denote the lowest and the highest points of arousal. The positive (that is, intrinsically rewarding) affects are enjoyment–joy and interest–excitement. The negative (or intrinsically punishing) affects are fear–terror, distress–anguish, anger–rage, shame–humiliation, disgust–contempt, and the "auxiliary" affect dissmell, distinguished somewhat later than the others. Finally, surprise–startle is described as a "resetting" affect, which simply interrupts any ongoing situation and requires the individual experiencing it to pay attention to something else. The intrinsically rewarding or punishing nature of the affects impels the one who experiences them either to put an end to something unpleasant, or to prolong something pleasurable. Taken together, the discrete affects form the primary human motivational system. Affect is also highly contagious, in part because of its tendency to form positive feedback loops in which more of the same affect is generated both in the individual experiencing it and in those who observe it.

Tomkins is at pains to point out that affects are both individual and social responses. He writes,

> [A]ffects are not private obscure internal intestinal responses but facial responses that communicate and motivate at once both publicly outward to the other and backward and inward to the one who smiles or cries or frowns or sneers or otherwise expresses his affects. (Tomkins 1962, p. 297)

In fact, Tomkins sees affects as central to human sociality – so much so that he speculates,

> Social contagion might precede self-contagion because the phenomenon of contagion within the organism is an indirect consequence of the similarity of one's own responses to social activators. Since it is known that the smile of the face of another is a specific activator of the smile of the one who sees it, the awareness of the smile in the self may release another smile either on the basis of the similarity of the smile in the visual and the smile in the proprioceptive modality, or on a learned basis, since one's own smile was often preceded by the smile of another. (p. 297)

Tomkins argues that the affects amplify the drives, so that, for example, sex is amplified by excitement, and hunger or thirst by distress. But unlike the drives, human affect can be provoked by absolutely anything at all. Its range of objects is limitless. It should be noted, however, that affect neither is simply a judgment nor preceded by a judgement, as some have suggested. Neither are the affects simply neurological or socially "constructed." Rather, in Tomkins's theory, they are a bio-psycho-social phenomenon, in which the corporeal and the cognitive are inescapably conjoined in ways which are contingent on experience.

Tomkins's Script Theory

Tomkins shows how the corporeal and the cognitive might be articulated by means of his script theory. Scripts are ways of managing and making sense of affect developed by individuals. A script is a set of rules for the interpretation, evaluation, prediction, production, and control of a set of scenes, while a scene is an event that renders a particular affect salient and endows it with meaning. Importantly, as Tomkins (1991) writes, "the socialization of affect [in families] is not independent of either the ideology of the larger society or the events of international relations." But, on the other hand, nor "are these interrelationships either simple, readily demonstrable, or unchanging" (p. 511).

Scripts dealing with negative affect will produce analogs (i.e. once you are alert to negative affect, you will see the potential for it everywhere, finding similarities in apparently different and increasingly remote scenes). Scripts dealing with positive affect, by contrast, aim to maximize it and will produce variants rather than analogs: for example, "one develops a talent by using it in many different ways or settings or a friendship grows through the sharing and rehearsal of diverse experiences" (Carlson 1981). But unlike at least some of the kinds of scripts produced by people, media scripts are not designed to make sense of or modulate affect, but rather to amplify (i.e. intensify) it and to manage it in the service of the media's own purposes, which may be many, varied, and contradictory, since they include the purposes of advertisers, program makers, networks, and the corporations that own the networks or the internet sites and software.

Because it offers an account of the way complexity is generated from a few very simple parameters, script theory is able to move easily between theory and empirical instance, and between the global and the local. It is also extremely useful in trying to account for the diversity of reactions of both individuals and groups to images in general, and for why some images remain individually and culturally memorable and resonant, while others are eventually forgotten.

Complexity is increased because scripts not only organize affect but also "co-assemble" it with cognition.[1] Cognitions "coassembled with affects become hot and urgent. Affects coassembled with cognitions become better informed and smarter" (Tomkins 1992). While the affect system *amplifies* whatever seizes attention, the cognitive system performs the work of *transformation*, so that "[a]ll information is at once biased and informed" (Tomkins 1992). Scripts, then, are like stories, but with the difference that they are designed to be put into action. Most importantly, these processes of scripting can be either individual or social, and they help to account for the diversity of reactions of both individuals and groups to images in general.

Corporeality and Belief

Because affect and cognition are always coassembled in consciousness, there can be no ideas without affect: we always have ideas about feelings and feelings about ideas. What contribution, then, does affect make to the generation, hold, and sway of ideas in contemporary society? In other words, how are affects implicated in the formation of *belief*? Belief is crucial to *all* aspects of the functioning of the social order, most obviously and visibly during election campaigns and during episodes of controversy when they are often held and stated explicitly over particular issues or personalities. The issue of weapons of mass destruction (WMD) in Iraq (which provided the publicly stated rationale for the US, British, and Australian invasion of that country) furnishes an example of one such instance. Why is it that, even after no such weapons were found and the self-styled Coalition of the Willing has formally admitted there were none, do as many as 30 percent of Americans still believe Iraq had WMD? One reason may be that the potential use of such weapons, had they existed, generated a high level of fear in the United States. Massumi (2005) theorizes that the affective reality of the fear created by the threat of something that hasn't yet happened forms what he calls an "affective fact," so that the "threat that does not materialize is not false," but simply deferred ... it could always happen, so the fear it generates can never be abolished by being proved groundless. In addition to this, I would argue that images in particular – and especially the way they are used in news reportage – play a very particular part in the creation of affective facts. It seems that people generally have difficulty in remembering negation – especially when they are distracted – so that, if something is wrongly asserted and then later corrected, the correction often fails to register. Images of silos said to contain WMD not only accompanied news reports in which some experts were critical of what was being claimed about the existence of such weapons, but also accompanied some reports in which it was later admitted that the belief in their existence had been proven wrong. Today, however, it seems testimony to the power of the adage that "seeing is believing" that so many Americans still believe Iraq had WMD. This is one reason why televisual images especially may function as a form of suggestion, having a power and immediacy greater and more compelling than that of speech.

Televisual close-ups of faces in particular communicate a continuous flow of affect, regardless of what is being said, as the televising of the US presidential campaign debate between Nixon and Kennedy in 1960 dramatically demonstrated. Polls of television audiences after the debate declared Kennedy – who appeared calm and composed – the winner over the profusely perspiring Nixon, while radio listeners had Nixon a little in front (Sifry and Rasiej 2008).[2] As this debate showed, affect is not always aligned with verbal expression in visual media. Even more telling, perhaps, is that verbal correction of false information seems to count as repetition that reinforces the original information: at least, this seems to be the case when levels of skepticism are low (Lewandowsky et al. 2005). Images seem to possess a facticity that may continue to provoke anxiety, even in the face of better knowledge.

Belief, in this optic, is the "affective force of thought" (Massumi 2010): it is created by a feeling about an idea, especially when that feeling is amplified with every successive mediatized repetition of the idea, and magnified by its attachment to different contexts as it circulates between different media platforms and different media genres, giving rise to commentary in current affairs programs or on blogs, or to sketches on radio or television comedy shows, or as it makes its way into advertisements or the plotlines of television dramas. The idea may be contradicted, questioned, or parodied in these different situations, but the original affect aroused by it persists, consciously or unconsciously, in the bodies of many, and may even be strengthened by repetition, regardless of the diversity of contexts in which this occurs.

In fact, the formation both of particular beliefs and of belief itself as an attitude depends on the embodied aspect of affect, on its power to make the heart beat faster, or the muscles to tense, or the skin to grow cold and clammy or to burn with a blush. The corporeal origin of affect and its power to transform the physiological state of the body in response to ideas is what makes belief feel real, both sustaining conviction and lending it urgency. Created only in the performative process of avowal, belief depends on linking language and ideas with the somatic dispositions that produce it as an affective reality.

Moreover, just as the tendency of any one component of affective response is to trigger the other neurological and physiological components comprising the entire pattern of response, the body, language, and attitudes become associated with each other over time in ways that mean that activation of any one component will very likely call up the others. As Bourdieu (1992) writes,

> Every social order systematically takes advantage of the disposition of the body and language to function as depositories of deferred thoughts that can be triggered off at a distance in space and time by the simple effort of re-placing the body in an overall posture which recalls the associated thoughts and feelings, in one of the inductive states of the body, which, as actors know, give rise to states of minds. (p. 73)

This is because the "body believes in what it plays at: it weeps if it mimes grief" (1992, p. 73). Belief, therefore, can be seen to be intimately bound up with affect, and dependent on the somatic dispositions associated with particular affects, each of which correlates with a precise physiological profile and a particular physical posture – which may be abbreviated (the lowered eyes instead of the head bowed in shame, for example) or might remain incipient, as when the angry impulse to clench the fist does not result in the production of the gesture.

Affect Contagion

Most importantly for audience studies, however, affect is implicated in the media-tized forms of subjectivity spawned by affective epidemics in response to public events such as the televising of the Gulf War, the death of Princess Diana, or the global financial crisis. As pointed out earlier, some discrete affects in particular (anger–rage, fear–terror, and enjoyment–joy) are highly contagious, tending to produce positive feedback loops which amplify the affect in question, while others might be more likely to give rise to complementary affective responses (the shame response to contempt, for example). However, some individuals are more suscep-tible than others to the contagious powers of particular affects. This is because of the different *ideo-affective postures* produced by different forms of familial and cul-tural affect socialization.

An ideo-affective posture is a loosely organized ensemble of feelings and ideas about feelings. Tomkins sees a polarity in Western cultures between what he calls "normative" and humanist ideo-affective postures. One item on the polarity scale he constructed to distinguish between these postures furnishes an example of what it might mean to have ideas about particular kinds of feelings. To find it disgusting to see an adult cry is more likely to be associated with normative attitudes, while to find it distressing to see an adult cry is more likely to be associated with humanistic attitudes. These ideo-affective postures are to be distinguished from specifically ideological postures, which arise when ideo-affective postures resonate strongly with the more precisely articulated sets of beliefs that compose an ideology (Tomkins 1995).

An ideo-affective posture, then, roughly corresponds with what we might more colloquially call an *attitude*. It represents a disposition – implying both an arrangement or organization, and a tendency to particular forms of expression. I have argued elsewhere that extreme right-wing Australian former politician Pauline Hanson's media-amplified tendency to give expression to distress (especially in her voice) resonated with people who might already be feeling distress because of their personal circumstances, or be sensitive to it by virtue of their affect socialization, even if they might otherwise have had little sympathy for Hanson's politics (Gibbs 2001). On the one hand, Hanson's distress produced an affective resonance in those whose own distress had apparently found no response from individual politicians or any public policy. This was a group composed of white, predominantly male, little educated, older blue-collar workers from rural or outer suburban areas whose political representatives were felt by them to have failed them. This group had lost not only the economic security it once enjoyed, provided by protectionist policies of successive postwar governments, but also its status as iconic Australians, ideal representatives of a certain familiar ethos, of which mateship is a metonym. The distress of this group of people found both echo and amplification in Hanson's voice, and it found a form of legitimization in her attitudes, as well as a prescription for remedial action in her campaign for election. On the other hand, however, Hanson's distress also resonated with people who didn't fit the usual profile of a One Nation voter: for example, retired people who experienced their situation as a loss of belonging and a loss of power also seemed to be susceptible, as did people who resented protestors preventing people from attending One Nation meetings. Hanson's distress seemed to increase whenever she found herself confronted and challenged by unsympathetic journalists or audiences, and this distress, communicated by televisual close-up and most affectingly by tone of voice, was a highly contagious affect that attached itself to the idea that individual freedoms were being restricted because protestors at One Nation rallies made attendance potentially dangerous, and Hanson's meetings were picketed by demonstrators who sometimes clashed with police as well as with her supporters. This perceived restriction of freedom in turn resonated with the government policies to which Hanson objected, such as so-called special treatment for Aboriginal people, which was believed by some to entail disadvantage to non-Aboriginal people. However, the idea (or the feeling) that freedoms were being curtailed actually belonged to another, more immediately personal, context (for her addressees) than to the wider, more public and political one that Hanson explicitly claimed to evoke. The amplification of these already existing affects, the anger and distress felt by people who no longer necessarily represented the universal idea of an Australian, made these affects powerful enough to be transposed from one context into another more public one, where they became attached to *ideas* which seemed to give legitimate voice to them (see Gibbs 2001).

Cultural theorist Lawrence Grossberg (1992), addressing the circulation of anger in the American New Right, describes an "affective epidemic" as a "series of trajectories or mobilities which, while apparently leading to specific concerns, actually constantly redistribute and displace investments. Affective epidemics define empty sites which, as they travel, can be contextually rearticulated" (p. 284).

This makes clear that while affect can thus be seen as a medium for the propagation of affectively laden attitudes by processes of contagion, the propagation of more specific ideas is both less certain and more fleeting, since it is not possible to forge permanent links between affects and objects – it is in the nature of affect that it readily transfers itself from object to object. Fear, for example, now alights on the fear of running out of water, and now on bird flu or white powder turning up in the mail. Whether these fears are well founded or not has little to do with this process of *magnification*, by which fear becomes increasingly salient as an affect, and must therefore be dealt with by any number of possible strategies enabled by scripts for dealing with the fear itself: it can be avoided (e.g. by turning off the television, or by tuning out and refusing to listen to politicians), cognitively controlled (e.g. by seeking out information on the internet), counteracted (by taking political action), and so on.

Imitation and Suggestion

Whether it is spontaneous or managed (as in viral marketing), the process of contagion ultimately relies on affect contagion, which can be thought of as a corporeally based form of mimetic communication. Mimetic communication is organized in terms of a shifting dynamic between "imitation" and "suggestion" first cogently theorized as such by nineteenth-century French sociologist Gabriel Tarde,[3] who saw this dynamic as the basis of sociality. "Society is imitation and imitation is a kind of somnambulism," he famously claimed (1962). While Tarde's work was taken up in America by sociologists such as George Herbert Mead, Franz Boas, James Baldwin, and others, his work was eventually eclipsed by that of his rival, Durkheim, and then by Durkheim's followers, critically in the United States by Talcott Parsons (Leys 1993). As Ruth Leys makes clear, the reasons Tarde fell out of favor in the United States rested on his particular conception of subjectivity which, organized and driven by forces outside of conscious awareness (*somnambulism*), was conceived by Tarde somewhat as a fluctuating field in which boundaries between self and other were constantly shifting. This view of the subject ran counter to the strength of the American belief in the strength and autonomy of the ego (1993).

Tarde conceived subjectivity as a center of action that receives and transmits movements. It both is prone to suggestion from the outside, which is what gives rise to its imitations, and, conversely, can transmit suggestions to others. For Tarde, imitation is not a process resulting in the production of second-rate copies, as the Platonic tradition in Western thought often implies, but a forming "senso-motorial memory" (Lazzarato 1999), or memory in the form of habit, what we would now call *procedural memory* – or, more broadly, *semantic memory*. Such memory is not simply cognitive, but involves nerves, muscles, and affects. Imitation is "suggested," then, both by the force of habit (the force of the past) and, more immediately, by the force of the sympathy that is the response to what is suggested by other bodies. Moreover, imitation has an exponential force, since

> [t]his very will to imitate has been handed down through imitation. Before imitating the act of another we begin by feeling the need from which this act proceeds, and we feel it precisely as we do only because it has been suggested to us. (Tarde 1962, p. 193)

The social state, then, is like a dream in which one seems to have control, but in which attitudes and courses of action that seem original and spontaneous are in fact the result of suggestion, not necessarily of individuals, but of environments, and for Tarde, cities are preeminent among environments; they are "rich in suggestion."

Imitation is a necessary process fundamental to social continuity and stability: it is the means by which novel inventions are taken up and formed into habit, custom, and fashion as modes of social aggregation. Imitation, as Tarde conceives it, represents the conservation of the past and the preservation of a social bond. But it is not democratic in character. It is always suggested by prestige: it flows along hierarchical lines of force from center to margins, from city to provinces, and from the nobility to the lower social orders (Zourabichvili 2003). As the rise of mass media (during Tarde's lifetime, this meant the press) began to render publics more significant than crowds both in reality and in Tarde's work, Tarde came to see imitation as a process that is lateral and sometimes mutual as well as hierarchical (Borch 2005). While it is still produced by prestige, prestige doesn't preexist its conferral by the other (Zourabichvili 2003). Suggestibility, then, means the attribution of prestige, power, and superiority to the other: it is this action on our part that makes those imitated desirable.

Audiences: Crowds, Publics, and Beyond

Audiences, like crowds, have been superseded in many ways by publics. The birth of publics – which Tarde was among the first to identify and describe – would seem to augur a social life less prone to contagion and suggestion than that of the age of crowds, because, among other things, publics are believed to be more disembodied than crowds (Warner 2002). Tarde, however, clearly predicates the suggestibility of publics on the relationship between bodies: in the first place on the human sensitivity to the gaze of others (especially in the density of urban life). This develops into sensitivity to the mere thought of this gaze and the attention that accompanies it. Similarly, the susceptibility to the voice of authority sensitizes the reader to the voice of the text, and even to the imagined authority of other readers, whether that authority means the weight of numbers or the selectivity of an elite (Tarde 1901). The suggestibility of publics is, finally, a kind of "contagion without contact," but Tarde seems to struggle to find a vocabulary to talk about the kind of influence exerted at a distance. He refers to it as "ideal," speaks of the "mental cohesion" of publics, and finally refers to it as "interspiritual" (Tarde 1901, p. 6) Perhaps the other most important characteristic of publics (as opposed to crowds) for Tarde is their degree of self-consciousness of themselves as a public which may militate against suggestibility. The tendency of individuals to belong to more than one public simultaneously will make publics less prey to panic than crowds, though this will tend to produce a media milieu in which multiple concerns create a certain incoherence (Tarde 1901). Michael Warner, a contemporary theorist of publics, argues that dominant conceptions of "the human" privilege and depend on an idea of the private reader as rational and critical and that this restricts our idea of their agency (2002). Tarde's view of reading as a locus of suggestion evinces a view of it which is less disembodied, and less rational, than the view described by Warner. Tarde emphasizes the irrationality of publics, provoked and amplified by the press as it creates a "fuss" about something (Tarde 2003). To analyze this fuss making as "moral panic" is to treat it primarily as a discursive and textual phenomenon, but Tarde's analysis of publics as susceptible to suggestion takes more fully into account the affective dimension of media engagement, and he does not necessarily see panic as the most important affective state created by media "fuss." Equally significant for Tarde is the creation of fads which often involve the pleasures of consumption of luxury goods. The newspaper – via the power of repetition rather than by rational argument or even by rhetoric – succeeds in making the reader "hallucinate" (2003). If Tarde sees publics as "less extremist than crowds, less despotic or less dogmatic," he also believes that their despotism or dogmatism will be "far more tenacious and chronic" (2003). The most cursory consideration of the role of opinion polls in contemporary Western politics would seem to confirm this.

The term *publics*, more than *audiences*, implies active participation consonant with the way in which we now speak of users (or, in some new media circles, *prosumers*) of media. Media still depend on human participation, but now users are also supplying content. And they are doing so free of charge to media owners who profit from their labor in blogs, vlogs, social-networking sites, citizen journalism, and even advertising. (Subway's recent campaign piggybacked on the television dance craze – *Strictly Dancing, So You Think You Can Dance, Dancing with the Stars,*

Kids' TV Dance Party, America's Best Dance Crew, Dance Your Ass Off, etc., etc. – with ads that featured actors doing the Subway Shuffle and enjoined viewers to post their own versions of the dance on a website with a promise that the best one would feature in a broadcast ad.)

Tarde's interest in fads rather than panics seems prescient not only because the attempt to maximize positive affects (which Tomkins saw as the overriding human motivation, along with minimizing negative ones) ensures our continuing participation in media while too strong a reliance on negative affects risks creating disaffection, but also because it alerts us to the need to consider an affect dynamics of publics and media in which the specific motivational force of each of the affects is taken fully into consideration. Contemporary affect theory now makes conceivable an epidemiological mapping of affective flows and a way of accounting for differential rates of transmission according to which particular discrete affects are in play.

Opinion and Conversation

Conversation and the press (which is a major producer of public conversation and largely controls its agenda) are two important channels for the formation of opinion (Tarde 1901). Tarde distinguishes between "opinion proper, a totality of judgements" and what he calls "the general will, a totality of desires" (1901), though he admits that in practice these two things intermingle. I want to suggest that they combine in the production of belief (which I discuss at more length in Gibbs 2008). Tarde focuses mainly on the former, which he sees as potentially a threat to tradition (whose sources are familial socialization, professional apprenticeship, and formal instruction) and reason (whose sources may be philosophical, scientific, judicial, or religious), as it may be a threat to individual judgement, though whether this is for good or ill depends on whether it is the "reasoning elite" or the "first comers" that control it. Tradition runs deeper and is more stable than opinion, and, while it is national in character, opinion ("something as light, as transitory, as expansive as the wind") always "strives to become international, like reason." Moreover, by its very nature, opinion gives rise to an inchoate consciousness of some similarity or agreement between the individual and others who share it – and the more "violently" an opinion is held to, the more it creates this awareness. It is the press (media) that produces this similarity (1901).

Tarde views conversation as divisible into pleasurable everyday sociability between equals or peers (or those rendered as such by virtue of the type of conversation in which they engage in certain situations – for example, Sydney's much vaunted democracy of Bondi Beach) on the one hand (voluntary conversation), and as a social institution which regulates relations within social hierarchies (obligatory conversation) on the other. While the latter is codified, the former is the medium for contagion and imitation. It is not immune, however, to the influence of "the monologues pronounced by superiors" – and, in fact, the media's active agenda setting takes over this function to some extent, while it also provides a channel for those superiors in the form of political leaders and experts of various kinds. The press unifies such conversation in space and diversifies it in time, and its reach extends, through conversation, to those who have no direct contact with it (Tarde 1901). Conversation and the press act in concert with each other: in Tomkins's terms, each "amplifies" (increases in intensity) the other, and also "magnifies" (renders more salient by connecting it to other scenes or topics) the other (1992). For Tarde (and contemporary social psychology would concur), the power of conversation to instigate imitation derives from the face-to-face situation which increases attention on the other and the likelihood of affect contagion. While the media depend on novelty to attract human attention (hence the constantly changing agenda), they also harness this attention and transform it into obsession with particular items on the agenda, and newspapers and television in particular rely on establishing and maintaining everyday rhythms of familiar flow to ingrain media usage as habit.

Tarde also differentiates between adversarial, argumentative conversation (*conversation-lutte*), and conversation that involves mutual informing and discussion (*conversation-échange*) (1901). Electronic media today are able to appropriate some of the powers of face-to-face conversation by replicating it through concentration on the face and the voice. But the internet also appropriates some of the features of intimate conversation via discussion groups, giving the appearance of democracy in the face of the increasing power and control exercised by the media corporations who own both the sites and the user-provided content of them. Tarde argues that conversations between people with "hereditary friendships" in villages differ from those between strangers in large cities in that they deal more in gossip about acquaintances held in common, while those among denizens of the city have to reach further afield to find common interests, so the topics will be general, or, if gossip is involved, the subject of it will be a celebrity or politician. The internet appropriates both modes of conversation: internet bullying among schoolchildren targets a community shared between bully and victim, but also potentially reaches beyond it to contaminate future acquaintances. The rise of celebrity-oriented programs on television also represents an attempt to appropriate the conversation of cities – one which reduces mutuality while at the same time celebrating and marketing it as the technologically advanced feature of interactivity. Think, for example, of *Dancing with the Stars*, where the *conversation-échange* between viewers as it is reflected in the program is reduced to voting couples on or off. This is not to say, however, that such conversation doesn't take place elsewhere and doesn't affect the way the vote goes. In fact, this conversation "off" is essential to the creation of celebrity on which media now depend. Without such conversation, there can be no such thing as a public.

As media become more pervasive and more diverse, and feed more off each other (as television celebrity programs feed off gossip magazines and vice versa, and television series feed off web-based fandom and vice versa), they become even more pervasive in the everyday than they currently are. On the one hand, media contribute to the globalization of opinion in precisely the way that Tarde foresaw, to the extent that local and national conversation becomes dominated by global opinion. This is because the more numerous the proponents of public opinion become, the more pressure there is to conform to it. This does not represent a weakening of character, but, as Tarde succinctly points out, when "poplars and oaks are brought down by a storm, it is not because they grew weaker but because the wind grew stronger" (1901).

Conclusion

If audiences can now be conceived as a discontinuous series of emergent formations of affectively driven "collective intelligence" (Lévy 2000), this is nevertheless not the "wisdom of the crowd," as James Surowiecki (2004) has it, purported to lead to more intelligent solutions to problems. Rather, it means that populations are swept through by contagion without ever coming to form an aggregated force. What this ultimately calls for is audience research which takes the form of an epidemiology of affect (Gibbs 2001), involving the identification of vectors of contagion and the mapping of the affect-born migration of ideas, only some of which will be successfully propagated, while the process of propagation may itself produce intensifications, modulations, or modifications of the forms that do manage to take root – much as the phenomenon of Elvis imitation spawned Elvis Herselvis, when taken up by a woman in San Francisco, or when the screening of *Sex and the City* in Australia served as a pretext for advertising to represent Australian versions of the women in the series and their audiences. However, Massumi is certainly right when he argues that as we try to account for contemporary cultural forms and current events, we may have to abandon the concept of cause, and examine instead "effects and their interweavings" (1993). In other words, it is syndromes that must come to form the new object of knowledge. Syndromes "mark the limit of causal analysis. They cannot be exhaustively *understood* – only pragmatically altered by experimental interventions operating in several spheres of activity at once" (1993).

Notes

1   Importantly, cognition here is not reducible to thinking, but it involves, for example, in the act of crossing the street, "*relating* the cars as seen to the danger as felt, to the action of avoiding danger. It is a momentary, environmental, sensory, perceptual, memorial action sequence that is cognitive by virtue of the achieved organized connectedness of these part mechanisms and the *information and urgency* they conjointly generate"

(Tomkins 1992, p. 8). For a fuller discussion of how Tomkins conceives the cognitive system, see Gibbs (2002).

2 My thanks to Jill Bennett for this example.

3 I have discussed this dynamic in more detail in Gibbs (2008).

References

Alliez, E. 1999 Tarde et le problème de la constitution. In E. Alliez, ed. *Gabriel Tarde, Monadologie et Sociologie*. Institut Synthélabo, Paris, pp. 9–32.

Alliez, E. n.d. The difference and repetition of Gabriel Tarde. Retrieved from http://www.gold.ac.uk/media/alliez.pdf

Angel, M. and Gibbs, A. 2005 Media, affect and the face: biomediation and the political scene. *Southern Review: Communication, Politics and Culture*, 38, 3, pp. 24–39.

Bolter, J.D. and Grusin, R. 1999 *Remediation*. MIT Press, Cambridge, MA.

Borch, C. 2005 Urban imitations: Tarde's sociology revisited. *Theory, Culture and Society*, 22, 3, pp. 81–100.

Bourdieu, P. 1992 *The Logic of Practice*. Trans. Richard Nice. Polity Press, Cambridge.

Burnett, R. 2002 Context, technology, communication, and learning. *Educational Technology*, 42, 22, pp. 67–70.

Burnett, R. 2005 *How Images Think*. MIT Press, Boston.

Carlson, R. 1981 Studies in script theory: I. Adult analogs of a childhood nuclear scene. *Journal of Personality and Social Psychology*, 40, 3, pp. 501–510.

Clough, P. 2007 *The Affective Turn: Theorising the Social*. Duke University Press, Durham, NC.

Darwin, C. 1998 *On the Expression of the Emotions in Man and Animals*. Ed. Paul Ekman. Harper Collins, London.

Deleuze, G. and Guattari, F. 1987 *A Thousand Plateaus: Capitalism and Schizophrenia*. Trans. Brian Massumi. University of Minnesota Press, Minneapolis.

Gibbs, A. 2001 Contagious feelings: Pauline Hanson and the epidemiology of affect. *The Australian Humanities Review*, September. Retrieved from www.lib.latrobe.edu.au/AHR/archive/Issue-December-2001/gibbs.html

Gibbs, A. 2002 Disaffected. *Continuum*, 16, 3, pp. 335–341.

Gibbs, A. 2007 Horrified: embodied vision, media affect and the images from Abu Ghraib. In D. Staines, ed. *Interrogating the War on Terror*. Cambridge Scholars Publishing, London.

Gibbs, A. 2008 Panic! Affect contagion, mimesis and suggestion in the social field. *Cultural Studies Review*, 14, 2, pp. 130–145.

Grossberg, L. 1992 *We Gotta Get Out of This Place: Popular Conservatism and Postmodern Culture*. Routledge, London.

Lazzarato, M. 1999 *"Postface" to Gabriel Tarde, Monadologieetsociologie*. Institut Synthélabo, Paris.

Lévy, P. 2000 *Cyberculture*. Trans. R. Bononno. University of Minnesota Press, Minneapolis.

Lewandowsky, S., Stritzke, W., Oberauer, K. and Morales, M. 2005 Memory for fact, fiction, and misinformation: the Iraq war 2003. *Psychological Science*, 16, 3, pp. 190–195.

Leys, R. 1993 Mead's voices: imitation as foundation, or, the struggle against mimesis. *Critical Inquiry*, 19, 2, pp. 277–307.

Massumi, B. 1993 Everywhere you want to be: introduction to fear. In Brian Massumi, ed. *The Politics of Everyday Fear*. University of Minnesota Press, Minneapolis.

Massumi, B. 2003 Interview with Mary Zournazi. Retrieved from www.21cmagazine. com/issue2/massumi.html

Massumi, B. 2005 The future birth of the affective fact. In *Conference Proceedings: Genealogies of Biopolitics*. Retrieved from http://browse.reticular.info/text/collected/massumi. pdf

Mitchell, W. J. T. 2005 *What Do Pictures Want? The Lives and Loves of Images*. University of Chicago Press, Chicago.

Nightingale, V. 1997 Are media cyborgs? In A. Gordo-Lopez and I. Parker, eds. *Cyberpsychology*. Macmillan, London.

Sedgwick, E.K. and Frank, A. 1995 *Shame and Its Sisters: A Silvan Tomkins Reader*. Duke University Press, Durham, NC.

Seltzer, M. 1992 *Bodies and Machines*. Routledge, New York.

Sifry, M. and Rasiej, A.2008 Welcome to the age of the soundblast. Retrieved from http:// thebreakthrough.org/blog/2008/03/youtubes_political_revolution.shtml

Stiegler, B. 2006 The disaffected individual. Working paper for the ArsIndustrialis seminar, Suffering and Consumption, 25 February.

Surowiecki, J. 2004 *The Wisdom of the Crowd: Why the Many Are Smarter Than the Few*. Abacus, London.

Tarde, G. 1901 *L'Opinion et La Foule*. Félix Alcan, Paris.

Tarde, G. 1962 *The Laws of Imitation*. Trans. E. Clews Parsons. Peter Smith, Gloucester, MA.

Tarde, G. 2003 *Les Transformations du Pouvoir*. InstitutSynthélabo, Paris.

Tomkins, S.S. 1962 *Affect, Imagery, Consciousness: Vol. 1. The Positive Affects*. 4 vols. Springer, New York.

Tomkins, S.S. 1991 *Affect, Imagery, Consciousness: Vol. 3. The Negative Affects: Fear and Anger*. 4 vols. Springer, New York.

Tomkins, S.S. 1992 *Affect, Imagery, Consciousness: Vol. 4. Cognition*. 4 vols. Springer, New York.

Tomkins, S.S. 1995 Exploring affect: The selected writings of Silvan S. Tomkins. In E. Virginia Demos, ed. *Exploring Affect: The Selected Writings of Silvan S. Tomkins*. Maison des Sciences de l'Homme and Cambridge University Press, Cambridge, New York.

Warner, M. 2002 *Publics and Counterpublics*. Zone Books, New York.

Zourabichvili, F. 2003 Préface: le pouvoir en devenir: Tarde et l'actualité. In G. Tarde, *Les Transformations du Pouvoir*. Institut Synthélabo, Paris, pp. 17–37.

Part III
Researching Audiences

13

Toward a Branded Audience
On the Dialectic between Marketing and Consumer Agency

Adam Arvidsson

In recent decades social theory, and in particular cultural studies, have introduced a strong distinction between, on the one hand, the efforts of marketers, media companies, and advertisers to control, program, and direct consumer practice, and, on the other, the "agency" of consumers themselves. Such agency has generally been construed as the evasive expression of an authentic element of resistance – perhaps to be attributed to the mysterious "popular spirits" of which Foucault (1975) famously spoke – that permits the expression of alternative forms of identity in the face of marketing's attempts at control.

However, the relation between the formation of consumer agency and the evolution of marketing and market research is much more complex than that. This story can be viewed as a dialectical movement, where the development of marketing, media, and the institutions of consumer culture more generally have permitted new, more advanced, and empowered forms of consumer agency. This evolution of agency has, in turn, driven the development of new technologies of marketing and market research, which have fundamentally changed the power–knowledge relations through which marketing has construed its object: the consumer audience. In this chapter, I would like to review the most important traits of this development, leading up to today's emphasis within marketing on including consumer agency as an internal aspect of commodity production. In conclusion I will argue that this novel approach entails a different conception of the power of marketing and audience management, working not against, but with, the agency of consumers, and suggest what this might imply for a critical approach to consumer and audience studies.

The Handbook of Media Audiences, First Edition. Edited by Virginia Nightingale.

First, however, we need to take a closer look at the concept of cultural studies, as well as the development within academic marketing discourse that this discipline has inspired – for example, consumer culture theory puts "consumer agency" at the center of its analysis, yet practically never defines it (Arnold and Thompson 2005).

Mediatization and Consumer Agency

People in all societies seem to have used goods – objects with one form of use value or another – productively. Anthropologists have been stressing this for a long time now. Marcel Mauss's (1924/1954), Malinowski's (1932), and, more recently, Marilyn Strathern's (1988) work have all shown how the circulation of objects creates or underpins social relations in one manner or another. Mary Douglas and Brian Isherwood (1979) made the same claim for contemporary Western societies. They argued that consumer goods essentially work to give a tangible reality to "culture" and the social relations that support it. Pierre Bourdieu (1984) too has showed how the correct use of goods works to maintain social divisions, which ultimately translate into differential endowments of real resources, like power, status, and cultural and economic capital. Indeed, it seems close to a universal that, in Arjun Appadurai's words, "the trajectories of things pattern human societies" (1986, p. 5). But, there is a generally recognized difference between the effects of modern goods and those of their nonmodern counterparts. To put it a bit crudely, nonmodern goods are used to reproduce existing forms of sociality, and modern goods are used to produce new forms of sociality. This is by no means an absolute difference: one can find instances of innovative consumption in nonmodern societies, as much as one can find (many) instances of reproductive consumption in modern societies. But, tendentially:

> Modern consumers are the victims of the velocity of fashion as surely as primitive consumers are the victims of the stability of sumptuary law. From the point of view of demand, the critical difference between modern capitalist societies and those based on simpler forms of technology and labour is … that the consumption demands of persons in our own society are regulated by high turnover of criteria of appropriateness (fashion), in contrast to the less frequent shifts in more directly regulated sumptuary or customary systems. (p. 32)

In Appadurai's words, this is essentially *a difference in turnover time*. And that difference can be attributable to the impact of mediatization.

The distinguishing element of modern consumer goods is that they are mediatized. Goods are connected to the intertextual web of meanings, symbols, images, and discourses diffused by (mostly commercial) media like television, magazines, film, radio, the internet, and, most importantly perhaps, advertising – by "media culture" (Kellner 1995) for short. What, then, does mediatization do?

One way to begin to answer that question is to give some precision to this concept, that has become increasingly popular at least within media studies (see e.g. Schultz 2004). To some extent, all human communication is of course mediatized, at least to the extent that it makes use of a medium (be this spoken language or the language of gestures and bodily demeanor) that transforms or distorts the intended message of "the sender." Seen in this way, *communication* is not so much a matter of transmitting a message, as it is a matter of making something *common*, of producing something new and shared (Peters 1999). Because people cannot understand each other directly, they have to produce an intelligible world that they can have in common. In so far as this production of a common employs meaningful discourse, it necessarily produces a virtual double in retaining its own possibility of being different. Indeed, the particular feature of *meaning*, as brilliantly described by Niklas Luhmann (1990), is its ability to retain what has been negated as a possibility. Human communication thus necessarily produces a horizon of virtuality by implying that things, because they are as they are, could be different (cf. Lévy 1998, p. 170). This virtuality is real – it can have the power to affect social relations – although it is not actual: it is real in its potentiality. Media culture – by which we mean the culture of modern mass-mediated communications – extends this horizon of virtuality by connecting diverse communication processes to each other and thus making them unfold within a common informational ambience.

Gabriel Tarde (1901/1989) stressed this in his discovery of a new modern subjectivity, particular to the age of mass media, the public. In Tarde's version, the public consists in the connected affect of individual minds that come to act together. The public thus institutionalizes a collective production process the outcomes of which, shared perceptions of "truth," "beauty," or "utility" conferred on goods by the public, are beyond the control of any single agent or class of agents. Of course, certain members of a public can be more influential than others – Tarde distinguishes between innovative and repetitive forms of reception – but as a whole the public is an autonomous and socialized unit of immaterial production, of the production of "virtuality" (Lazzarato 1997). This argument has since been developed by Jürgen Habermas (1989), who – without quoting Tarde – shows how the networking of communication in the bourgeois public sphere created an autonomous form of rationality that could act as a political force in its own right, irreducible to the will of a single individual or elite. (Remarkably, Habermas has then gone on to posit the mediatization of social communication in opposition to the autonomy of reason, even though he claims that a media-networked bourgeois public was necessary for its emergence in the first place.) As is well known, the emergence of autonomous communication networks – publics – was a crucial factor behind the construction of real and influential virtualities like "the Nation" (Deutsch 1953; Anderson 1991). Drawing on Tarde (and a somewhat unconventional reading of Habermas), we can thus think of media culture as a sort of network of publics. This makes the outcome of a socialized productivity available for the single individual or small group. It provides a common meaningful horizon that can be employed as a productive resource in particular instances of communication. The availability of this resource serves both to empower the production of virtual alternatives to the actual and to provide a common horizon that can unify the communication process in new ways, across geographic and cultural boundaries, and make new forms of productive cooperation possible.

Historians have pointed at the connection between the extension of publics, through new forms of mediated communication, and the spread of consumer goods. Already Werner Sombart (1967) made this connection in his *Luxury and Capitalism*. He argued that the development of a dynamic demand for luxury goods, which Sombart considered crucial to the development of modern capitalism, developed around the institutions of the royal court. The court with its formalized interaction worked not only as a source of new fashions and styles. Its centrality and visibility also made it into a kind of proto-mediatic spectacle where new goods, through their connection to particular, visible courtly practices or personalities, could be given meanings that were generally recognized. However, as Chandra Mukerji (1983) has argued, it is the link to an emerging print culture that marks the first real step toward a consumer culture in the modern sense. Print, she argues, functioned to unify, and generalize tastes at the same time as expanding capitalism unified commerce.

Indeed, it is through their connection to media culture that modern consumer goods acquire the horizon of virtuality that is the source of much of the utility that they have for consumers. This also goes for relatively anonymous mass-produced objects like cigarettes and chewing gum, which now can acquire deep and complex meanings. For example, through associations to movies, sports (like baseball), and popular music, chewing gum became an integral element in the myth of the "American dream" (Redclift 2004). When smoked by movie stars like Marlene Dietrich and Humphrey Bogart, cigarettes came to represent an attractive and slightly challenging "modernity" (Hilton 2000). By thus being filled with meaning in media culture, consumer goods can enable their user to think him or herself different. *By means of cigarettes*, it becomes possible to imagine oneself a Marlene Dietrich or, to draw more freely on this ideal, to enact a challenging, modern femininity (cf. de Grazia 1992). Simmel (1905/1997) has famously argued that the connection between modern consumer goods and individuality has to do with the introduction of choice into what was previously a traditionally determined relation between objects and subjects. But one could add that this probably also has to do with the fact that mediatization *extends the capacities of objects themselves*. Not only does one now have a choice, but also one has a choice between objects that tell different stories. When mediatized, goods can become tangible embodiments of fantasy that have real effects insofar as they change the way everyday life is lived, or at least push in this direction.

In this sense we can argue that the arrival of a modern media culture changes something fundamental in the relations between people and goods. Although most people in most times have probably used objects with some degrees of creativity (the consumer as a passive "cultural dupe" never existed), modern media culture accomplishes two transformations of this creativity. First, individual consumer creativity is empowered by the very fact that the new virtual dimensions of objects transform them into *means of production* through which new kinds of identities or lifestyles or other forms of immaterial wealth can be created. In this sense, as Paolo Virno (2004) suggests, the "culture industries" have become the producers of means of production. Second, such individual creativity is connected into a public where participants can find others with similar interests and come together in subcultures, tribes, or other identity-based social formations where new forms of collective co-creation can take place, and where new forms of common knowledge, or what Marx called *general intellect*, can circulate. This new empowered and connected nature of object-related creativity – consumer agency in its modern form – is exactly what gave early marketing theorists their impression of modern consumer publics as unruly and undisciplined.

The Development of Marketing Knowledge

Market research developed as part of a wide attempt to control, and originally contain, this enhanced power of consumer agency. When serious research into consumer tastes, habits, and buying patterns took off in the years following World War I, the main enemy was the perceived mutability and "irrationality" of existing consumer patterns, which was attributed to the influence of media culture. Most early market researchers, like their marketing colleagues in general, were steeped in the then dominant paradigm of "scientific management," and they aimed at a "Taylorization" or even "engineering," to use Elmo Calkins's influential term, of consumer demand (Calkins and Holden 1905). As in the case of the "scientifically" managed work process, this entailed the use of market knowledge to break down consumer demand into clearly identifiable segments. These segments could then be targeted by advertising that sought to educate, rationalize, and shape attitudes and behavior. The aim was to construct particular practices and taste patterns and to tie them to particular physical or mediatic places, such as the home, the supermarket, or the women's magazine. Such "rationalizing" or disciplinary practices were deemed particularly necessary in relation to consumer segments that were thought to be prone to irrational tastes or preferences, like recently arrived immigrants (destined to be Americanized through advertising and market propaganda; Ewen 1976), women (Scanlon 1995), and youth (Palladino 1996). The "irrationality" of the latter categories was thought to be an effect of their excessive media consumption. It is noticeable that WASP men, whose consumer demand was substantial, figured very rarely in the discourse of the advertising and marketing profession (cf. Osgerby 2001). The segmentation of consumer demand thus worked to contain the potential diversity of consumer practice within workable categories. These categories developed in relation to the then dominant advertising medium: the weekly (or monthly) magazine.

Given the central role of information in the economics of advertising and the media industry, the theories and methods employed in producing information have been heavily influenced by the dominant media structure. Indeed, studies of consumer behavior did not really come about until the establishment of mass-circulating, advertising-financed weekly magazines attributed a central economic role to the commodification of audiences. Although systemic studies of the consumer market began in the United States already with industrialization, early market research nurtured a rather scant interest in consumers. Rather, early studies found their main inspiration in German institutional economics, as did early academic marketing in general (Bartels 1976; Jones and Monieson 1990). These studies were mainly concerned with the institutional dynamics of markets and distribution systems. Research on consumer behavior, attitudes, and motivations first developed elsewhere, in the field of advertising psychology, with experimental research on the effectiveness of this new medium of persuasion (Beale 1991; Chessel 1995; Arvidsson 2003). Magazine publishers, who had sold their publications under production costs and relied heavily on advertising revenue ever since the 1890s, were the first to begin to market its readership as an "audience of consumers." Originally this was done without any kind of "scientific" backing whatsoever. Based on letters to the editor or, like in *Ladies World*, photographs of the homes of subscribers, they sought to market their audience to advertisers as representative of a particular kind of consumer, usually defined in terms of social class. Thus *Harpers' Bazaar* was supposedly read in upper-class households, *Ladies Home Journal* represented an audience of rational and frugal middle-class housewives, and so on (Fox 1984; Scanlon 1995; Ohmann 1996). In the immediate postwar years, however, big publishers like Curtis (*True Story*, *Love Magazine*, and *Ladies Home Journal*) set up research departments, and a number of research consultancies, like the Eastman Company, developed to service small publishers. Eastman, for example, worked for the *Christian Herald* and *Cosmopolitan* magazine. All of these surveyed readers for data on income and demographic composition (Lockley 1950). In the 1930s, it became common for mass-circulating magazines (and for radio companies like CBS) to maintain readers' panels. *Woman's Home Companion*, for example, launched a panel in 1935, consisting first of 250 and then expanding to 1500. Panelists were selected to represent different ages, occupations, and income levels among the journal's readers, and they were asked to answer a survey on matters like family size, husband's occupation, type and size of home, furniture, equipment, gardens, domestic help, laundry methods, car ownership, income levels, interests, and hobbies. Panel members were frequently interviewed on topics such as "meal planning, food preparation, laundry fashions, household equipment, leisure time, home decoration, and child care." The CBS panel was checked in even more detail. Through so-called pantry checks, an interviewer visited the homes of housewives on the panel over a period of several weeks to observe which brand names had appeared and disappeared (Lazarsfeld 1938; Converse 1987, pp. 92ff.). Much data on consumer demographics, behavior, and purchasing patterns were thus generated. However, publishers still assumed that these data could be presented as representative of a particular group of consumers, whose characteristics largely coincided with the life-world presented by the magazine itself. As the Spanish American Publishing Company claimed in an ad for *Cinelandia*, a motion picture magazine directed to the Latin American market, "just a glance through the magazine shows you the type to whom it is directed" (*Export Advertiser* 1930). There was a general assumption that the cultural space of a magazine was a good representation of the practices and attitudes of its readers. When radio promoted the development of nationwide ratings research in the 1930s, class differences roughly coinciding with differences between magazines were reified into a standardized typology, the so-called ABCD system, used to differentiate households according to income. As we can see from the way the J. Walter Thompson Corporation's chief researcher, Paul Cherington (1924), recommended the operationalization of the ABCD system, income differences were understood to imply a lot more about lifestyles and outlook. To him the categories meant the following:

1. Homes of substantial wealth above the average in culture that have at least one servant. The essential point, however, in this class is that the persons interviewed shall be people of intelligence and discrimination.
2. Comfortable middle-class homes, personally directed by intelligent women.
3. Industrial homes of skilled mechanics, mill operators, or petty tradespeople (no servants)
4. Homes of unskilled laborers or in foreign districts where it is difficult for American ways to penetrate.

There were no research data on motivations and attitudes that could substantiate such claims. Rather, the ABCD typology worked as a way of giving "scientific" legitimacy to speculations about aspects of consumer behavior on which there were no data available. Indeed, as the ABCD typology was sedimented in the 1930s through its deployment in the Cooperative Analysis of Broadcasting's (CAB) nationwide ratings research (which became the standard measure in the 1930s), and later in the Nielsen Ratings Index (launched in 1942), it provided a convenient ground for such speculations. Indeed, in the CAB survey much was hypothesized (or "surmised," to use the actual expression) about the actual behavior of each group. The relatively small share of the radio audience pertaining to group A was supposed to be explained not only by economic factors but also by "them having ... a wide range of social interests and activities limiting time for listening [and] the fact that the average program is directed to lower income groups making them of little interest for the A group." Conversely, the C group's high index of listening was explained by "lower educational standards" making listening the "preferable way of getting information" (James 1937; Beville 1940, pp. 198ff.; cf. Bogart 1987).

As the ABCD typology was sedimented as the main basis for market and audience "nose counting," it came to work as a convenient sorting device. It permitted market and audience researchers to place consumers (and listeners) in established categories based on data, on income, and/or residence. Once placed in such a category, accompanying assumptions about relatively fixed motivations, attitudes, and lifestyles made it possible to legitimately deduce further ideas about consumers. This way, the ABCD typology worked to reduce or contain the complexity of consumer mobility into a relatively neat and simple typology that permitted a highly standardized and streamlined marketing effort. Indeed, with the ABCD typology, classifications originally derived from the structure of the magazine advertising market were developed into the general categories that were used to contain and manage a wide diversity of consumer practices.

Capturing Creativity

The ABCD typology is still used in market research. However, in the years following World War II, it began to be challenged, or at least discussed. Many market researchers and academics now argued that it no longer provided an adequate representation of consumer practice (if it ever had). Indeed, as early as 1949, W. Lloyd Warner (1949), at the influential Chicago research company Social Research Incorporated (SRI), argued that "advertising agencies and their clients often waste their money" because of their ignorance of the actual makeup of class cultures. This was particularly true for the lower middle class, which, according to Warner, was now undergoing substantial transformations (p. 30).

Indeed, a number of developments made marketers question, or seek to go beyond, the simple link between income and what Bourdieu (1984) would latter call class "habitus." First, American consumer culture was transformed in the postwar years. Rising standards of living, suburbanization, new materials like plastic, new designs, new objects, television sets and domestic appliances, and new institutions of consumption like the shopping mall all radically altered the material culture of middle-class life. Many consumer researchers, like Warner and his colleagues at SRI, were influenced by contemporary sociological talk of "mass society" and "other directions," and argued that geographically rooted, communitarian taste and consumption patterns had begun to matter less than before. In short, American consumer behavior seemed less determined by class-specific taste cultures, and more open to reflexive expressions of consumer agency.

Second, television brought about a thorough transformation of the media environment, surpassing the press as the main channel for advertising investments by the early 1960s (Turow 1997). As the sponsorship model was abandoned for the *scatter plan*, in which advertising time on television was sold in the now familiar spot format, the medium generated an increasing pressure for audience segmentation, and hence more detailed research. A similar pressure came from the production side, as corporations were anxious to discover new market niches to exploit.

Third, the new consumption and media environment was actively appropriated by consumers, and goods were deployed in new ways to generate new patterns of consumption and styles of life. Youth were particularly active in this, producing a range of new youth cultures from the mid-1950s on. But adult middle-class consumers also did their share, in part borrowing from youth culture, and in part transforming their own forms of demeanor and self-presentation. Hence, the 1960s saw the emergence of *Playboy*, the (emancipated) *New Housewife*, and later *The Single Girl*: adult middle-class styles that built chiefly around practices of consumption. During the 1970s, this development would continue as new consumer goods, and in particular affordable fashion clothing, further encouraged the performance of style and demeanor through consumption.

Finally, the market research sector itself boomed. The market research community grew all through the 1950s, and in 1963 the turnover of the research business was 10 times (in current dollars) that of 30 years before. The expansion of the research community also made the social scientist a common figure in marketing circles, and introduced social science terminology into marketing and advertising jargon (Bogart 1963). The result was a pressure to generate more detailed and deeper descriptions of consumer behavior, and a growing suspicion of the "natural" centrality of the ABCD system. As David Yankelovich, later to found the successful Yankelovich Monitor in the 1970s (see below), wrote as early as 1964, "We should discard the notion that demographics is the best segmentation technique."

The first significant break with the ABCD typology and the containment paradigm that it represented was motivation research (MR). Pioneered by Pierre Martineau (1957) and Ernest Dichter (1960), MR was a commercial adaptation of Freudian psychology that suggested that the real sources of consumer decisions lay in the hidden depths of their unconscious. By means of in-depth interviews, motivation researchers thus tried to reveal such hidden or unconscious real motives behind consumer decisions, and transform them into new market niches and advertising arguments. Established market researchers were extremely critical of the motivation researchers' apparently sloppy methodology. Politz (1956) claimed that often Dichter's writings, as well as his research reports, were rambling summaries of his own impressions. Yet this fresh angle and the new information the method provided proved commercially successful. In addition, motivation research provided a perhaps unconscious, though important, theoretical move away from the containment paradigm. Previously, it had been thought that tastes and consumer patterns were an effect of the social and/or cultural environment, and that consumers were therefore determined by their surroundings. Motivation researchers, however, looked for and found needs and desires that were independent of (indeed, often in opposition to) that environment. Theoretically, motivation research thus contributed to delinking consumers and their preferences from structural determination. Also, motivation research concentrated on the intimate or emotional relations that people had to goods. This contributed to generating a different conception of the relations between consumers and the goods they were surrounded with. Previously it had been thought that consumers bought and desired certain kinds of goods because their identity (or *personality*, to use the term in vogue at the time) predisposed them in a particular way. Now it became possible to think of consumer identity as an effect of purchase patterns. As Sydney Levy (also of SRI) would write in an influential article, "Symbolism and Life Style," "[A] consumer's personality can be seen as the peculiar total of the products he consumes" (1964, p. 149).

The real shift toward an interest in consumer mobility came with psychographics. This method grew out of the dynamics that motivation research had initiated (Demby 1974) Motivation research had opened up the possibility of viewing consumer subjectivity as (at least relatively) autonomous in relation to social structure and thus potentially mobile. However, MR was not methodologically capable of supplying valid and reliable information. Such methodological innovations came out of the work of SRI. Like Paul Lazarsfeld's Bureau of Social Research, SRI was a place where market researchers and sociologists interacted. The methodological tools it developed were employed in the emerging field of sociological studies of class, such as W. Lloyd Warner's *Yankee City* study, as well as in market research. Both sociologists and market researchers shared an interest in reliable quantitative instruments that could provide a picture of what was understood to be a changing American class landscape. In particular, it became imperative to understand the culture of the "classless" middle classes, the "White Collars" as C. Wright Mills would later describe them, who were understood to be delinked from traditional ethnic or geographically rooted communities and appeared to form a kind of free-floating mysterious entity (Mills 1953; Whyte 1955). In 1959, SRI sociologists Lee Rainwater, Richard Coleman, and Gerald Handel published what has become known as the first lifestyle study, *The Workingman's Wife: Her Personality World and Life Style* (1959). The study aimed to investigate empirically what advertisers hitherto had taken for granted: the cultural universe of their main advertising object, the middle majority housewife. Rainwater and his colleagues combined demographic data similar to those of the old ABCD categories (they called it the Index of Urban Status) with Thematic Appreciation Tests borrowed from consumer psychology and in-depth interviews borrowed from motivation research. The study generated an in-depth descriptive picture of the everyday life of the housewives, including information on their psychological attitudes and relations to consumer goods. Early studies like this produced detailed pictures of consumer cultures that were, however, still coupled to a particular class position. During the 1960s, however, the variables used by Rainwater and his colleagues were developed into what became known as *psychographic variables* usually encompassing the fields of "Attitudes, Opinions and Interests" (Wells and Tigert 1971; Demby 1974). At the same time, advances in computer technology made it possible to employ large numbers of variables (300 was not uncommon) and then use factor analysis to produce a number of variable clusters, to be represented theoretically as "life styles" (Digg 1966; Seth 1970). The methodological procedure was thus very different from what had been the case in the ABCD system. There, consumers had been segmented according to one variable (or one series of variables) denoting class position. Now, segments were no longer defined a priori, but rather deduced from the rich data material generated by extensive questioners. This meant that the overall picture that was generated was no longer a priori determined by class. Also, the number of variables relating directly to consumption, such as product, brand, or media choice, tended to increase during the 1970s as the lifestyle survey became standard marketing practice through the impact of successful services like Daniel Yankelovich's Yankelovich Monitor, founded in 1971, and later Arnold Mitchell and Stanford Research Institute's VALS, which began officially in 1978.

The inductive approach of psychographics meant that consumers were no longer depicted as structured according to some overriding principle. It also meant that the particular segments generated could change over time. As William D. Wells recognized in his foreword to the American Marketing Association's 1974 volume on *Lifestyle and Psychographics*, this dynamic approach had developed as a response to a social environment that was perceived to be increasingly dynamic and marked by "rapidly changing values" (Wells 1974, p. v; cf. Rathnell 1964). It was to prove successful in the following decade as a new middle class, Bourdieu's "new petite bourgeoisie" (1984, p. 311), appropriated the new possibilities offered by a richer consumption and media environment to continuously produce new styles and fashions as well as identities and solidarities (cf. Touraine 1973). To put it in the words of an advertising professional writing at midcentury (Ruth Ziff [1974], head of Benton & Bowles' research department):

> We are living in an era of pluralism, non-conformity and rapid change. Racial groups are seeking a new identity and proposing separation rather than assimilation. Social mores have changed rapidly. The women's movement is positing changes that may affect our basic family structure. Styles of living and dress are indeed varied. Consumerism has become a major force. These changes make more hazardous than ever reliance on our own pre-conceptions or on data on the consumer that is scanty or outmoded. This then is another reason for turning to psychographics. (p. 139)

Putting Consumer Agency to Work: The Brand

Psychographics developed as a technique able to deal with increasingly mutable consumer practices that threatened to overflow the boundaries of the old ABCD typology. Also, it produced a much farther-reaching picture of consumers than what had been available before. Indeed, with psychographics the creativity of consumers, their production of new symbolic and social relations through their deployment of consumer goods could be valorized. Previously this creativity had been seen as problem, a complexity to be contained and reduced. Now such "life factors," changing and diverse consumer practices beyond preestablished notions of the ABCD typology, could become "the most important factors influencing and shaping economic activity" (Lazer 1964, p. 132). This opening up of *life itself* as a source of productive diversity was the real innovation of psychographics. This principle was what drove the development of the kinds of "single-source" information services described in the introduction, as well as techniques like the bar code scan or internet-tracking software in the 1980s and 1990s. Tracking life as a generic, mobile productive power (rather than the particular life form of a socially anchored group) responded to what had become established as the new knowledge interest of marketing. During the 1980s, the growth and integration of the media industries produced a situation where classic distinctions like that between media message and advertising, or for that matter public or private, were increasingly blurred. Consumers began to appear as fragmented, nomadic individuals, moving around in a media-saturated lifeworld constantly on the look for ways to constitute themselves as subjects. Generation X (or later Generation Y), much debated by marketers and advertisers in the early 1990s, offered a theoretical embodiment of this new kind of consumer subjectivity. "X'ers" had grown up with and were marked by the virtually complete media saturation of everyday life. They had become accustomed to the increasingly diversified fare of network television in the 1970s and to cable and VCR in the 1980s. As children, they had lived the disintegration of the nuclear family through the expansion of media choices and the proliferation of multiset households. For them, watching television was a solitary activity rather than a family ritual. Media, and in particular television, made up their main resource for knowing about themselves and the world. Consequently, they were much more "media literate" than their parents and skilled in the art of dodging or evading advertising through "zapping" or "zipping." While Generation X consumers were difficult to persuade or seduce, their experience of growing up in a fluid and multifaceted media universe also made them existentially insecure. It was thought that Generation X consumers were on the look for discourses and consumer goods that could function as a kind of medium for their own nomadic self-construction. During the second half of the 1990s, this kind of subjectivity was generalized as a representation of the "postmodern" consumer in general (Firat and Venkatesh 1995; Holt 2004).

At the same time, marketing went through what has retrospectively been called the *branding revolution*. Beginning with the proliferation of customer relations management in the 1980s, brands began to be understood less as "symbolic extensions of products" and more as platforms for action in media space. The business of brand management became that of anticipating diverse manifestations of consumer agency and enabling them to unfold on a common branded platform, kept together by a common *ethos* (Lury 2004; Arvidsson 2006). Brand value was increasingly understood to derive not so much from the product itself as from the ability to give coherence and direction to such a range of disparate activities. In order to do this, brand management entailed anticipating consumer demand in such a way that it remains contained within the branded platform itself. This way a brand seeks to control the mobility of a media-empowered creative consumer public by anticipating the evolution of its agency and transforming it into a controlled form of modulation of the brand itself.

Conclusion

Marketing and market research emerged as a new discipline driven by the perceived need to control and contain the kinds of unruly manifestations of consumer demand that were the effect of new forms of mediatization of consumer society. The results of these efforts enabled a wider diffusion of consumer goods, and the establishment of the kinds of market segmentations that allowed a further expansion of the media framework of consumer culture. The further mediatization of consumption contributed to the emergence of new, lifestyle-oriented manifestations of consumer agency. Driven by this transformation, marketing began to change its paradigm. New disciplines like motivation research, new technologies like psychographics, and new managerial approaches like branding transformed the aim of marketing, from containing consumer agency into anticipating its evolution.

This transformation also points toward the adaptation of a new modality of power on the part of marketing. Given that external life process cannot be directly commanded, that you cannot order someone to be creative or cool, contemporary marketing power works by designing a context in which such processes quite naturally come to evolve in the right direction, *where people themselves quite naturally strive to become creative or cool*. It is an instance of power becoming "ontological" rather than "epistemological," to use Scott Lash's (2007) recent distinction. Older forms of "epistemological" power were based on the power–knowledge nexus identified by Foucault in his works like *Discipline and Punish* (1975), and characterized by representative, scientific discourses (like those of Lazarsfeld's media and market research). These discourses contained a particular model of life, which was subsequently imposed on its subjects through the institutional means at its command (in this case, advertising and consumer culture at large). Ontological power (which, as a concept, is closer to Foucault's later musings on biopolitics) does not build on representative knowledge, but on activist interventions, able to program, design, and build a reality where particular forms of actions and attachments have been preordained. It looks less like the nineteenth-century prison or school and more like the videogame: Lara Croft is free to do what she wants, but only certain actions make sense and add to the pleasure of the experience.

As I have argued elsewhere (Arvidsson 2006), contemporary brand management provides a good illustration of this modus operandi. The brand is essentially a mechanism for the reproduction of a particular pattern of affect and community, of *culture* for short. The status and function of the brand have changed radically in this respect. While brands originated as symbols of products (or producers) as referential markers that would enable consumers to differentiate between virtually similar mass-produced goods, cutting-edge brands today tend to function more as a kind of social media. They stand less for a product (often they stand for a wide range of products) and more for a particular cultural pattern –a particular experience or mode of relating, which is reproduced in a wide variety of different situations, involving many different actors. This is perhaps most evident in the case of recent successes like Facebook, MySpace, and YouTube. There the ability to accumulate value (chiefly on financial markets) is directly based on the ability to accumulate the kinds of attention, affect, and community – in other words, the culture – that consumers produce. But the trend is for more mainstream brands to move in the same direction. There is a growing emphasis on *customer-based brand equity* and a concomitant recognition of the active role of consumers in contributing to brand value, a growing attention to the sensory or experiential aspects of brand management, thus expanding the number of dimensions along which consumers can be involved, and a growing weight of attention and affect in the calculation and establishment of brand value. At least for some high-profile brands, financial values directly build on the ability to mobilize consumer agency in generating attention and affect – an ethical surplus to again use Lazzarato's (1997) term. This way, brand values tend to build ever more directly on a selective activation of consumer agency.

What does this imply for a "critical," as opposed to "administrative" (Gitlin 1978), approach to audiences and consumer culture, an approach that is interested in furthering more authentic forms of consumer agency and empowerment? It is clear that the prevailing emphasis on "identity" as a vehicle for critique is outdated. How can attempts at "celebrating" identity or furthering agency constitute a progressive theoretical politics in a situation where administrative power works precisely through the empowerment of such manifestations? At the same time, however, this implies that consumer agency is already being empowered. In its attempts to derive value form social cooperation – from brand communities, active audiences, networks of open innovation, and other forms of what Yochlai Benkler (2006) calls "social production" – marketing and brand management continuously empowers the potential of such new forms of productive cooperation. The result is the de facto creation, within consumer capitalism itself, of an extended space for an alternative mode of production, marked by self-organization, the reliance on predominantly common resources, and the prevalence of "social" motivations, like peer recognition and the accumulation of reputation. Seen this way, the main contradiction no longer stands between freedom and discipline, between authentic forms of identity and imposed forms, but between two distinctive modalities of agency: one subjected to the control of the institutions of consumer capitalism, and another subjected to a different regime of governance, implicit to the emerging new mode of production. Seen this way, the task of progressive social research in this field should be to try to tip the scales even further in the direction of social production, aiding this new mode of production in finding greater degrees of autonomy and resilience.

References

Anderson, B. 1991 *Imagined Communities: Reflections on the Origins and Spread of Nationalism*. Verso, London.

Appadurai, A. 1986 Introduction. In A. Appadurai, ed. *The Social Life of Things*. Cambridge University Press, Cambridge.

Arvidsson, A. 2003 *Marketing Modernity: Italian Advertising from Fascism to the Postmodern*. Routledge, London.

Arvidsson, A. 2006 *Brands: Meaning and Value in Media Culture*. Routledge, London

Arnold, E. and Thompson, C. 2005 Consumer culture theory (CCT): twenty years of research. *Journal of Consumer Research*, 31, 4, pp. 868–882.

Bartels, R. 1976 *A History of Marketing Thought*. Grid Publishing, Columbus, OH.

Beale, M. 1991 Advertising and the politics of public persuasion in France, 1900–33. Ph.D. dissertation, Department of History, University of California, Berkeley.

Beville, H.M. 1940 The ABCD's of radio audiences. *Public Opinion Quarterly*, June.

Benkler, Y. 2006 *The Wealth of Networks*. Yale University Press, New Haven, CT.

Bogart, L. 1963 Inside market research. *Public Opinion Quarterly*, 27, 4, pp. 562–577.

Bogart, L. 1987 Review: Bourdieu, P. "Distinction." *Public Opinion Quarterly*, 51, 1, pp. 131–134.

Bourdieu, P. 1984 *Distinction*. Routledge, London.

Calkins, E. and Holden, R. 1905 *Modern Advertising*. Appleton, New York.

Cherington, P.T. 1924 Statistics in market research. *Annals of the American Academy of Political and Social Science,* 115, pp. 130–135.

Chessel, M. 1995 L'Émergence de la publicité. Publicitaires, annonceurs et affichistes dans la France de l'entre-deux-guerres. Ph.D. dissertation, Department of History and Civilisation, European University Institute, Fiesole, Italy.

Converse, J.M. 1987 *Survey Research in the United States: Its Roots and Emergence, 1890–1960*. University of California Press, Berkeley.

de Grazia, V. 1992 *How Mussolini Ruled Italian Women*. University of California Press, Berkeley.

Demby, E. 1974 Psychographics, from whence it came. In D.W. Wells, ed. *Life Style and Psychographics*. American Marketing Association, Chicago.

Deutsch, K. 1953 *Nationalism and Social Communication*. MIT Press, Cambridge, MA.

Dichter, E. 1960 *The Strategy of Desire*. Boardman, New York.

Digg, A.T. 1966 Lintas in computerland. *Admap*, December.

Douglas, M. and Isherwood, B. 1979 *The World of Goods*. Allen Cone, London.

Export Advertiser. 1930 Advertisement: *Cinelandia*. July, p. 25.

Ewen, S. 1976 *Captains of Consciousness*. McGraw-Hill, New York.

Firat, F.A. and Venkatesh, A. 1995 Liberatory postmodernism and the re-enchantment of consumption. *Journal of Consumer Research*, 22, 4, pp. 239–266

Foucault, M. 1975 *Surveiller et Punir*. Gallimard, Paris.

Fox, S. 1984 *The Mirror Makers: A History of American Advertising and Its Creators*. Morrow, New York.

Gitlin, T. 1978 Media sociology: the dominant paradigm. *Theory and Society*, 6, pp. 205–253.

Habermas, J. 1989 *The Structural Transformation of the Public Sphere*. Beacon Press, Boston.

Hilton, M. 2000 *Smoking in British Popular Culture, 1800–2000*. Manchester University Press, Manchester, UK.

Holt, D. 2004 *How Brands Become Icons: The Principles of Cultural Branding*. Harvard Business School Press, Boston.

James, E.P.H. 1937 The development of research in broadcast advertising. *The Journal of Marketing*, 2, pp. 141–145.

Jones, B.D. and Monieson, D.D. 1990 Early development of the philosophy of marketing thought. *Journal of Marketing*, 54, pp. 102–111.

Kellner, D. 1995 *Media Culture: Cultural Studies, Identity and Politics between the Modern and the Postmodern*. Routledge, London

Lash, S. 2007 Power after hegemony: cultural studies in transition. *Theory, Culture and Society*, 24, 3, pp. 55–78.

Lazarsfeld, P. 1938 The panel as a new tool for measuring opinion. *Public Opinion Quarterly*, 2, 4, pp. 596–612.

Lazer, W. 1964 Life style concepts and marketing. In S.A. Greyser, ed. *Toward Scientific Marketing, Proceedings of the Winter Conference of the American marketing Association, December, 27–28, 1963*. American Marketing Association, Boston.

Lazzarato, M. 1997 *Lavoro Immateriale: Forme di Vita e Produzione di Soggettività*. Ombre Corte, Verona.

Lévy, P. 1998 *Becoming Virtual, Reality in the Digital Age*. Plenum Trade, New York.

Levy, S. 1964 Symbolism and life style. In S.A. Greyser, ed. *Toward Scientific Marketing, Proceedings of the Winter Conference of the American marketing Association, December, 27–28, 1963*. American Marketing Association, Boston.

Lockley, L. 1950 Notes on the history of marketing research. *The Journal of Marketing*, 14, pp. 733–736.

Luhmann, N. 1990 Meaning as sociology's basic concept. In N. Luhmann, *Essays on Self-Reference*, Columbia: Columbia University Press.

Lury, C. 2004 *Brands: The Logos of the Global Economy*. Routledge, London.

Malinowski, B. 1932 *The Sexual Life of Savages*. Routledge, London.

Martineau, P. 1957 *Motivation in Advertising*. McGraw-Hill, New York.

Mauss, M. 1924/1954 *The Gift: The Form and Reason for Exchange in Archaic Societies*. Trans. Ian Cunniston. Free Press, Glencoe.

Mills, C.W. 1953 *White Collar*. Oxford University Press, Oxford.

Mukerji, C. 1983 *From Graven Images: Patterns of Modern Materialism*. Columbia University Press, New York.

Ohmann, R. 1996 *Selling Culture: Magazines, Markets and Class at the Turn of the Century*. Verso, London.

Osgerby, B. 2001 *Playboys in Paradise: Masculinity, Youth and Leisure Style in Modern America*. Berg, Oxford.

Palladino, G. 1996 *Teenagers: An American History*. Basic Books, New York.

Peters, J.D. 1999 *Speaking into the Air: A History of the Idea of Communication*. University of Chicago Press, Chicago.

Politz, A. 1956 Motivation research form a research perspective. *Public Opinion Quarterly*, 20, 4, pp. 663–673.

Rainwater, L., Coleman, R. and Handel, G. 1959 *The Workingman's Wife: Her Personality, World and Life Style*. Oceana, New York.

Rathnell, J.M. 1964 Life style influences and market segmentation: an introduction. In S.A. Greyser, ed. *Toward Scientific Marketing, Proceedings of the Winter Conference of the American marketing Association, December, 27–28, 1963*. American Marketing Association, Boston.

Redclift, M. 2004 Chewing gum: taste, space and the "shadow-lands". Presented at Consumption, Modernity and the West, 16–17 April, California Institute of Technology, Pasadena.

Scanlon, P. 1995 *Inarticulate Longings: The Ladies Home Journal, Gender and the Promise of Consumer Culture*. Routledge, London.

Schultz, W. 2004 Reconstructing mediatization as an analytical concept. *European Journal of Communication*, 19, 1, pp. 87–101.

Seth, J. 1970 Multivariate analysis in marketing. *Journal of Advertising Research*, 10, 1.

Simmel, G. 1905 / 1997 Philosophie der mode. In D. Frisby and M. Featherstone, eds. *Simmel on Culture*. Sage, London.

Sombart, W. 1967 *Luxury and Capitalism*. University of Michigan Press, Ann Arbor.

Strathern, M. 1988 *The Gender of the Gift*. University of California Press, Berkeley.

Tarde, G. 1901 / 1989 *L'opinion et La Foule*. Presses universitaires de la France, Paris.

Touraine, A. 1973 *La Production de la Societé*. Editions du Seuil, Paris.

Turow, J. 1997 *Breaking Up America: Advertisers and the New Media World*. University of Chicago Press, Chicago.

Virno, P. 2004 *A Grammar of the Multitude*. Verso, London.

Warner, W.L. 1949 *Social Class in America*. Harper, New York.

Wells, W.D. 1974 Foreword. In W.D. Wells, ed. *Life Style and Psychographics*. American Marketing Association, Chicago.

Wells, W. and Tigert, D. 1971 Activities, interests and opinions. *Journal of Advertising Research*, 11, pp. 27–35.

Whyte, W.H. 1955 The consumer in the new suburbia. In L.H. Clark, ed. *Consumer Behaviour. The Dynamics of Consumer Reaction*. New York University Press, New York.

Yankelovich, D. 1964 New criteria for market segmentation. *Harvard Business Review*, Spring.

Ziff, R. 1974 The role of psychographics in the development of advertising strategy and copy. In D.W. Wells, ed. *Life Style and Psychographics*. American Marketing Association, Chicago.

14

Ratings and Audience Measurement

Philip M. Napoli

One commonly used, though controversial, approach to conducting research on media audiences involves ratings analysis. Ratings analysis is the analysis of the audience size and composition data produced by audience measurement firms for use in both the commercial and noncommercial media sectors. Ratings data primarily are used by media outlets and advertisers to determine advertising rates, to assess the performance of media content, and to develop and assess strategies related to the production and placement of content. Ratings data are also are used by policy makers to assess media market dynamics and (most important to this chapter) by academics to develop and test theoretical perspectives regarding the dynamics of how audiences consume media and how media institutions navigate the audience marketplace (Stavitsky 2000; Napoli 2003; Webster, Phalen, and Lichty 2005).

Perhaps the best-known types of audience ratings that have been used in academic research are the television ratings produced by measurement firms such as The Nielsen Company and TNS Media Intelligence, and the radio ratings produced by measurement firms such as Arbitron and RAJAR (Radio Joint Audience Research). And, increasingly, internet audience ratings, produced by firms such as comScore and Nielsen//NetRatings, are being utilized in academic research (see e.g. Webster and Lin 2002; Bermejo 2007).

As these examples suggest, the term *ratings* is most often associated with audiences for the electronic media, though print media also utilize audience data produced by commercial measurement firms that indicate the number and demographic characteristics of readers of individual publications. Firms such as Simmons and MRI (Mediamark Research Inc.) produce data for a wide range of print publications. However, for whatever reason (perhaps a comparative lack of academic interest in print media audiences), academic ratings analyses have overwhelmingly focused on electronic media audiences. Thus, electronic media ratings,

The Handbook of Media Audiences, First Edition. Edited by Virginia Nightingale.
© 2014 John Wiley & Sons, Ltd. Published 2014 by John Wiley & Sons, Ltd.

and the mechanisms for the measurement of electronic media audiences, will be the focus of this chapter.

In considering ratings analysis as a tool for studying media audiences, this chapter will first provide an overview of the methodologies employed by the audience measurement firms. Unlike other academic approaches to researching audiences, ratings analysis involves the analysis of data previously gathered by third parties (audience measurement organizations). Consequently, it is important to understand how these data are gathered, as well as the strengths and weaknesses of these data. As this discussion will make clear, ratings data have been criticized on both methodological and theoretical grounds. These critiques will illustrate how some dimensions of audience behavior have been well illuminated by ratings data, while others have not.

This chapter will then provide an overview of the types of academic analyses that have been conducted using ratings data. As this discussion will illustrate, ratings data can be employed not only to understand certain aspects of media audiences, but also to understand certain aspects of media institutions and how they approach their audiences. That is, ratings data can be used not only to gain insights into the dynamics of audience behavior, but also to gain insights into the institutional dynamics surrounding the various marketplaces for audiences and the behaviors of various marketplace participants under changing competitive conditions (e.g. Napoli 2003). In this discussion of the analytical paths that have been pursued via ratings data, this section also will draw particular attention to the issue of access and the challenges associated with obtaining ratings data for use in academic research.

Finally, this chapter will consider the future of ratings analysis in an era in which the media environment is undergoing dramatic technological change, and, consequently, in which analytical approaches to audiences employed by media outlets, advertisers, and audience measurement firms are undergoing dramatic change as well. This section will consider the potentially diminishing analytical utility of traditional ratings data and the resultant new directions in audience measurement that are being pursued.

The Production of Ratings Data

There is a long and interesting history surrounding media industries' efforts to understand their audiences (see Napoli 2011). For the purposes of this chapter, the key element of this history is the emergence of ratings services, which first came into being during the development and commercialization of radio in the 1930s, as radio programmers and advertisers sought to accurately assess the size of the radio listening audience (Chappell and Hooper 1944). Many of the techniques and terminologies associated with radio ratings subsequently were transferred to television in the 1940s and 1950s (Beville 1988) and have since migrated to the internet as well (Bermejo 2007).

Today we are in something of a period of flux in relation to the methodologies for producing audience ratings. New technologies that are increasingly fragmenting media audiences and that are increasingly empowering audiences in terms of how, when, and where they consume content – and the advertisements embedded within this content – are making the production of sufficiently accurate and reliable audience ratings more difficult. At the same time, these technological developments are presenting alternative approaches to the measurement of media audiences and the production of ratings data (Napoli 2008). These technological developments will be discussed in greater detail below. The focus here is on the current state of affairs in the production of audience ratings.

Sampling

First, it is perhaps most important to recognize that ratings traditionally have been produced via the observation of a (presumably) representative sample of the population as a whole. Electronic media ratings have been, and largely continue to be, produced via the recruitment of a sample of individuals to take part in the measurement process. Samples are generated for each relevant unit of analysis. Thus, for instance, the measurement of international or national radio, television, and internet audiences is accompanied by the generation of international and national audience samples. Local samples similarly are generated for the measurement of local markets (in the United States, the Nielsen Company is working toward merging its local and national television audience samples). Of course, for any sample to accurately reflect the behavior of the population as a whole, it is essential that this sample be sufficiently large and representative of the population as a whole across as many key attributes as possible. Audience measurement firms expend substantial resources in their efforts to recruit representative samples to take part in the measurement process. According to basic sampling theory, samples need not be particularly large to be sufficiently generalizable to the population as a whole. Thus, for instance, Nielsen's sample of US television households for use in its national television audience ratings service consists of 12,000 of the over 100 million television households in the United States. Nielsen plans to expand this sample size to 37,000 homes by 2011.

Questions surrounding the extent to which such samples are sufficiently representative of the population as a whole have been a focal point of critiques of contemporary ratings services. The implications of nonrepresentative samples in audience measurement are of particular significance given that ratings data are the key tool that media outlets use to judge the performance of their content, and to eliminate content that is underperforming. Therefore, if certain audience segments are not adequately represented in the sample, then the ratings for the content preferred by these segments are likely to underrepresent that content's true popularity. As a result, certain audience segments can find themselves in a situation in which content serving their particular needs and interests is no longer available.

These concerns have been at the core of stakeholder battles over the Nielsen Company's ongoing introduction of the local people meter in the United States for the measurement of television audiences (Napoli 2005), as well as Arbitron's ongoing effort to introduce its portable people meter for the measurement of radio audiences. Both devices introduce electronic measurement technologies into local markets that previously were measured via paper diaries that participants filled out and returned for tabulation on a weekly basis. In both instances, however, the new ratings data produced by the new measurement technologies indicate levels of popularity for stations and programming targeting minority audiences that are in some instances significantly lower than those depicted via the old measurement system (see Napoli 2005). Debate persists as to whether the new ratings are a function of inadequate samples of minority audiences, or whether they simply represent a correction to inflated ratings data produced by the shortcomings of the paper diary methodology. In either case, these debates illustrate the strong connection between audience ratings, audience representation, and the availability of content serving a diverse array of audience interests. These debates also illustrate a fundamental aspect of audience ratings – as the technologies and methodologies for generating ratings data change, so to do the portraits of the audience contained within these data, a phenomenon that poses challenges for both academic researchers and industry decision makers (Napoli and Andrews 2008).

As this discussion suggests, effective sampling often is integral to accurate and reliable ratings data. Today, however, we are seeing the development of systems capable of moving beyond samples and measuring the media consumption of the population as a whole – essentially conducting a census of media consumption. Consider, for instance, the technique of *server log analysis* employed in some circles for the measurement of online audiences (Bermejo 2007). With server log analysis, the data come not from individual panelists, but from the servers of individual websites, which retain information about each individual visitor to the websites. In this way, every web surfer who visits a site is contributing to the site's ratings data, not just those individuals who are part of a measurement service's panel. Similarly, in television, efforts are underway to gather viewing data via the set-top boxes that are integral to virtually all multichannel video-programming delivery services (e.g. cable, DBS, etc.). Every set-top box can provide data back to the service provider about the viewing patterns taking place in every home receiving programming.

There are shortcomings to such approaches as well. One is that, unlike with panels, it is much more difficult to gather the highly desirable demographic data from audience members when data are being gathered via web server logs or television set-top boxes (Bermejo 2007). Under these approaches, the typical audience member is often not even aware that she is taking part in the audience measurement process, and may or may not be willing to provide accurate demographic information if asked. But without an accompanying effort to gather demographic data, set-top boxes and server logs provide only very basic information about audience exposure – essentially, how many computers visited a particular websites, or how many televisions tuned into a particular program.

A second significant issue that arises from such measurement approaches involves privacy. Web server logs and television set-top boxes have the capacity to gather basic media consumption data (if not demographic data) from all web and television users, regardless of whether they approve of having such data gathered about them; and techniques are being developed to ascertain more detailed demographic data – in many cases, once again, without the audience members' knowledge or permission. Particularly online, privacy concerns related to the gathering of web usage data are becoming increasingly pronounced, and we may see regulations put in place that directly address (and perhaps curtail) this kind of audience data gathering (Napoli 2011). The key, at this point, however, is to recognize that alternatives to the traditional sample-based panel approach to audience measurement are emerging, with many current measurement efforts oriented toward developing ways of integrating panel and census data.

Measurement technologies

Moving beyond sampling, the other key aspect of the audience measurement process that affects the accuracy and reliability of the underlying data involves the technology employed for gathering the data. A wide variety of data-gathering tools are employed around the world today to gather ratings data, ranging from paper diaries to television set-top meters (i.e. people meters), to wristwatch- and pager-style devices (often called *portable people meters*) that pick up audio signals. The different technologies for gathering data have different strengths and weaknesses, particularly in terms of the types of audience members for which they are best able to gather data. Older audience members, for instance, do quite well with traditional methods such as paper diaries, but have difficulties interacting with more technologically sophisticated systems such as people meters. Younger audience members, in contrast, tend not to be as conscientious in their keeping of paper diaries, but are more comfortable with more technologically sophisticated systems. Such tendencies again illustrate the means by which different measurement systems can produce very different ratings estimates.

More sophisticated ratings systems generally involve higher costs. Set-top and portable people meters are much more expensive to deploy and maintain than paper diaries. Generally, the greater the subscriber revenue potential for the measurement firm in any particular media market, the more advanced will be the measurement system deployed. Lower revenue media markets tend to have measurement systems that are less advanced, and thus less accurate and reliable, than higher revenue markets (Webster and Phalen 1997).

There are a number of elements to an effective data-gathering system that have been identified over time. Perhaps most important is the extent to which the system is "passive," that is, the extent to which it requires minimal work and input on the part of the participant. Thus, for instance, the time, effort, and recall involved in the completion of paper diaries are generally seen as sources of measurement error, as participants may inaccurately recall their viewing or listening behaviors, or may intentionally misrepresent them. Systems such as those used in online audience measurement, in which the participant needs only to download measurement software that records all of the participant's online activity, require much less of the participant and therefore offer far fewer opportunities for participant-induced error.

But even more advanced systems, such as people meters or portable devices, do require some work on the part of the participant. In the case of people meters, the participant must, at minimum, remember to log in and log out appropriately, so that a people meter can accurately record the demographic characteristics of the television viewers. Portable meters require that the participant remember to carry the meter around all day, so that all media exposure is accurately recorded. A related concern involves the issue of *fatigue* – the extent to which participants tire of taking part in the measurement process over time. Obviously, the more time and effort required by the participant, the greater the likelihood of fatigue. Generally, there is a reasonably rapid turnover in audience measurement samples in order to combat such fatigue.

As should be clear, ratings data are likely far from perfect in terms of the extent to which they accurately represent the size and composition of the audiences consuming electronic media content. However, they do gather such data on a scale that seldom, if ever, can be matched in academic research; and so in many instances they represent by far the best available option when it comes to information on audience exposure to electronic media content, particularly if the researcher is seeking to conduct analyses that compare audience behavior patterns across multiple media markets and / or over time.

Theoretical Critiques

Many critics have argued that the emphasis on audience size and demographics in the measurement of electronic media audiences is itself a fundamental problem (e.g. Ang 1991). According to this perspective, the reduction of the complex dynamics of media consumption into simplistic exposure metrics, in which demographic characteristics are used as proxies for product purchasing behaviors, represents a myopic conceptualization of the media audience. As many of these critics note, this reductionism reflects the economic imperatives of the commercial media industries, and is particularly reflective of the needs of advertisers and media buyers, who long have measured success in terms of ad *exposures* or *impressions*, and seek first and foremost to maximize such exposures and impressions amongst those segments of the audience that they perceive as likely to respond to their particular advertising message (Meehan 1984). It is from this perspective that the well-known notion of the audience as "commodity" emerged, with scholars recognizing that not only is the production of audiences a key objective of advertising-supported media (Smythe 1977), but also, more narrowly, it is the production of ratings that is in fact their key objective, with those audiences that contribute to the calculation of ratings data being the only audience members of real concern to ad-supported media (Meehan 1984).

As should be clear, the approach to the media audience reflected in ratings data is one in which questions of how or if audiences interpret, appreciate, are affected by, or respond to the content they consume have traditionally been marginal, at best. In some instances, ratings data have been analyzed in ways that seek to infer some of these dimensions of audience behavior (see e.g. Barwise and Ehrenberg 1988). In other instances, there have been efforts to construct ratings services that simultaneously capture not only traditional audience demographic and exposure data, but also data on aspects of media consumption such as audience appreciation of the content they consume (Mitgang 2002). Such efforts have, however, gained traction in only a few countries.

Ratings Analysis

Clearly, there are many aspects of audience behavior that are not well captured by ratings data. Nonetheless, there are a wide range of analyses related to the processes of audience exposure to media content that can be fruitfully conducted using ratings data. In addition, to the extent that ratings data reflect the strategic and economic imperatives of media institutions, they also can be used to glean insights into the behavior of these institutions. It is important to emphasize that the discussion below focuses on the uses of ratings data in academic research (see Webster, Phalen and Lichty [2005] for an overview of the uses of ratings data in industry settings). Although it is beyond the scope of this chapter to provide a comprehensive review of this literature, this section will provide a basic overview of the types of analyses that have been conducted. For a more detailed typology of the uses of ratings data in academic research, see Stavitsky (2000).

Audience behavior research via ratings analysis

Ratings analyses have been used in a wide range of studies related to audience exposure to media content. Many ratings analyses involve identifying stable and predictable patterns of audience behavior, in an effort to better understand the dynamics of media consumption. Scholars across a variety of disciplines, including sociology, communications, and economics, long have been interested in developing predictive and explanatory models of audience behavior that identify persistent patterns related to audience exposure to media content (Webster and Phalen 1997). Work in this vein, for instance, has empirically identified persistent patterns such as the "double jeopardy effect" (Barwise and Ehrenberg 1988), which depicts how content that attracts a small audience (source of jeopardy #1) also tends to attract audiences that are not particularly loyal, in terms of the frequency with which they consume the content (source of jeopardy #2).

Much of this work has been concerned with examining how content characteristics are related to exposure patterns. Thus, for instance, research in the media economics tradition has looked at how factors such as production budgets relate to audience exposure patterns in an effort to develop theoretical models of program choice (see Owen and Wildman 1992). One particularly important finding of this line of research is the extent to which media consumption appears to be first and foremost a function of audience availability, with general consumption patterns (i.e. the percentage of the population using television, radio, or the internet at a particular point in time) proving relatively stable and predictable, but the distribution of audience attention across available content options proving much more difficult to predict (Webster and Phalen 1997).

Other studies examining patterns of audience exposure have focused on "audience flows" across content options (see Cooper 1996), in an effort to understand the factors that affect if and how audiences transition from one content option to the next. Such analyses have illuminated behavioral patterns that are at the core of much of the "programming theory" employed by content providers (Eastman 1998). Examples of this type of work include studies of inheritance effects (analyses of the extent to which audiences for one program flow into the next program) and channel loyalty (the extent to which audiences return to individual channels) (Dick and McDowell 2004). Research in this vein is, of course, highly reflective of efforts by programmers to develop strategies to aid in the scheduling of programming in ways that maximize audience exposure.

Another important point of focus of ratings analyses has been on how audience exposure patterns are affected by technological change. A deeper understanding of the effects of new communications technologies can be obtained by examining how new technologies affect the dynamics of audience exposure to media content. Thus, for instance, ratings analyses have been used to examine how the introduction of cable television, and the associated growth of television channel capacity, affected the dynamics of audiences' television consumption (see Heeter and Greenberg 1988). More recently, a number of studies have examined how the distribution of audience attention is affected by the tremendous fragmentation of the media environment (particularly in the online realm), and have sought to determine whether audiences' behavioral patterns exhibit similarities across old and new media platforms (Webster and Lin 2002; Hindman 2007).

Such analyses can inform not only our basic understanding of the dynamics of the consumption of media products, but also policy questions related to how new technologies affect audience exposure patterns to content considered socially beneficial, such as news or public affairs programming (Webster 1984), or, for that matter, content considered harmful, such as violent programming (Hamilton 1998). The question of how the new media environment affects *exposure diversity* – the extent to which audiences are exposed to a diverse array of content types and/or sources (Napoli 1997) – has been a particular point of focus of recent ratings analyses (Yim 2003; Webster 2007; Yuan 2008). This issue has become an increasingly common component of contemporary media policy debates (see Napoli and Gillis 2006), given the widely held presumption that the diversity of content offerings available in the new media environment only achieves their full social value if audiences partake of the diversity of viewpoints, ideas, and content forms available to them.

Media institutions research via ratings analysis

Ratings data are useful not only for understanding media audiences, but also for understanding the institutions involved in the attracting and monetizing of media audiences. To the extent that ratings serve as the currency in the marketplace for media audiences, analyzing how these data are used by participants in this marketplace is a useful window into the operation of media outlets, content producers, advertisers, and media buyers. For example, a key use of ratings data for understanding media institutions has been the growing body of research that has examined the value that media industry stakeholders place on different audience segments (Koschat and Putsis 2000; Coffey 2008). Research in this vein typically melds ratings data with revenue or ad rate data in an effort to determine the valuations that are assigned to different audience groups. Such analyses not only provide insights into the logics that are guiding the audience marketplace, but also can illuminate patterns that may raise or inform policy issues. Thus, for instance, studies indicating low valuations of minority audience segments have been a focal point of policy discussions about possible mechanisms for promoting or preserving minority-targeted media outlets (Napoli 2003). Here again, as was the case in regard to the issue of minority representation in audience measurement panels (see above), the key concern involves the effect on the availability of minority-targeted content. If advertisers tend to undervalue minority audiences, then media outlets will not have sufficient economic incentives to provide content of interest to minority audiences, and the diversity of available content is subsequently diminished. Analyses of ratings data also have been used to explore the underlying economic logic of the production of violent programming (Hamilton 1998), as well as to investigate how variations in competitive conditions affect the distribution of audience attention and advertising revenues within individual media markets (Webster and Phalen 1997).

Access to Ratings Data

Regardless of whether a researcher is looking to examine media audiences or media institutions via the analysis of ratings data, a key hurdle that the researcher needs to overcome is obtaining such data. As was noted above, ratings data are produced by commercial audience measurement firms. The primary revenue stream for these firms is subscriptions from media outlets, content producers, advertisers, and media buyers. That is, these measurement firms typically are in the business of producing and selling syndicated ratings reports – aggregations of ratings data in a unified format to all subscribers. Increasingly, measurement firms also are providing subscribers with access to the underlying raw data in addition to standardized ratings reports.

The price that subscribers pay for the data, however, is anything but uniform. Pricing for commercial audience data is opaque. It is a function of factors such as the size of the organization seeking the data, the number of users of the data within the organization, or the number of computer terminals via which the data will be accessible (Napoli and Karaganis 2007). Thus, the amount paid by different subscribing organizations for the same data can vary widely. And, because there has historically been very little competition in the provision of ratings data, prices tend to be quite high. Because ratings function as the "currency" in the audience marketplace, there seldom has been sufficient commitment from media outlets or advertisers to financially support competing measurement services to provide alternative currencies. The lower prices arising from the arrival of competitors would likely be offset by the corresponding costs of having to subscribe to multiple ratings services. The need to analyze, and haggle over, multiple potentially conflicting ratings reports for the same piece of content would add greater uncertainty and analytical burdens to the audience marketplace. Based on these tendencies, one might even argue that the ratings business is a natural monopoly.

Typically, a subscription to a commercial audience ratings service (or even the purchase of a single data set) includes a contract that prohibits the subscriber from even discussing the terms under which she received access to the data. Such nondisclosure clauses facilitate maximum price discrimination by the measurement firm amongst its client base (i.e., the less a potential subscriber knows about how much others paid for the data, the easier it is for that measurement firm to charge that potential subscriber as much as possible). These contracts also typically prohibit the sharing of data with nonsubscribers (see Napoli and Seaton 2007).

Academic researchers, needless to say, seldom have substantial resources with which to purchase ratings data. Thus, if they are to obtain ratings data, they are most likely to do so via receiving the data for free or at a substantially discounted price from a sympathetic representative of the audience measurement firm. In some instances, the data provider may provide access primarily out of an interest in supporting academic research, out of a desire to see the data implicitly validated or endorsed by its use in academic research, or out of the desire to capture the additional, relatively small amount of revenue associated with serving an academic client. However, data access may be conditional upon the nature of the research project being proposed. Proposed projects that have the potential to produce results that would be unflattering to the measurement firm or to its clients are less likely to result in access to the data. Ratings firms recognize the problems that can arise for them should their more important clients learn that their high subscription fees essentially are subsidizing discounted access to ratings data for academics producing work critical of their activities.

It should be noted that this bottleneck of control over ratings data has most likely limited the nature of the academic analyses that have historically been conducted with ratings data. It is probably in part for this reason that much of the audience research that has been conducted utilizing ratings data has frequently been described as "administrative" research (i.e. research focused primarily on providing insights useful to the various sectors of the media industry; see Webster and Phalen 1997). Academic research projects of this type are much more likely to obtain access to ratings data.

The Future of Ratings Analysis

Technological changes have been gradually damaging the foundations upon which the traditional markets for audiences (i.e. ratings) have operated (Napoli 2003). Factors such as the increasing fragmentation of the media environment and the increasing control audiences have over the process of media consumption are serving to simultaneously undermine traditional audience ratings systems and, ironically, facilitate the creation and adoption of alternatives to this system.

In understanding this process, first, it is important to note that the greater the number content options (i.e. channels) available, the more challenging it is to accurately and reliably determine the ratings for these channels when relying on traditional panel-based measurement systems. This is because panels need to become larger and larger to adequately account for the number of channels. Consider, for instance, that Nielsen/NetRatings' web audience measurement panel for Australia consists of 4000 people. There are, in contrast, literally millions of websites available to these 4000 people. The odds are that many of these websites are not being visited by any of the members of the Nielsen panel, which would therefore mean that these sites would generate a rating of zero in Australia, despite the many Australians who might actually be visiting these sites. This is an extreme example meant to illustrate that as audiences become more widely dispersed across available content options, the ratings are less likely to accurately or reliably reflect the size or composition of the audience consuming the content. This same problem has become quite pronounced in the television realm, where channel capacity has expanded faster than sample sizes can keep up. Many of the over 500 television networks available in the United States today have average ratings that are too small for Nielsen to even report.

And, while one could argue that the measurement firms simply should increase their sample sizes, we must keep in mind that increasing sample sizes is costly. The addition of these new channels, with their very small audiences (and thus very small revenue streams), does not always add enough subscription revenues to the measurement firms' bottom line to sufficiently incentivize such sample size increases.

This situation is further complicated by the fact that content can now be consumed across multiple media platforms. Thus, for instance, a television program can be watched on television when it is aired by a broadcast or cable network, recorded on a DVR and watched later, watched online via a streaming media service, downloaded and watched on an iPod, or even watched via a cellular phone. The point here is that the platforms via which audiences consume media are increasing, and it is becoming increasingly difficult for ratings services to accurately and reliably capture all of these contact points, particularly given the traditional history of ratings firms operating in individual silos, with different firms and different methodological approaches independently handling the measurement of different content delivery platforms.

For the academic researcher, this situation means that ratings data likely are becoming an increasingly inadequate representation of audiences' media consumption – particularly if the researcher is interested in audience attention across the full range of content options, as opposed to just the most popular ones (which still are measured comparatively well by traditional measurement approaches).

The counterbalance to this decline in the reliability and comprehensiveness of traditional ratings data as a result of media and audience fragmentation is the institutionalization of alternative metrics for media consumption resulting from the increased interactivity of the new media environment. That is, while the new media environment makes it increasingly difficult to determine exposure-based audience ratings, it makes it easier to capture and aggregate other aspects of media consumption, such as audience engagement, audience appreciation, or audience recall of the content they have consumed.

Because new media technologies are increasingly interactive, various forms of audience response can now be captured and analyzed. Now, audience feedback and participation via interactive television set-top boxes, audience discussion in online forums and chat rooms, and behavioral responses in terms of ad-clicking or product-purchasing behaviors can be immediately gathered, aggregated, analyzed, and, ultimately, used as criteria for setting advertising rates and making strategic decisions about content production and placement.

Measurement firms are developing measures of audience engagement with media content that are beginning to be used in addition to traditional exposure-based audience ratings in the analysis of content performance and in the setting and negotiation of advertising rates (Napoli 2011). One recent trade publication described how smaller, niche cable networks – exactly those networks that are not well served by traditional exposure data – are beginning to employ "engagement" data as an "alternative currency" with advertisers (Crupi 2008, p. 12). Another recent analysis boldly declared that ratings "no longer matter" (Pilotta 2008, p. 1). Such developments suggest that we may be entering into what Napoli (2011) has described as a postexposure media environment, in which the basic criteria for success upon which the marketplace for media audiences operates are changing dramatically, and in which traditional exposure-focused audience ratings data likely will play a diminished role.

Redefining Ratings Analysis?

The obvious question that arises, then, is how do these developments affect our definition of ratings analysis? Is the focal point of the definition the aspect of media consumption that is being analyzed? That is, is ratings analysis defined in terms of the measurement and analysis of audience exposure via syndicated data sources? If so, then the academic utility of ratings analysis may be in decline, given the developments described above. Or, should ratings analysis be defined in terms of the source and purpose of the data being analyzed? That is, is ratings analysis defined as the analysis of the data (whatever their orientation) used by media industry stakeholders to assess performance and success in the audience marketplace? If this is the case, then we simply are at the beginning of an evolutionary stage in ratings analysis. The nature of the ratings is likely changing – or, more accurately, expanding – and the nature of the questions that can be investigated by ratings analysis will need to expand accordingly. In light of this, this is a very exciting time to be engaged in ratings analysis, as this research tradition is essentially in a period of reinvention.

What is particularly striking about this ongoing transition is the extent to which the media industry appears to be moving toward embracing dimensions of media consumption that have been the province of those scholars who have been critical of traditional ratings analysis and its use in both industry and academic settings (e.g. Ang 1991). Concepts such as engagement, appreciation, and response may soon challenge the primacy of exposure. This transition suggests that a window of opportunity may be open for those scholars who have been examining these aspects of audience behavior that traditionally have resided at the margins of media industry concerns to offer input into how the industry's ongoing reconceptualization of media audiences should take shape.

From an academic standpoint, these developments would also seem to represent an opportunity for a bridging of the gulf that has developed between those audience researchers who engage in ratings analysis and those who engage in more qualitative approaches to audience behavior, given the greater congruence (at least superficially) that appears to be developing in the aspects of audience behavior under examination in these historically divergent research traditions. If the nature of this gulf is purely methodological (i.e. quantitative versus qualitative), then the developments taking place likely will have no effect in terms of unifying the audience research field, as the "new" ratings systems still will cater to the media and advertising industries' established (and likely unchangeable) desire for quantitative data and performance metrics. Similarly, if the nature of the gulf is primarily ideological (i.e. focused around opposition to, versus cooperation with, the interests of commercial media organizations), then there is once again relatively little likelihood of seeing a coming together of these research traditions, as the data utilized in ratings analysis still will reflect the commercial imperatives of media industries.

However, if the nature of this gulf is more theoretical (i.e. involving the appropriate conceptualizations of audiences' media consumption), then it would seem that the move within the media industries and audience measurement organizations to look beyond exposure has the potential to narrow, at least somewhat, the divide separating these two research traditions. This prediction presumes that scholars currently engaged in ratings analysis will be flexible and adaptable in response to changes taking place in the realm of audience measurement, and will embrace the new audience metrics emerging alongside the declining exposure metrics. To the extent that such researchers tend to often approach their subject from a standpoint grounded in the economics of media industries or the behavior of media institutions, this would seem to be a safe presumption. Scholars with such an analytical orientation often are concerned less with understanding the audience per se than in understanding media industries and institutions via their engagement with audiences – whatever analytical form these audiences take.

In any case, the future of ratings analysis seems to be in a state of flux. New audience ratings are emerging to stand alongside the old. Opportunities are developing for the academic researcher to work with very different forms of ratings data; to investigate new and different questions related to both media audiences and media institutions with these data; and, ultimately, to expand the parameters of ratings analysis in the years to come.

References

Ang, I. 1991 *Desperately Seeking the Audience*. Routledge, London.

Barwise, P. and Ehrenberg, A.S.C. 1988 *Television and Its Audience*. Sage, London.

Bermejo, F. 2007 *The Internet Audience: Constitution and Measurement*. Peter Lang, New York.

Beville, H.M., Jr. 1988 *Audience Ratings: Radio, Television, Cable*. Lawrence Erlbaum, Hillsdale, NJ.

Chappell, M.N. and Hooper, C.E. 1944 *Radio Audience Measurement*. Stephen Daye, New York.

Coffey, A.J. 2008 The case for audience isolation: language and culture as predictors of advertiser investment. *International Journal on Media Management*, 10, 2, pp. 81–90.

Cooper, R. 1996 The status and future of audience duplication research: an assessment of ratings-based theories of audience behavior. *Journal of Broadcasting and Electronic Media*, 40, 1, pp. 96–111.

Crupi, A. 2008 It pays to be gay: logo tops key demos in Simmons engagement study. *Mediaweek*, April 28, pp. 10, 12.

Dick, S.J. and McDowell, W. 2004 Estimating relative audience loyalty among radio stations using standard Arbitron data. *Journal of Radio Studies*, 11, pp. 26–39.

Eastman, S.T. 1998 Programming theory under stress: the active industry and the active audience. *Communication Yearbook*, 21, pp. 323–377.

Hamilton, J.T. 1998 *Channeling Violence: The Economic Market for Violent Television Programming*. Princeton University Press, Princeton, NJ.

Heeter, C. and Greenberg, B.S. 1988 *Cable-viewing*. Ablex, Norwood, NJ.

Hindman, M. 2007 A mile wide and an inch deep: measuring media diversity online and offline. In P.M. Napoli, ed. *Media Diversity and Localism: Meaning and Metrics*. Lawrence Erlbaum, Mahwah, NJ, pp. 327–348.

Koschat, M.A. and Putsis, W.P. 2000 Who wants you when you're old and poor? Exploring the economics of media pricing. *Journal of Media Economics*, 13, pp. 215–232.

Meehan, E.R. 1984 Ratings and the institutional approach: a third answer to the commodity question. *Critical Studies in Mass Communication*, 1, 2, pp. 216–225.

Mitgang, L. 2002 *Big Bird and Beyond: The New Media and the Markle Foundation*. Fordham University Press, New York.

Napoli, P.M. 1997 Rethinking program diversity assessment: an audience-centered approach. *Journal of Media Economics*, 10, 4, pp. 59–74.

Napoli, P.M. 2003 *Audience Economics: Media Institutions and the Audience Marketplace*. Columbia University Press, New York.

Napoli, P.M. 2005 Audience measurement and media policy: audience economics, the diversity principle, and the local people meter. *Communications Law and Policy*, 10, 4, pp. 349–382.

Napoli, P.M. 2008 Toward a model of audience evolution: new technologies and the transformation of the media audience. Paper presented at the annual meeting of the International Association for Media and Communications Research, Stockholm, Sweden.

Napoli, P.M. (2011). *Audience Evolution: New Technologies and the Transformation of Media Audiences*. Columbia University Press, New York.

Napoli, P.M. and Andrews, K. 2008 Managing innovation in audience measurement. In C. dal Zotto and H. van Kranenburg, eds. *Management and Innovation in the Media Industry*. Edward Elgar, Cheltenham, UK, pp. 263–285.

Napoli, P.M. and Gillis, N. 2006 Reassessing the potential contribution of communications research to communications policy: the case of media ownership. *Journal of Broadcasting and Electronic Media*, 50, 4, pp. 671–691.

Napoli, P.M. and Karaganis, J. 2007 Toward a federal data agenda for communications policymaking. *CommLaw Conspectus: The Journal of Communication Law and Policy*, 16, pp. 53–96.

Napoli, P.M. and Seaton, M. 2007 Necessary knowledge for communications policy: information asymmetries and commercial data access and usage in the policymaking process. *Federal Communications Law Journal*, 59, pp. 295–329.

Owen, B.M. and Wildman, S.S. 1992 *Video Economics*. Harvard University Press, Cambridge, MA.

Pilotta, J.J. 2008 Why ratings no longer matter. *Radio Business Report/Television Business Report Intelligence Brief*, February 15.

Smythe, D. 1977 Communications: blindspot of Western Marxism. *Canadian Journal of Political and Social Theory*, 1, pp. 1–27.

Stavitsky, A.G. 2000 By the numbers: the use of ratings data in academic research. *Journal of Broadcasting and Electronic Media*, 44, 3, pp. 535–539.

Webster, J.G. 1984 Cable television's impact on the audience for local news. *Journalism Quarterly*, 61, pp. 419–422.

Webster, J.G. 2007 Diversity of exposure. In P.M. Napoli, ed. *Media Diversity and Localism: Meaning and Metrics*. Lawrence Erlbaum, Mahwah, NJ. pp. 309–326.

Webster, J.G. and Lin, S.F. 2002 The Internet audience: web use as mass behavior. *Journal of Broadcasting and Electronic Media*, 46, 1, pp. 1–12.

Webster, J.G. and Phalen, P.F. 1997 *The Mass Audience: Rediscovering the Dominant Model*. Lawrence Erlbaum, Mahwah, NJ.

Webster, J.G., Phalen, P.F. and Lichty, L.W. 2005 *Ratings Analysis: The Theory and Practice of Audience Research*, 3rd edn. Lawrence Erlbaum, Mahwah, NJ.

Yim, J. 2003 Audience concentration in the media: cross-media comparisons and the introduction of the uncertainty measure. *Communication Monographs*, 70, 2, pp. 114–128.

Yuan, E.J. 2008 Diversity of exposure in television viewing: audience fragmentation and polarization in Guangzhou. *Chinese Journal of Communication*, 1, 1, pp. 91–108.

15

Quantitative Audience Research
Embracing the Poor Relation

David Deacon and Emily Keightley

Introduction

*I am not what I am supposed to be. I am quite another thing. Perhaps before I go
further, I had better glance at what I AM supposed to be.*

Charles Dickens, *The Poor Relation's Story* (1852)

The claim that quantitative research is a "poor relation" in audience studies is only
sustainable from particular disciplinary and historical vantage points. Certainly,
plenty of quantitative audience research is still conducted, most noticeably by
researchers from other disciplines who are interested in questions of media
influence. For example, political scientists regularly use surveys for assessing the
electoral impact of the media (e.g. Freedman and Goldstein 1999; Anderson and
Carnagey 2003), and experimental methods are still used routinely in social
psychology to ascertain the existence and extent of independent media effects
(e.g. Coyne and Nelson 2008; Fischer, Guter, and Frey 2008; Ridout, Grosse, and
Appleton 2008).

However, in critical approaches to communication and media studies, particularly those of a culturalist orientation, quantitative audience research has long been
viewed with considerable suspicion, even disdain. Furthermore, this represents a
considerable change in fortunes, given it was once described as constituting a
"dominant paradigm" in the field (Gitlin 1978). In this chapter, we consider the
reasons for this marginalization and question its legitimacy. It is our contention that
this rejection is sustained by dubious "simple histories" of audience research that

The Handbook of Media Audiences, First Edition. Edited by Virginia Nightingale.
© 2014 John Wiley & Sons, Ltd. Published 2014 by John Wiley & Sons, Ltd.

misrepresent the character of much quantitative audience research and overstate the antimony of quantitative and qualitative methods and findings. This doctrinal "othering" of statistical methods detrimentally affects both the scale and scope of audience research, obstructing opportunities for the fruitful combination of methods.

Before addressing these matters, it is necessary first to describe the main characteristics of the quantitative methods that have been used in investigating media effects and reception.

The Twin Pillars

From its inception, surveys and experimental methods have been the twin pillars of quantitative audience research. Surveys are used to describe the behaviors, attitudes, and beliefs of audiences and their relations with media and patterns of media consumption. They do so by presenting standardized questions in a systematic manner administered either as self-completion forms (mail or online) or as standardized interviews. One of the core objectives of the method is to analyze associations, correlations, and significant differences either within or across research samples, using a range of bivariate and multivariate statistical methods (see Deacon et al. 2008, pp. 91–115). Surveys can provide both cross-sectional and longitudinal data. Cross-sectional surveys provide information about particular phenomena at the time the survey is conducted. Longitudinal surveys examine the relationship between variables over time and as a result can allow the exploration of the changing relationship between audiences and media over time. Gunter identifies three kinds of longitudinal surveys: trend studies, cohort studies, and panel studies (2000, pp. 243–245).

Surveys are extensive in range and deploy formal sampling strategies designed to gain a representative sample of a broader population (for a summary of the main forms of survey sampling, see Deacon et al. 2008, pp. 43–54). The idealized form of sampling is randomized, sometimes referred to as *probability sampling*, where all members of a population have an equal and random chance of being selected. This randomization offers justification for a range of statistical projections that either (a) make population estimates on the basis of sample data or (b) estimate the likelihood that observed relationships and associations between sample variables are likely to exist in the population as a whole (aka *hypothesis testing*). Where it is not possible to employ randomized sampling techniques, for example due to the absence of an adequate sampling frame or because of time constraints, nonrandom quota sampling techniques are used to achieve representative samples. According to the strict precepts of statistical theory, such purposive sampling prohibits probability testing; but in reality, this principle is honored more in the breach than the observance.

Experiments have been considered to be the preserve of psychology rather than sociology, as it is claimed that they are only suitable for the examination of the behavior, cognitions, and attitudes of individuals, rather than any assessment of social groups or processes. In challenging this assumption, Ann Oakley identifies the long history of random control testing research in sociological studies (1998), highlighting the potential of experimental research to contribute to the theorization of social and cultural life. Experimental design has also been used in research into the agenda-setting capacity of the media (e.g. Iyengar et al. 1982, 1984).

Studies using experimental methods are generally concerned with ascertaining causal influences rather than the coincidence and correlations between variables that are commonly sought in surveys. The use of laboratory experiments, in particular, allows the isolation, manipulation, and control of variables that is crucial to the establishment of causality. These experiments generally involve testing a hypothesis by applying a stimulus in a particular situation and then repeating this with changed or modified variables. There are numerous variations in design (for a more detailed elaboration of these, see Gunter 2000, pp. 29–35), but a classic design involves several groups of participants, not all of whom are subjected to experimental conditions. Participants will be randomly divided into experimental and control groups. Pretesting is conducted, perhaps using a questionnaire, to assess their preexisting attitudes, beliefs, and patterns of behavior. One group is then exposed to a stimulus or intervention, and the control group is not. Both groups are then post tested to assess any changes that may have been elicited by the stimulus. Conclusions about the effect of the stimulus or intervention are then inferred from the difference between pre- and posttest results for the experimental group, in contradistinction from the lack of change in the pre- and posttest results from the control group. The sampling used in laboratory-based experimental research is, like surveys, ideally randomized, although often on a smaller scale using smaller samples of populations for logistical reasons.

Laboratory-based experiments of this kind are commonly criticized for their artificiality and lack of ecological validity. The control over the research environment and the deliberate isolation and manipulation of variables necessarily involve a deliberate divergence from the everyday contexts of media consumption. Certainly, in these artificial conditions, matters of internal and external validity require careful management (see Wimmer and Dominick [1991, pp. 29–36] for a more detailed discussion). *Field experiments* are less vulnerable in this respect as they are conducted in more naturally occurring environments. For instance, a researcher concerned with the effects of internet use may test a prison population who have limited access to the internet with another high-use group such as university students. The difficulty here is that gains in ecological validity are traded for losses in control as real-life conditions are rarely as measureable in terms of exposure to a stimulus as can be determined by researchers in laboratory conditions. Taking advantage of naturally occurring groups is also difficult as they tend to occur by chance and are not always stable over time, making opportunities for comparison contingent on external circumstances.

The Early Years of Quantitative Audience Research

The history of audience research is often presented in a simple and straightforward manner, with the pioneers of quantitative methods cast as abstracted empiricists whose "effects" research is hermetically sealed from subsequent "discoveries" of the importance of social context and audience activity enabled by qualitative methods. However, this simple history overlooks the methodological variety of early studies and the considerable insights they provided into the audiences' role in the processes of communication. As a result, their significant contribution to understanding of audience power and autonomy is underappreciated.

The first sustained efforts to investigate systematically the relationship between media and their audiences were the Payne Fund Studies (PFS) in the United States, which were produced between 1929 and 1932 and examined the influence of movies on children. These studies broke new ground by transforming the key questions concerning the influence of mass communications and culture into a researchable form. At the time, there was a widespread belief in the vulnerability of mass audiences to manipulation by propagandists and the cultural industries, which was broadly informed by mass society theory and the empirical observation of the rapid development and prevalence of new forms of mass communication. The Payne Studies were the first to subject what McQuail terms "the best guess in the circumstances" (1987) to empirical scrutiny.

The research program used both experiments and surveys, although they inclined to the former. For example, one study measured whether children translated knowledge gained by watching films into changed behavior by measuring the teeth-cleaning habits of children exposed to a number of information films about dental care, and a control group which had not watched the films (Freeman 1933). Another experiment in the series measured physical responses to movies as an indicator of their influence on emotion (Ruckmick 1932).[1]

These initial forays into the application of experimental methods in audience research were refined and extended in the late 1930s and 1940s by the Yale University program of research headed by Carl Hovland.

This program was primarily concerned with the persuasive role of communications, and the means by which their efficacy could be optimized. With the United States about to enter the Second World War, Hovland's early work, conducted on his secondment to the Information and Educational Division of the War Department, used field experiments to test the impact of information films on soldiers' motivation (Hovland, Lumsdaine, and Sheffield 1949). As well as using questionnaires to pre-and posttest both experimental and control groups, these and subsequent studies conducted at Yale made significant methodological developments, such as the incorporation of demographic information and camouflaged tests within the questionnaires to distract respondents from the researcher's central interests (Hovland, Lumsdaine, and Sheffield 1949).

Around the same time, political research using sample surveys contributed further insight into the nature and extent of media influence. The pioneering study in this paradigm was Lazarsfeld, Berelson, and Gaudet's research into the 1940 American election campaign, published under the title *The People's Choice* (1944). In this project, Lazarsfeld and his colleagues investigated key influences on voting behavior by conducting a panel study with a sample of 600 people who were inter-viewed at measured intervals. The study highlighted the relative marginality of media influence in voter decision making, particularly when compared with the significant influence of other people. Instead of an atomized, anomic wasteland, the modern United States was revealed as a myriad of micro primary groups containing opinion leaders who actively surveilled the media and political arena and who communicated their views and opinions to less engaged and informed members of the group.

This research, conducted at the Bureau for Applied Social Research, Columbia University, was part of an ongoing program of research into the influence of mass communication, and had previously been located at Princeton University. The communications research program at Columbia expanded considerably over subsequent years, both in refining the initial model of media influence developed in *The People's Choice* and in exploring other approaches to the analysis of media audiences. For example, Columbia University hosted Herta Herzog's pioneering "uses and gratifications" research into the popularity of radio soap operas – an approach which famously inverted the question as to what the media "do" to people into examination of what people "do" with the media.[2]

It is not possible in the confines of this chapter to do full justice to the range of research that was conducted during these early years and utilized experimental and survey methods. Certainly, there are dangers in overstating the compatibility and coherence of these disparate research projects, initiatives, and programs. Nevertheless, it is possible to define some broad commonalities that legitimize the description of these early studies as a distinctive paradigm of research.

First, these studies shared a clear administrative orientation, and their empha-ses were shaped by the agencies that funded them. For example, the Payne Fund was a private foundation informed by a distinctly conservative moral agenda (Jowett, Jarvie, and Fuller 1996). US military needs gave a powerful impetus to the experimental studies at Yale University in the 1940s, and the program was also able to rely on considerable funding from the Rockefeller Foundation. Corporate funding underwrote Lazarsfeld's research ongoing work at Princeton and then Columbia, revealing the extent of private sector interest in exploiting the com-mercial potentialities of new forms of mass communication. This administrative orientation has been used subsequently by some critics as a means of rejecting this work, casting these researchers as unquestioning servants of capitalist and state interests. This is both simplistic and unfair. It is evident that the Payne Studies suffered from an inability to extricate themselves from the conservative moral agenda associated with their funding sources. But the academics involved were well aware of the difference between social science research and social policy, and made self-conscious attempts to distance themselves from the prevailing morals of the time, albeit unsuccessfully (Jowett, Jarvie, and Fuller 1996). Similarly, Lazarsfeld was well aware of the tensions between critical and administrative research, and was interested in the connections that could be established between the two (see Lazarsfeld 1941; Morrison 1998; Bruhn-Jensen 2002). For example, his appointment of the Frankfurt school theorist Theodore Adorno as musical director of the Princeton Radio Project in the late 1930s was both an act of com-passion (Adorno was a refugee from Nazism) and an expression of the serious-ness of his interest in establishing some commonality between administrative and critical traditions.[3] The collaboration may have ended in failure, but the very fact of its initiation challenges the ready portrayal of Lazarsfeld as a gung-ho, free market pluralist.[4]

Second, although surveys and experiments were the mainstays of these early studies, they were often more methodologically eclectic than is commonly appre-ciated. Hovland was receptive to the insights from a variety of disciplines, includ-ing anthropology, which he saw as crucial to a holistic theory of communication (Hovland, Janis, and Kelley 1953, p. 3), and his experimental work was underwrit-ten by methodological pragmatism rather than a blind faith in the laboratory method, as is often insinuated (e.g. Gitlin 1978, p. 211).[5] Similarly, the reductive methodological typecasting of the Payne Fund program ignores their considerable use of qualitative data.[6] Despite accusations to the contrary (e.g. Boudon 1972; Rex 1973), Lazarsfeld, too, was methodologically sophisticated and, in common with many of his contemporaries, was "tolerant of a whole variety of methodologies" (Morrison 1998, p. 2). Thus, here again, we can see a major discrepancy between the actual research practices of these early pioneers of audience research and their subsequent caricature as puritanical exponents of "brutal hard-headed, behaviour-istic positivism" (Hall 1982, p. 59).

Third, these studies cumulatively provided significant correctives to the initial untested assumptions about the omnipotence of media power. The Payne Fund Studies have been broadly maligned in histories of audience research and not completely without reason. There was an undeniably inadequate conceptu-alization of social and historical contexts of media consumption underlying the PFS which remains deeply problematic. However, criticism of nonexistent the-oretical framework is often conflated with their criticism of their methodologi-cal approaches. In fact, it was the data emerging from the use of these methods that made the theoretical shortcomings of the research painfully obvious as the data were largely inconclusive and were in many instances unable to provide clear answers to such decontextualized research questions (Jowett, Jarvie, and Fuller 1996). Their implicit conclusions about the limited nature of direct media influence on behavior and attitudes became far more evident in the work of researchers like Hovland and Lazarsfeld. The Yale studies evidence demanded the jettisoning of notions of direct model of media effects and of an unvarie-gated "mass" audience, by revealing conclusively that persuasive media cannot unilaterally impose ideas and attitudes and that audience are "active partici-pants" in the communication process (Hovland, Janis, and Kelley 1953, p. 278). In a similar way, the voting studies indicated the relative unimportance of mass communications in shaping individuals' voting in comparison with other key sources information such as friends and family. The importance of social characteristics such as class, were also identified as crucial in predicting voting behavior.

The new orthodoxy about audience power and media influence was famously summarized by Joseph Klapper in 1960 in his book the *Effects of Mass Communication*, in which he concluded,

> Mass communication ordinarily does not serve as a necessary and sufficient cause of audience effects, but rather functions among and through a nexus of mediating factors and influences.... These mediating factors are such that they typically render mass communication a contributory agent, but not the sole cause, in a process of reinforcing the existing conditions. (p. 8)

Such was the sanguinity of conclusions of this kind that some were even writing obituaries for the field on their basis (e.g. Berelson 1959). However, no sooner had this orthodoxy been established than its conclusions were called into profound question.

The Partial Death of the Dominant Paradigm

This new phase of media and audience analysis revitalized interest in questions of media influence by reconceptualizing its nature. This change had various origins. One particularly significant element was the development of new radical approaches to communication and media analysis. The emergence of cultural studies during this period was a major expression and accelerant of this change, but this was not the only location for developing critical perspectives. For example, new sociological approaches also gained prominence that argued for more socio-logically informed analyses of the broader political economy of communication and cultural production. These developments reflected wider transformations in the humanities and social sciences during this period, as, across the disciplines, earlier hermeneutic and radical traditions were rediscovered, reasserted, and extended (Hall 1982; Morrison 1998, ch. 4).

Tensions between culturalist and political economy approaches were to increase over the years, but there was at least a strong initial unity in their rejection of the earlier audience research paradigm. These studies were criticized for conceptualizing media influence too narrowly and behavioristically, and, in their fixation with measuring short-term attitudinal and behavioral change, ignoring wider questions about the configuration of social power and longer term media influence, in particular in legitimizing existing power structures and preventing change. Questions of ideology and reality construction moved to center stage, and the "dominant paradigm" of quantitative audience research (Gitlin 1978) was attacked not just for its lack of explanatory engagement with such matters, but also for its implicit ideological values. For example, in an influential critique published in the early 1980s, Stuart Hall (1982) claimed,

> The approach, though advanced as empirically-grounded and scientific, was predicated on a very specific set of political and ideological presuppositions. These presuppositions, however, were not put to the test, within the theory, but framed and underpinned it as a set of unexamined postulates. It should have asked 'does pluralism work?' and 'how does pluralism work?' Instead, it asserted, 'pluralism works' – and then went on to measure, precisely and empirically how well it was doing. This mixture of prophecy and hope, with a brutal hard-headed, behaviouristic positivism provided a heady theoretical concoction which, for a long time, passed itself off as 'pure science'. (p. 59)

This quotation reveals both the vehemence of the rejection of earlier empirical audience research approaches and the extent to which their methodological preferences were seen as a core part of the problem. Many within this radical paradigm saw methodology and epistemology as existing in an iron embrace, and, thus, a core element of the renunciation of positivism was the denunciation of the methods at its foundation. This rejection of quantification was particularly evident in critiques originating from within cultural studies (Deacon 2008). For example, in a chapter outlining the conduct of media studies at the Birmingham Centre for Contemporary Cultural Studies in the late 1970s, Stuart Hall (1980) asserted, "Audience-based survey research, based on the large statistical sample using fixed-choice questionnaires, has at long last reached the terminal point it deserved – at least as serious sociological enterprise" (p. 120).

And yet, obituaries of this kind were premature. As noted in our introduction, many researchers working in other disciplines have continued conducting audience research based on experimental and survey research. More significantly, confident assertions about the absolute redundancy of quantitative audience research within communication, media, and cultural studies ignored the emergence of a new direction in "pluralist" audience research from the 1960s onward that, in its own way, mounted as significant challenge to the orthodoxies of personal influence models as the critical paradigm. These studies were empirically orientated, like their predecessors, but reopened questions of media influence by relocating the search. Instead of focusing upon attitudinal or behavioral change, they shifted their analysis to cognitive influence.

The most influential manifestation of this neopluralist paradigm was agenda setting. The origins of this approach is sometimes ascribed to McCombs and Shaw's (1972) study of the relationship between the composite definitions of the mainstream US media during the 1968 presidential election campaign and the concerns of floating voters located in five electoral precincts of Chapel Hill, North Carolina. Although this study offered persuasive provisional evidence of a media agenda-setting effect, it was by no means the first to consider this aspect. Indeed, earlier communication researchers had anticipated this cognitive turn, from Walter Lippman's interest in the 1920s in the pseudo-environments created by the media and their impact upon "the images in our heads" (1925), through Lazarsfeld's acknowledgment in his 1944 election study of the media's influence in structuring political issues (Bruhn Jensen 2002, p. 146), to Bernard Cohen's (1963) now epigrammatic statement, made in the early 1960s, that "[t]he press may not be successful much of the time in telling people what to think, but it is stunningly successful in telling its readers what to think about" (p. 13).

McCombs and Shaw's study was significant because it offered a model for research in this area and, more importantly, a label for what had been, to that point, an underdeveloped aspect. It sparked an explosion of agenda-setting studies in Europe and North America, some of which sought to integrate with uses and gratifications research, which was itself experiencing something of a renaissance during this period, in an attempt to understand the contingent conditions of agenda-setting influence (e.g. *salience of affect* and *need for orientation*). Agenda setting has remained an influential concept and research approach and has stimulated and connected with some significant new directions in communication research, for example "agenda building" (Lang and Lang 1983; Roger and Dearing 1988), "priming," and "framing" (Weaver 2007).

Although it was the most prominent aspect, agenda-setting research was just one manifestation of a cognitive shift in audience research from the 1960s onward. For example, in 1970 Tichenor, Donohue, and Olien advanced their *knowledge gap hypothesis* that posited that the increased ubiquity of information available through media outlets was increasing rather than reducing information divisions within society. Structural inequalities in cultural and economic capital lie at the root of these divisions, in that those who are most socially and educationally advantaged are best positioned to utilize the increased ubiquity of information provided by the media for personal advantage and advancement. Consequently, although media-derived knowledge gains are evident across social strata, the greater gains of the already advantaged increase the relative deprivation of the "information poor." Knowledge gap research proliferated during the 1970s and 1980s (see Gaziano 1983) and has contributed significantly to wider exploration of news learning and information processing by media audiences. See, for example, the work of Doris Graber (1988) on schema theory and the ways the media can influence the mental maps (schemata) we develop to assimilate, manage, and order new information in an information-saturated world.

Two other significant developments in audience research during this period were Gerbner et al.'s work on cultivation analysis (Gerbner and Gross 1977; Gerbner et al. 1978, 1979) and Noelle-Neumann's spiral of silence theory (1974, 1984). The core hypothesis of cultivation analysis is that entrenched and enduring patterns in television representations have a mainstreaming effect on people's perceptions of the world (particularly those who watch television most intensively) – cultivating, but not creating, conservative belief systems that cater to the interests of commercial, political, and social elites. The spiral of silence theory also addresses the conservative ideological effects of media coverage, examining how people's intrinsic fear of isolation and propensity to identify with prevailing opinion can make them accept the dominant definitions of social consensus offered in mainstream media coverage (Noelle-Neumann 1974, 1984). Both of these theories of media influence share an interest in cognitive effects, but are distinguished by their emphasis upon their longer term, accretive manifestations.

It would be mistaken to assume there was complete theoretical coherence and empirical consistency within this neopluralist paradigm, even within its component aspects. For example, writing in the 1980s, Denis McQuail (1987) judged that, for all the research endeavor, "agenda-setting" remained "a plausible but unproven idea" (p. 276), and Oscar Gandy argued that the profusion of micro studies in agenda setting threatened to lead the paradigm into an empiricist cul-de-sac (1982). In a similar vein, and at a similar time, Gaziano's review of knowledge gap studies found conceptual and empirical discrepancies (1983). Nevertheless, the broad complementarity in the concerns of these theories and studies, and their historical convergence, played a significant role in revitalizing what had previously been seen as an increasingly moribund research field.

Three points are of relevance to our review of quantitative audience research. First, all of these new wave of studies used quantitative research methods extensively, sometimes exclusively (particularly survey research). Second, despite their reliance on methods deemed by some as an anathema to "serious sociological enterprise," the theoretical concerns and empirical findings of this neopluralist paradigm were remarkably cognate with many of the issues foregrounded by critical researchers during the same period. For example, Justin Lewis (1997) points out that agenda setting's focus on reality construction helpfully shifted attention from "the more overly ideological discourse of attitudes and opinions" toward "deep ideological structures – the social encyclopaedia of common knowledge" (p. 93). Additionally, several of these new approaches engaged with questions of longer term influence. In the opinion of Elihu Katz, cultivation analysis "brilliantly" inferred "a long term effect from a short-run methodology" (2008 p. xix), and in Lewis's judgment it "remains the only comprehensive body of research to have systematically demonstrated that television plays a clearly defined hegemonic role in contemporary society" (p. 93). [7] Third, this paradigm did not just continue traditions of quantitative audience research – for many years, it was the principal location for audience research per se, as most critical researchers switched their attention towards deconstructing the complexities of cultural texts or the political economic conditions that circumscribed their creation.

A Strange Twist ...

This near monopoly of pluralist audience research did not remain unchallenged. By the early 1980s, a significant reengagement with audience research gained momentum from within cultural studies. There were distinct but related phases to this new approach (see Morley 1998; Alasuutari 1999). In the first wave, analysis focused principally upon the complex ways that media audiences decoded media texts. In the second, attention was directed to the social locations, functions, and uses of the media which purported to show that "the social worlds of the audience encompass far more than their continuing efforts, as a dominated class or situated subjects, to decode the messages sent to them by the mass media" (Jensen and Pauly 1998). Both phases emphasized the agency and creativity of media audiences, and some working within this frame, influenced by new developments in post-structuralist and postmodernist theory, began to argue that previous assumptions about the ideological power of texts were misguided and that audience research should recognize that it is the media consumers who are the most powerful producers of meaning and pleasures.

Not all working within this paradigm are euphoric celebrants of the semiotic autonomy of the media consumer and the inherent democratic nature of her symbolic world. James Curran (1990) acknowledges that some of these studies take care "to situate cultural consumption in the broader context of social struggle" (p. 153), and Justin Lewis (1999) notes that several of the classic reception analyses of this period contain insights into the limits of audience resistance as well as its extent. Nevertheless, Brigitte Höijer (2008) identifies a profound "situationalism" shared by many of these studies which demonstrates "[a]n underlying ontological assumption ... that social life is extremely plural, shifting and unpredictable; it varies and changes from situation to situation and moment to moment" (p. 282). The obvious implication of this situationalism is an adamant and absolute rejection of quantitative research methods. For example, Ien Ang (1991) has claimed,

> The situational embeddedness of audience practices and experiences inevitably undercuts the search for generalizations that is often seen as the ultimate goal of scientific knowledge. In a sense, generalizations are necessarily violations to the concrete specificity of all unique micro-situations. (p. 164, quoted in Höijer 2008)

The methodological purism that inevitably follows from this ontological position is demonstrated by the enthusiasm with which many of these new audience studies label their work as *ethnographic*. These claims have not gone unchallenged.

For example, Virginia Nightingale (1989) notes that the term is used carelessly as a badge of allegiance to indicate a particular style of analysis that is "cultural, community-based, empirical and phenomenal" (p. 56). Graham Murdock (1989) argues that many self-styled audience ethnographies actually provide rather "thin descriptions" of the social and psychological dynamics of reception that come nowhere near the ideal of the "thick descriptions" outlined by Clifford Geertz in his classic exposition of ethnographic methods (see Geertz 1972). In our view, a further concern about the free and imprecise invocation of the term *ethnography* is its rhetorical function in perpetuating and extending the doctrinal "othering" of quantitative methods in audience research.

However, controversies about the methodological preferences and pretences of this paradigm pale by comparison to the disputes created by the wider conclusions that were sometimes drawn about the relative distribution of power within the circuit of mass communication. Indeed, these disagreements drove a considerable wedge between the sociological and culturalist components of the radical paradigm. For, whereas in the 1970s the major points of tension related to classic materialist-idealist arguments about the significance and determinants of ideological power, from the mid- to late 1980s the disputes transformed into whether questions of hegemony and ideology retained any validity whatsoever.

Those who expound the semiotic democracy of media consumption have been attacked for their "sociological quietism" (Corner 1991), for jettisoning "power as a central concept" (Barker and Beezer 1991), and for their "cultural compliance" in celebrating rather than critiquing capitalist culture (Philo and Miller 1997; see also Gitlin 1978; Murdock 1989). In an influential and trenchant critique, James Curran attacked two aspects of the most optimistic articulations of active audience theory. First, he held that there is little in this work that has not already been established by the earliest effects research. Citing examples from several pioneering studies of the 1940s and 1950s, he showed the effects tradition had already amply demonstrated "the multiple meanings generated by texts, the active and creative role of audiences and the ways in which different social and discourse positions encourage different readings" (1990, pp. 149–150). Second, he argued that aspects of the new audience paradigm replicated the failings of the original effects paradigm by neglecting questions of cognitive influence. In his judgment, "By a curious irony, revisionist celebrants of semiotic democracy are thus moving towards a position that pluralists are abandoning ... they are reverting to the discredited received wisdom of the past" (1990, p. 153).

With respect to our discussion here, Curran's first observation has considerable significance as it provides a convincing challenge to the situationalism and methodological purism so readily accepted by many reception analysts and audience "ethnographers." For, here again, one can see remarkable congruity between pluralist and radical perspectives, but, unlike the compatibility evident in neopluralist and radical perspectives in the 1970s we noted earlier, this emerged from two historically distinct, and supposedly antithetical, traditions of *primary audience research*.

Conclusion: The Compatibility Thesis

This chapter has examined the history of quantitative audience research and its complex interrelationship with more radical, interpretative trajectories. In this review, we have said little about the limitations of quantitative methods, and we are concerned that our failure to do so should not be taken as evidence of our belief that quantification represents a preferable or superior mode of analysis. This is not the case, as we reject epistemic prioritization of any kind. We accept that quantitative methods lack flexibility and are not suited to intensive analysis of audiences and their worlds *on their own terms*. We agree that excessive concern with establishing causality can lead to inappropriate media centrism and an artificial decontextualization of media use and consumption. (Although it is worth noting in passing that, while critical communication scholars are well schooled about the artificiality and asociality of laboratory experiments, and the way their demand characteristics may affect the processes they are analyzing, far less attention has been given to the impact these same processes may have on focus group interviews.)

However, awareness of the deficiencies of quantitative methods needs to be balanced by appreciation of their strengths. Losses of depth are compensated by gains in range, difficulties in dealing with particularities are compensated by more robust and convincing grounds for comparison and extrapolation, and so on. It follows from this that there are several significant gains to be made in incorporating extensive and intensive methods in audience research. Considerations of internal and external validity no longer need to be cast in either/or terms. Detailed qualitative engagement with audience beliefs and activity can continue to explore their dimensions and complexities and provide a vital corrective to overgeneralized and deterministic structural accounts of power. More extensive methods, on the other hand, provide a more robust basis for extrapolating beyond the particular, which remains a latent impulse in many qualitative studies, whatever might be said about the evils of generalization. Furthermore, quantification offers a means to identify structural patterns and inequalities in media consumption, and as such helps guard against excessive celebrations of the significance of micro agency. As Ann Oakley (1999) has noted with regard to feminist research,

> Women and other minority groups, above all, need 'quantitative' research, because without this it is difficult to distinguish between personal experience and collective oppression. Only large-scale comparative data can determine to what extent the situations of men and women are structurally differentiated. (p. 251)

We are not alone in recognizing and recommending the virtues of multimethod research in audience research (see Hansen et al. 1998; Bruhn Jensen 2001). Moreover, to do so would connect the field with a broader Zeitgeist in the humanities and social sciences. For example, the sociologist Alan Bryman has been at the forefront of debates about the reconcilability of qualitative and quantitative methods for several decades (Bryman 1988) and in a recent study examined (a) the prevalence of multimethod studies in refereed journal articles, and (b) the views of senior academics on the dangers and benefits of combining methods. On this basis he concluded that, although pockets of resistance remain,

> [T]he paradigm wars [of previous decades] have been replaced by a period of paradigm peace. In this new era, there is a tendency to stress the compatibility between quantitative and qualitative research and a pragmatic viewpoint which prioritises using any approach that allows research questions to be answered regardless of its philosophical presuppositions. (2006 p. 124)

An excellent example of the benefits of combining qualitative and quantitative methods is offered by Livingstone et al.'s research into audience reception of audience participation talk shows. In the first part of the research, textual analysis and focus groups were combined to explore the complex relations between "reader, text and context" in this genre (Livingstone and Lunt 1994). These were followed up by a large-scale sample survey of viewers of these programs (Livingstone, Wober, and Lunt 1994). The questionnaire design was informed by insights generated by the initial qualitative phase, and the survey was used to assess the general applicability and representativeness of the initial findings. Although the different methods produced many complementary insights, in some areas they generated unique insights. On the one hand, "the focus group interviews identified more complex connections between text and reception [and] identified contradictions within audience readings" (Livingstone, Wober, and Lunt 1994, p. 376). On the other hand, the self-completion questionnaire survey "highlighted what had been missed in the focus group analysis, namely, the importance of viewers' age compared to, say, gender or social class" (p. 376).

Despite examples such as these, the incompatibility thesis (Howe 1988, p. 10) retains considerable currency within the field, in which qualitative and quantitative methods are assumed to ontologically and epistemologically irreconcilable. Our challenge to this position is to request evidence as to where and how these presumed divisions have produced profoundly and consistently discrepant conclusions about the nature of media audiences and their media reception and use. The historical review provided in this chapter shows areas of remarkable consanguinity in qualitative and quantitative research conclusions and that there is no evidence that methodological choices have an a priori effect upon the kind of conclusion one might reach about media influence or audience activity. It was quantitative audience research, for all its supposed crudity and reductionism, that first discovered the "active audience," the contingent conditions of reception, and the significance of social location and relations in viewing practices. Quantitative methods have also played a significant role in charting the limits to audience power; indeed, for many years they offered the only source of empirical grist to the mill of ideological and cultural critique.

The unavoidable conclusion is that assessment about audience agency and media influence are not decided by methodological choice but by the different theoretical frameworks, implicit or otherwise, that inform research design, implementation, and interpretation. This is the level where discussion, evaluation, and critique should be focused. The failure to acknowledge and exploit the potential of quantitative methods in communication and cultural studies needs to be remedied. Simple histories need to be discarded. It is time to embrace the poor relation.

Notes

1   The Payne Studies were criticized subsequently on research design grounds, for example in relation to their sampling deficiencies, problems in measurement, and lack of control groups (Lowery and DeFleur, 1995, p. 382).
2   The credit for being the foundational uses and gratifications study was Hadley Cantril's study of the panic that ensued in the United States after Orson Welles's radio dramatization of H. G. Welles's *War of the Worlds* (Cantril, Gaudet, and Herzog 1940). This research was conducted at the Office of Radio Research, Princeton University, which was established in the mid-1930s with Paul F. Lazarsfeld as director, and Frank Stanton and Hadley Cantril as associate directors. Lazarsfeld moved the Radio Bureau to Columbia in 1940, following personal and professional conflicts with Cantril.
3   Interestingly, one can find connections between this aspect of Lazarsfeld's work, and the arguments of some cultural studies theorists who argue the need for a closer relationship between academic research and its policy application are evident within the field of cultural studies (e.g. Bennett 1992; McRobbie 1996).
4   Neither were Lazarsfeld and his colleagues entirely sanguine about the limited influence of media in society. See, for example, Lazarsfeld and Merton's concerns about the "narcoticising dysfunction" of the media, in which they speculated that the constant bombardment of news, information, and entertainment colonizes and deenergizes the life worlds of the audience (Lazarsfeld and Merton 1948).
5   Experiments were not presented as the only mode of investigation into communication, as Hovland et al. go as far as to say that it would be "presumptuous, of course, to expect all problems to be amenable to investigation in this fashion" and that "extensive case study analysis and opinion surveys" are also valuable (1953, p. 5).
6   For example, autobiographical accounts were collected to assess the role of movies in shaping sexual attitudes and behaviors (Jowett et al. 1996, pp. 242–280).
7   Not all commentators concur about the theoretical and empirical credibility of cultivation analysis. For a recent critical review, see Bruhn Jensen (2002, pp. 150–151).

References

Alasuutari, P. ed. 1999 *Rethinking the Media Audience: The New Agenda*. London: Sage.

Anderson, C. and Carnagey, N. 2003 Exposure to violent media: the effects of songs with violent lyrics on aggressive thoughts and feelings. *Journal of Personality and Social Psychology*, 84, 5, pp. 960–971.

Ang, I. 1991 *Desperately Seeking the Audience*. Routledge, London.

Barker, M. and Beezer, A. 1992 Introduction. In M. Barker and A. Beezer, eds. *Reading into Cultural Studies*. Sage, London.

Bennett, T. 1992 Putting policy in cultural studies. In L. Grossberg, C. Nelson and P. Treichler, eds. *Cultural Studies*. Routledge, New York.

Berelson, B. 1959 The state of communication research. *Public Opinion Quarterly*. 23, 1, pp. 1–6.

Boudon, R. 1972 An introduction to Lazarsfeld's philosophical papers. In P. Lazarsfeld, ed. *Qualitative Analysis: Historical and Critical Essays*. Allyn & Bacon, Boston.

Bruhn-Jensen, K. 2002 Media reception: quantitative traditions. In K. Bruhn-Jensen, rd. *A Handbook of Media and Communication Research: Qualitative and Quantitative Methodologies*. Routledge, Abingdon, UK.

Cantril, H., Gaudet, H. and Herzog, H. 1940 *The Invasion from Mars*. Harper & Row, New York.

Cohen, B. 1963 *The Press and Foreign Policy*. Princeton University Press, Princeton, NJ.

Corner, J. 1991 "Influence": the contested core of media research, In J. Curran and M. Gurevitch, eds. *Mass Media and Society*. Edward Arnold, London.

Coyne, S. and Nelson, D. 2008 The effects of viewing physical and relational aggression in the media: evidence for a cross-over effect. *Journal of Experimental Social Psychology*, 44, 6, pp, 1551–1554.

Curran, J. 1990 The new revisionism in mass communication research: a reappraisal. *European Journal of Communication*, 5, 2, pp. 135–164.

Deacon, D. 2008 Why counting counts. In M. Pickering, ed. *Research Methods for Cultural Studies*. Edinburgh University Press, Edinburgh.

Deacon, D., Pickering, M., Golding, P. and Murdock, G. 2008 *Researching Communications: A Practical Guide to Media and Cultural Analysis*, 2nd edn. Arnold, London.

Fischer, P., Guter, S. and Frey, D. 2008 The effects of risk-promoting media on inclinations toward risk taking. *Basic and Applied Social Psychology*, 30, 3, pp. 230–240.

Freedman, P. and Goldstein, K. 1999 Measuring media exposure and the effects of negative campaign ads. *American Journal of Political Science*, 43, 4, pp. 1189–1208.

Freeman, F. 1933 The technique used in the study of the effect of motion pictures on the care of teeth. *Journal of Educational Sociology*, 6, 5, pp. 309–311.

Gandy, O. 1982 *Beyond Agenda Setting: Information Subsidies and Public Policy*. Ablex, Norwood, NJ.

Gaziano, C. 1983 The knowledge gap: an analytical review of media effects. *Communication Research*, 10, 4, pp. 447–486.

Geertz, C. 1972 *The Interpretation of Cultures*. Basic Books, New York.

Gerbner, G. and Gross, L. 1976 Living with television: the violence profile. *Journal of Communication*, 26, pp. 173–199.

Gerbner, G., et al 1978 Cultural indicators: violence profile no. 9. *Journal of Communication*, 28, pp. 176–207.

Gerbner, G., et al. 1979 The demonstration of power: violence profile no. 10. *Journal of Communication*, 29, pp. 177–196.

Gitlin, T. 1978 Media sociology: the dominant paradigm. *Theory and Society*, 6, pp. 205–253.

Graber, D. 1988 *Processing the News: How People Tame the Information Tide*, 2nd edn. Longman, New York.

Gunter, B. 2000 *Media Research Methods*. Sage, London.

Hall, S. 1982 The rediscovery of "ideology": return of the repressed in media studies. In M. Gurevitch, T. Bennett, J. Curran and S. Woollacott, eds. *Culture, Society and the Media*. Methuen, London.

Höijer, B. 2008 Ontological assumptions and generalizations in qualitative (audience) research. *European Journal of Communication*, 23, 3, pp. 275–294.

Hovland, C.A., Janis, I.L. and Kelley, H.H. 1953 *Communication and Persuasion: Psychological Studies of Opinion Change*. Yale University Press, New Haven, CT.

Hovland, C.A., Lumsdaine, A.A. and Sheffield, R.D. 1949 *Experiments in Mass Communication*. Princeton University Press, Princeton, NJ.

Howe, K. 1988 Against the quantitative-qualitative incompatibility thesis or dogmas die hard. *Educational Researcher*, 17, 8, pp. 10–16.

Iyengar, S. et al. 1982 Experimental demonstration of the "not-so-minimal" consequences of television news programmes. *American Political Science Review*, 76. pp. 848–858.

Iyengar, S. et al. 1984 The evening news and presidential evaluations. *Journal of Personality and Social Psychology*, 66, pp. 778–787.

Jensen, J. and Pauly, J. 1998 Imaging the audience: losses and gains in cultural studies. In M. Ferguson and P. Golding, eds. *Cultural Studies in Question*. Sage, London.

Jowett, G., Jarvie, I. and Fuller, K. 1996 *Children and the Movies: Media Influence and the Payne Fund Controversy*. Cambridge University Press, Cambridge.

Katz, E. 2008 Foreword. In M. Baily, ed. *Narrating Media History*. Routledge, London.

Klapper, J. 1960 *The Effects of Mass Communication*. Free Press, New York.

Lang, G. and Lang, K. 1983 *The Battle for Public Opinion: The President, the Press and the Polls during Watergate*. Columbia University Press, New York.

Lazarsfeld, P. 1941 Remarks on administrative and critical communications research. *Studies in Philosophy and Social Science*, 9, 1, pp. 2–16.

Lazarsfeld, P., Berelson, B. and Gaudet, H. 1944 *The People's Choice*. Columbia University Press, New York.

Lewis, J. 1997 What counts in cultural studies. *Media, Culture and Society*, 19, 1, pp. 83–97.

Lewis, J. 1999 Reproducing political hegemony in the United States. *Critical Studies in Mass Communication*, 16, pp. 251–267.

Lippmann, W. 1925 *The Phantom Public*. Harcourt, Brace, New York.

Livingstone, S. and Lunt, P. 1994 *Talk on Television: Audience Participation and Public Debate*. Routledge, London.

Livingstone, S., Wober, B. and Lunt, P. 1994 Studio audience discussion programmes: an analysis of viewers' preferences and involvement. *European Journal of Communication* 9, 4, pp. 355–380.

Lowery, S. and DeFleur M. 1995 *Milestones in Mass Communication Research: Media Effects*, 3rd edn. Longman, New York.

McCombs, M. and Shaw, D. 1972 The agenda-setting function of mass media. *Public Opinion Quarterly*, 36, pp. 176–185.

McQuail, D. 1987 *Mass Communication Theory*. Sage, London.

Morley, D. 1998 So-called cultural studies: dead-ends and reinvented wheels. *Cultural Studies*, 12, 4, pp. 476–497.

Morrison, D. E. 1998 *The Search for a Method: Focus Groups and the Development of Mass Communication Research*. University of Luton Press, Luton.

Murdock, G. 1989 Critical enquiry and audience activity. In B. Dervin, L. Grossberg, B.J. O'Keefe and E. Wartella, eds. *Rethinking Communications: Vol. 2. Paradigms and Exemplars*. Sage, London.

Nightingale, V. 1989 What's "ethnographic" about ethnographic audience research? *Australian Journal of Communication*, 16, pp. 50–63.

Noelle-Neumann, E. 1974 The spiral of silence: a theory of public opinion. *Journal of Communication*, 24, pp. 43–51.

Noelle-Neumann, E. 1984 *The Spiral of Silence: Public Opinion – Our Social Skin*. University of Chicago Press, Chicago.

Oakley, A. 1998 Experimentation and social interventions: a forgotten but important history. *British Medical Journal* 317, pp. 1239–1242.

Oakley, A. 1999 Paradigm wars: some thoughts on a personal and public trajectory. *International Journal of Social Research Methodology* 2, 3, pp. 247–254.

Philo, G. and Miller, D. 1997 *Cultural Compliance: Dead Ends of Media/Cultural Studies and Social Science*. Glasgow Media Group, Glasgow University, Scotland.

Rex, J. 1973 *Discovering Sociology: Studies in Sociological Theory and Method*. Routledge & Kegan Paul, London.

Ridout, T., Grosse, A. and Appleton, A. 2008 News media use and Americans' perceptions of global threat. *British Journal of Political Science*, 38, pp. 575–593.

Roger, E.M. and Dearing, J. 1988 Agenda-setting research: where has it been, where is it going? In J. Anderson, ed. *Communication Yearbook 11*. Sage, Newbury Park, CA.

Ruckmick, C. 1932 How do motion pictures effect the attitudes and emotions of children? *Journal of Educational Sociology* 6, 4, pp. 210–216.

Tichenor, P., Donohue, G. and Olien, C. 1970 Mass media flow and differential growth of knowledge'. *Public Opinion Quarterly*, 34, pp. 159–170.

Weaver, D. 2007 Thoughts on agenda setting, framing and priming. *Journal of Communication*, 57, 1, pp. 142–147.

Wimmer, R.D. and Dominick, J.R. 1991 *Mass Media Research: An Introduction*. Wadsworth, Belmont, CA.

16

Media Effects in Context

Brian O'Neill

Introduction

The media effects tradition occupies a hugely influential and dominant role within mainstream communications research. It is unquestionably the longest running tradition within the field of audience studies, spanning nearly its entire history, yet it continues to divide opinion, both methodologically and with regard to its fundamental approach toward the study of media audiences. Its influence extends well beyond the academy, and the powerful influence exerted by its research agenda on public and political understanding of the impact of media is perhaps one of its most significant achievements. The body of research is also voluminous and beyond the scope of any one review for a serious critical appraisal. The media effects research tradition has been extensively reviewed in the literature, and a number of excellent surveys of the field exist (McQuail 1983; Livingstone 1996; McDonald 2004). Accordingly, this chapter confines itself to a contextual discussion of effects research from the point of view of the audience researcher, exploring the diversity of the tradition, and assessing its contribution to an understanding of audience engagement and media–audience relationships.

The entire study of mass communication, according to McQuail (1983), is based on the premise that there are effects from "the media," though what precisely these effects are and the means by which they can be identified and measured has been the subject of extensive debate (p. 175). The foundational position given to the study of effects is present in Lasswell's famous formulation of communications as the study of "Who says what to whom in which channel and to what *effect*?" (Lasswell 1948, emphasis in original). Katz (1980) characterized the history of communications theory as an oscillation between active and passive audiences, between minimal or powerful effects. Later, Lowery and DeFleur (1995) proposed the preeminent

The Handbook of Media Audiences, First Edition. Edited by Virginia Nightingale.
© 2014 John Wiley & Sons, Ltd. Published 2014 by John Wiley & Sons, Ltd.

question of communications research as "What do mass communications actually do to us, both individually and collectively?" Their landmark collection, *Milestones in Mass Communication Research: Media Effects*, maps the development of research from the 1920s on, consolidating a tradition and delineating its key historical parameters. At the same time, effects research findings are frequently contested in quite fundamental ways. For long disparagingly referred to as the "dominant paradigm" (Gitlin 1978), its methods and hypotheses have been subject to extensive critique (Gauntlett 1998; Barker and Petley 2001), and as a tradition it is often associated with a narrow and conservative approach to communications research.

This chapter approaches the subject of effects research somewhat differently. It argues that knowledge of the effects research tradition is important for audience researchers for two main reasons. First, effects research provides a valuable insight into the historical development of central research questions about audiences and media in a way not afforded by any other branch of communications study. As various surveys of the field attest, the history of effects research coincides to a great extent with the history of the discipline of mass communication and media theory, in particular as it became institutionalized in North America (Schramm 1997). As such, the history of media effects research is important not only for the fact that it consists of an extraordinary range of empirical and theoretical output on all dimensions of media–audience relations, but also because it constitutes a social history of thinking about the media and their impact on society from the early twentieth century to the present. For all audience researchers, such knowledge is indispensable to formulating a historically informed approach to media development and audience engagement. A second reason for supporting a wider understanding of the effects tradition is that it provides an insight into how media research and its dissemination can be socially relevant and meaningful. Again, irrespective of the research approach involved, greater accessibility to and public applicability of research findings are centrally important to the research endeavor as a whole. The following discussion, therefore, places the ongoing relevance of effects research in the context of public discourses – popular, political, or policy oriented – concerning the pervasive impact of media in everyday social processes. This is illustrated through a discussion of thematic issues in media effects research, principally the rise of new media forms and their impact on distinct audience groups such as children and young people. Media effects play a crucial role in emerging debates concerning media literacy and regulation of the new media environment, and in this context audience researchers need to be attuned to the methodological limits and possibilities of new knowledge creation in this tradition.

Effects Research in Historical Context

Effects research is itself a shorthand for research consisting predominantly of quantitative empirical investigation of measurable behavioral attributes, usually conducted on a large scale, and based on methodological approaches drawn from the physical sciences. Yet, effects studies have also come to characterize an entire domain of communication research which is resolutely empirical, broadly quantitative in nature, interdisciplinary, and with a "conspicuous absence of theory" (Bryant and Cummins 2007, p. 2). Its combined output over some 70 years of communication scholarship has been widely represented in the form of a historical narrative of the evolution of the discipline as a whole.

The received history

Historical perspectives on the foundation and development of communications research have become an important feature of the literature of effects studies, ranging from the "natural history" of media effects research (McQuail 1983) to the "founding fathers" mythology (Berelson 1959; Schramm 1997), the "milestones" in the development of the discipline (Lowery and DeFleur 1995), and the more historiographic enquiry in Dennis and Wartella (1996). To some extent, this debate has been confined to the United States and to scholarly discussion within journals and communication departments in North American institutions, where questions of curriculum and disciplinary boundary division have been to the fore. It is also, however, despite its often exclusively American frame of reference, a profoundly international issue given the nature of communication research and the global reach of the methodological and theoretical issues involved.

The outlines of this received history typically describe the effects tradition as falling into three distinct historical phases, each coinciding with significant periods of development in mass media communication and representing a paradigm shift in media–audience relations. The first phase, in the decades following World War I, was the period of perceived powerful media effects illustrated through the widespread use of propaganda in mass society, increasingly sophisticated forms of advertising and public relations, and concern about the lowering of cultural standards through cheapened forms of mass cultural production. The second phase is marked by the beginnings of more formal, scientific investigation of media audiences and by the establishment of noted university-based research centers. It articulates a view of "limited" or "minimal" effects in that fears of brainwashing were seen to be exaggerated, and opinion formation was a complex social process in which the media played a constitutive but not determining role (Klapper 1960). A third phase from the 1960s on marks a return to a concept of more powerful mass media and continues to the present, dealing with issues of the effects of media violence, functions of the media in socialization, diffusion, and ideological formation (McQuail 1983, p. 178). As Carey and others have noted (Rowland 1982; Carey 1996, p. 24), while there is some truth in the above narratives as a standard history, it is also misleading in a number of important ways, excluding some elements from the narrative. The following discussion, however, focuses less on the completeness of the narrative than on the emergent thinking about the nature of audience experience and how it might be studied.

Powerful media effects

Early thinking about the impact of mass media on society is represented in the conventional history by the prevailing view of powerful media exercising direct, immediate, and powerful effects upon relatively powerless and passive audiences. Variously described as the *magic bullet*, *stimulus–response*, or *hypodermic needle* model of media effects, it assumed the mass media were so powerful that they could "inject" their messages into the audience, or that advertising messages could be precisely targeted at audiences like a magic bullet. While the accuracy of this representation is disputed (Dennis and Wartella 1996, p. 169), it is widely understood that the then "new" mass media of communication were seen to have extraordinary powers of persuasion and ideological control on seemingly passive and powerless audiences. Katz and Lazarsfeld (1955) described this first phase as follows:

> The image of the mass communication process entertained by researchers had been, firstly, one of 'atomistic mass' of millions of readers, listeners and movie-goers, prepared to receive the message; and secondly … every Message was conceived of as a direct and powerful stimulus to action which would elicit immediate response. (p. 16)

The "powerful media" effects approach was supported conceptually by mass society theory, imputing the rise of alienating social structures to large-scale industrialization, the division of labor, urbanization, the centralization of decision making, and the growth of mass political movements all supported by the rise of sophisticated communications systems (DeFleur and Ball-Rokeach 1982). In a similar vein, the Frankfurt school critique of the culture industry – Adorno's excoriating critiques of popular music, for instance – portrayed audiences as helpless dupes of industrialized cultural production designed to engender passivity and compliance to a repressive economic regime (Adorno 2001).

The effects of propaganda as studied by the political scientist Harold Lasswell, to whom the hypodermic needle model of media influence is attributed, are a pivotal element of the powerful media effects paradigm. Lasswell's (1971) study of propaganda techniques during the First World War provided some of the first modern scientific research on mass persuasion, a central feature of which was the manipulation of a symbol's multiple associations to produce desired effects, whether "to mobilize hatred against the enemy, to preserve the friendship of allies, to preserve the friendship and, if possible, to procure the co-operation of neutrals and to demoralize the enemy" (p. 195). The study of propaganda therefore became an investigation of these manipulation efforts. Mass persuasion and the use of psychological, stimulus–response techniques in communication coincided likewise with the rise of advertising as an industry and modern public relations techniques. Mass communication techniques of the interwar period, whether it was the use of radio and mass media during the Nazi era, Lenin's use of film as a promotional tool following the Bolshevik Revolution, or the use of propaganda techniques to educate the public for democracy as advocated by John Grierson, stemmed from the belief that mass media had an overwhelming influence on behavioral and attitudinal change. Lasswell's account of the "garrison state," an imagined future where skilled communicators manipulating information would be immensely powerful, was a further expression of this vision. Conceived again during the dark era of World War II, he argued that experts in technology and symbolic manipulation would in the future be key elements of the apparatus of state-sponsored violence. Accordingly, the role of communication and political science is to identify policy that will avoid the least desirable features of elite-ruled states (Schramm 1997, p. 38).

While claims for powerful media effects were rarely substantiated by empirical research, a number of studies did emerge to test the approach. The now infamous 1938 broadcast of H. G. Wells's *The War of the Worlds* and the attending audience panic stand as the iconic example of the "powerful media" paradigm. Hadley Cantril, a psychologist then based at Princeton University, used the opportunity to conduct an investigation of the "mass panic" experienced during and after the broadcast. In collecting audience accounts in the immediate aftermath, he sought to place the events of that night into the context of the larger political and social upheavals of the times (Cantril 1940). While the scale of the panic is known to have been exaggerated (Heyer 2005), Cantril was interested in exploring the variability of listeners' experiences, factors that may have inhibited critical ability for some, and the contradictory accounts, pointing toward how the same information heard by individual listeners was processed in very different ways. Cantril's (1940) claim was that neither educational level nor the circumstances in which the broadcast was heard were sufficient to explain the susceptibility to suggestion or the different "standards of judgement" displayed by individuals (p. 68). Rather, he argued that a combination of psychological personality traits – self-confidence, fatalism, or deep religious belief – predisposed individuals to uncritically believe what they were hearing.

Cantril and Allport's earlier study, *The Psychology of Radio*, published in 1935, was one of the first comprehensive treatments of radio and its effects. Describing the new "mental world" created by radio, a medium that in less than a generation had come to dominate popular entertainment, they developed a systematic behavioral study of radio listening in response to growing concerns about its influence. The most important questions of radio listening, they argued were psychological ones: why do people like to listen for hours on end, what do they like to hear, how much do they understand, what is the most effective way to persuade listeners, and are listeners influenced more by what they hear, what they read, or what they see on the screen? The clear assumption was that radio had effects. As a medium of communication, "It was pre-eminent as a means of social control and epochal in its influence on the mental horizons of men" (p. vii). Yet, at the same time, they argued, the purpose of research should be a guide to better regulation and control to ensure radio achieved its greatest social usefulness.

Concern about the negative effects of powerful new media was also expressed in a series of studies about the rise of cinema as a form of mass entertainment. The so-called Payne Fund Studies, conducted between 1928 and 1933, adopting a similar social psychological approach, consisted of a series of studies of potential effects of motion pictures, particularly on children. Identifying patterns of learned behavior, researchers documented effects including imitation of both positive and negative role models, and the association of high cinema attendance with what were perceived as declining morals and delinquent behavior. Concluding that there was no simple cause-and-effect relationship, the research pointed toward a reciprocal relationship in that high-attendance cinema was thought to have negative effects, though those attracted were also predisposed by virtue of existing social problems. Despite methodological and theoretical shortcomings, the significance of such research was one of documenting a process of learning that takes place in media consumption and that what is learned has an impact on people's lives (McDonald 2004, p. 186).

Studies from the era of the powerful effects paradigm retain an intrinsic interest as a social history of thinking about the then "new media" in a social context. Why the media were accorded such powerful and persuasive influence in this particular historical juncture has been explained in a number of different ways. For one, the rise of new media systems, including the press, radio broadcasting, and cinema, applied new technologies and techniques to reach mass audiences on an unprecedented scale (Gurevitch and Bennett 1990, p. 12). Second, it was also the case that the social context in which mass communications technologies flourished was one of significant upheaval, extensive urbanization, and industrialization in which individuals appeared to be less rooted and more open to manipulation and persuasion. Media effects studies, more generally then, particularly in this North American context, can be seen to reflect a broader consideration of the impact of mass communication systems on the polity and political landscape of early twentieth century society. A diverse range of theorists such as Cooley, Lippman, Dewey, and Lasswell, all associated with pioneering political and social thought in the immediate postwar period of the 1920s, were concerned with the function and impact of communications in democracy and how new communications systems were becoming increasingly constitutive of social and political life. Walter Lippmann's highly influential *Public Opinion* (1922), for instance, raised concern about the dangers arising from the "manufacture of consent" through mass communication and journalistic processes of selection and interpretation, and yet believed the art of persuasion that depended on powerful media influence was necessary to a functioning democracy. Drawing on his insights about propaganda techniques, Lasswell (1971) and other researchers were convinced that communications research required the rigor and discipline of scientific behavioristic models:

> Modern public opinion and communications research developed in response to a
> remarkable convergence of favorable conditions. The social sciences were in a spasm

of inferiority when they compared themselves with their brothers, sisters, and cousins in the physical and biological sciences. Many of the leading figures were convinced that, unless the specialists on society were able to 'quantify' their propositions, they were doomed to the permanent status of second class citizens in the universe of secular knowledge. (Quoted in Schramm 1997, p. 28)

While powerful, direct, and unmediated effects of the kind assumed in this first conceptual formation are often exaggerated, at least in their historical retelling, an important emphasis which is clearly consolidated in the effects paradigm as a whole is the emphasis on message-based studies, that is, an approach which moves from analysis of the content of messages to their effects on audiences. This is an approach which Morley (1992) later contrasted with audience-based studies that focus on the "social characteristics, environment and, subsequently, needs which audiences derived from, or brought to the message" (p. 62). The tension between these approaches becomes apparent in the next phase of effects research.

Limited effects

Against the view that powerful media induce effects on unsuspecting audience members, research in the second phase of communications research lent support for a much more nuanced model of influence, the so-called *limited effects* or *indirect effects paradigm* that dominated research from the 1940s to the 1960s. Klapper (1960), summarizing the limited effects position and claiming that media influence had hitherto been exaggerated, argued, "Mass communication ordinarily does not serve as a necessary and sufficient cause of audience effects, but rather functions among and through a nexus of mediating factors and influences" through interpersonal communication, social context, and influence of opinion leaders (quoted in Perse 2001, p. 25). The central contribution to the development of the limited effects perspective was the work of Paul Lazarsfeld at the Bureau for Applied Social Research at Columbia University, encompassing groundbreaking studies into patterns of radio listening and subsequently media influence in election campaigns, culminating in Katz and Lazarsfeld's landmark *Personal Influence* (1955).

Lazarsfeld is a towering figure in the history of communications research, bridging the European roots of social research with experience of North American media systems. His organizational influence contributed to the consolidation of academy-based research on institutional and media audiences processes (Cole 2004). His legacy is an extraordinary one: he occupies a pivotal position in the development of industry techniques of research, whilst influencing the inclusion of industry and government interests in the audience research agenda (Rowland 1982, p. 392). A Rockefeller Foundation grant in 1937 initiated the first of a series of large-scale studies of the social effects of radio, examining audiences, radio programming, and preferences of radio listeners, the purpose of which was to study "what radio means in the lives of the listeners." Research methods employed included secondary data analysis, content analysis, and use of the Lazarsfeld-Stanton Program Analyzer, the device developed with Frank Stanton of CBS for recording the instantaneous likes and dislikes of "experimental" audiences. Subsequent large-scale studies of the effects of newspapers, magazines, radio, and motion pictures on society effectively created the field of mass communications research, and focused detailed attention on why messages are introduced into the media and why people attend to them – that is, what gratifications or rewards people get from the media and what functions the media serve in their lives. Among Lazarsfeld's major accomplishments and contributions to the field were the use of sophisticated survey techniques in audience research, at a time when no formal recording of listening was being undertaken, and extending the reach of the "opinion poll" to include measurement of the impact of radio upon attitudes. Further, the extensive range of social topics and issues studied – including audience reports and campaign studies – set the agenda for a whole generation of communications scholars in the postwar period.

This social research oriented approach stands in contrast to a different tradition centered on the social psychology of Carl Hovland, whose experimental approach to studying media effects became an alternative reference point for the discipline. Hovland's study of the effects of social communication on attitudes, beliefs, and concepts, initially at the US War Department and subsequently at Yale University, laid the foundation for numerous studies of persuasion and communication effectiveness. Between 1942 and 1945, Hovland studied the effectiveness of military training films and information programs, and especially audience resistance to persuasive communications and methods of overcoming it. This work formed the basis of his influential *Experiments on Mass Communication* (Hovland, Lumsdaine, and Sheffield 1949). Through controlled field experiments, they assessed differences between channels of communication and sought to generalize effects across media, including motion pictures, radio, and newspapers. A widely cited experiment on opinion change tested the effects of a one-sided versus a two-sided presentation of a controversial issue. The results contradicted contentions of totalitarian propagandists who claimed that a communication that presents only one side of the issue will generally be more successful than one that mentions the opposing side of the argument. Following World War II, Hovland developed his research on attitudes further by exploring their capacity to influence the effectiveness of persuasive communication, selecting issues such as the influence or "sleeper effect" of the communicator's prestige and the ways prestige effects disappear over time (Hovland, Janis, and Kelley 1953).

However, it was Katz and Lazarsfeld's *Personal Influence* (1955) that did most to introduce and consolidate the new paradigm of "limited" media effects. Reappraising its significance some 50 years later, Simonson (2006) writes,

> *Personal Influence* was perhaps the most influential book in mass communication research of the postwar era, and it remains a signal text with historic significance and ongoing reverberations … more than any other single work, it solidified what came to be known as the dominant paradigm in the field. (p. 6)

This field study of media influence in the midwestern community of Decatur, Illinois, questioned the ability of radio and print media to directly influence important political or consumer decisions and argued that the media had in fact limited persuasive power. What little influence media did possess operated through leaders in the community, who, in turn, influenced their followers. Katz and Lazarsfeld proposed that media's effects are diffused through "opinion leaders" who explain and diffuse media content to others. Thus, the two-step flow theory of the media's influence arose. This was an approach that placed a new emphasis on human agency in the process of media effects. It argued that between media and audiences lay a series of intervening variables, including selectivity on the part of the audience and on the basis of preexisting opinions and preferences, as well as interpersonal and small group relations whereby messages are filtered through social networks according to social norms. The two-step flow model of communication, introduced by Katz and Lazarsfeld, claimed that the impact of the media was limited by key influencers within social networks who mediated the flow of information from media sources. The main impact of the media was thus more likely to be one of reinforcement than direct influence, and as a result a research agenda with a focus on the part played by people in the study of mass media effects was instituted.

Reflecting on this work some 50 years later, Katz commented that this research agenda supplanted the "powerful media" and "mass persuasion" concerns associated with early radio with the enduring research question of "What do people do with the media?" (Katz 2006, p. xviii), a question shared by diverse approaches to audience study, including uses and gratifications research, active audience theory, and reception studies. The "powerful media" effects paradigm, according to Katz, suggested that the audience was undifferentiated, and that reception was simultaneous and otherwise unmediated. In the limited effects model, this was replaced by an understanding that audiences are selective, that they consume media over time, and reception happens in the context of mediating social groups and networks. In this way, the study of media effects became part of a broader sociological investigation of decision making and diffusion of ideas in which the media played an integral though not dominant role. Rescuing the study of effects from a purely psychologistic approach to messages and responses, the emphasis became one of media in a societal context, raising questions of the relationship between the media system and the social system, and how media influence interacts with the persuasive power of interpersonal influence in the transmission of ideas at both the individual level of decision making and at the collective level of diffusion of ideas.

A return to powerful effects

There was a contention in the early 1960s that the field of mass communication effects research had effectively run its course and that the key contributions of Lasswell's political-historical and survey research into media effects, Lewin's studies of small group communication, and Hovland's psychological analysis of messages and their effects had solved the principal issues in effects research (Shafer 1961, p. 197). In a wide-ranging debate on the future of the field, Berelson (1959) famously predicted that the field of communications effects was "withering away" and that research would revert to more important matters of social and public welfare. For Schramm and others in the mainstream tradition, the achievement of limited effects studies was founded upon "a more realistic concept of the audience" and a revised notion of the relationship between mass and interpersonal communication (Schramm and Roberts 1971). The resulting research agenda involved programmatic studies of audiences' social knowledge alongside limited and focused research on public information campaigns, and the development of eclectic and varied modeling of the role persuasive messages play in changing people's attitudes or behaviors. This shift coincided with Merton's (1967) preference for middle-range theory over grand social theory and a generally functionalist emphasis in social research that balanced good and bad effects in a static, value-neutral way within the overall social system (Baran and Davis 2006, p. 178). Yet, the dominance enjoyed by the limited effects model stood in marked contrast to the rise of dynamic and powerful media institutions and posed obvious dilemmas for researchers and media observers. Wartella framed the dilemma as follows: "How could media researchers demonstrate the seemingly obvious power of the mass media, in the face of the equally well-demonstrated obstinate audience?" (Wartella and Middlestadt 1991, p. 209). One dimension of a more powerful media effects paradigm was represented by the work of McCombs and Shaw (1972), who, in the context of research into political communication and voting behavior, advanced their agenda-setting hypothesis of media influence. In the context of US presidential election campaigns in 1968 and 1972, they examined the role played by newspaper and broadcast journalists and editors in shaping political reality for their readers and viewers. Through the information sources available to them, audiences learn about not only a given issue in a political campaign but also, according to McCombs and Shaw, how much importance to attach to that issue based on the prominence given to it by the media. In this way, the media's re-presentation of what politicians say during an election may well set the agenda for the campaign by determining what it considers of most importance. As a central issue on research into the relationship between media and society, focusing on the cognitive rather than the behavioral aspects of media effects, agenda-setting research has maintained an important position in communications and uniquely one that has arisen from within the media specialization of journalism rather than from mainstream disciplinary fields like sociology or psychology (Lowery and DeFleur 1995, p. 288).

The return to a research agenda based on a more powerful and direct version of media effects is largely associated with the changed media environment of the 1960s, when renewed public concern about the impact of television and its apparent negative social influence arose. The rapid and widespread adoption of television in the middle part of the twentieth century was by any standards extraordinary: between 1950 and 1965, television ownership in the United States had gone from just 9 percent of homes to 92.6 percent (Perse 2001, p. 21). Television had become the dominant medium, replacing radio listening, cinema attendance, and newspapers as the most consumed and trusted medium. In this context, the question was whether selective exposure was feasible in such a television-saturated media environment. The influence of television was studied and debated on competing grounds and with contrasting approaches. For example, one of the first major studies of television in a North American context was an investigation of the impact of the new medium on the lives of children. Schramm, Lyle, and Parker's *Television in the Lives of Our Children* (1961) consisted of a series of studies from 1958 to 1960, focusing on the functions of television in the lives of children rather than its direct effects, attempting to move away from the idea of "what television does to children" toward a concept of "what children do with television." Thus, they sought to document television's role and function in children's everyday lives, examining data on how and when television was viewed, how it acted as a source of both entertainment and information, and how it provided social utility as an event in itself. Responding to widespread popular concerns about the content of television and its possible effects on children, they concluded,

> For *some* children, under *some* conditions, *some* television is harmful. For *other* children under the same conditions, or for the same children under *other* conditions it may be beneficial. For *most* children, under *most* conditions, most television is probably neither harmful nor particularly beneficial. (Schramm, Lyle, and Parker 1961, p. 13, emphasis in original)

In Lowery and DeFleur's (1995) reading of the study, the implied or implicit theory (of the middle range) was that television as a medium did not have an overly negative impact on the world of childhood, and that responsible effective parenting provided the required safe social context for television consumption (p. 263). Yet at the same time, Schramm's colleague at Stanford, the psychologist Albert Bandura, was carrying out the now classic "Bobo doll" experiments to investigate how imitation and social learning might affect aggressive behavior in children. The laboratory-based experiments suggested that children, boys in particular, were encouraged to imitate aggressive behavior by viewing role models both in real life and through television. The important question was therefore whether such role models' use of violence was depicted in terms that rewarded or punished the use of violence.

Studies of television and violence have been of central importance within the tradition of media effects. Landmark studies in the 1960s laid the foundations for ongoing empirical investigation into the wide-ranging issues of how media content impacts society in both direct and indirect ways. The deep divisions of American society during that decade and the media's reflection of a turbulent and troubled period found expression in a series of government-funded studies designed to investigate the role of the media in public affairs more generally, but especially its role in contributing to the experience of violence and disorder in everyday life (Lowery and DeFleur 1995; Ball-Rokeach 2001). The 1968–1969 Commission on the Causes and Prevention of Violence, the so-called Eisenhower Commission, contained an extensive review of research of how audiences are affected by portrayals of violence in the mass media and incorporated a detailed content analysis of mediated violence as well as surveys of public attitudes toward violence as experienced in the real world and through television. The report concluded that TV portrayals of violence had short-term effects and were "one major contributory factor which must be considered in attempts to explain the many forms of violent behavior that mark American society today" (Baker and Ball 1969, p. 375) and that, more generally, "Exposure to mass media portrayals of violence over a long period of time socializes audiences into the norms, attitudes, and values for violence contained in those portrayals" (p. 376). This, it was noted, was the first time a government inquiry had come off the fence on the media-and-violence debate and supported a view of television as a potent effects agent (Ball-Rokeach 2001, p. 11).

The Violence and the Media Task Force report laid the foundations for ongoing research and public debate throughout the 1970s interrogating television and its regulation, on the basis of the supposed long-term socialization effects of mediated representations of violence and antisocial behavior. The Task Force report was quickly followed by a further presidential commission in 1972 of a series of individual studies contained in the Surgeon General's report *Television and Social Behavior* (Comstock and Rubinstein 1972) and *Television and Growing Up* (Surgeon General 1972), with follow-up studies 10 years later (Pearl and Bouthilet 1982). Such studies brought together extensive discussion and evidence of media violence and contributed to a growing consensus among academics and policy makers on the role played by television violence in antisocial behavior. This was accompanied by further research on the effects of pornography and sexual violence in the media, leading to the conclusion that prolonged exposure to sexual violence also had undesirable effects, including "emotion desensitization to violence and its victims" (Ball-Rokeach 2001, p. 13). These research efforts culminated in calls for greater levels of media regulation in the public interest and for media institutions to intervene in positive ways to solve the social problems identified.

An overview of the social cognitive theory of mediated violence was summarized by Bandura in 1994, when he argued that audiences "acquire lasting attitudes, emotional reactions, and behavioural proclivities towards persons, places, or things that have been associated with modelled emotional experiences" (p. 75). This is not, however, a reinvention of powerful effects and passive audiences; on the contrary, embedded within contemporary approaches to the study of mediated violence or harmful content across diverse media is a shared concept of active viewing and reading in which audiences actively and consciously work to understand content (Baran and Davis 2006, p. 190). While audience activity is an ongoing and shared emphasis across diverse research traditions, in the context of models of social learning and social cognition, the research focuses on the empirical testing of effects on individual audience members and the relationship between media content and acquired behaviors and attitudes. In such relationships, the question arises as to whether the level of active cognitive engagement of audiences is sufficient to overcome the reactive and passive role induced by exceptionally powerful media influences. This sense of a return to powerful media effects is a familiar feature of some recent studies of new media, particularly those focusing on children's use of new media, gaming technologies, and the internet, many of which replicate past research designs with different media in a newer technological setting (McDonald 2004).

Children and Media Effects

Current research concerning media effects on vulnerable subjects reflects an ongoing public interest on in the impact of media and significance of emergent patterns of media consumption. It also provides an important illustration of the use of research findings in contributing to and shaping public opinion. Reflecting on the sensitive subject of violent media content, Gentile (2003) offers this summary of some 40 years of research in the field: "A clear and consistent pattern has emerged from over decades of research on the effects of media violence. It is therefore surprising that people still resist the idea that media violence has negative effects" (p. ix). Now classic texts such as Postman's *The Disappearance of Childhood* (1994) and Elkind (1998) lament the erosion of the distinction between childhood and adulthood brought about by media. Drawing on well-established patterns of effects research, evidence is marshaled to support the view that new media and ICTs – whether this means mobile phones, video games consoles, internet use, or new modes of communication through social networking – have a negative impact on family life, on health and lifestyle, and on communication, creativity, and imagination, learning, and social development. Some researchers suggest the impact of effects of new media forms such as video games should theoretically be stronger given their interactive and immersive nature (Dill and Dill 1998).

In reality, the research evidence may be more mixed (Sherry 2007), and there are many contrasting and contradictory examples in the literature on topics linking different aspects of children's lives – academic performance, independent mobility, creative expression, aggressive behavior, and so on – to media use. Barker and

Petley (2001) suggest that the claims about the "possible effects of violent content" are mischievous, while Gauntlett (1998) argues that it is a "circuitous and theoretically undernourished line of enquiry." Cumberbatch (2004) concludes that "the real puzzle is that anyone looking at the research evidence in this field could draw any conclusions about the pattern." Clearly, the role that violence plays in media entertainment and the question of why viewers are drawn to it are complex, multilayered, and need to be studied in context.

Children's emotional responses to television, video, or computer games and their effects on children's imagination comprise another important theme in effects studies. Asking whether screen-based media stimulate or constrain children's imaginative responses, their story making, and their ability to creative imaginary play worlds, Belton (2001) argues that the ubiquity and ease of access to television and screen content does have implications for the development of children's imaginative capacity by constantly demanding responses to external agendas. Others have argued, however, that new media, particularly educational applications using adventure or fantasy role-playing games, can foster imagination and encourage children's creative capacities, though the research is incomplete and inconclusive (Valkenburg and Cantor 2001).

An enduring image of the addictive or obsessive dangers posed by new media technology and its effects is that of the *otaku*, the Japanese term for the technology-obsessed "stay at home tribe," typically young males who spend most of their days and nights at home at their computers, and whose virtual, online relationships are more real to them than face-to-face ones. Building on the notion of virtual reality and cyberculture as a distinct cultural formation, the *otaku* have been described as follows:

> This subculture of kids [trading] information, trivia and corporate passwords in their bedrooms via modem while their parents downstairs think they are studying. But they have abandoned schoolwork, sometimes becoming so immersed in the world of computer networks, cracking corporate security codes and analysing algorithms that they can never come back. (Tobin 1998)

An underlying concern of effects research in relation to children's media culture, echoing much public concern, is the idea that the media act as a surrogate parent by virtue of the fact that children tend to spend more time each week with media than they do with their parents or teachers. Illustrating how children may be presented with adult images of sex, commercialism, and violence, Steyer (2003) is one of a number of recent texts aimed at educating parents about children's media experiences and the need to consider a balanced and "healthy" media diet. There is widespread concern about the large-scale commercial interests involved in the production of toys and their marketing to children. Linn (2004) likens marketing and merchandising to children to the hostile takeover of childhood, underpinned by the resources of a $15 billion global industry, a view echoed in Steinberg and Kincheloe (1997), who criticize what they call the corporate construction of childhood. Similarly, Kinder (1991) argues that the domination of the children's toy market by multinational corporations with cross-media interests represents a dangerous colonization of children, indoctrinating them in the values of consumerism and instilling an illusory sense of empowerment. The underlying theme of the widespread suspicion surrounding the children's marketing industry is that children are seen as helpless victims and that without their consent or that of their parents, the experience of childhood has been transformed into an experience of prefabricated consumerism.

Many researchers in the area of children's media have tended to reject such accounts as giving too little credit to children's critical autonomy or their ability to actively negotiate meaning with the symbolic resources of contemporary culture. Fleming (1996), for example, has argued that toys, branded and otherwise, help children make sense of their worlds and are essential to their development. Unquestionably, toys are increasingly products of a global consumer culture but, he suggests, in children's hands have the capacity to escape the stereotypes of gender and power which they sometimes apparently reproduce. Similarly, Dyson's (1997) study of children's story making using superheroes and media characters suggests that these act as a prism in which images of power and of gender are translated into the child's world, rendering it more complex but helping them deal with the contradictory pressures of growing up in a multicultural society. However, what such research does point to is the extensive nature of public engagement in the topic beyond the actual research community, and the important role that may be played by research outcomes in formulating and influencing public policy in the media environment. Seiter (1999) comments how "lay theories of media effects" play a major role in how parents negotiate and seek to maintain a particular relationship with the broader media environment, echoed by Hoover and Schofield Clark's (2004) study of families' sense of media identity and based on derived notions of media effects discourse and normative positions on contemporary media culture, ranging from the oppositional to fully integrationist.

Conclusion: The Uses of Effects Research

Despite the obvious potential for scholarly contribution to public debate, on the whole media effect researchers resist this type of engagement. A longstanding critique of the effects paradigm is that it reinforces a functionalist approach, vigorously maintaining its methodological adherence to quantitative surveying and measurement, and retaining an individualistic rather than societal focus. Effects research has always labored under the criticism of maintaining an "administrative" research agenda (Lazarsfeld 1941), reflecting the interests and power structures of the media that it purports to survey and contributing, even unwittingly, to the rational control of the media over individuals. Its concern for short-term, predictive media effects, defined and produced in accordance with the priorities of media industries, lacks, according to Gitlin's classic critique (1978), a structural perspective on the media's role in society and reduces power to discrete behavioral shifts and attitude changes. As the media become ever more pervasive in everyday life, so the dominant paradigm stresses pluralism and variability, "the recalcitrance of audiences, their resistance to media generated messages, and not their dependency, their acquiescence, their gullibility" (p. 205). Rowland's 1982 study of the US debates about media violence similarly criticized effects studies for complicity with industry interests, exonerating media of any accountability based on the assumption that their impact is always a function of the social environment, and that media merely reinforce preexisting dispositions, eschewing any form of causal explanation (p. 388). In the heyday of limited effects studies, Klapper's influential review (Klapper 1960) was, for instance, published when he was director of social research at CBS, and was used by television networks as an argument against any form of regulation (Perse 2001, p. 21). By contrast, at least within the received historical accounts, "critical" research traditions have contributed to a ferment in the field (Gerbner 1983; Nordenstreng 2004), breaking with the behavioral focus of effects studies by introducing a more critical reflection on the relations of media and power in society and how research interests served to unwittingly support the needs of industry rather than the public interest.

Additionally, the themes of media effects research circulate widely in popular discourse about media impact on society. In the context of a rapidly changing communications landscape where the impact of media on citizens is to the fore in policy discussions, research findings of the kind produced within the discipline have a value in serving an evidence-based approach to media regulation (Braman 2003). An exception is that of Elihu Katz, one of the tradition's central figures, and for whom the legitimation of academic research serving policy purposes was an important emphasis (Livingstone 1997). While Katz's first major work (Katz and Lazarsfeld 1955) laid the foundation for empirically grounded administrative research emphasizing media diffusion through interpersonal communication, it is, Livingstone claims, unfairly placed as a programmatic "administrative" block to an emerging critical perspective in communications research. On the contrary, Katz's career-long objective was to make research available in a form that is accessible and useful for the purposes of informing public debate and shaping policy from a variety of political perspectives. A consideration of this position suggests, as Livingstone argues, a need to move beyond such dualisms as active and passive viewing, or powerful effects or less powerful media, and to seek a greater convergence in audience research which synthesizes questions of effects within the "diverse kinds of power relations between media and audiences, the contexts within which the media is influential, and the relation between effects, however reconceived, and pleasure, identity, everyday practices, citizenship." (1997, p. 15).

Against a background of profound technological and social change, media effects as constituted within mainstream mass communication theory is undoubtedly undergoing substantial reorganization. Charting an evolution from mass communication theory to media theory, Chaffee and Metzger (2001) highlight the fact that audiences in new media environments are harder to identify and monitor, and effects studies, as traditionally conceived, become more problematic when audiences "are not as well assembled or accessible to researchers as they once were" (p. 371). In this context, the challenge for effects researchers will be to meet policy makers' expectations for straightforward answers with intellectually rigorous policy guidance, while remaining faithful to the real complexity of the subject and the highly varied perspectives on media influence (Livingstone 2007). This may require moving beyond the narrow disciplinary focus that has defined much of the effects tradition and relinquishing the resistance to greater levels of theoretical debate and critical engagement.

References

Adorno, T. W. 2001 *The Culture Industry*. Routledge, London.

Baker, R. K. and Ball S. J. 1969 Mass media and violence: a report to the National Commission on the Causes and Prevention of Violence. National Commission on the Causes and Prevention of Violence, Washington, DC.

Ball-Rokeach, S. J. 2001 The politics of studying media violence: reflections 30 years after the violence commission. *Mass Communication and Society*, 4, 1, pp. 3–18.

Bandura, A. 1994 Social cognitive theory of mass communication. In J. Bryant and D. Zillman eds. *Media Effects: Advances in Theory and Research*. Lawrence Erlbaum,Hillsdale, NJ.

Baran, S. J. and Davis, D. K. 2005 *Mass Communication Theory: Foundations, Ferment, and Future*, 4th edn. London, Thomson Wadsworth.

Barker, M. and J. Petley 2001 *Ill Effects: The Media Violence Debate*. Routledge, London.

Belton, T. 2001 Television and imagination: an investigation of the medium's influence on children's story-making. *Media Culture and Society* 23, 6, p. 799.

Berelson, B. 1959 The state of communication research. *Public Opinion Quarterly* 23, 1, pp. 1–6.

Braman, S. 2003 *Communication Researchers and Policy-Making*. MIT Press, Boston.

Bryant, J. and Cummins R. G. 2007 Traditions of mass media theory and research. In R. W. Preiss, B. M. Gayle, N. Burrell, M. Allen and J. Bryant, eds. *Mass Media Effects Research: Advances through Meta-analysis*. Lawrence Erlbaum, Mahwah, NJ, pp. 1–13.

Cantril, H. 1940 *The Invasion from Mars: A Study in the Psychology of Panic*. Princeton University Press, Princeton, NJ.

Cantril, H. and Allport G. W. 1935 *The Psychology of Radio*. Harper & Brothers, New York.

Carey, J. 1996 The Chicago School and mass communication research. In E. E. Dennis and E. Wartella, eds. *American Communication Research: The Remembered History*. Lawrence Erlbaum, Mahwah, NJ, , p. 21–38.

Chaffee, S. H. and Metzger, M. J. 2001 The end of mass communication? *Mass Communication and Society*, 4, 4, pp. 365–379.

Cole, J. R. 2004 Paul F. Lazarsfeld: his scholarly journey. Presented at an International Symposium in Honor of Paul Lazarsfeld, Brussels, Belgium.

Comstock, G.A.E. and Rubinstein, E.A.E. 1972 *Television and Social Behavior: Reports and Papers, Volume I: Media Content and Control* (DHEW Pub. No. HSM 72-9057). Superintendent of Documents, US Government Printing Office, 20402, Washington, DC.

Cumberbatch, G. 2004 *Video Violence – Villain or Victim? A Review of the Research Evidence concerning Media Violence and Its Effects in the Real World with Additional Reference to Video Games*. Video Standards Council, London.

DeFleur, M. L. and Ball-Rokeach S. 1982 *Theories of Mass Communication*. Longman, New York.

Dennis, E. E. and Wartella, E., eds. 1996 *American Communication Research: The Remembered History*. Lawrence Erlbaum, Mahwah, NJ.

Dill, K. E. and Dill J. C. 1998 Video game violence: a review of the empirical literature. *Aggression and Violent Behaviour*, 3, 4, pp. 407–428.

Dyson, A. H. 1997 *Writing Superheros: Contemporary Childhood, Popular Culture, and Classroom Literacy*. Teachers' College Press, New York.

Elkind, D. 1998 *Reinventing Childhood: Raising and Educating Children in a Changing World. New York*. Modern Learning Press, Rosemont, NJ.

Fleming, D. 1996 *Powerplay: Children, Toys and Popular Culture*. Manchester University Press, Manchester, UK.

Gauntlett, D. 1998 Ten things wrong with the "effects model." In R. Dickinson, R. Harindranath and O. Linné, eds. *Approaches to Audiences: A Reader*. Hodder Arnold, London.

Gentile, D. A. 2003 *Media Violence and Children: A Complete Guide for Parents and Professionals*. Praeger, London.

Gerbner, G. 1983 Ferment in the field. *Journal of Communication*, 33, p. 3.

Gitlin, T. 1978 Media sociology – the dominant paradigm. *Theory and Society*, 6, 2, pp. 205–253.

Gurevitch, M. and Bennett, T., eds. 1990 *Culture, Society and the Media*. London, Routledge.

Heyer, P. 2005 *The Medium and the Magician: Orson Welles, the Radio Years, 1934–1952*. Rowman & Littlefield, London.

Hoover, S.M. and Schofield Clark, L. 2004 *Media, Home and Family*. London, Routledge.

Hovland, C.A., Janis, I.L. and Kelley, H.H. 1953 *Communication and Persuasion: Psychological Studies of Opinion Change*. Yale University Press, New Haven, CT.

Hovland, C.A., Lumsdaine, A.A. and Sheffield, R.D. 1949 *Experiments on Mass Communication*. Princeton University Press, Princeton, NJ.

Katz, E. 1980 On conceptualising media effects. *Studies in Communication*, 1, pp. 119–141.

Katz, E. 2006 Introduction to the Transaction edition. In E. Katz and P. F. Lazarsfeld, eds. *Personal Influence: The Part Played by People in the Flow of Mass Communications*. Transaction, New Brunswick, NJ.

Katz, E. and P. F. Lazarsfeld 1955 *Personal Influence: The Part Played by People in the Flow of Mass Communications*. Free Press, New York.

Kinder, M. 1991 *Playing with Power in Movies, Television and Video Games*. University of California Press, Berkeley.

Klapper, J. 1960 *The Effects of Mass Communication*. Free Press, New York.

Lasswell, H. D. 1948 The structure and function of communication in society. In L. Bryson, ed. *The Communication of Ideas*. Harper & Brothers, New York.

Lasswell, H. D. 1971 *Propaganda Technique in World War I*. MIT Press, Boston.

Lazarsfeld, P. F. 1941 Remarks on administrative and critical communications research. *Studies in Philosophy and Science*, 9, pp. 3–16.

Linn, S. 2004 *Consuming Kids: The Hostile Takeover of Childhood*. New Press, New York.

Lippmann, W. 1922 *Public Opinion*. Harcourt, Brace, New York.

Livingstone, S. 1996 On the continuing problem of media effects. In J. Curran and M. Gurevitch, eds. *Mass Media and Society*, 2nd edn. Arnold, London.

Livingstone, S. 1997 The work of Elihu Katz: conceptualizing media effects in context. In J. Corner, P. Schlesinger and R. Silverstone, eds. *International Media Research: A Critical Survey*. Routledge, London.

Livingstone, S. 2007 Do the media harm children? *Journal of Children and Media*, 1, 1, pp. 5–14.

Lowery, S. and DeFleur, M. L. 1995 *Milestones in Mass Communication Research: Media Effects*, 3rd edn. Longman, New York.

McCombs, M.E. and Shaw, D.L. 1972 The agenda-setting function of mass media. *Public Opinion Quarterly*, 36, 2, pp. 176–187.

McDonald, D.G. 2004 Twentieth century media effects research. In J. Downing, D. McQuail, E. Wartella and P. Schlesinger, eds. *The Sage Handbook of Media Studies*. Sage, Thousand Oaks, CA, pp. 183–200.

McQuail, D. 1983 *Mass Communication Theory: An Introduction*. Sage, London.

Merton, R. K. 1967 *On Theoretical Sociology*. Free Press, New York.

Morley, D. 1992 *Television, Audiences and Cultural Studies*. Routledge, London.

Nordenstreng, K. 2004 Ferment in the field: notes on the evolution of communication studies and its disciplinary nature. *Javnost The Public*, 11, 3, pp. 5–18.

Pearl, D. and Bouthilet, L. 1982 *Television and Behavior: Ten Years of Scientific Progress and Implications for the Eighties*. National Institute of Mental Health, Washington, DC.

Perse, E. M. 2001 *Media Effects and Society*. Lawrence Erlbaum, Mahwah, NJ.

Postman, N. 1994 *The Disappearance of Childhood*. Vintage, New York.

Rowland, W. D. 1982 The symbolic uses of effects: notes on the television violence inquiries and the legitimation of mass communications research. In M. Burgoon, ed. *Communication Yearbook 5*. Transaction, London, pp. 385–404.

Schramm, W. 1997 *The Beginnings of Communication Study in America: A Personal Memoir*. Sage, Thousand Oaks, CA.

Schramm, W., Lyle J., and Parker, E. 1961 *Television in the Lives of Our Children*. Stanford University Press, Palo Alto, CA.

Schramm, W. and D. F. Roberts, eds. 1971 *The Process and Effects of Mass Communication*, rev. edn. University of Illinois Press, Urbana.

Seiter, E. 1999 *Television and New Media Audiences*. Oxford University Press, Oxford.

Shafer, R. E. 1961 Mass communication. *Review of Educational Research*, 31, 2, pp. 197–207.

Sherry, J. L. 2007 Violent video grames and aggression: why can't we find effects. In R. W. Preiss, B. M. Gayle, N. Burrell, M. Allen and J. Bryant, eds. *Mass Media Effects Research: Advances through Meta-analysis*. Lawrence Erlbaum, Mahwah, NJ,.

Simonson, P. 2006 Introduction. *Annals of the American Academy of Political and Social Science*, 608, 1, pp. 6–24.

Steinberg, S. R. and Kincheloe J. L. 1997 *Kinderculture: The Corporate Construction of Childhood*. Westview Press/Harper Collins, Oxford and Boulder, CO.

Steyer, J. P. 2003 *The Other Parent: The Inside Story of the Media's Effect on Our Children*. Atria Books, New York.

Surgeon General's Scientific Advisory Committee on Television and Social Behavior. 1972 *Television and Growing Up: The Impact of Televised Violence. Report to the Surgeon General*. US Public Health Service, Washington, DC.

Tobin, J. 1998 An American otaku (or, a boy's virtual life on the net). In J. Sefton-Green, ed. *Digital Diversions: Youth Culture in the Age of Multimedia*. UCL Press, London.

Valkenburg, P. M. and Cantor, J. 2001 The development of a child into a consumer. *Journal of Applied Developmental Psychology*, 22, 1, pp. 61–72.

Wartella, E. and Middlestadt, S. 1991 The evolution of models of mass communication and persuasion. *Health Communication*, 3, 4, pp. 205–215.

17

Cultivation Analysis and Media Violence

Andy Ruddock

Introduction

Originally developed by George Gerbner and Larry Gross (Gross 2009), cultivation analysis (CA) was a method of audience research that argued that television violence reflected the structural nature of media power. Studies conducted by Gerbner and his colleagues in the 1970s at the University of Pennsylvania found that primetime television vastly exaggerated how common violence was. This finding suggested that a person's chances of being assaulted in some way were far greater than they actually were. Using surveys that compared the beliefs and opinions of light, moderate, and heavy television viewers, Gerbner et al. (1980) argued that this hyperbole made people scared rather than aggressive, and this mainly affected political attitudes. Primetime television encouraged "first-order" judgments, where Americans who watched a lot were significantly more prone to overestimate how dangerous society was and how likely they were to experience danger. These beliefs led to "second-order" attitudes about how society should be managed. Ideologically, television violence encouraged audiences to acquiesce to the gender-, class-, and race-biased political values of US corporate culture. The act of watching "cultivated" right-of-center attitudes to society and social policy. Gerbner et al. (1980) called this effect "mainstreaming." Regardless of gender, class, race, or location, heavy viewers tended to have less trust in others and be less tolerant of difference, less supportive of civil rights, and more accepting of authoritarian governance that would protect them from a "mean world." The lesson that the world was a dangerous place was particularly directed at women, the elderly, and nonwhite audiences. However much violence there was onscreen, white, middle-aged, middle-class men were least likely to be victims (Gerbner 1996).

The Handbook of Media Audiences, First Edition. Edited by Virginia Nightingale.
© 2014 John Wiley & Sons, Ltd. Published 2014 by John Wiley & Sons, Ltd.

Media representation plays an important role in sanctioning certain forms of political violence (Emantian and Delaney 2008). For this reason, the question of what media violence "does" is one that concerns qualitative and quantitative scholars alike. In a survey on the Iraq War, Lewis, Jhally, and Morgan (1991) noted how enthusiasm for military intervention among people who watched a lot of television went hand in hand with gross underestimations of the casualties inflicted by American foreign policy; casualties that news media tend to shy away from reporting. Even fan studies recognize that many audiences live in dangerous worlds, where media's role in making these worlds more or less inhabitable is far from trivial (Gray, Harrington, and Sandvoss 2007). Given this, all audience researchers should know something about cultivation analysis. The paradigm has been a major player in methods debates, particularly the possibilities of studying cultural processes with statistics (see Lewis 1997; Ruddock 2001; Morley 2006 for the use of cultivation methods with cultural theory). Cultivation analysts have explicitly discussed the relationship between causality and influence that lies behind the difficulties faced when looking for media effects (Gerbner 1983; Potter 1993; Shanahan and Morgan 1999; Shrum 2007, 2009). They have also argued that data generated by content analysis and audience surveys have to be interpreted against the recognition that any "effects" of media violence are "caused" by many things (Gerbner 1983; Shrum 2007). Numbers, then, are not "findings" that speak for themselves. Qualitative audience researchers have identified cultivation analysis as the part of mass communications research that is most in tune with culture-based understandings of what media "do." The argument that the repetitive features of television, such as violence, probably shape how audiences understand social reality is widely accepted as compelling (Newcomb 1978; Gauntlett 2005, 2007; Morley 2006).

Cultivation analysis developed a language that productively dissects what media violence says about the politics of popular media. As scholars from a variety of backgrounds become interested in how the uses and effects of violence are entangled in its media representation (and absence), the insights of Gerbner, Gross, and those who followed remain relevant. Cultivation analysis *is* a form of critical research. It focuses on systemic media power while remaining sensitive to the importance of reviewing *why* questions about media influence are asked and how we seek answers to them. Violence was central to the paradigm's efforts to understand television's social impact beyond the confines of behavioral effects. Criticisms that cultivation analysis paid insufficient attention to what violence meant to audiences have contributed to a second generation of cultivation studies that have engaged with interpretation, audience action, and the conflicting influences of changing media environments. The status of cultivation analysis as a form of critical research can be shown by using it in combination with fan studies to investigate new forms of media violence, combining theories and methods from both fields.

What Is Cultivation Analysis?

Cultivation analysis challenged many mass communications orthodoxies. Growing political interest in television's capacity to aggravate social unrest boosted funding for media effects research in the United States during the late 1960s (Ball-Rokeach 2001). Yet many mass communications scholars submitted that any such effects were at best limited, since they were mediated by audience selection, perception, and motivation. For Gerbner (1973, 1983), this conclusion demanded a redefined notion of media power connected to the industrialization of cultural production. The key concern, for him, was the effects that followed when storytelling was out-sourced to profit-driven corporate media. Gerbner confronted the idea that media influence was directed by viewing choices. Choice meant little, Gerbner argued, since primetime television constantly traded in stories of an ultraviolent world where people needed protection, regardless of what the viewer chose to watch (1983). Gerbner likened television to a Trojan horse which wrapped insidious ide-ologies in the guise of simple entertainment, then smuggled them in to audience consciousness. He tried the same trick, using behaviorist anxieties to sneak a nuanced political argument into the debate on what violence did (Shanahan and Morgan 1999).

CA began when Gerbner and his colleagues received funding from the US Surgeon General's Office to literally count episodes of violence on American television (Gross 2009). Defining media violence as "the overt expression of physical force, with or without a weapon, against self or other, compelling action against one's own will on pain of being hurt or killed, or actually hurting or killing" (Gerbner et al. 1978, p. 179), the researchers found that television was very violent, and moreover the violence had a symbolic pattern. White, middle-class, middle-aged male characters were least likely to be victimized. Violence therefore symbolized the "order of things," and its "effect" was the production of "a sense of fear and the need for protection" (p. 184). Other patterns also became apparent. It was noted, for example, that older people were vastly underrepresented on television, which led to studies on how television watching associated with attitudes toward aging (Gerbner 1998). The model became the basis for research on television and ideas about families, health, and the environment (Morgan, Shanahan, and Signorelli 2009). However, the matter of how violence provokes fear and conservatism has continued to occupy center stage in understanding what cultivation analysis is about.

Gerbner and colleagues used data collected by the University of Michigan's National Opinion Research Center (NORC) from 1975 to 1979 to investigate what audiences learned from these patterns. The team knew it was hard to show the influence of a medium whose power hid in plain sight, simply because it was so pervasive. They argued, however, that quantifying differences between television and social reality, and differentiating, in relative terms, between light, medium, and heavy viewers, might give a glimpse of television's social influence. Gerbner distinguished his violence research from behaviorism by locating media effects in the systemic biases of media industries rather in than audience psychologies. Television was to be understood as "the cultural arm of the industrial order" (1976, p. 151). "Mainstreaming" was not something that only happened to "weak" viewers: it was the predictable outcome of a cultural scene dominated by a medium with a vested interest in presenting audiences with a narrow and biased picture of reality (Gerbner et al. 1982).

In his essay "On Being Critical – in One's Own Fashion," included in the classic 1983 *Ferment in the Field* edition of the *Journal of Communication*, Gerbner aligned himself with broadly Marxist approaches to media critique and against "fractured positivistic fantasies based on real data abstracted from their historical context" (1983, p. 362). Gerbner *struggled* with questions of causality. This began in his conviction that qualitative and quantitative research were complementary, since "Qualitative distinctions and judgments (as in labelling or classifying) are prerequisites to quantitative measurements; the two are inseparable" (p. 161). Certain as he was that television's influence always pulled for corporate capitalism, Gerbner acknowledged that fear and resentment were also motivated by "unemployment, poverty, neo-colonial wars, immorality in higher circles, and repressive activities of police and armies" (p. 356), and that media effects could not be studied or described in isolation from such things. His intention was not to dismiss audiences, but to develop a "new critique (and) research tasks that can be seen (or used) to empower ... people" (p. 358). He therefore grounded CA in the need to avoid unidirectional models of media power. This is not to say he was successful in doing so, but it does illustrate that Gerbner considered that he shared conceptual territory with the critical, qualitative audience research of the time.

Criticisms of Cultivation Analysis and the Question of Interpretation

Some researchers dismissed the cultivation case as empirically weak and methodologically unsound. Gerbner and his colleagues conceded that in most studies, attitudinal differences between light and heavy viewers were small, even if they were statistically significant. Doob and MacDonald (1979) went further, dismissing mainstreaming as spurious. Their analysis of the same NORC data found that fear of crime and heavy viewing were most prevalent among those living in high-crime areas. Unsurprisingly, people for whom violence was a real threat were more afraid than the average person, and tended to stay at home more. Naturally, at the time, they ended up watching more television. The criticism that cultivation effects could be explained away by other social factors was repeated by Hughes (1980) and Hirsch (1980, 1981). These criticisms were largely empirical. The argument was that closer interrogation of the NORC data did not support the case for cultivation. This prompted an empirical defense from Gerbner et al. They countered that the statistical evidence could only ever be weak given television's ubiquity, and that Doob and MacDonald had found a specification, where television violence was especially frightening for people who lived with the real thing. This specification was termed *resonance* (Gerbner et al. 1981; Shanahan and Morgan 1999).

Horace Newcomb's "humanistic critique" of 1978, however, challenged the conceptual fit between cultivation theory and method. Newcomb's thoughts, and the response to them from cultivation analysis, illuminate what the model shares with qualitative forms of audience research like fan studies. Newcomb considered cultivation analysis to be interesting but methodologically misconceived, since its *method* fitted neither its *claims* nor *concepts* when it comes to *audiences* and the question of how they made sense of media. *Mainstreaming* assumed that television had a coherent political manifesto that audiences uniformly understood. Having predetermined what television was "like" and "for," Gerbner et al. failed to interrogate the alternative and variant meanings of media violence –in terms of either what they expressed or how they were interpreted. According to Newcomb, this meant that cultivation analysis's conclusion that violence was the dominant feature of television because it served industrial ends was a contradiction. Cultivation analysis claimed media violence affected mental states because it expressed meaning, but then stopped looking for the meanings that audiences saw in violence. Gerbner's was simply an elegant effects argument: the more television came under centralized control, the more racist, sexist, classist, and gendered values dominated. The mainstreaming case depended on being able to show that the greater the exposure, the greater the likelihood that viewers would accept these values. Whatever the intentions, in effect cultivation analysis was only interested in how much influence audiences absorbed. Newcomb did not see why television necessarily concentrated the power of the already powerful. The medium created a rich and widely accessible symbolic culture. Newcomb suspected that Gerbner et al. were ultimately unable to account for this because of the limitations inherent in surveys and content analysis. Culture, he argued, was not a thing that could be measured.

But Newcomb acknowledged that numbers had their uses. He credited the violence profiles for describing the symbolic gap between television and social reality. This surely expressed something about culture and society – even if it was not clear what. Potter (1993) developed this positive reading. Potter thought that the problem with cultivation analysis was that it looked for television's overall effect instead of asking how interactions between industries, viewers, and content worked among different audience groups. His view reconciles cultivation analysis with culture-based audience studies, since it effectively frees the former from the assumption that more watching always means more persuasion.

Potter agreed that the cultivation case was hampered by the assumptions that viewing was nonselective, that television content was homogenous, and that the meaning of violence had nothing to do with genres, narratives, or viewing habits. This contradicted the findings of qualitative researchers who watched audiences watching television. David Morley (1989), Anne Gray (1992), and James Lull (1990) found viewers did all sorts of things while "watching television." This meant that the experiences of "heavy viewers" who watched 30 hours or so of television per week could be very different according to who they were, why they were watching, where they were watching, and their level of attention. Knowing how people watched television, the assumptions that more watching meant more exposure to and acceptance of dominant ideas had to be dismissed. Each element in the "heavy viewing" equation (exposure, nonselectivity, and homogeneity) could be queried, and thus become especially troublesome in combination.

Potter suggested using "nonglobal" measures of influence related to genre and audience segments. This new approach needed nonlinear models, where television was a necessary but not sufficient cause of social attitudes. Certainly the mainstreaming thesis turned on the capacity to show that audiences were drawn toward television rather than the social world. But it was equally possible that television was a necessary condition for "influence" that only worked for some viewers. For example, suppose a study dismissed mainstreaming on the basis that "moderate" viewers were just as fearful of the real world as "heavy viewers." According to the strict application of statistical measure, this would mean "no effect." Yet it was just as feasible to think that television had "threshold" effects wherein audiences reached a certain "saturation" point, where "moderate" amounts of viewing – which could be quite heavy in absolute terms – were that point. Posing queries like this meant humanistic reservations about cultivation, particularly surrounding differing contexts and interpretations of violence, could be addressed in closer explorations of how certain sorts of content provided by certain genres exercised various forms of influence among *different* audiences. Potter's critique allowed researchers to think of television violence as an *ingredient* rather than a cause in the production of social outcomes.

Cultivation, Context, and Interpretation

Cultivation analysts accepted the need to consider interpretation and context in their work. By the 1980s a "second generation" of researchers was looking at how developments like the appearance of VCRs and multichannel cable systems influenced mainstreaming (see Morgan and Signorelli 1996). However, television today demands going beyond the idea that "context" modifies influences that still flow from media to audience. This opposes accounts from qualitative studies showing that media content can be pulled in the direction of experience. John Fiske (1993), for example, watched homeless men "rewriting" the Bruce Willis cop blockbuster *Diehard* by reading it as a tale of urban anarchy. *Diehard* is the tale of a lone cop who restores order when terrorists occupy the headquarters of a Los Angeles–based Japanese corporation. Unless, as Fiske's homeless men did, you stop watching halfway through. For this audience, *Diehard* is about the chaos that follows a successful assault on the institutions of law and finance. This appealed to men who felt like victims of both. Watching half of the film offered some sort of symbolic revenge in keeping with Newcomb's view of the possibilities opened by popular media. For many years, when presented with evidence like this, cultivation analysts argued that these moments were irrelevant when set against the generally conservative "gravitational pull" that media violence exerted (Morgan and Shanahan 1999). This has been the nub of differences between fan studies and cultivation analysis. The former has objected to the idea that more watching means more influence. Close studies of how fans use media in everyday life have shown that people who watch a lot of television often have a better understanding of the medium and are therefore more critical of media industries (Harris 1998). The point becomes compelling as fans become involved in television production, often being consulted on matters such as plot and character development.

It is tempting to think that this disagreement is driven by conflicts between quantitative methods that look for what is common across audiences, and qualitative techniques that are more alert to difference. However, this case stumbles because cultivation analysts have generated data disproving the idea that the politics of violence only work in one direction. According to Appel (2008), television violence makes the world *less* mean and scary for German and Austrian viewers, because it is mostly found in narratives where justice is restored. Kolbeins (2004) found the same dynamic in Iceland. Violence no longer teaches viewers across the board that the world is a scary place (if it ever did), and its political "outcomes" have changed.

Cultivation analysts still believe that media violence molds perceptions of social reality. Television's capacity to make people afraid and politically conservative is still investigated. The distinction between first- and second-order effects remains meaningful. What has changed is that researchers now explore how media violence has many outcomes, sometimes driven by how audiences "play" with television content; as James Shanahan (2004) notes, "types of violence, their relation to social context, and audience reactions to such violence need to be theorized more in connection to each other to be able to make sense of the social functions played by violence on TV" (pp. 292–293). Nevertheless, violence continues to define what CA is "about" as a form of critical media research.

Hetsroni and Tukachinsky (2006), for example, altered the mainstreaming thesis on the topic of the first order effect. Originally, "mainstreamed" viewers had attitudes that accurately matched what they saw onscreen. Hetsroni and Tukachinsky's surveys of Israeli students, however, showed evidence of "overcultivation." Here, heavy viewers *also* exaggerated how much violence they had watched. The authors hypothesized that what viewers remember about content might say more about what they pay attention to than what is there. On one hand, the study presented a conventional cultivation finding: screen violence made viewers crave strong law-and-order policies because they were afraid. But, on the other hand, these attitudes could not have been caused by television because they were based on a first-order *misperception* of what they had seen. And so cultivation does not only happen because viewers move toward television's version of events, and the political influence of its violence is shaped by audience interpretation.

Varying cultivation patterns can also be expected since viewers can now make meaningfully different choices (Bilandzic 2006). Studies of how audiences react to crime genres have lent empirical support to this hypothesis. Grabe and Drew (2007) found numerous generic variations in how violence was shown in drama, reality television, and news, and corresponding differences in how the audiences for each reacted to what they saw. Content analysis showed that black men were the most frequent perpetrators of violent crime on television news, whereas in dramas white men were most likely to offend. Police reality shows exaggerated crime levels and arrest rates. People who watched a lot of reality shows were more likely to buy guns than were those who watched a lot of crime dramas. On the other hand, the former had more faith in the criminal justice system. Grabe and Drew speculated that this was because plots involving institutional corruption are common in shows like *Law and Order*. Whether or not this is true, their surveys led to the conclusion that overall exposure to television was a poor predictor of second-order beliefs because different genres taught different lessons. Grabe and Drew thus supported Potter's belief that the media influence could be seen more clearly by comparing subgroups rather than searching for general effects.

Fan studies, therefore, turns to questions of political violence just as cultivation analysis has significantly revised many of its core assumptions, and recognizes that audiences do things with media violence. The grounds for interaction between the paradigms is now possible for the following reasons:

- Cultivation is now understood as a conditional process that depends on context and interpretation.
- The case for cultivation may be strengthened by arguing that it happens not only when television shapes ideas about the real world, but also by conditions under which, for reasons that are still to be explored, the interpretation of television content is "bent toward" audience circumstance (as when viewers exaggerate the amounts of violence onscreen).
- "Heavy" viewers draw conflicting inferences about what reality is like according to genre. Indeed, cultivation analysts have found conflicting data on fictional media; sometimes drama makes people feel safer, and sometimes it does not. The differences matter because, in the example of crime drama, "fans" sometimes arrive at counterhegemonic conclusions about social institutions, where those who like reality shows appear happier with how society is governed.

Cultivation analysts are unclear on why this happens, but it does open the possibility for dissent and debate among heavy viewers.

- The idea that television influence moves in many directions has opened the possibility for mixed-method approaches. Rossmann and Brosius (2004) point out that cultivation analysis' methodological flaws turn on matters of causality that are fundamental to the selection of methods across the discipline. They propose a multimethodological approach, and therefore open a dialogue with qualitative studies. This makes sense within Gerbner's recognition that quantitative procedures are grounded in numerous interpretative judgments. In mixed-method studies, where surveys comparing light and heavy viewers would no longer be as central as they were in the original violence profiles, cultivation theory, and the insights offered by past studies, would be as important as its methods.

- Cultivation analysis needs to engage with other forms of audience and user studies because it presently remains focused on reception. Fan studies outlines how audiences often participate in media production. This is useful as it addresses how audiences may *produce* the mainstream.

- The continued prevalence of media violence *within* these changes makes it important, as Shanahan (2004) suggests, to consider anew what it means and *expresses*. Nevertheless, the original empirical conclusions on the ideology of violence provide a useful language in considering its current political significance.

The fact that the world is dangerous for many people cannot be divorced from evidence that feeling safe and using media are associated. Public support for the wars in Iraq and Afghanistan depends on fear of terrorism. For most people, these feelings depend on media. In this way, the safety that television viewers feel affects the dangers that soldiers and civilians face in warzones. Yet we can make this claim without castigating either media or their audiences. Appreciating the need to explore diverse television experiences, cultivation analysts study what audiences learn from certain genres, shows, and even discrete media events.[1]

Within this, it is recognized that sometimes audiences learn because they want to learn (Dutta 2007). In these moments, television performs a positive social function where we can speak of relations between first- and second-order judgments without relying on naïve "media-as-mirror" metaphors.

The key question today is how the lessons learned from past studies apply to a current situation where media violence is politicized in many ways by as-yet-unstudied communications processes. Now would be a spectacularly bad time to abandon the idea that television violence dramatizes power and is either a force or resource guiding the political judgments that viewers make. Since genre, context, and interpretation are recognized across the spectrum of audience research as things that affect influence, it is clear that we need to study how particular audiences are attracted to media violence as it plays in specific political spaces.

Ross Kemp in Afghanistan: A Case Study

Consider the case of UK actor-turned-investigative journalist Ross Kemp, and his series *Ross Kemp in Afghanistan* (hereafter *RKIA*; Tiger Aspect Productions 2008). Kemp is well known for playing "hard man" military roles. In 2007, Sky One, a UK satellite television station, embedded the actor with the Royal Anglian Regiment as they trained for and deployed in Helmand province. Kemp and his production team lived on the frontline, noting the Spartan realities of life in the field, the difficulties of fighting a war with inadequate equipment, and the financial challenges experienced by ranking soldiers and their families. Kemp reported being teased for his performance as Sergeant "Henno" Henderson in the UK television SAS drama *Ultimate Force*. He accepted this in good humor; after all, *he* had parodied the role whilst playing "himself" on Ricky Gervais' *Extras*. The praise *RKIA* received from soldiers, veterans, and their families suggests that in playing the space between Henno Henderson and Ross Kemp, the actor successfully created an authentic celebrity persona. And so Kemp embodied the main "lesson" of television violence described by George Gerbner (1996):

> If you are a white male in the prime of life, although your chances of getting into a violent situation are frequent on television, your chances of getting away with it, your chances of being the winner rather than the victim, are the greatest. (n.p.)

In *RKIA*, Kemp "got away with it" twice. First, he survived a war zone where the risk of being killed was very real. Second, he emerged as a credible investigative journalist despite doubts on his ability to carry a fictional tough-man persona into an arena that demanded real physical courage. At the same time, the fact that he was afforded such an opportunity also says something about the changing structures of British television. Kemp made his name playing a Falklands war veteran on *EastEnders*, a show which bears the distinction of being the first television soap produced by the publicly funded BBC. In the early 2000s, he left the BBC to star in a number of dramas produced by its oldest commercial rival, ITV. *RKIA* explicitly drew on Kemp's familiarity and star persona in efforts to attract an audience to satellite and cable platforms. Kemp's celebrity has therefore been drawn into the conflict over how British television should be structured in the twenty-first century.

Kemp *is* a figure who can be analyzed using both fan and cultivation studies. He is a *celebrity* whose *fan base* was used to draw *attention* to a *story about violence* serving institutional needs. He was also a modern exemplar of Gerbner's thesis that media violence is a narrative about white male power, this time applied to the production of entertaining war news. Audience reactions to the show verified the value of looking for influence within subgroups. *RKIA*'s official fan website caught the eye of women who wanted to draw attention to the domestic violence they suffered. This illustrated the varying and contradictory influences that violence could have on *the same* viewers. *RKIA* was hegemonic, in terms of its institutional rationale and role in reinforcing gendered impressions of victimization, and empowering in what it allowed viewers to say about the personal damage caused by British foreign policy. Here, audiences were involved in the production of the show as a media event, and participated in media practices that shaped its significance vis-à-vis the war in Afghanistan. *RKIA* is therefore noteworthy as a case study in how cultivation theory can learn from fan studies, where media effects come to pass through the actions of audiences who use and create media content.

Nevertheless, this observation is couched in *RKIA*'s strategic value to Sky One. Reviewing for *The Spectator*, James Delingpole (2008) worried that *RKIA*'s heroism and technology only worked when viewers had firsthand combat experience or had loved ones in harm's way. With no real-life referent, finding out that bullets whistle and bombs go bang was neither moving nor surprising. If Delingpole's was a common reaction, *RKIA* fundamentally showcased Sky One's capacity to deploy new media technologies, with content remaining secondary. But what did audiences say about this content?

This matter is partly a fan question since *RKIA* involved fans in the political economy of media violence. Writing for *PR Week UK*, Caroline Dickinson (2008) attributed the show's success to synergies of digital technologies, Kemp's star persona, and his fan base. Sky One had hired the PR company Way to Blue to market the show online. The campaign also capitalized on the work that Kemp fans were willing to do. Intent on drumming up positive "word-of-mouth" publicity, WTB targeted moderators of Facebook's Ross Kemp Appreciation Society and the *EastEnders* fan site as the vanguard for a wider marketing effort. Eventually the campaign reached almost 6 million people, of whom 2 million tuned in to the show's Sky debut. *RKIA* went on to become Sky's highest ranking show, often gathering a larger audience than its BBC competitors (Dickinson 2008). Kemp's capacity to draw the attention of an audience through his "history of violence" solved a long-running institutional problem: the need to prove that Sky One is more in tune with viewers than its terrestrial competitors (King 1998).

Audience Reactions

But what did audiences say and do about the show? The following data were drawn from Sky One's *RKIA* site (http://www.skyone.co.uk/SKYONEFORUM/ShowForum.aspx?ForumID=119), containing 444 posts spread across 92 threads.

Each post was coded using the NVIVO 8 database. The aim of the coding was to assess how far *RKIA* worked hegemonically, insofar as it was perceived as a credible

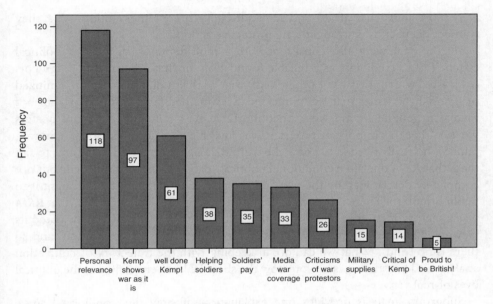

Figure 17.1 Why did viewers post to the RKIA website?

account of the war that bolstered support for military operations in Afghanistan and faith in the veracity of television's account of that war. Evidence was sought for why viewers found the show credible, informative, or entertaining (or not). The results shown in Figure 17.1 support the case for multidirectional cultivation. Here, the positions viewers occupied were neither entirely determined by nor entirely free of media content, and it was possible to argue for associations between opinions, actions, textual structures, and the forces that made *RKIA* available to the public. What is new, here, is the observation that audiences were meaningfully involved in the production of those structures.

In some ways, the results painted a picture that showed how "mainstreaming" still operates through digital media. For this sample, *RKIA* worked because Kemp was someone they could relate to as either veterans or people with loved ones in the armed forces, and because he showed the war as they imagined it was. About a quarter of the posts simply wished to congratulate Kemp on a stellar job. *RKIA* encouraged politicized debate on soldiers' living conditions (35 posts complained about poor pay, and 15 about inadequate battlefield supplies) and tried to organize actions that could improve life in the field (writing letters, protesting pay and conditions, sending supplies, fundraising, and participating in welcome home celebrations). As unhappy as they were about conditions for the British Army in Afghanistan, posters had no time for those who protested about the war itself, especially if they criticized troops. According to this reading, *RKIA* had an influence that resembled "mainstreaming." These viewers wanted more honest accounts of the war, but also demanded better logistical support and victory. They were more angry than afraid, and demanded government intervention. What they wanted, in effect, was stronger state protective action.

Yet the data were also consistent with a multidimensional view of political effects. *RKIA*'s credibility as a reliable foundation for first-order reality judgments contrasted with criticisms of other media that, in this audience's opinion, sanitized or ignored the issues that Kemp tackled. Viewers had faith in this show, but not media in general. Some were uncomfortable with satellite television: posters worried that this important program was invisible to a nonsubscribing, ignorant public who really needed to know the truth that Kemp imparted. It is fairer to say, then, that *RKIA* opened a conditional political space which was influenced but not completely determined by the text and the television platform that brought it to public attention. There is little value in interrogating the data to "prove" that *RKIA* was a victory for Kemp and Sky, or that, alternatively, the show emancipated its viewers. The war continues, as does Kemp's adventures in syndication, and so there is no "end." What we can do, in keeping with the trajectory of cultivation analysis and fan studies, is explore how the show became enmeshed in the political lives of real viewers.

Subgroup analysis provides one explanation of how *this* conditional space worked to contrasting ends. Women formed the largest subgroup within the 188 "personal relevance" posts, with 38 from those with serving partners. Set against the millions who watched the show, these viewers are clearly not representative. Certainly they do nothing to dismiss Delingpole's concern that *RKIA* probably meant little to most of its audience. Yet neither qualification changes the fact that Kemp became hugely important here to a subgroup within a subgroup; the women who liked the show. The fact that *RKIA* mattered to women who were coping with the war justifies a closer examination of what drew their attention, and the ensuing political consequences.

The show's associations with realities lived by viewers created a critical space where the key variable was how Kemp was absorbed into the lives of women at the frontline of dealing with Afghanistan's domestic fallout. Posts by these women did support the conclusion that the structure of the show affected the responses it evoked. Across all 444 responses, posts were generally "embedded" in a soldier's view of the war – as was Kemp. The ferocity normally directed at any "antisoldier" post was consistent with a program that was very much "on their side." This trend was complemented by the fact that some women posters with partners in action were struggling through stressful situations, where asking why British troops are in Afghanistan did nothing to help day to day. Nevertheless, the sentiment that the women were also victims of the real war was clear. As "CVG" stated,

Being back home … you try to live as normal as life as possible whilst your loved 1 is away, they are always on your mind, you keep as strong and as positive as you can to support them, whilst on their tour. Everyday normal things go on, you just want to let the whole world know that your loved one is away on tour. (CVG 200)

In this, the show became part of the domestic campaign to prepare postwar lives. Much as some women may have wanted to simply "get on with things," in this dimension it did become evident that television's capacity to show real violence was valued, and so it was disappointing that most of the time it failed to do so. This had an effect, insofar as other people were ignorant of the suffering endured by military families. The outcomes of representations that were deemed to be accurate could be reassuring, alarming, and frightening all at the same time. Some women thought that *RKIA* provided an emotional bridge between women and men who will, inevitably, return traumatized (if at all).

> I count on Ross to keep us all in the picture about what is really going on out there, it has prepared me for what to expect when he gets posted to Afghanistan.... I would rather sit and watch the episodes Ross makes rather than read the letters I get sent about what will happen to my fiancé when he goes out there what he will get up to.... I hope that one day he will get recognition for what he has done to help us get through it all.

However, one poster feared that "getting through it" was likely to continue long after deployment. In a thread titled "Not All Soldiers Are Heroes," "EmDubs" reveals a different sort of war reality:

> Fair enough a soldier goes out to places like Iraq and Afghanistan and puts his life on the line. I know I wouldn't like to do it. However, I was the wife at home with our child while he was out there. I had to suffer when he got home. I was threatened with violence, pulled down the stairs whilst pregnant, our dog was beaten up and our daughter was put at risk because of him and his anger problem which the Army refused to recognise. There were times when I was locked in the Army quarter with no access to a phone, isolated from friends and family.... Everybody is quick enough to pat them on the back for a job well done but what about us back at home who really take a beating...? Sometimes quite literally.

As is common with posts critical of troops, this was met with initial hostility:

> This is a message board regarding our troops in Afghanistan, not some place to vent your personal problems. There are many other places to do that. Trying to tarnish a group for your situation, shame.

However, this was the only occasion on which a moderator intervened in favor of a critical comment:

> It saddens and worries me that a person can push aside someone's problem and give a generic reply of saying its a national problem.... Although I am extremely sad to hear what has happened to the OP, her post is valid as it about Afghanistan and what can happen to our troops when they aren't looked after properly.

Thereafter, EmDubs receives support from other women posters, and eventually an offer of offline help from someone claiming to be a serving soldier.

> Although I can't comment on the problems with the army welfare system as my dealings have always been pleasant, I can say this is not the first story like this I have heard … please talk to the unit's Padre if you can find him, and tell him to pull his finger out and get busy on your behalf. He will do this if he is half decent. Mention the unit and I will get busy on them.

Emdubs takes the "victim" idea in a new direction. In her account, the general suffering inflicted by the misery of having a loved one in harm's way ended in direct physical menace. Here, *RKIA* did not resonate with her real experience of violence, which, in her view, even Kemp failed to represent. Emdubs was scared by a reality that Sky would not show.

Emdubs showed why the enduring relevance of Gerbner's ideas are best appreciated through close attention to processes of reception as "live" encounters with content crossing multiple platforms. Attention is needed to the ongoing tendency to equate "immersion" in media with "influencability," a traditional anathema to fan studies (Harris 1998). Bilandzic's (2006) work on cultivation and learning updates the immersion = influence equation by arguing that audiences work to lose themselves in television. Bilandzic combines "activity" and "cultivation" by arguing that audiences work to "transport" themselves into media narratives, whose plausibility depends on the absence of "disconfirmation." Although this idea gives audiences a more active role, it cannot explain how we can argue that Emdubs was "cultivated." Although she was afraid, and her fear was somehow invoked by *RKIA*, this viewer was far from "transported" into the show's reality. Quite the reverse!

Within fan studies, the problem with "transportation" is that it locates influence squarely in reception. Mark Andrejevic's study of online cult television fans (2008) argues that the gap between television and fans is closed by the fact that some fans are a part of television's world. Andrejevic's study of posts to *Television without Pity* concludes that the main "effect" of online fandom is to draw greater attention to television by making viewers producers of cultural value. "Bad" television is "good" as the raw material viewers can use to do their duty; making better television by providing considered feedback, since they have a fundamental faith in the medium. This stands very close to the original cultivation thesis. Gerbner was convinced that what mattered most were the metanarratives of television itself, which were mostly effective in changing *nothing* (1998). According to Andrejevic, *Television without Pity* teaches the same lesson.

> A savvy identification with producers and insiders facilitated by interactive media fosters an acceptance of the rules of the game. In an era of interactive reflexivity, the media turn back on themselves: new media mock the old while tellingly failing to deliver on the promised transformative shift in power relations. (p. 24)

Andrejevic's comments are entirely in keeping with the idea that television's cardinal lesson is to accept things as they are. However, his version of "mainstreaming" is driven by what audiences do rather than what they think or accept. In the new television world, groups like the *RKIA* fans may be small and unrepresentative, but they are also powerful people who quite literally produce and police meanings in ways that go beyond the "producerly" aspects of interpretation. Yet their power is not always something they control, nor are they always its primary beneficiaries. The power held by this group began in the observation that *RKIA* became influential when it was "transported" into the experience of living the war from a distance. The meanings of *RKIA*'s violence for these women were greatly determined by their context. The uses they found for that content, on many levels, had little to do with industrial design. Kemp's celebrity was largely irrelevant to the viewer-posters. Nor, as we have seen, did they embrace Sky's ideology.

However, the attention they drew to the show served institutional purposes. The data outlined a "third-person" cultivation effect, where Kemp was gifted the power to transport other people with no direct war experience into the world in which the soldier's partners lived. There was a tension between praising the show and worrying that its positive effects ("letting the whole world know that your loved one is on tour") were limited by its unavailability to terrestrial viewers. The effects that "connected" viewers hoped the show might have had on general audiences depended as much on distribution as content; hence the wish that such an important show could be available on the BBC.

The judgment, coming from fans, that *RKIA* did tell a tale that no one else could was hugely valuable to a satellite corporation desperate to prove its public service credentials. The judgment also influenced how other viewers could speak, which is why we can say that its mainstreaming effect came from both the show and its fans. Emdubs was clearly not "transported" into *RKIA*'s world, but her words had to be chosen carefully among people who were effectively producing a heavily politicized media event. The political significance of the violence on *RKIA* can be seen in Emdubs, her efforts to make her domestic world less scary, and the subject of how media would fit in that better world. It was "scary" for her that *RKIA* embedded hegemonic masculinity through the tripartite of Sky's ambitions, Kemp's persona, and digital technologies. But at least the online forum created a space where concern for *other* victims could be voiced, allowing her to "bend" violence to her own purposes. Emdubs was anti-Army, not antisoldier, making others more willing to listen to her. This mirrored the structure of a show whose ground's-eye view fixed on soldiers being failed by the military establishment. While the women clearly expected to suffer as partners of soldiers, they did not expect that suffering to come from poor pay, inadequate insurance arrangements, deaths that functional equipment would prevent, or violence inflicted by traumatized men denied the aftercare they deserved.

Some of the "effects" of *RKIA*, therefore, depended on its resonance with the lifestyles of women for whom life was on hold. However, as these women coped with their situation by watching television and conversing on web fansites, media were a *part* of their lifestyle. The matter of what the women thought about the war was less important than what they could express within a media community who were largely convinced that Ross Kemp and Sky television had presented a story of violence they could take to be true. And so, the political economy of media violence had a direct impact on communication and care for people who lived on a different frontline. The *RKIA* data demonstrate what can happen within the political and media mainstream when fans are recruited to draw the attention of other audiences. Although certain things effectively could not be said on the site, the theme of violence raised, in an overdetermined way, a situated political critique connecting media, beliefs about the real world, political positions, offline efforts to make the world less mean, and even commentary on the sort of media systems that could support these endeavors (public and terrestrial, not commercial and digital). A conditional model of influence results that is explicable in the language of cultivation analysis and fan studies. Gerbner's original framing of what media violence is for remains a powerful analytical device. Where longstanding curiosity about what politics violence cultivates and how it does so remain live issues, fan perspectives answer "how" questions in the contexts that now interest cultivation analysts such as Bilandzic. Fan methods also reconnect cultivation with its history as a component of a "cultural indicators project" which also examined how media industries work (Gerbner 1998). Fan studies place audiences within industries, and specify the value of engaging with localized political activism.

It is hard to overestimate the reasons why the models should be used in combination. Michele Emanatian and David Delaney (2008) have recently written of the need to confront the mediation of the wars in Iraq and Afghanistan, where violence is consistently presented as an act of communication rather than destruction. The theme of what media violence means, and how it is understood, has a political gravitas that is at the very least equal to that of the 1960s. Given this, the reasons why media scholars should use all of the tools at their disposal to analyze these meanings is transparent. CA is a valuable place to begin the work.

Note

1 Soaps (Carveth and Alexander 1985; Perse 1986), talk shows (Rössler and Brosius 2001; Woo and Dominick 2003; Glynn et al. 2007), and different sorts of news (Lett, DiPietro, and Johnson, 2004) have all been examined for their powers to cultivate. Individual shows such as *Grey's Anatomy* (Quick 2009) and *Sex and the City* (Gray 2007) have been studied for their influence on knowledge and attitudes toward health issues. Nabi (2007) found a small but significant relationship between watching makeover shows and the desire to undergo cosmetic surgery.

References

Andrejevic, M. 2008 Watching *Television without Pity*: the productivity of online fans. *Television and New Media*, 9, 1, pp. 24–26.

Appel, M. 2008 Fictional narratives cultivate just-world beliefs. *Journal of Communication*, 58, 1, pp. 62–83.

Ball-Rokeach, S. 2001 The politics of studying media violence: reflections 30 years after the Violence Commission. *Mass Communication and Society*, 4, pp. 3–18.

Bilandzic, H. 2006 The perception of distance in the cultivation process: a theoretical consideration of the relationship between television content, processing experience and perceived distance. *Communication Theory*, 16, pp. 333–355.

Carveth, R. and Alexander, A. II 1985 Soap opera viewing motivations and the cultivation process. *Journal of Broadcasting and Electronic Media*, 29, pp. 259–273.

Delingpole, J. 2008 The pity of war. *The Spectator*, January 26, p. 46.

Dickinson, C. 2008 Sky One puts Ross Kemp on the front line. *Brand Republic*. Retrieved from http://www.brandrepublic.com/News/803009/MEDIA-CAMPAIGN-Sky-One-puts-Ross-Kemp-front-line/?DCMP=ILC-SEARCH

Doob, A. and Macdonald, G. 1979 Television viewing and fear of victimization: is the relationship causal? *Journal of Personality of Social Psychology*, 37, 2, pp. 170–179.

Dutta, M. 2007 Health information processing from television: the role of health orientation. *Health Communication*, 21, 1, pp. 1–9.

Emanatian, M. and Delaney, D. 2008 What message does "send a message" send? *Journal of Language and Politics*, 7, 2, pp. 290–320.

Fiske, J. 1993 *Power Plays, Power Works*. Routledge, London.

Gauntlett, D. 2005 *Moving Experiences: Media Effects and Beyond*. John Libbey, London.

Gauntlett, D. 2007 *Creative Explorations: New Approaches to Identities and Audiences*. Routledge, London.

Gerbner, G. 1976 *Studies in Mass Communication*. Unpublished monograph.

Gerbner, G. 1983 The importance of being critical – in one's own fashion. *Journal of Communication*, 33, 3, pp. 355–362.

Gerbner, G. 1996 Fred Rogers and the significance of story. *Why Public Broadcasting?* Retrieved from http://www.current.org/why/why609gerbner.shtml

Gerbner, G. 1998 Cultivation analysis: an overview. *Mass Communication and Society*, 1, 3–4, pp. 175–195.

Gerbner, G., Gross, L., Jackson-Beck, M., Jeffries-Fox, S. and Signorelli, N. 1978 Cultural indicators: violence profile no. 9. *Journal of Communication*, 28, 3, pp. 176–207.

Gerbner, G., Gross, L., Morgan, M. and Signorelli, N. 1980 The mainstreaming of America: violence profile no. 11. *Journal of Communication*, 30, pp. 10–29.

Gerbner, G., Gross, L., Morgan, M. and Signorielli, N. 1981 Final reply to Hirsch. *Communication Research*, 8, 3, pp. 259–280.

Gerbner, G., Gross, L., Morgan, M. and Signorelli, N. 1982 Charting the mainstream: television's contributions to political orientations. *Journal of Communication*, 32, pp. 100–127.

Glynn, C., Huge, M., Reineke, J., Hardy, B. and Shanahan, J. 2007 When Oprah intervenes: political correlates of daytime talk show viewing. *Journal of Broadcasting and Electronic Media*, 51, 2, pp. 228–244.

Grabe, M. and Drew, D. 2007, Crime cultivation: comparisons across media genres and channels. *Journal of Broadcasting and Electronic Media*, 51, 1, pp. 147–171.

Gray, A. 1992 *Video Playtime*. London, Routledge.

Gray, J. 2007 Interpersonal communication and the illness experience in the *Sex and the City* breast cancer narrative. *Communication Quarterly*, 55, 4, pp. 397–414.

Gray, J., Sandvoss, C. and Harrington, C.L. (2007). Introduction: why study fans? In J. Gray, C. Sandvoss and C.L. Harrington, eds. *Fandom: Identities and Communities in a Mediated World*. New York University Press, New York, pp. 1–16.

Gross, L. 2009 My media studies: cultivation to participation. *Television and New Media*, 10, 1, pp. 66–68.

Harris, C. 1998 A sociology of television fandom. In C. Harris, ed. *Theorizing Fandom: Fans, Subculture and Identity*. Hampton Press, Cresskill, NJ, pp. 41–53.

Hetsroni, A. and Tukachinsky, R. 2006 Television-world estimates, real-world estimates, and television viewing: a new scheme for cultivation. *Journal of Communication*, 56, 1, pp. 133–156.

Hirsch, P.M. 1980 The scary world of the non-viewer and other anomalies. *Communication Research*, 7, pp. 403–456.

Hirsch, P.M. 1981 On not learning from one's own mistakes. *Communication Research*, 8, pp. 3–37.

Hughes, M. 1980 The fruits of cultivation analysis. *Public Opinion Quarterly*, 44, pp. 287–302

King, A. 1998 Thatcherism and the emergence of Sky Television. *Media, Culture and Society*, 20, 2, pp. 277–293.

Kolbeins, G. 2004 The non-finding of the cultivation effect in Iceland. *Nordicom Review*, 25, 1–2, pp. 309–314.

Lett, M., DiPietro, A., and Johnson, D. 2004 Examining effects of television news violence on college students through cultivation theory. *Communication Research Reports*, 21, 1, pp. 39–46.

Lewis, J. 1997 What counts in cultural studies. *Media, Culture and Society*, 19, 1, pp. 83–97.

Lewis, J., Jhally, S. and Morgan, M. 1991 *The Gulf War: A Study of the Media, Public Opinion and Public Knowledge*. Center for the Study of Communication, University of Massachusetts, Amherst.

Lull, J. 1990 *Inside Family Viewing*. Routledge, London.

Morgan, M. and Signorelli, N. 1996 Cultivation analysis: conceptualization and methodology. In N. Signorelli and M. Morgan, eds. *Cultivation analysis: new directions in media effects research*. Sage, Newbury Park CA, pp. 13–34.

Morgan, M., Shanahan, J. and Signorelli, N. 2009 Growing up with television: cultivation processes. In J. Bryant and M. Oliver, eds. *Media Effects: Advances in Theory and Research*, 3rd edn. Lawrence Erlbaum, Mahwah, NJ, pp. 34–49.

Morley, D. 1989 *Family Television*. BFI, London.

Morley, D. 2006 Unanswered questions in audience research. *The Communication Review*, 9, 2, pp. 101–121.

Nabi, R. 2009 Cosmetic surgery makeover programs and intentions to undergo cosmetic enhancements: a consideration of three models of media effects. *Human Communication Research*, 35, 1, pp. 1–27.

Newcomb, H. 1978 Assessing the violence profile studies of Gerbner and Gross: a humanistic critique and suggestion. *Communication Research*, 5, 3, pp. 264–282.

Perse, E. 1986 Soap opera viewing patterns of college students and cultivation. *Journal of Broadcasting and Electronic Media*, 30, 2, pp. 175–193.

Potter, W. J. 1993 Cultivation theory and research: a conceptual critique. *Human Communication Research*, 19, 4, pp. 564–602.

Quick, B. 2009 The effects of viewing *Grey's Anatomy* on perceptions of doctors and patient satisfaction. *Journal of Broadcasting and Electronic Media*, 53, 1, pp. 38–55.

Rössler, P. and Brosius, H. 2001 Do talk shows cultivate adolescents' views of the world? A prolonged-exposure experiment. *Journal of Communication*, 51, 1, p. 143.

Rossmann, C. and Brosius, H. 2004 The problem of causality in cultivation research. *Communications: The European Journal of Communication Research*, 29, 3, pp. 379–397.

Ruddock, A. 2001 *Understanding Audiences*. Sage, London.

Shanahan, J. 2004 A return to cultural indicators. *Communications: The European Journal of Communication Research*, 29, 3, pp. 277–294.

Shanahan, J. and Morgan, M. 1999 *Television and Its Viewers: Cultivation Theory and Research*. Cambridge University Press, Cambridge.

Shrum, L. 2007 The implications of survey method for measuring cultivation effects. *Human Communication Research*, 33, 1, pp. 64–80.

Shrum, L. 2009 Media consumption and perceptions of social reality: effects and underlying processes. In J. Bryant and M. Oliver, eds. *Media Effects: Advances in Theory and Research*, 3rd edn. Lawrence Erlbaum, Mahwah, NJ, pp. 50–73.

Slater, M. 2007 Reinforcing spirals: the mutual influence of media selectivity and media effects and their impact on individual behavior and social identity. *Communication Theory*, 17, 3, pp. 281–303.

Woo, H. and Dominick, J. 2003 Acculturation, cultivation, and daytime TV talk shows. *Journalism and Mass Communication Quarterly*, 80, 1, pp. 109–127.

18

Creative and Visual Methods in Audience Research

Fatimah Awan and David Gauntlett

As readers of this *Handbook* may notice, much of the fieldwork in media audience research is conducted through language-based events, in particular in focus groups and interviews where participants are expected to be able to generate more or less immediate verbal accounts of their feelings and experiences. However, alongside this in recent years there has been a growing interest in creative and visual research methods, in which participants are asked to make things such as videos, collage, drawings, or models to express their feelings or impressions. These methodologies often, in fact, come back to language at some point, as it is usually considered necessary to access the participants' own commentary on the thing that they have produced. Nevertheless, it is argued that by asking research participants to go through a reflective process, taking time to consider an issue and to create a visual response, we receive more carefully thought-through responses which can offer rich insights into what a particular issue or representation really means to an individual.

The Origins of Creative Methods

Creative methods have developed out of a confluence of sources. These include various projects in "visual sociology" which are not actually concerned with media audiences; some of this background is discussed toward the end of this chapter. Within media audience research, we can see some of the roots in studies such as *Watching Dallas* (Ang 1985) and *TV Living* (Gauntlett and Hill 1999) which broke away from the typical kind of interview encounters and instead asked people to

The Handbook of Media Audiences, First Edition. Edited by Virginia Nightingale.
© 2014 John Wiley & Sons, Ltd. Published 2014 by John Wiley & Sons, Ltd.

write about their relationship with television. These projects showed that asking audience members to engage in a process which requires some time and reflection could pay dividends – although asking people to write about their relationship with television at any length is such a strange and time-consuming task for many people that willing volunteers had a tendency to be atypical.

The question of how such material could be *interpreted* also raised its head at an early stage: Ang (1985) warns, "What people say or write about their experiences, preferences, habits, etc., cannot be taken entirely at face value" (p. 11). Considering the letters which people had sent to her about the soapy US drama series *Dallas*, in response to an advert which she placed in a magazine, Ang asserts that "we cannot let the letters speak for themselves … they should be read 'symptomatically': we must search for what is behind the explicitly written, for the presuppositions and accepted attitudes concealed within them" (p. 11). Unsurprisingly, Ang does not actually have a method by which she can achieve this. An attempt to "read behind the lines" which wanders away from what is actually written leads the researcher into speculation and guesswork – a challenge which later researchers in this field would face in different ways. Meanwhile, the subfield of visual sociology was beginning to take root, and media researchers were starting to see what happened when "audiences" were given the opportunities and tools to make media, in larger and smaller ways, themselves. This chapter will chart the rise of these methods and consider their contribution, and potential contribution, to media audience studies.

Audience Research: Pictures as Prompts

The studies mentioned above have highlighted how the production of written materials by audience members can be used to elicit a more comprehensive range of views and responses to media texts than would have been possible had the participants been required to give instant verbal responses. The Glasgow Media Group has used this notion to explore media influences (Kitzinger 1990; Philo 1990). In their book *The Mass Media and Power in Modern Britain* (1997), John Eldridge, Jenny Kitzinger, and Kevin Williams acknowledge that although audiences are able to articulate a critical awareness of media messages, this awareness does not negate the possibility of the media's influences (p. 160). To explore this notion, a research technique which they called "the news game" was devised in which "research participants were actively engaged in trying to write and criticize a media report" (p. 161). In order to achieve this, participants were provided with materials such as news photographs and headlines, and asked to write an accompanying text that could take the form of a newspaper report, news broadcast script, or headline. These studies claimed to find that although participants apparently presented their own perspectives on these issues, in practice they replicated the ideological discourses predominant in the initial news reports. (However, it seems possible that when participants reproduced dominant ideological discourses in their own media texts, they did so not because they agreed with these ways of thinking, but because they may have thought that this was what they were being asked to do.) In Kitzinger's study *Understanding Aids* (1993), participants were given 13 photographs around which they produced a news report on AIDS that then became the focus of a group discussion. In these reports, it was found that the participants reproduced the terminology and attitudes circulated by the mainstream press, such as "promiscuous, irresponsible drug users or gay people" and "innocent victims" (p. 277). Furthermore, her analysis also highlighted the forcefulness of visual representations in the participants' understandings of AIDS:

> television and newspaper representations are, for many people, the lens through which they view the reality of AIDS. Media images of the visible ravages of disease thus form the template for their perceptions of the world and of the people in it. (Eldridge, Kitzinger, and Williams 1997, p. 163)

Consequently, according to Kitzinger, media representations may dictate how audiences perceive an issue, even though this may contradict "informed" opinion and observations based on personal experience. Therefore, as this study demonstrates, the use of strategies that integrate both the creative production and discussion of media texts can arguably provide the researcher with a more thorough understanding of the attitudes held by audience members – attitudes that may not have become apparent within more conventional interviews or focus group discussions.

Audience Research: Editing News Footage

Expanding on this theme, Brent MacGregor and David Morrison's study (1995) of audience responses to coverage of the 1990–1991 Gulf War sought to overcome limitations which they felt were imposed by focus group–based research, believing that a research method was required that would bring "respondents into closer contact with the text ... enabling them to articulate their response in an appropriate manner" (p. 143). This was achieved by asking participants to edit existing audiovisual news footage to create "a report that you would *ideally* like to see on TV, not what you think others would like to see, not what you think journalists would produce" (p. 146, emphasis in original).

MacGregor and Morrison noted that prior to editing the footage, participants all claimed that they aimed to produce "an ideal, impartial, neutral account" (1995, p. 146) by selecting what they considered to be the more reliable material. Importantly, the researchers observed that although there was considerable similarity between participants' comments made before and after editing, crucial nuanced differences were noted as a result of the editing process itself: "Positions articulated in discussion which would have been reported as definitive in focus groups were modified as a result of the active engagement with the text" (p. 147). For example, MacGregor and Morrison note that participants described one text as having "an undesirable emotional tone" (p. 147) but were unable to identify why this was the case. However, on engaging in the editing process, the participants were able to suggest how this feeling had been created by presentation techniques. Therefore, the employment of this method seems to have enabled MacGregor and Morrison to access more significant and meaningful results than would have been made available by traditional methods. The researchers state that this method is

> not a methodological solution looking for a research problem, but a real tool capable of producing significant results in any situation where tangible viewer contact with the text can unlock new insights into the dynamic of how audio-visual texts are read. (p. 148)

Audience Research: Making Video

In an attempt to move further beyond the reliance on interviews and focus groups in qualitative research, David Gauntlett's *Video Critical* (1997) aimed to evaluate audience responses to mass media material by engaging participants in the creation of their *own* original texts, rather than merely modifying or discussing existing sources. For this project, Gauntlett worked with groups of children aged 7–11, from seven primary schools; they used video equipment to make documentaries on the issue of "the environment" over a period of several weeks each. In the first meeting, a focus group–style discussion identified that for children at that time, television was the primary source of information and commentary on environmental matters (pp. 96–97). It also appeared to show that, in each group, children were overwhelmingly enthusiastic about "green" issues – but, significantly, the research process over subsequent weeks would reveal that this was only patchily the case.

The study recorded the children's conception of the impact of environmental issues on their lives, and facilitated an understanding of how these beliefs were informed by media messages on this topic. The method enabled the researcher to amass a substantial amount of ethnographic data through observation and discussions with the participants throughout the video production project, in addition to the completed videos themselves – which Gauntlett states should be read as "constructed, mediated accounts of a selection of the perceptions of the social world held by the group members" (p. 93).

In line with the principles proposed by MacGregor and Morrison, Gauntlett (1997) highlights that initial discussions with participants were not necessarily indicative of their more deeply felt attitudes or beliefs, but rather they "represented a kind of 'brain dump' of *potential* interests and concerns, which in subsequent weeks were sifted and filtered to reveal the more genuinely-felt opinions" (p. 150, emphasis in original). The researcher suggests that the video-making process constitutes a significant departure from more traditional techniques, which often confined the participants within a predetermined structure that only allowed for limited responses. Video making enabled the participants to influence the research process itself: participants were able to construct a free and open response to the research brief which Gauntlett encourages as a productive strategy, stating that "the video project researcher celebrates their own inability to predict what will happen – a 'risk' worth taking" (p. 93). He also notes Stuart Hall's observation about the value of enabling everyday people to produce mediated representations:

> [I]t is important to get people into producing their own images because … they can then contrast the images they produce of themselves against the dominant images which they are offered, and so they know that social communication is a matter of conflict between alternative readings of society. (Hall 1991, quoted in Gauntlett 1997, p. 92)

In another video study, Gerry Bloustein (1998) explored how 10 Australian girls constructed their gendered identities by inviting the participants to record what they believed were salient elements of their lives in an attempt to investigate "everyday lived experience … *through their own eyes*" (p. 117, emphasis in original). During this work she claimed that the film-making process facilitated an arena in which the girls were able to experiment with the way in which they represented their identities, whilst also paradoxically revealing the restrictions and difficulties encountered in their quest to articulate "alternative selves" (p. 118). According to Bloustein, then, the film-making process *as well as* the actual completed videos reflected the social and cultural frameworks and limitations impacting the girls' perceptions of themselves. Indeed, she claimed that the use of the camera empowered the participants, the camera becoming "a tool for interpreting and redefining their worlds" (p. 117). (We should note, however, that claims that studies of this kind are "empowering" for participants are usually overegging their value: taking part may be interesting and enjoyable, and may offer some insights, but cannot reasonably be expected to be a life-transforming experience.)

Research by Horst Niesyto (2000; see also Niesyto, Buckingham, and Fisherkeller 2003) has highlighted the ever increasing proliferation of media materials in young people's lives and how these are integral to the construction of social worlds and self-perception. He further noted that although there are a vast number of films that focus on youth which have provided the basis for critical analysis, very few of these films are produced by the young people themselves. In consideration of these factors, Niesyto developed a method which has been utilized within a number of projects in Germany, where "young people had the chance to express *personal images of everyday experience* in self-produced films" (2000, p. 137, emphasis in original). Within these studies, Niesyto observed how different modes of filming revealed different perspectives of representation. For example, the "collage-like video films" gave insight into emotional and ambivalent aspects of identity through association and metaphor (p. 143), and this was a particularly rewarding mode of expression utilized by the participants that he described as "marginal," as in many cases their media literacy exceeded their competence in more conventional forms of expression, such as talking and writing (p. 144). Niesyto makes his point with gusto:

> In view of media's increasing influence on everyday communication, I put forward the following thesis: If somebody – in nowadays media society – wants to learn something about youth's ideas, feelings, and their ways of experiencing the world, he or she should give them a chance to express *themselves* also by means of their own self-made media products! (p. 137, emphasis in original)

These principles are evident and further developed in the more recent international project Children in Communication about Migration (CHICAM), which sought to explore the lives and experiences of migrant and refugee children in a number of European countries (see www.chicam.org). This collaborative project, coordinated by David Buckingham, established "media clubs" in six European countries (England, Italy, Sweden, Germany, the Netherlands, and Greece) in which a researcher and a media educator worked with recently arrived refugee and migrant young people to make visual representations of their lives and experiences (De Block, Buckingham, and Banaji 2005). The material was shared and discussed between the groups over the internet. The children made videos, collages (with cut-up magazines), arrangements of photographs with music, and specific photo tasks (such as a photo essay on likes and dislikes, or on national symbols), all of which were shared and discussed internationally via an online platform.

This method provided the researchers with a wealth of valuable data – or "thick description" (Geertz 1973/1993) – generated not only from the products produced by the children, but also from observations, written reflections, and discussions by both researchers and children throughout the entirety of the project. Hence, in this formulation verbal data are not abandoned in favor of the visual, but rather they are considered complementary factors. As two of the project researchers, Peter Holzwarth and Björn Maurer (2003), state:

> In an era when audio-visual media play an increasingly influential role in children's and adolescents' perceptions, it is important that researchers not only rely on verbal approaches alone, but also give young people the opportunity to express themselves

in contemporary media forms. Audio-visual data should not be considered an alternative to verbal data but rather a source of data with a different quality. (p. 127)

Audience Research: Young People's Literacies

The methodological principles underpinning such work are demonstrated in a significant body of work on children's media literacy undertaken by David Buckingham (1987, 1993a, 1993b, 1996, 2000, 2003). In his collaborative research with Julian Sefton-Green (1994), which discussed the pedagogic practices of media studies, they used a wide variety of methods in their analysis, including observations, interviews, and surveys; and, importantly, they examined the students' creations of, and reflections upon, their own media productions. In so doing, the students were not considered solely as consumers but also as *producers* of popular culture. Furthermore, they questioned established cultural studies approaches to popular culture in which texts are symptomatically "read"; rather, they considered students' material as a form of *social action* in relation to the environment in which it was created:

> [W]hat students say about popular culture, and the texts they produce, are part of the process by which they construct their own social identities. Although this process, inevitably, is defined in terms of social power – for example, of social class, gender, ethnicity and age – we would see the meanings of these categories not as predetermined but as actively constructed in social relationships themselves. (p. 10)

In addition, Buckingham and Sefton-Green (2004) rejected the notion of "theoreticism" (p. 11) – the privileging of theory – and aimed instead to explore the interrelation between theory and lived experience. Consequently, they attempted to foreground their own position as researchers, thus revealing rather than disguising epistemological issues inherent in the power relations between researchers and the students, identifying themselves instead as *"participant* observers" (2004, p. 11, emphasis in original).

An example of their approach is a discussion which specifically focuses on the work of two GCSE Media Studies students, giving particular attention to "the relationship between practical work and written reflection, and the students' own perspectives on this issue" (p. 146). Integral to this exercise was the production of posters by the students in which they expressed their identity, these in turn becoming the subject of written reflections. Buckingham and Sefton-Green (2004) report that the written feedback ostensibly appeared to be limited in scope, observing that one student did not comment upon the fact that the only image of a black person in his poster was his own (p. 157). Furthermore, they noted that the students themselves found the writing of a log a frustrating and pointless task (p. 160). However, Buckingham and Sefton-Green suggested that the written logs served as a springboard for revealing *and* valuable discussions with the students, claiming that the students themselves came to recognize the role of the written reflections as the project continued (pp. 159–162). Hence, they maintained that the combined process of production and reflection can uncover valuable information that was not made available by any one element alone. In this formulation, they argued that writing facilitates what they termed a "'metacognitive' function" (p. 160), that is to say,

> [The writing] made explicit those cognitive developments which are largely implicit in the production process itself. In other words, by writing things down in the log, the student 'translates' those understandings arrived at empirically into a more abstract, theoretical understanding of media production. (pp. 160–161)

Therefore, this study demonstrated the value of research that exploits the interconnections between creative processes and evaluative reflections, a notion which is developed further in subsequent studies.

David Buckingham and Sara Bragg's (2004) study of young people aged 9 to 17 aimed to explore their attitudes toward representations of sex and personal relationships in the media. To achieve this, the researchers utilized a number of methods: the completion of a diary or scrapbook in which the children documented their personal responses to media representation; interviews where they expanded upon the statements made in their diaries; group discussions that centered on a selection of video clips; further interviews discussing extracts from tabloid newspapers and magazines; and, finally, surveys that extrapolated further information about their opinions and social lives (pp. 18–19). Importantly, Buckingham and Bragg state, "Research is not a natural conduit that extracts the 'truth' about a topic or about what participants 'really' feel and think about it" (p. 17). Rather, they acknowledge that their findings would be determined by the methods employed, the environment in which the study was conducted, relationships between the participants predating and developed during the research, as well as their own chosen system of analysis. Ostensibly, although this position may appear to limit the potential scope of the research, it may in fact broaden the range of possibilities available to the researcher. As Buckingham and Bragg highlight, tasks were specifically arranged so they would prompt either "personal" or "public" responses from the participants depending upon the nature of the individual task, such as writing or speaking in a group (p. 22). Thus, by locating participants in varying discursive fields, they were more able to elicit "different voices" which facilitated a more complex and arguably more comprehensive understanding of the students involved.

Indeed, use of these methods meant that the researchers were able to offer a range of findings including: that young people utilize the media – particularly teenage magazines and soap operas – as a resource for learning about love, sex, and relationships and use the media to facilitate discussion on potentially embarrassing and sensitive issues with parents and peers; that although young people are aware of media regulation, such as the film classification system, and use it to inform their own media consumption, they believe they are capable of self-regulation and making autonomous judgments regarding their own viewing; and that young people consider sex within the context of their own morality and highlight the importance of trust, loyalty, and respect in discussions about sex and relationships in the media, rather than demonstrating that the media have "morally corrupted" them (pp. 236–241).

In their analysis, Buckingham and Bragg

> aimed at what Laurel Richardson (1998) has described as a 'crystal' structure or a range of viewpoints, none of which is necessarily more transparent or true than any others, but where we can learn from the contradictions and differences between them to develop more complex ways of seeing issues. (2004, p. 22)

Furthermore, as Buckingham has noted elsewhere (1993c, p. 92), talk functions as a *social act*, that is to say, talk is not merely a statement of held beliefs and attitudes, but rather is a behavior or process which draws upon available cultural concepts to fulfill specific functions: "people achieve identities, realities, social order and social relationships through talk" (Baker, 1997, quoted in Buckingham and Bragg, 2004, p. 23).

In consideration of this, Buckingham and Bragg emphasize the significant role of reflexivity in their approach – "that is the role of researchers in interpreting, representing and producing knowledge from the voices of research subjects" (2004, p. 38) – to promote an informed understanding of how their standpoints may influence and impact the research process. Noting, then, how their methods have molded their work, they assert that *all* research is limited by the methods applied. However, they maintain that their methods will enable researchers to gain a greater insight into children's understandings and uses of the media that are not provided by other techniques. This, Buckingham and Bragg state, is due to the systematic, multifaceted, and holistic approach of their own work:

> [R]eaders should be wary of the extent to which *all* methods necessarily constrain what research is able to show or prove…. We would strongly contest the idea that qualitative research is automatically more 'subjective' than quantitative research, or more subject to interpretation. The methods we have used enable us to be systematic and rigorous, both in ensuring the representativeness of the data we present and analyse, and in comparing material gathered through different methods and in different contexts. (p. 41, emphasis in original)

Examples from the Broader Sociological Context

These approaches are not unique to media audience studies: an interest in the use of still and moving images to understand the social world is steadily becoming more common in the social sciences generally. This is reflected in a small but growing body of literature on visual research methods by sociologists and anthropologists (Prosser 1998; Emmison and Smith 2000; Banks 2001; Pink 2001, 2003; Van Leeuwen and Jewitt 2001; Knowles and Sweetman 2004). Indeed, the cause of visual sociology has been promoted for a quarter of a century through the activities, conferences, and publications of the International Visual Sociology Association (IVSA), established in 1981. The founders of the IVSA were primarily photographers who took their own photographs to record aspects of social life that would otherwise go unremarked and unrecorded. In these early days of visual sociology, the idea of the researcher handing over the camera, or other tools, had not really dawned. More recently, however, a new generation of researchers has started to join the IVSA and fostered some diversity of methods.

Visual research, as the sources listed in the last paragraph typically note, is not an independent, self-contained approach; rather, it is methodologically and theoretically diverse, utilizing a variety of analytical perspectives (e.g. anthropology, sociology, and psychology) to study a broad spectrum of issues. Thus, visual research methods are regarded as complementary to existing approaches and, as Christopher Pole (2004) has suggested, have "the capacity to offer a different way of understanding the social world" (p. 7). However, despite the potential value offered by visual research methods, the approach remains reasonably marginal within existing qualitative practice.

In his discussion of image-based research, Jon Prosser (1998) claimed that the limited status of images within social research was attributable to the employment of "scientific" paradigms, as well as established qualitative strategies which give primacy to the written word. His study of ethnographic and methodological texts found that visual methodologies were given minimal coverage; rather, he says, they tended to suggest that "images were a pleasant distraction to the real (i.e., word-orientated) work that constituted 'proper' research" (p. 98). There are, of course, some honorable exceptions, a selection of which we will discuss below.

Making Drawings and Diagrams in Sociological Studies

In 1972, Noreen Wetton first presented her "draw and write" technique, which was originally developed as part of a project to explore emotional literacy in 7- to 8-year-old children. This work established that although children could express particular emotions visually – using both drawing *and* writing – they lacked this ability when relying solely on written or spoken words:

> It became apparent that the children experienced and empathized with a wide range of emotions including anger, frustration, despair, remorse, guilt, embarrassment and relief as well as delight, enjoyment, excitement. The children differed only from adults in that they did not have the vocabulary to express themselves. (Wetton and McWhirter 1998, p. 273)

Wetton and her colleagues (1998) argue that this approach can reveal how children conceptualize particular issues in areas such as health and safety, and that the combined process of drawing and writing enables researchers to access aspects of children's knowledge that elude conventional techniques.

Also within the field of health research, Marilys Guillemin (2004) employed a similar strategy with adults in order "to explore the ways in which people understand illness conditions" (p. 272) – specifically, women's experience of the menopause and of heart disease. Participants were asked to "draw how they visualised their condition" (p. 276). They were typically reluctant at first, but eventually drew an image, "sometimes hesitatingly and at times with such intent and force that I and they were taken aback" (p. 276). The researcher asked each participant to describe and explain their drawing. The study revealed the many and diverse ways in which the women experienced these conditions. For example, menopause was represented as a life transition (such as one part of a staircase, or as "a sun setting and the moon coming up"), as a lived experience (often chaotic), or as loss and grief.

These studies have highlighted how the use of drawings can be used to elicit a broader and richer range of data than would have been possible through traditional word-orientated approaches. Other projects have also confirmed the value of asking participants to generate visual material. For instance, Lorraine Young and Hazel Barrett's study of Kampala streetchildren (2001) adopted similar strategies in an attempt to understand the children's "socio-spatial geographies in relation to their street environments and survival mechanisms" (p. 142). Young and Barrett recognized that existing methods are not devised to provide an accurate reflection of the child's perspective, and fail to allow them any influence on the research design and process. Therefore, Young and Barrett specifically aimed to develop procedures which fostered a high degree of child-led participation in order to produce "research 'with children' rather than research 'about children'" (p. 144). They therefore utilized a number of visual methods which included drawing-based exercises (mental and "depot" maps, thematic and nonthematic drawings, and daily timelines) as well as the production of photo diaries. The children were engaged by these unusual tasks, and the practical nature of these activities facilitated a space in which the children could communicate their thoughts freely, with time being given to consider and formulate their responses. Furthermore, the visual material served as useful prompts during discussion in order to gain a greater insight into their lives.

Indeed, Young and Barrett claimed that photographic images were particularly valuable in this instance, as even the seemingly weakest pictures conveyed a wealth of information gained through the children's own interpretation of their photographs. The use of visual methods seems to have enabled the children to maintain a degree of ownership over the research exercises and, as Young and Barrett explain, "proved to be particularly important for developing gainful insight into the street child's urban environment from the child's perspective" (p. 142).

Making Photographs and Videos in Sociological Studies

In a similar way, Michael Schratz and Ulrike Steiner-Löffler (1998; see also Raggl and Schratz 2004) used photographic images produced by children in an attempt to evaluate the "inner world" of school life from the pupils' standpoint. Participants were invited to photograph what they "liked or disliked" about the school environment (1998, p. 235), and these images were used as the basis for group discussions. Significantly, the pictures instigated a dialogue amongst pupils and teachers about issues which had not formerly been discussed, including personal reflections of schooling.

A study by Alan Radley, Darrin Hodgetts, and Andrea Cullen (2005) asked homeless adults to photograph places and activities of personal significance, in order to "collect a series of glimpses of the city as seen through their eyes" (p. 276). The researchers then discussed the images produced with the participants, leading to insights into homeless life. The photographs did not constitute an object of study in themselves but served to engender communication, which itself became intrinsic to the analysis:

> We used photography in this research so that homeless people could show us their world as well as interpret it. Rather than see the photographs as bounded objects for interpretation, they are better understood as standing in a dialectical relationship with the persons who produced them. Their meaning does not lie in the pictures, except in so far as this is part of the way people talk about them. To talk about the photographs one has taken is to make claims for them – to explain, interpret and ultimately take responsibility for them. (p. 278)

Hence, Radley, Hodgetts, and Cullen claimed that this kind of interview can be conceptualized as a *dialogic* relationship between researcher and participant, through which meaning is produced in a dialectic process, and therefore not imposed by either party.

Still photography, then, has proved to be valuable as a research tool (and see also Harper 1998; Prosser and Schwartz 1998; Banks 2001; Collier 2001; Bolton, Pole, and Mizen 2004; Wright 2004). In keeping with these principles, video production has also demonstrated the advantages of combining discussion *and* visual work (e.g. Dowmunt 1980, 2001; Pink 2001, 2004; Noyes 2004). For example, in a study conducted between 1998 and 2000, Ruth Holliday's (2004) exploration of queer performances employed video diaries in order to evaluate their potential "for capturing some of the complex nuances of the representation and display of identities" (p. 1597). This was enabled by lending video cameras to participants and requesting them to detail how they represented themselves in differing everyday environments – "work, rest (home), and play (the scene)" (p. 1598) – both verbally and visually. Holliday specifically achieved these aims by encouraging respondents to film themselves in the appropriate settings whilst wearing, discussing, and commenting upon the suitability of their typical clothing for each occasion. In doing so, she maintained that this approach allowed her to "chart the similarities and differences in identity performances" (p. 1598). Significantly, Holliday established that the use of video diaries helped amass information on "identity performances" in ways that are unique to this method. On the one hand, she suggested that, as opposed to a tape-recorded interview which can only express what the participants *say*, the videos provided a *visual illustration* that allowed for a more "complete" image of self-representation; on the other hand, not only did the act of making a video generate a visual representation, but also these were supported by the individual's own narrative. Moreover, Holliday stated that the process of video making permitted participants to choose, alter, and refine their presentations of self, thus affording them a more reflexive role within the research process:

> Against other methods that focus on 'accuracy' or 'realism', then, this approach affords diarists greater potential to *represent* themselves; making a video diary can be an active, even empowering, process because it offers the participant greater 'editorial control' over the material disclosed. (p. 1603, emphasis in original)

Using Metaphor in Social and Media Research

The increased focus on reflexivity within qualitative enquiry (see Denzin and Lincoln 2005) has been central to developments in visual research methodologies and, it is argued, helps advance a fuller understanding of participants' experiences of their social worlds. More recently, the use of metaphor has emerged within social research as an effective means of exploring individuals' experiences and identities. These ideas are highlighted in Russell Belk, Güliz Ger, and Søren Askergaard's (2003) analysis of consumer desire which engaged participants from

Denmark, Turkey, and the United States in a series of tasks to investigate "the thoughts, feelings, emotions, and activities evoked by consumers in various cultural settings when asked to reflect on and picture desire, both as their particular idea of a general phenomena and as lived experiences" (p. 332). Within these exercises, a proportion of the participants were instructed to complete a journal detailing their own accounts of fulfilled or unfulfilled desires and interviewed on the issues raised; remaining participants undertook tasks specifically designed to provoke meta-phorical representations of desire, including collage making, drawing, and writing stories (p. 332). Although Belk, Ger, and Askergaard acknowledged that the jour-nals and interviews provided valuable *descriptive* information, they maintained that the projective tasks revealed a greater depth of data. This is best exemplified in the collage-making activities, where participants not only represented what they desired but also created metaphors for desire's dualistic nature by juxtaposing abstract images (pp. 333–340). Therefore, they claimed the combination of meta-phoric expressions as well as participants' explanations enabled them to construct a thematic portrait of desire that exceeded constraints of language, and would not have been possible through any one method alone:

> We found the projective and metaphoric data to be very rich in capturing fantasies, dreams, and visions of desire. The journal and depth interview material was espe-cially useful for obtaining descriptions of what and how desire was experienced. Although this is useful data, especially concerning the things people desire, it also showed some evidence of repackaging in more rational-sounding terms. Some informants found it difficult to elaborate on their private desires or did not want to reveal those desires. Hence, the projective measures sought to evoke fantasies, dreams, and visual imagination in order to bypass the reluctance, defence mecha-nisms, rationalizations, and social desirability that seemed to block the direct verbal accounts of some of those studied. (p. 332)

Research by Brandon Williams (2000) on interprofessional communication in health care has also highlighted the usefulness of metaphors within collage mak-ing, as a means for developing a more complex and comprehensive understanding of individuals.

The use of visual metaphors was further developed in Gauntlett's more recent work (2007, and see 2006) that engaged participants in building metaphorical models of their identities using Lego bricks. This method was a development of Lego Serious Play, a metaphorical consultancy process developed by Lego (see www.seriousplay.com), the Danish toy company that Gauntlett collaborated with. The approach draws some of its inspiration from Seymour Papert's theory of con-structionism (see Papert and Harel 1991), which maintains "that people learn effectively through *making* things" (Gauntlett 2006, p. 7, emphasis in original), and argues against mind–body distinctions, claiming that our perceptions and experi-ences of the world are mediated bodily *as well as* mentally (see Merleau-Ponty

1945/2002). Therefore, physical engagement with our environment activates somewhat different cognitive procedures from those triggered by purely cerebral activity. Thus, Gauntlett claims, by building metaphors of their identities prior to discussion, not only are participants granted *time* to *reflect* on what they create, but also this process engages a *different type* of thinking about the issue itself. He suggests that this approach can therefore avoid some of the problems inherent in approaches which aim to elicit an immediate reaction, by allowing a considered and reflective response to the research task.

Of course, Gauntlett readily admits, asking a participant at the start of a research workshop to "build a metaphorical model of your identity in Lego" would seem rather baffling. Rather, participants go through a series of exercises which get them acquainted with Lego building, and then with building in metaphors, before this ultimate task is reached in the second half of a workshop session which is at least 4 hours long.

Importantly, Gauntlett says, the method allows for a more complex representation of identity that does not presume an individual's self is a fixed, discernable artifact which can be described in a linear manner, but acknowledges its multifarious, amorphous, and changeable nature more suited to symbolic expression. Furthermore, he states that the process of building a Lego model is particularly appropriate in this instance as it entails improvisation and experimentation, hence providing diverse forms of conceptualization. As Gauntlett explains, the *process* offers "an alternative way of gathering sociological data, where the expressions are *worked through* (through the process of *building* in Lego, and then talking about it) rather than just being spontaneously generated (as in interviews or focus groups)" (2006, p. 5, emphasis in original). Consequently, the researcher concludes that the method affords individuals time and opportunity to build a *whole* presentation of their identity that can be presented "all in one go" (Gauntlett, 2007, p. 183) – rather than the linear, one-thing-then-another-thing pattern necessary in speech – and so enables participants to present a rounded and satisfyingly "balanced" view of their identity. Of course, it must be remembered that this is only a selected view of what a participant thinks of as their "identity" – but this thoughtfully selected representation is the very focus of the study. It is a mere snapshot, not only of a point in time but also of a point in time where the person was in an unusual research situation, making something out of Lego to explain to other participants and a university researcher. In spite of all these necessary caveats, however, Gauntlett maintains that the participants were presenting something which felt "true" to them, and which they uniformly asserted was a reasonable presentation of their sense of "who they were".

The findings of the study (2007, pp. 182–196) suggest that the use of metaphors in social research techniques can be powerful, as they enable participants to make thoughtful representations of intangible concepts (such as emotions, identities, and relationships), including the fruitful additional meanings which metaphors naturally suggest. In relation to how people think about their identities, the study found that there was in all cases a degree of tension between the desire to be a distinctive individual (not wanting to be the same as everybody else) and the desire to be a member of the community (wanting to fit in). People negotiated this in a range of different ways. In terms of media influences, the study found that the most significant role of the media was in circulating *stories* – in every form from "real-life" and celebrity magazine stories to news and advertising *as well as* movies and TV dramas – narratives which people used as framing devices to understand aspects of their lives and their overall "journey" (which was a common metaphor).

On a similar theme, Fatimah Awan's PhD study, "Young People, Identity and the Media" (2008), sought to exploit and develop the value of metaphors in social research by directing participants to create metaphorical collages on how they perceived their identities in order to examine how the media is used to shape their conceptions of self. For this project, the researcher invited 111 young people aged 13 to 14 – of contrasting class and ethnic backgrounds – drawn from seven schools across Dorset, Hampshire, and London to produce identity collages using media materials which expressed "How I see myself" and "How I think other people see me," and to provide their own interpretations of this work within unstructured interviews. From this process, Awan was able to identify a number of findings about the young people's identities and their relationship with the media. In terms of how the young people conceptualized their identities, the study revealed that whilst the participants appeared to construct their sense of self in accordance with traditional notions of masculinity and femininity, on closer reading their comments demonstrated that they did not wholly conform to these gendered positionings; rather, both boys and girls made forceful assertions of "individualism" which seemed to transgress any gender differences and instead aimed to articulate a unique identity.

In relation to the media, the study found that the participants' perceptions of ethnic minority representations were determined, to some degree, by their social worlds: the diversity intrinsic to multicultural milieus facilitated participants' negotiations of media representations alongside their actual understandings of ethnic minority individuals and cultural products encountered daily in these environments, and a lack of diversity within the predominantly white areas producing and perpetuating stereotyped notions of ethnicity. In addition, the media's influence was most apparent in participants' accounts of media celebrities and pop stars as role models. For the young people, role models did not exclusively perform a positive or negative function, or operate as figures whom individuals sought to imitate directly; rather, role models acted as a "tool kit" which enabled participants to utilize specific facets of these figures within the formations of their self-identities, and were adapted and/or negotiated in accordance with their aspirations, values, and social context.

Importantly, Awan notes that within the collages, constituent elements of these works functioned as metaphors to represent aspects of participants' identities, but the completed pictures operated as a metaphor on another plane through revealing contradictions, relationships, and patterns within the *whole* image. This was possible as the task itself required participants to produce an entire visual representation of their identity, "all in one go," as Gauntlett has put it (2007, p. 183), with individuals' reflections on their collages exploring each image independently whilst moving toward an explanation of what was shown by the overall piece. Consequently, viewing the collages enabled participants to consider their whole presentation of identity in relation to their responses to the constituent parts; the metaphors providing participants with an opportunity to express and share creative interpretations of their personal and social worlds.

Summary

Creative and visual research methods offer unique methodological advantages for considering individuals' identities and their relationships with the media. For example, Kitzinger's (1993) analysis of media influences on people's understanding of AIDS highlighted that although participants articulated a critical awareness of the media's rhetoric, they replicated the dominant discourse of the medium. Thus, the use of the "news game" technique enabled Kitzinger to elicit attitudes that may not have been uncovered by more traditional methods. Similarly, by asking participants to create their own original videos, Gauntlett (1997) revealed that children were influenced by existing media coverage, but could create their own stories with their own emphases. In particular, it was the very process of the children's active engagement in producing the videos that granted the researcher access to more comprehensive and worthwhile data. Developing this point, Buckingham and Bragg's (2004) work on young peoples' attitudes toward sex and relationships in the media specifically sought to draw out participants' responses through the adoption of a variety of methods, including diaries, interviews, and group discussions. In doing so, the study facilitated a more complex and reflexive understanding of the students' thoughts and beliefs. Expanding on this theme, Belk, Ger, and Askergaard's (2003) work revealed that metaphors could overcome the limitations of language to convey ambivalent emotional and intuitive responses. In addition, Gauntlett's (2007) more recent study, in which metaphors of personal identity were constructed using Lego, established that this process exercises different modes of thinking which can produce more nuanced representations of the self.

These studies have then started to trace a trajectory of research that employs creative and visual methods in the process of their investigations. The researchers discussed have argued that these methodological approaches offer crucial and distinct benefits over more traditional techniques, providing a rich and varied supply of data for analysis. To date, these methods have been applied in a relatively small number of quite specific research projects, and we can anticipate that visual and creative research techniques may be put to diverse and fascinating uses in the future.

References

Ang, I. 1985 *Watching* Dallas: *Soap Opera and the Melodramatic Imagination*. Methuen, London.

Awan, F. 2008 Young people, identity and the media: a study of conceptions of self-identity among youth in southern England. Retrieved from http://www.artlab.org.uk/fatimah-awan-phd.htm

Banks, M. 2001 *Visual Methods in Social Research*. Sage, London.

Belk, R.W., Güliz, G. and Askegaard, S. 2003 The fire of desire: a multisited inquiry into consumer passion. *Journal of Consumer Research*, 30, 3, pp. 326–351.

Bloustein, G. 1998 "It's different to a mirror 'cos it talks to you": teenage girls, video cameras and identity. In S. Howard, ed. *Wired Up: Young People and the Electronic Media*. UCL Press, London, pp. 115–133.

Bolton, A., Pole, C. and Mizen, P. 2001 Picture this: researching child workers. *Sociology*, 35, 2, pp. 501–518.

Buckingham, D. 1987 *Public Secrets: Eastenders and its Audiences*. BFI, London.

Buckingham, D., ed. 1993a *Reading Audiences: Young People and the Media*. Manchester University Press, Manchester, UK.

Buckingham, D. 1993b *Children Talking Television: The Making of Television Literacy*. Falmer Press, London.

Buckingham, D. 1993c Boy's talk: television and the policing of masculinity. In D. Buckingham, ed. *Reading Audiences: Young People and the Media*, Manchester University Press, Manchester, UK, pp. 89–115.

Buckingham, D. 1996 *Moving Images: Understanding Children's Emotional Responses to Television*. Manchester University Press, Manchester, UK.

Buckingham, D. 2000 *The Making of Citizens: Young People, News and Politics*. Routledge, London.

Buckingham, D. 2003 *Media Education: Literacy, Learning and Contemporary Culture*. Polity, Cambridge.

Buckingham, D. and Bragg, S. 2004 *Young People, Sex and the Media: The Facts of Life?* Palgrave Macmillan, Basingstoke.

Buckingham, D. and Sefton-Green, J. 1994 *Cultural Studies Goes to School: Reading and Teaching Popular Media*. Taylor & Francis, London.

Collier, M. 2001 Approaches to analysis in visual anthropology. In T. Van Leeuwen and C. Jewitt, eds. *Handbook of Visual Analysis*. Sage, London, pp. 35–60.

De Block, L., Buckingham, D. and Banaji, S. 2005 Children in Communication about Migration (CHICAM) – final report, funded by the European Commission (Contract No: HPSE – CT2001-00048). Retrieved from http://www.chicam.org/reports/download/chicam_final_report.pdf

Denzin, N.K. and Lincoln, Y.S., eds. 2005 *The Sage Handbook of Qualitative Research*, 3rd edn. Sage, Thousand Oaks, CA.

Dowmunt, T. 1980 *Video with Young People*. Inter-Action Imprint, London.

Dowmunt, T. 2001 Dear camera: video diaries, subjectivity and media power. Paper presented to ICA preconference "Our Media Not Theirs," American University, Washington, DC, 24 May. Retrieved from http://ourmedianetwork.org/files/papers/2001/Dowmunt.om2001.pdf

Eldridge, J., Kitzinger, J. and Williams, K. 1997 *The Mass Media and Power in Modern Britain*. Oxford University Press, Oxford.

Emmison, M. and Smith, P. 2000 *Researching the Visual: Images, Objects, Contexts and Interactions in Social and Cultural Inquiry*. Sage, London.

Gauntlett, D. 1997 *Video Critical: Children, the Environment and Media Power*. John Libbey, Luton, UK.

Gauntlett, D. 2006 Creative and visual methods for exploring identities: a conversation between David Gauntlett and Peter Holzwarth. *Visual Studies*, 21, 1, pp. 82–91. Retrieved from http://www.artlab.org.uk/VS-interview-2ps.pdf

Gauntlett, D. 2007 *Creative Explorations: New Approaches to Identities and Audiences*. Routledge, London.

Gauntlett, D. and Hill, A. 1999 *TV Living: Television, Culture and Everyday Life*. Routledge, London.

Geertz, C. 1973/1993 *The Interpretation of Cultures*. Fontana, London.

Guillemin, M. 2004 Understanding illness: using drawings as a research method. *Qualitative Health Research*, 14, 2, pp. 272–289.

Harper, D. 1998 An argument for visual sociology. In J. Prosser, ed. *Image-Based Research: A Sourcebook for Qualitative Researchers*. Falmer Press, London, pp. 24–41.

Holliday, R. 2004 Filming "The Closet": the role of video diaries in researching sexualities. *American Behaviour Scientist*, 47, 12, pp. 1597–1616.

Holzwarth, P. and Maurer, B. 2003 CHICAM (Children in Communication about Migration): an international research project exploring the possibilities of intercultural communication through children's media productions. In M. Kiegelmann and L. Gürtler, eds. *Research Questions and Matching Methods of Analysis*. Ingeborg Huber Verlag, Tübingen, Germany.

Kitzinger, J. 1990 Audience understandings of AIDS media messages: a discussion of methods. *Sociology of Health and Illness*, 12, 3, pp. 319–335.

Kitzinger, J. 1993 Understanding AIDS: researching audience perceptions of acquired immune deficiency syndrome. In J. Eldridge, ed. *Getting the Message: News, Truth and Power*. Routledge, London, pp. 272–304.

Knowles, C. and Sweetman, P. eds. 2004 *Picturing the Social Landscape: Visual Methods and the Sociological Imagination*. Routledge, London.

MacGregor, B. and Morrison, D. 1995 From focus groups to editing groups: a new method of reception analysis. *Media, Culture and Society*, 17, 1, pp. 141–150.

Merleau-Ponty, M. 1945/2002 *Phenomenology of Perception*. Routledge, London.

Niesyto, H. 2000 Youth research on video self-productions: reflections on a social-aesthetic approach. *Visual Sociology*, 15, pp. 135–153.

Niesyto, H., Buckingham, D. and Fisherkeller, J. 2003 VideoCulture: crossing borders with young people's video productions. *Television and New Media*, 4, 4, pp. 461–482.

Noyes, A. 2004 Video diary: a method for exploring learning dispositions. *Cambridge Journal of Education*, 34, 2, pp. 193–201.

Papert, S. and Harel, I. 1991 *Constructionism*. Ablex, Norwood, NJ.

Philo, G. 1990 *Seeing and Believing: The Influence of Television*. Routledge, London.

Pink, S. 2001 *Doing Visual Ethnography*. London, Sage.

Pink, S. 2003 Interdisciplinary agendas in visual research: re-situating visual anthropology. *Visual Studies*, 18, 2, pp. 179–192.

Pink, S. 2004 Performance, self-representation and narrative: interviewing with video. In C. Pole, ed. *Seeing Is Believing? Approaches to Visual Research, Studies in Qualitative Methodology*, vol. 7. Elsevier JAI, Oxford, pp. 61–77.

Pole, C., ed. 2004 *Seeing Is Believing? Approaches to Visual Research, Studies in Qualitative Methodology*, vol. 7. Elsevier JAI, Oxford.

Prosser, J., ed. 1998 *Image-Based Research: A Sourcebook for Qualitative Researchers*. Falmer Press, London.

Prosser, J. and Schwartz, D. 1998 Photographs within the sociological research process. In J. Prosser, ed. *Image-Based Research: A Sourcebook for Qualitative Researchers*. Falmer Press, London, pp. 115–130.

Radley, A., Hodgetts, D. and Cullen, A. 2005 Visualizing homelessness: a study in photography and estrangement. *Journal of Community and Applied Social Psychology*, 15, 4, pp. 273–295.

Raggl, A. and Schratz, M. 2004 Using visuals to release pupils' voices: emotional pathways into enhancing thinking and reflecting on learning. In C. Pole, ed. *Seeing Is Believing? Approaches to Visual Research, Studies in Qualitative Methodology*, vol. 7. Elsevier JAI, Oxford, pp. 147–162.

Richardson, L. 1998 Writing: a method of inquiry. In N.K. Denzin and Y.S. Lincoln, eds. *Collecting and Interpreting Qualitative Materials*, vol. 3. Sage, London, pp. 345–371.

Schratz, M. and Steiner-Löffler, U. 1998 Pupils using photographs in school self-evaluation. In J. Prosser, ed. *Image-Based Research: A Sourcebook for Qualitative Researchers*. Falmer Press, London, pp. 235–251.

Van Leeuwen, T. and Jewitt, C. 2001 *Handbook of Visual Analysis*. Sage, London.

Wetton, N.M. and McWhirter, J. 1998 Images and curriculum development in health education. In J. Prosser, ed. *Image-Based Research: A Sourcebook for Qualitative Researchers*. Falmer Press, London, pp. 263–283.

Williams, B. 2000 Using collage art work as a common medium for communication in interprofessional care. *Journal of Interprofessional Care,* 16, 1, pp. 53–58.

Wright, T. 2004 *The Photographic Handbook*, 2nd edn. Routledge, London.

Young, L. and Barrett, H. 2001 Adapting visual methods: action research with Kampala street children. *Area*, 33, 2, pp. 141–152.

19

Locating Media Ethnography

Patrick D. Murphy

What are the qualities and distinguishing features of media ethnography? Certainly, in developing research designs and reporting findings, ethnography has a history of being guided by an identifiable range of investigative activities, such as participant observation, conversational interviews in naturalistic settings, observation and the recording of speech-in-action, and detailed field note documentation (Spradley 1979, 1980; Fetterman 1989; Sanjek 1990; Wolcott 1995; Denzin and Lincoln 1998). As this range of investigative activities attests, what ethnography has historically done best is "make direct contact with social agents in the normal courses and routine situations of their lives to try to understand something of *how* and *why* these regularities take place" (Willis 2000, p. xiii, emphasis in original). It is therefore fair to say that participation in and the witnessing of activities and events over time to form a research record lie at the qualitative heart of what ethnography does, and does well. But despite a large and growing body of scholarship from which to draw, these qualifying characteristics are not always salient in media ethnography, making it difficult to describe the contours and confines of what is meant by *ethnography* in media ethnography.

This chapter is an attempt to explore and identify what qualities and distinguishing features are used to define and give shape to media ethnography. To pursue this charge, I want to revisit Nightingale's (1993) question of "What's ethnographic?" about media ethnography. Although Nightingale originally offered the question rather pithily by casting into doubt the ethnographic credentials of ethnographic research focused on media audiences, I think it is useful to return to her query, albeit this time taking it as an exploratory challenge. In fact, I want to engage this challenge by taking up a second, more recent set of questions posited by Coman and Rothenbuhler (2005), who ask, "Where is the dividing line between doing ethnography in the classic sense and doing research that is ethnographic in

The Handbook of Media Audiences, First Edition. Edited by Virginia Nightingale.
© 2014 John Wiley & Sons, Ltd. Published 2014 by John Wiley & Sons, Ltd.

some respects? How important is that line?" (p. 2). Guided by these questions, I draw from past and present work in media ethnography and examine it in relation to a broader history of ethnography and some of the key methodological and representational issues that have defined it. Through this approach, I hope to tease out a clearer portrait of what might be said to constitute media ethnography.

Ethnographic Roots and Trajectories

Eminent ethnographer Harry F. Wolcott (1995) notes that one of the problems surrounding the definition of *ethnography* is that the term

> refers to both the *processes* for accomplishing it – ordinarily involving original fieldwork and always requiring the reorganization and editing of material for presentation – and to the presentation itself, the *product* of that research, which ordinarily takes its form in prose. (pp. 82–83, emphasis in original)

It is precisely along these two lines that I'd like to consider how the tensions within and converging forces outside the ethnographic enterprise have shaped the formation of media ethnography's own practice and prose.

Ethnography has, of course, long been associated with doing research in "the field." Indeed, for much of anthropology's history, doing fieldwork has constituted a sort of rite of passage, and the field is conceptualized as a place "out there," often in faraway locations where the "natives" dwell, practicing traditional, authentic culture. Since Malinowski yanked anthropology "off the veranda," doing ethnography has involved the immersion of the researcher in the lives of research subjects as a means to observe their behavior in naturalistic settings. This commitment was perceived as essential for gaining access to the patterns, pressures, constraints, and incentives of local cultures, and thus necessary for unlocking the native's point of view in order to produce ethnographic descriptions rigorous enough to be considered scientific.

While being in the field has remained important, in more recent years ethnographers from various disciplines have wrestled with both fieldwork's problematic origins in empire and colonization – for example, travel writing as a reflection of exploration and expansionist enterprises (Clifford 1983; Pratt 1992) – and ethnography's tendency to exoticize "the Other" while suppressing the ethnographer's own presence in the completed text. From the latter half of the 1960s on, the internal conflict inherent in participant observation began to produce epistemological fissures along these lines, most notably in anthropology with the publication of transformative texts such as Malinowski's (1967) *A Diary in the Strict Sense of the Term* (released 25 years after his death) and Claude Lévi-Strauss's *Tristes Tropiques* (1955 in French and 1961 in English). These texts and others that followed, such as

Dumont's (1978) *The Headman and I* and especially Clifford and Marcus's (1986) seminal edited collection, *Writing Culture*, began to move ethnographic description toward more confessional, reflexive, and eventually experimental writing styles as ways to recast the notion of epistemological validity in fieldwork and reject the scientization of research subjects, advocating instead more dialogical, contingent, and even autobiographic accountings of the field experience. These descriptive turns were meant, in short, to resuscitate the intimacies and vulnerabilities of fieldwork and make them part of an ethnographic record that had, up to that point, been defined by distance and objectivity but that increasingly seemed artificial and exploitative.

As a product, ethnography's passage through this transformative process has been characterized as a series of identifiable phases of aesthetic reformations, which Lincoln and Denzin (1998) label as *traditional, modernist, blurred genres*, and the *crisis of representation and legitimation*. They assert that this progression has led to a "fifth moment" of representational "bricolage" capable of better addressing the inner tensions and ongoing dialectics of ethnographic practice (Lincoln and Denzin 1998). But while most agree that the concerns over ethnographic authority and the political implication of representation (e.g., who gets to speak for whom) have forced a reconsideration of the basis of ethnographic knowledge, not all observers are convinced of the currency of a paradigmatic interlacing. Hammersley (1999), for instance, points to the problem of merely binding together dissimilar ideas and the indiscriminate mixing of paradigms implied by ethnographic bricolage. Drawing from German sociologist Otto Neurath, he argues instead for a reconceptualization of ethnography closer to the art of boat building while at sea, "sailors who on the open seas must reconstruct their ship but are never able to start afresh from the base. Where a beam is taken away a new one must at once be put there, and for this the rest of the ship is used for support" (p. 577). Ethnography, like boatbuilding, can replace constructs but must keep enough from its past to remain intact and "seaworthy." As these contrasting visions of ethnography's path into the future underscore, the elaboration of an epistemologically agreeable way to translate the ethnographic experience appears to remain very much a work in progress.

As if this challenge to ethnography were not enough, the contentious debates and competing visions surrounding the translative process between fieldwork and ethnographic text have been followed by a "deep reassessment of the nature of fieldwork" and a realization that the mise-en-scène of ethnography is being profoundly altered by the deterritorialization of culture (Marcus 1998, p. 107). Here various writers have called into question the need for traditional, Evans-Pritchard-style immersion in one cultural site as a means to explain the entire cultural and social life, focusing instead on elaborating ethnographies that explore how "large scale forces work themselves out in everyday life" (Ortner 1993, p. 413). This was precipitated by a sense that the gaps between the cultural worlds of informants and ethnographers were closing, and how (if they ever were) "the natives" were no longer limited in experience to local lifeways, their worldviews being expanded (disrupted?) by a host of interrelated phenomena (migration, tourism, international trade policies, urbanization, natural resource exploitation, war, mass media, personal communication devices, etc.). Within this context, several prominent theorists have called for a shift from the more classical notion of "being there" in the field (singular and over time) to a less fixed, temporally emergent "multisited ethnography" focused, if not on cultural completeness, then on linkages and connections (Hannerz 2003a; Marcus 1998). This shift in locational emphasis implies to some extent a less deliberate selection of the research site, and indeed Hannerz (2003b) confesses, "I wonder if it is not a recurrent character-istic of multi-sited ethnography that site selections are to an extent made grad-ually and cumulatively, as new insights develop, as opportunities come into sight, and to some extent by chance" (p. 207).

The implications for this reconsideration of what constitutes fieldwork (and where and how long) and, by extension, "the field" itself is of particular relevance for ethnographers of media reception as the participant observation of media use has always been a problematic endeavor, not to mention the more recent challenge of studying the communities and cultural practices of cyberspace. In fact, in some media ethnography the notion of clearly defined geographic borders and cultural boundaries of a situated field gave way to a more open "network" of localities, flows, and movements of people, capital, and ideas (Castells 1996). For "new media" ethnographers in particular, this recasting of ethnographic inquiry as a means to study the heterogeneous complexity of networks has necessitated a rethinking of the nature of fieldwork, especially as cyberspace becomes both the "place" and medium through which research is conducted.

However, I don't want to give the impression that the degree to which the reas-sessment of the field or the force of the various cycles of epistemological purpose and ontological doubt emerging out of anthropology and elsewhere has been transferred to media ethnography's own formation in an easily identifiable line. On the contrary, even when traces of influence are discernable, that influence is quite fragmented and uneven for various reasons. For instance, media and cultural studies' own ethnographic turn was seeded at the height of ethnography's "crisis in representation" (Murdock 1997; Murphy 1999), whereas anthropology, though slow to come to mass media as a serious object of study, was already intimately immersed in the rethinking of the parameters of ethnographic theory and method when it finally did (Spitulnik 1993; Ginsburg, Abu-Lughod, and Larkin 2002). Broadly speaking, the result was that while media and cultural studies took up the issue of reflexivity to spark a robust and theoretically productive debate, it didn't immediately translate that debate into more complex, thickly descriptive media ethnographies because researchers seemed to be unsure as to how to negotiate the pitfalls of representing "the Other" without reproducing traditional ethnography's dual legacy of objectification and exploitation.

Meanwhile, anthropology's own capacity to weather its "crisis" was affected in some interesting ways by its concurrent engagement of broader issues of national and transnational power. This involved the pressing need to consider how human agency and local cultures were suspended within and expressed in relation to larger webs of subnational and transnational networks that were comprised, in no small measure, via "imagined communities" (Anderson 1991) and profoundly shaped by "mediascapes" and "ideoscapes" (Appadurai 1996). Within this context, it was not hard to make the short leap from ethnography to media ethnography, as the collection *Media Worlds: Anthropology on New Terrain* (Ginsburg, Abu-Lughod, and Larkin 2002) most clearly illustrates. In contrast, the vast majority of the more social scientifically driven news production ethnographies, established in the 1970s and now experiencing a "second wave" (see Paterson and Domingo 2008), have been grounded in a social construction- ist orthodoxy that has demonstrated little serious interest in the sort of methodological or epistemological introspection (Cottle 2000) found in media cultural studies and anthropology.

These different historical moments in the conception, development, and transformation of media ethnography have led in some interesting ways to parallel and intersecting research traditions. Indeed, the various strategies that media ethnographers in the different camps have employed as ethnographic methods (participant observation, observation, conversational interviews, group interviews, time use diaries, letters, and family albums and other personal documents) and as approaches to fieldwork and its related constructs (the field, immersion, rapport, researcher–subject relations, fieldnotes, etc.) are as diverse as they are revealing. But it is precisely because of these disparate trajectories of ethnographic research that it becomes difficult to talk about "media ethnog- raphy" in the singular, and so we might be better served to think in terms of "media ethnographies." That said, it is also worth noting that various visions of media ethnography, and I am thinking particularly here of media and cultural studies and anthropology, have also criss-crossed, mingled, and broken free of each other at various times, giving the impression of a cross-disciplinary dialogue at the same moment that they somehow seem to float free of one another.

By way of analogy, we could think of the fabric of media ethnography as something resembling more an unfinished quilt than a tightly woven tapestry of ideas, as the various traditions and methods used to approach media-related issues often appear like a patchwork of stitched-together materials. That is, as part of a longer ethnographic tradition, media ethnography displays reoccurring patterns and intersections, but much of what has been cut from other cloths often seems not to match. In an effort to trace some threads that lace together this creation, in the remainder of the chapter I attempt to present a clearer picture of media ethnography's contours and limits by focusing on that key concept so central to ethnography's origins: fieldwork.

Media Ethnographies and the Field

First, it should be noted that as a research strategy, ethnography has been enlisted to answer different kinds of media-related problems. Broadly speaking, most media ethnographies fall into one of two categories: audience ethnography or media production ethnographies. These, in turn, can be defined in various subareas of study, such as media reception ethnographies (focused on meaning making), media use (emphasizing media technologies and the rites and rituals that surround them at home and elsewhere), and fan studies. Production ethnographies have pursued questions concerning media professionals in the contexts of the cultural industries, creative personnel involved in the production of "alternative" media (e.g., blogs, indy music, or film), or noncommercial citizens' media (local community radio stations, indigenous video, etc.). Production and reception are not necessarily mutually exclusive areas of investigation, and some studies have collapsed two or more of the above foci (e.g. Juluri 2003; Abu-Lughod 2005). While it would be impossible in one chapter to take up a full examination of these different trajectories within the expanding range of media ethnography, it is useful to provide a few notes on general tendencies within media ethnography and look at some specific studies to help illustrate differences as well as overlapping points of methodological engagement and presentation.

Media Ethnographies and the Study of Production

In many respects, the study of the cultural context of media production, which has a rather established history in journalism studies, reflects the most deliberate vision of what constitutes the field. Classic studies of news production, such as Tuchman's (1973) *Making News* and Gans's (1980) *Deciding What's News*, have as their focus very concrete field sites: newspaper newsrooms. These studies were developed via long-term observation of newsroom culture and its relationship to decision making in order to establish how news was made. Ethnographic observation of newsroom routines helped these researchers gain a fuller, more intimate understanding of how news was, in essence, manufactured via divisions of labor, bureaucratic hierarchies, and professional norms and ideological pressures (e.g., the place of "objective" and "authoritative" sources) (Cottle 2007). More recent work has extended this tradition of focusing on routines and decision-making practices in newsrooms, as journalists respond to technological determinants and new market pressures and adjust their craft to online environments (Paterson and Domingo 2008). Producing ethnographies that aspire to provide a "dispassionate look" that "real online journalists face" (pp. x–xi), Paterson and Domingo's edited collection draws from and extends the lessons of past media production ethnography produced in sociology and early cultural studies, as well as its tradition of epistemological realism.

Though the methodology used is referred to as *participant observation*, both past and recent news production ethnography have emphasized the objective nature of data collection and thus clearly lean toward observation and away from the emic-etic interpretative work necessitated when participation is given full partnership in methodological practice. In fact, Gans (1999) fully advocates detachment in the field, asserting that "once researchers fail to distance themselves from the people they are studying, however, or fail to allow them the same distancing, the rules of qualitative reliability and validity are side stepped" (pp. 542–543). To punctuate this emphasis on distance and analytical control, Gans goes on to say that "the rule I used in fieldwork was to be friendly to and with the people you were studying and to form friendships only after the research was done" (p. 547 n. 4). Such declarations underscore that within this literature there is little interrogation of the politics of the field and that the ethnographies are authenticated through cool distance that is textually inscribed by adopting a decidedly "expository" descriptive style (see Murphy 2008).

Anthropology has provided a related yet distinct corpus of ethnographic work on media production. In keeping with anthropological tradition, some of this research has been carried out with indigenous communities and other marginalized groups, often in terms of self-definition and activism via the use of video cameras. Others, however, have moved more into the realm of the cultural industries. Illustrative of this pool of scholarship is Arlene Dávila's (2002) study of the production of *latinidad* in advertising targeted to Hispanics, Tejaswini Ganti's (2002) examination of the Bombay film industry, and the previously referenced work on foreign news correspondents by Hannerz (2003a). Though focused on very distinct questions about media production, collectively these studies nevertheless tell us something about how ethnographic method has been employed to pursue issues related to media production as a cultural force, particularly within the context of globalization. It should be noted, however, that ethnographically these studies bear some striking differences, especially with regard to self-reflexivity and the relationship between the field experience and the ethnographic text.

This is particularly the case of media ethnographies that have primarily been elaborated via interviews with only passing attention to participant observation. For instance, interacting with foreign news correspondents in Johannesburg, Tokyo, Jerusalem, and elsewhere, Hannerz provides a thickly descriptive study grounded in the personalities of foreign correspondents. Significantly, unlike the work of sociologists of journalism sketched out above, Hannerz (2003b) focuses on agency over bureaucratic structures, describing and interpreting the lives and experiences of individual correspondents by "studying sideways" (pp. 3–4) – a notion meant to underscore his affinity with and professional similarity to his research subjects. It is within the context of this research that Hannerz (2003b) waxes reflexive over his relationships with correspondents and his choice to call his interviews with them "conversations" rather than interviews, going into some detail as to why and how his approach to the multisited study of news correspondents took shape. In short, through *Foreign News* and its companion article, Hannerz (2003a, 2003b) clearly attempts to make salient and textually inscribe those aspects of his research that were messy and not easily resolved, and one gets the feeling that he is oddly ambivalent about doing fieldwork in a multisited field despite his advocacy for it. This sense of discomfort, however, does not come across as contradictory. On the contrary, his reflections are revealing and productive, and in my view comprise one of the things that helps evoke a richer, more textured sense of his research experience in the final text and thus why multisited media ethnography has value.

Conversely, fellow anthropologist Arlene Dávila (2002) simply makes the assertion that her interviews with the staffs of 16 Hispanic advertising agencies are part of "current anthropological research on the media's role in the construction and expression of identities through ethnographic analyses" (p. 264) without any further methodological reflection or interpretation. In her book on marketing and Latinos (Dávila 2002), she does supply a few notes on entrée, immersion, and participant observation (pp. 17–20), but these are quite limited and provide strikingly little detail. As such, though in many ways just as descriptive as Hannerz's, her study actually reads much more in line with past cultural studies work which evokes ethnography while refusing the often untidy work of delving into details of how or why it is necessarily ethnographic. This is not to suggest that Dávila's interviews are any less conversational or rapport generating than Hannerz's, or that her observations of meeting and attendance of events and conventions are any less participatory. But whereas Hannerz provides ongoing narrative connections with his subjects and moments of reflexivity that give a sense of his ethnographic habitus, Dávila largely retreats from such efforts.

To this observation some might respond, so what? But the point that I think needs to be made is that if ethnographers dismiss the chore of methodological self-interrogation or fail to provided detailed renderings of the field experience, how are readers able to identify the "ethnographicness" of what is labeled media ethnography? That is, if ethnography is in fact both "process" and "product," than how can we, as readers, fully appreciate the latter without a clear sense of the former?

Indeed, simply stating that something is ethnographic instantiates a trading on the currency of the ethnographic tradition and an allegiance to an academic heritage by declaration. As Nightingale wrote some 20 years ago about cultural studies, the application the term *ethnographic* "acts to legitimate the research, to denote its cultural, phenomenal and empirical methods, and even to signify its emphasis on 'community'" (p. 154). In short, media ethnography that doesn't invoke the "complex specificness" (Geertz 1973, p. 23, quoted in Walcott 1995, p. 96) of the research process and communicate in some substantial and candid way the grain of the field ultimately undermines "ethnographic validity" – a quality that Sanjek (1990) argues lies at the heart of good ethnography and is contingent upon explicit choices made in the field (e.g. decisions to link and follow events and activities), the range and variety of field relationships (e.g., key informants and friendships), and direct evidence from fieldnotes and interview transcripts.

Ethnographic Identity in Fieldwork

In my view, many of the most insightful media ethnographies that provide the kind of fodder for ethnographic validity identified by Sanjek are those of anthropologists and media studies scholars engaging questions of reception and meaning making who have as their field sites geographically identifiable communities (e.g., Michaels 1994; Gillespie 1995; Mankekar 1999; Tufte 2000; Parameswaran 2002; LaPastina 2003; Abu-Lughod 2005; Miller 2006; Podber 2007). These studies are fully anchored in immersion and long-term participant observation, and tied to the examination of "local culture." These have provided some of the most detailed and compelling insights into the politics and practices of doing media ethnography. In asserting this, I also think it should be said that the kinds of tales from the field told by these writers are quite diverse in both descriptive style and ethnographic detail. What they share, however, is a sense of how the field experience shapes the direction of the research and how "being there" not only provides opportunities for detailed fieldnotes but also forms the more sensually understood (and thus remembered) "headnotes" from which to draw interpretations.

It is, therefore, not surprising perhaps that the negotiation of ethnographic identity, the centrality of community, the importance of surprise, and the embodied field experience surface as central points of interpretive struggle across the range of these long-term studies. For instance, Brazilian media ethnographer Antonio LaPastina (2003, 2006) has published several essays detailing some of the field dilemmas that have shaped his study of telenovela reception in "Macambira," a small town in northeastern Brazil. In "Now That You're Going Home, Are You Going to Write about the Natives You Studied?" a title inspired by a community member's utterance days before his departure from the field, LaPastina (2003) interprets his ethnographic presence as something that reinforced his subjects' own sense that their lives were quite distant from that of the "modern" Brazil they encountered on television. This feeling of difference and "otherness," however, facilitated his conversations with followers of *The Cattle King*, a popular telenovela about rural life, adultery, and redemption in which a husband confronts his own faults and reconciles with his wife, who was driven to adultery by her feeling of abandonment within the marriage. Most of the viewers rejected the notion that a man would take back an adulterous wife, but through this and other ongoing discussions about televisual relationships, LaPastina was able to engage a full range of issues related to local versus urban gender roles and practices, family life, perceptions about the influence of television on local culture, and the line between public and private life. Moreover, in discussing gender roles and adultery as played out in a telenovela, LaPastina was able to position his difference as a way to ask increasingly provocative questions and access the inner workings of gender roles and relations typically kept private. In such a way, his ethnography presents a contextually grounded study of meaning within an interpretive community, though that interpretive community is understood not first and foremost by its ties to a particular media text, but rather in terms of how a particular media text revealed something about how the community saw itself in relation to modernity.

In a related but more intimate and self-reflexive article, LaPastina (2006) examines, via his own experiences in the field, how avoiding disclosure shapes the personalities of gay and lesbian ethnographers fearful of the consequences should their sexual identities be revealed in the communities where they work. Counter to the experiences of gay, lesbian, bisexual, or transgender (GLBT) researchers who draw from their own sexual orientation as a tool for researching GLBT issues, LaPastina (2006) crafts a "story of unfulfilled erotic tension, of moving back into the closet and choosing celibacy for fear of the repercussions my sexuality might have on my work and my life" (p. 728). Through this essay, LaPastina confesses that though he is Brazilian, much of his childhood experiences in São Paulo (where he grew up) and elsewhere shaped his "expectations, norms, anxieties, and fears" about "remote lands of the interior of northeastern Brazil" (p. 729). These profoundly framed his encounter with the community, filling him with presuppositions that caused a great deal of trepidation as he approached fieldwork. But it was not until he lied about his own marital status that he confessed, "I felt like a fraud and a coward, distanced from this culture I had begun to grow accustomed to" (p. 732).

Reflecting on this intense negotiation of ethnographic identity within this small community "where everybody knows everyone and notions of privacy are illusory" (p. 730), he acknowledges that he felt he had to use deception to be accepted. And though he is convinced this decision may have had implications for his data collection, he doesn't believe that it negatively affected the quality of his data. What did surface and remain, however, was a sense that he had compromised his ethical mantra and in the process became somewhat objectified. "Although I was the one empowered, at least in the ethnographic sense, I was also the one feeling vulnerable. It was an anthropophagic encounter. I consumed them through my gaze and regurgitated them through my writing while they devoured the outside world, the externality of urban modern society, through me" (p. 730).

Along a similar line, another Brazilian media ethnographer, Heloisa Buarque de Almeida (2003), found that her field relationships with people of the rural community where she conducted her research were initially shaped by *their* objectification of *her*, via television images of São Paulo, as a big-city woman. This imposed ethnographic identity was difficult to negotiate as it often negatively "sexuated" her field experience.

However, she also found that, unlike most local women, her field identity as a *paulista* (a woman from São Paulo) allowed her to transgress local cultural norms to engage questions across gender about dominant representations and their interpretations.

Within this context of ethnographic production, I'd like to turn, momentarily, to my own work. Some might argue that, as a white male US scholar whose ethnographic work has taken place primarily in Mexican working-class communities, my emphasis on the necessity of immersion and on the productive discomfort of wrestling to come to terms with something not properly my own is by definition a product of ethnographic distance as well as an extension of anthropology's "trade in curiosities, bringing 'home' accounts of exotic and unsettling practices from unfamiliar places" (Murdock 1997, p. 180). There is, of course, a long history behind this perception, and elsewhere I have examined at length my own burden of authorship in relation to representation, power–knowledge networks, and the ethical conundrums now recognized as a largely insoluble part of what ethnography based on fieldwork in "traditional societies" must contend with (Murphy 1999, 2002). However, while acknowledging that issues of location profoundly shape epistemological and political elements of the ethnographic encounter, I have found that even in my recent work with people and places very similar to my own background and place of origin, entrée, rapport, spontaneous conversations, and the surprise of the field experience remain essential dynamics in the gathering of data. These field-related, experiential processes engender an interpretive vitality that I find hard to imagine emerging through studies that draw from a more dissolved, ephemeral, phantom-like sense of the field or that spring from quasi-ethnography that assumes rather than establishes ethnographic proximity.

Along these lines, I am skeptical of the notion that "concept near" ethnographers simply "begin ethnography years before," and hence bypass the difficulties of establishing rapport and credibility in the field. In fact, the contrary may be true as what might be called a renegotiation of ethnographic identity is often a thematically defining characteristic of "native" ethnographies, particularly when media ethnographers "go home" to conduct research (e.g., Kraidy 1999; Mankekar 1999; Parameswaran 2002; Akindes 2003; Acosta-Alzuru 2005; Kim 2005, 2006). For instance, Maronite-Lebanese researcher Marwan Kraidy (1999) has detailed the renegotiation of his ethnographic identity through the study of his own community, and in fact put the process of reimmersion into a productive dialogue with his fellow Maronites' struggles to come to terms with their own hybrid ethnicity within a highly politicized and increasingly globalized, fragmented, and media-saturated cultural environment. Even more deliberate is the tenor of Kim's (2005, 2006) work, whose focus on reflexivity in ethnographic practice involves exposing not only her own experiences studying women of different generations from two apartment complexes in Seoul, but also how imported televisual texts operated as a resource for those women's reflexivity about a changing world and their place within it. Interestingly, it is via her own profile as a Korean woman with Western credentials (degrees and time lived in the West) that Kim (2006) was able to develop

"TV talk" sessions where the women "*'enthusiastically'* engaged in a process of self-discovery" (p. 237, emphasis in original) and where she was expected to participate by drawing from and sharing her own experiences in the West.

The host of reflexive work produced by Kim (2005, 2006), Kraidy (1999), Buarque de Almeida (2003), LaPastina (2003), and others (e.g., Darling-Wolf 2003; Mayer 2005), underscore LaPastina's (2005) assertion that ethnographic research on audiences "allows the examination of the phenomena not only in its immediate social, political, and economic contexts but also in a larger historical framework, as well as its insertion in the broader regional, national and global context" (LaPastina 2005, p. 141). Though LaPastina is primarily referring here to ethnography's capacity to engage the cultural and social dynamics between community life and popular (hegemonic-commercial) culture, as Kim and Kraidy both show, what tales from the field contribute to media ethnography is a sense of situated knowledge and how that knowledge can draw attention to the link between the local and the global via the interpretive struggles associated with the field experience, ethnographic identity, representation, and objectification. That is, descriptive interpretations that implicate the ethnographic encounter make the rendering of field research with audiences an opportunity (though often an uncomfortable one) to bring to the surface that which has been masked or simply edited out in traditional ethnography: field dilemmas and personal tensions tied to hegemonic issues of power (e.g. race, gender, sexuality, age, social class, religion, and nationalism). Grappling with instead of discarding the tensions, contradictions, and dilemmas of the field experience within the ethnographic process and through the writing of the ethnographic text can lead to the elaboration of more revealing, insightful, and, well, more "humane" research, or at least the kind that ethnography is uniquely equipped to deal with if the ethnographer is willing.

In recognizing these qualities, the point I want to underscore is that the value of ethnographies which privilege personal experience and investment in the field not only is a simple matter of sharing a good story (though they should be that) but also, rather, serves as an avenue through which to articulate "ethnographicness" along three important lines. First, going back to Sanjek (1990), they can evoke the range and variety of field relationships, help the reader understand decisions made in the field, and tell us something about direct evidence from fieldnotes and interview transcripts. Second, they can help address in some very interesting ways Spitulnik's (2002) question "Does culture (place) matter?" – a question meant to return inquiry to the context of the local and a "sociocentric" as opposed to subject-centric interrogation of media reception (pp. 338–339). Third, they can help speak to broader issues about the social world, which Geertz (1973) argued involves drawing "large conclusions from small, but densely textured facts" that ethnographically emerge from the "particularity" of a given context but yet tell us something about the "normalness" of a people's culture (p. 28). In my view, these three labors of textualization are the criteria through which the value of media ethnographies of communities should be elaborated and judged.

The Dissolving Field?

Despite this track record of field-based contextually grounded media ethnography, and the compelling tales of situated knowledge that it has conceived, the future of long-term participant observation as a central component of media ethnography appears in serious question. As more than one scholar has observed (Murdock 1997; Hammersley 1999; Murphy and Kraidy 2003), fieldwork, at least as traditionally envisioned, is time intensive, often quite expensive, and typically a solitary endeavor (the lone ethnographer), and does not necessarily lend itself to the tight production schedules or multiple multiauthored papers for those seeking numerous publications for tenure and promotion. This makes it, at least at the level of self-interest on the part of many researchers, a less attractive option for engaging issues of media consumption and culture.

But this doesn't mean that media ethnography is just dying via its own cumbersome methodological weight. Rather, not unlike other kinds of ethnographic inquiry, media ethnography has been undergoing, perhaps even from its inception, a reconceptualization of "the field" and fieldwork. This is visible in the very language now used by media ethnographers, as indicated by terms like "opportunistic ethnography" (Bird 2003, p. 5), "passing ethnographies" (Couldry 2003), and "rhizomatic ethnography" (Akindes 2003). In earlier times, such approaches might have fallen under the banner of *microethnographies* in that they tend to present interpretations of data drawn from relatively abbreviated research periods (Wolcott 1995). But it would be a mistake to think such descriptive turns are just responses to time logged in the field. In the particular case of audience ethnographers, the new translations of the terms of fieldwork are as much as anything a response to a number of interrelated issues that have served to shape and define "reception," such as the advent of "dispersed audiences" and "nomadic subjects" (Radway 1988), and the identification of "partial truths" (Clifford and Marcus 1986), the rise of complex "networks" (Castells 1996), and the need to study media and "translocality" ethnographically within globalization (Kraidy and Murphy 2008).

Within this academic context, it is perhaps not surprising that the rites and rituals of what were once the relative valences of fieldwork – entrée, rapport, and immersion – have given way to "complicity," "lurking," and "embodied subjectivities." These adjustments signal more than just a trading of descriptive tropes, as doing fieldwork and the field itself begin to dissolve into a fluid, even ephemeral, sense of context and situatedness. And, of course, this sense of relocating the parameters of fieldwork is demanded by the ethnographic study of cultural exchanges (chatting, surfing, emails, tweeting, etc.) and social ties taking shape in cyberspace, but it should not be understood as something limited to virtual networks.

Couldry (2003), for example, asserts that since people live increasingly mediated lives, research needs to study people in action to reveal patterns of thinking. This requires doing research in multiple contexts which have to be grasped as *rhetorical* context – as contexts of arguments and negotiation – which is not the same as knowing the total life-contexts in which those arguments took place. Listening closely and effectively to people's talk *need not* require a full ethnographic contextualization for that talk. (p. 52, emphasis in original)

For Couldry, rather than "being there" in one site to capture media's myth-making power, such "listening in" requires a dispersed notion of ethnography and must be elaborated across a range of contexts in order to capture patterns of thought and action that teach us something about the naturalizing power of media discourses.

Equally abstract is Bird's (2003) rendering of fieldwork, which literally disappears via her efforts to develop "researcher-absent" methods (p. 17), arguing that one should not worry so much about "insignificant" issues such as time in the field (p. 8). Bird is, though, fully committed to an "ethnographic way of seeing" (p. 12) which places emphasis on asking the right questions and communication with participants over immersion. To pursue this, she charts ways in which ethnographic intimacy can be engendered without some of the more threatening and time-intensive aspects of the field encounter. These have included group chat room exchanges, solicited letters, and "ethnographically-based" telephone interviews, all of which have been adopted to help answer different questions and create situations where "the participant is invited to define the terms of the encounter" (p. 12).

Based on her past body of work, it is clear that Bird's researcher-absent methods can foster ethnographically dense interactions and rich exchanges, especially as they seem to have been highly effective in facilitating participants' interest in the research process by engaging them in ways that respected their communicative practices and cultural boundaries. So it is hard to argue with the fact that Bird's scholarship not only has been methodologically creative and lucidly mapped, but also has shaped a better, fuller sense of the possibilities of ethnography for the study of media. But there are severe contextual limitations to these contributions as well, as it would be difficult to imagine soliciting letters and conducting conversational phone interviews in parts of the world where letters sent rarely reach their destinations and only a privileged part of the populace may have access to phones. And these are important considerations, because as more media ethnography in the "periphery" has shown (Juluri 2003; Fung 2008), newly industrialized regions are also the places where the biggest audiences are, who are entering in a massive scale into the culturally complex and politically loaded world of "audiencehood."

The work of Bird, Couldry, and other media scholars underscores the observation that ethnographic method is in a time of transition, and that "fieldwork is not what it used to be" (Faubion and Marcus 2009). This assertion is punctuated by the work of Hills (2002), whose ethnography on fandom has moved perhaps furthest beyond the conventional boundaries of situated method, and offers one of the most "internal" visions of doing media ethnography. Hills is motivated by an empirically salient dilemma: that ethnographers need to question the currency of the fan's own interpretations of their relationship with media texts. He contends that media studies has been hesitant to fully engage the "auto-legitimation within fan culture," depicting instead fans' personal investment in and articulation of their relationship with particular texts as "knowledgeability" (p. 66). But is "asking the audience" enough? Indeed, Hills argues that this deferment to fans' vested, insider knowledge helps create an ethnographic alibi: "given the fan's articulate nature, and immersion in the text concerned, the move to ethnography seems strangely unquestioned, as if it is somehow grounded in the fan's (supposedly) preexistent form of audience knowledge and interpretive skill" (p. 66). Methodologically grounded in conversational interviews, this move to place fans' own interpretations at the center of analysis is problematic as it serves to legitimize fan ethnography while disconnecting it from its own discursive justification. In short, since fan ethnographies take at face value fan discourses, they lead to inherently weak interpretations of fan culture.

So, then, how should one study fandom? Hills (2002) suggests a provocative albeit surprisingly personalized ethnographic adjustment: "ethnography of the self" as constituting both the heuristic device and the field itself. This requires, instead of suspending theoretical debate about the epistemological and ontological pitfalls of doing ethnography (e.g. Couldry 2003), an ethnographic inquiry for the study of fandom that lunges straight into the interpretive dilemmas of the self and experience. Hills's decision to take this dive necessarily makes "the field" an internal place, and self-interrogation a pursuit of how the "personal is culture" as well as the ethnographic chore of wrestling to come to terms with one's own tendency to provide narrative closures (e.g., the ethnographer's own self-justifications and displays of common sense). As such, he argues passionately that this exercise in autoethnography is not, as critics have charged, the narcissistic pursuit of navel gazing, but rather offers a path to achieve something which past fan ethnographies (e.g., Bacon-Smith 1992; Jenkins 1992) have neglected: "how multiple fandoms are linked through the individual's realization of self-identity" (Hills 2002, p. 81).

This desire to link together various moments of fandom is an attempt to move away from single-text fan cultures (e.g. *Star Trek*; *Yo soy Betty, la fea*; and *Doctor Who*) and intertextual networks of "telefantasy," placing emphasis instead on fans' often long, interlaced histories attached to different fandoms of different programs or genres that gain and lose relevance through a person's lifetime. It is also an acknowledgment of the very dispersed and increasingly fluid relationship that people have with media as a response to the sheer volume of texts encountered through everyday life. Within this mediated context of an ethnographer-fan's biography, Hills (2002) places great emphasis on the fruits of autoethnography's productive tension and performative contradiction:

> I am methodologically and theoretically obliged to concede that my account of my own fandoms arrives at a point of narrative closure which privileges (present) academic reflection on the non-academic (past) self. The only possible way to disrupt

this narrative closure may be to interpret fan culture (and the self) through alternative theoretical positions. (p. 88)

In such a way, the field becomes a question of personal experience, and fieldwork a chore bound by and expressed through one's own identities and affiliations in relation to media cultures.

Hills's (2002) autoethnographic privileging of the self clearly casts the personal-locational as "the" ethnographic center, capable of questioning the naïve celebration of the "native's point of view" and overcoming the interpretive limitations of low-tech, face-to-face ethnography when charged with making sense of the multiple theaters of reception. These points of interrogation are certainly needed in the ethnographic adjustment to people's relationship with new media environments and textual convergence, but they are not unproblematic. In short, researchers trying to craft personal and meaningful ethnographies of the self will inevitably be faced with the difficult dilemma of trying to direct inquiry to sociocentric issues that resonate more broadly, as opposed to just settling on the subject-centric issues that autoethnography invites. Moreover, lost in the emphasis on the self and virtual is ethnography's longstanding, fruitful, and, one might add, concrete commitment to observation (Nightingale 2008).

Making Ethnographic Media Ethnography

Since Malinowski moved anthropology off of the veranda and into the field, the enterprise of ethnography has traveled far. Indeed, media ethnographers have been invited to watch TV in living rooms, follow nomadic audiences, and "study sideways" media professionals. They have stretched the field translocally, hung out at passing media events, wandered through media worlds of production and reception, interfaced with fellow fans, and lurked in cybersites. Collectively, in no small measure this multicontextual tour of field sites has quite deliberately trespassed well beyond the boundaries of traditional ethnography to the extent that it would probably not be recognizable to many of its founders. So it is within this context that we might return to Nightingale's (1993) query of "What's ethnographic about media ethnography?" and Coman and Rothenbuhler's (2005) questions, "Where is the dividing line between doing ethnography in the classic sense and doing research that is ethnographic in some respects? How important is that line?" (p. 2).

Though partial, my mapping of the visions, practices, and politics of fieldwork in media ethnography suggests a number of underlying themes that begin to reveal not only what is ethnographic about media ethnography, but also some points of unresolved tensions that might be seen as dividing lines. First and foremost, in considering the above questions it is important to recognize that in an effort to cover the full (and expanding) range of people's relationship with consuming and/or making media, many media researchers have adjusted ethnography's aperture. This methodological recalibration has led to a sense that "the field" is a considerably less concrete and empirically "knowable" place, and that the *there* in "being there," so foundational to traditional ethnography, has been fundamentally transformed in relation to media-centric issues of flow and fluidity of information within a networked society. Though the implications for this migration into the fluid, situational, virtual, and even ephemeral challenge ethnography's longstanding commitment to studying cultural patterns through long-term immersion and participant observation, it has not stopped researchers from conducting "old-school" fieldwork. Nor has it meant that the new castings of media ethnography, where media events and networked communities seem to replace the field, fail to meet ethnographic standards of validity. In fact, the ethnographic value of this transmutation has been demonstrated by various researchers in different but quite significant ways (e.g. Hills 2002; Bird 2003; Hannerz 2003a). Through the articulation of process (methodology) and presentation of product (the ethnographic text), these studies have not only pointed to new strategies through which to empirically adjust ethnographic method to expand or alter our notion of the field, but also refine standard methods (e.g. interviews, group discussions, and personal diaries) to do research that is responsive to new ways in which people interact with, use, and make media, not to mention as well as with each other.

So, we must acknowledge that within the evolving elasticity and application of the term *the field*, there are very real reasons for this reconceptualization of ethnographic practice. A central one, in my view, can be understood through Abu-Lughod's (1997) observation that, pace Geertz, media "renders more and more problematic a concept of cultures as localized communities of people suspended in shared webs of meaning" (p. 123). That is to say, since people, even in the most isolated communities, are increasingly connected to the cultural capital of cosmopolitanism via mass media, ethnographers have to be prepared and willing to venture beyond the situated boundaries of local culture to make sense of how members of that community might use media (whether as audiences or producers) to alter, renew, and reinvest in it. While this may cause some difficulties when trying to determine ethnographic validity along Sanjek's (1990) previously outlined criteria, such as time in the field, it does not mean that we should stop looking for ethnographic rendering of "field" decisions, the textual explication of the range and variety of researcher–subject relationships, or evidence from fieldnotes and interview transcripts as measures of ethnographicness.

Within the move to networked communities, multiple sites, virtual lurking, and the internal field for the self, there is, I believe, a sense that we not wander too easily and comfortably into the virtual and the networked at the great expense of losing track of fieldwork's former requisite: the embodied experience. To do so is to embrace a vision of ethnography that would be in my view concomitant with moving back onto the "veranda." Or, stated another way, does a shift away from the situated and sensual experience of being in the field (e.g. village, neighborhood, or production center) carry naturally with it a return to transcription of what people say over inscription of what they do? In networked ethnography, do participation and conversation necessarily trump observation and the embodied experience? I think that in the ethnographic challenges ahead when considering the full cultural force of media convergence, we need to think hard about these questions. Certainly for whatever the shortcomings of his own ethnography were, Malinowski tried hard to overcome the Boas-esque limitations of transcription by attempting to "dislodge it from center stage in favor of participant-observation: getting away from the table on the verandah and hanging around the village as instead, chatting, questioning, listening in, looking on – writing it all up later" (Clifford 1990, p. 51) – lessons that, however old, we cannot afford to lose.

Finally, because of these somewhat contradictory directions of elaborating a more mobile, opportunistic, and arguably less concretely fixed vision of ethnography for the study of media, it seems that, regardless of how the field might be conceptualized, the articulation of the ethnographic experience through thick description carries a heavier burden than ever. Indeed, it is through the telling of tales from the field that we, as readers of media ethnographies, are able to get a sense of whether a researcher has between doing ethnography or doing research that is somehow ethnographic in nature. By this, I do not mean to suggest that for research to qualify as ethnographic, it merely needs to indulge in the appropriate stylistic maneuvering. Certainly there are plenty of writers who can produce what Sanjek (1990) has dubbed "slick description" (p. 404) without necessarily immersing themselves in the experiential and interpretive work of ethnographic method. What I want to assert instead is that media ethnographers need to labor more purposely with *bringing the process to the product* in an effort to evoke a fuller sense of place, context, community, intercultural exchange, and, yes, the consciousness that is articulating that experience.

Stylistically speaking, whether we see our work as residing in a fifth moment or as labor in a process of boat building while at sea is less important than if we are able to tap into the lessons from past ethnographic cycles of representation and description to write thick accounts of media reception or production that tell us something about the communities with whom we worked and how they view themselves, as well as, in the process, relay to us a sense of their "ethnographic-ness." In my view, only by taking this descriptive chore seriously are ethnographers in a position to translate the field, however defined, into ethnographies that are, well, ethnographic. And if they do that, then the readers of those ethnographies will be better able to identify and judge whether or not the person who crafted the media ethnography was truly able, echoing Geertz, to interpret the possible meanings of a wink of an eye (virtual ;-) or otherwise) or the linguistic double entendre in the context of a media event, exchanges in fan speech, or the creation of alterative media. Indeed, if our media ethnographies do not labor to communicate such things, then maybe they are simply not worthy of being called ethnography.

References

Abu-Lughod, L. 1997 The interpretation of culture(s) after television. *Representations*, 59, pp. 109–134.

Abu-Lughod, L. 2005 *Dramas of Nationhood: The Politics of Television in Egypt*. University of Chicago Press, Chicago.

Acosta-Alzuru, C. 2005 Home is where my heart is: reflections on doing research in my native country. *Popular Communication* 3, 3, pp. 181–193.

Akindes, F. 2003 Methodology as lived experience: rhizomatic ethnography in Hawai'i. In P. Murphy and M. Kraidy, eds. *Global Media Studies: Ethnographic Perspectives*. Routledge, London, pp. 147–216.

Anderson, B. 1991 *Imagined Communities: Reflections on the Origins and Spread of Nationalism*. Verso, London.

Appadurai, A. 1996 *Modernity at Large: Cultural Dimensions of Globalization*. University of Minnesota Press, Minneapolis.

Bacon-Smith, C. 1992 *Enterprising Women: Television Fandom and the Creation of Popular Myth*. University of Pennsylvania Press, Philadelphia.

Bird, S. E. 2003 *The Audience in Everyday Life*. London, Routledge.

Buarque de Almeida, H. 2003 On the border: reflections on ethnography and gender. In P. Murphy and M. Kraidy, eds. *Global Media Studies: Ethnographic Perspectives*. Routledge, London, pp. 165–183.

Castells, M. 1996 *The Rise of the Network Society: The Information Age: Economy, Society and Culture*. Blackwell, Cambridge.

Clifford, J. 1983 On ethnographic authority. *Representations*, 1, pp. 118–146.

Clifford, J. 1990 Notes on (field)notes in fieldnotes. In R. Sanjek, ed. *Fieldnotes: The Making of Anthropology*. Cornell University Press, Ithaca, NY, pp. 47–70.

Clifford, J. and Marcus, G., eds. 1986 *Writing Culture: The Poetics and Politics of Ethnography*. University of California Press, Berkeley.

Coman, M. and Rothenbuhler, E. 2005 The promise of media anthropology. In E. Rothenbuhler and M. Coman, eds. *Media Anthropology*. Sage, Thousand Oaks, CA, pp. 1–13.

Cottle, S. 2000 New(s) times: towards a "second wave" of news ethnography. *Communications*, 25, 1, pp. 19–41.

Cottle, S. 2007 Ethnography and news production: news(s) developments in the field. *Sociology Compass* 1, 1, pp. 1–16.

Couldry, N. 2003 Passing ethnographies: rethinking the sites of agency and reflexivity in a mediated world. In P. Murphy and M. Kraidy, eds. *Global Media Studies: Ethnographic Perspectives*. Routledge, London, pp. 40–56.

Darling-Wolf, F. 2003 Negotiation and position: on the need and difficulty of developing "thicker descriptions." In P. Murphy and M. Kraidy, eds. *Global Media Studies: Ethnographic Perspectives*. Routledge, London, pp. 109–124.

Dávila, A. 2002 Culture in the ad world: producing the Latin look. In F. D. Ginsburg, L. Abu-Lughod and B. Larkin, eds. *Media Worlds: Anthropology on New Terrain*. University of California Press, Berkeley, pp. 264–280.

Denzin, N. and Lincoln, Y. S. eds. 1998 *Collecting and Interpreting Qualitative Materials*. Sage, Thousand Oaks, CA.

Dumont, J. P. 1978 *The Headman and I: Ambiguity and Ambivalence in the Fieldworking Experience.* University of Texas Press, Austin.

Faubion, J. D. and Marcus, G. F., eds. 2009 *Fieldwork Is Not What It Used to Be: Learning Anthropology's Method in a Time of Transition.* Cornell University Press, Ithaca, NY.

Fetterman, D. M. 1989 *Ethnography: Step by Step.* Sage, Newbury Park, CA.

Fung, A. 2008 *Global Capital, Local Culture: Transnational Media Corporations in China.* Peter Lang, New York.

Gans, H. 1980 *Deciding What's News: A study of CBS Evening News, NBC Nightly. News, Newsweek, and Time.* Vintage, New York.

Gans, H. 1999 Participant observation in the era of "ethnography." *Journal of Contemporary Ethnography,* 28, 5, pp. 540–547.

Ganti, T. 2002 "And yet my heart is still Indian": the Bombay Film Industry and the (H) Indianization of Hollywood. In F. D. Ginsburg, L. Abu-Lughod and B. Larkin, eds. *Media Worlds: Anthropology on New Terrain.* University of California Press, Berkeley, pp. 281–300.

Geertz, C. 1973 *The Interpretation of Cultures.* Basic Books, New York.

Gillespie, M. 1995 *Television, Ethnicity and Cultural Change.* Routledge, London.

Ginsburg, F. D., Abu-Lughod, L. and Larkin, B. 2002 Introduction. In F. D. Ginsburg, L. Abu-Lughod and B. Larkin, eds. *Media Worlds: Anthropology on New Terrain.* University of California Press, Berkeley, pp. 1–36.

Hammersley, M. 1999 Not bricolage but boatbuilding: exploring two metaphors for thinking about ethnography. *Journal of Contemporary Ethnography,* 28, pp. 574–585.

Hannerz, U. 2003a *Foreign News.* University of Chicago Press, Chicago.

Hannerz, U. 2003b Being there … and there … and there! Reflections on multi-site ethnography. *Ethnography,* 4, 2, pp. 201–216.

Hills, M. 2002 *Fan Cultures.* Routledge, London.

Jenkins, H. 1992 *Textual Poachers: Television Fans and Participatory Cultures.* Routledge, London.

Juluri, V. 2003 *Becoming a Global Audience: Longing and Belonging in Indian Music Television.* Peter Lang, New York.

Kim, Y. 2005 Experiencing globalization: global TV, reflexivity and the lives of young Korean women. *International Journal of Cultural Studies,* 8, 4, pp. 445–463.

Kim, Y. 2006 The body, TV talk and emotion: methodological reflections. *Cultural Studies/ Critical Methodologies,* 6, 2, pp. 226–244.

Kraidy, M. 1999 The global, the local, and the hybrid: a native ethnography of glocalization. *Critical Studies in Mass Communication,* 16, 4, pp. 456–476.

Kraidy, M. and Murphy, P. D. 2008 Shifting Geertz: toward a theory of translocalism in global communication studies. *Communication Theory* 118, 3, pp. 335–355.

LaPastina, A. 2003 Now that you're going home, are you going to write about the natives you studied? Telenovela reception, adultery and the dilemmas of ethnographic practice. In P. Murphy and M. Kraidy, eds. *Global Media Studies: Ethnographic Perspectives.* Routledge, London, pp. 125–146.

LaPastina, A. 2005 Audience ethnographies: a media engagement approach. In E. Rothenbuhler and M. Coman, eds. *Media Anthropology.* Sage, Thousand Oaks, CA, pp. 139–148.

LaPastina, A. 2006 The implications of an ethnographer's sexuality. *Qualitative Inquiry,* 12, pp. 724–736.

Lévi-Strauss, C. 1961 *Tristes Tropiques*. Atheneum, New York. (Original work published in 1955)

Lincoln, Y. S. and Denzin, N. 1998 The fifth moment. In N. K. Denzin and Y. S. Lincoln, eds. *The Landscape of Qualitative Research*. Sage, Thousand Oaks, CA, pp. 407–429.

Malinowski, B. 1967 *A Diary in the Strict Sense of the Term*. Routledge & Kegan Paul, London.

Mankekar, P. 1999 *Screening Culture, Viewing Politics: An Ethnography of Television, Womanhood and Nation in Postcolonial India*. Duke University Press, Durham, NC.

Marcus, G. 1998 *Ethnography through Thick and Thin*. Princeton University Press, Princeton, NJ.

Mayer, V. 2005 Research beyond the pale: whiteness in audience studies and media ethnography. *Communication Theory*, 15, 2, pp. 148–167.

Michaels, E. 1994 *Bad Aboriginal Art and Other Essays*. Minnesota Press, Minneapolis.

Miller, D. 2006 *The Young and the Restless* in Trinidad: a case of the local and the global in mass consumption. In E. Rothenbuhler and M. Coman, eds. *Media Anthropology*. Sage, Thousand Oaks, CA, pp. 163–226.

Murdock, G. 1997 Thin descriptions: questions of method in cultural analysis. In J. McGuigan, ed. *Cultural Methodologies*. Sage, London, pp. 178–192.

Murphy, P. D. 1999 Doing audience ethnography: a narrative account of establishing ethnographic identity and locating interpretive communities in fieldwork. *Qualitative Inquiry*, 5, pp. 479–504.

Murphy, P. D. 2002 The anthropologist's son (living and learning the field). *Qualitative Inquiry*, 8, 3, pp. 246–260.

Murphy, P. D. 2008 Writing media culture: representation and experience in media ethnography. *Communication, Culture and Critique*, 1, pp. 267–285.

Nightingale, V. 1993 What's "ethnographic" about ethnographic audience research? In J. Frow and M. Morris, eds. *Australian Cultural Studies*. University of Illinois Press, Urbana, pp. 149–161.

Nightingale, V. 2008 Why observing matters. In M. Pickering, ed. *Research Methods for Cultural Studies*. Edinburgh University Press, Edinburgh, pp. 105–122.

Ortner, S. 1993 Ethnography among the Newark: the class of '58 of Weequahic High School. *Michigan Quarterly Review*, 32, pp. 411–429.

Parameswaran, R. 2002 Feminist media ethnography in India: exploring power, gender, and culture in the field. *Qualitative Inquiry*, 7, pp. 69–103.

Paterson, C. and Domingo, D., eds. 2008 *Making News Online: The Ethnography of News Production*. Peter Lang, New York.

Podber, J. 2007 *The Electronic Front Porch: An Oral History of the Arrival of Modern Media in Rural Appalachia and the Melungeon Community*. Mercer Press, Macon, GA.

Pratt, M. L. 1992 *Imperial Eyes: Travel Writing and Transculturation*. Routledge, London.

Radway, J. 1988 Reception study: ethnography and the problems of dispersed audiences and nomadic subjects. *Cultural Studies* 2, 3, pp. 359–367.

Sanjek, R., ed. 1990 *Fieldnotes*. Cornell University Press, Ithaca, NY.

Spitulnik, D. 1993 Anthropology and mass media. *Annual Review of Anthropology*, 22, pp. 293–315.

Spitulnik, D. 2002 Mobile machines and fluid audiences: rethinking reception through Zambian radio culture. In F. D. Ginsburg, L. Abu-Lughod and B. Larkin, eds. *Media Worlds: Anthropology on New Terrain*. University of California Press, Berkeley, pp. 337–354.

Spradley, J. P. 1979 *The Ethnographic Interview*. Holt, Rinehart & Winston, New York.

Spradley, J. P. 1980 *Participant Observation*. Holt, Rinehart & Winston, New York.

Tuchman, G. 1973 *Making News*. Free Press, London.

Tufte, T. 2000 *Living with the Rubbish Queen: Telenovelas, Culture and Modernity in Brazil*. University of Luton Press, Luton, UK.

Willis, P. 2000 *The Ethnographic Imagination*. Polity Press, Cambridge.

Wolcott, H. 1995 Making a study "more ethnographic." In J. Van Maanen, ed. *Representation in Ethnography*. Sage, Thousand Oaks, CA, pp. 79–111.

Part IV
Doing Audience Research

20
Children's Media Cultures in Comparative Perspective

Sonia Livingstone and Kirsten Drotner

Introduction

Children's agency, their social engagements and participation are catalyzed by the combined developments of global communication networks and digital media technologies, thereby catapulting children's media cultures to the center of public attention and shaping children's everyday lives and the conception of childhood in many parts of the world. Debates are rife over the regulation of children's media fare, for this is increasingly more personalized, more global, and certainly more volatile and versatile than, for example, the more familiar print media have been. Arguably, globalizing media processes favor new forms of cosmopolitanism by providing opportunities for children to encounter and engage with greater cultural and social diversity or, at least, to know that such possibilities exist. On the other hand, it appears that the commercial basis of these media downplays such diversities in order to mass cater to mass audiences across spatial boundaries.

Yet, while audience researchers have long analyzed children's media culture, too often they have asked disconnected questions about the impacts of particular media on particular groups of children, often framed in terms of moral panics, and with a predominant focus on American children as the implicit prototype for children everywhere. This chapter offers a new framework for understanding child audiences, grounded in the complex and changing cultural environments within which children live and contextualizing specific research questions regarding media interpretations and appropriations within a broad account of children and young people's lifeworlds.

We argue that research must move beyond familiar discourses of celebration or concern and develop multidisciplinary and multisited understandings of the complex relations among children, media, and culture. Our *International Handbook of Children, Media and Culture* (Drotner and Livingstone 2008) includes telling cases of

The Handbook of Media Audiences, First Edition. Edited by Virginia Nightingale.

children's media culture in "other" parts of the world, supporting the argument that the dominant English language research tradition must now "de-Westernize" (Curran and Park 2000), recognizing the importance of globalization or transnationalism, and prioritizing comparative analysis in terms of method. Only thus can we counter universalistic (or even imperialistic) assumptions about "childhood" or "media" as homogeneous phenomena.

More concretely, in what follows, our aim is to highlight the range of recent research on children's media engagement, conducted across all continents of the globe, thus revealing the cultural commonalities and diversities that characterize children's mediated cultures around the world. We conclude that children and young people play a key role in contemporary processes of mediatized globalization, with notable implications for relations between generations, for local and national cultures, and for transnational media flows.

From Protectionism to Empowerment

Historically, it has often been public, moral or media panics that have catapulted children's media uses into the public eye, this providing the major motivation for conducting and, certainly, funding research on children and media over decades. As has long been the case (Drotner 1992), questions of media harm become drawn into urgent debates over the regulation and governance of both media and childhood, with the laudable desire to protect children from harm uneasily balanced against both adult freedom of expression and, less noticed but equally important, children's own rights to expression, exploration, and even risk taking (Millwood Hargrave and Livingstone 2009). It is the pessimism inherent in these moral panics, uneasily combined with society's idealistic optimism regarding the new, which has long informed the dominant – and highly ambivalent – frameworks for researching children's media, especially within media and communication studies.

Yet critics of the uneasy historical connection between moral panics and administrative research on children's media (we refer here to Lazarsfeld's [1941] classic contrast between critical and administrative schools of communication research) have long observed that both the moral panics over potentially harmful media and the excitement over potentially empowering media are not really, or not simply, debates over media. Rather, what is at stake are more profound debates over the cultural values that society should promulgate to its children (Rowland and Watkins 1984; Critcher 2008). These concern, in short, the potential and actual meaning-making processes of communication and social interaction, and the ways in which they shape the cultural dimension of life. A parallel debate in childhood studies, revitalized by Philippe Ariès's (1960/1962) classic text *Centuries of Childhood*, has centered on the historically, culturally, and psychologically fraught relations between adults and children. For both academics and the wider public, children's cultural articulations, whether self-styled or mediatized, are obvious entry points for playing out an array of concerns, because they are tangible manifestations of children's everyday practices and priorities. Given the increasing prominence of the media in children's everyday cultures, the social concerns over children often revolve around media as a symptom or pretext for discussion and debate. Indeed, publicly expressed concerns over children and media are often not, at heart, about media, but rather they concern sociocultural relations of authority and the negotiation of cultural and social boundaries (Drotner 1999).

But analysis of the latter requires a multidisciplinary approach, and this is precisely what is excluded when pediatricians and clinical psychologists capture, to the near-exclusion of alternative perspectives, the public agenda on matters concerning children. Consider the widespread attention devoted to the American Academy of Pediatrics' (2001) claim that children should not be allowed to watch more than two hours of television per day irrespective of the substance of programs or contexts of use. The result is often that little attention is paid to the more subtle and contextualized insights of educationalists, let alone sociologists, cultural theorists, media scholars, and others with expertise in children's lifeworlds (e.g. Corsaro 1997). However, in advocating the importance of these multidisciplinary approaches, we must also acknowledge the relative paucity of research on children's media cultures in many countries and within many disciplines, notwithstanding consistently high levels of public interest in children's media engagement. This is particularly problematic for the two primary fields on which the analysis of children and media draws, as already signaled above, namely, media studies and childhood studies.

Traditionally, in media studies, economic structures, textual articulations, and historical trajectories take center stage, relegating children to the contextual margins of interest, a specialist topic of interest only to the few. Conversely, in childhood studies, children (and youth) as social agents, psychological subjects, or cultural producers are positioned as key areas of interest, but here the media are accorded only a minimal role, being defined as a narrow area of applied research rather than a substantive focus in their own right. So, although each approach has much to offer, research on children and media has suffered from this restricted vision (Livingstone 1998). Partly, this problem arises because implicit in the relative neglect of children's media cultures by both media studies and childhood studies is the assumption that these media cultures can be safely relegated to the domains of the private rather than the public, of leisure rather than work, and of entertainment rather than "serious" engagement with society. This assumption is no longer tenable – not that we would agree it ever was. Today, young people's uses of new communication technologies have far greater significance than their traditional relation to audiovisual technologies, all too easily marginalized as "mere" entertainment, for – as has in fact always been the case for print media – they represent crucial new routes to education, civic participation, work, and the wider world.

For example, when disadvantaged children in India with little or no schooling get the opportunity to take up computing, access the internet, and enter game worlds, questions begin to be asked about these children's position in (or exclusion from) public life, the material and symbolic resources which (might) grant them a voice and a new visibility, and the institutional consequences of such "digital inclusion." When highly profitable transborder flows of marketing and media products push the boundaries between local and global forms of representation, questions arise regarding children's identity development and sense of belonging to a community. And when, with the rise of the knowledge society (Stehr 1994; Mansell 2004) or network society (Castells 1996), children's literacies assume a new urgency – should they be media literate, computer literate, multimedia literate, information literate, or something completely different? – new questions of convergent and critical literacies become ever more pressing in a complex media environment. The debate over children's media must therefore shift, belatedly but crucially, from a primarily protectionist to a primarily emancipatory or empowerment frame. Since children's media engagements are key to their present and future social engagements, the task is no longer to work out how to restrict or control children's media uses so as to minimize risks but, crucially to work out how best to enhance and guide children so as to maximize opportunities. This is not to say the risk of harm no longer exists, but rather that a protectionist approach must be balanced against, and understood only in relation to, the more important empowerment agenda.

In the remainder of this chapter, we argue that the importance of contextualizing children's media culture within a multidimensional account of societal change cannot be overestimated, for only thus can we avoid the narrow and decontextualized impact analysis of technological determinism (Smith and Marx 1994) in evaluating the social, cultural, and personal consequences of media and information technologies. This means analyzing children's media culture as it shapes and is shaped by the dimensions of space, time, and social relations (as Thompson [2005] does in his account of media and modernity, but as is so rarely extended to include children; although see Meyrowitz 1984). It also means recognizing that these dimensions are themselves culturally and historically contingent. So, rather than emphasizing the one-way impact of media on children, we urge the importance of asking when and why different children use different aspects of media; how these uses are shaped by family circumstances, educational expectations, economic pressures, and cultural values; and whether such media uses enable or impede children's opportunities in terms of knowledge, action, or resources. To address these questions, it should by now be obvious that we welcome contributions from a diversity of academic disciplines also – sociology, anthropology, literary studies, history, cultural studies, pedagogy, and more. Only with this wider lens can a greater diversity of research come into view, opening up some exciting prospects for the field.

Everyday Culture Matters

For many researchers, then, the investigation of the changing place of media in childhood is grounded in a specialist focus on children and childhood. For others, the analysis of media, communications, and culture comes first, this being adapted and developed in relation to children and young people in particular. Notwithstanding the marginalization of this intersection of fields already noted above, it is undoubtedly the case that both approaches are valuable, potentially combining to offer a rich understanding of the specificities of children's life contexts combined with more general perspectives from the analysis of media, culture, and society.

How shall we identify, analyze, and understand children's media cultures around the world? The American anthropologist Clifford Geertz (1973) cogently defines *culture* as "a system of inherited conceptions expressed in symbolic forms by means of which people communicate, perpetuate, and develop their knowledge about and attitudes toward life" (pp. 89). The "symbolic forms" noted by Geertz can be words, images, written text, or numbers – that is, a range of semiotic sign repertoires – and this process of sense making, or signification, is increasingly mediated by global media such as satellite television, the internet, and mobile communication. This foregrounding of the cultural dimension is encapsulated by Robertson (1992), who argues that cultural globalization serves to accelerate everybody's notion of living in "a single place." Yet this accelerated interdependence also brings about confrontations among different, even clashing worldviews. So, globalization involves "comparative interaction of different forms of life" (pp. 6, 27).

Detailed observational and ethnographic work readily reveals that, in their everyday lives, children and young people weave together practices involving a wide range of media and cultural forms and technologies, generating a rich symbolic tapestry in a manner which is in some ways deliberate or agentic but in other ways accidental, part of the sheer serendipity of childhood (Corsaro 1997; Schroeder et al. 2003). But, since the relations among play and learning, and toys and media, are increasingly intersecting, being managed and marketed as part of the regulation and the commercialization of children's culture, a critical perspective informed by a political economic analysis of children's media is vital. Only then can we judge how far children's culture is being transformed into promotional culture, as we examine ways in which modern marketing directs flows of popular culture, identity becomes refashioned through consumption, and the citizen (or viewer) becomes transformed into the consumer (Kenway and Bullen 2001).

Further, only a critical perspective can investigate the question of inequalities – the degree to which some children gain access to certain kinds of meanings and practices, along with certain kinds of opportunities or dangers, while others lack such opportunities, restricted by certain social arrangements of time, space, and cultural norms and values, as well as personal preferences and lifestyles. For this, the analysis of the micro practices of childhood – what de Certeau (1984) called the "tactics" of everyday life – must be complemented by an analysis of the structures of family, school, community, and society that encompasses them in multiple circles of influence and constraint (Bronfenbrenner 1980).

In short, our advocacy of a focus on children's everyday cultures does not imply, by any means, a license to become primarily either descriptive or celebratory on the part of children or media. Rather, the more empirical research generates a body of new material detailing the specifics of children's engagement with media cultures around the world, the more an integrative and critical lens on the relations between specific cultural practices and the broader social analysis of processes of power becomes necessary. Cultural studies has proved successful here in grounding its analysis in particular cultural forms in particular contexts in order both to reveal the power relations embedded in those experiences, forms, and contexts and to guide theoretical conclusions that transcend the particular (du Gay et al. 1997; Buckingham 2008; Seiter 2008). Other approaches also integrate the micro and macro of cultural and political economy approaches (e.g. Kenway and Bullen 2001; Kraidy and Khalil 2008; Wasko 2008). As Buckingham argues, the "cultural circuit" linking processes of the production and consumption of mediated meanings demands a multidimensional and multilevel analysis that respects people's agency while recognizing the significant degree to which institutions, culture, and political economy shape the contexts within which people – including children – act. So, although the constraints of children's media provision are largely set institutionally, children's interpretations may reflexively reposition them as childish, or as patronizing those texts considered appropriate for them by adults; one consequence is the emergence of children's tastes which, as Jenkins (2003) has shown, may then be reappropriated by profit-hungry content providers.

This question of children's agency is gaining increasing interest, especially in relation to new media, where they are seen not only as the creative reappropriators of imported or dominant media but additionally as the "pioneers" in the new media world, popularly dubbed "digital natives" by comparison with the "digital immigrant" adults who seek, often ineffectively, to guide, teach, or manage children's relations with media (Prensky 2001). Drotner (2000) proposes three key ways in which young people may specifically be said to be "cultural pioneers" in their use of new media technologies, centering on innovation, interaction, and integration. Under *innovation*, she notes how young people combine multiple media, multitask, blur production and reception, and so make creative use of the opportunities available. By *interaction*, she points to how young people engage with each other within and through different media and media contents, opening up opportunities for intertextuality and connectivity. And by *integration*, she points to the transformation of the distinction between primary (or face-to-face) and secondary (mass-mediated) socialization, resulting in diverse and hybridized forms of mediated communication.

There is, it seems, an intriguing reverse generation gap opening up, in which children may become the leaders, and their parents and teachers followers in relation to emerging mediated cultures. While not wishing to overstate the case – for children too have much to learn – their enhanced and much-valued expertise in this regard challenges the traditional approach of media researchers toward their child subjects, forcing a reflexive reappraisal of just what adults, including researchers, may suppose they know "better" than children, hastening some "catching up" (e.g. checking out social-networking services or other web 2.0 applications in advance of conducting interviews with children) and – joining with other developments in the study of children and childhood – reframing research methodology from that of doing research "on" children to doing research "with" children (Lobe et al. 2008).

Another instance of children's potentially pioneering role in relation to the globalization of media, one that illustrates Drotner's analysis above, can be found in the exploration of diasporic peoples and media. Often, it is the media that move as part of transnational and global flows, while children stay where they have always been, in local settings defined largely by local traditions and cultures. However, following Appadurai's ethnoscape, in addition to the (in this context) more obvious mediascape, the transborder flows of people also contribute to globalization, and here it is ordinary families and communities whose activities shape their mediated culture, sometimes by constructing diasporic media in new cultural contexts so as to retain a connection with their original "home," building mediated diasporic connections in the host culture, or reappropriating the media of their new "home" (Robins and Morley 1989; Georgiou 2001; Silverstone 2005). The particular position of children – often quickest to find mediating strategies between original and host cultures, between generations, and across linguistic and cultural contexts – in leading these transnational processes is only just beginning to be sufficiently recognized (Elias and Lemish 2008).

Children's agency in relation to media is not always publicly welcomed. On the contrary, often this is precisely what gives rise to adult concerns. Examples include contemporary conflicts with teachers and other adults of authority over time spent texting or gaming. These are in fact part of a long-term struggle over who has the right to control children's leisure time and for what reasons (Seiter 2008). Ling and Haddon (2008) note how the mobile phone operates as an ambivalent mediator between private and public spaces according to differing social arrangements. In some countries, such as Britain, perceived fears of public violence have served to domesticate and supervise children's leisure time, and so the mobile offers both a parental "umbilical cord" and a lifeline to public space. In countries such as Finland and Japan such fears are less pronounced, and here the mobile helps structure and coordinate children's public activities. The variations in negotiating children's activities in public and private spaces are clear indications of the ambivalent ways in which media speak to, and impinge upon, particular tensions in changing definitions of childhood. To take another example, Hoover and Clark (2008) chart how, in the United States, parental articulations of normative values are forms of claims making in terms of perceived cultural hierarchies and ideals of family life, articulations that are at odds with both their own and their children's actual media practices as these could be followed through observation. Such insights help unpack prevalent notions of media discourses as monolithic givens and point to the need for more detailed studies and analytical sensitivity to contextual aspects, attuned to the often imperceptible, but significant, ambivalences involved in family negotiations over media.

Consumption is another key area in which cultural norms of child–adult relations are played out. In their chapter on child consumerism, Kenway and Bullen (2001) describe how advertising and entertainment aimed at children are currently converging, creating new ambivalences between parents and their offspring. In line with Kinder (1999), they note that commercial media and advertising industries position children as discrete, independent consumers with a "right" to make independent choices, while at the same time cultivating adult hedonism with a "right" to have fun. As we hope to have made clear, a rigorous recognition of the importance and complexities of the everyday circumstances in which children engage with media provides good grounds for caution against taking normative public debates on media at face value, instead pointing to the necessity for contextualized empirical studies pursued across demarcations of discipline and region.

Difference and Diversity in Children's Media Cultures

A central premise of this chapter is that difference and diversity are central to childhood. Understanding the importance of media and culture in the lives of children and young people, therefore, demands an engagement with theories of globalization and transnational media flows, and with the methods of cross-national comparative and ethnographic research (Alasuutari 1995; Morley and Robins 1995; Tomlinson 1999; Rantanen 2004). Children, childhood, and, further, processes of learning and development, family dynamics, peer relations, consumption, media engagement, and play are not the same everywhere. Nor, evidently, are the institutions, forms, and practices associated with the media and communication environment. So, what are children's experiences of media and culture in different countries? Are there commonalities across cultures? And what are the significant or intriguing points of divergence?

For many, the hotly contested theory of media imperialism remains a common starting point, if only to challenge this through empirical investigation. For example, Strelitz and Boshoff (2008) observe that for South African youth, there is no unified national identity to be challenged, undermined, or reshaped by imported media. In South Africa, class and ethnicity remain closely linked, marking major social divisions in – among other things – the interpretative resources with which young people interpret media contents. For example, a young black man reinterprets American rap music in terms of his turbulent experience in Soweto, while middle-class white students read techno music as offering an identity of "global whiteness" which they prefer to a specifically African identity.

Strelitz and Boshoff (2008) suggest that youth's pleasurable engagement with imported media is often due to an intense negotiation with local contexts of experience, resulting in both a reimagining of life's possibilities and, simultaneously, a reaffirmation of the traditional. So, although one group of black working-class students in Grahamstown rejects global media for lacking "cultural proximity," instead preferring local drama as offering a "haven" from the threat of the modern, others, positioned at the hybrid intersection of the global and local, use media to negotiate competing identities. Examples include the Indian students in South Africa who try to reconcile traditional family values with the pleasure of watching the American series *Friends* or, involving a different kind of cultural negotiation, Bollywood movies. Consider too the interpretative demands on South African youth as American television confronts them, sometimes for the first time, with images of successful middle-class black people or of young women with the right to publicly voice their experiences.

To those on the margins of the Arctic North, the critique of globalization as a cultural and economic threat to a traditional way of life receives sparse attention. Moreover, debates that resonate elsewhere – should children watch national or imported television programs, for example – make little headway in a country such as Greenland, where the costs of producing domestic content for a population of 57,000 are prohibitive, making imported content the norm. Notwithstanding a centuries-long history of imperialism, for young people in Greenland the prospect of the globalization of culture and lifestyle is welcomed as an exciting opening up to the world, even though, for the rest of the world, Greenland barely figures on the map. Rygaard's (2008) portrait of youth culture in Greenland reveals that, as so often, it is youth who lead the way, particularly grasping the global connections afforded by the internet. She concludes that, although globalization carries distinct risks for so small a population, this is far outweighed by the frustrations of being located within so marginal a context.

While youth "lead the way" in cultural globalization, the media and culture provided by a nation for its children often focus contestation over social values, especially when the society is itself under pressure to change. The values embedded in children's media culture have been termed by Heller (2008) the "hidden curriculum". She shows how childhood games reinforce social roles, societal hierarchies, and the importance of winning, whether they prioritize inventiveness and intellectual mastery, memory and knowledge, warfare and opposition, or even, as in Snakes and Ladders, the very course of human life with its path of trials and successes, accompanied by good and evil. Individual economic competition – epitomized by

Monopoly – posed a particular problem for socialist Hungary when the game was first marketed there in the 1960s, and the refashioning of the game (with the board divided into the "good" socialist institutions of pedagogy, culture, and trade unions and the "bad" places of bars, tobacconists, and pubs) captures the tacit recognition that children's play matters. Youthful resistance to such ideology is equally well demonstrated by the case of Monopoly, for Heller notes the secret and pleasurable circulation of the original capitalist version among Hungarian households.

Control over media, culture, and, of course, education by the state shapes children's experiences in many parts of the world. Donald (2008) traces the Chinese state's efforts to socialize children through education and media to fulfill a vision of a new and sustainable modernity, for example through the insistence on broadcasting children's programs in Mandarin despite the plethora of languages and dialects spoken at home. Rejecting the othering of Asia implied by the dominance of Western approaches in the (English language) research literature, Donald examines children and media in the Asia-Pacific region through the idea of "regional modernity," seeking to understand the negotiation between local and global through its contextualization in the geography, culture, and politics of the region. This brings into focus some of the tensions in Asia's modernity that fit poorly with a Western modernity centered on individualism, secularism, freedom of speech, and equality, and allows us to avoid what Donald terms "the lure of ungrounded cosmopolitanism." Revealing a strongly antimodern tendency in China, Australia, and elsewhere, Donald is concerned to show that Asian modernity is characterized significantly by stark and growing differences in social class, typically mapped onto the crucial geographic distinction between urban and rural and thus dividing the experiences and life chances of children across the region.

Responding to rapid change in India is equally demanding, as Nayar and Bhide (2008) note when scoping children and young people's relation to the media in a country in which they represent some half of the population. The potent combination of youthfulness, social change, and new media developments has several consequences in India – one is "the politics of anxiety," in Salman Rushdie's phrase, and another is the generational divide between parents and their children in terms of their experiences of media in childhood (see Kraidy and Khalil 2008). Like other researchers cited here, Nayar and Bhide trace the connection between geography and consumption, contextualizing consumption, lifestyle, and youth culture in relation to both world geography and also the spaces of the nation, especially the urban-rural divide so striking in Asia. Too often, they argue, the world's image of Indian youth – as fast changing, successfully integrating Western and traditional values, ready to adapt to global capitalism, and wired via the internet cafés – is an urban image, barely touching the daily experience of millions of rural youth, though their aspirations may be very similar. It is also, to a considerable degree, a masculine one in India (and, arguably, elsewhere), though the signs of a new image of technologically skilled Indian womanhood can also be discerned in the emerging discourse of mediated modernity. This demands some clever footwork from young women (and their families), for as Nayar and Bhide observe, they remain the bearers of traditional values but added to this is today's expectation of achievements commensurate with a globalized and commercialized individualism. This is exemplified by *Indian Idol*, a popular televised singing competition which is a far cry from the call for a Spartan lifestyle expected of youth by Nehru's government half a century ago.

Similar demands fall on the shoulders of Arab youth, although as elsewhere, the opportunities offered by new media technologies are enthusiastically welcomed by these young people as they seek to participate in global youth culture. Kraidy and Khalil (2008) argue that the consequence is less cultural homogenization but rather a cultural hybridity, albeit one marked by the growing "detraditionalization" or individualism of family life (especially insofar as global influences are locally appropriated by Islamic culture – examples include the growth of religious channels on satellite television and the emergence of religious stars or *tele-muftis*). Such a hybridization is hampered, however, by the paucity of indigenous cultural production for children in many Arab states, making reliance on Western imagery and ideas a practical necessity. Kraidy and Khalil trace how one Lebanese program, *Mini Studio*, pioneered a multilingual cultural space for children but combined this with an equally pioneering approach to encouraging the advertising industry to target children – leading to the program being popularly dubbed *Mini Market*. They are more optimistic about Al Jazeera Children's Channel and its promise to counter the relentless commercialization of children's culture by harnessing the interactive potential of the media to educate, engage, and empower children.

What is meant here by *global youth culture*? Giddens (1991) argues that young people are, in globalized late modernity, fundamentally absorbed in "the project of the self," a continual biographization of identity for which today's complex, intertextual, and reflexive media environment provides the symbolic resources for the never-completed task of drafting and redrafting. Acknowledging Buckingham's insistence on the recognition of structure, especially political economic and institutional constraints, as well as on the dynamics of the creative reappropriations of given meanings, Wildermuth (2008) integrates audience reception analysis of interpretative practices with a notion of the mediated imagination in his rich, ethnographic account of youth's creative appropriation of media resources in Brazil in order to "draft" and redraft the self. Again, this is a far from comfortable account, for Brazilian youth suffer the contradictory demands of a "periphery country" expected to "progress" rapidly, especially via new media technologies, while still being caught in the familiar trap of inequality, poverty, and a considerable underclass. As ever, these tensions are made visible through the stratified acquisition and display of media goods and in the far greater choices available to middle-class youth, whose possessions and media activities thereby mark – and perpetuate – social distinction. As Wildermuth concludes, these inequalities are all but impossible to escape from, despite the deployment of media by underprivileged young people to seek individual tactics for identity, resistance, and social mobility.

What immediately stand out when surveying these studies are the differences found in children's media cultures around the globe. As we argue, media scholars need to acknowledge these differences and act on them in analytical terms. Additionally, we also need to look beyond the richness and diversities in these cultures in order to seek for possible commonalities. In doing so, we may begin to detect economic, legal, and social inequalities of power between adults and children, structuring generational interactions in most parts of the world. Perhaps these inequalities also help explain the pervasive public concerns over children's media engagements, since in relation to media especially, young users may exercise some form of independence. Also common across many cultures is the importance of gender in orchestrating genre preferences to a degree that class, ethnicity, and age, arguably, do not (Livingstone and Bovill 2001). The often complicated pull and push between differences and commonalities in children's media cultures raises urgent questions about more global approaches to research.

The Emerging Research Agenda

What, then, of future directions for research? In the *International Handbook of Children, Media and Culture* (Drotner and Livingstone 2008), we mapped out some fruitful paths ahead. We began with Ito's (2008) account of the emerging lineaments of the interactive, participatory digital environment, apparently so welcoming to today's youth though often less so for today's researchers. Blurring the online/offline, mediated/face-to-face boundaries on which the analysis of media and communication has traditionally relied, the contemporary conceptual toolkit centers on the prefix *re-*, as in, remixing, reconfiguring, remediating, reappropriating, and recombining (Bolter and Grusin 1999; Dutton and Shepherd 2004; Lievrouw and Livingstone 2006). The familiar and the new are thus integrated, innovation being both continuous with and distinct from that which has gone before, simultaneously remediating the familiar with a shake of the kaleidoscope. The result is a convergent media culture – epitomized by the Japanese phenomena of Pokemon, Yugioh, and Hamtaro, and broadly characterized by personalization, hypersociality, networking, and ubiquity. This offers new "genres of participation" engaging the collective imagination, indeed positively requiring creativity on the part of its typically youthful users and raising many questions in the process (Jenkins 2006).

The implications of such an engagement for people's life chances have yet to be traced. Takahashi (2008) looks beyond Japanese media to the anthropological analysis of Japanese society and its modernity. A de-Westernized media studies cannot simply reject Western theory, asserting the uniqueness of Japan (or anywhere else). Rather, she argues, it should identify concepts from diverse intellectual traditions and consider, question, and apply them in particular contexts, thereby enriching the conceptual toolkit for the analysis of society as well as for new media. For example, the public-private distinction central to Western thinking provokes questions about visibility, sharedness, and the public sphere. In Japan, a key distinction is that between *uchi* (an intimate interpersonal realm, e.g. within couples, friendships, and workplace camaraderie, now extended by the advent of peer-to-peer networking) and *soto* (a notion of "outside" closely aligned with "them" and so distinct from the Western "public sphere"). Learning from the concepts and frameworks developed within the academy, and the society, of different countries poses an as yet little reflected upon challenge for many of us, for though we are willing to consider empirical findings internationally, we remain implicitly reliant on familiar theories and concepts with which to analyze them.

Literacy is just such a concept, commonly used in the English-speaking world, that only imperfectly matches concepts from other linguistic traditions (Livingstone 2008). Understood in a context of empowerment and human rights – for media literacy enables civic participation, cultural expression, and employability – it is certain that most cultures hope children will be critical media consumers, though not all provide, or can provide, the educational resources to enable this. However, the need for vigilance remains. In Europe, for example, media literacy is being repositioned as a strategic counterbalance to deregulatory moves to liberalize a converging market – put simply, if children can discern good content from bad, use media to express themselves, and protect themselves from mediated harm, then the burden of regulation on firms can be lessened. Though debates over the purposes of media literacy are not new (Luke 1989), what is new is the importance accorded to "new media literacies" beyond the domains of entertainment, values, and personal expression to encompass also educational success, competitive workplace skills, and civic participation (Hobbs 1998). Spurred on by pervasive discourses of knowledge societies and knowledge economies, policy makers and private stakeholders in many parts of the world are now urgently trying to identify and facilitate the human drivers of knowledge formation and sharing. Consequently, we can also see an academic reframing of what was once a rather specialized area for media practitioners and educators as a central issue for all concerned with people's (and especially children's) interpretative and critical engagement with all forms of media and communication. Media literacy will surely occupy a central place on the future agenda for children, media, and culture. However, arguably too, (media) literacy is one form of cultural capital, as theorized by Bourdieu (1984), a means of conceptualizing not only children's potential but also the means of their exclusion, for literacy relies on cultural and economic resources, and these serve to divide or coerce as much as – perhaps more than – they enable (see Pasquier 2008).

While several researchers have long stressed the importance of the family in mediating children's relation with the media (e.g. Heller 2008; Hoover and Clark 2008; Lemish 2008), Pasquier raises a new question, namely the way that the family itself is changing in late modernity. Is this a story of growing individualism, as families become less hierarchical and more democratic, enabling the plurality of individual tastes rather than inculcating traditional values; or, on the contrary, do the media open the door to an increasing tyranny of the peer group, as teenagers fear the social stigma of failing to follow the latest fad or fashion? Perhaps these arguments are compatible, just as the multiplicity of – especially personal and mobile – media permits some escape from parental supervision only to become subject to the scrutiny of one's peers (as suggested by Beck and Beck-Gernsheim 2002; see also Drotner 2005). We need simultaneously to analyze trends in media and trends in childhood and the family if we are to explain, and evaluate, social change in a meaningful fashion, avoiding the reductionisms of both technological and social determinism.

Political economists are keen to point out that the market benefits considerably from teenagers' constant desire to have the latest product, to try the newest service, and to seek out the niche media that make them both "individual" and "cool." For those contemplating any celebration of youthful creativity or active media engagement, Wasko (2008) offers a salutary check (see also Kenway and Bullen 2001). Children not only are bombarded with advertising and marketing for the latest commodity but also, arguably, as a new and profitable market, have themselves been commodified, sold to advertisers as "tweenies," "kids," and "teens" (Smythe 1981; Seiter 1993). Wasko's analysis of Disney and Neopets, to take two among many prominent cases of children's brands, develops the cultural circuit argued for by Buckingham and others integrating audience, text, production, and market analyses. Yet here again, and notwithstanding Wasko's depressing conclusions, the debate remains open. For Jenkins (2003) and perhaps Ito (2008), Buckingham (2008), and others, the circuit is not closed. To be sure, the market capitalizes on children's creative appropriations, but then children reappropriate, the market watches and responds, and children again get their turn. Perhaps the next stage of research is not to analyze the popular brands or their reappropriation by children, but rather to scope the (possibly narrowing) range of available choices, thus developing a critique of choice itself.

Intriguingly, the climate of academic opinion appears to be turning from distanced to engaged forms of critique, reflecting a normative turn in theory and research (Bennett 2000; Habermas 2006). Although emerging forms of critical engagement differ significantly from the administrative tradition long in evidence, especially in research on children's media (as overviewed e.g. in Singer and Singer 2001), both forms would concur that, as "experts" on questions of children's play, learning, participation, and literacy, it is incumbent on us, first, to ensure that good research reaches those stakeholders who might act on it constructively and, second and perhaps more contentiously, to ensure that particular outcomes which we judge to be in children's interests are supported. For example, Oswell's (2008) critical reflections on the regulation of children's media, especially but not only in the domain of advertising, highlight the risk that current regulatory developments may bypass democratic scrutiny, tending to devolve the burden of regulation from states or public institutions to either commercial bodies (i.e. self-regulation) or parents (i.e. media literacy and domestic regulation). However, for academic researchers of children, media, and culture, the interface with regulatory and policy debates is fraught with pitfalls, partly because these deliberations – though increasingly conducted in public – are often highly specialized in terms of both legal and technological matters, as well as fast moving; moreover, the translation from evidence to policy, notwithstanding the stress on "evidence-based policy," is far from straightforward.

There are further domains where critical engagement from children's media researchers is both much in demand from policy makers and less contentious within the academy. The potential for media, especially new media, to stimulate and sustain youthful contributions to the civic sphere is one such domain. Dahlgren and Olsson (2008; see also Bennett 2008) review attempts to use interactive media to facilitate political participation among a supposedly apathetic and disconnected youth. A further domain is the relation between human rights, children's rights, and communication rights, as represented in Hamelink's (2008) advocacy of a communications rights agenda for children, in the context of the UN Convention on the Rights of the Child. Extending the circuit of culture into the civic domain, Dahlgren and Olsson propose a circuit of civic culture driven by the dynamic interrelations among knowledge, values, trust, spaces, practices, and identities. They conclude that we must see beyond the formal political system if we are to recognize youthful civic engagement, for a traditional lens brands youth as passively distanced from politics.

However, less optimistically, it seems to be youth who are already active for whom the combination of new media and alternative politics is especially potent, possibly because so many are socialized – by media and other means – not into a culture of activism but rather into one of inefficacy and distrust. For these issues also, a comparative perspective is especially important, for societies vary in their approach to freedom of expression, norms of public engagement, and, in consequence, expectations held of children and young people. Noting the fundamental relation between mediation and cultural or individual rights, Hamelink advocates children's rights to express themselves, to be listened to, to privacy, to good-quality information, to the avoidance of mediated harm, and to see their culture reflected and valued by others. In a statement that surely every researcher of children's media culture would sign up to, we quote from UNICEF's Oslo Challenge, issued on the tenth anniversary of the UN Convention on the Rights of the Child:

> [T]he child/media relationship is an entry point into the wide and multifaceted world of children and their rights – to education, freedom of expression, play, identity, health, dignity and self-respect, protection … in every aspect of child rights, in every element of the life of a child, the relationship between children and the media plays a role. (UNICEF n.d.)

In support of an agenda for a globalized approach to children's media culture, this is a stimulating rallying call.

Conclusion

We hope to have convinced readers of this chapter that children's media culture matters. It matters not simply because children comprise a quarter of the population in developed countries, while in developing countries as much as half of the population is under 15 years old. Nor is it simply because they are "the future," as popular wisdom blandly pronounces. But also because, in the here and now, children and young people represent a vast economic market, a focus of both political despair and hope, a test bed for innovators in technology and design, and, last but certainly not least, a creative, emotional, and ethical force shaping continuities and change in values for societies everywhere. Children and young people cannot be contained in the domestic sphere, and in many parts of the world children have a keen public presence. They should not be rendered invisible by any wider or more abstract lens.

We have argued that universalistic claims about children and media must be critically interrogated, for the "same" phenomenon evidenced in different contexts often requires a different explanation. And we have shown how, in practice, this opens the way to an exciting terrain of new (and old but neglected) research on children's media culture. This means sidestepping – or contextualizing as itself historically and culturally particular – the dominant American research tradition on children and media (Singer and Singer 2001), in order to both recognize the diversity of our research domain and to avoid obscuring or "othering" the non-American experience (Curran and Park 2000; Lemish 2007). Donald offers some stern injunctions to the research community, warning against uncritically applying findings from one culture or subculture to another, or against building assumptions into our methodologies that blind us to certain dimensions of children's experience or ignore the values embedded in language when we translate – literally or figuratively – across contexts. Nor can the contemporary researcher take their own experience as primary and project this unwittingly onto the rest of the world (Livingstone 2003).

In order to both substantiate these real differences and look for possible connections and commonalities across boundaries of place and social demarcations, we need comparative studies and what may be called *contextualized conceptual developments*. And while such larger studies are not easily conducted (or funded), the careful hedging of claims with qualifications and contextualization is, perhaps, a necessary and realistic strategy for individual researchers in a fast-globalizing space of knowledge production. But at its best, a view that spans cultures, balancing both range and depth, offers the excitement of new questions and insights, critical reflections, and challenging problems that stimulate a rethinking of long-held assumptions regarding children, media, and culture.

Acknowledgment

This chapter reprises and rewrites the introductory and editorial texts originally published in Drotner and Livingstone (2008).

References

Alasuutari, P. 1995 *Researching Culture: Qualitative Methods and Cultural Studies*. Sage, London.

American Academy of Pediatrics Committee on Public Education. 2001 Children, adolescents and television. *Pediatrics*, 107, 2, pp. 423–426.

Ariès, P. 1962 *Centuries of Childhood: A Social History of Family Life*. Trans. R. Baldick. Vintage, New York. (Original work published in 1960)

Beck, U. and Beck-Gernsheim, E. 2002 *Individualization*. Sage, London.

Bennett, T. 2000 Acting on the social: art, culture, and government. *American Behavioral Scientist*, 43, 9, pp. 1412–1428.

Bennett, W. L. 2008 Changing citizenship in the digital age. In W. L. Bennett, ed. *Civic Life Online: Learning How Digital Media Can Engage Youth*, vol. 1. John D. and Catherine T. Macarthur Foundation Series on Digital Media and Learning, MIT Press, Cambridge, MA, pp. 1–24.

Bolter, J.D. and Grusin, R. 1999 *Remediation: Understanding New Media*. MIT Press, Cambridge, MA.

Bourdieu, P. 1984 *Distinction: A Social Critique of the Judgement of Taste*. Harvard University Press, Cambridge, MA.

Bronfenbrenner, U. 1980 Ecology of childhood. *Social Psychology Review*, 9, 4, pp. 294–297.

Buckingham, D. 2008 Children and media: a cultural studies approach. In K. Drotner and S. Livingstone, eds. *International Handbook of Children, Media and Culture*. Sage, London, pp. 219–236.

Castells, M. 1996 *The Rise of the Network Society*. Blackwell, Oxford

Corsaro, W. A. 1997 *The Sociology of Childhood*. Pine Forge, Thousand Oaks, CA.

Critcher, C. 2008 Making waves: historic aspects of public debates about children and mass media. In K. Drotner and S. Livingstone, eds. *International Handbook of Children, Media and Culture*. Sage, London, pp. 91–104.

Curran, J. and Park, M. eds. 2000 *Dewesternising Media Studies*. Routledge, London.

Dahlgren, P. and Olsson, T. 2008 Facilitating political participation: young citizens, internet and civic cultures. In K. Drotner and S. Livingstone, eds. *International Handbook of Children, Media and Culture*. Sage, London, pp. 493–507.

De Certeau, M. 1984 *The Practices of Everyday Life*. University of California Press, Los Angeles.

Donald, S. H. 2008 Children, media and regional modernity in the Asia Pacific. In K. Drotner and S. Livingstone, eds. *International Handbook of Children, Media and Culture*. Sage, London, pp. 299–313.

Drotner, K. 1992 Modernity and media panics. In M. Skovmand and K. C. Schroder, eds. *Media Cultures: Reappraising Transnational Media*. Routledge, London, pp. 42–62.

Drotner, K. 1999 Dangerous media? Panic discourses and dilemmas of modernity. *Paedagogica Historica*, 35, 3, pp. 593–619.

Drotner, K. 2000 Difference and diversity: trends in young Danes' media use. *Media, Culture and Society*, 22, 2, pp. 149–166.

Drotner, K. 2005 Media on the move: personalised media and the transformation of publicness. In S. Livingstone, ed. *Audiences and Publics: When Cultural Engagement Matters for the Public Sphere*. Intellect, Bristol, UK, pp. 187–212.

Drotner, K. and Livingstone, S. 2008 *The International Handbook of Children, Media and Culture*. Sage, London.

du Gay, P., Hall, S., Janes, L., Mackay, H. and Negus, K. 1997 *Doing Cultural Studies: The Story of the Sony Walkman*. Sage and Open University Press, London.

Dutton, W.H. and Shepherd, A. 2004 *Confidence and Risk on the Internet*. Oxford Internet Institute, Oxford.

Elias, N. and Lemish, D. 2008 When all else fails: the internet and adolescent-immigrants' informal learning. In K. Drotner, H. S. Jensen and K. C. Schrøder, eds. *Informal Learning and Digital Media*. Cambridge Scholars Publishing, Cambridge, pp. 138–154.

Geertz, C. 1973 *The Interpretation of Cultures: Selected Essays*. Basic Books, New York.

Georgiou, M. 2001 Crossing the boundaries of the ethnic home: media consumption and ethnic identity construction in the public space: the case of the Cypriot community centre in north London. *Gazette*, 63, 4, pp. 311–329.

Giddens, A. 1991 *Modernity and Self-identity: Self and Society in the Late Modern Age*. Polity Press, Cambridge.

Habermas, J. 2006 Political communication in media society: does democracy still enjoy an epistemic dimension? The impact of normative theory on empirical research. *Communication Theory*, 16, 4, pp. 411–426.

Hamelink, C. J. 2008 Children's communication rights: beyond intentions. In K. Drotner and S. Livingstone, eds. *International Handbook of Children, Media and Culture*. Sage, London, pp. 508–519.

Heller, M. 2008 Games and media: the acquisition of social structure and social rules. In K. Drotner and S. Livingstone, eds. *International Handbook of Children, Media and Culture*. Sage, London, pp. 271–298.

Hobbs, R. 1998 The seven great debates in the media literacy movement. *Journal of Communication*, 48, 1, pp. 6–32.

Hoover, S. and Clark, L. S. 2008 Children and media in the context of the home and family. In K. Drotner and S. Livingstone, eds. *International Handbook of Children, Media and Culture*. Sage, London, pp. 105–120.

Ito, M. 2008 Mobilizing the imagination in everyday play: the case of Japanese media mixes. In K. Drotner and S. Livingstone, eds. *International Handbook of Children, Media and Culture*. Sage, London, pp. 397–412.

Jenkins, H. 2003 Quentin Tarantino's Star Wars? Digital cinema, media convergence, and participatory culture. In D. Thorburn and H. Jenkins, eds. *Rethinking Media Change: The Aesthetics of Transition*. MIT Press, Cambridge, MA. pp. 281–312.

Jenkins, H. 2006 *Confronting the Challenges of Participatory Culture: Media Education for the 21st Century*. John D. and Catherine T. Macarthur Foundation, Chicago.

Kenway, J. and Bullen, E. 2001 *Consuming Children: Education-Entertainment-Advertising*. Open University Press, Buckingham, UK.

Kinder, M., ed. 1999 *Kids' Media Culture*. Duke University Press, Durham, NC.

Kraidy, M. and Khalil, J. 2008 Youth, media and culture in the Arab world. In K. Drotner and S. Livingstone, eds. *International Handbook of Children, Media and Culture*. Sage, London, pp. 336–350.

Lazarsfeld, P.F. 1941 Remarks on administrative and critical communications research. *Studies in Philosophy and Science*, 9, pp. 3–16.

Lemish, D. 2007 Setting new research agendas. *Journal of Children and Media*, 1, 1, pp. 1–4.

Lemish, D. 2008 The mediated playground: media in early childhood. In K. Drotner and S. Livingstone, eds. *International Handbook of Children, Media and Culture*. Sage, London, pp. 152–167.

Lievrouw, L. and Livingstone, S., eds. 2006 *Handbook of New Media: Social Shaping and Social Consequences*, updated student edn. Sage, London.

Ling, R. and Haddon, L. 2008 Mobile emancipation: children, youth and the mobile phone. In K. Drotner and L. Livingstone, eds. *International Handbook of Children, Media and Culture*. Sage, London, pp. 137–151.

Livingstone, S. 1998 Mediated childhoods: a comparative approach to young people's changing media environment in Europe. *European Journal of Communication*, 13, 4, pp. 435–456.

Livingstone, S. 2003 On the challenges of cross-national comparative media research. *European Journal of Communication*, 18, 4, pp. 477–500.

Livingstone, S. 2008 Engaging with the media: a matter of literacy? *Communication, Culture and Critique*, 1, 1, pp. 51–62.

Livingstone, S. and Bovill, M., eds. 2001 *Children and Their Changing Media Environment: A European Comparative Study*. Lawrence Erlbaum, Mahwah, NJ.

Lobe, B., et al. 2008 *Best Practice Research Guide: How to Research Children and Online Technologies in Comparative Perspective*. EU Kids Online Deliverable D4.2 the EC Safer Internet Plus Programme. LSE, London.

Luke, C. 1989 *Pedagogy, Printing and Protestantism: The Discourse on Childhood* State University of New York Press, Albany.

Mansell, R. 2004 Political economy, power and new media. *New Media and Society*, 6, 1, pp. 96–105.

Meyrowitz, J. 1984 The adultlike child and the childlike adult: socialization in an electronic world. *Daedalus*, 113, 3, pp. 19–48.

Millwood Hargrave, A. and Livingstone, S. 2009 *Harm and Offence in Media Content: A Review of the Evidence*. Second edition. Intellect, Bristol, UK.

Morley, D. and Robins, K. 1995 *Spaces of Identity: Global Media, Electronic Landscapes and Cultural Boundaries*. Routledge, London.

Nayar, U. and Bhide, A. 2008 Contextualizing media competencies amongst young people in Indian culture: interface with globalization. In K. Drotner and S. Livingstone, eds. *International Handbook of Children, Media and Culture*. Sage, London, pp. 328–335.

Oswell, D. 2008 Media and communications regulation and child protection: an overview of the field. In K. Drotner and S. Livingstone, eds. *International Handbook of Children, Media and Culture*. Sage, London, pp. 475–492.

Pasquier, D. 2008 From parental control to peer pressure: cultural transmission and conformism. In K. Drotner and S. Livingstone, eds. *International Handbook of Children, Media and Culture*. Sage, London, pp. 448–459.

Prensky, M. 2001 Digital natives, digital immigrants. *On the Horizon*, 9, 5, pp. 1–2.

Rantanen, T. 2004 *The Media and Globalization*. Sage, London.

Robertson, R. 1992 *Globalization: Social Theory and Global Culture*. Sage, London.

Robins, K., and Morley, D. 1989 Spaces of identity: communication technologies and the reconfiguration of Europe. *Screen*, 30, 4, pp. 11–34.

Rowland, W.D. and Watkins, B. 1984 *Interpreting Television: Current Research Perspectives*. Sage, London.

Rygaard, J. 2008 Let the world in! Globalization in Greenland. In K. Drotner and S. Livingstone, eds. *International Handbook of Children, Media and Culture*. Sage, London, pp. 254–270.

Schroeder, K. S., Drotner, K., Kline, S. and Murray, C. 2003 *Researching Audiences*. Arnold, London.

Seiter, E. 1993 *Sold Separately: Children and Parents in Consumer Culture*. Rutgers University Press, New Brunswick, NJ.

Seiter, E. 2008 Practicing at home: computers, pianos, and cultural capital. In T. McPherson, ed. *Digital Youth, Innovations, and the Unexpected*, vol. 4. John D. and Catherine T. Macarthur Foundation Series on Digital Media and Learning, MIT Press, Cambridge, MA, pp. 27–52.

Silverstone, R. 2005 *Media, Technology and Everyday Life in Europe: From Information to Communication*. Ashgate, Aldershot, UK.

Singer, D.G. and Singer, J.L., eds. 2001 *Handbook of Children and the Media*. Sage, Thousand Oaks, CA.

Smith, M.R. and Marx, L. 1994 *Does Technology Drive History? The Dilemma of Technological Determinism*. MIT Press, Cambridge, MA.

Smythe, D. W. 1981 *Dependency Road: Communications, Capitalism, Consciousness and Canada*. Ablex, Norwood, NJ.

Stehr, N. 1994 *Knowledge Societies: The Transformation of Labour, Property and Knowledge in Contemporary Society*. Sage, London.

Strelitz, L. and Boshoff, P. 2008 The African reception of global media. In K. Drotner and S. Livingstone, eds. *International Handbook of Children, Media and Culture*. Sage, London, pp. 237–253.

Takahashi, T. 2008 Japanese young people, media and everyday life: towards the de-Westernising of media studies. In K. Drotner and S. Livingstone, eds. *International Handbook of Children, Media and Culture*. Sage, London, pp. 413–430.

Thompson, J. B. 2005 *The Media and Modernity: A Social Theory of the Media*. Polity Cambridge.

Tomlinson, J. 1999 *Globalization and Culture*. Chicago: University of Chicago Press.

UNICEF n.d. Oslo Challenge. Retrieved from http://www.unicef.org/magic/briefing/oslo.html

Wasko, J. 2008 The commodification of youth culture. In K. Drotner and S. Livingstone, eds. *International Handbook of Children, Media and Culture*. Sage, London, pp. 460–474.

Wildermuth, N. 2008 Constrained appropriations: practices of media consumption and imagination amongst Brazilian teens. In K. Drotner and S. Livingstone, eds. *International Handbook of Children, Media and Culture*. Sage, London, pp. 351–370.

21

Fan Cultures and Fan Communities

Kristina Busse and Jonathan Gray

Introduction

When Henry Jenkins (1992b) started his discipline defining *Textual Poachers* by describing an infamous *Saturday Night Live* skit in which William Shatner tells *Star Trek* fans to "get a life," he raised and then rejected the stereotype of fans as socially awkward, maladjusted losers living in a fantasy world. Thus began academic fan studies' more earnest attempt to make sense of fan communities, identities, and textual play. Jenkins famously described fans as "scribbling in the margins" and as reinterpreting and responding to media texts, not simply accepting them as presented. Following various scholars' early insistences on the importance of studying rather than caricaturizing, much of fan studies' subsequent work has attempted to map out fans' intricate and thoughtful engagements with popular culture texts, and with each other. Marking a major shift in this project, though, Jenkins's recent *Convergence Culture* (2006a) focuses more on the mainstreaming of fannish behavior, and on fans as the new trailblazers of a "convergence culture" based on "collective intelligence." Much of fan studies has occurred in between these two positions of fans as fundamentally othered (for better and worse) and fans as early adapters and adopters of particular audience behaviors that have become widespread.

In this chapter, we trace the methodological and theoretical implications of this trajectory of fan studies. Aware that Jenkins is also contributing to this volume, though, our prime concern will not be to detail convergence culture; rather, it will be to examine fan communities. In particular, we ask what happens to fans and fan studies when a combination of increased interest in fan psychology and in fans as *individuals* and the industry's "discovery" of fans, again often as individuals, might seem to abandon former interests in fan *communities* and audience formations.

The Handbook of Media Audiences, First Edition. Edited by Virginia Nightingale.
© 2014 John Wiley & Sons, Ltd. Published 2014 by John Wiley & Sons, Ltd.

Thus, beginning with a brief historical overview that connects theoretical frameworks and methodologies with the audience groups studied and defined as fans, we look at the shifts and changes in fan studies and how these various approaches have political and social implications for audience studies.

While we are invested in acknowledging the range of fans and fannish behaviors, most of our discussion focuses on *fans* as members of *fandom*, and on fandom as a particular identity that affects and shapes its members in ways beyond shared media consumption. For example, an intense emotional investment in a text that is wholly singular may create a fan but does not make the individual part of a larger fandom, where its members are characterized not only by their affect and engagement with the source text but also by their engagement with one another. Of course, there are no clearly defined lines, but we find it useful to consider the overlapping but not necessarily interdependent axes of investment and involvement as two factors that can define fannish engagement. So even though we look at individual fans, it is the community and the social interaction we want to foreground, both as important characteristics of members of fandom (as opposed to casual viewers who display fannish interests or behaviors) and as two of the structural models that now many social networks are displaying.

Discussing what fans are and are not is important not only for the developing field of fan studies but also for audience studies in general. On one hand, fans so often stand in for audiences more generally in research studies. Even though fans are still derided and often invisible in public, for media scholars they are ever present. Fans are some of the easiest and most interesting subjects to study: proactive, self-theorizing, and invested in their texts in ways that few other audiences are, they offer a dangerously ideal research subject as they welcome inquiries, readily describe and explain their own affect, and overshadow other – less visible and less vocal – types of audience engagement (Gray 2003). On the other hand, since fans and fan communities exist on a spectrum of media consumption that more generally includes *all* audiences, findings about fans stand to tell us a great deal about audiences as a whole.

Looking at the way these communities have changed over the past four decades and how they both anticipate and respond to current technologies and varying interfaces allows us to see how and why these more narrowly defined groups of fans can remain exemplary audience subjects. At the same time, this chapter will also address new frontiers for fan research, namely, other forms of strongly affective engagements such as in antifans, "high-culture" fandom, global fandom, and their respective audience formations. But even as the field of fan studies expands and definitions of fans and fandoms become ever more diverse, we ultimately maintain in this chapter that there remains value in looking at the self-identifying, self-analyzing, often quite well-defined and activist groups of fans that in some cases trace themselves back to pre-internet, pre-convergence days of fannish identity formation.

History

As a field, fan studies grows for the most part out of audience studies (and, to a lesser degree, reader response theory) and cultural studies' embracing of popular culture.[1] One of the central influences to all of cultural theory but especially audience studies was Stuart Hall's (1973/1991) incorporation/resistance model: refuting the notion that all viewers automatically take the intended dominant reading, Hall instead suggested that reading or viewing constitutes a complex negotiation that creates multiple interpretation. This more complex understanding of the role of the viewer or reader mirrored literary theory's turn to the role of the reader (see e.g. Iser 1978; Fish 1980), and its insistence (quickly backed up by Morley and Brunsdon's audience research [1999]) that all cultural consumption can involve both negotiation with and outright resistance to meanings within texts.[2] As a result, cultural studies turned to the qualitative examination of popular cultural consumption. At the same time, Dick Hebdige's *Subculture* (1979) foregrounded the political role played by countercultural readings and appropriations. Often the most compelling and rhetorically powerful act for audience researchers was to turn to those whom society had deemed the least thoughtful, most "passive" consumers. Frequently, this led to the examination of fans.

Hence, for instance, Janice Radway's *Reading the Romance* (1984) began with a critical feminist examination of romance literature, but Radway's interviews with romance fans found multiple points of resistance to patriarchy. Similarly, working with a model of reading as resistance borrowed in part from Michel de Certeau (1984), John Fiske (1989) studied how teenage Madonna fans used their own reading "tactics" to oppose and work against the culture industry's "strategies" for the use of Madonna. Fiske infamously pronounced a "semiotic democracy," in which "active audiences" made sense of texts in creative, personally, and communally meaningful ways, frequently writing and talking back to established power hierarchies in the process. Indeed, cultural studies' encounter with audiences was intrinsically about power. Pierre Bourdieu's highly influential book *Distinction* (1984) had argued that taste and cultural consumption were always also acts of performance, of class, and of power. It is thus no surprise that those cultural products generally regarded by society as the lowest were those of the masses, the working class, women, children, and minorities; likewise, those consumers regarded as the most passive and mindless were those at the bottom of social hierarchies. As such, the early study of fans was a political act as cultural studies scholars sought to redeem "low" or "mass" culture and its consumers by showing the texts to be as complex as those of high culture, and the consumers to be as thoughtful and intelligent as any opera denizen or aficionado of European art cinema (see Jensen 1992).

Media fans had often been derided and mocked, seen as perennial losers to a dominant media system, following a subpar pied piper. Celebrity, soap, and *Star*

Trek fans attracted particular scorn, becoming the poster children for rabid attachment to supposedly insignificant, fluffy items of mass culture. In gaining such status, though, they also became ripe for discussion by the first wave of fan studies – and even paradigmatic for future work. Three key early fan studies examinations that grew out of this period were Henry Jenkins's *Textual Poachers* (1992), Camille Bacon-Smith's *Enterprising Women* (1992), and Constance Penley's "Feminism, Psychoanalysis, and the Study of Popular Culture" (1992), later expanded into *NASA/Trek* (1997). Even though Jenkins, Bacon-Smith, and Penley used different approaches (textual, ethnographic, and psychoanalytic, respectively), all three foregrounded the community that fandom creates and the relationship among the fans as well as between the fans and the texts. Fans, as all three showed, not only were extremely well organized due in several cases to their community roots in science fiction fandom with its well-organized cons, amateur press associations (APAs), and fanzines, but also tended to be quite self-reflexive and able to analyze their own behavior.

Given the predominance of Hall's (1973/1991) incorporation/resistance paradigm, a central task for early fan studies was to show the subversive nature of fan productions. In that reading, fans became exemplary resistant readers who not only critically analyzed the texts but also actively wrote back, creating their own narratives that filled the plots, characters, and emotions they found lacking in the source text. Building off Michel de Certeau's (1984) notion of the "textual poacher," Jenkins posited fans as those who squat on products not of their creation, yet ultimately make of them what they wish. Bacon Smith's title, meanwhile, employed its pun to suggest an intrinsic act of production and worth (*enterprise*) in fannish activities, and Constance Penley likened fandom to the giving of a vigorous massage that might hurt the text in the short run, yet ultimately was done for that text's sake (1997, p. 3). All three writers offered a picture of fandom as never necessarily passive and compliant, as thoughtful and deliberative, as happening in and through communities of engaged and intelligent individuals, and as a legitimate source of production of meaning and value in and of itself. While the cultural studies of the 1980s and early 1990s endeavored to chart resistance, after all, it also examined how culture was produced by those who live it, not simply passed down a chute from the cultural industries, and thus early fan studies began to explore fandom as a culture and as an audience formation.

Following on from this, Abercrombie and Longhurst (1998) critiqued Hall's (1973/1991) incorporation/resistance model as often automatically (even if unintentionally) framing audience reactions as purely reactive. Instead, they attempted to initiate a new era of audience and fan studies with their *spectacle performance paradigm* that regarded the act of being an audience as performative and as constructive of identity.[3] Also revising fan studies' focus, Matt Hills (2002) and Cornel Sandvoss (2005) somewhat shifted emphasis in their object of study from fan communities to fans as individuals, from social interaction to psychological motivation, and from a focus on resistance to one on affect and individual engagements with texts. While both still looked at communities, these communities often were constructed in the minds of individuals only or relevant primarily insofar as they reflect or constitute the individual fan's relationship to the fannish object. For instance, Hills (2002) defines fan cultures as

> Formed around any given text when this text has functioned as a *pto* [primary transitional object] in the biography of a number of individuals who remain attached to this text by virtue of the fact that it continues to exist as an element of their cultural experience. (p. 108)

Much as a child turns to a favorite blanket for security and as a substitute for the mother, noted Hills, fans imbue their beloved texts with feelings of warmth and ontological security. Thus, he drew from D. W. Winnicott's theories on child psychological development (1974) and Roger Silverstone's subsequent application of an understanding of the individual's relationship to television as a transitional object (1994) as the kernel of a theory of fan communities.

Sandvoss (2005), likewise, focused on the individual fan and actually redefined fandom for his purposes:

> In a broader understanding of "fandom," as on a most basic level the state of being a fan, this focus on communities and tightly networked fans fails to conceptualize important aspects of the relationship between the modern self, identity and popular culture which forms my particular concern here.... I define fandom as the regular, emotionally involved consumption of a given popular narrative or text. (pp. 5–6, 8)

Drawing from Walter Marcuse's theory of the "one dimensional man" (1964), using texts in a narcissistic manner to mirror his own images of the world back at him, and from Wolfgang Iser's theories of textual reception (1978), Sandvoss exhibited particular interest in the engagement between individual fan and individual text, to explore fan texts as a projection of individual fan meanings. For instance, he observed sports fans' ability to fashion their beloved team in their image, seeing it as nationalistic if they see themselves as nationalists, or as diverse and multicultural if they see themselves that way. Sandvoss argued that, as can any text, a team can become a canvas for a fan to project meanings that affirm his or her own values and sense of self. Hence, where previous fan studies had often considered the fan as one part of a greater whole, Abercrombie and Longhurst (1998), Hills, and Sandvoss all offered means by which one can examine the fan as an individual unit too or, rather, redefine the larger whole as a function of the individual. Moreover, this focus on individual subjects, with its larger scope of what constitutes fannish objects and activities, also permitted an approach that connected the multiple ways in which an individual engages fannishly with different objects, intensities, and levels of community involvement.

Convergence and New Media Culture

Just as academic theories of fandom have changed in recent years, so has the relationship between fans as communities and/or individuals, technology, and the cultural industries. Most notably, recent years have witnessed an expansion of fannish activities into more mainstream audiences and a concurrent industry focus on viral marketing and the immense profitability of encouraging and exploiting fannish behaviors. It is this type of fannish behavior that is at the center of much of Jenkins's recent work (2006a), where he traces the interactions and engagements traditionally associated with well-defined and often subcultural fan communities and finds them in more easily accessible and often industry-sponsored arenas. The rise of the internet has led to a revolution in how individuals can access the fan community, and hence in how fan and nonfan "collective intelligence" (Lévy 1997) can be mobilized.

New technologies have facilitated creating one's own content at the same time as social networks provide spaces in which to easily share this content with others. Meanwhile, the increased specialization within the entertainment industry and fragmentation of the audience have required that producers follow the rules of what Jenkins calls "affective economics," capitalizing on (and frequently disciplining) fan practices in order to ensure a loyal audience base. Both developments – in technology and cultural practice and in industry and marketing practice – have given much mainstream consumption a fannish look. Thus, for instance, today's fan of any given television program can access the program's official website, which will likely include a discussion forum, computer wallpapers and screensavers, extra video and webisodes, and perhaps even links to other sites within the show's diegetic frame, spinoff books, comics, merchandise, and/or competitions for fan creations. In *Convergence Culture* (2006a), Jenkins addresses mainstream and subcultural discourses, suggesting their similarities in terms of practices and behaviors. In fact, in his analysis, the communities that spring up spontaneously either with or without the help of industry-sponsored spaces and activities would appear to mimic the fan-created magazines, listservs, and conventions that carried the responsibility of keeping fan communities alive in earlier years, yet were decidedly subcultural.

Whereas a decade ago, fans were easily identified and defined as those more intense and invested media audiences who engaged and connected with one another, media convergence, new technologies, and transmedia marketing have all created new types of fans who exhibit many similarities and yet may not be quite the same. At first glance, convergence culture seems to facilitate being a fan, with new technologies making it easier to access media, engage with others, and create one's own content. Only a few years ago, downloading an episode one might have missed the night before required at least a certain degree of computer savvy and often connections to a network of other fans; with legal downloads and online streaming, it is now possible for anyone with high-speed internet access to keep up fairly easily with any show. Likewise, for instance, creating fanvids in the 1980s and early 1990s was a lengthy, exhausting, and expensive endeavor, using two VCRs and keeping track of the song via stopwatch (see Coppa 2008). Today, every computer comes with a simple movie maker program that allows anyone within minutes to edit digital media files with immediate results. The cultural industries, for their part, have recognized the marketing potential of both transmedia products and user-generated content as forms of viral marketing, and they often openly encourage its development, thereby moving previously marginalized fan behavior into the mainstream.

However, the similarity in terms of behavior and textual productions obscures the clear differences between traditional fan communities and new industry-driven fans: fandoms as specific social and cultural formations – as communities – have a history, a continuity, and a sense of identity that are at times profoundly distinct from contemporary convergence culture. Our interest here is in the sense of identity at the center of our approach to fans, fan communities, and fandom as a specific audience formation. Indeed, it is one that is often threatened by convergence culture. While we do not want to negate or exclude other forms of fan engagement, we suggest that there are particular insights that can be gained by focusing on more organized fan communities as we have chosen to do in this chapter: their members function as exemplary viewers as they self-consciously and freely interpret and share their responses. More importantly, focusing on traditional fan communities may allow us to pinpoint exactly where they differ from more casual fans, individual fans, or other forms of fan engagement, thus offering further understanding of the emotional engagements and cultural attachments of all fans.

After all, there remain central differences between fandom as social community and congregates of individual fans, between what fans would call *fan works* and what the industry has termed *user-generated content*.[4] Some of it may be measurable in intensity and investment, not just emotionally but also in terms of time and length of involvement. These differences, of course, have always existed. Fans humorously distinguish between Fandom-Is-a-Way-of-Life (FIAWOL) and Fandom-Is-Just-a-Goddamned-Hobby (FIJAGH): the former denotes fans for whom their fannishness is a central facet of their identity, affecting all aspects of their lives; and the latter is used by fans who feel that liking something is one among many of their hobbies that do not shape their identity and that may be temporarily limited. Whereas for a long time, fans tended to mostly fall into the Way-of-Life category, more and more fans are now actively created, not only by more exposure of fandoms themselves but also by the media industry actively interpellating viewers as fans (see Stein 2010).

And yet, unless the industry actually creates online spaces for fans to meet – often with quite clear rules and guidelines – it still requires committed fans to create and sustain that infrastructure. Such spaces then allow other users to gather and use the offered materials and spaces. For example, many casual fans may visit a wiki, and some may even add material and thus create user content, but it still requires someone more dedicated to provide server space, maintain the wiki, and assure its continuance. Fan film, machinima, and vids may be *watched* by thousands on Youtube.com, but a much smaller band of fans actually dedicates the significant time and creative energy needed to *make* such films. In fact, the media industry often seems to be more interested in large numbers of low-level users than it is in the fewer, more dedicated fans – more often than not tied to organized fandom – that tend to control the noncommercial spaces.

When the industry itself steps in to create such spaces for fans to gather and communicate, and to share their ideas and creations, they often curtail the more unusual and extreme forms of fan responses, which is one of the biggest fears many members of fan communities express. Often fan material is critical or completely re-envisions the purview of the show – many fan communities are adamant in maintaining their own spaces to continue to create material that might not be approved of or condoned by the industry itself. Whereas so-called coloring within the lines is something encouraged and desired by industry, it is the very limitation of those "lines" that has many members of traditional fan communities rejecting these more legal and endorsed spaces (see Cupitt 2008). Anne McCaffrey, for example, encourages stories told in her Pern universe, but for the longest time, such stories could not expand existing story lines she herself might still use, and even today she continues to impose limits on fanfictional worlds.[5] Furthermore, one contentious issue is the often adult nature of many fan productions, especially when the source text is geared toward children and teens. J. K. Rowling, thus, encourages fan fiction as long as it remains sexually nonexplicit.[6]

Even in cases where rating and authorial competition are no concerns, critical commentary may still be: many fan creations pay homage to the sources that inspired them and expand their universes, but others offer biting critique. Yet whereas a film critic or book reviewer can safely criticize, creative responses' citations may threaten to violate copyright of the very texts they so bitterly critique. George Lucas, for example, supported *Star Wars* fan film contests, but set firm rules as to what story lines and genres were permitted, encouraging parodies while preventing the public showing of more critical engagements.[7] Since fandom often questions, pushes, or removes a show's "lines,"[8] tensions between fans and those entrusted with entrenching such lines are inevitable, yet through intellectual property laws and/or posturing, the media industries attempt to lay claim to the power to silence critics. At various times, numerous media companies have sent cease-and-desist letters to fan fiction writers and other fan creators, despite the at best questionable validity of their legal claims to own characters and universes (see Tushnet 2007). Or, they have also excluded such productions from the walled gardens of their official sites. Yet the question remains as to what degree such acts are motivated largely by the urge to silence criticism.

The question of what should ultimately constitute the central object of fan studies is a crucial one. Critics, in fact, debate whether the focus should remain on or be shifted from heavily engaged and active fans and cult aficionados, that is, fans who may have higher status within a given fan community due to their particular engagement with the fannish object (Hills 2002, pp. ix–x). In other words, can fan studies be relevant to audience studies only if they shift focus to the individual fan whose fan engagements are parts of their everyday lives? Or can the study of the more defined fan *communities* become useful even if their members' behavior may not be easily extrapolated or generalized? Moreover, even if fandom communities turned out to be more different than similar to casual viewers and those differences are qualitative rather than merely quantitative, would those differences still afford us insight into all viewers and the way they engage with texts?

Fan Communities: Exemplary or Exceptional Audiences

We would like to suggest that fan communities should be of particular interest to current media and especially new media scholars for the way they employ and create social publics, and manipulate and alter social network engines to their needs. Given the wide range of what might be defined as *fans*, we focus on the fan as a member of a fan community, for a number of reasons:

- There are specific ways in which those fans engage that are more explicit and useful for audience studies in general.
- Even where their responses differ from casual audiences, we would argue, their communities are still a useful object of audience studies.
- The recent focus on media convergence, user-generated content, and individual fan risks replacing or overshadowing these fans and their particular infrastructures and modes of engagements.

Fans hold interest for literary scholars as an example of intertextual engagement on multiple levels: fan works are created in dialogue with their respective source text, but they also in many cases respond to other fan textual productions – be they theoretical or creative (see Derecho 2006; Stasi 2006; Tosenberger 2007). As such, many fans create in a complex intersection where meaning production is highly dependent on shared interpretations and interpretive communities. As fannish artifacts gain wider mainstream popularity, some if not many are misread as they lose their specific contexts of shared interpretive frameworks (see Busse 2007). For audience studies, fan communities and their audience responses remain exemplary cases of active readers, involved respondents, and an interactivity that creates a co-imaginary fan community that may be present but that is often far less pronounced in casual or individual fans. Finally, fans use wiki software, blogging platforms such as LiveJournal.com, or bookmarking sites like Delicious.com in very specific ways: Livejournal.com, for example, was never intended to serve as a story archive, yet many fans developed specific workarounds such as newsletters, announcement communities, and particular tagging and bookmarking systems to customize the site for their particular use.

In order to better describe differences between types of fans, we want to suggest a way to categorize levels of fannishness, drawing from but expanding upon previous models such as Abercrombie and Longhurst (1998). Fans, we argue, function along two central lines of involvement and investment, and it is this particular matrix that defines the more intense fan of the Fandom-Is-a-Way-of-Life variety. Both community interaction and affect exist on a continuum (changing between different people and even within a person over time). Conceptualizing fan identity along these two axes allows us to cover those who may be quite unevenly aligned along the two axes: the fan who may be singular but heavily emotionally invested as well as the member of a community who may refuse to self-identify as a fan. Moreover, it also allows for understanding the lone noninteracting fan who is nevertheless emotionally invested in community.

Fan psychology has long been read within the context of mass psychology; as a result, the psychology of audiences has often, falsely, generalized or simply asserted a given response of an imaginary ideal viewer that then gets assumed to function for all. Of course, research of actual viewers indicates that their levels of engagement and emotional and intellectual investment are often quite different and indeed change over time, even within a given viewer. Matt Hills (2002) and Cornel Sandvoss (2005) have both focused on the psychology of individual viewers: Hills foregrounds how every viewer creates his or her own matrix of fan objects that often overlap and affect one another. For Hills, the transitional object, then, can very much be communal, and even though it is a concept that begins with the individual, it takes on extra meaning when it is communal. Likewise, even as Sandvoss's fans may be by themselves, their fandom of one creates an imaginary space that is shared with others. After all, psychological engagement with a text can be intense, even in the absence of others to share that particular sentiment, that obsessional focus. Thus, the lonely fan reading, watching, and/or enjoying fannish products is in fact often participating in an imagined community of other fans – even when they are not explicitly interacting as part of a community per se, they may think of themselves as part of that community, in a way creating parasocial relations with other fans.

Focusing on fan communities allows us to foreground the highly intertextual aspects of fan works and the way community and artifact are in constant communication with one another. This, in turn, helps us look at how communities then get created (even if imaginarily) in the fan's affective space. In a way, fandom often literalizes otherwise more subtle engagements. For example, much audience reception and reader response are concerned with trying to understand and describe the particular and individual textual reception, often attempting to generalize large audience groups or constructing ideal readers. Looking at creative fan communities, though, can show us how varied individual responses really are. In fact, one could argue that viewers or readers often voice readings that are more similar and normative than the ones they may personally have. Fan fiction writers, for example, suggest that more aggressive (and at times more subversive) readings are not unusual but part of the spectrum of audience responses. In particular, fan fiction discourse evokes Barthes's notion of writerly texts where "[t]he reader [is] no longer a consumer, but a producer of the text" (1974, p. 4), and where individual readings indeed are *written* – where readers are writers.

More generally, using reader response with a clear awareness of individual readers as distinct fan writers, actual readers of literary texts can and ought to be studied, and fan studies is a particularly apt venue in which to do so. Literary studies – even in its guise of reader response criticism and reception aesthetics – has mostly focused on the "ideal" or "implied" readers constructed by the text (see Iser 1978; Fish 1980; Suleiman and Crosman 1980; Tompkins 1980; Jauss 1982; Eco 1992); in turn, since readers attempt to become ideal readers, they tend to imagine the text as an artifact that needs to be deciphered. Fan readers and writers, however, provide us with an approach to reading that is more personal and more idiosyncratic, thus offering an approach to the text that is more immediate and less normative. After all, reader response criticism has yet to fully account for the multiple personal variations and levels of identification and personal investment involved in reading texts, an issue central to fan fiction studies and any attempt to analyze the dialectical reading processes practiced within fan communities. Liking or hating a character, feeling kinship to one, or identifying with a situation has little place in academic discourse. In fannish discourse, however, personal investment is crucial to any reading process. So, whereas it may be much harder to question individual fans' idiosyncratic, aggressive counterreadings, fandom's creative artifacts testify to these readings, offering traces of the particular affective engagement and the personalized engagement with the text.

Moreover, fandom can also offer us a more intense understanding of how viewers employ intertextual clues and interpret within an intertextual cultural field, again, by literalizing this community. All texts are created and read in context (see Kristeva 1980; Bakhtin 1981), but most contexts either are fairly general (i.e. feminist readings of Joyce, or the reception of *Knight Rider* in Germany) or tend to be quite individualistic (i.e. as readers or viewers, we bring our own experiences and ideological background to texts as we interpret them). While these large-scale ideological and personalized individualist contexts exist for fannish readers as well, fan texts also contain more limited shared interpretive spaces. Clearly, fan creations are commentary on only the source text, and thus their readers or viewers tend to share that interpretive framework that reads the fan text with and against the text to which it responds. More interestingly, however, all these texts and conversations create a fannish space so that fan texts also tend to be intertextual with the fan community in which they are produced and circulated. In a way, they can be seen to respond to all the other texts, all the interpretations and debates. As the internet in particular allows fans to share their work and communicate with one another easily, creative fans often tend to be part of a community. Thus, fans engage in an emotionally invested negotiation not only with the source text they analyze, criticize, and expand, but also with their fan community and its discourses.

Drawing from reader response criticism, we can think of such groups of fans as what Stanley Fish has called *interpretive communities*. Fish (1980) defines interpretive communities as being "made up of those who share interpretive strategies not for reading (in the conventional sense) but for writing texts, for constituting their properties and assigning their intentions" (p. 171). It is important, however, to realize that unlike Fish, for whom interpretive communities denote a collection of interpretive strategies rather than *actual* readers, fan fiction readers and writers create actual *communities*. Likewise, Fish does not mean *writing* literally but instead uses it in a Barthesian sense of active interpretation. In fact, it is interesting how he chooses terms that come to life within the fan fiction community, that is, fans read texts by writing their critical and creative responses within an actual community, thus literalizing Fish's metaphors. This writing is seen most obviously in fan fiction and online fan discussion forums, but also visually in fanvid creation, in how one dresses and/or decorates, and in daily spoken discussions. Fish describes the struggle between varying interpretive stances and the communities they create:

> The assumption in each community will be that the other is not perceiving the "true text," but the truth will be that each perceives the text (or texts) its interpretive strategy demands and calls into being. This, then, is the explanation both for the stability of interpretation among different readers (they belong to the same community) and for the regularity with which a single reader will employ different interpretive strategies and thus make different texts (he belongs to different communities).... Interpretive communities grow large and decline, and individuals move from one to another; thus while the alignments are not permanent, they are always there, providing just enough stability for the interpretive battle to go on. (1980, pp. 171–172)

Again, these words ring all too true in describing fandom and the way fannish disagreements about the source text tend to get played out in terms of having access to the "true" reading rather than as competing interpretations. Members of an interpretive community share certain "articles of faith" about the definition of "good writing," as well as a "repertoire of interpretive strategies" with respect to canon. In other words, they tend to agree on central interpretive choices and values. Relationship pairings are one of the clearest markers of interpretive communities; in fact, many fans identify themselves primarily as fans of one or another pairing. As such, they agree on particular events, characteristics, and interpretations of the actual texts. An unconventional relationshipper, for example (i.e. a fan who reads or writes stories where a particular pair of characters – not romantically connected on screen – is, has been, or will be a couple), will read certain canonical events with a particular lens toward supporting this pairing choice; the interpretation will be inflected by the shared presupposition.

Moreover, as Fish suggests figuratively, fandom exemplifies literally that readers can simultaneously or consecutively belong to various interpretive communities (in Fish's sense) as they choose different approaches for the same or differing texts. Likewise, actual readers are members of various interpretive communities. As such, they can celebrate a particular reading of their preferred pairing for one story and accept a vastly different interpretation in another. These communities are diverse in what they consider and emphasize as shared values: some place a high emphasis on formal concerns, such as grammar and spelling in writing or editing techniques and matching aspect ratios in fanvids; others focus on specific characters or pairings; and others yet congregate around a preference for particular genres such as Alternate Universes or Constructed Reality vids, or subgenres such as transformation stories or fanart. At times, the interpretive communities simply comprise a reading consensus, whereas at others they may be an explicitly defined society, group, or community. Given that such affiliation can revolve around issues as diverse as pairings, character interpretations, or even style, it is clear how a fan could simultaneously be part of several interpretive communities.

Fans are exemplary in the ways they literalize theories of reading and actively talk back to the text and thus allow easy access to interpretive as well as affective strategies. Fans, however, are also exceptional in the intensity of their attachment and the particular ways they communicate, share, and thus mutually affect their audience responses. Even as these mechanisms are taken up by more mainstream viewers and often consciously encouraged by media producers (as described above), we need to be careful to acknowledge that members of fan communities may exhibit exemplary audience behavior but simultaneously that we cannot always extrapolate from it, and that there exists a certain affective surplus that does not easily transfer onto individual or casual fans. In turn celebrated as aficionado knowledge and derided as fanaticism, it is not only the level of investment and the quantitative time and effort poured into supporting fannish infrastructures and creating paratexts but also the way the community (as opposed to the fannish object itself) affects the fan's identity. And yet fans literalize the virtual and imaginary senses of belonging (see Sandvoss 2005) by actually embodying the imagined community and turning them into something more viable: a couch space for visiting strangers, a postcard to cheer up a friend, a collection for a fan in need, and encounters at a con or even long-term relationships.

So, to fully understand fannish reading practices, it is important to always remember that they are inextricably connected to the communities from which they arise and the way fans define themselves vis-à-vis these texts and communities. Of course, the social and cultural structures of fan communities are interesting and important to study on their own, but we would like to suggest that they are also a fruitful subject of research for audience studies, simply because their use of intertextuality and their quite explicit and literal writing back to the source text allow insight into at least one particular engagement with texts.

Beyond Communities

Since Jenkins, Bacon-Smith, and Penley's opening salvos in the early 1990s, fan studies has developed considerably as a subfield of media and cultural studies, and its ranks have also developed within literary studies. In a 2001 interview with Matt Hills for *Intensities*, Henry Jenkins (2006b) describes a natural shift, if not evolution, in his work: whereas his early work was dominated by a rhetorical imperative to place fans on the map and to write back against the pervasive pathologization of fans that took place throughout popular culture and academia, Jenkins's more recent work – reflecting fan studies more generally since then – has explored a larger range of issues and agendas. As it has done so, various traditions and theoretical foundations have been utilized, often in contradiction to one another, as fan studies has become as contestatory a space as are many of the fan communities it discusses. For instance, in the summer of 2007, Jenkins's personal blog, Confessions of an Aca-Fan, hosted a series of discussions over the place (or lack thereof) of gender in academic discussions of fandom, and it was frequently fraught with disagreement. Without wishing to diminish the importance of the issues discussed there, or to overlook the discussions' unresolved tensions, one might also step back and observe that such an occurrence attests to the vitality of fan studies, which in 2010 finds itself setting out in various directions with a wide range of questions to examine, and little consensus on which theoretical toolboxes to bring along, or even on who counts as a fan anymore.

With this in mind, here we survey a few of fan studies' new frontiers. As alluded to above, a growing rift within fan studies stems from the media industries' own relative and contingent embracing of fans in what Jenkins dubs "affective economics." Fandom has traditionally been a subcultural entity, existing outside mainstream audience practices and responses. However, as *some* of those practices are now stamped with approval by the media industries, and as *some* of them are allowed or even openly encouraged, fans and fandom are being balkanized. The front door is enticingly left wide open for those fans willing to play within the confines of the industry-set rules, but that legitimation reifies the subcultural existence of those not playing in the proper sandbox and/or with the proper tools – whether it involves fan fiction of stories whose authors publicly decry fannish creations, photo manipulations that draw from copyrighted material, or fanvids that use songs whose owners have not permitted their use. Moreover, given the uncertain legal status of many fan works, there is a real danger that critical or seemingly offensive material gets singled out and targeted for copyright violations as the media industries interpret them. Thus, a key danger for fan studies in particular is that many within the field might find the seeming promise of an affective economics that allows participatory culture so attractive that they too follow the more socially acceptable forms of fandom through the open door, leaving an interest in the full range of fandom behind. Certainly, research of all types is required, but whereas fan studies began with a concern for the disempowered in society, and for their creative responses to mainstream and cult media, a fan studies that follows industry-sanctioned fans too closely may lose much of its critical edge.

At the same time, though, a renewed and reinvigorated fan studies will need to pay greater attention to race, ethnicity, and global practices of fandom. The overwhelming majority of fan studies have come from the United States, the United Kingdom, and Australia, examining middle-class audiences in developed nations. Notable exceptions exist, as with, most prominently, the ever-growing field of anime studies that examines Japanese and other East Asian fandoms (Napier 2007). But fan studies have for too long rendered the white middle-class Western fan as normative. As Bertha Chin (2007) argues, fandoms around the world may operate in wholly different ways, with entirely different relationships posited between fan, fan object, industry, and the surrounding society. Not only could a great deal be learned by studying fans of local media around the world, but also more work on fans of transnational media could tell us much of audience formations globally. Indeed, Aswin Punathambekar (2007) notes that global media studies have traditionally focused on issues of production and trade, meaning that a close study of global fandom could add multiple layers of depth to global media studies. Fan studies has proven a powerful lens through which we can examine the practices of power through media transmission and reception in the West, so let us use fan studies to examine similar processes internationally. Let us also use fan studies to examine minority racial and ethnic communities within the West. If the middle-class white American posting comments about an American network drama on *Television without Pity* is rapidly becoming the hegemonically normative fan in *some* accounts of fandom, a global and racially sensitive fan studies could further help to destabilize this odd norm, returning fan studies' focus to issues of power.

Finally, if fan studies began in part as a reaction against taste hierarchies, and hence developed by examining the fans of culturally "suspicious" and derided texts – whether soaps, teen television, sci-fi, pop music, or sports – we pose that it is time for fan studies now to apply its methods to the study of high-culture fans or "aficionados." Joli Jensen's early and influential essay "Fandom as Pathology" (1992) argued persuasively that we all have our fandoms, whether of *Buffy the Vampire Slayer* or Mozart, slasher films or James Joyce, and 15 years later Roberta Pearson (2007) suggested many similarities between fans of *Star Trek*, *Sherlock Holmes*, and Bach. But neither piece was borne out by much audience research, nor have many studies in the intervening years taken up either polemic with hard data. As a result, many still tend to see fandom as a practice endemic to "low culture" and to modern mass media. Should fan studies turn to the "scribbling women" and subcultural, sometimes subversive consumption practices of aficionados and fans of high culture, though, much of the ground that social hierarchies of values posit themselves as resting upon could be exploded, perhaps demanding a more accurate accounting of the varying forms and cultures of consumption that exist across the class and cultural spectrum. Fan studies, in other words, still has much to study and still may have much to say about the politics of taste.

A continuing issue for fan studies in all its diverse and propagating variations regards the representativeness or uniqueness of fans. Simply put, are fans important because their practices are indicative of general processes of consumption, or are they important because their differences are illustrative? As fan studies becomes a field in its own right, drawing from myriad disciplines, and as the subjects and objects of inquiry become less easily placeable in single categories or definitions, it becomes clear that fans are both and that any inquiry from here on needs to be less concerned with large-scale claims and instead look at particular scenarios, specific fandoms, and individual fannish expressions.

Notes

1   Given the framing of this book, we choose to discuss fan studies within the context of film, television, and media studies only. For a contrast between media and sports fans and a discussion of disciplinary differences, see Schimmel, Harrington, and Bielby (2007).
2   Whereas audience- and reader-focused theories responded to models that had advocated singular readings, they do not suggest that all readings are equally valid or that a given text supports any interpretation. What they do, however, is acknowledge audiences as part of the interpretive framework of texts.
3   Though neither writer finds their theoretical footing in Abercrombie and Longhurst (1998)'s work, Lancaster (2001) and Coppa (2006) both provide examples of work that focuses on fan engagement as intrinsically performative.
4   The different approaches and cultures are mirrored in terminology. A group of fans of creative responses to media recently found Organization for Transformative Works, part advocacy group, part legal council, with the purpose to create a permanent archive for fan works. Many fans supporting the organization articulate their separate community space by making icons and banners proclaiming, "I am not your user-generated content." See http://transformativeworks.org. See also Russo (2009) on the differences between music videos made in response to a sponsored contest and fan vids in *Battlestar Galactica* fandom.
5   See http://en.wikipedia.org/wiki/Dragonriders_of_Pern/; http://chillingeffects.org/fanfic/notice.cgi?NoticeID=143/; http://web.archive.org/web/19981111191431/http://pern.dreamhaven.org; and http://annemccaffrey.net/index.php?page_id=20/.
6   See http://www.chillingeffects.org/fanfic/notice.cgi?NoticeID=534/ and http://www.guardian.co.uk/print/0,3858,4814875-103680,00.html.
7   See http://en.wikipedia.org/wiki/The_Official_Star_Wars_Fan_Film_Awards/; http://web.archive.org/web/20051231065227/; http://www.chron.com/disp/story.mpl/ae/movies/jump/1381119.html/; and http://news.cnet.com/Star-Wars-and-the-fracas-over-fan-films/2008-1008_3-5690595.html.
8   This aggressive reading and pushing of boundaries are most comprehensively studied in slash fiction. See Jenkins (1992), Bacon-Smith (1992), and Penley (1992) for early accounts, and Jones (2002), Willis (2006), and Kohnen (2008) for more recent ones.

References

Abercrombie, N. and Longhurst, B. 1998 *Audiences: A Sociological Theory of Performance and Imagination*. Sage, Thousand Oaks, CA.

Bacon-Smith, C. 1992 *Enterprising Women: Television Fandom and the Creation of Popular Myth*. University of Pennsylvania Press, Philadelphia.

Bakhtin, M. 1981 *The Dialogic Imagination*. Trans. Caryl Emerson and Michael Holquist. University of Texas Press, Austin.

Barthes, R. 1974 *S/Z*. Trans. Richard Miller. Noonday, New York.

Bourdieu, P. 1984 *Distinction: A Social Critique of the Judgment of Taste*. Trans. Richard Nice. Routledge, London.

Busse, K. 2007 Intense intertextuality: derivative works in context. Conference Presentation at "Media in Transition," April 27–29, Cambridge, MA. Retrieved from http://kristina-busse.com/cv/research/mit07.html

Chin, B. 2007 Beyond kung-fu and violence: locating East Asian cinema fandom. In J. Gray, C. Sandvoss, and C.L. Harrington, eds. *Fandom: Identities and Communities in a Mediated World*. New York University Press, New York, pp. 210–219.

Coppa, F. 2006 Writing bodies in space: media fan fiction as theatrical performance. In K. Hellekson and K. Busse, eds. *Fan Fiction and Fan Communities in the Age of the Internet*. McFarland, Jefferson, NC, pp. 225–244.

Coppa, F. 2008 Women, *Star Trek*, and the early development of fannish vidding. *Transformative Works and Cultures*, 1. Retrieved from http://journal.transformative-works.org/index.php/twc/article/view/44

Cupitt, C. 2008 Nothing but net: when cultures collide. *Transformative Works and Cultures 1*. Retrieved from http://journal.transformativeworks.org/index.php/twc/article/view/55

de Certeau, M. 1984 *The Practice of Everyday Life*. University of California Press, Berkeley.

Derecho, A. 2006 Archontic literature: definition, a history, and several theories of fan fiction. In K. Hellekson and K. Busse, eds. *Fan Fiction and Fan Communities in the Age of the Internet*. McFarland, Jefferson, NC, pp. 61–78.

Eco, U. 1992 *Interpretation and Overinterpretation*. Cambridge University Press, Cambridge.

Fish, S. 1980 *Is There a Text in This Class? The Authority of Interpretive Communities*. Harvard University Press, Cambridge, MA.

Fiske, J. 1989 *Reading the Popular*. Routledge, New York.

Gray, J. 2003 New audiences, new textualities: anti-fans and non-fans. *International Journal of Cultural Studies*, 6, 1, 64–81.

Hall, S. 1991 Encoding/decoding (1973). In S. Hall, D. Hobson, A. Lowe, and P. Willis, eds. *Culture, Media, Language: Working Papers in Cultural Studies, 1972–79*, rev. edn. Hutchinson, London, pp. 128–138.

Hebdige, D. 1979 *Subculture: The Meaning of Style*. Methuen, London.

Hills, M. 2002 *Fan Cultures*. Routledge, New York.

Iser, W. 1978 *The Act of Reading: A Theory of Aesthetic Response*. John Hopkins University Press, Baltimore.

Jauss, H.R. 1982 *Toward an Aesthetic of Reception*. Trans. Timothy Bahti. University of Minnesota Press, Minneapolis.

Jensen, J. 1992 Fandom as pathology: the consequence of characterization. In A. Lewis, ed. *The Adoring Audience*. Routledge, New York, pp. 9–29.

Jenkins, H. 1992 *Textual Poachers: Television Fans and Participatory Culture*. Routledge, New York.

Jenkins, H. 2006a *Convergence Culture: When Old and New Media Collide*. New York University Press, New York.

Jenkins, H. 2006b Excerpts from "Matt Hills interviews Henry Jenkins." In H. Jenkins, *Fans, Bloggers, and Gamers*. New York University Press, New York, pp. 9–36.

Jenkins, H. 2007 Confessions of an aca-fan. Retrieved from http://www.henryjenkins.org

Jones, S.G. 2002 The sex lives of cult television characters. *Screen*, 43, 79–90.

Kohnen, M. 2008 The adventures of a repressed farm boy and the billionaire who loved him: queer spectatorship in Smallville fandom. In S.M. Ross and L.E. Stein, eds. *Teen Television: Essays on Programming and Fandom*. McFarland, Jefferson, NC, pp. 207–223.

Kristeva, J. 1980 *Desire in Language: A Semiotic Approach to Literature and Art*. Ed. Leon Roudiez, trans. Thomas Gora et al. Oxford: Blackwell.

Lancaster, K. 2001 *Interacting with Babylon 5: Fan Performances in a Media Universe*. University of Texas Press, Austin.

Lévy, P. 1997 *Collective Intelligence: Mankind's Emerging World in Cyberspace*. Perseus, Cambridge.

Marcuse, H. 1964 *One-Dimensional Man: Studies in the Ideology of Advanced Industrial Society*. Beacon Press, Boston.

Morley, D. and Brunsdon, C. 1999 *The Nationwide Television Studies*. Routledge, London.

Napier, S. 2007 *From Impressionism to Anime: Japan as Fantasy and Fan Cult in the Mind of the West*. Palgrave, New York.

Pearson, R. 2007 Bachies, Bardies, Trekkies, and Sherlockians. In J. Gray, C. Sandvoss and C.L. Harrington, eds. *Fandom: Identities and Communities in a Mediated World*. New York University Press, New York, pp. 98–109.

Penley, C. 1992 Feminism, psychoanalysis, and the study of popular culture. In L. Grossberg, C. Nelson and P.A. Treichler, eds. *Cultural Studies*. Routledge, New York, pp. 479–500.

Penley, C. 1997 *NASA/Trek: Popular Science and Sex in America*. Verso, New York.

Punathambekar, A. 2007 Between rowdies and rasikas: rethinking fan activity in Indian film culture. In J. Gray, C. Sandvoss, and C.L. Harrington, eds. *Fandom: Identities and Communities in a Mediated World*. New York University Press, New York, pp. 198–209.

Radway, J. 1984 *Reading the Romance: Women, Patriarchy, and Popular Literature*. University of North Carolina Press, Chapel Hill.

Russo, J.L. 2009 User-penetrated content: fan video in the age of convergence. *Cinema Journal*, 48, 4, 125–130.

Sandvoss, C. 2005 *Fans: The Mirror of Consumption*. Polity Press, Cambridge.

Schimmel, K.S., Harrington, C.L. and Bielby, D. 2007 Keep your fans to yourself: the disjuncture between sport studies and pop culture studies' perspectives on fandom. *Sport in Society*, 10, 580–600.

Silverstone, R. 1994 *Television and Everyday Life*. Routledge, New York.

Stasi, M. 2006 The toy soldiers from Leeds: the slash palimpsest. In K. Hellekson and K. Busse, eds. *Fan Fiction and Fan Communities in the Age of the Internet*. McFarland, Jefferson, NC, pp. 115–133.

Stein, L. 2010 "Word of mouth on steroids": hailing the millennial fan. In *The Flow Anthology* M. Kackman, M. Binfield, M. T. Payne, A. Perlman, and B. Sebok, eds. Flow TV: television in the age of media convergence. Routledge, New York, pp. 128–143.

Suleiman, S.R. and Crosman, I., eds. 1980 *The Reader in the Text: Essays on Audience and Interpretation*. Princeton University Press. Princeton, NJ.

Tompkins, J., ed. 1980 *Reader-response Criticism: Form Formalism to Post-structuralism*. Johns Hopkins University Press, Baltimore.

Tosenberger, C. 2007 Potterotics: Harry Potter fanfiction on the World Wide Web. Unpublished doctoral dissertation, University of Florida.

Tushnet, R. 2007 Copyright law, fan practices, and the rights of the author. In J. Gray, C. Sandvoss and C.L. Harrington, eds. *Fandom: Identities and Communities in a Mediated World*. New York University Press, New York, pp. 60–71.

Willis, I. 2006 Keeping promises to queer children: making space (for Mary Sue) at Hogwarts. In K. Hellekson and K. Busse, eds. *Fan Fiction and Fan Communities in the Age of The Internet*. McFarland, Jefferson, NC, pp. 153–170.

Winnicott, D.W. 1974 *Playing and Reality*. Penguin, Harmondsworth.

22

Beyond the Presumption of Identity?

Ethnicities, Cultures, and Transnational Audiences

Mirca Madianou

For a long time, ethnicity and cultural differences were mainly studied at the level of representation and, hence, the text. Following the intensification of global migration and the parallel proliferation of transnational media in the past 15 years, research began to focus on the ethnic and cultural diversity of audiences, both within the nation and transnationally. However, apart from empirical reasons, there are strong theoretical reasons why it matters to study questions of ethnicity, identity, and difference from a bottom-up, or an audience-centered, perspective: this is the only way in which the dynamic nature of ethnicities and identities (as they are articulated in relation to the media texts) can be captured. A bottom-up perspective guards against essentializing the "ethnic" or "national" audience, and against assuming one overarching cultural or ethnic identity that is shared by all its members.

This chapter will review those studies which have explored ethnicity and culture at the level of the audiences. It will include classic reception (such as Liebes and Katz 1990/1993) and ethnographic studies (Gillespie 1995; Madianou 2005a, 2005b), while the media covered range from small media (Abu-Lughod, 1989) and television (Miller 1992; Gillespie 1995; Robins and Aksoy 2001; Madianou 2005b) to new media such as the internet (Miller and Slater 2000) and mobile phones (Horst and Miller 2006; Madianou and Miller 2011b), thereby extending the notion of audience to include that of user and consumer, as well as producer of content (in the case of the internet). The chapter will also highlight the shift from studies of audience reception to ethnographies of media consumption among transnational audiences and will argue for the advantages of ethnography in studying processes of identity and culture.

The Handbook of Media Audiences, First Edition. Edited by Virginia Nightingale.

Crucially, this chapter argues that it is impossible to research ethnically and culturally differentiated audiences without theorizing the concepts of culture and identity. Recent studies on media consumption in the context of diasporas and immigrant groups have pointed to the changing and dynamic nature of ethnic and cultural identities. In reviewing the literature on media and transnational audiences, we will highlight several common findings such as the diversity within ethnic groups, the multiplicity of belongings, and their nonexclusively ethnic use of media. Media consumption emerges as a process of negotiation and ambivalence, often revealing tensions among affiliations, generations, and genders. The chapter will also consider the boundary-making role of the media in creating communicative spaces (Madianou 2005a) that can either include or exclude.

A special section will focus on the ways in which new media, such as the internet and mobile phones, reconfigure transnational belongings. Here we will address some popular views about the role of ethnic media in consolidating and potentially radicalizing ethnic identities as exemplified in Anderson's "long distance nationalism" (Anderson 2001). Although research has pointed out the role of mainstream media in contributing to processes of exclusion which can give rise to phenomena of disaffection and reaction (Madianou 2005a, 2005b), most research has shown that the majority of ethnic media consumption is characterized by banality and sociality rather than radicalization and the growth of fundamentalism (see Robins 2000; Robins and Aksoy 2001; Madianou 2005b; Kosnick 2007; Madianou and Miller 2011a). In so doing, the chapter will offer an alternative framework in examining transnational audiences not from the point of view of identity, which remains a bounded concept, but rather from the point of view of transnationalism and transnational relationships. For example, the chapter will discuss recent and current research on new communication technologies in the context of migration (Wilding 2006; Madianou and Miller 2011a and 2011b) and considers whether the concept of relationships and sociality needs to be given more attention in the field of transnational audience research.

The Export of Meaning

The study which has been very influential in shifting the attention of audience researchers to the issues of ethnicity and culture was *The Export of Meaning* (Liebes and Katz 1990/1993), which was originally intended as a response to the media imperialism thesis and attendant fears of cultural homogenization. Liebes and Katz studied the reception of *Dallas* (widely considered at the time as synonymous with American cultural imperialism) among different ethnic groups in Israel, as well as with American and Japanese audiences, and showed that audiences appropriated the program in different ways according to their ethnic and cultural background. For instance, the study observed how Israeli Arabs and Moroccan Jews emphasized family relations in their interpretations of the soap opera, while Russian émigrés saw characters as manipulated by the writers and producers of the program. On the other hand, kibbutz members and American viewers' interpretations were characterized as critical as they interpreted the program in psychological terms, as an ongoing saga of interpersonal relations and intrigue. Finally, they observed how Japanese audiences found it difficult to deal with *Dallas'* inconsistencies, which was one of the factors that contributed to the early axing of the soap opera in Japan.

Despite the study's paradigmatic status as a response to the limitations of the cultural imperialism thesis, it seems that in *The Export of Meaning* differences in interpretations are grounded in ethnicity and culture, with no further analysis of how they themselves are shaped and determined by other social, economic, and political factors. This criticism is not to deny that there *were* differences among the groups in question, but rather to question the way these differences are accounted for. It seems that the authors argue that people interpret *Dallas* in particular ways *because* of their identities as Arab Israelis, Russian émigrés, Californians, or Japanese. Such an approach glosses over other parameters that also shape media reception, such as gender, age, class, and the text itself. By attributing explanatory power to cultural difference, culture is reified and taken for granted, instead of something that needs to be explained. A quote from the book (Liebes and Katz 1990/1993) illustrates these points:

> The two more traditional groups – Arab and Moroccan Jews – prefer linearity. They retell the story in a modified Proppian form. They select the action-oriented subplot for attention, defining a hero's goals and his adventures in trying to achieve them.... The Russians ... ignore the story line in favour of exposing the overall principles which they perceive as repeated relentlessly, and which in their opinion, have a manipulative intent. Like the Arab Moroccans, their retellings are closed and deterministic, but the ideological force is ideological rather than referential.... Americans and kibbutzniks tell the story psychoanalytically.... Their retellings are open, future oriented, and take into account the never-ending character of the soap opera. (pp. 80–81)

Explanations which rely solely on culture or ethnicity sometimes sit uncomfortably close to perspectives that favor race or biological differences. In other words, by attributing explanatory power to *culture*, a term that is not thoroughly theorized in *The Export of Meaning*, other numerous (political, social, and economic) factors that shape the experience of being an Arab, a Jew, or an American are neglected. Despite *The Export of Meaning*'s paradigmatic refutation of the cultural imperialism thesis and the essentialism inherent in that approach, it becomes apparent that Liebes and Katz's study also inadvertently falls prey to some of the same limitations.

Essentializing Culture – Essentializing Essentialism

We, therefore, need to begin by theorizing culture and identity. It is hard to think of a more contested concept than culture in the social sciences. Its greatest advantage was that it shifted the explanation of difference away from the notions of race and nature and the biological connotations they entail. Yet, as the post-modernist critiques in the 1980s pointed out, despite its anti-essentialist intent, culture implies a homogeneous, coherent, timeless, and discrete whole (Abu-Lughod 1991, p. 147) and "tends to freeze difference" in much the same way as the concept of race (Abu-Lughod 1991, p. 144). Cultures seem frozen in time as distinct entities, whereas in fact as research has forcefully demonstrated they are always the result of a "mish-mash, borrowings, mixtures that have occurred, though at different rates, ever since the beginning of time" (Levi-Strauss 1961, cited in Kuper 1999, p. 243). It seems, then, that there is an inherent paradox in the concepts of culture and multiculturalism. The irony of stressing difference as a means of refuting primodialist perspectives, according to which identities are complete and natural wholes, is that one reproduces the same ideology one purports to question. As Kuper has noted, "[T]he insistence that radical differences can be observed between people serves to sustain them" (1999, p. 239). Furthermore, another related issue is that of cultural determinism, where culture, instead of being something that requires description, analysis, and explanation, "is treated instead as a source of explanation in itself" (Kuper 1999, p. xi). By reducing everything to cultural differences, the researcher falls into the trap of essentialism, of "imputing a fundamental, basic, absolutely necessary constitutive of quality to a person, social category, ethnic group, religious community, or nation" (Werbner 1997, p. 228).

The threat of essentialism, however, can in its extreme form lead to a research paralysis. Moreover, the acknowledgment that difference can (and has been) manipulated should not make us deny difference altogether, as this would risk colluding with problematic views which refuse the recognition of minority rights to those who feel different. Therefore, to recognize the pernicious effects of essentialism in social science should not erase our awareness of the fact that it is part and parcel of social life. Both majorities and minorities use essentialist categories, as much as the media and the official discourse do. To address essentialist discourse is not the same as endorsing essentialism. We will return to these debates later on in the chapter, but for the time being it seems that as long as culture and identity are not treated as real things, but rather as open-ended processes and sets of performances which require explanation rather than assume explanatory power, then it seems that the concepts can survive the backlash. As Hall (1992) eloquently put it,

Identity is actually formed through unconscious processes over time, rather than being innate in consciousness at birth. There is always something 'imaginary' or fantasised about its unity. It always remains incomplete, is always 'in process', always 'being formed'.... Thus rather than speaking of identity as a finished thing, we should speak of identification and see it as an ongoing process. (p. 287)

Domesticating the Global

In the 1990s, a generation of studies drawing on theories of globalization (Giddens 1991; Tomlinson 1999) and cultural consumption stressed the dialectic relationship between local cultures and the global media, without privileging either of the two. Examples include the studies by Abu-Lughod (1989, 1993), Miller (1992), and Sreberny-Mohammadi and Mohammadi (1994). An influential paradigm here has been the "domestication" thesis (Miller 1987; Silverstone and Hirsch 1992; Silverstone 1994) which highlighted the processes through which local cultures make the unfamiliar familiar. A paradigmatic study within this context is that by Miller (1992), who observed the local appropriation of a US soap opera, *The Young and the Restless*, in Trinidad. Trinidadians interpreted the soap opera through the key term for Trinidadian culture, *bacchanal*, which connotes scandal, confusion, and truth (pp. 170–176). Miller's argument involves not just the appropriation of the soap opera as Trini, but also its role in the refinement of the concept of Trinidad itself as a culture of "bacchanal." In a later study on the internet in Trinidad, Miller together with Slater (2000) similarly argued that the internet is appropriated and domesticated locally, while at the same time reconfiguring Trinidad as a transnational entity encompassing its large diaspora.

In her fieldwork among the Bedouins of Western Egypt, Abu-Lughod (1989) also observed the dialectic relationship between the global and the local through media consumption. For example, she argued that the introduction of media technologies did not undermine everyday social interaction as had been feared, but rather enhanced sociability as people came together to listen to the radio or watch television (p. 8). However, this is not to say that media technologies had no impact: for example, Abu-Lughod discusses the "democratising effect" of television as household members of different genders gathered together for the first time to watch programs. She also argued for soap opera's emancipatory potential for the Bedouin women, who for the first time became exposed to different worlds and narratives (1989, 1993). So, again, both media technologies and texts are simultaneously domesticated by the local culture, but in turn also contribute to the transformation of that very culture.

Transnational Audiences: Ambivalence and Reflexivity

Parallel to the studies of local appropriation of global products another area of research emerged in the 1990s which focused on the media consumption of transnational audiences in the context of their everyday lives (Silverstone 1994). Several studies have argued against the homogeneity of immigrant communities and their monolithic consumption of ethnic media. Gillespie (1995), Hargreaves and Mahjoub (1997), and Madianou (2005b) have observed significant differences among different generations of immigrants, while Georgiou (2006) has stressed gender differences. Similarly, in her study of Iranians living in London, Sreberny (2000) has observed not only generational or gender divisions, but also those relating to political factionalism, waves of migration, and internal linguistic and ethnic differentiation (p. 195).

One assumption which the existing literature has dispelled is that diasporas or ethnic groups have exclusive belongings and thus consume media in an exclusively ethnic way. On the contrary, research has pointed to the multiplicity of belongings which extend beyond the diaspora with transnational subjects moving across different media landscapes (Robins and Aksoy 2001; Madianou 2005a; Sreberny 2005; Georgiou 2006, p. 149). Because of their exposure to multiple points of cultural reference, transnational people can be more cosmopolitan than the sedentary national audiences (Robins and Aksoy 2001). Gillespie (1995), in her ethnographic work with Punjabi families in a London neighborhood, argued that the consumption of a range of transnational television programs and films, from both the United Kingdom and India, has "accelerated processes of cultural change" while in parallel reaffirming and reinventing Punjabi cultural traditions (p. 76). Encounters with a plethora of media texts, both national and transnational, seem to intensify reflexivity and contribute to the symbolic project of the self (Thompson 1995).

Television viewing is a process of negotiation and often contestation. In Gillespie's work (1995), watching Indian films and dramas was seen by the parents as essential for the language training of their children and part of their socialization into what they considered as traditional Indian values. Whilst children participated – albeit with some resistance – in the "devotional viewing" of serialized versions of sacred texts such as the *Mahabarata*, they were also devoted viewers of Western soaps typically consumed by teenagers globally. Gillespie argued that soap opera consumption intensified the young Punjabis' awareness of their position in UK society and encouraged aspirations for change (p. 174). At the same time, soap operas such as *Neighbours* were filtered through the local. Gillespie observed that in Southall, domestication took place through the practice of gossip, which, like Miller's concept of Trinidadian "bacchanal" (1992), came to symbolize the whole neighborhood. Television viewing practices are contested as revealed through the intergenerational and gender tensions to which they give rise.

Other studies have also documented the ambivalence that characterizes transnational media consumption as an act of negotiation and increased reflexivity. Mai (2005), for example, in his research with Albanian migrants in Italy observed the near absence of consumption of Albanian media and the dominance of Italian media. Yet, Italian media were also responsible for stigmatized representations of Albanians, thus contributing to their experience of social exclusion (Mai 2005, p. 588). Apart from identity, the other concept which has emerged as relevant is that of citizenship since transnational audiences, through consumption, make a symbolic statement about their public connection (Couldry, Livingstone, and Markham 2007). When transnational audiences choose media from within their country of residence, this is often a statement about their citizenship and desire for participation in public life (Madianou 2005a). This is particularly the case with news programs, according to research with a Turkish-speaking group in Greece, as news viewing is understood as a form of expressing one's presence and participation in public life. However, the same study has shown that this consumption was characterized by "ruptures" when people felt that news was misrepresenting their neighborhood or religion (Madianou 2005a, 2005c).

Robins and Aksoy (2001; and Robins 2000), drawing from their fieldwork among Turkish-speaking groups in London, have argued that media consumption is not determined ethnically but, rather, socially. In other words, there isn't anything particularly Turkish about the way television is consumed. Television culture is ordinary, they argue, thus implying a universality in the practices of television watching that transcends ethnic categories, thereby refuting arguments about Turkish media being responsible for the growth of Islamic fundamentalism (Robins 2000; for a discussion of the prevalence of these debates in Germany, see Kosnick 2007). Similar findings were reported by Madianou, who in her research with Turkish speakers in Greece found that the most popular Turkish channel programs amongst her informants were sports programs, Hollywood movies (dubbed into Turkish), and globally recognizable game show formats such as *Who Wants to Be a Millionaire?* and *Wheel of Fortune* (Madianou 2005a). Based on similar findings, Aksoy and Robins (2000) argue for a shift of focus from "identity" and "community" to "experience" and "resources" in an attempt to find a new and more pertinent language to describe processes of migration, belonging, and media consumption (p. 705).

Although Robins and Aksoy have a point in wanting to overcome the problems associated with bounded concepts such as identity, I have found that it is harder to dispense with these concepts altogether so long as audiences themselves continue to use them in their everyday and media-related talk. We have so far indicated that other concepts such as citizenship are relevant in understanding the media consumption of transnational audiences. Moreover, *identities* are understood in the plural, recognizing their diversity, ambivalence, and incompleteness. The following section examines the question of identity further by returning to the problem of essentialism and the strategies for addressing it.

The Boundary-Making Role of Media

If both majorities and minorities use essentialist categories to describe themselves, how can we then address this as social scientists? Recently, researchers have identified two strategies. The first is to understand identities as social relations, acknowledging that all identities are relational, that is, articulated in relation to some one or something else. This particular strand, which was recently developed by Madianou (2005b), draws on older anthropological work by Barth (1969), who had argued for ethnicity as a form of social organization that results from the interaction between group and environment. This meant that "the critical focus for investigation [becomes] the ethnic boundary that defines the group rather than the cultural stuff that it encloses" (p. 15). Barth argued that ethnic group membership must depend on ascription and self-ascription, rather than possession of a certain cultural inventory. In transposing this theory to media studies, Madianou (2005b) focused on the mediated processes that create boundaries and thus difference.

The other strategy to deal with the problem of essentialism is, instead of focusing on groups and identities as complete wholes, to focus on the ways in which people describe, redescribe, and argue who they are (Madianou 2005b). This description and redescription are performative, including discursive as well as material practices. In her research with national and transnational audiences in Greece, Madianou (2005a, 2005b), drawing on Baumann's ethnography of the multicultural London suburb of Southall (1996), focused on discourses and practices about identity rather on identity itself. Like Baumann, Madianou identified two discourses about culture and identity: a dominant discourse that reifies culture and identity, and a demotic discourse that challenges and works against existing reifications. Although these are separate discourses, they coexist as people fluctuate between the two according to context. Baumann describes how the same people who contest the rigid boundaries of the official discourse will revert to it when it suits their interests.

So, for example, although my informants expressed openness and reflexivity in their narratives about identity, when they were confronted with "closure" in the media they adopted an essentialist, "closed" discourse themselves (Madianou 2005a, 2005b). This was particularly the case in their encounters with news media, which would oscillate between engaged viewing which signified desire for participation in public life, and switching off – and anger – whenever they encountered distorted representations of their neighborhoods in the news. This boundary-making role of the media has been confirmed by other researchers (Gillespie 1995; Matar 2007; Ong 2009). It is interesting that it is the genre of news which often has the power to raise boundaries, as suggested by these studies (Gillespie 1995; Madianou 2005b; Mai 2005; Matar 2007; Ong 2009). This points to the power of representation as well as the symbolic power that news programs still popularly enjoy (Madianou 2008).

New Media and Transnational Audiences:
Lifting the Boundaries?

New media deserve a separate section as they have allowed for the proliferation of
channels and content, thereby increasing the potential of the representation and
visibility of ethnic groups. In this sense, ethnic groups are not only consumers of
content but also producers themselves. Its relative low cost combined with other
structural features such as interactivity have made the internet particularly attractive to those who want to produce content directed to particular ethnic or transnational groups. But this section also addresses something more fundamental, which
is the convergence of transnational movements of populations and the fundamentally transnational nature of the internet and other new media, such as mobile
phones. These two phenomena – the *ethnoscapes* and the *technoscapes/mediascapes*,
to borrow Appadurai's terms (1990) – feed one another and contribute to the
intensification and perhaps even to the reconfiguration of the overall phenomenon of transnationalism as a set of processes in which migrants establish social
fields that cross geographic, cultural, and political borders (Glick Schiller, Basch,
and Blanc Szanton 1992).

This section will focus on research with migrant transnational consumers of
new media in order to understand the ways in which the experience of transnationalism is affected. In so doing, the section also contributes to the discussion of
the reconfiguration of audiences in the light of new media.

One of the well-documented uses of the internet by migrants is instrumental.
An example is migrants using the media for practical information – this is crucial
in the premigrant and postmigrant phase, that is, in the period that precedes the
actual migration and the early stages of migrant settlement, when practical information is invaluable for obtaining information about one's host country and
integrating into the new environment (Hiller and Franz 2004). According to Elias
and Lemish (2009), the internet has the potential to close knowledge gaps amongst
immigrants.

Research on the later stages of settled migration has documented that the internet
becomes pivotal in researching connections to one's place of origin (Hiller and Franz
2004, pp. 739–740). Migrants use the internet for increasing social capital in terms of
reinvigorating lost connections (Miller and Slater 2000), maintaining existing ties
(Vertovec 2004; Horst and Miller 2006; Miller and Madianou 2011a and 2011b;
Wilding 2007), and forming new relationships (Hiller and Franz 2004). The recent
explosion of social-networking sites (such as Facebook and Twitter) also contributes
to the reinvigoration and maintenance of social ties at a distance. Friendster, a social-
networking site which is particularly popular in the Philippines, a country where
more than 10 percent of the population live and work abroad, is heavily used to
maintain transnational relationships (Madianou and Miller 2011a). Similarly, Multiply,
another social-networking site which particularly targets families, is very popular

for uploading and sharing photographs and is used by Filipino transnational families in order to keep in touch despite prolonged physical separation because of work (Madianou and Miller 2011a).

Research on new media and transnationalism needs to include mobile phones not only because of the evident technological convergence, but also because they are pivotal in forming transnational networks amongst migrants. One of the reasons for the boom of mobile phone telephony in the developing world is because of the scarcity of landlines (Vertovec 2004; Ling and Donner 2008). The lack of landline infrastructure as well as the high cost of mobile internet access also partly explain the low internet rates in developing countries. As Horst and Miller (2006) have shown, mobile phones are crucial in maintaining relationships amongst transnational families. In Jamaica, almost all low-income households are economically dependent upon phone contacts to diaspora relations, which means that people ask for, and increasingly send, remittances through their mobile phones (Horst and Miller 2006; Madianou and Miller 2011a). Mobile telephony is also crucial for transnational families and in particular for those who experience separation because of the international division of labor. The increasing feminization of international migration and the increasing demand for care and domestic workers from the global South mean that millions of women are now separated from their children because of work (Parreñas 2005). Cheap calls have intensified connectivity, supplying what Vertovec (2004) calls the "social glue of transnationalism" so that family members can feel and function as a family. However, Madianou and Miller (2011a and 2011b), in a current ESRC-funded study on family separation among Filipino families, have found that although new media such as the internet and mobile phones present some solutions to the problems faced by transnational families, they are not always successful in addressing the problems of separation and are experienced in different ways by the migrating mothers and their children left behind. However, the opportunities opened up by new media for transnational communication seem to be valued by all those who can afford them; and judging from the amount of time and income spent on new media (Madianou and Miller 2011b), it is easy to see that both migrants and those left behind are affected by the possibility of "perpetual contact" (Katz and Aakhus 2002).

A lot of discussion has taken place over whether the use of the internet among transnational groups has any impact on identity. One influential perspective in this regard has been Anderson's concept of "long distance nationalism" to capture the way that nationalist sentiment and identities are being reconfigured in a new deteritorrialized fashion which is underpinned by electronic media (Anderson 1998, 2001). However, although phenomena of long-distance nationalism do occur, research of internet activity has so far revealed that the majority of transnational usage is for rather more banal, social, and personal purposes such as those described in the previous paragraph. This is not to say that the political dimension of transnational internet consumption is irrelevant in this analysis, or that its consequences for identity are insignificant. For example, it is well supported that the internet gives voice (Mitra 2001) and visibility to otherwise marginalized groups. Relatively low costs allow migrant groups to participate in public life and take responsibility for the representation of their own communities (something that is structurally less possible in the mainstream media; and given that migrants feel stigmatized by them, as observed earlier in the chapter, the significance of the internet is obvious). Apart from the more publically and politically oriented uses of the internet among transnational groups, research has also pointed out how the internet can create new outlets for expressing ethnicity, especially amongst those who already have some ethnic consciousness, as Panagakos (2003) found out in her research with Greek communities in Canada. However, the highly politicized and radical activity which, as some contend, can be facilitated by the internet (Brinkerhoff 2009) seems to be the exception rather than the rule.

Methodological and Theoretical Implications for Audience Studies

This chapter has observed how the study of audiences and ethnicity has moved from studies of reception to more ethnographic studies of media consumption. This move has theoretical implications, as the ethnographic perspective can facilitate the dynamism and nuances of identities to emerge. The bottom-up perspective of ethnographic inquiry guards against essentializing audiences, especially when these are ethnically or nationally defined. In my ethnography of media consumption in Greece, as part of a wider concern with the question of the reproduction of nationalism and identities (Madianou 2005b), instead of presupposing people's identities as fixed, I adopted a perspective from the bottom up which allowed for the dynamic nature of people's identifications to come to light. Because this perspective allowed for people's own discourses and practices about belonging to emerge, it became possible to observe the ways in which people moved from one identity positioning to another according to context, whether mediated or not. The observation of such shifts over time was again made possible through the long-term nature of ethnographic inquiry. As it is in relation to someone or something else (including the media text) that identities are articulated, this dynamic and relational understanding of identity highlighted the boundary-making capacity of the news media to create symbolic communicative spaces that either include or exclude (Madianou 2005a, 2007).

This call for an ethnographic shift in the study of transnational audiences does not imply that the text and its reception are no longer important areas of research. The study of the text matters in understanding processes of representation, inclusion and exclusion, and boundary work, which, as has already been argued, are central to processes of identity. Ultimately, focusing on texts is one important method to examine media power. Some of the ethnographically inspired studies discussed in this chapter have included the study of media texts and their reception (Gillespie 1995; Madianou 2005b).

Also, this chapter has observed a move from the study of identity and culture within the nation-state to the study of such processes transnationally. This move follows empirical transformations with unprecedented levels of human mobility which need to be investigated systematically. However, this move also has theoretical implications as it calls for an approach and a set of concepts that can be applied to these dynamic processes and escape the "methodological nationalism" which has imprisoned social research, as Beck (2007) has argued. The review of the literature presented here suggests that although identity is still relevant when dealing with processes of ethnic and culturally differentiated audiences – so long as people themselves refer to their identities – it can often be too bounded a concept for the understanding of transnational processes. The methodological bias with asking questions about identity in a project on transnational media consumption is that one can presuppose the importance of identity from the outset while overlooking other practices that are equally important for the people in question. In other words, if one sets out to explore the consequences of the media for identity, then they will come up with such findings. Recent research on transnational relationships and connections can be considered as one alternative framework through which to understand transnationalism.

Finally, a note on terminology: the chapter has addressed audiences, viewers, consumers, and users of new media – and also, marginally, producers, acknowledging the increasingly blurred boundaries between production and consumption in respect to new media. Parallel to these terms, we have also referred to nations, ethnic groups, diasporas, transnational subjects, and migrants. Which should be the term that best describes these processes, and can there be consensus on this? If we follow an ethnographic perspective, the answer is easy, and it is to adopt the ways in which people define themselves. If these definitions vary, then the shifts may have something to reveal about the overall context of everyday life and mediation. However, we also need to recognize that these terms come loaded with theoretical assumptions. In this chapter I have chosen to use the term *transnational* because I find that it suggests a more diffused notion of belonging that cuts across national affiliations in contrast to *diaspora*, which implies an imaginary homeland as a national center and can be, thus, interpreted as a more bounded concept.

Conclusions

In this chapter, we have reviewed the studies of media reception and consumption by ethnically and culturally differentiated audiences. We have argued that in order to understand the consequences of media for transnational audiences, it is important to theorize the concepts of identity and culture and to recognize their diffused, processual, and multiple character. The chapter identified some common themes in the literature on transnational audiences, namely, the diversity within ethnic groups, the multiplicity of belongings, the local appropriation of media texts, and the way in which consumption is a process of negotiation and increased reflexivity. We also discussed the boundary-making role of media in order to describe the processes in which the media, national or transnational, influence the ways in which people describe and redescribe who they are, thereby pointing to the power of the media in raising boundaries for inclusion and exclusion. Finally, the chapter considered the challenges posed by information and communications technologies (ICTs). It was argued that new communications technologies allow for different forms of sociality and intimacy which transform the wider transnational experience. The internet also has consequences for the visibility and political participation of minority groups, and while some research supports the ways in which identities are reconfigured, there is less evidence to suggest that internet-mediated communication sustains phenomena such as long-distance nationalism (Anderson 2001). In conclusion, the chapter has also made an argument for studying processes of culture and identity from an audience-centered (or people-centered) ethnographic perspective, which is the only way to avoid the pitfalls of essentialism and to allow for the dynamism and multiplicity of identities to unfold.

References

Abu-Lughod, L. 1989 Bedouins, cassettes and technologies of public culture. *Middle East Report*, 159, 4, pp. 7–11.

Abu-Lughod, L. 1991 Writing against culture. In R. Fox, ed. *Recapturing Anthropology*. School of American Research Press, Santa Fe, NM, pp. 137–161.

Abu-Lughod, L. 1993 Finding a place for Islam: Egyptian television serials and the national interest. *Public Culture*, 5, 3, pp. 493–513.

Aksoy, A. and Robins, K. 2000 Thinking across spaces: transnational television from Turkey. *European Journal of Cultural Studies*, 3, 3, pp. 343–365.

Anderson, B. 1998 *The Spectre of Comparisons*. Verso, London.

Anderson, B. 2001 Western nationalism and eastern nationalism: is there a difference that matters? *New Left Review*, 2, 9, pp. 31–42.

Appadurai, A. 1990 Disjuncture and difference in the global cultural economy. *Theory, Culture and Society*, 7, pp. 295–310.

Barth, F. 1969 Introduction. In F. Barth, ed. *Ethnic Groups and Boundaries: The Social Organisation of Culture Difference*. Allen & Unwin, London, pp. 9–38.

Baumann, G. 1996 *Contesting Culture: Discourses of Identity in Multi-ethnic London*. Cambridge University Press, Cambridge.

Beck, U. 2007 The cosmopolitan condition: why methodological nationalism fails. *Theory, Culture and Society*, 24, 7–8, pp. 286–290.

Brinkerhoff, J. 2009 *Digital Diasporas: Identity and Transnational Engagement*. Cambridge University Press, Cambridge.

Couldry, N., Livingstone, S. and Markham, T. 2007 *Media Consumption and Public Engagement: Beyond the Presumption of Attention*. London: Palgrave.

Elias, N. and Lemish, D. 2009 Spinning the web of identity: the roles of the internet in the lives of immigrant adolescents. *New Media and Society*, 11, 4, pp. 533–551.

Georgiou, M. 2006 *Diaspora, Identity and the Media*. Hampton Press, Cresskill, NJ.

Giddens, A. 1991 *Modernity and Self-Identity: Self and Society in the Late Modern Age*. Polity Press, Cambridge.

Gillespie, M. 1995 *Television, Ethnicity and Cultural Change*. Routledge, London.

Glick Schiller, N., Basch L. and Blanc Szanton, C. 1992 Towards a definition of transnationalism. In L. Basch, N. Glick Schiller and C. Blanc Szanton, eds. *Towards a Transnational Perspective on Migration: Race, Class, Ethnicity and Nationalism Reconsidered*. Academy of Sciences, New York, pp. ix–xiv.

Hall, S. 1992 The question of cultural identity. In S. Hall et al., eds. *Modernity and its Futures*. Polity Press, Cambridge, pp. 274–325.

Hargreaves, A. and Mahjoub, D. 1997 Satellite television viewing among ethnic minorities in France. *European Journal of Communication*, 12, 4, pp. 459–477.

Hiller, H. and T. Franz 2004 New ties, old ties and lost ties: the use of the internet in diaspora. *New Media and Society*, 6, 6, pp. 731–752.

Horst, H. and Miller, D. 2006 *The Cell Phone: An Anthropology of Communication*. Berg, Oxford.

Katz, J. and E. Aakhus, eds. 2002 *Perpetual Contact: Mobile Communication, Private Talk, Public Performance*. Cambridge University Press, Cambridge.

Kosnick, K. 2007 *Migrant Media: Turkish Broadcasting and Multicultural Politics in Berlin*. Indiana University Press, Bloomington.

Kuper, A. 1999 *Culture: The Anthropologist's Account*. Harvard University Press, Cambridge, MA.

Lévi-Strauss, C. and Pouillon, J. 1961 *Race et Histoire*. Editions Gonthier, Paris.

Liebes, T. and Katz, E. 1990/1993 *The Export of Meaning: Cross-Cultural Readings of Dallas*. Oxford University Press, New York.

Madianou, M. 2005a Contested communicative spaces: identities, boundaries and the role of the media. *Journal of Ethnic and Migration Studies*, 31, 3, pp. 521–541.

Madianou, M. 2005b *Mediating the Nation: News, Audiences and the Politics of Identity*. London: UCL Press.

Madianou, M. 2005c The elusive public of television news. In S. Livingstone, ed. *Audiences and Publics: When Cultural Engagement Matters to the Public Sphere*. Intellect Press, Bristol, UK.

Madianou, M. 2007 Shifting identities: banal nationalism and cultural intimacy in Greek television news and everyday life. In R. Mole, ed. *Discursive Constructions of Identity in European Politics*. Palgrave, London pp. 95–118.

Madianou, M. 2008 Audience reception and news in everyday life. In K. Wahl-Jorgensen and T. Hanitzsch, eds. *Handbook of Journalism Studies*. Routledge, New York.

Madianou, M. and Miller, D. 2011a. *Migration and new Media: transnational families and polymedia*. Routledge, London.

Madianou, M. and Miller, D. 2011b. Mobile phone parenting: reconfiguring relationships between Filipina migrant mothers and their left-behind children. *New Media and Society*, 13, 2.

Mai, N. 2005 The Albanian diaspora in the making: media, migration and social exclusion. *Journal of Ethnic and Migration Studies*, 31, 3, pp. 543–562.

Matar, D. 2007 The Palestinians in Britain, news and the politics of recognition. *International Journal of Media and Cultural Politics*, 2, 3, pp. 317–330.

Miller, D. 1987 *Material Culture and Mass Consumption*. Blackwell, Oxford.

Miller, D. 1992 *The Young and the Restless* in Trinidad. In R. Silverstone and E. Hirsch, eds. *Consuming Technologies*. Routledge, London, pp. 163–182.

Miller, D. and Slater, D. 2000 *The Internet: An Ethnographic Approach*. Berg, Oxford.

Mitra, A. 2001 Marginal voices in cyberspace. *New Media and Society*, 3, 1, pp. 29–48.

Ong, J. C. 2009 Watching the nation, singing the nation: London-based Filipino migrants' identity constructions in news and karaoke practices. *Communication, Culture and Critique*, 2, 2, pp. 160–181.

Panagakos, A. 2003 Downloading new identities: ethnicity, technology and media in the global Greek village. *Identities: Global Studies in Power and Culture*, 10, 2, pp. 201–219.

Parreñas, R. S. 2005 *Children of Global Migration: Transnational Families and Gendered Woes*. Stanford University Press, Stanford, CA.

Robins, K. 2000 Introduction: Turkish (television) culture is ordinary. *European Journal of Cultural Studies*, 3, 3, pp. 291–295.

Robins, K. and Aksoy, A. 2001 From spaces of identity to mental spaces: lessons from Turkish-Cypriot cultural experience in Britain. *Journal of Ethnic and Migration Studies*, 27, 4, pp. 685–711.

Silverstone, R. 1994 *Television and Everyday Life*. Routledge, London.

Silverstone, R. and Hirsch, E. eds. 1992 *Consuming Technologies: Media and Information in Domestic Spaces*. Routledge, London.

Sreberny, A. 2000 Media and diasporic consciousness: an exploration among Iranians in London. In S. Cottle, ed. *Ethnic Minorities and the Media*. Open University Press, Buckinghamshire, UK, pp. 179–196.

Sreberny, A. 2005 "Not only, but also": mixedness and media. *Journal of Ethnic and Migration Studies*, 31, 3, pp. 443–460.

Sreberny-Mohammadi, A. and Mohammadi, A. 1994 *Small Media, Big Revolution: Communication, Culture and the Iranian Revolution*. University of Minnesota Press, Minneapolis.

Thompson, J. B. 1995 *The Media and Modernity*. Polity Press, Cambridge.

Tomlinson, J. 1999 *Globalisation and Culture*. Polity Press, Cambridge

Vertovec, S. 2004 Cheap calls: the social glue of migrant transnationalism. *Global Networks*, 4, 2, pp. 219–224.

Werbner, P. 1997 Essentialising essentialism, essentialising silence: ambivalence and multiplicity in the constructions of racism and ethnicity. In P. Werbner and T. Modood, eds. *Debating Cultural Hybridity: Multi-Cultural Identities and the Politics of Anti-Racism*. Zed Books, London, pp. 226–254.

Wilding, R. 2006 "Virtual" intimacies? Families communicating across transnational contexts. *Global Networks*, 6, 2, pp. 125–142.

23

Participatory Vision
Watching Movies with Yolngu

Jennifer Deger

This chapter is about tracking culture through the affective processes, and imaginative dynamics, of watching films. It's about how I have used my senses in the work of audience research, instead of relying solely on talk and exegesis – an approach that's harder than it sounds, especially when trying to apprehend the ways people from a very different cultural lifeworld uses televised stories from distant places to make sense of their own lives.

Over the past 15 years, I've worked in with Aboriginal people in northern Australia as media trainer, collaborator, and ethnographer. Like so many Aboriginal communities across the country, Gapuwiyak (the settlement of about 900 people where I spend most of my time) has increasingly become a place of suffering and struggle. Poverty, illness, boredom, widening intergenerational gaps, premature death and suicide, unemployment, and the repeated failures and blunt intrusions of state policies – all have incrementally taken their toll, undoing certainties and unmooring purpose. Yet even as disappointment, frustration, and fury ripple under the surface of the everyday, local languages and ceremonies remain strong – defiantly so – especially in comparison to many other parts of indigenous Australia. What strikes me constantly about this cultural context is the way in which the work of imagination buoys, propels, and sustains the social. Both within and beyond the ceremony ground, Yolngu animate ancestral events and mythic relations with a playful imaginative vitality that can imbue even the most apparently everyday or incidental events with layers of potential meaning and significance.

Such generative moments of creativity and world making also inflect the ways Yolngu watch movies.[1]

This chapter describes how I have come to recognize – to see and therefore know for myself – something of these largely invisible processes. By offering a few stories

The Handbook of Media Audiences, First Edition. Edited by Virginia Nightingale.
© 2014 John Wiley & Sons, Ltd. Published 2014 by John Wiley & Sons, Ltd.

about my often clunky attempts at audience research, I want to show how Yolngu taught me to pay closer attention to sensuous and feeling ful relationships between the screen and the social, so that I might begin to watch films with something akin to what I now think of as "Yolngu eyes." As I will describe, my growing appreciation of Yolngu audiences as particular kinds of imaginative and affectively attuned viewers led me to abandon textual models of analysis, with their emphasis on resistant readings, and reframe my research in terms of developing a capacity for "participatory vision."[2]

There is not the space here to provide a thorough ethnographic-theoretical analysis of Yolngu forms of media spectatorship. I can merely offer suggestive glimpses of a cultural imaginary that has its own stakes in the social productivities of engaging with screen-based stories originating from elsewhere. In the process, I want to claim – in fact, to insist upon – the productivities of long-term fieldwork as a means of finding new paradigms for appreciating the new kinds of social dynamics that media generate and enable. One thing I have learned in Gapuwiyak is that audience research (although, as I will indicate below, I have a growing ontological quibble with the term *audience*) is productive in such contexts exactly because the audiences are coming from somewhere quite different – ontologically, epistemologically, as well as geographically – from the middle-class, text-based milieu of media studies and associated disciplines. By saying this, I do not intend to impose a blanket separation between "here" and "there" (or, for that matter, "us" and "them") at a time when communications technologies are, more than ever, mediating all kinds of new relations between places such as Arnhem Land and Hollywood (albeit in uneven directions). Nonetheless, as I want to argue, there can be significant differences between the ways that different cultural imaginaries take up the possibilities generated by television. My aim in this chapter is to use my ethnographic experience to gesture toward new ways to think about the power and potencies of such engagements, while insisting on the culturally and historically specific manner in which audiences respond to – and elaborate their experience of – technologically mediated stories and images.

For my purposes here, I've narrowed my discussion to a very specific group of people and a specific style of viewing or media engagement, namely, my adopted Yolngu family's relationships to their favorite Hollywood films as viewed in their homes on video, DVD, or cable.[3] Most of all, I'm interested in why *Rambo* remains a favorite figure in these homes, even as his star is on the wane elsewhere.[4]

Mediated Relations

Even if I hadn't been a self-identified media-visual anthropologist, I would still have spent more than my fair share of time over the past 15 years watching television with my adopted Yolngu kin. The television is on constantly, especially in the wet seasons when there can be up to 13 people living in the small three-bedroom fibro house that is now also my home away from home. In the mornings I'm generally up first, soon to be joined by my 2-year-old *gayminyarr* (grandson), who, after kicking off his nappy, hunts out the remote control so that I can turn on the cartoons before sprinkling milk powder and sugar over his bowl of Weet-Bix. As older members of the family wake up, my nieces and their mother select an action *bitcha* (picture, film) to watch as they sit cross-legged on the floor smoking cigarettes and drinking tea. (I have particularly vivid memories of repeats of Robert Rodriguez's *From Dusk Til Dawn* with its sleazy vampires filling my days during one long, wet summer. Adults sat with children pointing and laughing at a level of violence and killings that I had to turn my eyes away from. If there are concerns about the "impact" of media, it certainly isn't in relation to violence.)[5] During my workdays in the midst of various video projects, I sometimes drop by to linger in the air-conditioned cool of the Women's Centre, joining the ladies on the settees as they laugh, again and again, at Jim Carrey emerging from a rhino's arse in *Ace Ventura 2*. The evenings after dinner we spend on the living room floor, propped up on pillows, watching shop-bought videos or DVDs under clanky ceiling fans while the children sleep besides us.[6]

On many such nights, I too would find myself falling asleep in front of the television set, lulled by films that I'd already seen many times (and that, if I'm honest, held little interest in the first place). But as time passed, I began to struggle against my tiredness. It was becoming clear that that these laidback moments of familial sociality posed a greater intellectual and methodological challenge than almost any of my other research pursuits. I began to realize that they offered a key to understanding broader contemporary social dynamics in Gapuwiyak.

The Allure of the Unspoken

From early on in my research, comments that Yolngu made while watching films indicated to me that Yolngu see no necessarily distinct separation between screen worlds and their own lives. On the contrary, Yolngu talk about the television screen as if it were permeable, as if the image extended beyond that which is visible, and as if there is no intrinsic distinction between film and audience. They say things like "That's me in that film," "When I watch that film I go right inside it," "I see myself and my sisters in that film," or "Really, when I watch, I'm the director." Such statements – combined with the ways in which Yolngu would seek out and watch certain films over and over again – raise questions about agency, identification, and the ontology of the image that I initially didn't know how to approach with my ready-made theories of representation and textual resistance. But as is so often the case in my research in Gapuwiyak, asking direct questions in order to follow up these kinds of statements didn't get me far.

Although people would occasionally elaborate a little for my benefit about a film, telling me about when they first saw it, and who they used to watch it with (thus providing a clue to the ways that the social contexts of viewings become part of how people remember and recall a film), I mostly found people unable (or unwilling) to describe why they responded strongly to a particular film beyond statements like "It's an interesting story" or "It's funny." As time went on and my grasp of local language improved, I began to pick up on the ways in which people make overt links between local characters, family stories, and the on-screen action. Over time I started to also recognize references to ancestral events being made as passing comments during the viewings of Hollywood films. But still, asking direct questions did not help me understand more. When the insistences and intrusions of my questions transformed our viewings into awkward, silent events, I gave up asking. I found it no more productive to ask questions at later times in other contexts, whether in general conversation or in more formal interviews.

Such reactions reinforced my growing sense of how the see-it-for-yourself epistemology that underpins Yolngu culture required me to find a way to approach these questions without recourse to either formal or informal interviews. But how could I get a better sense of what they were seeing – and what engaged them in these multiple viewings – if not through questioning? Part of the problem for me in accessing the deeper significances and effects of films for Yolngu – especially the favorite films that might be watched twice or three times in a row – was that they often had a place within people's lives and memories that predated my own relations in Gapuwiyak. In trying to understand why and how my Yolngu family particularly loved *Rambo*, I needed to know deep and personal family histories as well as something of their clan narratives of ancestral drama.

It soon became clear that I could only come to understand the ways that Yolngu watch movies – and the ways they use these films to inflect their lives with meaning – by participating in all dimensions of everyday life. I had to learn to wait for the moments in which people would offer explanations *that I was in a position to understand*. To this end, I had to acquire language skills, learn genealogies and kinship, study ritual structures and mythic narratives, dance in ceremonies, undertake bush trips to ancestral sites, charter flights for shopping and funerals, cook dinners, and drive the kids to school. At the same time I had to build up my movie knowledge to encompass a back catalogue of action flicks, musicals, and melodramas that I had spent much of my life avoiding.

Seeing Similitude

It's impossible to provide a thorough inventory of the films that have circulated through Yolngu homes and hearts since television (and VCRs) became commonly available in Gapuwiyak in the late 1980s.[7] From spending time talking to people about their favorite films, it's clear that the specifics people like and choose to view vary with individual tastes, ages, gender, and access to televisions and DVD players (and, now, mobile phone accounts). Having said that, because of the degree to which viewing movies operates as a deeply enjoyable *social* activity – certain popular movies are shared, circulated widely, and watched many times by various configurations of family in private homes, or sometimes screened at the basketball court – as a result, there is something of a shared filmic repertoire that informs and infuses the cultural imaginary. The most popular genre, by far, is action films (including martial arts films). The *Rambo* films are probably amongst the most universally well known in the region (especially given the recent release of box sets on DVD), although, as I will describe, the specific ways vary in which people attach meaning and find emotional resonance and satisfaction.

When a film catches their imaginations, Yolngu prove to be deeply attentive and sentimental audiences, cheering, swooning, and gasping out loud as screen events unfold. If people know a film well, they might sometimes recite the dialogue, or mimic the gestures of characters; others will call out the name of actors when they appear on screen in an act of recognition and welcome. A pair of middle-aged sisters I know hoot with laughter as they berate heroes and bad guys alike for violent behavior or swearing (causing their children and grandchildren much merriment). *Rambo III* is their favorite movie for this kind of viewing (a film in which, because of their own relationship to the Dhalwangu clan who have "adopted" him, Rambo can be claimed as their husband or son).

The more times people have seen a movie, the greater the range of social contexts and connections it encompasses, and the deeper the pleasure of this kind of participation. Clearly, familiarity generates a certain pleasure: there is the pleasure of anticipation and the affective payoffs that come with giving oneself over to the emotional arc of a film (a form of identification and participation that no doubt all movie fans appreciate). But what I want to argue here is that Yolngu not only bring certain kinds of culturally attuned bodies and imaginations to the viewing – they also harness the potential for filmic identifications, pleasures, and participations to particular cultural effect.

The thing that people do talk about easily and avidly in front of the TV screen – often with much laughter – are the relationships between on-screen characters. Because of the degree to which kinship structures relationships and motivations in Yolngu society – every one in the community lives in kin-based relations which determine the way they act with each other, what and how people speak to each other, and who they can have relationships with – it makes sense that plot and motivation are discussed by Yolngu viewers in terms of their kinship, whether or not such relations are made explicit in the actual film. (Other nonkin categories such as *best friend* or *boss* are also these days accepted defining and recognizable relationships.) This sense of the importance of relationships as structuring story and motivations often extends beyond the frame of the film to include viewers who, in certain movies, "adopt" characters as kin. "That's me, that's you; they are our sisters," I might be told by someone pointing at the screen or DVD cover as I settle down to watch a local favorite for the first time. In just this simple move, we all gain preassigned "viewing positions." These playful maneuvers mean that everyone present becomes related (the Yolngu, the anthropologist, and the characters on screen) so that the patterning of the social through kinship extends into the dynamics of the film itself. Not surprisingly, it is mostly the heroes who are adopted first, from whom other relations with other minor characters follow. (So, for instance, the rest of the "gang" would be seen as his brothers or brothers-in-law; the romantic interest would be identified in ways that locate her as his classificatory "right skin," or wife; etc.) When we watch in an audience with both brothers and sisters present, the *yongbellas* (good guys) are often claimed as our clan brothers. (Girls and women have to be extremely careful of openly positioning themselves as lead romantic characters if their brothers are present because of strict cultural rules prohibiting women from displaying desire in the company of their brothers.) The bad guys or *gurrkman* might also be playfully assigned a clan identity that reflects current tensions between the group watching and other clans in the community. (When this happens, it is very much on the quiet, so as not to stir things up more.)

An actor's physical traits and the disposition of their character can also influence these adoptings and identifications. For instance, the figure of Rambo, especially in his incarnation in *Rambo III* in which he wears a red headband, can be imaginatively "seen" as a manifestation of a powerful local ancestral figure who is identified with the color red and the use of knives. Once I realized this, I began to hear afresh allusions to film characters and actors in everyday conversation and to recognize nicknames drawn from television as based on playful but astute corporeal identifications. I became acquainted with Bruce Lee, Wesley Snipes, and an old woman called Pinky after the cartoon panther from the Inspector Clouseau films. (The resemblance, now that I see it, is striking yet so difficult to put into words.) In recent years, I've been introduced to the chubby and wide-eyed toddler Ugly Betty.

Seeing Stories

Just as visible similitudes open a space of mimetic resonance, stories themselves can open a space for identifications and elaborations on local terms. For Yolngu, stories are not simply linear. They have layers. They are profoundly a matter of perspective (see e.g. Keen 1994). Again, then, the model of textual reading is not adequate to an epistemological drive which privileges not simply the agency of the viewer, but also understandings and truths uncovered beneath the appearance of things. Yolngu epistemology turns on see-for-yourself veracities, but the general assumption is that what you can literally perceive is not necessarily all there is to be seen (see Deger 2006). In terms of knowledge transmission, the onus is on each person putting things together for themselves; a higher truth value is placed on insights that are gained by bringing a broader and deeper contextual knowledge to bear on the "readings" of situations. Likewise, stories, immanent with meaning, await discovery by those who have developed the capacity to "see." This is a cultural context in which ancestral stories (the stories that continue to give structure and meaning to the lives of Yolngu) lie embedded within places; they can be "found" by individuals through dream and activated by ritual. Local epistemological imperatives drive audiences to look beneath the surface, to seek out similitudes (both narrative and visible) and use them to figure their own lives and relationships through them. (And so this work of finding meaning exceeds the epistemological. It is equally about the dynamics of becoming through the reconstitution of selves in constellations of relationship and narrative.)

But in the beginning I didn't know that. All I knew was that Yolngu seemed to latch onto aspects of the movie's story, or its overall themes and trajectories, but often weren't concerned with specific details or what seemed to me to be crucial plot points. Certainly, this might have been partially because of people's lack of English language competency, but there was a kind of narrative authority assumed by viewers that seemed particular – and more than a sign of playfully "filling in the gaps" of incomprehension. (One teenage girl takes this disregard for any "official" version of the film story to the extreme by authoritatively elaborating screen stories to younger children that have almost nothing to do with what is being said. Although other family members more proficient in English enjoy laughing at her "mistakes" and misreading, they acknowledge that they all participate in this kind of "story finding.") Generally, however, the more the on-screen story directly resonates with the shared story and meaning the better, and the more opportunity is created for a productive play of sameness and difference which holds the web of identification and embellished (but apparently immanent) significances in place. Thus, the narratives that mean the most (and give the most pleasure and offer, at least potentially, deeper insight into local events) are those that are constituted by the viewer themselves in specific relation to events, characters, and emotional patterns from their own lives. In these instances, viewing is a form of participatory revelation.[8]

Focus, Force, and Feeling

For many years now, I have been incrementally piecing together a sense of the visual, affective, and cognitive dynamics activated by Yolngu when they watch movies. Despite my progress, I still feel the need to develop visual research methods that access something closer to movies *as they play in people's minds*. Last year, I achieved something toward this goal when I encouraged people to make screen grabs from their favorite movies on my laptop. My aim here was twofold. First, I was trying to gain closer access to what it was that was catching people's eyes within the frame. Second, in keeping with local cultural dynamics, I wanted to use images, rather than my direct questions, as the prompts for discussion and the sources of (potential) revelation.

Although formalizing things somewhat, the method worked. Positioned by this set-up as the ones in the know (and this sense of knowing as a prerequisite for speaking about something is an important epistemological stance in this cultural context), my research subjects (or, as they would identify themselves, my adopted Yolngu kin) used the self-made video stills as the trigger for extensive narrative elaboration.

Joking and laughing as they explained, the young women embellished their identifications, enjoying seeing my understanding deepen as I brought my local knowledge about clandestine relationships, jealousies, and ongoing feuds into play. With just a few hints, I could see the resemblances between actors and local characters, make the connections between a love story and the ones currently preoccupying these girls, read colors as signifiers of local clan-based identities, and further appreciate locally and personally specific emotional undertones and implications found within the story, information that didn't need to be spelled out once I had my social bearings in the movie. We laughed the most when I offered up my own understandings, with eyebrow raised ("might be that's like that story about so and so"), feeling ourselves bound together in the moment by that which did not have to be spelled out. A knowing glance was all that was needed to share the pleasures of looking beneath the surface of the story, to discover our own stories and participate in the recognition of ourselves and others.

All along, though – and this too is in keeping with an epistemology that understands knowledge to be particular and partial – they stressed that this was just *their* way of seeing things, and others might make something quite different from the same visual and narrative elements. Most valuable of all, though, was that what they showed me on-screen trained me to pay attention to and recognize more of what was going on in everyday life, and how to learn how to open new spaces of resonance by flicking back and forth between screen images and stories and the "real" world.[9]

The freeze frame method allowed W., a shy and reticent research subject, to show me his specific corporeal identification with Sylvester Stallone and Bruce Willis as left-handed men. (From there, I could make my own connection between what I knew of his own character and personal history and these on-screen characters with their tendencies toward a combustive and physically expressed rage.) As we worked through his favorite film, *Rambo III*, the screen shots enabled me to see, for the first time, the direct links that could be made between Rambo's knife and the ancestral *yiki* (knife) that forms part of the sacred legacy of his Dhalwangu clan. Forced to look at the elements in the image, rather than focusing on narrative and dialogue (or lack thereof), I saw not only the hard, masculine body of magical potency that Kellner describes (1995) but also that, in local terms, Rambo's red headband, together with his knife and powerful (seemingly indestructible) body, added another layer of local potency and meaning which allowed Yolngu to play-fully, but at another level quite literally, incorporate him into Dhalwangu mythic structures (as well as Dhalwangu bodies and imaginations) as a manifestation of Birrinydji, the ancestor who never dies.[10]

This method also enabled me to understand that strong and overt identifications are not fixed, even during a single viewing. At other points in the same film, W. switched viewing positions (or perhaps he holds both points of view at once?). Pointing to a video still of the young boy who can be structurally seen as "son" to Rambo in the film, W. told me firmly, "This is me too." He then proceeded to explain how he had watched this film as a boy with his father (who, as a Dhalwangu man, could also take up the identification as Rambo). This information then enabled me to see – and to begin to feel into – his viewings as saturated with his own memories (including memories of previous viewings with his deceased father) and to appreciate this act of viewing and identification as a deliberate way of activating this relationship. Not only did his intimate knowledge from earlier viewings allow him to anticipate (and participate imaginatively with) the events on screen, but also this viewing enacted a form of ritualized remembrance as the unchanging temporality of the film – every shot remaining the same after all these years – provides a conduit for an encompassing of loss and an enactment of enduring connection between father and son. (Such identifications and connections became even more resonant, and more encompassing, when we sat together with W.'s own young son as he was captivated by the movie for the first time.)

Viewing from the Inside

What this kind of overtly relationally inclined viewing highlights is the ways in which Yolngu understand their own subjectivities as constituted through relationships – with people, places, and stories. Unlike the model of individuated selves that dominates Western cultural theories, Yolngu do not conceive of the self as inherently distinct or unitary (see Keen 2006). Rather, identities are constantly being constituted through particular constellations or patterns of embodied relations: one will emphasize a particular identity in order to emphasize a particular set of relations, or vice versa.

Appreciating this critical aspect of Yolngu identificatory dynamics helps me to understand how television screens offer Yolngu new ways of both perceiving and activating the ontological – and deeply affective – work of becoming-in-relation. With imaginations fueled by an epistemology that comprehends knowledge as multilayered and revelatory, and narratives as always inherently perspectival, Yolngu use certain films to trigger a sensorially charged participation in the uncovering and elaborating (whether out loud or internally) of connection. Through conscious acts of identification with other bodies and other stories, Yolngu work the charge of recognition and affective resonance, to reactivate their own stories and to re-immerse themselves in their own recontextualized narratives. They use these films to retell themselves to themselves – and to others – and, unlike rituals that offer ancestral identities that are potentially shared by all clan members, these moves to occupy positions beneath the surface of a movie allow for more individually personal identifications and narratives.

In all these ways, the *Rambo* plots (at least as they initially appear to me) can provide the grounds for local narrative, imagistic, and affective elaboration. Watching through the prism of their own dramas, projecting themselves and their relationships into the story image, and playfully claiming Rambo's power and resilience as manifestations of ancestral qualities, the family – in moments, comments, shared looks, memories, and understandings – reconstitutes itself at multiple levels (as both a group and a collection of individuals with their own private associations and fantasies) while relaxing in front of the television set. Uncluttered by wordiness (or the sophisticated word play that I favor in films but that is difficult for many Yolngu to follow or elaborate from), muscular violence and fantastic spectacles call bodies and imaginations into play as active forces, viscerally captivating – and activating – viewers who, by adding their own local layers of sentiment and narrative, enter and occupy the space of the film as a Yolngu space made and held within a Yolngu place. The result is a bringing forth and commingling of stories and selves – past and present, Balanda (non-Aboriginal) and Yolngu, and the ceremony ground and the lounge room floor – that locate Yolngu on the screen and Rambo in a Yolngu world in ways that work against any binaristic notions of the local and global, the traditional and the modern, and the "ancestral" and the "everyday," not to mention the audience and the film.

Toward a Participatory Vision

Doing ethnography requires one to become attentive to, and participate with, other lives at many levels. Even having made a commitment to long-term, live-in work in specific places with specific people, and having dedicated oneself to the work of attempting to understand the world from other perspectives, it is not easy to quell the relentless urge to ask for explanations and to live life as it unfolds on other people's terms. It is not easy to appreciate – much less do justice to – social dynamics that far exceed the bare facts of what is directly before one's eyes. It is, in fact, quite difficult to learn to look with instead of look at others.[11] Inevitably, there are times when this kind of cautious and yet necessarily experimental research method relies on the unintended productivities of misstep and cross-purpose, while always one works beholden to the generosities of others.

For all these reasons, I often feel my ethnographic method – for all its on-the-ground richness and inclusive social dramas – is a quite indirect route to understanding, and never more so than when one is called to account in the established terms and time scales of universities. Yet, the longer I do this work, the more convinced I am of the value of a research method that places us in situations that require a profound rethinking of not simply *what* we know but also *how* we know.

Undertaking audience ethnography with Yolngu has given me a new appreciation of the unspoken and the unspeakable, the indirect, and the imagined and the invisible as sources of filmic allure and efficacy. As a result, the shared viewing of films has increasingly become central to my embodied, affective, and imaginative participation in the lives and worlds of my adopted Yolngu kin – and theirs with mine.

With the benefits of accrued knowledge, experience, and relationships, I can now appreciate the degree to which the films of spectacle and melodrama that my Yolngu family chooses to view repeatedly provided force and focus to the everyday thrum of frustration and yearning in their lives. I now see movies like *Rambo* as a means of my adopted kin actively allowing the drama of their own lives (always figured in terms of a being-in-relationship to others, never in terms of the individuated self) to be re-encountered, examined, leaned into, and breathed through. While at one level, this conscious use of local identifications allows a witnessing (and potentially a sharing) of one's own struggles via the TV screen, there is more to it than that. In harnessing story, affect, and memory to the work of seeing themselves, their families, and their lives and longings on screen, Yolngu are actively constituting the social on local terms. And, in the process, they are affirming their own place in the world.[12]

Notes

1   Although I pursue an alternative theoretical trajectory to Eric Michaels, his article "Hollywood Iconography" (1987) must be acknowledged as an important and influential precedent in recognizing the highly creative uptake of nonlocal media by Aboriginal people.

2   The classic ethnographic method of participant observation is an approach to the production of knowledge that turns on the productive tensions of positioning oneself simultaneously inside and outside events. Over time, fieldworkers aim to position themselves in the thick of the things they are studying, actively participating alongside the people they are researching, and yet always – at least in the classic view – remaining at a critical distance. This distancing – and the forms of knowledge that are understood to arise from it – is achieved by assuming an observational stance: a modality of vision that is scientistic, detached, and appraising. Even in the heat of the moment – such as a ritual, a harvest, or a board meeting – the conscious act of observing (i.e. looking for data, for patterns, and for meaning beyond the everyday surface, filtering events through theoretical templates) places one at a critical remove from events. (Although I suspect the cool observational perspective relies on hindsight to a greater degree than

many writers credit.) In any case, this methodology assumes that one's outsider status provides the critical purview on the inside, that the visual modality of the researcher as observer is not only detached but also somehow positioned above, capable of generating overviews and insights unavailable to those on the ground. My argument here seeks to offer a quite different sense of the productivities of vision as an ethnographic research method.

3   My "adoption" into the clan was by no means unusual. Every outsider who stays for a length of time and engages at any meaningful level will be "adopted" and given a clan- and skin-based identity that prefigures and structures ensuing social relationships and responsibilities.

4   See Kellner (1995) on Rambo as a potent and divisive figure in social discourse in the 1980s.

5   In comparison, children were enjoined to cover their eyes or hide under the blankets when sex scenes came on.

6   Over the years, as DVD technologies have become more affordable and DVDs more accessible within the community, I have observed Yolngu watching far less free-to-air television, preferring, when possible, to watch films on DVD or cable. Although relatively few Yolngu have access to cable television in their homes, again I have observed in such situations an overall tendency to prefer the movie channels to news, documentary, television dramas, or infotainment programs.

7   Prior to that, film nights run by missionaries or enterprising Yolngu gave locals a taste for "action" genres from kung fu to cowboy.

8   Berndt (1976), when describing Yolngu songs from the 1940s, describes similar incorporative maneuvers whereby in songs dealing with characters and stories set beyond the home area of the singers, the "exotic is put into a local, traditional frame of reference" (p. xi).

9   Although I found this freeze frame method extremely useful, I don't think it would have worked in the early days of my research. Looking back, I wonder if it was really the making of still images that mattered to the elicitation process, or the fact that my methodology made my own problem with seeing explicit. This process demonstrated clearly to Yolngu that I needed some clues as to how to see and recognize the films on their terms. But at the same time, it also highlighted that I now had the imaginative framework – if not the specific biographic details – to make my own sense of what they might show me.

10 See McIntosh (2006) on Birrinydji; and see Deger (forthcoming) on the phenomenological and cultural potency of red in Yolngu society.

11 Indeed, it seems to me that ethnographic research is more experimental – more dependent the productivities of failure and adaptation – than generally acknowledged. Or at least it should be. The terms that describe what ethnographers do – *participant observation* and *fieldwork* – convey a certain surety and purposefulness that belies the necessarily tentative, reactive and adaptive dimensions of a research methodology that requires one to "fit in" in order to "find out."

12 In writing this chapter, I have tried to avoid the lure of the celebratory tone that has accompanied, and indeed vivified, so much of the active audience literature. I understand the urge to claim and affirm forms of resistance because I feel it too. How can one resist the subversive pleasure of turning *Rambo* to one's own underdog agenda?

This is surely what Yolngu themselves are doing at some level. The danger, though, it seems to me, lies in the researcher making these small moments of pleasure and fantasy stand metonymically for victories in a much more complex field of struggle over the grounds of the social and the impacts – and indeed the possibilities – of human agency.

References

Berndt, R. M. 1976 *Three Faces of Love*. Nelson, Melbourne.

Deger, J. 2006 *Shimmering Screens: Making Media in an Aboriginal Community*. University of Minnesota Press, Minneapolis.

Deger, J. Forthcoming. Pink cake, red rock, colour photos. In D. Young, ed. *Re-materializing Colour*. Sean Kingston, Oxon, UK.

Keen, I. 1994 *Knowledge and Secrecy in an Aboriginal Religion: Yolngu of North-east Arnhem Land*. Oxford University Press, Melbourne.

Keen, I. 2006 Ancestors, magic, and exchange in Yolngu doctrines: extensions of the person in time and space. *Journal of the Royal Anthropological Institute*, 12, 3, 515–530.

Kellner, D. 1995 *Media Culture: Cultural Studies, Identity and Politics between the Modern and the Postmodern*. Routledge, London.

McIntosh, I. 2006 The iron furnace of Birrinydji. In A. Rumsey and J. Weiner, eds. *Mining and Indigenous Lifeworlds in Australia and Papua New Guinea*. Sean Kingston, Oxon, UK.

Michaels, E. 1987 Hollywood iconography: a Warlpiri reading. In Drummond, P. and R. Patterson, ed. *Television and Its Audience*. British Film Institute: London.

24

The Audience Is the Show

Annette Hill

"People Produce Beliefs"

Researchers face a challenge in capturing the variety of people's relationships with a range of media and communications technologies.[1] The concept of audience participation is useful in exploring connections between production, content, and reception in multimedia environments. In a talk show, members of the public participate in the production itself, as guests interviewed by the host, as a studio audience, and by watching, listening to, and interacting with the show on TV, radio, mobile, and the web. This concept also captures the way new communication technologies give people opportunities for making and sharing their own media content, such as documentaries created and produced by members of the public and uploaded to the web, where they can then be downloaded to personal computers, mobiles, iPods, and so on. Audience participation addresses the complex dynamics of cultural practices.

Being an audience can be like participating in a show. A public performance, exhibition, or event shows people's cultural practices. At an agricultural show, for example, people make jams or grow vegetables to compete for prizes. A public demonstration can be a platform for people's professional or amateur interests in cars or airplanes. At a variety show, there are a range of performance styles from dance routines, songs, or comedy acts, to physical feats like juggling or acrobatics. A show includes the production of performances, sometimes by the performers themselves, but more often by others working backstage, such as the producers of television or radio programs. A show can go on without an audience; for example, there are full dress rehearsals which help performers and producers to perfect a production. But a show is designed to

The Handbook of Media Audiences, First Edition. Edited by Virginia Nightingale.
© 2014 John Wiley & Sons, Ltd. Published 2014 by John Wiley & Sons, Ltd.

work best with an audience, showcasing talent, skills, and interests to the public, family, and friends, who in turn show their reactions through appreciation, criticism, and interaction.

There is a style of entertainment and communication where the performer and audience create the show together. In an analysis of qualitative audience research, the idea of the audience as the show is explored in relation to historical and contemporary examples from public entertainment, in particular stage magic and medium demonstrations which involve a high degree of audience participation. A medium, or psychic, who performs in public needs an audience not only to watch, or listen, but also to actually make the performance happen. A magician, or mentalist, performs entertainment that is based on audience participation. Most singers or actors can still perform even if there is no audience, but a medium or mentalist must have an audience because their form of communication and entertainment is created with a high degree of public participation. As one research participant said, "People produce beliefs" (51-year-old female secretary). An audience with a medium co-produces belief in spirit communication; an audience with a magician co-produces a sense of wonder. In a live performance, the relationship between a medium, or magician, and the audience is like that between a conductor and his or her orchestra. They all have a role to play in the creation of a cultural experience. In a very real sense, the audience is the show.

The Attentive Audience

An audience that listens, watches, and engages closely with a performance has emerged over time. The word *auditorium* came into the English language after 1727 (Winston 2005, p. 225). Contemporary understanding of an auditorium as a place for appreciation of a performance is quite different from early examples of audiences at the opera or theater. Brian Winston comments,

> It was by no means the case at either theatrical or musical public entertainments that people were silent during the performance. In fact, aristocrats seemed to regard quiet attentiveness as an unforgivably bourgeois trait. Performances were social gatherings and the done thing was to circulate – exactly as is still done at modern parties. (p. 224)

And Donald Sassoon (2006) describes eighteenth-century opera goers as having been anything but attentive to the music:

> Before the 1800s, in popular theatres and in taverns some attention was paid to the action on the stage, but in the opera houses patronised by the upper classes bedlam reigned. At the Paris Opera, the system effectively made the subscribers tenants of

the theatre box, where they could do as they saw fit. Punctuality and silence were not thought to be necessary, or even desirable.... Attentiveness was a social *faux pas*.... The opera house was like a twentieth-century nightclub: people dropped in when it suited them, and would come and go during the performance. (p. 233)

The most sought-after seats in theaters were the ones on, or near, the stage. This was not because of the good view – in fact, it was worse in these seats because people were blinded by oil lamps – but because the rest of the audience could see them. "Visibility to others was crucial. The audience was the show" (p. 234).

Toward the end of the eighteenth century, "the more attentive behaviour which was characteristic of audiences at private performances of chamber music began to be adopted in the public arena" (Sassoon 2006, p. 235). And "[a]s theatres become more market-dependent ... watching the aristocracy provided only limited entertainment for the middle classes. When all was said and done, the bourgeois ethos consisted in getting value for money" (p. 239). The magic lantern show was an example of a transition from the inattentive to the attentive audience. Early lantern shows took place in an informal, domestic environment, with no fixed seating, where people circulated, chatted, and interacted with each other, paying little attention to the lantern show itself (Winston 2005). During the end of the eighteenth and the early nineteenth centuries, lantern shows shifted from the private soirée to the public theater. Robertson's *Fantasmagorie* were lantern shows where audiences sat in fixed rows in a public space. The design of these shows drew the audience into a macabre narrative, mixing single images or effects of ghosts and ghouls with stories. The *Fantasmagorie* were an early example of "narrative and non-narrative spectacle" (p. 226). They signaled a style of entertainment that involved an audience at a public show.

By the mid-nineteenth century, magic lantern shows were overtaken by the popularity of "attractions," which came to mean a mix of performance styles, including animal or aquatic dramas, panoramas and dioramas, or burlesque. These attractions were similar to what now would be called *variety shows*. They mixed images and sounds with stories. Attractions were part of a repertoire of family-friendly theaters. Managers had changed their policies to increase the comfort and safety of theater space by replacing the pit with civilized reserved seats. These theaters appealed to women by eliminating drink, tobacco, and prostitution. In the 1840s managers like P. T. Barnum introduced museum theaters, "adopting the manners of the middle class parlours and assuring a moral climate on and off stage" (Butsch 2008, p. 64). Barnum was one of the first to showcase the Fox sisters, public mediums who performed spirit rapping for a paying audience. As part of Victorian attractions, magicians, mediums, and lecturers showcased new visual and aural modes of experience – the telegraph, the photograph, panoramas, and stereoramas. Many such new attractions relied on fixed seating, for example Dr. Pepper's Ghost. Steinmeyer (2005) notes that the invention of optical illusions used in theatrical dramas influenced the way mediums and magicians performed in public, directing the audience to see specific images through complex use of lighting, sightlines, mirrors, and mechanics.

Richard Butsch (2008) points out that theater spaces, policies, and performances worked together in the emergence of nineteenth-century ideas of cultural appreciation. Etiquette manuals advised people on how to present themselves in public and private, with many cautions against spontaneous displays of emotion, or physical acts. These bourgeois theatergoers avoided rowdy working-class venues, favoring respectable places in newly developed areas. Etiquette rules on how to be a theatergoer emphasized "the duty of the audience to give full attention to the performance, in order to cultivate oneself" (p. 65). The right of audiences to speak and act out was considered working-class behavior and "an outrage against both performers and other members of the audience" (p. 65). Manuals warned against talking during the performance as ticket holders had a right to enjoy entertainment uninterrupted. Theatergoers were schooled to stay in their seats, not to eat peanuts, and to refrain from loud gestures or sounds. A children's etiquette book exemplified late Victorian attitudes to cultural appreciation and respectability: "perhaps nowhere are bad manners more disagreeable than in public places of amusement … [where people] are defrauded of the pleasure they have paid for by the conduct of those about them" (pp. 65–66).

Butsch (2008) argues that Victorian theatergoers represented different visions of audiences as crowds and publics. In early American theater, "revolutionary discourse framed audiences as engaging in legitimate actions in their roles as citizens, both exercising rights and participating in political debate" (p. 24). Depictions of working-class men in the city theaters of the 1830s and 1840s showed a vocal, boisterous crowd. This image changed with concerns about the incivility of the working classes. Nineteenth-century crowd psychology synthesized intellectual views about the "emotionality and suggestibility of subordinate groups" (p. 33). These theatergoers were thought to be lacking in reason, and quickly capable of becoming a dangerous mob. The influential writings of Gustave Le Bon (1875/1960) and Boris Sidis (1899) on crowd psychology drew upon ideas of mesmerism and hypnosis, both of which were popular in theaters as part of lecture tours or stage acts (see Melechi 2008). Early writings conceived the crowd as mobs: "the speaker or focus of the crowd was simply the trigger to unify it into one mind, making it more powerful; its emotionality and volatility then made it an agent of chaos and destruction" (Butsch 2008, pp. 36–37). Later writings represented "the crowd as dependent upon and under the control of the speaker" (p. 37). These were different constructions of an audience in Victorian theaters, one that was unruly and inattentive, and another that was too attentive to the manipulation of the speaker or performer.

The historical context of the attentive audience helps to explain the work of mediums and magicians. In the case of nineteenth-century mediums, many started out conducting private sittings in their own homes. The style of the séance provided an element of the experience of watching and listening to a private performance. The class distinctions of Victorian audiences and crowds were apparent in the different venues for demonstrations of séance phenomena. Prominent patrons of spiritualism organized private séances in their homes. Some mediums only worked in such spaces, never charging for their demonstrations but instead relying on patronage. Others worked in public theaters to a paying audience. In both types of performance spaces, the attention of the audience was crucial – these séances happened in the dark, with fixed seating, where the medium could control the performance and the participation of the audience. People had to pay attention, whether to catch fraudulent mediums in the act, as their critics suggested, or to witness proof of an afterlife. The scientist W. D. Carpenter coined the term "expectant attention" as an explanation for people's unconscious acts of movement or thought which helped to create séance phenomena (Lamont 2005, p. 41). For example, in the act of table tipping the questions posed by a medium were unconsciously answered by other participants in their effort to make the "table talk." Today this is commonly referred to as *ideomotor movement* and is one of the explanations used for the trickery associated with pseudo-psychics.

The vision of Victorian audiences of mediums as victims of a delusion fitted into crowd psychology of the time. It also suggested concerns about female audiences and performers, as many women were associated with public and private demonstrations of mediumship. The magician John Henry Anderson denounced spiritualism in a pamphlet which he sold for a shilling at his shows. He stated this delusion had driven 10,000 people mad, causing them to "become lunatics … and thousands of poor infatuated victims … have become melancholy misanthropes and imbecile tormentors" (cited in Lamont 2005, p. 62). In his shows in London, performed to a full house, he revealed the secrets of spiritualism – "The Homological Evaporation," "The Aqua-avial Paradox," and "The Mesmeric Couch" – to all be the product of mechanical methods. Anderson with grave tone "expatiated on the mischief done by pretended spirit media," and his performance was "received with applause equally serious" (cited in Lamont 2005, p. 63). The construction of audiences of mediums as dupes and imbeciles worked alongside the image of skeptical audiences as critical and sane. Lamont (2005) writes that "most of the public did not need convincing, their view of spiritualism being instinctively dismissive, and they were quite happy to accept the rhetoric and pseudo-explanations of the Wizard" (p. 65).

Such ideas of mediums and their audiences failed to capture the complexity of their performances and public responses. Fake mediums Charles Forster, Henry Slade, and the Davenports performed in public to paying audiences, and their "speciality feats … entered the repertoires of mainstream magicians" (Lamont 2006, p. 22). For example, Foster's speciality was to involve an audience member in billet reading, where the names of the recently departed would be mysteriously spelled out through spirit raps, or dramatically written in red on his body. Slade's speciality of slate writing directed the audience to look closely at a blank slate for the appearance of messages, drawing attention away from any hidden mechanisms. The Davenports would invite audience members to tie the ropes that secured them in their spirit cabinet, thus ensuring focus on the stage. Although these performances resembled those of conjurers, "[I]t was essential that … their feats were seen as genuinely supernatural" (p. 22). Thus, "[F]ake mediums had to fabricate both the phenomena and the performance as a whole" (p. 26). The strategies employed by fraudulent mediums enabled audiences to feel they were witnessing authentic séance phenomena. These included the use of novel effects not known as conjuring tricks by their audience. They added spiritual significance to these effects, for example by asking audience members for the names of recently departed loved ones, rather than simply to pick a random word. Unlike magicians, who performed conjuring with ease, mediums drew attention to their labor as spirit messengers:

> By fabricating both a desirable purpose and a lack of control, the medium was able to align himself with the audience and distance himself from the phenomena (both the implied source and the real source). Thus medium and sitter were in it together, neither in control of events yet both seeking success. (p. 27)

Lamont's analysis highlights how these mediums and their audiences produced alternative frames of interpretation that made fake spirit communication seem real.

The history of an attentive audience thus highlights how a specific style of live entertainment and communication emerged during the nineteenth century. The private experience of the salon transformed into public entertainment. Theater managers changed policies and business practices, installing fixed seating, electricity, and lighting in theaters, and producing narrative and nonnarrative spectacles, attractions, dramas, and public demonstrations. New styles of listening and watching performances emerged, with the appreciation of a performance characterized by attentiveness and respectability. In this environment, mediums and magicians created a type of public entertainment and communication that relied on audience participation. They used seating and lighting plans to their advantage, increasing control of audience reactions and concealing the means of producing these reactions. In magical entertainment and medium demonstrations, the audience was the show in a different sense than they had been a century before. Rather than ignore the performance, an audience made the performance possible.

Producing Beliefs

Magical entertainment is about audience participation. Take as an example the art of misdirection. This begins from the basis that an audience is attentive to the performer and therefore can be directed toward the magic effects and away from the methods behind them. Lamont and Wiseman (1999) explain that physical misdirection is all about directing the attention of the audience to what they see (the space, person, and object) and when they see it (timing, placement, and movement). Magicians have multiple methods of physical misdirection. They use passive diversion, which directs the audience to look at areas of interest which appear natural (contrasting colors, or light); and active diversion, which draws the audience to specially created areas of interest (e.g. deliberate use of the eyes or voice in the performance). Another diversion involves reducing or increasing attention at a specific moment in the performance (at the point of effect). A skilled magician regulates audience attention through focus and timing.

Psychological misdirection is about how a magician controls audience interpretation of a magic effect. This can be done by using natural actions that appear appropriate within the context of a performance (shuffling cards in the same manner each time during a card trick). Or a magician can make an inconsistent action appear consistent by using familiar actions (producing a false shuffle amongst many similar card shuffles). A ruse involves the false justification of an action as necessary to the performance (coughing to cover hand palming in a card trick). A convincing performer can divert suspicion by misrepresentation, using false solutions and expectations, or "sucker effects" (Lamont and Wiseman 1999, p. 75). This approach utilizes audience expectations about false traps, or the power of suggestion, to direct them to misinterpret a conjuring act.

To create a magical experience involves an understanding of audience participation as more than misdirection. Contemporary magician and mentalist Derren Brown (2006) says that "magic isn't about fakes and switches and dropping coins in your lap. It's about entering into a relationship with a person, whereby you can lead him[,] economically and deftly, to experience an event as magical" (p. 36). Hilary Mantel (2006) explains,

> When a trick is performed, the harder you watch, the more you may miss. You become committed to its process; you are complicit, and your attention moves as directed. It is natural, when we are surprised, to exaggerate the oddity and wonder of our experience. (p. 3)

Mentalist Paul Stockman uses terms like *audience handler* to signal the close relationship between performer and audience. He explains,

> Psychological entertainment for me is 90 per cent performance and 10 per cent method. It's all about the entertainment, and holding the attention of a large audience needs a lot of preparation as far as script and audience management techniques are concerned. (Quoted in Hey 2009, p. 13)

An audience with a mentalist knows that their participation is crucial. For example "Derren Brown always has somebody with him, somebody from the audience, just kind of randomly picked, that makes it more believable as well" (28-year-old male computer programmer). Brown makes his audience feel special: "it's like you want to believe it, you want to be the one" (26-year-old male student). "The joy is that, 'oh that could happen to me!' And he is kind of playing with the unknown parts of yourself – 'will I be able to do that?' It's a kind of joy of the mystery playing with minds" (28-year-old female public relations person). To experience an event as magical involves an audience investing in the process of playing with the mind.

In the following discussion, participants debated the process of participating in a magical experience:

> It's a kind of enlightenment experience.... If you look at it, we are kind of skeptical... the magic format is sort of old really, and for lots of people just not convincing. So this is just kind of the next level of that. (25-year-old male marketing assistant)

> Russian roulette. (20-year-old unemployed male)

> Also, he tricks minds. (28-year-old female volunteer manager)

> Recently magic became really sexy. Everyone is into magic. My mate started getting into it, and he works at bar and he does stuff like that. (19-year-old male student)

> And people really like it. Really, yeah it's become sexy. It's just become very popular. (28-year-old male civil servant)

> I don't think Derren Brown and David Blaine are anything to do with magic though. Really, truly... (28-year-old female volunteer manager)

> It's illusion. (19-year-old male student)

> But magic to me is like, I don't know, I can't explain it, but not to do with tricking someone's mind. The trick itself wouldn't be magic, but the person who watched it. (28-year-old female volunteer manager)

> I was watching Derren, I like using my own imagination more rather than trying to give scientific proof. (28-year-old male civil servant)

> He tries to explain things, how they could possibly happen... (25-year-old male marketing assistant)

> I don't rely on science to explain things to me, though. (28-year-old male civil servant)

> I don't understand, if science doesn't explain it... (25-year-old male marketing assistant)

> Well, to prove different things, the science of the mind, to sort of prove how people are doing it, I don't need exactly to know how hypnotherapy and alternative therapy works. I don't need any proof. (28-year-old male civil servant)

> I found, in a kind of way, it spoils it to know how they do it. Whenever I see a magic show, I guess it's interesting to see how they do it, but that's not how I watch it. I want to see what they can do, really. (24-year-old female teacher)

> I just found it's really disappointing. I really would want to know the answer, but when I did I wasn't really interested in it anymore. That's why I like Derren Brown because he doesn't give you answers, but he wants you to try to work it out, and that's part of it. And so you can have a bit, but you can't have all of it. (28-year-old female volunteer manager)

The context of magic is important. It has to be fresh and contemporary, to tap into what an audience thinks, drawing on shared expectations, practices, and beliefs. The kind of magic that is popular amongst this group is deliberately ambiguous, a form of psychological entertainment rather than trick conjuring. Popular psychology, alternative therapies, and pseudo-science form the backdrop to the construction of magic as psychological entertainment. A magician and mentalist, such as Brown, assumes a level of skepticism from his audience, not only about magic but also about related issues such as hypnotherapy. Rational thinking is the basis from which the magical experience is constructed, "a kind of enlightenment experience." This is why his style of performance focuses so much on explanations behind the magic effects, for example hypnotism works because of the power of suggestion. But, these explanations are part of psychological mis-direction. An audience follows twists and turns so that their own logical thinking leads them down the garden path. There is an understanding that the construction of a magic effect involves audience participation – "you try to work it out, and that's part of it." To achieve a sense of wonder in the magic effect is difficult to explain. And that is the point – a magical experience is beyond explanation.

The relationship between the production of beliefs in magic and the paranor-mal is of significance. In the case of magic tricks, the performer and audience work together to create an experience that lasts for as long as the act. Once outside the entertainment frame, the magic has gone. A medium is demonstrating what is thought to exist outside of the performance itself. Lamont (2006) comments that even though a medium constructs a performance on the basis of paranormal beliefs, it is not necessarily the case that audiences believe in them. Indeed, an audi-ence with a medium brings their own skepticism to the performance: "ostensibly psychic phenomena [are] not only unusual and surprising, but inherently anoma-lous. Few people view such events without suspicion and many reject them as highly unlikely if not impossible" (p. 25). The problems of belief in psychic phe-nomena signal one of the ways that paranormal experiences are created by a medium and their audience. The difficulties, contradictions, and unusual nature of the phenomena comprise a basis for the construction of the performance and experience. There is a shared understanding of the inherently anomalous nature of the phenomena.

There is a lot of detailed advice as to how to be the audience of a medium. One woman described psychics as dodgy plumbers. People offer advice routinely – pre-pare in advance, do your research, ask around, and when you meet the medium give nothing away, be nonresponsive, but also be alert and active. For example:

> Good mediums don't ask you questions. If you go into a medium, and say, I've got John here, you know a John, well, everyone knows a John somehow … then you say, no, no. Basically you don't feed them anything. Then they tell you. You don't tell them anything…. And a good medium doesn't tell you someone close to you is going to die. It could be your mum, or child, oh my god, someone is going to die, and it really makes you paranoid…. Word of mouth is the best way to get good

mediums. If you know people have been to a medium and verified them. (46-year-old female care worker)

All the advice is about being self-aware – looking at emotional, psychological, and spiritual responses. The problems of belief direct the attention of the audience toward themselves.

In her novel *Beyond Black*, Hilary Mantel (2005) writes of the relationship between a medium and their audience. The character Alison explains,

> This is how you handle them; you tell them the small things, the personal things, the things no one else could really know. By this means you make them drop their guard: only then will the dead begin to speak. On a good night, you can hear the skepticism leaking from their minds, with a low hiss like a tyre deflating. (p. 26)

Often when mediums perform in public, they make reference to the audience in the warm-up, explaining that they would like yes or no answers, as it is important to give accurate readings, and at the same time explaining that without audience participation nothing will happen. Thus, an audience with a medium is on double duty, giving out the energy and openness to spirits they are told is necessary for spirit communication to work and also keeping a tight rein on their responses so as not to give too much away. It is a curious open-and-closed feeling where audiences regulate their level of participation. As Mantel (2005) notes, the punters for a medium "entertain any number of conflicting opinions. They could believe … and not believe … both at once" (p. 31).

The medium Gordon Smith (2007) describes the experience of a live performance:

> Every event is absolutely unique and I don't really know what's going to happen any more than the audience does. It's a real act of faith … my name may be on the bill, but it's not my show. The word 'medium' comes from the same root as 'media'. I am a messenger, a carrier of messages. (p. 78)

Audiences also carry messages: their own responses, the collective responses from the crowd, and the responses of absent others brought to life by an audience and medium together. Although people attend a public demonstration of a medium's skills, it is also a demonstration of the skills of a live audience, alert to their emotions and psychological processes, critical of themselves and others, and at the same time open to experiences and producing beliefs.

Participation

Audience participation signals the merging of ideas around an active audience with production research and with social and cultural theory. The active audience model promotes a complex understanding of how people think, feel, and act. For example, studies on soap operas or households explored issues of gender, power, and ideology (see Hobson 1982; Morley 1986; Lull 1990, amongst others). The relations between audiences and everyday life highlighted the way the media was part of broader cultural and social practices (see Silverstone 1994; Gauntlett and Hill 1999, amongst others). Researchers have studied media reception at home, in the workplace, on trains, and in waiting rooms; they have looked at individuals, households, and crowds (see McCarthy 2001; Hermes 2005, amongst others). As the active model developed, multiple methods were used, from interviews, focus groups, and participant observation to surveys and conversation analysis. Multiple approaches were adopted, from a basis in social science, to work in cultural anthropology and geography, visual sociology, and social psychology. Participation is a natural progression in understanding audiences today.

Participation can mean different things. One approach can mean participation as citizenship and consumer rights, drawing on broader notions of the public knowledge project (see Hill 2007). Participation is framed by social and cultural theories regarding the normative concept of the public sphere, subsequent variations of these theories as public spheres, and alternative publics. Cultural citizenship includes a connection between the individual, audience, and public and their participation or avoidance of political matters within public and private spheres (Hermes 2005). This puts the citizen at the heart of understanding audience participation, within the broader framework of the media and democracy (Dahlgren 2009). Another related approach considers the individual, audience, and public as agents of change, engaged in dynamic practices (e.g. Bird 2003, amongst others). The promise of web environments as participatory can be a tool for empowerment, and different styles of cultural production can offer multiple modes of engagement (Gauntlett 2007, amongst others). This sees participation as practices that evolve within media and cultural environments.

Live performances are powerful moments of participation. There is participation on several levels, such as sitting, standing, clapping, or going on stage. There is participation through thinking, feeling, looking, and listening. Architect and designer Frederick Kiesler wanted his theater audiences to "recognise the act of seeing, or receiving, as participation in the creative process no less essential than the artist's own" (cited in Pringle 2002, p. 344). In the case of a magician or medium, the performer and audience commit to participation in the creative process. Their relationship is like, as mentioned above, that of a conductor and orchestra. A magician conducts their audience as if they are members of an orchestra. They create the performance together. When magicians are good at what they do, there is a collective pleasure in their skills to conduct the audience; some participants perform solos, some perform as part of an orchestral section, and at key moments the entire live audience performs together. There are tonal qualities to audience experiences of a live performance with a magician where they are participating in major and minor moments in the show. Magicians want their audience to tune in to the magic of the moment, to produce a belief in something they are skeptical of. A live demonstration with a medium involves a similar relationship. An audience comes to a demonstration alternating between skepticism in paranormal claims and belief in what they personally see as evidence of life after death. A medium conducts the audience as they orchestrate their own skepticism and belief. Their participation shows great investment in the process. An audience with a medium is committed to performing or playing out their beliefs both within and outside of the live show.

In different contexts, the audience as show highlights the power of live or seemingly live performances and events. Televangelists are charismatic leaders. From the stage, they conduct the audience as an orchestra, with a theatrical performance of emotions and religious beliefs. A regular part of their stage show includes the dramatic transformation of the skeptic to believer. Rather like a solo act, one participant comes on stage and performs in tandem with the televangelist. Together they co-produce the transformative act of skeptic to believer and in doing so reinforce a collective experience of religious belief. Televangelists cannot do this alone; their performance is based on audience participation. There are similarities with the psychology of mediums and their audiences. There is a demonstration of skills, and a live audience produces the belief that makes possible an interpretation of such skills as genuine. High-profile fakery scandals indicate that some televangelists are frauds. To say that audiences of televangelists are gullible misses the power of the live performance of charismatic leaders and their audiences. Derren Brown's television show *Messiah* (Channel Four, UK 2005) specifically addressed the ways in which a magician can masquerade as a charismatic leader, using the professional skills of mentalism to produce the appearance of a spiritual experience. When Brown explains how magicians enter into a relationship with a person or audience, whereby they can lead them "economically and deftly to experience an event as magical" (2006, p. 36), this is also true of certain types of charismatic leaders and their relationship with their audiences.

Another example is politics. Politicians in Britain and the United States construct their performance on the basis that audiences do not trust them. They address their audience as skeptics, disillusioned by the modern style of Western politics, by high-profile scandals involving corruption in money or sex, and by the slick ways politicians spin issues to their advantage. Rather like a medium, most people assume a lot of politicians are frauds, even criminals, and come with a prior degree of skepticism in the claims of a politician to act on the public's behalf for the public good. Also, rather like a magician, people expect a politician to deceive them. The difference between a good and bad politician can be in the way they use these expectations of deception to their advantage. A politician can use an audience's skepticism in the construction of political performances. For example, when politicians attempt to reduce public suspicion, they can do so by controlling the interpretation of a political act. Some use false explanations as psychological misdirection. Some use charisma and a personal style to regulate and control the public's attention. Research by Peter Dahlgren (2009) and John Corner and Dick Pels (2003) shows how ideas of performance are part of understanding modern politics. Work by Couldry, Livingstone, and Markham (2007) highlights how audiences critically engage with celebrity politics in the wider political arena. Successful politicians understand the psychology of their audience and construct a performance based on a high degree of public participation. In order to win votes, a politician has to lead the public, economically and deftly, to experience an event as democratic even when that same public is suspicious of politicians. It is a transformative act where even in the most hostile of environments people can produce beliefs.

In the case of media experiences, the audience as show works in different ways, depending on the degree of participation in terms of both a collective, live audience and the participative frame used by producers. As Livingstone and Lunt (1992) suggested in their research on talk shows, certain styles of production invite participation by the studio and television audience. The type of talk shows that include ordinary people and their stories are filmed as live, and include a participative frame that invites a studio audience to vocally and emotionally engage with the performances; indeed, it is a co-performance carefully produced by the program makers and host. In turn, but to a lesser degree, television audiences are invited to participate with the studio audience, what Daniel Dayan (2005) describes as "collective attention" or "watching with," where "audiences embody a fundamental dimension of social experience" (p. 55). In a similar way to the early experiences of opera goers, there is a rowdy, noisy audience in these talk shows that is just as much a part of the performance as anybody else. But, this is an audience as show, where the incivilities of a live crowd are orchestrated by the talk show host and producers to shape a collective cultural experience. The audience as show works best on television when a live show is transformed into a collective participatory act.

Dayan (2005) argues that publics emerge through co-production: "to go public in our societies means going on air, or in print, more often than taking to the streets," and this "involves being allowed or encouraged to do so" (p. 63). In the case of web environments, publics emerge through the participative frame of digital media which encourages people to perform, participate, and produce content to be shared by a few or many around the world. David Gauntlett comments that the web 2.0 environment encourages users to be the show (personal communication, December 12, 2009). If aristocratic audiences of early opera acted like tenants because of the theater policies of the time, now web users act like the performers, crowds, managers, owners, and architects of the show. The idea of attention is ever more important in a web environment, where bloggers actively encourage specific links to increase the flow of users to their sites. Whilst the web is known for its "always, anytime, anywhere" function, where content is available for people when they want it, there are elements which relate to live participatory acts. For example, web discussions are scheduled live after a TV show, with actors or journalists going online to participate in a live debate. Flash mob experiences, such as dancing at a crowded train station in London at a particular moment, are organized beforehand through the use of the web and mobile communications, but the point is to create a live event with a high degree of participation where the audience is the show.

Reality entertainment formats involve both live television performances and web engagement which encourage participatory acts for audiences and users. The broadcasting success stories of the past decade are shows like *Idol*, *X Factor*, *Got Talent*, or *Strictly Come Dancing* (also known as *Dancing with the Stars*). All of these shows are filmed live with a studio audience. The show consists of variety acts: professionals and nonprofessionals singing, dancing, or performing comedy, acrobatics, or magic acts. A panel of expert judges rates the performances and invites the public to vote for their favorite performers. The show could be filmed without a live audience in the studio, but this would miss the point. The producers want to create a show that involves audience participation. To do so, they must invite the audience to co-produce the outcome of the show through their votes. What is so successful about these reality shows is the way the excitement of the live performance and the close involvement of the studio audience are communicated to the broadcast audience. This is a moment of televised entertainment where the public participate in an extraordinary way. At a time of dwindling shares and fragmented audiences, these shows get the attention of the nation. With record shares of over 50 percent of broadcast audiences, shows like *Idol* or *X Factor* outperform their rivals because they capture the feeling of being in the moment at a live performance. The studio audience is a stand-in for the public, and their reactions are important to the televised event; but they cannot vote, and that power is reserved for the audience at large, participating via their telephones, TVs, computers, and mobiles. The relationship between the producers of *X Factor* and their audience is not the same as that between a conductor and an orchestra. The YouTube Orchestra was produced by Google to promote the wonders of digital media and creative collaboration. A leading composer wrote a new piece, "Internet Symphony No 1," and a selection of YouTube users was chosen to perform the symphony at Carnegie Hall in New York, broadcast live across the World Wide Web. The producers of reality entertainment shows have found a way to make live entertainment feel like a creative collaboration between performers and audiences. It is the next generation in the production of entertainment experiences.

Conclusion

The idea of audience as show relates to notions of participation. For example, elite audiences at the opera in the eighteenth century were inattentive to entertainment performances. When Sassoon (2006) says that "the audience was the show," he is referring to the framing of the upper classes as the focus of attention at the opera in the late eighteenth century. This was an early example of audience management where an elite few directed the majority view. It was also an example of audience participation in a cultural experience where sociability was more important than appreciation of a performance. Another notion of the audience as the show utilized the attentive audience as part of the performance. Etiquette rules on how to be an attentive audience were an example of audience management, where a middle-class crowd co-produced an environment for cultural appreciation. During the nineteenth century, the profession of magicians and mediums developed in tandem with the idea of an attentive audience. Magic acts were constructed around an understanding of audience participation and management. Public demonstrations of mediums were shaped around an attentive audience that helped to produce beliefs in the skills of the performer. The nineteenth century saw a particular type of live entertainment and communication experience emerge where the audience was the show.

Ways of understanding audiences with magicians or mediums have included psychology and mass communication theories concerning media influences and effects. Nineteenth-century crowd psychology explicitly referenced mesmerism and mass hypnosis as explanations for the reactions of working-class audiences in theaters or at public events. Suggestion and emotion, irrationality and uncritical thinking – these would become hallmarks of some early idea of mass audiences. Another way of understanding audiences is that of participation. Magicians are audience handlers with a high degree of knowledge and skills in participatory experiences. In turn, audiences know their participation is crucial to the production of a magic show. A relationship between a magician and his or her audience is like that between a conductor and an orchestra. They co-perform and co-produce the cultural experience together. Both magicians and mediums are professions that deal with audience skepticism, and these performers have learned how to trans- form skepticism into belief, even if only for a brief moment.

There are several key issues that arise from the idea of the audience as the show. The first is the power of live performances as moments where performers and audi- ences produce a memorable experience. In the case of some professions, magicians, mediums, or, for example, televangelists and politicians, the live performance is a powerful moment where the charismatic leader on stage attempts to transform the skepticism of their audience into the production of beliefs. In this way, an audience becomes committed to the process and the production of their own experience. As ways of participating in live events, televised live shows, and multimedia environ- ments develop, audiences evolve. Through various acts of participation, people breathe life into a show. In so doing, audiences embody the culture they experience.

Note

1   A note on methods: this project used a combination of a deductive and inductive approach to the sociology of the paranormal in popular culture. Theoretical and empirical studies on media audiences, popular culture, media and communication

theory, cultural history, media and religion, social psychology, cultural geography, anomalous psychology, and parapsychology worked alongside the data design, collection, and analysis of cultural practices. The two informed each other and led to a specific approach that combines qualitative media audience research with critical social and cultural theory.

The study was based on an audience research project conducted by the author and two research assistants, Dr. Koko Kondo and Dr. Lizzie Jackson. The project included a combination of qualitative research methods. There are 18 focus group interviews with 104 participants (aged 18–65+), and in-depth interviews with 70 participants in 27 households in southeast England. Both of these methods allow for semistructured interviews with a range of people from working- to middle-class backgrounds who are viewers or users of paranormal media and related programs about illusionism, and who held a range of attitudes and beliefs about paranormal phenomena. The project also involved participant observation of ghost-hunting events at three selected sites. There were also interviews with a range of experts in the media industry, academic researchers, paranormal professions, and members of psychic and folklore societies in order to extend contextual knowledge.

References

Bird, S.E. 2003 *The Audience in Everyday Life*. Routledge, London.

Brown, D. 2006 *Tricks of the Mind*, Channel Four Books, London.

Butsch, R. 2008 *The Citizen Audience: Crowds, Publics and Individuals*. Routledge, London.

Corner, J. and Pels, D. eds. 2003 *Media and the Restyling of Politics*. Sage, London.

Couldry, N., Livingstone, S. and Markham, T. 2007 *Media Consumption and Public Engagement: Beyond the Presumption of Attention*. Palgrave Macmillan, Basingstoke.

Dahlgren, P. 2009 *Media and Political Engagement: Citizens, Communication and Democracy*. Cambridge University Press, Cambridge.

Dayan, D. 2005 Mothers, midwives and abortionists: genealogy, obstetrics, audiences and publics. In S. Livingstone, ed. *Audiences and Publics: When Cultural Engagement Matters for the Public Sphere*. Intellect Books, Bristol, UK, pp. 43–76.

Gauntlett, D. 2007 *Creative Explorations: New Approaches to Audiences and Identities*. Routledge, London.

Gauntlett, D. and Hill, A. 1999 *TV Living: Television, Culture and Everyday Life*. Routledge, London.

Hermes, J. 2005 *Re-reading Popular Culture*. Blackwell, London.

Hey, G. 2009 Paul Stockman: from drummer to mentalist on a roll. *Magicseen* 5, 4, pp. 12–15.

Hill, A. 2007 *Restyling Factual TV: Audiences and News, Documentary and Reality Genres*. Routledge, London.

Hobson, D. 1982 *Crossroads: the Drama of a Soap Opera*. Methuen, London.

Lamont, P. 2005 *The First Psychic: the Peculiar Mystery of a Notorious Victorian Wizard*. Abacus, London.

Lamont, P. 2006 Magician as conjuror: a frame analysis of Victorian mediums. *Early Popular Visual Culture*, 4, 1, pp. 21–33.

Lamont, P. and Wiseman, R. 1999 *Magic in Theory*. University of Hertfordshire Press, Hertfordshire.

Le Bon, G. 1960 *The Crowd*. Viking Press, New York. (Original work published in 1875).

Lull, J. 1990 *Inside Family Viewing: Ethnographic Research on Television Audiences*. Routledge, London.

Mantel, H. 2005 *Beyond Black*. Harper Perennial, London.

Mantel, H. 2006 Magical thinking: Hilary Mantel studies the self-deprecating master of debunking: *Tricks of the Mind* by Derren Brown. *The Guardian*, Saturday Review, Cultural Studies, 16 December, p. 3.

McCarthy, A. 2001 *Ambient Television*. Duke University Press, Durham, NC.

Melechi, A. 2008 *Servants of the Supernatural: The Night Side of the Victorian Mind*. Heinemann, London.

Morley, D. 1986 *Family Television: Cultural Power and Domestic Leisure*. Routledge, London.

Pringle, T. 2002 The space of stage magic. *Space and Culture 5*, 4, pp. 333–345.

Sassoon, D. 2006 *The Culture of the Europeans: From 1800 to Present*. Harper Press, London.

Sidis, B. 1899 *The Psychology of Suggestion*. Appleton, New York.

Silverstone, R. 1994 *Television and Everyday Life*. Routledge, London.

Smith, G. 2007 *Life Changing Messages*. Hay Publishing, London.

Steinmeyer, J. 2005 *Hiding the Elephant: How Magicians Invented the Impossible*. Arrow Books, London.

Winston, B. 2005 *Messages: Free Expression, Media and the West from Gutenberg to Google*. Routledge, London.

25

Seeking the Audience for News
Response, News Talk, and Everyday Practices

S. Elizabeth Bird

Introduction: News as a Cultural Phenomenon

We know surprisingly little about audiences for news.[1] Public opinion research gives us broad pictures of what people think about issues, and we have gained important insights about how people process information psychologically, or what surveys can tell us about reception of specific news stories. In other words, we do have a social scientific body of literature about the relationship of texts and reception, although it comprises a small portion of the scholarship on other aspects of journalism. As Hartley (2008) writes, "Journalism research tends to prioritise the perspective of the producer (the professional, the industry, the firm)" (p. 680), with emphasis on texts, production, and so on. For instance, a recent *Handbook of Journalism Studies* (Wahl-Jorgenson and Hanitzsch 2008) devotes only one of its 30 chapters directly to audiences.

Given that we live in a world in which much of what we know is learned through various kinds of news (leaving aside for the moment the thorny question of exactly what constitutes news), the neglect is striking. We are all news audiences at one time or another, and journalism of course depends on having an audience. But the neglect is also understandable, in light of the difficulty involved in identifying an "audience" to study, and then actually exploring people's relationship to news in anything approaching a natural setting. In trying to conceptualize this relationship, I find it useful to think of it in several connected but rather different ways. These might be framed by questions, all of which are worth investigating: "How does

The Handbook of Media Audiences, First Edition. Edited by Virginia Nightingale.
© 2014 John Wiley & Sons, Ltd. Published 2014 by John Wiley & Sons, Ltd.

news consumption fit into everyday life?" or "How do people directly respond to news?" or "How do people talk about news?" or indeed "How does news directly affect people?" In this chapter, I explore these questions, focusing especially on interpretive, cultural approaches to news audiences, rather than on the social scientific research that has been more common in journalism studies. And in doing so, I address some of the methodological challenges that come with asking these questions. My disciplinary starting point is anthropological and ethnographic, which I define as looking at news as a form of cultural meaning making – its creation, content, and reception and dissemination. Cultural analyses include the study of news production and content (see Bird 2009), but in this context, my focus is on the way that news circulates among audiences. I am not suggesting that interpretive perspectives are "better" than others; cultural analyses of audiences can and should be productively informed by other approaches.

As Hartley suggests, cultural approaches to news audiences have not been extensive, especially in the journalism studies literature. Ethnographic audience studies have flourished in the domain of cultural studies, and more recently in anthropology, but news has largely been neglected in favor of work with entertainment media – even though some of the earliest work in British cultural studies by Stuart Hall and others had an intense interest in the decoding of news.[2] The reasons, I believe, lie primarily in the difficulty of capturing the news audience for study (as opposed to the audience for specific entertainment programs or genres), because news is received and circulated almost constantly – even more so today with the rise of social media. In addition, when one moves away from definitions of news that are producer oriented, and begins with the consumer, the very understanding of what constitutes news begins to blur, thus making it harder to conceptualize the relationship between news and audience. In a small project I did on audience reception and understandings of news in the United States (reported in Bird 1998, 2003), I found there was not even agreement on what news is – for some people, news includes talk shows, late-night comedians, parody news shows, tabloids, or reality TV, while for others it is confined to "straight news" and does not even encompass magazine shows like *60 Minutes* or newsmagazines like *Time*. Journalists' often rigid definitions of news have much less salience among the public. And a key conclusion of my study was that culturally, news is not really even about text – it is about process. In my study, I invited readers and viewers to talk, in a kind of contrived natural setting, about the news. People found it difficult to talk about specific texts in detail, but rather used them to frame a story that emerged in conversation. Explaining this process, a participant said, "When you watch by yourself, you have ideas that you have unsolved because you can't converse with other individuals." Another agreed that "it helps others in the community feel a part of the news world.... The community or the listeners get to contribute to the story and make the news effective and be part of the results." The rise of the internet and its multiple forums for such sharing has greatly expanded and complicated this process, of course. Thus the cultural significance of news emerges through everyday interaction. Second, people pay attention to news very selectively. In my study, I found that some news stories were especially significant because they spoke to people of different demographics in very different ways. In an analysis of online discussion of a news story about revelations that the Reverend Jesse Jackson had fathered an illegitimate daughter, I concluded that the story was used, not as a text with a clear meaning, but as an opportunity to interrogate issues, from morality, to religion, to race (Bird 2003). People do not evaluate news stories in isolation, but incorporate them into their already-established worldviews. Traditional journalistic concerns, such as whether the "message is clearly understood," tend to dissolve when one starts with the audience. However, a consequence of all these complications is that journalism scholars rarely tackle the reception of news in other than quantitative, text–response ways, and cultural studies scholars and anthropologists continue to focus primarily on entertainment genres.

News in Everyday Life: The News Habit

At this point, I turn attention to the questions posed earlier about the different ways we might look at news audiences, and what we can learn through these various approaches. First, we might consider the ways in which news is inserted in everyday routines, in ways that go beyond textual content. For many people, discussions about current events are an important part of their daily routines; for others, the importance of news is more personal and less shared, but may nevertheless help structure their lives. As newspaper readership declines, some fear that the news habit may die, yet more recent work is suggesting that while the habit may change with media, the need to stay connected does not.

As ethnographically informed scholarship on media audiences extends beyond studies of direct engagement with texts toward a consideration of broader cultural context, this approach is increasingly being framed in terms of media practices – what people do and say around and about media (Couldry 2004; Bird 2010). These arguments echo Carey (1975), who long ago advocated a ritual model of communication, arguing similarly that much media consumption is less about textual content and more about activities surrounding reception. As he wrote then, "[C]ulture must first be seen as a set of practices" (p. 19), some of which are the habitual activities surrounding news.

Academic interest in the news habit has a long history, dating back before Carey to Berelson's classic study of "what missing the newspaper means" (1949). Berelson researched people's sense of emotional loss when their morning newspapers disappeared because of the 1945 newspaper strike, concluding that the loss was less about missing specific information and more about an interruption in their daily schedule, and a sense of being disconnected from public discourse. Berelson talks about a "non-rational" attachment to news that prefigured more recent discussions of practices around news (although later interpretations would not frame this is in such overtly psychological terms). Decades later, Bentley (2001) conducted in-depth interviews with people who for various reasons had not received their daily paper. He summarizes older literature that explored the daily functions of news, from the uses and gratifications approach in which Berelson was working, through media dependency theory, ritual theory, and play theory. He concludes that while people find it very difficult to articulate what reading the newspaper really means to them,

> The unifying function of the newspaper buried in the comments of the respondents was of social integration. Whether it was by providing them news of their neigh-bors, helping them cope with the death of a friend or simply telling them that tuna was on sale at the market, the newspaper made survival in their community much easier and more enjoyable, a function of the community building ability of the press. (p. 14)

Jeffres et al. (2007) develop this notion of the unifying function of news reading, concluding that those who read newspapers and talk regularly about current events reported in the media are much more connected to their community, more politi-cally active, and more socially tolerant, a point also made by Norris (2000). Anthropologist Mark Peterson (2009) uses a more ethnographic approach to explore this broader context of news consumption as a habit with a significant social dimension – in this case, in urban India. He draws attention to

> the wide range of possible discoveries ethnography of news consumption may pro-duce once we abandon the nearly ubiquitous a priori assumption that news con-sumption is primarily about the transmission of content, and that contexts of consumption merely affect the nature of reading and interpretation. Instead … con-texts of consumption constitute social fields in which people engage in narrative and performatory constructions of themselves, reinforce social relations with other actors, negotiate status, engage in economic transactions, and imagine themselves and others as members of broader imagined communities. (p. 181)

Peterson shows how news consumption habits need to be understood in spe-cific cultural contexts; in India, particular habits connect with class, gender, and the postcolonial legacy. His work reminds us that news and its meanings are not the universals that Western journalists and journalism scholars often assume. Spitulnik (2009) makes a similar point in discussing her long-term ethnography in Zambia, where she explores the complexity of what news really is in a radio envi-ronment where "urgent private announcements" about funerals and other events have traditionally been a major part of the news landscape. Do people wanting to make these announcements constitute news makers or news audiences, or perhaps advertisers who should pay? How (if at all) is the circulation of such personal news connected to the news of the elite that we associate with journalism? Here, the news habit encompasses participation in practices that link media with interpersonal communication, and blur the distinction between news maker, text, and audience, while showing how dependent people are on the sense of connectedness provided by radio news.

Like newspapers and radio, television news has also been described as maintaining connections and a sense of community. Bourdan (2003), in an unusual study, used life history techniques to show how consumption of television, including news, has moved in predictable cycles:

> Changes in viewing habits are associated with major changes in the life cycle. Being a child, coming of age, leaving one's parents, marrying, divorcing, losing one's spouse: all these changes are naturally evoked by viewers when they recall changes of viewing habits. (p. 17)

In particular, attention to news increases with maturity. Bourdan's respondents recalled special news flashbulb moments, when major news events were first known, often in a communal setting. Gauntlett and Hill's (1999) unique longitudinal study, using self-reported diaries, shows that watching the news is frequently very much part of a daily routine. Within the family, teenagers and young adults develop an interest in the news from the example of parents, and eventually take up the news habit as they mature.

Today, however, we know that both newspaper reading and TV news viewing are declining, as younger generations are abandoning both and turning to the Internet. Barnhurst and Wartella (1998) suggest that the traditional life stages of news consumption, as people move to newspapers and serious TV news later in life, no longer hold true. Indeed, the changing news environment has precipitated something of a crisis for the profession of journalism, with grand assumptions being made about new generations of uninformed, distracted young people. Other research is suggesting that what may be happening is a reconceptualization about what news is and how it is delivered, rather than a rejection of news in itself. Barnhurst and Wartella (1998) argued that changes do not necessarily mean young people do not want the sense of connectedness that news provides: "Whatever it means to them to be citizens, to be political does not seem to require the services of television news" (p. 304). More recently, Meijer (2007) acknowledges that young people are not likely to become traditional news consumers, because they live in a totally different news environment:

> Because young people are almost permanently in contact with their peers, siblings or parents through various new means of communication, they feel no need to watch the news all the time. They will soon be informed about important news anyway. (p. 105)

Thus the habitual patterns of morning newspaper reading or evening TV newscast viewing are disappearing because they are no longer necessary to stay informed. Meijer (2007) studied news habits in a large sample of Dutch young people, using an impressive array of techniques that ranged from surveys to diaries, and concluded,

> Young people do not watch news as part of a daily routine.... Instead, young people watch news because TV is on and others are watching, because they happen to have nothing else to do at that moment. If while zapping they happen to run into news, some may watch it for a few minutes, but most will move on to another station after they have seen the headlines. (p. 104)

Meijer's respondents still have a clear sense that news is important to keep them informed about what is going on in the world. However, in a media environment in which almost every form of communication comes virtually (whether through computers, cell phones, or other devices), genres are even more blurred than on other media; news, entertainment, gossip, reality programming, and so on are all intertwined. Young people, like older generations, link citizenship and community with news, but may express it very differently, depending, for example, on virtual communities for support and action on political issues, rather than connecting with their immediate geographical neighbors.

News in Everyday Life: News Talk

The study of news reading as a habit or a practice is one way to approach the role of news in everyday life. From this perspective, the content of the news itself is less important than the various activities and social connections that come with attention to the news. The news habit can be studied most effectively by long-term ethnography, of the kind used by Peterson (2009), Spitulnik (2009), or Dracklé (2009), but it can also be approached quite effectively through self-reporting. Thus people can be asked to report how and how often they access news, with the emphasis being on the routine, rather than the content. At the same time, as both Madianou (2010) and Martin (2008) point out, there is a tendency for people to enhance self-reported news consumption. Observation may well contradict the reports of frequent attention to serious news and public affairs that many people feel obliged to claim; in-depth, qualitative forms of reporting that involve a more personal relationship between researcher and participant are more likely to avoid that problem, which is endemic with large-scale surveys.

As Madianou (2010) argues, a richer (and perhaps more accurate) understanding of news reception can be reached by using a variety of methods. One would be an analysis of how people engage with news, through what we might call *news talk* – the informal and often very active way that news stories are communicated among people, and meanings are made that may have more or less to do with the original intent of the journalist who created the text. In my own work (Bird 1992, 1998, 2003), I suggest that the "stories" of news emerge as much through interpersonal communication as from the specific texts.[3] However, there is relatively little scholarship done in this area, partly because of the difficulty of actually capturing everyday news conversations in natural settings. Once again, long-term ethnography is probably the ideal tool, as conversations about news emerge naturally in the course of observation. However, this is rarely a practical way for most scholars with limited time; one could imagine hours passing before any significant "data" emerged! Self-reporting methods, such as the diaries used by Gauntlett and Hill (1999) or Markham and Couldry (2007), go some way to addressing this gap, but do tend to shed light more on the "habit" than the actual engagement with news. A few researchers (myself included) have tried to create situations that as far as possible mimic everyday conversations, in an attempt to capture the often ephemeral everyday interactions with news. My way of doing this was to attempt to remove myself from the interaction, by setting up an admittedly artificial situation in which viewers watched some recorded news programs, and then conversed on tape about them. While focusing primarily on news as a routine, Martin (2008) created opportunities for people to gather and talk about news, such as in book clubs. She noted, for instance, that people tend not to discuss political news in the workplace, reserving that kind of discussion for close family and friends.

McCallum (2009) uses a form of discourse analysis to look at how news on indigenous affairs is received by Australians. Having already mapped the framing of news reporting on Indigenous issues, she does not ask participants to respond directly to specific news accounts. Rather,

> My fieldwork entailed recording, in participants' local settings, over 50 conversations with groups and individuals about a wide range of Indigenous issues. Using qualitative grounded theory techniques to analyse the data, it was established that participants spoke about Indigenous issues using four main narrative themes and 12 distinct narratives. (p. 152)

Her subtle approach shows how media frames are understood, but transformed and added to by the everyday talk of people who are both media audiences and members of their own discursive communities. However, capturing somewhat natural talk about news is extremely difficult and time-consuming; as Tewkesbury (2003) writes, "The upshot of all this is that communication researchers have an incomplete picture of how people receive the news" (p. 695).

Perhaps the most exciting development in capturing everyday news talk has been the rise of the internet. As Tewkesbury (2003) comments, "New technologies are changing the nature of news reading and providing new opportunities for studying ... behavior" (p. 695). As newspaper reading and TV news watching decline, and people move to the internet, there may be fewer opportunities for people to talk in person about news – internet news consumption use is generally solitary, is not tied to specific times, and is often tailored closely to individual tastes and interests. At the same time, the rise of newsgroups and other online forums offers new possibilities for everyday news-related interactions. Some scholars have suggested that the future of newspapers lies in encouraging reader involvement through interactive environments associated with virtual versions of their print edition. An interesting study by Gray (2007) suggests that news fan communities are vibrant forums where news is energetically discussed, and where civic awareness and interest in trivial news may not be mutually exclusive.

Can the internet, then, provide us with an opportunity to peek into the everyday news talk that has shifted from the living room to the virtual world? Is it possible that the decline of newspaper reading and TV news watching can actually lead to the creation of new, informed communities in which news has a different but equally significant role? Gray's work suggests that, and Rosen (2006) argues, "Now the horizontal flow, citizen-to-citizen, is as real and consequential as the vertical one."

While optimistic about this possibility, I would also like to sound a note of caution, based on some preliminary study of online comment sections associated with newspaper sites. I found these forums interesting because they appear to resemble everyday conversations about news, possibly akin to the kind of water cooler conversations we might seek to capture through ethnographic observation. However, my analysis of both the content and tone of the online discourse suggests that they are very different from face-to-face conversation.

I use two groups of data to discuss this. First, I use data gathered as part of a larger ongoing study of public discourse on the teaching of human evolution in US public schools. Public debate about this peaked in the state of Florida as its State Board of Education debated whether to mandate the teaching of evolution as part of revised science standards in schools – an action it approved in February 2008, against considerable opposition. This decision was then followed by attempts by conservative legislators to introduce bills allowing teachers to offer both their own criticisms and alternative positions (such as "intelligent design") in the classroom. In addition to doing interpretive content analysis of news stories, I also studied online comment sections in two newspapers, the *St. Petersburg Times* and the *Tampa Tribune*, in the months following the decision. A total of 23 stories were analyzed. Second, I have also been studying the online comments associated with generally popular stories in *the Tribune*. My goal in both cases was to try to develop a sense of the nature of this news talk. Did the commenters engage with the content of the stories and debate them, and what was the quality of that debate? How was online discussion like or unlike personal conversation? And, more broadly, can we learn anything from this about the future of civic engagement?

In both cases, I found there was relatively little discussion of news content. Indeed, many contributors do not even address the particular story, but simply use it as a catalyst to express an opinion. Stories about evolution, for instance, consistently caused contributors to divide into distinct evolution and creation camps. A typical example is a *Tampa Tribune* story from April 24, 2008 (White 2008), that reported on the narrow passage in the Florida Senate of the bill to allow "academic freedom" to teachers to criticize evolution (the measure was later defeated by the entire legislature). The story triggered four pages of comments that remained on the site, as well as many more that were removed because of abusive language. Almost none debate the central issue of the article; instead, participants begin stating and restating their existing positions on evolution generally, in identical terms as they use in all stories about the topic. Many postings are quite long – the longest is 495 words – as representatives from each camp detail their "evidence," as well as their characterizations of their opponents. Some excerpts illustrate the way the insults develop (online screen names removed):

- Why are Darwinists so afraid of debate when they can't even prove their theory in a scientific laboratory? Evolution is a religion in itself.
- Do you folks never tire of the same tedious and specious arguments?… C'mon, think a little. If you bring preexisting beliefs about invisible intelligences, you don't get to play.
- By stating that the Theory of Evolution is a religion, you have proven your ignorance of science and said theory. You should be ashamed of yourself for your un-American behavior. It is this exact kind of thing that caused the Founding Fathers to include the clause prohibiting the establishment of a state religion. You would undo the history of America and its founding principles. You, sir, are a traitor.
- The anti-Godly Theory of Evolution relies quite a bit on "belief" and could not be taught without Freedom of Speech … the anti-Godly want to deny Freedom of Speech in the classroom so that those theories cannot be heard or taught. Sounds like Soviet Communism all over again.
- Perhaps you should go to a creationist doctor and tell him you do not wish to be availed of any medical technology that has grown out of science…. It was nice of you to provide an article showing how vicious, underhanded so-called Christians will do anything to suppress the truth.
- I guess all that talk about being tolerant of others views was really just baloney just like the theory of evolution is baloney.
- The Truth will make you free…. For those of you who really believe in the bubbles of Evolution because it was taught as fact in school, I'm sorry for popping your bubbles but the truth will make you free… for those of you who are anti-God zombies marching to Marxist/Leninist Communism, I pity you.

Although I have presented these comments in a kind of point–counterpoint format, these comments are not being traded between one pair of posters, but actually represent several contributors. The tone of the debate is not collaborative, building on the various views expressed. Rather it resembles the type of debate structure often seen between US political candidates – each one states a position, and neither engages directly with the other.

The evolution–creation issue is perhaps atypical because the opposing positions have become so entrenched in US culture, and in this case news does not function to enlighten but simply to stimulate constant restating of the same discussion, often in abusive terms. What about the more random, daily flow of stories that are read and commented on each day in the *Tampa Tribune* and online editions of other newspapers across the country? First, the lists of most viewed stories are revealing. Tewkesbury (2003), like other researchers, notes that while people typically report paying most attention to news about public affairs, when tracked online, this is not the case. Rather, readers seek out stories about entertainment, crime, and various human interest topics. That certainly is true on the *Tribune*, which regularly lists the "most viewed" and "most commented" stories.

To reach a sense of the most popular kinds of stories, I read all the "top three" stories in the Metro (city news) section of the paper for the month of October 2008, along with the accompanying comments (I avoided the national news section, which was dominated by coverage of the upcoming presidential election; local and state elections, however, were the domain of the Metro section). In the interests of space, I will discuss here only the top three (not rank-ordered) stories for October 31, which seemed very typical. None was about public affairs. These were

- "Tampa Woman Charged with Felony Child Neglect," a brief story that reported on the arrest of a woman whose home and children were reportedly found in a filthy and neglected state;
- "Missing Teeth Gum Up Relationship," which described a knife fight between a woman and her live-in boyfriend, whom she accused of stealing her false teeth; and
- "Gunman Robs Girl at School Bus Stop," about an armed robber stealing from a 15-year-old girl waiting at a bus stop.

It could certainly be argued that none of these stories was especially informative, but each was apparently quite entertaining. In fact, they are very much like the stories that participants in my earlier study (Bird 2003) found most memorable and that spurred them into enthusiastic conversation. As I wrote then, "[F]rom an audience point of view, the best stories are those that leave room for speculation, for debate, and for a degree of audience 'participation'" (p. 41). And, to some extent, we see the same process online, as people bring their own experiences to bear on the story at hand. However, it was striking that the collaborative quality of face-to-face communication seems to disappear online. In my earlier study, participants talked about how their sense of the story was reached through conversation. As one participant noted, "I want to hear everyone's opinion about what's going on in the news. There's something in their view that I can use, and hopefully there's something in my view that can contribute to making theirs better" (p. 42).

The tone of the online discussions is markedly different – much more aggressive, and quite often hateful. The most vitriolic comments are typically removed by site staff almost immediately, especially those that are overtly racist, but many still remain. I will look briefly at each of the "top three" stories to illustrate this. Comments on the first story are characterized by assumptions about the woman's status as a welfare freeloader, and frequently address race indirectly (the accompanying photo shows that she is African American):

- She's a filthy nasty two-bit ho!
- Thank god they arrested her today, on Tuesday we will be sharing the wealth with her [this refers to the November 4, 2008, US presidential election; black candidate Barack Obama had made a widely quoted comment about the need to "share the wealth" through tax changes].
- By "socializing with friends" do ya mean, hookin?... I have no doubt she's been on the receiving end of our redistributed wealth for a couple generations already. I'll bet she gets her nails done every week!

The second story elicited nine pages of comment, all derisory in the extreme.

- This took place in a mobile home? Hmmmm??
- Can you imagine the fracas if she had misplaced her diaphragm?
- What a typical bunch of trailer trash ... do any of them see a shrink?

While the commenters were united in their mockery, they also began to snipe at each other, with people claiming that "white trash" people like this are natural Obama voters, while others noted the plethora of signs for Republican candidate John McCain in such "trailer trash" areas. Thus the discussion moves away from the story itself, and into often mean-spirited characterizations of fellow contributors, based on stereotypes.

The third story, perhaps unexpectedly, became a major opportunity for political name calling and insults. A few commenters began with fairly innocuous comments about the need to be vigilant while waiting alone at dawn or dusk, or simply bemoaned the declining state of civility. The tone soon changed:

- When Obama isn't elected, the thugs will all be coming for you. Lock and load.
- If Obama is not elected no one will have any money to steal, we will be in a depression waiting for jobs and wages to trickle down, just like workers in China, we will probably have to join the Buddhist religion too.
- It's fortunate this girl wasn't hurt or killed. Since Obama wants to "spread the wealth around" the middle class will be supporting more people. "Spreading the wealth" – isn't that the same as living in a commune? Everyone better run, not walk, to your nearest gun store....
- When McCain wins the election, all the Obama supporters will riot & claim bias against the candidate. The foolishness of the school bus robbery is just the beginning.

One might argue that this story became an opportunity to debate politics – but in reality, it simply devolved into a flurry of virtual insults that one could not imagine happening "around the water cooler." This pattern occurs repeatedly in the online comments. A story about a civic award for a person working with migrant families spurs readers to vitriolic attacks on the supposed evils of illegal immigration. Stories about crime routinely produce racist diatribes, and so on. Such forums actually free people to talk in ways they would not do face-to-face, which of course has some advantages in terms of facilitating open discussion. However, it does tend to change the nature of talk about news, producing rapid polarization rather than thoughtful discussion – or even the empathetic, personal responses I found in my earlier study. As noted above, both Martin (2008) and Madianou (2010) point out that in a face-to-face environment, people are very careful about the topics and tone of news talk, reserving hot button topics for those with whom they feel most familiar and comfortable. The online environment – especially on open forums in which there is no sense of community rules – often removes these constraints. While Jeffres et al. (2007) correlate traditional newspaper reading and interpersonal news talk with greater levels of tolerance, might we expect to see a correlation between participation on online sites and increased intolerance? At this point it is too early to tell.

In any event, I would caution against too easily treating online news talk as an unproblematic surrogate for face-to-face talk. This can often be tempting because of the rich data that can easily be gathered – how much simpler to monitor news forums than set up focus groups or observe people's everyday interactions! Yet we sometimes forget that online communication varies very much according to context. There is much written about virtual groups and whether they really nurture a sense of community. I believe they can – but not all online communication encourages the collaborative, constructive interaction that leads to shared action. When it comes to news, news fan groups with regular contributors (like the ones Gray studied) seem to produce a different kind of measured and respectful discourse than the more random, scattered comments that appear on general newspaper sites and quickly escalate to hostility. Just as we have to understand offline activities as happening within specific contexts with particular rules and expectations, we should be careful about understanding the precise context of online interactions before concluding that they represent news reception in general.

Direct Audience Response to News

So far, I have focused attention more toward audience practices around news and less toward direct response to specific news texts (although, of course, news talk does comprise response, if often in fairly diffuse ways). Does this mean we should not study direct response? I would say absolutely not. One of the very valid critiques of the entire tradition of active audience research is that it can lead to a perception that people can make any meaning from texts – that audience response is infinitely polysemous. To some extent the meaning of news actually is somewhat independent of content, as my discussion above suggests. People use news as a catalyst for much broader, social discussions, which is one reason why people tend to attend more to human interest news than important stories. I have long argued that in its ritualistic, community-building role, trivial news allows us to interrogate morality and dialogue with others about shared values. News is not just about the successful transmission of information.

However, people do engage directly with textual content. They use news to seek out information, to learn about what is happening in the world, and to make important decisions. Almost everyone rejects the idea that they are influenced by media; the notion of individual autonomy is powerful. And yet where else can we get information about the state of the world than from the media, especially the news media? Indeed, although Hall's influential model of encoding and decoding was the spark that ignited the explosion of active audience work, he himself did not argue for complete polysemy, being deeply interested in the ideological power of media, especially of news. Nevertheless, his model of the active audience was embraced enthusiastically, especially by those studying entertainment or fictional media.[4]

The idea of true polysemy has been less convincing when applied to news. Morley's pioneering *Nationwide* study (1980) has been regarded as the closest attempt to show the many meanings that can be made from television news, as focus groups comment directly about specific news stories. Morley shows that audience readings of news do vary, as people bring their own identity, experience, and personal knowledge to the table. Martin (2008) continues this tradition, showing how racial identity is a key filter through which news is passed, and drawing on earlier work by Lind (1996). Philo (2010) notes that Morley's work "focused attention on how class and cultural factors could produce different responses to encoded messages" (p. 414). Yet, at the same time, the model "underestimates the power of the media in shaping 'taken for granted' beliefs" (p. 414). Speaking as a member of the influential Glasgow Media Group, one of the few research collaborations that has addressed the power of news over an extended period, Philo (2010) writes,

> We have not in our work underestimated the capacity of audiences to engage actively with texts. But nonetheless, there is a powerful body of evidence which shows the influence of media messages on the construction of public knowledge as well as the manner in which evaluations are made about social action and what is seen as necessary, possible and desirable in our world. For us, media power is still very much on the research agenda. (p. 542)

As Philo and others point out (see Bird and Dardenne 2008; Ruddock 2008), audiences can only engage with the texts they are given; dominant meanings are inscribed. From this, it follows that when we seek to explore how audiences interact in their daily lives with news, an important dimension must be to investigate direct response to specific texts. Analysis of news content can show how stories are framed, but what are the consequences of this for readers and viewers? In fact, we know little about how journalism narratives enter daily life and consciousness. We may argue, for example, that the European press framed the Iraq War in terms of civilian tragedy rather than heroic military success, because scholars find it in the texts (Bird and Dardenne 2008). But is that translated by those who use the media into everyday perceptions and, more important, into action? And if so, how and with what result? These questions are very difficult to answer; most scholars now agree that a simple cause–effect relationship between text and response/ action is almost impossible to demonstrate, even as we all know that media do impact our lives in profound ways.

There is some work that directly addresses this issue and sheds light on the ways specific news frames are received and interpreted. Philo's extensive work is exemplary in this regard. For example, Philo and Berry (2004) showed that news stories on the Palestinian–Israel conflict are often read in ways that simply confirm audience members' existing beliefs, a point also made by Liebes (1997). Yet when given new information about the conflict, individuals modified their views – what is included or excluded in the dominant narrative is important. In the absence of competing narratives, or (importantly) personal experience that contradicts the dominant story (Madianou 2007), the ability of audiences to produce oppositional readings is much less than the semiotic democracy celebrated by such "active audience" proponents as Fiske (1987).[5] Morley himself (1992) argues that while the audience can reinterpret texts, the power of the audience cannot compete with the "discursive power of centralized media institutions to construct the texts" (p. 31).

However, we still know very little about this crucial question, and there is much to be done. As Madianou (2008) argues, "News is the main means for the mediation of conflict and war, as well as for the mediation of otherness ... There is a moral and ethical argument to be made about researching the place of news in a transnational world" (p. 332). There are signs of newer work that addresses close readings of Otherness in interesting ways. For example, Mendelson and Darling-Wolf (2009) explore the neglected area of how text and images are received by readers. Using a *National Geographic* illustrated story about Saudi Arabia as a case study, they presented readers with the complete story (with photos), the text alone, or the photos alone before conducting qualitative interviews. They found that the text and images essentially told separate and often contradictory stories, with the power of the rather stereotypical images (of camel races and "warriors") often drowning the much more nuanced narrative of the text. They productively draw on social psychological work on mental processing while reaching provocative conclusions that speak at a more cultural level and invite more studies of this type. Combined with news production studies of how images are selected (e.g. Gürsel 2009), we might learn much about the circulation and normalization of dominant narratives of difference.

The News Audience in the Digital World

As we enter the second decade of the twenty-first century, many people continue to get most of their news through mainstream corporate media, and it is still important that we interrogate not only the stories provided to us but also how people receive them, talk about them, and insert them into their daily lives. At the same time, the news habit, as documented by researchers with a primary interest in newspapers and television news, is drastically changing, and the situation offers many new opportunities to explore the audience for news.

First, we need to learn more about what the news habit means for new generations. As noted above, younger people are consuming their news differently, and, as Meijer (2007) and Martin (2008) suggest, they are not necessarily making the same kind of generic distinctions between news and other forms of information that older generations and journalists find familiar. They simply absorb and disseminate information all the time. As Deuze (2005) comments, "The bottom line: as media become inescapably pervasive in the everyday lives of people in modern nations ... their day-to-day use tends to disappear." In other words, being a media audience member is basically what people do continually; Deuze mentions that in new studies, people find it almost impossible to accurately state how much time they spend with media. What are the implications of this? On the one hand, perhaps it will lead to an empowered, informed citizenry who will know more about the world than ever before. On the other, some fear that information overload, and a demonstrated preference for celebrity gossip and YouTube trivia over serious issues, will result in a world of distracted and self-absorbed consumers, for whom serious news is an anachronism.

Second, we might look at the increased power and voice that the digital world offers the audience, should they choose to engage. Robinson (2009), for instance, provides a careful case study of the Spokane, Washington, *Spokesman Review*'s coverage of a pedophilia scandal involving its mayor. She described a coherent, conventional story that fit familiar narrative frames emerging over the course of a month-long investigation. However, simultaneous with the printed story, a "cyber newsroom" on the paper's own website made available interviews, documents, and multiple forms of information, and people dissected and analyzed the information, often offering their own sometimes radically different versions of the "official" stories. Readers, interacting with journalists, the news content, and other readers, helped form an online news narrative:

> If readers took issue with the coverage, they had the newspaper's own space to criticize the journalism.... Like reporters, readers utilized quotation marks and hyperlinks to source the material.... This sharing of information production changed the dynamics of the journalism resulting in a re-negotiation of the news paradigm within cyberspace. (pp. 417–18)

A cacophony of narratives increasingly competes with mainstream journalism to define the day's stories. News audiences pick and choose stories they want to attend to and believe, and select from a seemingly endless supply of information to assemble their own versions. This too has caused alarm; Keen (2007), for example, argues that the rise of the amateur, online audience is disastrous, stripping journalists of authority to shape stories, which creates a relativistic world devoid of "the telling of common stories, the formation of communal myths, the shared sense of participating in the same daily narrative of life" (p. 80).

Third, and developing from the second point, the digital environment now allows audiences not only to respond more richly, but also to actually generate news themselves. Rosen (2006), in a much-blogged statement, claims that the new context has finally destroyed the concept of "the audience" for news:

> The people formerly known as the audience are those who *were* on the receiving end of a media system that ran one way, in a broadcasting pattern, with high entry fees and a few firms competing to speak very loudly while the rest of the population listened in isolation from one another – and who *today* are not in a situation like that *at all*. (2006, emphasis in original)

Jenkins (2006) has become the champion of convergence culture, in which the audience and producer are one, with audiences themselves creating news through blogs, wikis, Twitter, and so on. This image of the "produser" is several steps beyond the idea of online "news talk"; what does it mean for the study of news audiences? In my view, we should not too hastily abandon more traditional approaches or conceptualizations of news reception. We are by no means all produsers of news, given the vast economic disparities that affect global access to the virtual world. Much online news is not particularly profound or creative, with much of it simply recycling existing opinion and information. Can citizen journalism adequately replace the role of the professional investigative journalist once the new media environment drives newspapers out of business? On the other hand, some argue that the rise of the amateur opens rich new possibilities for cooperative partnerships between journalism and the people who once were traditional "audiences" (Gillmor 2006). In any event, these new contexts offer us opportunities to study "audiencing" in new and ever-mutating forms.

Finally, a topic ripe for renewed scholarly attention is audience interpretation and use of visual images, which have always played key roles in defining journalistic narratives, from Matthew Brady's Civil War photos and those from Vietnam and Iraq, to the Rodney King video, images of Tiananmen Square defiance, planes striking the Twin Towers, and the toppling of a statue of Saddam Hussein. Case studies like that of Mendelson and Darling-Wolf (2009) are illuminating, but their study is positioned in the traditional context of printed story and audience. Today, both professionals and citizens easily create, manipulate, and instantaneously transport digital images across the world through various and ubiquitous technologies (Taylor 2000), as we have seen dramatically in the cases of dissent in Iran and the 2010 Haiti earthquake. What story would have emerged from Abu Ghraib without digital snapshots taken by amused soldiers with cell phones? What have been the consequences of "protecting" Americans from horrifying images, common elsewhere in the world, of mutilated Iraqi children? The creation, manipulation, and dissemination of images; their combination with words; the public's interpretation of them; and their roles in the way dominant narratives gain ascendancy offer enormous potential for important, interesting, and necessary research.

Conclusion

News is among the most difficult genres to define, and its audience difficult to identify for study. News comprises texts and images that people see, read, and interpret, and we need to continue to develop ways to investigate that interaction. And news is also unformed snippets of information that pass through our communities and eventually coalesce into opinions that produce action. Darnton (2000) describes the dissemination of news in eighteenth-century Paris, where to stay informed,

> You went to the tree of Cracow. It was a large, leafy chestnut tree, which stood at the heart of Paris in the gardens of the Palais-Royal.... Like a mighty magnet, the tree attracted *nouvellistes de bouche*, or newsmongers, who spread information about current events by word of mouth. They claimed to know, from private sources (a letter, an indiscreet servant, a remark overheard in an antechamber of Versailles), what was really happening in the corridors of power and the people in power took them seriously, because the government worried about what Parisians were saying. (p. 2, emphasis in original)

The internet may have replaced the tree of Cracow, but the dissemination and reception of news today are similarly diffuse and perhaps even harder to capture. But it is equally important that the "people in power" do not have a monopoly of information, and that we continue to study the day-to-day messiness of the complex and varied relationships of news and its audiences.

Notes

1 This chapter, although significantly lengthened, incorporates most of the material published as Bird, S.E. 2010 News practices in everyday life: beyond audience response. In S. Allan, ed. *The Routledge Companion to News and Journalism.* Routledge, London, pp. 417–427.

2   There are notable exceptions, particularly the work of both David Morley and the Glasgow Media Group, to which I will return.
3   Hall (1980) defined the "encoding-decoding" model, having used it in Hall (1976). Morley (1980) is the best-known early application of the approach.
4   As much of my previous work indicates, I do not mean to suggest that there is a clear difference between "news" and "entertainment." However, I do believe that audiences maintain a conceptual distinction between "reality" and "fiction," however frayed that may have become in today's media environment, and thus they do feel much freer to remake fictional texts, which can indeed become genuinely polysemous in the hands of the audience-producer.
5   For a more detailed critique, see the conclusion of Bird (1992), in which I take issue with Fiske and others' celebration of the liberating potential of tabloids, which often publish absurd interpretations of scientific subjects.

References

Barnhurst, K.G. and Wartella, E. 1998 Young citizens, American TV newscasts and the collective memory. *Critical Studies in Mass Communication*, 15, 279–305.

Bentley, C. 2001 No newspaper is no fun – even five decades later. *Newspaper Research Journal*, 22, 4, pp. 2–15.

Berelson, B. 1949 What "missing the newspaper" means. In P.F. Lazarsfeld and F.N. Stanton, eds. *Communications Research, 1948–1949*. Harper, New York.

Bird, S.E. 1992 *For Enquiring Minds: A Cultural Study of Supermarket Tabloids*. University of Tennessee Press, Knoxville.

Bird, S.E. 1998 News we can use: an audience perspective on the tabloidisation of news in the United States. *Javnost: Journal of the European Institute for Communication and Culture*, 3, pp. 33–50.

Bird, S.E. 2003 *The Audience in Everyday Life: Living in a Media World*. Routledge, New York

Bird, S.E. 2009 The anthropology of news and journalism: why now? In S.E. Bird, ed. *The Anthropology of News and Journalism: Global Perspectives*. Indiana University Press, Bloomington, pp. 1–18.

Bird, S.E. 2010 Mediated practices and the interpretation of culture. In J. Postill and B. Braeuchler, eds. *Theorising Media and Practice*. Berghahn, Oxford.

Bird, S.E. and Dardenne, R.W. 2008 News as myth and storytelling: lessons and challenges. In K. Wahl-Jorgenson and T. Hanisch, eds. *Handbook of Journalism Studies*. Routledge, London, pp. 205–217.

Bourdan, J. 2003 Some sense of time: remembering television. *History and Memory*, 15, 2, pp. 5–35.

Carey, J.W. 1975 A cultural approach to communication. *Communication*, 2, pp. 1–10, 17–21.

Couldry, N. 2004 Theorising media as practice. *Social Semiotics*, 14, 2, pp. 115–132.

Darnton, R. 2000 An early information society: news and the media in eighteenth-century Paris. *The American Historical Review*, 105, 1, pp. 1–35.

Deuze, M. 2005 Toward professional participatory storytelling in journalism and advertising. *First Monday*, 10, 7. Retrieved from http://firstmonday.org/htbin/cgiwrap/bin/ojs/index.php/fm/article/viewArticle/1257/

Dracklé, D. 2009 Gossip and resistance: local news media in transition, a case study from the Alentejo, Portugal. In S.E. Bird, ed. *The Anthropology of News and Journalism: Global Perspectives*. Indiana University Press, Bloomington, pp. 199–214.

Fiske, J. 1987 *Television Culture*. Routledge, London.

Gauntlett, D. and Hill, A. 1999 *TV Living*. Routledge, London

Gillmor, D. 2006 *We the Media: Grassroots Journalism by the People, for the People*. O'Reilly Media, Sebastopol, CA.

Gray, J. 2007. The news: you gotta love it! In J. Gray, C. Sandvoss and C.L. Harrington, eds. *Fandom*. New York University Press, New York.

Gürsel, Z.D. 2009 US Newsworld: the rule of text and everyday practices of editing the world. In S.E. Bird, ed. *The Anthropology of News and Journalism: Global Perspectives*. Indiana University Press, Bloomington, pp. 35–53.

Hall, S. 1976 The determination of news photographs. In S. Cohen and J. Young, eds. *The Manufacture of News: Social Problems, Deviance and the Mass Media*. Constable, London, pp. 176–190.

Hall, S. 1980 Encoding/decoding. In S. Hall, D. Hobson, A. Lowe and P. Willis, eds. *Culture, Media, Language: Working Papers in Cultural Studies, 1972–1979*. Hutchinson, London, pp. 128–138.

Hartley, J. 2008 The supremacy of ignorance over instruction and of numbers over knowledge. *Journalism Studies*, 9, 5, pp. 679–691.

Jeffres, L.W., Lee, J., Neuendorf, K. and Atkin, D. 2007 Newspaper reading supports community involvement. *Newspaper Research Journal*, 28, 1, pp. 6–23.

Jenkins, H. 2006 *Convergence Culture*. New York University Press, New York.

Keen, A. 2007 *The Cult of the Amateur: How Today's Internet Is Killing Our Culture*. Doubleday, New York.

Lazarsfeld, P., Berelson, B. and Gaudet, H. 1944 *The People's Choice*. Columbia University Press, New York.

Liebes, T. 1997 *Reporting the Israeli–Arab Conflict: How Hegemony Works*. Routledge, London.

Lind, R. 1996 Diverse interpretations: the "relevance" of race in the construction of meaning in, and the evaluation of, a television news story. *Howard Journal of Communications*, 7, pp. 53–74.

Madianou, M. 2007 Shifting identities: banal nationalism and cultural intimacy in Greek television news and everyday life. In R. Mole, ed. *Discursive Constructions of Identity in European Politics*. Palgrave, London, pp. 95–118.

Madianou, M. 2008 Audience reception and news in everyday life. In K. Wahl-Jorgensen and T. Hanitzsch, *The Handbook of Journalism Studies*. Routledge, London, pp. 325–337.

Madianou, M. 2010 Living with news: ethnographies of news consumption. In S. Allan, ed. *The Routledge Companion to News and Journalism*. Routledge, London, pp. 428–438.

Markham, T. and Couldry, N. 2007 Tracking the reflexivity of the (dis)engaged citizen: some methodological reflections. *Qualitative Inquiry*, 13, 5, pp. 675–695.

Martin, V. 2008 Attending the news: a grounded theory about a daily regimen, *Journalism*, 9, 1, pp. 76–94.

McCallum, K. 2009 News and local talk: conversations about the "crisis of indigenous violence" in Australia. In S.E. Bird, ed. *The Anthropology of News and Journalism: Global Perspectives*. Indiana University Press, Bloomington, pp. 151–167.

Meijer, I.C. 2007 The paradox of popularity. *Journalism Studies*, 8, 1, pp. 96–116.

Mendelson, A.L. and Darling-Wolf, F. 2009 Readers interpretations of visual and verbal narratives of a *National Geographic* story on Saudi Arabia. *Journalism: Theory, Practice, and Criticism*, 1, 6, pp. 798–818.

Morley, D. 1980 *The "Nationwide" Audience: Structure and Decoding*. British Film Institute, London.

Morley, D. 1992 *Television, Audiences, and Cultural Studies*. Routledge, London.

Norris, P. 2000 *A Virtuous Circle: Political Communications in the Post-industrial Democracies*. Cambridge University Press, New York.

Peterson, M.A. 2009 Getting the news in New Delhi: newspaper literacies in an Indian mediascape. In S.E. Bird, ed. *The Anthropology of News and Journalism: Global Perspectives*. Indiana University Press, Bloomington, pp. 168–181.

Philo, G. 2010 News, audiences, and the construction of public knowledge. In S. Allan, ed. *The Routledge Companion to News and Journalism*. Routledge, London, pp. 407–416.

Philo, G. and Berry, N. 2004 *Bad News from Israel*. Pluto, London.

Robinson, S. 2009 The cyber newsroom: A case study of the journalistic paradigm in a news narrative's journey from a newspaper to cyberspace. *Mass Communication & Society*, 12, 4, 403–22.

Rosen, J. 2006 The people formerly known as the audience. Retrieved from http:journalism.nyu.edu/pubzone/weblogs/pressthink/2006/06/27/ppl_frmr.html

Ruddock, A. 2008 Media studies 2.0? Binge drinking and why audiences still matter. *Sociology Compass*, 2, 1, pp. 1–15.

Spitulnik, D. 2009 Personal news and the price of public service: an ethnographic window into the dynamics of production and reception in Zambian state radio. In S.E. Bird, ed. *The Anthropology of News and Journalism: Global Perspectives*. Indiana University Press, Bloomington, pp. 182–198.

Tampa police: gunman robs girl at school bus stop. 2008 *Tampa Tribune*, 31 October. Retrieved from http://www2.tbo.com/content/2008/oct/31/tampa-police-gunman-robs-girl-school-bus-stop/news-metro/

Tampa police: Missing teeth gum up relationship. 2008 *Tampa Tribune*, 31 October. Retrieved from http://www2.tbo.com/content/2008/oct/31/311634/tampa-police-womans-missing-teeth-gum-relationship/news-metro/

Tampa woman charged with felony child neglect. 2008 *Tampa Tribune*, 31 October. Retrieved from http://www2.tbo.com/content/2008/oct/31/tampa-woman-charged-felony-child-neglect/c_2/#comments

Taylor, J. 2000 Problems in photojournalism: realism, the nature of news, and the humanitarian narrative. *Journalism Studies*, 1, 1, 129–143.

Tewkesbury, D. 2003 What do Americans really want to know? Tracking the behavior of news readers on the Internet. *Journal of Communication*, 694–710.

Wahl-Jorgensen, K. and Hanitzsch, T. 2008 *The Handbook of Journalism Studies*. Routledge, London.

White, N.M. 2008 Senate approves evolution bill. *Tampa Tribune*, 24 April. Retrieved from http://www2.tbo.com/content/2008/apr/24/me-senate-approves-evolution-bill/

26

Sport and Its Audiences

David Rowe

Introduction: An Audience for and with Sport

Writing in April 1970, seemingly in the late evening, the eminent cultural theorist Raymond Williams was disenchanted with the state of British television. Still, he consoled his readers in his regular newspaper column on television in the BBC's weekly journal *The Listener*, "There's always the sport. Or so people say, more and more often, as they become sadder about what is happening to the rest of television" (Williams 1970/1989, p. 95). Williams saw that, if television was failing to realize its promise in other genres and for other purposes, it could be relied upon to deliver sport to good effect. Television, he noted a few years later, had not created spectator sport – urban industrialized leisure had done that – but it had stimulated interest among spectators and provided a new mode of watching sport, because "some of the best television coverage of sport, with its detailed close-ups and its variety of perspectives, has given us a new excitement and immediacy in watching physical action, and even a new visual experience of a distinct kind" (Williams 1974, p. 68). While for Williams television had taken up the practice of engaging in "sporting gossip" long evident within newspapers and among sport supporters and fans, its métier was that it could inexpensively "transmit something that was in any case happening or had happened" (p. 30).

It is useful to reflect, from the current vantage point, on Williams's brief account of the relationship between sport and media, and to consider the continuities and ruptures within media sport over the last four decades, especially with regard to audiences. It is clear that sport is still crucial to television – and that television is vital for sport. Of all the forms of media sport, television is still dominant because of its as-yet-unrivalled capacity to represent "live" events to vast, widely dispersed audiences in a manner that plausibly simulates a sense of "having been there"

The Handbook of Media Audiences, First Edition. Edited by Virginia Nightingale.
© 2014 John Wiley & Sons, Ltd. Published 2014 by John Wiley & Sons, Ltd.

(Whannel 1992; Brookes 2002; Rowe and Stevenson 2006). Television also constitutes a sprawling media space where, as Williams notes, sport and sport-related matters can be endlessly discussed, previewed, and reviewed (Boyle and Haynes 2000; Rowe 2004a). Thus, television and the media that preceded and then accompanied it have been central to the extension of sport audiences beyond the stadium, in the process refashioning media audiences. It is to these formations – which are multiple rather than singular – that the focus of this chapter will turn.

Audience Formation Pre- and Post Mediatization

Sport and sport spectatorship first emerged within an almost entirely place-based experiential framework. Indeed, what we call *sport* – in the sense of regular, regulated physical competitive activity with a paying audience and paid performers – is, as Williams observed above, a product of modernity, industrialism, capitalism, and urbanization. Importantly, what is recognizable in the twenty-first century as sport is of Western European (specifically British) origin, and emerged out of folk games of a highly ritualized, episodic nature where there was no rigid distinction between performer and audience (Elias and Dunning 1986). What we today call sport is the product of two principal forces of modernity – the development of common rules and of organizations responsible for the governance of sport (Miller et al. 2001), and the commoditization of physical pastimes producing professional performers and spectators who supported them through payment to enter enclosed performances spaces (stadia) in local, then national and international contexts. At this point, the print media became important both to service the developing sport audience and to help recruit new adherents to sport (recording the results of contests, describing and discussing them for those who were both present and absent, and advertising forthcoming sport events and associated activities such as drinking and gambling) through text and still photography.

The subsequent development of audiovisual media, including newsreels in cinemas and domestic radio sets, rendered striking visual images of past sport events in the case of the former and often compelling "as-it-happened" commentary regarding the latter. When television became a regular feature of homes in the West in the middle of the twentieth century, these features could be combined and, with the development of color, replay, multicamera, and slow motion televisual technologies (Whannel 1992), could claim to replicate and even better the experience of in-stadium spectatorship. Here the sport audience was divided in two – the physically present engaged in a monetary exchange and the mediated audience that gained access without significant charge (apart from the cost of a set, power, and perhaps a state-imposed TV license). It is unsurprising that sports organizations were at first suspicious of television, seeing it as a potential drain on paying spectators who could feel that they were present without incurring the cost and inconvenience of watching in real time and space. The political economy of sport and television adjusted to this rivalry between types of audience when television companies began competing commercially for the rights to broadcast sport.

In Europe, this commodification of the representation rather than simply the performance of sport saw a shift from the pioneering public service broadcasters like the BBC who had established sport television (in the United States, a task that was always discharged by the commercial networks NBC, ABC, and CBS, and later Fox) toward commercial terrestrial broadcasters who could use mass sport audiences to sell to advertisers. Rapid inflation in the sport TV rights market made the TV audience the most powerful force in contemporary sport (Rowe 2004b), leading in time both to rule changes to accommodate television schedules (such as tie breaks in tennis) and to the timing of events (like the daytime marathons and morning swimming finals in the Olympics). The most valuable media sport texts are live to air, given the premium that can be demanded for watching a unique event unfold in real time. However, the cost of purchasing and staging such events requires risk minimization strategies. Such "event" television, with the unpredictability of the quality of the contest and the considerable length of viewing time, is reliant on the quality of the spectacle.

A key element of the spectacular quality of live sport is the in-stadium audience, whose noisy passion, colorful appearance (signified through contrasting team or country regalia), and often innovative performance of spectatorship are integral to a sense of occasion and of "having been there" for the distant, mediated audience. The sports television viewer, therefore, enlists in-stadium spectators for the purposes of both identification and differentiation if disposed to partisanship (usually supporting one competitor or the other is a key aspect of sport appreciation or, less commonly, enjoying the contest for its own sake as a matter of cultural taste). For those uncommitted to sport, the televised crowd can provide a spectacular element that may engender a temporary interest in what is occurring on screen. In her discussion of ethnographic approaches to media audiences in everyday life, S. Elizabeth Bird (2003) notes the uncertain and high variability of audience encounters with media:

> [W]e experience media in non-predictable and non-uniform ways. One can be a proud TV avoider, yet still be also physically dependent on recorded music. One can watch TV most of the time as a casual, passive viewer, but be a knowledgeable, active 'fan' of a particular program. The images and messages wash over, but most leave little trace, unless they resonate, even for a moment, with something in our personal or cultural experience. (p. 2)

One key way of making the sporting text "resonate" involves the dispersed media audience gazing at the audience in the specific sports site. When for some reason that element of the spectacle is absent – a poor in-stadium attendance, the banning of one sport fan group or of all fans, or the disruption caused by stadium refurbishment – the sport spectacle is widely felt to be much diminished (Rowe 2004a). Thus, in televised sport, the co-present audience (routinely described as *the crowd* in differentiating it from the fragmented "mass" of dispersed, distant viewers) is an indispensable element of the text itself.

But this audience is also aware that it is part of the text, and itself insists on dual audience status – that of both the viewer and viewed. In other words, the in-stadium audience is also part of the media sport audience because it has become accustomed to the advantages of televised sport that in some ways exceed those of physical attendance. Dayan and Katz (1992), in their analysis of the live broadcast-ing of major events, have noted how the experience of "being there" may be disap-pointing given the physical constraints imposed on crowds, such as a single point of view, as opposed to the multiperspectival, multispeed visual experiences one may have through television. The original concern about televising sport, as noted above, was that potential paying spectators would calculate rationally that free-to-air, two-dimensional sound and vision experience, either live or delayed, would be preferable to actual attendance of sport events. The financial compensation of broadcast rights, though, did not take into account spectators who were present but also wanted to take advantage of television's perspectives. At first, this need was satisfied by watching replays at home and, after the introduction of domestic video technology, accessing home recordings. But such arrangements could not take account of the instantaneity or rapid response of television, meaning that large screens were introduced within many large sport stadia in order, ironically, to compensate co-present spectators for the shortcomings of the visual spectacle for which they had paid. This transportation of the domestic technology to the out-side, collective world made audiences both the subject and object of the televisual gaze. As a result, there was an increased emphasis on performance for, and com-munication through, television (Rinehart 1998).

Thus, large crowds could perform both for those outside the stadium and to themselves and their co-present rivals within it. It then became possible for attend-ees to use the developing technique of personalization within television – picking out members of the crowd for dramatic expressions of emotion; eliciting empathy, sympathy, or hostility in a concrete way; highlighting particularly attractive traits; and so on – to "talk back" to television itself. Some audience members have become skilled at attracting camera attention and even, as in the case of the Australian Open and Wimbledon tennis tournaments, paid by sponsors to promote their goods and services under the guise of spontaneous, unselfconscious sport fandom. On other occasions, sport television broadcasters run competitions (often with cross-promotional tie-ins) whereby the cameras scan stadia for the best examples of a crowd banner or element of fan style. Not uncommonly, when fans are caught unaware and then see themselves on giant stadium screens, they immedi-ately wave and call out to those at home. Crawford (2004) notes this dual audience–performer role as directed both to those present and to television in a combination of the "scripted" and the carnivalesque:

> In particular, sport audiences are often among the most performative, where sup-
> porters will often dress-up, sing, play instruments and generally perform to those
> around them.... Moreover, the advent of large screen televisions at many sport
> performances allows *key performances* to become *key spectacles*; as these are selected
> by the venue's cameras and displayed on the screens and scoreboards....
>   ... Generally, individuals who are selected and shown on the screens appear to be
> having a good time. Most wave when they see themselves on the screens, while
> some may shy away and hide. However, others continue performing undeterred or
> even increase their activity, as though the camera provides an opportunity to extend
> their display. Many will 'play' to the cameras, by bringing banners, or dressing-up in
> costumes in an attempt to get on the screen. (p. 86, emphasis in original)

This relatively innocuous audience activity contrasts with "playing to the cameras" while engaging in violent and antisocial behavior, with television accused of offering the "oxygen of publicity" and an (inter)national stage for, in the case of European association football, expressions of status competition between violent fan groupings or "firms" (Giulianotti 1999). Such behavior within football stadia has been reduced by stricter policing, more vigorously enforced fan segregation, and what can generally be called an *embourgeoisifica-tion* of the game with the introduction of seating in place of standing terraces, higher admission prices, and an emphasis on middle-class "family viewing" and corporate-sanctioned leisure at the expense of territorial, working-class, male-dominated cultural practices that prevailed until the final years of the twentieth century (King 1998).

In a further indication of how audience practices have shifted to accommo-date telecommunications and media development, it is now also routine for sport fans to communicate by mobile phone with significant others while sta-dium cameras are turned toward their section of the crowd, and even to take and upload their own camera shots from the same devices. Of course, the purpose of such "user-generated content" is highly variable, and may also incorporate the violent and antisocial behavior – diminishing but by no means extinguished in such areas as racial and other forms of abuse – that was mentioned above. By such means, formerly solid distinctions between present and mediated audiences are redrawn. They are still maintained in some respects – the cultural capital pertaining to "being there" is still significant, and co-presence necessarily rationed (Rowe and Stevenson 2006) – but it is now clear that all sport audiences are also media audiences to a greater or lesser degree. But media sport is not always freely available to all citizens, thereby raising questions of audience equity and access.

Citizenship and Media Sport Audiences

Accompanying the erosion of the binary distinction between stadium and home audience has been the proliferation of media-viewing sites and so the recomposition of media sport audiences. This trend has been stimulated by a number of developments, not least among which has been the extension of the primary cost of admission to witness on-site sport contests to the media sphere. The cause of this shift was the remodeling of sport television structures. After the first wave of public and commercial free-to-air television carriage of sport between the 1950s and the 1980s, in an era when television monopolies transmuted into highly regulated oligopolies, a second wave of change occurred that was organized around the political ascendancy of broadcasting privatization and deregulation, the availability of (increasingly digitized) multichanneling, and the growth of subscription television. Cable television developed early in the United States, but so had network television's domination of, and reliance on, sport (Chandler 1988). In countries with strong public service broadcasting histories, such as the United Kingdom, most of continental Europe, and much of Asia, satellite and cable television became available in the late 1980s, but in the context of an untried market model relating to audiences accustomed to receiving major sport events, especially those involving national representatives and a sample of nationally significant tournaments and events, live and without charge (Rowe 2004c). Subscription television promised to offer audiences many improvements – more sports events in total; more live sports events among them; and a range of technical innovations, including customized viewing and interactivity. In return for this promise, though, was the imposition of a fee to view, with its obvious consequences for cultural inclusion.

The United Kingdom is the most (in)famous case study of the making of a new sport television audience on a subscription television sport platform. The assent of the state was gained through the politically sympathetic relationship between the Conservative Thatcher–Major governments (1979–1997) and the media proprietor Rupert Murdoch (Goodwin 1998). After an aggressive and debilitating struggle between rival start-up companies Sky and BSB, Murdoch's company Sky was victorious and formed BSkyB in 1990. It then in 1992 outbid all rivals to secure exclusive live rights to the nascent English Premier League (EPL) of association football, with Murdoch believing that sport was the "battering ram" that would break down the barriers to new audiences and media applications (Rowe 2004a). Since then, the EPL has become the world's richest sport league and a major television export around the world, especially in the rapidly developing Asian market (Rowe and Gilmour 2008). Its relationship with Sky is a clear case of carrot-and-stick audience formation wherein enhanced televisual access to a new competition (in this case, essentially a rebadging of an old one) within a popular sport (here Britain's most popular by far) is provided through the essentially coercive mechanism of "pay to see." This formation of media sport audiences as electronically reconfigured versions of those charged at the stadium turnstile has prompted keen cultural political debate. At one pole is the construction of the audience as a class of consumers freely exercising their rights to purchase or to refuse a premium service of sport television. At the opposing pole is the audience positioned as a citizenry whose rights of cultural citizenship include free access to televised events of national cultural significance. It is notable that, when there have been attempts to codify such events in individual countries such as Australia and within a collective, federated network like the European Union through such mechanisms as "antisiphoning provisions" and "event listing" (the proscription of exclusive capture of specified tournaments and events by pay television), the vast majority (over 90 percent) of such events has involved a sporting contest or ritual (such as the Opening Ceremony of the Olympic Games) (Rowe 2004c). Within such discursive struggles, media sport audiences come to stand for whole nations and their cultural rights, and access to sport television translated into a measure of the health of public culture in the face of the marketization of everyday life.

Below the level of government and intergovernmental policy and public debate, media sport providers and audiences operate on a diurnal basis in negotiating modes of watching sport. For example, in the aforementioned case of viewing association football in Britain, the introduction of subscription television involves not only homes but also licensed premises. It therefore has created a new leisure option of attending pubs and clubs to watch live games whose reception was paid for by "mine hosts," once again encouraging the foundational relationship between professional sport, gambling (here in the form of gaming machines), and alcohol consumption. While "attendance" at such events is nominally free of charge, it is not possible to enter commercial space without requirement or encouragement to consume. Ironically, therefore, the cost of attendance through the purchase of alcohol, food, and other products might exceed that of a pay TV subscription or even a singular "pay per view" (Rowe 2004a). However, beyond strictly financial considerations there are the benefits of extended sociality to be derived from a collective sport-viewing experience outside the home.

This new sector of the media audience adapted an established practice of drinking socially before and after a game, or within the stadium itself, by drinking within licensed premises and watching the event on one of the screens provided in an often-boisterous context that, drawing simultaneously from the on-screen crowd and the co-present pub and club patrons, to a substantial extent simulates the in-stadium experience. It also created the possibility not only to "get out of the house," but also for one or more members of the household to absent themselves from it while others remained at home (no doubt, in some cases, including households that subscribe to the pay television service delivering the live match). In this sense, sport television in licensed premises can attend to the demands of audiences for whom sport is a pretext for forms of sociality centered on, in the sociological language of an earlier era but one with some contemporary relevance, "conjugal role segregation." At the same time, the domestic context itself – especially in the era of the home stadium – is also frequently a key site for social interaction among residents and visitors organized around viewing major live sports events (Rowe and Stevenson 2006).

Beyond the spaces of commercial licensees and viewers' homes, in major sport tournaments, especially those of an international nature such as the World Cup of association football and the Olympics, a new media audience mode was created. The conditions favorable to this viewing innovation were stimulated by a range of factors: the unmet demand caused by the necessary capacity limitation of stadia (in an event final, for example, almost never more than 120,000 people); the social democratic impulse to cater to those excluded from major events by economic and other circumstances; the heightened importance of sport tourism, and the growing practice of marketing whole cities around major sports events and exploiting urban sites beyond main, enclosed stadia; and the institutional politics entailed by the intense competition for mega-media sports events requiring a commitment that all citizens and visitors should be able to feel a legitimate part of the event and so membership of its audience or "family" (Roche 2000; Weed and Bull 2004). The proliferation of what have been called *live sites* – assembly points in public spaces with large screens where sports events can be watched in a "crowd" setting – demonstrates how screen technologies can be combined with a traditional emphasis on collective co-presence in creating different manifestations of media sport audiences. New sites of audience assembly are, furthermore, also being created between and within the media themselves.

Other Media, Other Audiences

In the discussion so far, there has been a concentration on sport television and the shift from fixed place-based sport audiences to those dispersed but largely confined to domestic environments. The subsequent splintering of media sport audience modes – coexisting, it should be recalled, with both the foundational in-stadium and ensuing home-based modes – was shown, albeit in shorthand form, to have been created by social, political, cultural, economic, and technological changes. Returning to Raymond Williams (1977), whose reflections on television sport set the tone for this chapter, media sport and its audience relationships can be said to display, simultaneously, "dominant," "residual," and "emergent" cultural forms. Mass broadcast sport remains "structured in dominance," although there are persistent elements of previous eras when media sport was much more local and low-key, and, if not strictly amateur, evidenced a form of professionalism that contrasts strikingly with the more distanced arrangements of celebrity-athlete and media-dependent fan that predominate in the contemporary era (Whannel 2008).

There are also new media sport formations that are emerging that, as is noted, challenge the performer–spectator dyad itself. Before examining one such instance, it is necessary go beyond the exclusive concern with sport television to recognize other media and their audiences. In this way, a deeper appreciation of the "media sports cultural complex" (Rowe 2004a) can be gained which enhances understanding of the ways in which media sport audience relations might be in the process of change and rearticulation. Predating and feeding into television have been a range of media with overlapping and distinct audiences.

As in other areas of media, there is no singular media sport audience, but a range of sites and practices within the media sports cultural complex characterized by very different possibilities and levels of engagement. It is especially important to recognize that, to a significant extent, the membership of media sport audiences is not voluntary. This is because it has been structured into the very fabric of everyday life, to the extent that some knowledge of sport events, institutions, personnel, and issues is routinely presented and circulated through a range of media. To take some brief examples, a person who is listening to a radio news bulletin may be interested in a parliamentary debate, but the lead story might be about a national sporting triumph or scandal. Indeed, perhaps the parliamentary debate concerns sport, such as how much in the way of public funding should be committed to an Olympic bid, or whether there should be a boycott of a sports tournament in another country because of human rights abuses there. In any case, structured into the bulletin, along with the stock market and the weather reports, there is likely to be a sport update. Such experiences are replicated across media – sport news may have migrated from the back to the front page of newspapers because, say, a cyclist or sprinter has won a gold medal or been detected as using performance-enhancing drugs. The sport news on television may have been avoided, only for there to be a primetime sport quiz show, documentary, or live event. Indeed, Ruddock's (2001, p. 13) general wondering "if it really makes any sense to talk about non-viewers [of television] in the contemporary media environment" may be specifically applied to the domain of media sport. Even if the highly dubious proposition is accepted that some inhabit a postbroadcast universe, leaving the small screen behind for the even smaller one of the computer, pop-up advertisements on web pages might invite sport ticket purchase, while film trailers in multiplex cinemas may promote the latest sports "biopic" or rags-to-riches drama. Even people encountered in the street may function as a sport medium, wearing fan merchandising or leading sportswear brands (Horne 2006).

The extension of the media sport audience became a clear political economic imperative as saturation – in terms of sport, as well as media – became an impediment to both the industrial development of sport and its utilization to sell other products. The constitution of sport performers and audiences as predominantly male established an enduring, intergenerational core constituency, but at the same time limited its horizons. Attracting more females to media audiences by promoting identification with female athletes has, notably, not been a major strategy – indeed, female athletes have suffered substantial media neglect unless consenting and/or being subjected to sexual objectification for a predominantly heterosexual male gaze (Hargreaves 1994). For "glamorous" sportswomen such as now-retired Russian tennis player Anna Kournikova (Evans 2001), sexuality and actual or fantasized personal relationships may virtually obliterate sport performance in the construction of a highly sexualized and lucrative media image (handsomely compensating, in Kournikova's case, for relative underperformance on the international tennis circuit). The invention by *Sports Illustrated* of "Simonya Popova," a virtual, fashion-conscious, 17-year-old Uzbekistani tennis player, is a parodic reflection of the enduring media preoccupation with the sexuality of sportswomen. The spoof article (Wertheim 2002), complete with an image of Simonya in a colorful halter top, short skirt, and bare midriff, prompted many media inquiries to the Women's Tennis Association about the mysterious (and fictional) tennis player. The irony, of course, is that *Sports Illustrated* is best known for an annual swimsuit issue using professional models that is squarely aimed at a heterosexual male audience and pays no more than cursory interest to any sport, let alone that performed by women (Davis 1997).

The orthodox media industry "wisdom" is that, except with regard to a limited number of sports (such as tennis) and events (like the Olympic Games), women's sport is unattractive to large male and female audiences (Hargreaves 1994). Hence, media sport audiences are in most cases imagined as men and women gazing on men, with an emphasis on "recruiting" women who have not been socialized, like many men, into sport culture from childhood, or on "feminizing" elements of media sport texts. One such technique regarding the latter is a "reverse" sexual objectification of men (Miller 2001), or the mobilization of a celebrity discourse that was once largely confined to so-called gossip and celebrity magazines targeted at younger women. The most often-cited case of the "celebritization" of sport is that of the British footballer David Beckham and his pop singer wife, Victoria (formerly Posh of the Spice Girls). As Whannel (2008) notes of male sport stars such as Beckham, now retired basketballer Dennis Rodman, and retired boxer Mike Tyson, "The visual appearance of sport performers has come to constitute a significant factor in the marketing and promotional strategies of sporting organizations" (p. 186). But such strategies would be futile without the involvement of the media in producing the requisite level of recognition. The audience for male sport stars such as Beckham may have only a tangential relationship with his performance on the field of play. Indeed, while his standing as a professional footballer has made him available to a public at large, it is quite possible to follow his activities as a model, endorser of products, attendee of gala events, and so on without ever being part of an orthodox media sport audience. Not only do such sport celebrity phenomena problematize what might be said to constitute a media sport audience, but they also question what counts as sport itself. If performance sport is, literally, the "pre-text" of media coverage, it might be argued that the cultural forms and practices that surround, intersect with, and lightly touch upon sport as regulated, competitive physical culture might be regarded as more important than the "strictly sporting" cultural elements precisely because of their capacity to produce larger, multiple audience formations.

For example, the British television drama *Footballers' Wives*, which went to five series between 2002 and 2006, produced an American pilot (though it was not "picked up") and has been broadcast in every continent in the world, draws on the world of sport, but requires little if any knowledge of, or interest in, that world. Described by Wills (2002, pp. 4, 7) as "not so far-fetched" in representing "footballers' lives" and yet "like a car crash. You don't want to look, but you just have to," the program concentrates on the relationships, travails, and conspicuous consumption of sportsmen and the women that they live with and encounter. While there are some specific elements concerning sport within its stories – form on the field of play, injury, transfers between clubs, conflicts between players on the same team, and so on – they are subordinated to a conventional television soap opera format of sexual intrigue. While audiences may have been attracted to watch the show by the cultural visibility of association football (soccer) across media, sport per se is at least one remove from it, and it is not necessary to be a sport fan to be part of the television audience of *Footballers' Wives* or of any other such "secondary" sports media text.

Concentration on the significant others of sportsmen occurs not only in televisual dramas but also in everyday news, especially within tabloid media. The category of the WAG (wives and girlfriends), first used in the middle of the first decade of the twenty-first century as the English Premier League boomed, was deployed intensively in the British tabloid press during the World Cup in Germany in 2006. Particular attention was given to such issues as fashion, consumption (especially shopping), and status competition between women within this identified group (Wong 2006). Again, the audience for this media coverage need not have been much interested in football, and, while their husbands and boyfriends were of significance and renown, a parallel sphere could be said to exist in which the WAGS themselves were or became celebrities. This phenomenon may also be detected in other sports – for example, Elin Nordegren, the girlfriend (and now ex-wife) of the world's best golfer, Tiger Woods, was once described, bizarrely, as "one of the hottest properties in world sport" (Mcclure 2002, p. 6). The justification for this claim was that there was more general interest in Woods's relationship – albeit including its effect on his sporting performance – than in his golf (Rowe 2009). This focus on the Woods–Nordegren union reached fever pitch in late 2009, when there was an apparent confrontation between them over Woods's infidelity and he crashed his vehicle near their home in the early hours. There followed massive media coverage of their marital problems and Woods's sexual conduct, much of which had little bearing on golf and which could readily connect with audiences who neither knew nor cared about his sporting prowess. In such cases, an entire audience can form around a prominent scandal involving high-profile sportspeople and their personal lives for whom the sport is quite incidental.

The key point being advanced here is that media sport audiences have highly variable orientations toward what is conventionally regarded as sport. It is increasingly difficult to maintain a purist definition of sport as athletic performance, given that, however important it might ultimately be, it could not be sustained without all of the other modes of media representation and the involvement of constantly shifting audience formations. The entire edifice of professional sport is dependent on an economics of high visibility that sustains its frequently extravagant costs of organization and labor. The protean nature of sport as a cultural form that can pass across and through different media and domains of everyday life has enabled it to occupy a discursive space encompassing such pivotal reference points as identity, gossip, work, leisure, the body, style, and intercultural dialogue. The logic of this cultural economy is classically capitalistic in that it is "compelled" to grow by reaching new cultural sites, social groups, and geographical regions in the face of alternative, competing popular forms. It is for this reason that, among major Western sports and media, there have been stringent attempts to develop audiences in other places, especially in the Asian-Pacific region, with its vast population and un- or underexploited market potential.

Professional sport, as argued above, is a Western invention, and the media sport apparatus first developed there. Internationalization and then globalization (Maguire 1999; Miller et al. 2001) demanded a move beyond this sphere, not least because of market saturation and the development of sport as a major form of content in the development of worldwide subscription television platforms (Miller et al. 2003). The staging of mega-media sport events like the Summer and Winter Olympics (e.g., in Tokyo in 1964, Sapporo in 1972, Seoul in 1988, Nagano in 1998, and Beijing in 2008) and the World Cup of Association Football (Korea-Japan in 2002) can be seen as both a form of geographical sporting "equity" and a means of developing the reach of the media sport industry (Roche 2000; Tomlinson and Young 2006). The two principal techniques of audience attraction involve the promotion of sporting nationalism – both very prominent, for example, in Korea and China in 2002 and 2008, respectively – and of an internationalist form of cosmopolitan brand association (Rowe and Gilmour 2008) connecting Asian-Pacific consumers with Western sports brands, such as leading European football teams Manchester United, Liverpool, Chelsea, AC Milan, Juventus, Barcelona, and Real Madrid, or US basketball teams like the Chicago Bulls, Boston Celtics, and Los Angeles Lakers. In turn, these sport team brands are further associated with major consumer brands, mostly Western in origin, such as Visa, Pepsi, Coca Cola, Nike, Rolex, Adidas, McDonalds, and Reebok. The nationally constituted media sport audience is one of the most powerful means of symbolically creating collective identity and materially fashioning a commodifiable entity. But within the nation itself, local competitions in sports like basketball and football often suffer in comparison with more glamorous, cleverly marketed competitions like the English Premier League, the European Champions League, and the National Basketball Association. Horne (2006) notes,

As global flows increase, an awareness of differences between nations and national identities also increases. Becoming aware of other cultures sharpens people's consciousness of their own domestic world and their distinctive national and cultural identities. Other identities apart from national are also developed through the consumption of sport and leisure. (p. 132)

The consequences of the globalization of sport culture are, therefore, ironic in terms of audience formation. The national audience emphasizing national cultural difference is, at the same time, initiated into a Western-dominated cultural form linked with Western sport and general brands. This is not, though, universally the case – in the sport of cricket, the sheer size of the Indian subcontinent audience and its variety of media opportunities have shifted the balance of power from England, the former colonial power, to India, which freed itself from that power in the 1940s but retained the introduced cultural attachment to cricket, which it has now come to dominate by means of the economic power of its television audience. This shift occurred not only through the relative powers of forms of cricket – most dramatically, through the promotion of the short, spectacular, television-friendly Twenty20 version of the game – but also through such event-based innovations as the Indian Premier League (IPL, launched in 2008), which created synthetic team franchises of international and local players based in such cities as Mumbai, Delhi, and Kolkata. More than in most "mobile" contemporary sports, the IPL has created complex options for, and dilemmas of, audience identification, as different combinations of teammates and opponents in other competitions came together for this single purpose. At the same time, in drawing on both local and introduced elements from entertainment and sport – such as Bollywood film and American-style cheerleaders – an hybridic audience appeal has been fashioned that again problematizes what constitutes sport, its audiences, and its followers.

The type of media audience that sports broadcasters and organizations have tried to develop has typically been passive and consumption oriented (Rowe and Gilmour 2008). For example, in the aforementioned English Premier League – the richest in the world – sport fans have been required to pay more to watch games at the stadium and at home, pay for overpriced fan merchandise with only a short shelf life, watch favorite clubs and players traded on the market with little sense of tradition and loyalty, and so on. As a result, some sport audiences have engaged in acts of resistance and sometimes develop and use their own media. The first expressions of this resistance could be found in fanzines during the 1980s and 1990s (Haynes 1995) and in local takeovers of clubs (sometimes because of financial collapse), but of particular interest today is the possibility of using new media to constitute an audience that is also involved in the ownership and management of sports clubs.

Debates within audience studies have frequently hinged on polar conceptions of audiences as either disempowered and manipulated or empowered and agentic

(Ruddock 2001). In sport, there has been considerable interest in "fan power" movements, which usually operate on the basis that the "sportsbiz" – and, especially, the commercial media that wield most power within it – have corrupted and debauched sport by detaching it from its local, community roots and making it into a plaything of international corporate capitalism and placed in the service of bourgeois consumerism. This grassroots resistance to the commodification of sport is highly romantic, seeking to return it to a (substantially illusory) golden age of "authentic" sport, while also being heavily dependent on those modern sport developments – especially, its televisual representation – that are felt to represent its contemporary "evils." But one recent case of the "active audience" that invites attention is that of MyFootballClub (MFC), which has used new media and computing technologies in seeking to redraw the lines between audience membership and club ownership. In late 2007, MFC was launched through a UK-based website (www.myfootballclub.co.uk), recruiting members willing to pay an annual fee of £35 and for it to be used to purchase the controlling interest in a football club. Drawing on the liberatory discourse of fan organizations such as the Football Supporters' Association, the founder – journalist Will Brooks – proposed a democratic reform by means of the motto "Own the club, pick the team." This statement of intent meant that all major decisions of the club – from team formation, shirt design, and sponsorship to player transfers and employee remuneration – would be made through a ballot process on the website. In due course, 30,000 members were recruited and a team, Ebbsfleet United, purchased, thereby allowing fans to move from relatively passive audience status to a more active role as multiple co-managers (Hutchins, Rowe, and Ruddock 2008).

It should be emphasized that this "experiment" is by no means established and that by late 2010, the club and the remaining membership of 3,000 faced a financial crisis. But, irrespective of its ultimate success or failure, the MFC "experiment" highlights significant trends in media sport audience formation. First, it reveals the high level of dependency of sport on media, irrespective of its prelapsarian discourse of football innocence lost and of hyperlocalism. The location of the physical team, in a small, unglamorous ground in Gravesend, to the southeast of London, is a matter of symbolic importance, but most members have not visited it or rarely do so (with average home attendances well below 2,000). It also indicates the importance of media convergence and proliferation, as a combination of website communication – with multiple forums and votes (including elections of members of the board), email, web-based match and club interview videos (classified on the website as a "watching" activity), radio podcasting ("listening"), chat ("talking"), and Wiki ("reading"), as well as considerable "external" coverage in broadcast and print media (including the BBC, ABC, FoxSports [Australia], ESPN, *Guardian, Economic Times* [India], and *Time*) – enables an enormous amount of media- and computer-based audience contact and exchange. This interactive capability is especially significant given that, according to the MFC website "Stats" section (http://members.myfootballclub.co.uk/stats, 19 October 2008), numerical membership by country ranged (when it was at its highest point) from the top three of 20,229 (UK), 3231 (USA), and 957 (Australia) (over 80 percent of total membership) to only 1 in such places as Malawi, Cuba, and Ecuador.

The sport–entertainment nexus is also emphasized through such means as the song "Beat the Weather," performed by the Stonebridge Road groundsman, Peter Norton, which is sold on iTunes and has an accompanying YouTube video (both produced by members who are also media professionals). Especially striking is the similarity between MFC and sport management and simulation computer games, a link made stronger by the MFC website's sponsorship by EA Sports, the major sport gaming company. MFC, therefore, encapsulates many of the issues surrounding contemporary media sport audiences. The audience is spatially dispersed but connected through media (although it is concentrated mainly in the United Kingdom); displays residual elements of earlier, place-based audience formations but uses new converged media, telecommunications, and computing technologies to construct and reconstitute audiences; spills out into other, formerly separate cultural domains, such as those that surround gaming and even those of "reality" television programming involving voting participants "on" or "off"; and engages with questions of audience activism and knowledge, using such contemporary management communication concepts as *crowd sourcing* and the *wisdom of crowds*. Most ambitiously, it suggests the possibility of an epochal shift from the notion of media *and* sport, to that of media *as* sport (Hutchins, Rowe, and Ruddock 2008). Media sport audiences, then, can be seen to be much more than readers of sport reports, listeners to radio commentary, and viewers of televised action, all of which once dominated, in turn, media sport audience practice.

Conclusion: The Sportization of Media and Their Audiences

As this chapter was being initially drafted, the author broke off to watch a television news bulletin. The 2008 crisis on financial markets was in full swing, and the news broadcast moved around the world to major stock markets and received an update from a correspondent on the statistical movement of composite share prices that day. The bulletin then switched into the business segment, during which more detailed financial figures and trends were presented, including in tabular format, and then was followed by the sport segment. A striking similarity between the presentation and style of the "scores" of the financial report and those addressed in the sport segment was evident. The convergence of the sport and business reports may have occurred in both directions, but the interpellated audience of a major, free-to-air television news program would be likely to recognize the style accompanying the sports results as common to both. With systematic attempts to enliven television in the face of pressures on audience time and competition from other media, it is apparent that the viewing audience was being "cued" to recognize the state of the share market in much the same way as it was being informed of the latest sport scores: the upward and downward movements on sports league or medal tables, and the affective atmosphere (sentiment) pertaining to "winners" and "losers" – and prospects of success and failure. Media audiences across a range of topics, from parliamentary fortunes to the international trading health of a nation's currency, from public policy debates to the condition of the labor market, are being oriented to the world within the familiar framework of sport contests. "Reality" and "quiz" show formats similarly share familiar elements of the mediated sport contest.

It has often been noted that audiences are not just out in the world waiting to be discovered and quantified, but also subject to a constant process of "mobilization" (Balnaves, O'Regan, and Sternberg 2002). It is apparent that media sport audiences form, re-form, and dissolve in myriad ways, with highly variable orientations toward sport in the restricted sense of competitive physical activity. Sport-related media texts and practices have become so ubiquitous as to suggest a wide-ranging process of "sportization" not just of sport and exercise (Elias and Dunning 1986) but also of the whole field of contemporary culture and its significations. As a result, sport audience membership, once restricted and voluntary, has through a series of unavoidable and proliferating engagements with media become increasingly open and conspicuously compulsory.

Acknowledgments

The research on which this chapter draws has been supported by two Australian Research Council Discovery Grants that address, respectively, broadcast and "postbroadcast" media sport: *Handling the "Battering Ram": Rupert Murdoch, News Corporation and the Global Contest for Dominance in Sports Television*, and *Struggling for Possession: The Control and Use of Online Media Sport* (with Dr Brett Hutchins).

References

Balnaves, M., O'Regan, T. and Sternberg, J., eds. 2002 *Mobilising the Audience*. University of Queensland Press, Brisbane.

Bird, S. E. 2003 *The Audience in Everyday Life: Living in a Media World*. Routledge, New York.

Boyle, R. and Haynes, R. 2000 *Power Play: Sport, the Media and Popular Culture*. Pearson Education, Harlow, UK.

Brookes, R. 2002 *Representing Sport*. Arnold, London.

Chandler, J.M. 1988 *Television and National Sport: The United States and Britain*. University of Illinois Press, Urbana.

Crawford, G. 2004 *Consuming Sport: Fans, Sport and Culture*. Routledge, London.

Davis, L.R. 1997 *The Swimsuit Issue and Sport: Hegemonic Masculinity in Sports Illustrated*. State University of New York Press, Albany.

Dayan, D. and Katz, E. 1992 *Media Events: The Live Broadcasting of History*. Harvard University Press, Cambridge, MA.

Elias, N. and Dunning, E. 1986 *Quest for Excitement: Sport and Leisure in the Civilising Process*. Basil Blackwell, Oxford.

Evans, K. 2001 Commodified bodies: sport, image and gender. Unpublished master's thesis, Monash University, Australia.

Giulianotti, R. 1999 *Football: A Sociology of the Football Game*. Polity, Cambridge.

Goodwin, P. 1998 *Television under the Tories: Broadcasting Policy 1979–1997*. British Film Institute, London.

Hargreaves, J. 1994 *Sporting Females: Critical Issues in the History and Sociology of Women's Sports*. Routledge, London.

Haynes, R. 1995 *The Football Imagination: The Rise of Football Fanzine Culture*. Arena, Aldershot.

Horne, J. 2006 *Sport in Consumer Culture*. Palgrave Macmillan, Basingstoke, UK.

Hutchins, B., Rowe, D. and Ruddock, A. 2008 "It's fantasy football made real": networked media sport, the internet, and the hybrid reality of myfootballclub. *Sociology of Sport Journal*, 10, 4, pp. 354–370.

King, A. 1998 *The End of the Terraces: The Transformation of English Football in the 1990s*. Leicester University Press, Leicester, UK.

Maguire, J. 1999 *Global Sport: Identities, Societies, Civilizations*. Polity, Cambridge.

Mcclure, G. 2002 Sporting life. *The Age*, 23 April, p. 6.

Miller, T. 2001 *Sportsex*. Temple University Press, Philadelphia.

Miller, T., Lawrence, G., McKay, J. and Rowe, D. 2001 *Globalization and Sport: Playing the World*. Sage, London.

Miller, T., Rowe, D., Lawrence, G. and McKay, J. 2003 The over production of US sport and the new international division of cultural labour. *International Review for the Sociology of Sport*, 38, 4, pp. 427–440.

MyFootballClub. 2008 [Home page]. Retrieved from http://www.myfootballclub.co.uk

Rinehart, R.E. 1998 *Players All: Performances in Contemporary Sport*. Indiana University Press, Bloomington.

Roche, M. 2000 *Mega-Events and Modernity: Olympics and Expos in the Growth of Global Culture*. Routledge, London.

Rowe, D. 2004a *Sport, Culture and the Media: The Unruly Trinity*, 2nd edn. Open University Press, Maidenhead, UK.

Rowe, D. 2004b Sports and television. In H. Newcomb, ed. *Museum of Broadcast Communications Encyclopedia of Television*, vol. 4, 2nd edn. Routledge, New York, pp. 2172–2177.

Rowe, D. 2004c Fulfilling the cultural mission: popular genre and public remit. *European Journal of Cultural Studies*, 7, 3, 381–399.

Rowe, D. 2009 Attention la femme! Intimate relationships and male sports performance. In L. K. Fuller, ed. *Sexual Sports Rhetoric: Global and Universal Contexts*. Peter Lang, New York, pp. 69–81.

Rowe, D. and Gilmour, C. 2008 Contemporary media sport: de- or re-Westernization? *International Journal of Sport Communication*, 1, 2, pp. 177–194.

Rowe, D. and Stevenson, D. 2006 Sydney 2000: sociality and spatiality in global media events. In A. Tomlinson and C. Young, eds. *National Identity and Global Sports Events: Culture, Politics, and Spectacle in the Olympics and the Football World Cup*. State University of New York Press, New York, pp. 197–214.

Ruddock, A. 2001 *Understanding Audiences: Theory and Method*. Sage, London.

Tomlinson, A. and Young, C., eds. 2006 *National Identity and Global Sports Events: Culture, Politics, and Spectacle in the Olympics and the Football World Cup*. State University of New York Press, New York

Weed, M. and Bull, C. 2004 *Sports Tourism: Participants, Policy and Providers*. Butterworth Heinemann, London.

Wertheim, L. J. 2002 Who's that girl? *Sports Illustrated*, September 2. Retrieved from http://sportsillustrated.cnn.com/si_online/news/2002/09/04/popova/

Whannel, G. 1992 *Fields in Vision: Television Sport and Cultural Transformation*. Routledge, London.

Whannel, G. 2008 *Culture, Politics and Sport: Blowing the Whistle, Revisited*. Routledge, London.

Williams, R. 1989 There's always the sport [1970]. In A. O'Connor, ed. *Raymond Williams on Television: Selected Writings*. Routledge, London, pp. 95–99.

Williams, R. 1974 *Television: Technology and Cultural Form*. Fontana, London.

Williams, R. 1977 *Marxism and Literature*. Oxford University Press, Oxford.

Wills, J. 2002 Home and away. *The Guardian Guide*, 19–25 January, pp. 4–7.

Wong, S. C. 2006 Gender bias in World Cup 2006 coverage: the men still don't get it? Presentation to the Media Asia Conference, Perth, Curtin University of Technology November.

Index

The Handbook of Media Audiences, First Edition. Edited by Virginia Nightingale.
© 2014 John Wiley & Sons, Ltd. Published 2014 by John Wiley & Sons, Ltd.